A Different Mirror

RONALD TAKAKI

A
DIFFERENT
MIRROR

A History

of

Multicultural

America

LITTLE, BROWN AND COMPANY

BOSTON NEW YORK TORONTO LONDON

FIRST PAPERBACK EDITION

Copyright acknowledgments appear on page 507.

Library of Congress Cataloging-in-Publication Data
Takaki, Ronald T., 1939–
    A different mirror : a history of multicultural America / Ronald
Takaki. — 1st ed.
        p.   cm.
    Includes bibliographical references and index.
    ISBN 0-316-83112-3 (HC)   0-316-83111-5 (PB)
    1. Minorities — United States — History.   2. United States — Race
relations.   3. United States — Ethnic relations.   I. Title.
E184.A1T335   1993
973'.04 — dc20   92-33491

10 9 8

MV-NY

Published simultaneously in Canada by
Little, Brown & Company (Canada) Limited

PRINTED IN THE UNITED STATES OF AMERICA

AUTHOR'S NOTE

I N HIS APPRAISAL of *Strangers from a Different Shore: A History
of Asian Americans*, Edgar Wickberg of the *San Francisco Chronicle*
concluded: "What is needed now is an entirely different way of
studying and teaching American history — one in which 'different
shores' are seen as equal points of departure in a story of multidimen-
sional ethnic interaction. Takaki's book will surely provide one of the
basic sources." What I have written in the following pages is an attempt
to respond to this reviewer's challenge. For *A Different Mirror: A History of Multicultural America*, I have chosen only two of the Asian
immigrant groups — the Chinese and Japanese — in order to illustrate
Asian-American history, and have drawn from my previous work for
many of their voices and stories. In this new study, I seek to present
their experiences within a more inclusive multicultural context. This
broader and comparative approach opens the possibility of understanding and appreciating our racial and cultural diversity — Native Americans as well as peoples from different "points of departure" such as
England, Africa, Ireland, Mexico, Asia, and Russia. This is the story of
our coming together to create a new society in America.

CONTENTS

CONTENTS

CONTENTS

A DIFFERENT MIRROR

1

A DIFFERENT MIRROR

I HAD FLOWN FROM San Francisco to Norfolk and was riding in a taxi to my hotel to attend a conference on multiculturalism. Hundreds of educators from across the country were meeting to discuss the need for greater cultural diversity in the curriculum. My driver and I chatted about the weather and the tourists. The sky was cloudy, and Virginia Beach was twenty minutes away. The rearview mirror reflected a white man in his forties. "How long have you been in this country?" he asked. "All my life," I replied, wincing. "I was born in the United States." With a strong southern drawl, he remarked: "I was wondering because your English is excellent!" Then, as I had many times before, I explained: "My grandfather came here from Japan in the 1880s. My family has been here, in America, for over a hundred years." He glanced at me in the mirror. Somehow I did not look "American" to him; my eyes and complexion looked foreign.

Suddenly, we both became uncomfortably conscious of a racial divide separating us. An awkward silence turned my gaze from the mirror to the passing landscape, the shore where the English and the Powhatan Indians first encountered each other. Our highway was on land that Sir Walter Raleigh had renamed "Virginia" in honor of Elizabeth I, the Virgin Queen. In the English cultural appropriation of America, the indigenous peoples themselves would become outsiders in their native land. Here, at the eastern edge of the continent, I mused, was the site of the beginning of multicultural America. Jamestown, the English settlement founded in 1607, was nearby: the first twenty Africans were brought here a year before the Pilgrims arrived at Plymouth Rock. Several hundred miles offshore was Bermuda, the "Bermoothes" where William Shakespeare's Prospero had landed and met the native Caliban in *The Tempest*. Earlier, another voyager had made an Atlantic crossing and unexpectedly bumped into some islands to the south. Thinking he had reached Asia, Christopher Columbus mistakenly identified one of the islands as "Cipango" (Japan). In the wake of the admiral, many peoples would come to America from different shores, not only from Europe but also Africa and Asia. One of them would be my grandfather. My mental wandering across terrain and time ended abruptly as we arrived at my destination. I said good-bye to my driver and went into the hotel, carrying a vivid reminder of why I was attending this conference.

QUESTIONS like the one my taxi driver asked me are always jarring, but I can understand why he could not see me as American. He had a narrow but widely shared sense of the past — a history that has viewed American as European in ancestry. "Race," Toni Morrison explained, has functioned as a "metaphor" necessary to the "construction of Americanness": in the creation of our national identity, "American" has been defined as "white."[1]

But America has been racially diverse since our very beginning on the Virginia shore, and this reality is increasingly becoming visible and ubiquitous. Currently, one-third of the American people do not trace their origins to Europe; in California, minorities are fast becoming a majority. They already predominate in major cities across the country — New York, Chicago, Atlanta, Detroit, Philadelphia, San Francisco, and Los Angeles.

This emerging demographic diversity has raised fundamental questions about America's identity and culture. In 1990, *Time* published a cover story on "America's Changing Colors." "Someday soon," the magazine announced, "white Americans will become a minority group." How soon? By 2056, most Americans will trace their descent to "Africa, Asia, the Hispanic world, the Pacific Islands, Arabia — almost anywhere but white Europe." This dramatic change in our nation's ethnic composition is altering the way we think about ourselves. "The deeper significance of America's becoming a majority nonwhite society is what it means to the national psyche, to individuals' sense of themselves and their nation — their idea of what it is to be American."[2]

Indeed, more than ever before, as we approach the time when whites become a minority, many of us are perplexed about our national identity and our future as one people. This uncertainty has provoked Allan Bloom to reaffirm the preeminence of Western civilization. Author of *The Closing of the American Mind*, he has emerged as a leader of an intellectual backlash against cultural diversity. In his view, students entering the university are "uncivilized," and the university has the responsibility to "civilize" them. Bloom claims he knows what their "hungers" are and "what they can digest." Eating is one of his favorite metaphors. Noting the "large black presence" in major universities, he laments the "one failure" in race relations — black students have proven to be "indigestible." They do not "melt as have *all* other groups." The problem, he contends, is that "blacks have become blacks": they have become "ethnic." This separatism has been reinforced by an academic permissiveness that has befouled the curriculum with "Black Studies" along with "Learn Another Culture." The only solution, Bloom insists, is "the good old Great Books approach."[3]

Similarly, E. D. Hirsch worries that America is becoming a "tower of Babel," and that this multiplicity of cultures is threatening to rend our social fabric. He, too, longs for a more cohesive culture and a more homogeneous America: "If we *had* to make a choice between the *one* and the *many*, most Americans would choose the principle of unity, since we cannot function as a nation without it." The way to correct this fragmentization, Hirsch argues, is to acculturate "disadvantaged children." What do they need to know? "Only by accumulating shared symbols, and the shared information that symbols represent," Hirsch answers, "can we learn to communicate effectively with one another in our national community." Though he concedes the value of multicultural education, he quickly dismisses it by insisting that it "should not be allowed to supplant or interfere with our schools' responsibility to ensure our children's mastery of American literate culture." In *Cultural Literacy: What Every American Needs to Know*, Hirsch offers a long list of terms that excludes much of the history of minority groups.[4]

While Bloom and Hirsch are reacting defensively to what they regard as a vexatious balkanization of America, many other educators are responding to our diversity as an opportunity to open American minds. In 1990, the Task Force on Minorities for New York emphasized the importance of a culturally diverse education. "Essentially," the *New York Times* commented, "the issue is how to deal with both dimensions of the nation's motto: 'E pluribus unum' — 'Out of many, one.'"

Universities from New Hampshire to Berkeley have established American cultural diversity graduation requirements. "Every student needs to know," explained University of Wisconsin's chancellor Donna Shalala, "much more about the origins and history of the particular cultures which, as Americans, we will encounter during our lives." Even the University of Minnesota, located in a state that is 98 percent white, requires its students to take ethnic studies courses. Asked why multiculturalism is so important, Dean Fred Lukermann answered: As a national university, Minnesota has to offer a national curriculum — one that includes all of the peoples of America. He added that after graduation many students move to cities like Chicago and Los Angeles and thus need to know about racial diversity. Moreover, many educators stress, multiculturalism has an intellectual purpose. By allowing us to see events from the viewpoints of different groups, a multicultural curriculum enables us to reach toward a more comprehensive understanding of American history.[5]

What is fueling this debate over our national identity and the content of our curriculum is America's intensifying racial crisis. The alarming signs and symptoms seem to be everywhere — the killing of Vincent Chin in Detroit, the black boycott of a Korean grocery store in Flatbush, the hysteria in Boston over the Carol Stuart murder, the battle between white sportsmen and Indians over tribal fishing rights in Wisconsin, the Jewish-black clashes in Brooklyn's Crown Heights, the black-Hispanic competition for jobs and educational resources in Dallas, which *Newsweek* described as "a conflict of the have-nots," and the Willie Horton campaign commercials, which widened the divide between the suburbs and the inner cities.[6]

This reality of racial tension rudely woke America like a fire bell in the night on April 29, 1992. Immediately after four Los Angeles police officers were found not guilty of brutality against Rodney King, rage exploded in Los Angeles. Race relations reached a new nadir. During the nightmarish rampage, scores of people were killed, over two thousand injured, twelve thousand arrested, and almost a billion dollars' worth of property destroyed. The live televised images mesmerized America. The rioting and the murderous melee on the streets resembled the fighting in Beirut and the West Bank. The thousands of fires burning out of control and the dark smoke filling the skies brought back images of the burning oil fields of Kuwait during Desert Storm. Entire sections of Los Angeles looked like a bombed city. "Is this America?" many shocked viewers asked. "Please, can we get along here," pleaded Rodney

King, calling for calm. "We all can get along. I mean, we're all stuck here for a while. Let's try to work it out."[7]

But how should "we" be defined? Who are the people "stuck here" in America? One of the lessons of the Los Angeles explosion is the recognition of the fact that we are a multiracial society and that race can no longer be defined in the binary terms of white and black. "We" will have to include Hispanics and Asians. While blacks currently constitute 13 percent of the Los Angeles population, Hispanics represent 40 percent. The 1990 census revealed that South Central Los Angeles, which was predominantly black in 1965 when the Watts rebellion occurred, is now 45 percent Hispanic. A majority of the first 5,438 people arrested were Hispanic, while 37 percent were black. Of the fifty-eight people who died in the riot, more than a third were Hispanic, and about 40 percent of the businesses destroyed were Hispanic-owned. Most of the other shops and stores were Korean-owned. The dreams of many Korean immigrants went up in smoke during the riot: two thousand Korean-owned businesses were damaged or demolished, totaling about $400 million in losses. There is evidence indicating they were targeted. "After all," explained a black gang member, "we didn't burn our community, just *their* stores."[8]

"I don't feel like I'm in America anymore," said Denisse Bustamente as she watched the police protecting the firefighters. "I feel like I am far away." Indeed, Americans have been witnessing ethnic strife erupting around the world — the rise of neo-Nazism and the murder of Turks in Germany, the ugly "ethnic cleansing" in Bosnia, the terrible and bloody clashes between Muslims and Hindus in India. Is the situation here different, we have been nervously wondering, or do ethnic conflicts elsewhere represent a prologue for America? What is the nature of malevolence? Is there a deep, perhaps primordial, need for group identity rooted in hatred for the other? Is ethnic pluralism possible for America? But answers have been limited. Television reports have been little more than thirty-second sound bites. Newspaper articles have been mostly superficial descriptions of racial antagonisms and the current urban malaise. What is lacking is historical context; consequently, we are left feeling bewildered.[9]

How did we get to this point, Americans everywhere are anxiously asking. What does our diversity mean, and where is it leading us? *How* do we work it out in the post–Rodney King era?

Certainly one crucial way is for our society's various ethnic groups to develop a greater understanding of each other. For example, how can

African Americans and Korean Americans work it out unless they learn about each other's cultures, histories, and also economic situations? This need to share knowledge about our ethnic diversity has acquired new importance and has given new urgency to the pursuit for a more accurate history.

More than ever before, there is a growing realization that the established scholarship has tended to define America too narrowly. For example, in his prize-winning study *The Uprooted,* Harvard historian Oscar Handlin presented — to use the book's subtitle — "the Epic Story of the Great Migrations That Made the American People." But Handlin's "epic story" excluded the "uprooted" from Africa, Asia, and Latin America — the other "Great Migrations" that also helped to make "the American People." Similarly, in *The Age of Jackson,* Arthur M. Schlesinger, Jr., left out blacks and Indians. There is not even a mention of two marker events — the Nat Turner insurrection and Indian removal, which Andrew Jackson himself would have been surprised to find omitted from a history of his era.[10]

Still, Schlesinger and Handlin offered us a refreshing revisionism, paving the way for the study of common people rather than princes and presidents. They inspired the next generation of historians to examine groups such as the artisan laborers of Philadelphia and the Irish immigrants of Boston. "Once I thought to write a history of the immigrants in America," Handlin confided in his introduction to *The Uprooted.* "I discovered that the immigrants *were* American history." This door, once opened, led to the flowering of a more inclusive scholarship as we began to recognize that ethnic history was American history. Suddenly, there was a proliferation of seminal works such as Irving Howe's *World of Our Fathers: The Journey of the East European Jews to America,* Dee Brown's *Bury My Heart at Wounded Knee: An Indian History of the American West,* Albert Camarillo's *Chicanos in a Changing Society,* Lawrence Levine's *Black Culture and Black Consciousness,* Yuji Ichioka's *The Issei: The World of the First Generation Japanese Immigrants,* and Kerby Miller's *Emigrants and Exiles: Ireland and the Irish Exodus to North America.*[11]

But even this new scholarship, while it has given us a more expanded understanding of the mosaic called America, does not address our needs in the post–Rodney King era. These books and others like them fragment American society, studying each group separately, in isolation from the other groups and the whole. While scrutinizing our specific pieces, we have to step back in order to see the rich and complex portrait they compose. What is needed is a fresh angle, a study of the American past from a comparative perspective.

While all of America's many groups cannot be covered in one book, the English immigrants and their descendants require attention, for they possessed inordinate power to define American culture and make public policy. What men like John Winthrop, Thomas Jefferson, and Andrew Jackson thought as well as did mattered greatly to all of us and was consequential for everyone. A broad range of groups has been selected: African Americans, Asian Americans, Chicanos, Irish, Jews, and Indians. While together they help to explain general patterns in our society, each has contributed to the making of the United States.

African Americans have been the central minority throughout our country's history. They were initially brought here on a slave ship in 1619. Actually, these first twenty Africans might not have been slaves; rather, like most of the white laborers, they were probably indentured servants. The transformation of Africans into slaves is the story of the "hidden" origins of slavery. How and when was it decided to institute a system of bonded black labor? What happened, while freighted with racial significance, was actually conditioned by class conflicts within white society. Once established, the "peculiar institution" would have consequences for centuries to come. During the nineteenth century, the political storm over slavery almost destroyed the nation. Since the Civil War and emancipation, race has continued to be largely defined in relation to African Americans — segregation, civil rights, the underclass, and affirmative action. Constituting the largest minority group in our society, they have been at the cutting edge of the Civil Rights Movement. Indeed, their struggle has been a constant reminder of America's moral vision as a country committed to the principle of liberty. Martin Luther King clearly understood this truth when he wrote from a jail cell: "We will reach the goal of freedom in Birmingham and all over the nation, because the goal of America is freedom. Abused and scorned though we may be, our destiny is tied up with America's destiny."[12]

Asian Americans have been here for over one hundred and fifty years, before many European immigrant groups. But as "strangers" coming from a "different shore," they have been stereotyped as "heathen," exotic, and unassimilable. Seeking "Gold Mountain," the Chinese arrived first, and what happened to them influenced the reception of the Japanese, Koreans, Filipinos, and Asian Indians as well as the Southeast Asian refugees like the Vietnamese and the Hmong. The 1882 Chinese Exclusion Act was the first law that prohibited the entry of immigrants on the basis of nationality. The Chinese condemned this restriction as racist and tyrannical. "They call us 'Chink,' " complained a Chinese immigrant, cursing the "white demons." "They think we no good! America cuts us off. No more come now, too bad!" This precedent later provided a basis for the restriction of European immigrant groups such as Italians, Russians, Poles, and Greeks. The Japanese painfully discovered that their accomplishments in America did not lead to acceptance, for during World War II, unlike Italian Americans and German Americans, they were placed in internment camps. Two-thirds of them were citizens by birth. "How could I as a 6-month-old child born in this country," asked Congressman Robert Matsui years later, "be declared by my own Government to be an enemy alien?" Today, Asian Americans represent the fastest-growing ethnic group. They have also become the focus of much mass media attention as "the Model Minority" not only for blacks and Chicanos, but also for whites on welfare and even middle-class whites experiencing economic difficulties.[13]

Chicanos represent the largest group among the Hispanic population, which is projected to outnumber African Americans. They have been in the United States for a long time, initially incorporated by the war against Mexico. The treaty had moved the border between the two countries, and the people of "occupied" Mexico suddenly found themselves "foreigners" in their "native land." As historian Albert Camarillo pointed out, the Chicano past is an integral part of America's westward expansion, also known as "manifest destiny." But while the early Chicanos were a colonized people, most of them today have immigrant roots. Many began the trek to El Norte in the early twentieth century. "As I had heard a lot about the United States," Jesus Garza recalled, "it was my dream to come here." "We came to know families from Chihuahua, Sonora, Jalisco, and Durango," stated Ernesto Galarza. "Like ourselves, our Mexican neighbors had come this far moving step by step, working and waiting, as if they were feeling their way up a ladder." Nevertheless, the Chicano experience has been unique, for most of them have lived close to their homeland — a proximity that has helped reinforce their language, identity, and culture. This migration to El Norte has continued to the present. Los Angeles has more people of Mexican origin than any other city in the world, except Mexico City. A mostly mestizo people of Indian as well as African and Spanish ancestries, Chicanos currently represent the largest minority group in the Southwest, where they have been visibly transforming culture and society.[14]

The Irish came here in greater numbers than most immigrant groups. Their history has been tied to America's past from the very beginning.

Ireland represented the earliest English frontier: the conquest of Ireland occurred before the colonization of America, and the Irish were the first group that the English called "savages." In this context, the Irish past foreshadowed the Indian future. During the nineteenth century, the Irish, like the Chinese, were victims of British colonialism. While the Chinese fled from the ravages of the Opium Wars, the Irish were pushed from their homeland by "English tyranny." Here they became construction workers and factory operatives as well as the "maids" of America. Representing a Catholic group seeking to settle in a fiercely Protestant society, the Irish immigrants were targets of American nativist hostility. They were also what historian Lawrence J. McCaffrey called "the pioneers of the American urban ghetto," "previewing" experiences that would later be shared by the Italians, Poles, and other groups from southern and eastern Europe. Furthermore, they offer contrast to the immigrants from Asia. The Irish came about the same time as the Chinese, but they had a distinct advantage: the Naturalization Law of 1790 had reserved citizenship for "whites" only. Their compatible complexion allowed them to assimilate by blending into American society. In making their journey successfully into the mainstream, however, these immigrants from Erin pursued an Irish "ethnic" strategy: they promoted "Irish" solidarity in order to gain political power and also to dominate the skilled blue-collar occupations, often at the expense of the Chinese and blacks.[15]

Fleeing pogroms and religious persecution in Russia, the Jews were driven from what John Cuddihy described as the "Middle Ages into the Anglo-American world of the *goyim* 'beyond the pale.' " To them, America represented the Promised Land. This vision led Jews to struggle not only for themselves but also for other oppressed groups, especially blacks. After the 1917 East St. Louis race riot, the Yiddish *Forward* of New York compared this anti-black violence to a 1903 pogrom in Russia: "Kishinev and St. Louis — the same soil, the same people." Jews cheered when Jackie Robinson broke into the Brooklyn Dodgers in 1947. "He was adopted as the surrogate hero by many of us growing up at the time," recalled Jack Greenberg of the NAACP Legal Defense Fund. "He was the way we saw ourselves triumphing against the forces of bigotry and ignorance." Jews stood shoulder to shoulder with blacks in the Civil Rights Movement: two-thirds of the white volunteers who went south during the 1964 Freedom Summer were Jewish. Today Jews are considered a highly successful "ethnic" group. How did they make such great socioeconomic strides? This question is often reframed by neoconservative intellectuals like Irving Kristol and Nathan Glazer to read: if

Jewish immigrants were able to lift themselves from poverty into the mainstream through self-help and education without welfare and affirmative action, why can't blacks? But what this thinking overlooks is the unique history of Jewish immigrants, especially the initial advantages of many of them as literate and skilled. Moreover, it minimizes the virulence of racial prejudice rooted in American slavery.[16]

Indians represent a critical contrast, for theirs was not an immigrant experience. The Wampanoags were on the shore as the first English strangers arrived in what would be called "New England." The encounters between Indians and whites not only shaped the course of race relations, but also influenced the very culture and identity of the general society. The architect of Indian removal, President Andrew Jackson told Congress: "Our conduct toward these people is deeply interesting to the national character." Frederick Jackson Turner understood the meaning of this observation when he identified the frontier as our transforming crucible. At first, the European newcomers had to wear Indian moccasins and shout the war cry. "Little by little," as they subdued the wilderness, the pioneers became "a new product" that was "American." But Indians have had a different view of this entire process. "The white man," Luther Standing Bear of the Sioux explained, "does not understand the Indian for the reason that he does not understand America." Continuing to be "troubled with primitive fears," he has "in his consciousness the perils of this frontier continent. . . . The man from Europe is still a foreigner and an alien. And he still hates the man who questioned his path across the continent." Indians questioned what Jackson and Turner trumpeted as "progress." For them, the frontier had a different "significance": their history was how the West was lost. But their story has also been one of resistance. As Vine Deloria declared, "Custer died for your sins."[17]

By looking at these groups from a multicultural perspective, we can comparatively analyze their experiences in order to develop an understanding of their differences and similarities. Race, we will see, has been a social construction that has historically set apart racial minorities from European immigrant groups. Contrary to the notions of scholars like Nathan Glazer and Thomas Sowell, race in America has not been the same as ethnicity. A broad comparative focus also allows us to see how the varied experiences of different racial and ethnic groups occurred within shared contexts.

During the nineteenth century, for example, the Market Revolution employed Irish immigrant laborers in New England factories as it expanded cotton fields worked by enslaved blacks across Indian lands toward Mexico. Like blacks, the Irish newcomers were stereotyped as "savages," ruled by passions rather than "civilized" virtues such as self-control and hard work. The Irish saw themselves as the "slaves" of British oppressors, and during a visit to Ireland in the 1840s, Frederick Douglass found that the "wailing notes" of the Irish ballads reminded him of the "wild notes" of slave songs. The United States annexation of California, while incorporating Mexicans, led to trade with Asia and the migration of "strangers" from Pacific shores. In 1870, Chinese immigrant laborers were transported to Massachusetts as scabs to break an Irish immigrant strike; in response, the Irish recognized the need for interethnic working-class solidarity and tried to organize a Chinese lodge of the Knights of St. Crispin. After the Civil War, Mississippi planters recruited Chinese immigrants to discipline the newly freed blacks. During the debate over an immigration exclusion bill in 1882, a senator asked: If Indians could be located on reservations, why not the Chinese?[18]

Other instances of our connectedness abound. In 1903, Mexican and Japanese farm laborers went on strike together in California: their union officers had names like Yamaguchi and Lizarras, and strike meetings were conducted in Japanese and Spanish. The Mexican strikers declared that they were standing in solidarity with their "Japanese brothers" because the two groups had toiled together in the fields and were now fighting together for a fair wage. Speaking in impassioned Yiddish during the 1909 "uprising of twenty thousand" strikers in New York, the charismatic Clara Lemlich compared the abuse of Jewish female garment workers to the experience of blacks: "[The bosses] yell at the girls and 'call them down' even worse than I imagine the Negro slaves were in the South." During the 1920s, elite universities like Harvard worried about the increasing numbers of Jewish students, and new admissions criteria were instituted to curb their enrollment. Jewish students were scorned for their studiousness and criticized for their "clannishness." Recently, Asian-American students have been the targets of similar complaints: they have been called "nerds" and told there are "too many" of them on campus.[19]

Indians were already here, while blacks were forcibly transported to America, and Mexicans were initially enclosed by America's expanding border. The other groups came here as immigrants: for them, America represented liminality — a new world where they could pursue extravagant urges and do things they had thought beyond their capabilities. Like the land itself, they found themselves "betwixt and between all fixed points of classification." No longer fastened as fiercely to their old countries, they felt a stirring to become new people in a society still being defined and formed.[20]

These immigrants made bold and dangerous crossings, pushed by political events and economic hardships in their homelands and pulled by America's demand for labor as well as by their own dreams for a better life. "By all means let me go to America," a young man in Japan begged his parents. He had calculated that in one year as a laborer here he could save almost a thousand yen — an amount equal to the income of a governor in Japan. "My dear Father," wrote an immigrant Irish girl living in New York, "Any man or woman without a family are fools that would not venture and come to this plentyful Country where no man or woman ever hungered." In the shtetls of Russia, the cry "To America!" roared like "wild-fire." "America was in everybody's mouth," a Jewish immigrant recalled. "Businessmen talked [about] it over their accounts; the market women made up their quarrels that they might discuss it from stall to stall; people who had relatives in the famous land went around reading their letters." Similarly, for Mexican immigrants crossing the border in the early twentieth century, El Norte became the stuff of overblown hopes. "If only you could see how nice the United States is," they said, "that is why the Mexicans are crazy about it."[21]

The signs of America's ethnic diversity can be discerned across the continent — Ellis Island, Angel Island, Chinatown, Harlem, South Boston, the Lower East Side, places with Spanish names like Los Angeles and San Antonio or Indian names like Massachusetts and Iowa. Much of what is familiar in America's cultural landscape actually has ethnic origins. The Bing cherry was developed by an early Chinese immigrant named Ah Bing. American Indians were cultivating corn, tomatoes, and tobacco long before the arrival of Columbus. The term *okay* was derived from the Choctaw word *oke*, meaning "it is so." There is evidence indicating that the name *Yankee* came from Indian terms for the English — from *eankke* in Cherokee and *Yankwis* in Delaware. Jazz and blues as well as rock and roll have African-American origins. The "Forty-Niners" of the Gold Rush learned mining techniques from the Mexicans; American cowboys acquired herding skills from Mexican *vaqueros* and adopted their range terms — such as *lariat* from *la reata, lasso* from *lazo,* and *stampede* from *estampida.* Songs like "God Bless America," "Easter Parade," and "White Christmas" were written by a Russian-Jewish immigrant named Israel Baline, more popularly known as Irving Berlin.[22]

Furthermore, many diverse ethnic groups have contributed to the building of the American economy, forming what Walt Whitman saluted as "a vast, surging, hopeful army of workers." They worked in the South's cotton fields, New England's textile mills, Hawaii's canefields,

New York's garment factories, California's orchards, Washington's salmon canneries, and Arizona's copper mines. They built the railroad, the great symbol of America's industrial triumph. Laying railroad ties, black laborers sang:

> Down the railroad, um-huh
> Well, raise the iron, um-huh
> Raise the iron, um-huh.

Irish railroad workers shouted as they stretched an iron ribbon across the continent:

> Then drill, my Paddies, drill —
> Drill, my heroes, drill,
> Drill all day, no sugar in your tay
> Workin' on the U.P. railway.

Japanese laborers in the Northwest chorused as their bodies fought the fickle weather:

> A railroad worker —
> That's me!
> I am great.
> Yes, I am a railroad worker.
> Complaining:
> "It is too hot!"
> "It is too cold!"
> "It rains too often!"
> "It snows too much!"
> They all ran off.
> I alone remained.
> I am a railroad worker!

Chicano workers in the Southwest joined in as they swore at the punishing work:

> Some unloaded rails
> Others unloaded ties,
> And others of my companions
> Threw out thousands of curses.[23]

Moreover, our diversity was tied to America's most serious crisis: the Civil War was fought over a racial issue — slavery. In his "First Inaugural Address," presented on March 4, 1861, President Abraham Lincoln declared: "One section of our country believes slavery is *right* and ought to be extended, while the other believes it is *wrong* and ought not to be extended." Southern secession, he argued, would be anarchy. Lincoln sternly warned the South that he had a solemn oath to defend and preserve the Union. Americans were one people, he explained, bound together by "the mystic chords of memory, stretching from every battlefield and patriot grave to every living heart and hearthstone all over this broad land." The struggle and sacrifices of the War for Independence had enabled Americans to create a new nation out of thirteen separate colonies. But Lincoln's appeal for unity fell on deaf ears in the South. And the war came. Two and a half years later, at Gettysburg, President Lincoln declared that "brave men" had fought and "consecrated" the ground of this battlefield in order to preserve the Union. Among the brave were black men. Shortly after this bloody battle, Lincoln acknowledged the military contributions of blacks. "There will be some black men," he wrote in a letter to an old friend, James C. Conkling, "who can remember that with silent tongue, and clenched teeth, and steady eye, and well-poised bayonet, they have helped mankind on to this great consummation. . . ." Indeed, 186,000 blacks served in the Union Army, and one-third of them were listed as missing or dead. Black men in blue, Frederick Douglass pointed out, were "on the battlefield mingling their blood with that of white men in one common effort to save the country." Now the mystic chords of memory stretched across the new battlefields of the Civil War, and black soldiers were buried in "patriot graves." They, too, had given their lives to ensure that the "government of the people, by the people, for the people shall not perish from the earth."[24]

Like these black soldiers, the people in our study have been actors in history, not merely victims of discrimination and exploitation. They are entitled to be viewed as subjects — as men and women with minds, wills, and voices.

> *In the telling and retelling*
> *of their stories,*
> *They create communities*
> *of memory.*

They also re-vision history. "It is very natural that the history written by the victim," said a Mexican in 1874, "does not altogether chime with

14

the story of the victor." Sometimes they are hesitant to speak, thinking they are only "little people." "I don't know why anybody wants to hear my history," an Irish maid said apologetically in 1900. "Nothing ever happened to me worth the tellin'."[25]

But their stories are worthy. Through their stories, the people who have lived America's history can help all of us, including my taxi driver, understand that Americans originated from many shores, and that all of us are entitled to dignity. "I hope this survey do a lot of good for Chinese people," an immigrant told an interviewer from Stanford University in the 1920s. "Make American people realize that Chinese people are humans. I think very few American people really know anything about Chinese." But the remembering is also for the sake of the children. "This story is dedicated to the descendants of Lazar and Goldie Glauberman," Jewish immigrant Minnie Miller wrote in her autobiography. "My history is bound up in their history and the generations that follow should know where they came from to know better who they are." Similarly, Tomo Shoji, an elderly Nisei woman, urged Asian Americans to learn more about their roots: "We got such good, fantastic stories to tell. All our stories are different." Seeking to know how they fit into America, many young people have become listeners; they are eager to learn about the hardships and humiliations experienced by their parents and grandparents. They want to hear their stories, unwilling to remain ignorant or ashamed of their identity and past.[26]

The telling of stories liberates. By writing about the people on Mango Street, Sandra Cisneros explained, "the ghost does not ache so much." The place no longer holds her with "both arms. She sets me free." Indeed, stories may not be as innocent or simple as they seem to be. Native-American novelist Leslie Marmon Silko cautioned:

> *I will tell you something about stories . . .*
> *They aren't just entertainment.*
> *Don't be fooled.*

Indeed, the accounts given by the people in this study vibrantly re-create moments, capturing the complexities of human emotions and thoughts. They also provide the authenticity of experience. After she escaped from slavery, Harriet Jacobs wrote in her autobiography: "[My purpose] is not to tell you what I have heard but what I have seen — and what I have suffered." In their sharing of memory, the people in this study offer us an opportunity to see ourselves reflected in a mirror called history.[27]

In his recent study of Spain and the New World, *The Buried Mirror,*

Carlos Fuentes points out that mirrors have been found in the tombs of ancient Mexico, placed there to guide the dead through the underworld. He also tells us about the legend of Quetzalcoatl, the Plumed Serpent: when this god was given a mirror by the Toltec deity Tezcatlipoca, he saw a man's face in the mirror and realized his own humanity. For us, the "mirror" of history can guide the living and also help us recognize who we have been and hence are. In *A Distant Mirror*, Barbara W. Tuchman finds "phenomenal parallels" between the "calamitous 14th century" of European society and our own era. We can, she observes, have "greater fellow-feeling for a distraught age" as we painfully recognize the "similar disarray," "collapsing assumptions," and "unusual discomfort."[28]

But what is needed in our own perplexing times is not so much a "distant" mirror, as one that is "different." While the study of the past can provide collective self-knowledge, it often reflects the scholar's particular perspective or view of the world. What happens when historians leave out many of America's peoples? What happens, to borrow the words of Adrienne Rich, "when someone with the authority of a teacher" describes our society, and "you are not in it"? Such an experience can be disorienting — "a moment of psychic disequilibrium, as if you looked into a mirror and saw nothing."[29]

Through their narratives about their lives and circumstances, the people of America's diverse groups are able to see themselves and each other in our common past. They celebrate what Ishmael Reed has described as a society "unique" in the world because "the world is here" — a place "where the cultures of the world crisscross." Much of America's past, they point out, has been riddled with racism. At the same time, these people offer hope, affirming the struggle for equality as a central theme in our country's history. At its conception, our nation was dedicated to the proposition of equality. What has given concreteness to this powerful national principle has been our coming together in the creation of a new society. "Stuck here" together, workers of different backgrounds have attempted to get along with each other.

> *People harvesting*
> *Work together unaware*
> *Of racial problems,*

wrote a Japanese immigrant describing a lesson learned by Mexican and Asian farm laborers in California.[30]

Finally, how do we see our prospects for "working out" America's racial crisis? Do we see it as through a glass darkly? Do the televised images of racial hatred and violence that riveted us in 1992 during the days of rage in Los Angeles frame a future of divisive race relations — what Arthur Schlesinger, Jr., has fearfully denounced as the "disuniting of America"? Or will Americans of diverse races and ethnicities be able to connect themselves to a larger narrative? Whatever happens, we can be certain that much of our society's future will be influenced by which "mirror" we choose to see ourselves. America does not belong to one race or one group, the people in this study remind us, and Americans have been constantly redefining their national identity from the moment of first contact on the Virginia shore. By sharing their stories, they invite us to see ourselves in a different mirror.[31]

PART ONE

Boundlessness

Before Columbus: Vinland

FROM THE SHORE, the small band of Indians saw the floating island pulled by billowy clouds and the landing of the strangers. Never before had they seen such people. The newcomers looked like animals — monstrous, hairy, and pale skinned, their eyes the color of the sea and their hair the color of the sun. In their hands, they carried shiny sharp sticks that looked like long vicious claws. Their foreign speech sounded like gabble. Confused and frightened, the Indians quickly hid beneath their skin-covered boats, hoping to appear like three mounds on the beach. They could hear footsteps approaching; suddenly their boats were violently overturned. All but one of them were captured. Paddling away frantically, the lone survivor looked back and saw red stains darkening the beach.[1]

Led by Thorvald Eiriksson, son of Eirik the Red, the Vikings had sailed from Greenland to the New World. He had been told about this land by his brother, Leif, who had sailed south from Iceland about the year 1000 and reached a place he called "Vinland," an old Norse term for grassland or pasture. In the wonderful country to the south, Thorvald had learned, the grass tasted "sweet" and the rivers teemed with salmon. "This is a beautiful place," Thorvald exclaimed when he first saw what is now known as Newfoundland. "I should like to build myself a home here." After their initial encounter with the Indians on the beach, Thorvald and his men pitched camp and went to sleep. Suddenly, they were attacked by Indians armed with bows and arrows; Thorvald was wounded. "You must carry me out to the headland where I thought it would be good to live," the dying leader told his men. "You must bury me there, and put a cross at my head and another one at my feet, and from then on you must call the place Krossanes [Cross Head]."[2]

Shortly afterward, another group of Vikings sailed to Vinland. Among them were Thorfinn Karlsefni and his wife, Gudrid. They found a land of great abundance: "Every stream was full of fish. They dug holes where sea and land met at high tide, and when the sea went down again, there was halibut lying in the holes. There were plenty of animals of all kinds in the forest." Then one day, the colonists were approached by some Indians. "Dark, ugly fellows, with ugly hair on their heads" with "large eyes and broad faces," the "Skraelings" came out of the forest and were frightened by the bellowing of the cattle. "They ran towards Karlsefni's farm and wanted to get into the houses; but Karlsefni had the doors bolted. Neither of the two groups understood the other's language. Then the Skraelings took their packs off and undid their bundles, and offered goods for sale; they wanted weapons more than anything else in exchange. But Karlsefni refused to sell any weapons." Instead, he offered them some cheese for pelts. Karlsefni "caught" two Skraeling boys, "taught them to speak the language, and had them christened."[3]

The next year, the Indians returned to the site, rowing around the headland from the south. "There were so many of them that it looked as if charcoal had been strewn on the water." They wanted to trade for red cloth and swords. Suddenly, one of the Indians was killed as he tried to steal some weapons. During the fierce battle, the Vikings retreated up the riverbank, where they successfully resisted the Indian attacks. "Now it's hard to know what to do," Karlsefni said, "because I think they will come back a third time, and then they will come as enemies and there will be very many of them." The following spring, Karlsefni and his fellow colonists abandoned their plans to settle the country and returned to Greenland. They realized that "although this was a good country, there would always be terror and trouble from the people who lived there."[4]

And so this first European settlement in the New World came to an end and remained virtually unknown to the Western world. The Norse people on Greenland had been cut off from their homeland, and when a Norwegian missionary arrived there in 1721, he found only the ruins of farms and churches. Only the Viking sagas, handed down orally and recorded in the fourteenth and fifteenth centuries, preserved the story of the first encounter. This Viking contact remained unacknowledged until 1960 when, on the northern point of Newfoundland at L'Anse aux Meadows, archaeologists found a group of overgrown housesites with ancient Norse tools and artifacts dated by carbon 14 analysis at about A.D. 1000.

About five hundred years after Leif Eiriksson's voyage to Vinland, Christopher Columbus made his crossing and changed the course of history. Unlike the Viking expeditions, his project was sponsored by the king and queen of Spain and was the focus of immense and wide interest throughout Europe. Moreover, the printing press was now available to spread the exciting news of Columbus's amazing "discovery." At first the admiral thought he had reached Asia. After he sighted land on October 21, 1492, the explorer wrote in his journal: "I am determined to go to the mainland and to the city of *Quisay* [Hangchow] and to present Your Highnesses' letters to the Grand Khan." Two days later, he recorded: "I wish to depart today for the island of Cuba, which I believe should be *Cipango* [Japan], according to the description that this people give me of its size and wealth. . . ." But soon he was astonished to realize that he had encountered a new land between Europe and Asia. This most momentous accident of history opened the way to efforts by Spain, Portugal, France, Holland, and England to colonize the continents that would be named the Americas. Unlike the Vikings, however, the new strangers stayed.[5]

2

THE "TEMPEST" IN THE
WILDERNESS

The Racialization of Savagery

I N THEIR FIRST encounters with Europeans, the Indians tried to
relate the strangers to what was familiar in their world. Traditional
Penobscot accounts had described the earth as flat and surrounded
by ocean, the "great salt water," *ktci-sobe-k*. Beyond this body of water,
there were other islands and countries inhabited by "tribes of strangers."
The Indians of Massachusetts Bay, according to early reports by the
English, "took the first ship they saw for a walking island, the mast to
be a tree, the sail white clouds, and the discharging of ordnance for
lightning and thunder. . . ." They were seized by curiosity. By word of
mouth, the fantastic news spread, and the "shores for many miles were
filled with this naked Nation, gazing at this wonder." Armed with bows
and arrows, some of them approached the ship in their canoes, and "let
fly their long shafts at her . . . some stuck fast, and others dropped into
the water." They wondered why "it did not cry." The native people were
struck by the "ugliness" and "deformity" of the strangers — their
"white" complexions, hair around their mouths, the eyes with "the color
of the blue sky." They tried to identify the visitors. According to Roger
Williams, the Indians in Rhode Island used the term *Manittoo*, meaning
"god," to describe excellence in human beings and animals. When they

saw the English arriving on their ships, they exclaimed: "*Mannittowock.*
They are Gods."[1]

Indian dreams had anticipated the coming of the strangers. In New
England, an old Wampanoag story told about a wise chief foretelling
the arrival of Europeans: "On his death-bed he said that a strange white
people would come to crowd out the red men, and that for a sign, after
his death a great white whale would rise out of the witch pond below.
That night he died . . . and the great white whale rose from the witch
pond." Another version of this story recounted how the old man was
describing his approaching death when suddenly "a white whale arose
from the water off Witch Pond." The chief said: "That's a sign that
another new people the color of the whale [would arrive], but don't let
them have all the land because if you do the Indians will disappear." In
Virginia, a Powhatan shaman predicted that "bearded men should come
& take away their Country & that there should be none of the original
Indians be left, within an hundred & fifty years." Similarly, an Ojibwa
prophet had a dream many years before actual contact between the two
peoples: "Men of strange appearance have come across the great water.
Their skins are white like snow, and on their faces long hair grows.
[They came here] in wonderfully large canoes which have great white
wings like those of a giant bird. The men have long and sharp knives,
and they have long black tubes which they point at birds and animals.
The tubes make a smoke that rises into the air just like the smoke from
our pipes. From them come fire and such terrific noise that I was frightened, even in my dream."[2]

Shakespeare's Dream about America

"O brave new world that has such people in't!" they heard Miranda
exclaim. The theatergoers were attending the first performance of William Shakespeare's *Tempest*. This play was first presented in London in
1611, a time when the English were encountering what they viewed as
strange inhabitants in new lands. The circumstances surrounding the
play determined the meaning of the utterances they heard. A perspica-
cious few in the audience could have seen that this play was more than
a mere story about how Prospero was sent into exile with his daughter,
took possession of an island inhabited by Caliban, and redeemed himself
by marrying Miranda to the king's son.[3]

Indeed, *The Tempest* can be approached as a fascinating tale that
served as a masquerade for the creation of a new society in America.

Seen in this light, the play invites us to view English expansion not only as imperialism, but also as a defining moment in the making of an English-American identity based on race. For the first time in the English theater, an Indian character was being presented. What did Shakespeare and his audience know about the native peoples of America, and what choices were they making in the ways they characterized Caliban? Although they saw him as "savage," did they racialize savagery? Was the play a prologue for America?

The Tempest, studied in relationship to its historical context, can help us answer these questions. While *Othello* also offers us an opportunity to analyze English racial attitudes, as Winthrop Jordan has demonstrated so brilliantly, our play is a more important window for understanding American history, for its story is set in the New World. Moreover, the timing of *The Tempest* was crucial: it was first performed after the English invasion of Ireland but before the colonization of New England, after John Smith's arrival in Virginia but before the beginning of the tobacco economy, and after the first contacts with Indians but before full-scale warfare against them. This was an era when the English were encountering "other" peoples and delineating the boundary between "civilization" and "savagery." The social constructions of both these terms were dynamically developing in three sites — Ireland, Virginia, and New England.[4]

One of the places the English were colonizing at the time was Ireland, and Caliban seemed to resemble the Irish. Theatergoers were familiar with the "wild Irish" onstage, for such images had been presented in plays like *Sir John Oldcastle* (1599) and *Honest Whore* (1605). Seeking to conquer the Irish in 1395, Richard II had condemned them as "savage Irish, our enemies." In the mid-sixteenth century, shortly before the beginning of the English migrations to America, the government had decided to bring all of Ireland under its rule and encouraged private colonization projects.[5]

Like Caliban, the Irish were viewed as "savages," a people living outside of "civilization." They had tribal organizations, and their practice of herding seemed nomadic. Even their Christianity was said to be merely the exterior of strongly rooted paganism. "They are all Papists by their profession," claimed Edmund Spenser in 1596, "but in the same so blindly and brutishly informed for the most part as that you would rather think them atheists or infidels." To the colonists, the Irish lacked "knowledge of God or good manners." They had no sense of private property and did not "plant any Gardens or Orchards, Inclose or improve their lands, live together in setled Villages or Townes." The Irish were described as lazy, "naturally" given to "idleness" and unwilling to work for "their own bread." Dominated by "innate sloth," "loose, barbarous and most wicked," and living "like beasts," they were also thought to be criminals, an underclass inclined to steal from the English. The colonists complained that the Irish savages were not satisfied with the "fruit of the natural unlaboured earth" and therefore continually "invaded the fertile possessions" of the "English Pale."[6]

The English colonizers established a two-tiered social structure: "Every Irishman shall be forbidden to wear English apparel or weapon upon pain of death. That no Irishman, born of Irish race and brought up Irish, shall purchase land, bear office, be chosen of any jury or admitted witness in any real or personal action." To reinforce this social separation, British laws prohibited marriages between the Irish and the colonizers. The new world order was to be one of English over Irish.[7]

The Irish also became targets of English violence. "Nothing but fear and force can teach duty and obedience" to this "rebellious people," the invaders insisted. While the English were generally brutal in their warfare practices at that time, they seemed to have been particularly cruel toward the Irish. The colonizers burned the villages and crops of the inhabitants and relocated them on reservations. They slaughtered families, "man, woman and child," justifying their atrocities by arguing that families provided support for the rebels. After four years of bloody warfare in Munster, according to Edmund Spenser, the Irish had been reduced to wretchedness. "Out of every corner of the woods and glens they came creeping forth upon their hands, for their legs would not bear them. They looked anatomies of death; they spake like ghosts crying out of their graves." The death toll was so high that "in short space there were none almost left and a most populous and plentiful country suddenly left void of man and beast." The "void" meant vacant lands for English resettlement.[8]

The invaders took the heads of the slain Irish as trophies. Sir Humphrey Gilbert pursued a campaign of terror: he ordered that "the heads of all those . . . killed in the day, should be cut off from their bodies and brought to the place where he encamped at night, and should there be laid on the ground by each side of the way leading into his own tent so that none could come into his tent for any cause but commonly he must pass through a lane of heads. . . . [It brought] great terror to the people when they saw the heads of their dead fathers, brothers, children, kinsfolk, and friends. . . ." After seeing the head of his lord impaled on the walls of Dublin, Irish poet Angus O'Daly cried out:

O body which I see without a head,
It is the sight of thee which has withered up my
strength.
Divided and impaled in Ath-cliath,
The learned of Banba will feel its loss.
Who will relieve the wants of the poor?
Who will bestow cattle on the learned?
O body, since thou art without a head,
It is not life which we care to choose after thee.[9]

The English claimed that they had a God-given responsibility to "inhabit and reform so barbarous a nation" and to educate the Irish "brutes." They would teach them to obey English laws and stop "robbing and stealing and killing" one another. They would uplift this "most filthy people, utterly enveloped in vices, most untutored of all peoples in the rudiments of faith." Thus, although they saw the Irish as savages and although they sometimes described this savagery as "natural" and "innate," the English believed that the Irish could be civilized, improved through what Shakespeare called "nurture." In short, the difference between the Irish and the English was a matter of culture.[10]

As their frontier advanced from Ireland to America, the English began making comparisons between the Irish and Indian "savages" and wondering whether there might be different kinds of "savagery."

The parallels between English expansionism in Ireland and America were apparent. Sir Humphrey Gilbert, Lord De La Warr, Sir Francis Drake, and Sir Walter Raleigh participated in both the invasion of Ireland and the colonization of the New World. The conquest of Ireland and the settlement of Virginia were bound so closely together that one correspondence, dated March 8, 1610, stated: "It is hoped the plantation of Ireland may shortly be settled. The Lord Delaware [Lord De La Warr] is preparing to depart for the plantation of Virginia." Commander John Mason conducted military campaigns against the Irish before he sailed to New England, where he led troops against the Pequots of Connecticut. Samuel Gorton wrote a letter to John Winthrop, Jr., connecting the two frontiers: "I remember the time of the wars in Ireland (when I was young, in Queen Elizabeth's days of famous memory) where much English blood was spilt by a people much like unto these [Indians]. . . . And after these Irish were subdued by force, what treacherous and bloody massacres have they attempted is well known."[11]

The first English colonizers in the New World found that the Indians reminded them of the Irish. In Virginia, Captain John Smith observed that the deerskin robes worn by the Indians did not differ much "in fashion from the Irish mantels." Thomas Morton noticed that the "Natives of New England [were] accustomed to build themselves houses much like the wild Irish." Roger Williams reported that the thick woods and swamps of New England gave refuge to the Indians engaged in warfare, "like the bogs to the wild Irish." Thus, in their early encounters, the English projected the familiar onto the strange, their images of the Irish onto the native people of America. Initially, "savagery" was defined in relationship to the Irish, and the Indians were incorporated into this definition.[12]

The Tempest, the London audience knew, was not about Ireland but about the New World, for the reference to the "Bermoothes" (Bermuda) revealed the location of the island. What was happening onstage was a metaphor for English expansion into America. The play's title was inspired by a recent incident: caught in a violent storm in 1609, the Sea Adventure had been separated from a fleet of ships bound for Virginia and had run aground in the Bermudas. Shakespeare knew many of the colonizers, including Sir Humphrey Gilbert and Lord De La Warr. One of his personal friends was geographer Richard Hakluyt, author of widely read books about the New World. The future of Englishmen lay in America, proclaimed Hakluyt, as he urged them to "conquer a country" and "to man it, to plant it, and to keep it, and to continue the making of Wines and Oils able to serve England."[13]

The scene of the play was actually the mainland near the "Bermoothes" — Virginia. "The air breathes upon us here most sweetly," the theatergoers were told. "Here is everything advantageous to life." "How lush and lusty the grass looks! how green!" Impressed by the land's innocence, Gonzalo of The Tempest depicted it as an ideal commonwealth where everything was as yet unformed and unbounded, where letters, laws, metals, and occupations were yet unknown. Both the imagery and the language revealed America as the site of Prospero's landing: it was almost as if Shakespeare had lifted the material from contemporary documents about the New World. Tracts on Virginia had described the air as "most sweet" and as "virgin and temperate," and it soil "lusty" with meadows "full of green grass." In A True Reportory of the Wracke, published in 1609, William Strachey depicted Virginia's abundance: "no Country yieldeth goodlier Corn, nor more manifold increase. . . . [W]e have thousands of goodly Vines." Here was an opportunity for colonists to enhance the "fertility and pleasure" of Virginia by "cleansing away her woods" and converting her into "goodly meadow."[14]

Moreover, the play provided a clever clue that the story was indeed about America: Caliban, one of the principal characters, was a New World inhabitant. "Carib," the name of an Indian tribe, came to mean a savage of America, and the term *cannibal* was a derivative. Shakespeare sometimes rearranged letters in words ("Amleth," the name of a prince in a Viking era tale, for example, became "Hamlet"), and here he had created another anagram in "Caliban."[15]

The English had seen or read reports about Indians who had been captured and brought to London. Indians had been displayed in Europe by Christopher Columbus. During his first voyage, he wrote: "Yesterday came [to] the ship a dugout with six young men, and five came on board; these I ordered to be detained and I am bringing them." When Columbus was received by the Spanish court after his triumphal return, he presented a collection of things he had brought back, including some gold nuggets, parrots in cages, and six Indians. During his second voyage in 1493, Columbus again sent his men to kidnap Indians. On one occasion, a captive had been "wounded seven times and his entrails were hanging out," reported Guillermo Coma of Aragon. "Since it was thought that he could not be cured, he was cast into the sea. But keeping above water and raising one foot, he held on to his intestines with his left hand and swam courageously to the shore. . . . The wounded Carib was caught again on shore. His hands and feet were bound more tightly and he was once again thrown headlong. But this resolute savage swam more furiously, until he was struck several times by arrows and perished." When Columbus set sail with his fleet to return to Spain, he took 550 Indian captives. "When we reached the waters around Spain," Michele de Cuneo wrote matter-of-factly, "about 200 of those Indians died, I believe because of the unaccustomed air, colder than theirs. We cast them into the sea."[16]

Similarly, English explorers engaged in this practice of kidnapping Indians. When Captain George Waymouth visited New England in 1605, he lured some Abenakis to his ship; taking three of them hostage, he sailed back to England to display them. An early seventeenth-century pamphlet stated that a voyage to Virginia was expected to bring back its quota of captured Indians: "Thus we shipped five savages, two canoes, with all their bows and arrows." In 1614, the men on one of Captain John Smith's ships captured several Indians on Cape Cod. "Thomas Hunt," Smith wrote, ". . . betrayed four and twenty of these poor savages aboard this ship, and most dishonestly and inhumanely . . . carried them with him to Maligo [Málaga] and there for a little private gain sold . . . those savages for Rials of eight." In 1611, according to a biographer of William Shakespeare, "a native of New England called Epnew was brought to England . . . and 'being a man of so great a stature' was showed up and down London for money as a monster." In the play, Stephano considered capturing Caliban: "If I can recover him, and keep him tame, and get to Naples with him, he's a present for any emperor. . . ." Such exhibitions of Indians were "profitable investments," literary scholar Frank Kermode noted, and were "a regular feature of colonial policy under James I. The exhibits rarely survived the experience."[17]

To the spectators of these "exhibits," Indians personified "savagery." They were depicted as "cruel, barbarous and most treacherous." They were thought to be cannibals, "being most furious in their rage and merciless . . . not being content only to kill and take away life, but delight to torment men in the most bloody manner . . . flaying some alive with the shells of fishes, cutting off the members and joints of others by piecemeal and broiling on the coals, eating the collops of their flesh in their sight whilst they live." According to Sir Walter Raleigh, Indians had "their eyes in their shoulders, and their mouths in the middle of their breasts." In *Nova Brittania*, published in 1609, Richard Johnson described the Indians in Virginia as "wild and savage people," living "like herds of deer in a forest." One of their striking physical characteristics was their skin color. John Brereton described the New England Indians as "of tall stature, broad and grim visage, of a blacke swart complexion."[18]

Indians seemed to lack everything the English identified as civilized — Christianity, cities, letters, clothing, and swords. "They do not bear arms or know them, for I showed to them swords and they took them by the blade and cut themselves through ignorance," wrote Columbus in his journal, noting that the Indians did not have iron. George Waymouth tried to impress the Abenakis: he magnetized a sword "to cause them to imagine some great power in us; and for that to love and fear us."[19]

Like Caliban, the native people of America were viewed as the "other." European culture was delineating the border, the hierarchical division between civilization and wildness. Unlike Europeans, Indians were allegedly dominated by their passions, especially their sexuality. Amerigo Vespucci was struck by how the natives embraced and enjoyed the pleasures of their bodies: "They . . . are libidinous beyond measure, and the women far more than the men. . . . When they had the opportunity of copulating with Christians, urged by excessive lust, they defiled and prostituted themselves." Caliban personified such passions. Prospero saw him as a sexual threat to the nubile Miranda, her "virgin-knot" yet untied. "I have used thee (filth as thou art) with humane care," Prospero scolded Caliban, "and lodged thee in mine own cell till thou didst seek to violate the honor of my child." And the unruly native snapped: "O ho, O ho! Would't had been done! Thou didst prevent me; I had peopled else this isle with Calibans."[20]

To the theatergoers, Caliban represented what Europeans had been when they were lower on the scale of development. To be civilized, they believed, required denial of wholeness — the repression of the instinctual forces of human nature. A personification of civilized man, Prospero identified himself as mind rather than body. His epistemology was reliant on the visual rather than the tactile and on the linear knowledge of books rather than the polymorphous knowledge of experience. With the self fragmented, Prospero was able to split off his rationality and raise it to authority over the "other" — the sensuous part of himself and everything Caliban represented.

But could Caliban, the audience wondered, ever become Christian and civilized? The Spanish lawyer Juan Gines de Sepulveda had justified the Spanish conquest of Indians by invoking Aristotle's doctrine that some people were "natural slaves." The condition of slavery, Sepulveda argued, was natural for "persons of both inborn rudeness and of inhuman and barbarous customs." Thus what counted was an ascriptive quality based on a group's nature, or "descent."[21]

On the other hand, Pope Paul III had proclaimed that Indians, as well as "all other people" who might later be "discovered" by "Christians," should not be deprived of their liberty and property, even though they were outside the Christian faith. Christopher Columbus had reported that Indians were "very gentle and without knowledge of . . . evil." He added: "They love their neighbors as themselves, and have the sweetest talk in the world, and gentle, and always with a smile." In *The Tempest*, Gonzalo told theatergoers: "I saw such islanders . . . who, though they are of monstrous shape, yet, note, their manners are more gentle, kind, than of our human generation you shall find many — nay, almost any." Thus, Indians were not always viewed as brutish by nature: they could be acculturated, become civilized through "consent."[22]

Indeed, Caliban seemed educable. Prospero had taught him a European language: "I . . . took pains to make thee speak, taught thee each hour one thing or other. When thou didst not, savage, know thine own meaning, but wouldst gabble like a thing most brutish." Defiantly, the native retorted: "You taught me language, and my profit on't is, I know how to curse. The red plague rid you for learning me your language." Clearly, Caliban was no mere victim: capable of acculturation, he could express his anger. A Virginia tract stated that the colonists should take Indian children and "train them up with gentleness, teach them our English tongue." In the contract establishing the Virginia Company in 1606, the king endorsed a plan to propagate the "Christian Religion to such people" who as yet lived in "darkness and miserable ignorance of the true knowledge and worship of God." Three years later, the Virginia Company instructed the colony's governor to encourage missionaries to convert Indian children. They should be taken from their parents if necessary, since they were "so wrapped up in the fog and misery of their iniquity." A Virginia promotional tract stated that it was "not the nature of men, but the education of men" that made them "barbarous and uncivil." Every man in the new colony had a duty to bring the savage Indians to "civil and Christian" government.[23]

All of these cultural constructs of Indians at this point in time were either the fantasy of Shakespeare or the impressions of policymakers and tract writers in London. What would happen to these images on the stage of history?

The first English settlement in the New World was in Virginia, the home of fourteen thousand Powhatans. An agricultural people, they cultivated corn — the mainstay of their subsistence. Their cleared fields were as large as one hundred acres, and they lived in palisaded towns, with forts, storehouses, temples, and framed houses covered with bark and reed mats. They cooked their food in ceramic pots and used woven baskets for storing corn: some of their baskets were constructed so skillfully they could carry water in them. The Powhatans had a sophisticated numbering system for evaluating their harvests. According to John Smith, they had numbers from one to ten, after which counting was done by tens to one hundred. There was also a word for "one thousand." The Powhatan calendar had five seasons: "Their winter some call *Popanow*, the spring *Cattaapeuk*, the sommer *Cohattayough*, the earing of their Corne *Nepinough*, the harvest and fall of the leafe *Taquitock*. From September until the midst of November are the chief Feasts and sacrifice."[24]

In Virginia, the initial encounters between the English and the Indians opened possibilities for friendship and interdependency. After arriving in 1607, the first one hundred and twenty colonists set up camp. Then, John Smith reported, came "the starving time." A year later, only thirty-eight of them were still alive, hanging precariously on the very edge of survival. The reality of America did not match the imagery of the New World as a garden; the descriptions of its natural abundance turned out to be exaggerated. Many of the English were not prepared for survival in the wilderness. "Now was all our provision spent . . . all help abandoned, each hour expecting the fury of the savages," Smith wrote. Fortunately, in that "desperate extremity," the Powhatans brought food and rescued the starving strangers.[25]

A year later, several hundred more colonists arrived, and again they quickly ran out of provisions. They were forced to eat "dogs, cats, rats, and mice," even "corpses" dug from graves. "Some have licked up the blood which hath fallen from their weak fellows," a survivor reported. "One [member] of our colony murdered his wife, ripped the child out of her womb and threw it into the river, and after chopped the mother in pieces and salted her for his food, the same not being discovered before he had eaten part thereof." "So great was our famine," John Smith stated, "that a savage we slew and buried, the poorer sort took him up again and ate him; and so did diverse one another boiled and stewed with roots and herbs."[26]

Hostilities soon broke out as the English tried to extort food supplies by attacking the Indians and destroying their villages. In 1608, an Indian declared: "*We hear you are come from under the World to take our World from us.*" A year later, Governor Thomas Gates arrived in Virginia with instructions that the Indians should be forced to labor for the colonists and also make annual payments of corn and skins. The orders were brutally carried out. During one of the raids, the English soldiers attacked an Indian town, killing fifteen people and forcing many others to flee. Then they burned the houses and destroyed the cornfields. According to a report by commander George Percy, they marched the captured queen and her children to the river where they "put the Children to death . . . by throwing them overboard and shooting out their brains in the water."[27]

Indians began to doubt that the two peoples could live together in peace. One young Indian told Captain John Smith: "[We] are here to intreat and desire your friendship and to enjoy our houses and plant our fields, of whose fruits you shall participate." But he did not trust the strangers: "We perceive and well know you intend to destroy us." Chief Powhatan had come to the same conclusion, and he told Smith that the English were not in Virginia to trade but to "invade" and "possess" Indian lands.[28]

Indeed, Smith and his fellow colonists were encouraged by their culture of expansionism to claim entitlement to the land. In *The Tempest*, the theatergoers were told: "I think he will carry this island home in his pocket and give it his son for an apple." Prospero declared that he had been thrust forth from Milan and "most strangely" landed on this shore "to be the lord on't." Projecting his personal plans and dreams onto the wilderness, he colonized the island and dispossessed Caliban. Feeling robbed, Caliban protested: "As I told thee before, I am subject to a tyrant, a sorcerer, that by his cunning hath cheated me of the island." But the English did not see their taking of land as robbery. In *Utopia*, Sir Thomas More justified the appropriation of Indian lands: since the natives did not "use" the soil but left it "idle and waste," the English had "just cause" to drive them from the territory by force. In 1609, Robert Gray declared that "the greater part" of the earth was "possessed and wrongfully usurped by wild beasts . . . or by brutish savages." A Virginia pamphlet argued that it was "not unlawful" for the English to possess "part" of the Indians' land.[29]

But the English soon wanted more than just a "part" of Indian territory. Their need for land was suddenly intensified by a new development — the cultivation of tobacco as an export crop. In 1613, the colony sent its first shipment of tobacco to London, a small but significant four barrels' worth. The exports grew dramatically from 2,300 pounds in 1616 to 19,000 the following year, and to 60,000 by 1620. The colonists increasingly coveted Indian lands, especially the already cleared fields. Tobacco agriculture stimulated not only territorial expansion but also immigration. During the "Great Migration" of 1618–1623, the colony grew from four hundred to forty-five hundred people.

In 1622, the natives tried to drive out the intruders, killing some three hundred colonists. John Smith denounced the "massacre" and described the "savages" as "cruel beasts," who possessed "a more unnatural brutishness" than wild animals. The English deaths, Samuel Purchas argued, established the colonists' right to the land: "Their carcasses, the dispersed bones of their countrymen . . . speak, proclaim and cry, This our earth is truly English, and therefore this Land is justly yours O English." Their blood had watered the soil, entitling them to the land. "We, who hitherto have had possession of no more ground than their [Indian] waste, and our purchase . . . may now by right of War, and law of Nations," the colonists declared, "invade the Country, and destroy them who sought to destroy us." They felt they could morally sweep away their enemies and even take their developed lands. "*We shall enjoy their cultivated places. . . . Now their cleared grounds in all their villages (which are situated in the fruitfulest places of the land) shall be inhabited by us.*"[30]

In their fierce counterattack, the English waged total war. "Victory may be gained in many ways," a colonist declared: "by force, by surprise, by famine in burning their Corn, by destroying and burning their Boats, Canoes, and Houses . . . by pursuing and chasing them with our horses, and blood-hounds to draw after them, and mastives to tear them." In 1623, Captain William Tucker led his soldiers to a Powhatan village, presumably to negotiate a peace treaty. After he concluded the treaty, he persuaded the Indians to drink a toast, but he served them poisoned wine. An estimated two hundred Indians died instantly, and Tucker's soldiers then killed another fifty and "brought home part of their heads." In 1629, a colonist reported, the English forced a hostile Indian leader to seek peace by "continual incursions" and by "yearly cutting down, and spoiling their corn." The goal of the war was to "root out [the Indians] from being any longer a people."[31]

What happened in Virginia, while terrible and brutal, was still based largely on the view that Indian "savagery" was cultural. Like the Irish, Indians were identified as brutal and backward, but they were not yet seen as incapable of becoming civilized because of their race, or "descent." Their heathenism had not yet been indelibly attached to distinctive physical characteristics such as their skin color. So far at least, "consent" was possible for Indians. What occurred in New England was a different story, however, and here again, the play was preview.[32]

Although the theatergoers were given the impression that Caliban could be acculturated, they also received a diametrically opposite construction of his racial character. They were told that Caliban was "a devil, a born devil" and that he belonged to a "vile race." "Descent" was determinative: his "race" signified an inherent moral defect. On the stage, they saw Caliban, with long shaggy hair, personifying the Indian. He had distinct racial markers. "Freckled," covered with brown spots, he was "not honored with human shape." Called a "fish," he was mockingly told: "Thy eyes are almost set in thy head." "Where should they be set else? He were a brave monster indeed if they were set in his tail." More important, his distinctive physical characteristics signified intellectual incapacity. Caliban was "a thing of darkness" whose "nature nurture [could] never stick." In other words, he had natural qualities that precluded the possibility of becoming civilized through "nurture," or education. The racial distance between Caliban and Prospero was inscribed geographically. The native was forced to live on a reservation located in a barren region. "Here you sty [to lodge, to place in a pig pen or sty] me in this hard rock," he complained, "whiles you do keep from me the rest o' the island." Prospero justified this segregation, charging that the "savage" possessed distasteful qualities, "which good natures could not abide to be with. Therefore wast thou deservedly confined into this rock, who hadst deserved more than a prison." The theatergoers saw Caliban's "sty" located emblematically at the back of the stage, behind Prospero's "study," signifying a hierarchy of white over dark and cerebral over carnal.[33]

This deterministic view of Caliban's racial character would be forged in the crucible of New England. Five years after the first performance of *The Tempest*, Captain John Smith sailed north from Virginia to explore the New England coast, where again he found not wild men but farmers. The "paradise" of Massachusetts, he reported, was "all planted with corn, groves, mulberries, savage gardens." "The sea Coast as you pass shews you all along large Corne fields." Indeed, while the Abenakis of Maine were mainly hunters and food gatherers dependent on the natural abundance of the land, the tribes in southern New England were horticultural. For example, the Wampanoags, whom the Pilgrims encountered in 1620, were a farming people, with a representative political system as well as a division of labor, with workers specializing in arrowmaking, woodwork, and leathercrafts.[34]

The Wampanoags as well as the Pequots, Massachusets, Nausets, Nipmucks, and Narragansets cultivated corn. As the main source of life for these tribes, corn was the focus of many legends. A Narraganset belief told how a crow had brought this grain to New England: "These Birds, although they do the corn also some hurt, yet scarce one *Native* amongst a hundred will kill them, because they have a tradition, that the Crow brought them at first an *Indian* Grain of Corn in one Ear, and an *Indian* or French bean in another, from the Great God *Kautantouwits* field in the Southwest from whence . . . came all their Corn and Beans." A Penobscot account celebrated the gift of Corn Mother: during a time of famine, an Indian woman fell in love with a snake in the forest. Her secret was discovered one day by her husband, and she told him that she had been chosen to save the tribe. She instructed him to kill her with a stone ax and then drag her body through a clearing. "After seven days he went to the clearing and found the corn plant rising above the ground. . . . When the corn had born fruit and the silk of the corn ear had turned yellow he recognized in it the resemblance of his dead wife. Thus originated the cultivation of corn."[35]

These Indians had a highly developed agricultural system. Samuel de Champlain found that "all along the shore" there was "a great deal of land cleared up and planted with Indian corn." Describing their agricultural practices, he wrote: "They put in each hill three or four Brazilian beans [kidney beans]. . . . When they grow up, they interlace with the corn . . . and they keep the ground very free from weeds. We saw there many squashes, and pumkins, and tobacco, which they likewise cultivate." According to Thomas Morton, Indians "dung[ed] their ground" with fish to fertilize the soil and increase the harvest. After visiting the Narragansets in Rhode Island, John Winthrop, Jr., noted that although the soil in that region was "sandy & rocky," the people were able to raise "good corn without fish" by rotating their crops. "They have every one 2 fields," he observed, "which after the first 2 years they let one field rest each year, & that keeps their ground continually [productive]." According to Roger Williams, when the Indians were ready to harvest the corn, "all the neighbours men and women, forty, fifty, a hundred," joined in the work and came "to help freely." During their green corn festival, the Narragansets erected a long house, "sometimes a hundred, sometimes two hundred feet long upon a plain near the Court . . . where many thousands, men and women," gathered. Inside, dancers gave money, coats, and knives to the poor. After the harvest, the Indians stored their corn for the winter. "In the sand on the slope of hills," according to Champlain, "they dig holes, some five or six feet, more or less, and place their corn and other grains in large grass sacks, which they throw into the said holes, and cover them with sand to a depth of three or four feet above the surface of the ground. They take away their grain according to their need, and it is preserved as well as it be in our granaries." Contrary to the stereotype of Indians as hunters and therefore savages, these Indians were farmers.[36]

However, many colonists in New England disregarded this reality and invented their own representations of Indians. What emerged to justify dispossessing them was the racialization of Indian "savagery." Indian heathenism and alleged laziness came to be viewed as inborn group traits that rendered them naturally incapable of civilization. This process of Indian dehumanization developed a peculiarly New England dimension as the colonists associated Indians with the Devil. Indian identity became a matter of "descent": their racial markers indicated inerasable qualities of savagery.

This social construction of race occurred within the economic context of competition over land. The colonists argued that entitlement to land required its utilization. Native men, they claimed, pursued "no kind of labour but hunting, fishing and fowling." Indians were not producers. "The *Indians* are not able to make use of the one fourth part of the Land," argued Reverend Francis Higginson in 1630, "neither have they any settled places, as Towns to dwell in, nor any ground as they challenge for their owne possession, but change their habitation from place to place." In the Puritan view, Indians were lazy. "Fettered in the chains of idleness," they would rather starve than work, William Wood of Boston complained in 1634. Indians were sinfully squandering America's resources. Under their irresponsible guardianship, the land had become "all spoils, rots," and was "marred for want of manuring, gathering, ordering, etc." Like the "foxes and wild beasts," Indians did nothing "but run over the grass."³⁷

The Puritan possession of Indian lands was facilitated by the invasion of unseen pathogens. When the colonists began arriving in New England, they found that the Indian population was already being reduced by European diseases. Two significant events had occurred in the early seventeenth century: infected rats swam to shore from Samuel de Champlain's ships, and some sick French sailors were shipwrecked on the beaches of New England. By 1616, epidemics were ravaging Indian villages. Victims of "virgin soil epidemics," the Indians lacked immunological defenses against the newly introduced diseases. Between 1610 and 1675, the Indian population declined sharply — from 12,000 to a mere 3,000 for the Abenakis and from 65,000 to 10,000 for the southern New England tribes.³⁸

Describing the sweep of deadly diseases among the Indians, William Bradford reported that the Indians living near the trading house outside of Plymouth "fell sick of the smallpox, and died most miserably." The condition of those still alive was "lamentable." Their bodies were covered with "the pox breaking and mattering and running one into another, their skin cleaving" to the mats beneath them. When they turned their bodies, they found "whole sides" of their skin flaying off. In this terrible way, they died "like rotten sheep." After one epidemic, William Bradford recorded in his diary: "For it pleased God to visit these Indians with a great sickness and such a mortality that of a thousand, above nine and a half hundred of them died, and many of them did rot above ground for want of burial."³⁹

The colonists interpreted these Indian deaths as divinely sanctioned opportunities to take the land. John Winthrop declared that the decimation of Indians by smallpox manifested a Puritan destiny: God was "making room" for the colonists and "hath hereby cleared our title to this place." After an epidemic had swept through Indian villages, John Cotton claimed that the destruction was a sign from God: when the Lord decided to transplant His people, He made the country vacant for them to settle. Edward Johnson pointed out that epidemics had desolated "those places, where the English afterward planted."[40]

Indeed, many New England towns were founded on the very lands the Indians had been living on before the epidemics. The Plymouth colony itself was located on the site of the Wampanoag village of Paw-tuxet. The Pilgrims had noticed the village was empty and the cornfields overgrown with weeds. "There is a great deal of Land cleared," one of them reported, "and hath beene planted with Corne three or foure yeares agoe." The original inhabitants had been decimated by the epidemic of 1616. "Thousands of men have lived there, which died in a great plague not long since," another Pilgrim wrote; "and pity it was and is to see so many goodly fields, and so well seated, without men to dress and manure the same." During their first spring, the Pilgrims went out into those fields to weed and manure them. Fortunately, they had some corn seed to plant. Earlier, when they landed on Cape Cod, they had come across some Indian graves and found caches of corn. They considered this find, wrote Bradford, as "a special providence of God, and a great mercy to this poor people, that here they got seed to plant them corn the next year, or else they might have starved." The survival of these pallid strangers was so precarious that they probably would have perished had it not been for the seeds they found stored in the Indian burial grounds. Ironically, Indian death came to mean life for the Pilgrims.[41]

However, the Puritans did not see it as irony but as the destruction of devils. They had demonized the native peoples, condemning Indian religious beliefs as "diabolical, and so uncouth, as if . . . framed and devised by the devil himself." The Wampanoags of Martha's Vineyard, wrote Reverend Thomas Mayhew in 1652, were "mighty zealous and earnest in the Worship of False gods and Devils." They were under the influence of "a multitude of Heathen Traditions of their gods . . . and abounding with sins."[42]

To the colonists, the Indians were not merely a wayward people: they personified something fearful within Puritan society itself. Like Caliban, a "born devil," Indians failed to control their appetites, to create boundaries separating mind from body. They represented what English men and women in America thought they were not — and, more important, what they must not become. As exiles living in the wilderness far from "civilization," the English used their negative images of Indians to delineate the moral requirements they had set up for themselves. As sociologist Kai Erikson explained, "deviant forms of behavior, by marking the outer edges of group life, give the inner structure its special character and thus supply the framework within which the people of the group develop an orderly sense of their own cultural identity. . . . One of the surest ways to confirm an identity, for communities as well as for individuals, is to find some way of measuring what one is *not*." By depicting Indians as demonic and savage, the colonists, like Prospero, were able to define more precisely what they perceived as the danger of becoming Calibanized.[43]

The Indians presented a frightening threat to the Puritan errand in America. "The wilderness through which we are passing to the Promised Land is all over fill'd with fiery flying serpents," warned Reverend Cotton Mather. "Our Indian wars are not over yet." The wars were now within Puritan society and the self: the dangers were internal. Self-vigilance against sin was required, or else the English would become like Indians. "We have too far degenerated into Indian vices. The vices of the Indians are these: They are very lying wretches, and they are very lazy wretches; and they are out of measure indulgent unto their children; there is no family government among them. We have [become] shamefully Indianized in all those abominable things."[44]

To be "Indianized" meant to serve the Devil. Cotton Mather thought this was what had happened to Mercy Short, a young girl who had been a captive of the Indians and who was suffering from tormenting fits. According to Mather, Short had seen the Devil. "Hee was not of a Negro, but of a Tawney, or an Indian colour," she said; "he wore an high-crowned Hat, with straight Hair; and had one Cloven-foot." During a witchcraft trial, Mather reported, George Burroughs had lifted an extremely heavy object with the help of the Devil, who resembled an Indian. Puritan authorities hanged an English woman for worshiping Indian "gods" and for taking the Indian devil-god Hobbamock for a husband. Significantly, the Devil was portrayed as dark complected and Indian.[45]

For the Puritans, to become Indian was the ultimate horror, for they believed Indians were "in very great subjection" of the Devil, who "kept them in a continual slavish fear of him." Governor Bradford harshly condemned Thomas Morton and his fellow prodigals of the Merrymount settlement for their promiscuous partying with Indians: "They also set up a maypole, drinking and dancing about it many days together, inviting the Indian women for their consorts, dancing and frisking together like so many fairies." Interracial cavorting threatened to fracture a cultural and moral border — the frontier of Puritan identity. Congress of bodies, white and "tawney," signified defilement, a frightful boundlessness. If the Puritans were to become wayward like the Indians, it would mean that they had succumbed to savagery and failed to shrivel the sensuous parts of the self. To be "Indianized" meant to be decivilized, to become wild men.[46]

But they could not allow this to happen, for they were embarking on an errand to transform the wilderness into civilization. "The whole earth is the Lord's garden and he hath given it to the sons of men [to] increase and multiply and replentish the earth and subdue it," asserted John Winthrop in 1629 as he prepared to sail for New England. "Why then should we stand starving here for the places of habitation . . . and in the meantime suffer a whole Continent as fruitful and convenient for the use of man to lie waste without any improvement."[47]

Actually, Indians had been farming the land, and this reality led to conflicts over resources. Within ten years after the arrival of Winthrop's group, twenty thousand more colonists came to New England. This growing English population had to be squeezed into a limited area of arable land. Less than 20 percent of the region was useful for agriculture, and the Indians had already established themselves on the prime lands. Consequently, the colonists often settled on or directly next to Indian communities. In the Connecticut Valley, for example, they erected towns like Springfield (1636), Northampton (1654), Hadley (1661), Deerfield (1673), and Northfield (1673) adjacent to Indian agricultural clearings at Agawam, Norwottuck, Pocumtuck, and Squakheag.[48]

Over the years, the expansion of English settlement sometimes led to wars that literally made the land "vacant." During the Pequot War of 1637, some seven hundred Pequots were killed by the colonists and their Indian allies. Describing the massacre at Fort Mystic, an English officer wrote: "Many were burnt in the fort, both men, women, and children. . . . There were about four hundred souls in this fort, and not above five of them escaped out of our hands. Great and doleful was the bloody sight." Commander John Mason explained that God had pushed the Pequots into a "fiery oven," "filling the place with dead bodies." By explaining their atrocities as divinely driven, the English were sharply inscribing the Indians as a race of devils. This was what happened during King Philip's War of 1675–76. While one thousand English were killed during this conflict, over six thousand Indians died from combat and disease. Altogether, about half of the total Indian population was destroyed in southern New England. Again, the colonists quickly justified their violence by demonizing their enemies. The Indians, Increase Mather observed, were "so *Devil driven* as to begin an unjust and bloody war upon the English, which issued in their speedy and utter extirpation from the face of God's earth." Cotton Mather explained that the war was a conflict between the Devil and God: "The Devil decoyed those miserable savages [to New England] in hopes that the Gospel of the Lord Jesus Christ would never come here to destroy or disturb His *absolute empire* over them."[49]

Indians, "such people" of this "brave new world," to use Shakespeare's words, personified the Devil and everything the Puritans feared — the body, sexuality, laziness, sin, and the loss of self-control. They had no place in a "new England." This was the view trumpeted by Edward Johnson in his *Wonder-working Providence*. Where there had originally been "hideous Thickets" for wolves and bears, he proudly exclaimed in 1654, there were now streets "full of Girls and Boys sporting up and down, with a continued concourse of people." Initially, the colonists themselves had lived in "wigwams" like Indians, but now they had "orderly, fair, and well-built houses . . . together with Orchards filled with goodly fruit trees, and gardens with variety of flowers." The settlers had fought against the Devil, who had inhabited the bodies of the Indians, Johnson observed, and made it impossible for the soldiers to pierce them with their swords. But the English had violently triumphed. They had also expanded the market, making New England a center of production and trade. The settlers had turned "this Wilderness" into "a mart." Merchants from Holland, France, Spain, and Portugal were coming here. "Thus," proclaimed Johnson, "hath the Lord been pleased to turn one of the most hideous, boundless, and unknown Wildernesses in the world in an instant . . . to a well-ordered Commonwealth."[50]

But, in a sense, all of these developments had already been acted out in *The Tempest*. Like Prospero, the English colonists had sailed to a new land, and many of them also felt they were exiles. They viewed the native peoples as savages, as Calibans. The strangers occupied the land, believing they were entitled to be "the lord on't."[51]

Still, in Shakespeare's fantasy, race as a social construction had not yet been firmly formed, and Caliban's qualities as "other" not yet definitely fixed by race. What happened in history, however, was a different story.

The English possessed tremendous power to define the places and peoples they were conquering. As they made their way westward, they developed an ideology of "savagery," which was given form and content by the political and economic circumstances of the specific sites of colonization. Initially, in Ireland, the English had viewed savagery as something cultural, or a matter of "consent": they assumed that the distance between themselves and the Irish, or between civilization and savagery, was quantitative rather than qualitative. The Irish as "other" was educable: they were capable of acquiring the traits of civilization. But later, as colonization reached across the Atlantic and as the English encountered a new group of people, many of them believed that savagery for the Indians might be inherent. Perhaps the Indians might be different from the English in kind rather than degree; if so, then the native people of America would be incapable of improvement because of their race. To use Shakespeare's language, they might have a "nature" that "nurture" would never be able to "stick" to or change. Race or "descent" might be destiny.[52]

What happened in America in the actual encounters between the Indians and the English strangers was not uniform. In Virginia, Indian savagery was viewed largely as cultural: Indians were ignorant heathens. In New England, on the other hand, Indian savagery was racialized: Indians had come to be condemned as a demonic race, their dark complexions signifying an indelible and inherent evil. Why was there such a difference between the two regions? Possibly the competition between the English and the Indians over resources was more intense in New England than in Virginia, where there was more arable land. More important, the colonists in New England had brought with them a greater sense of religious mission than the Virginia settlers. For the Puritans, theirs was an "errand into the wilderness" — a mission to create what John Winthrop had proclaimed as "a city upon a hill" with the eyes of the world upon them. Within this economic and cultural framework, a "discovery" occurred: the Indian "other" became a manifest devil. Thus savagery was racialized as the Indians were demonized, doomed to what Increase Mather called "utter extirpation." Once the process of this cultural construction was under way, it set a course for the making of a national identity in America for centuries to come.[53]

A World Turned Upside Down

Indians viewed these developments very differently. One of their legends told about a creature named Ki-wa-kwe-skwe, "woman wandering in

44

the woods." She was a cannibal, and a boy whom she called her brother lived with her. She always kept her back turned toward him to hide her face. She also taught him to hunt rabbits and offered him frequent meals in order to fatten him. Once a rabbit came to the boy and said: "You have already killed a great many of us. That is enough; don't hunt us too persistently or you will exterminate us. Henceforth do not obey that woman who is ordering you. She is not your sister. On the contrary, she is a bad magician who is only lying to you and just fattening you up until you are prime, when she will kill and eat you. For her food is human beings." That night the boy pretended to fall asleep, and he had a chance to see the woman's face, her true cannibalistic self. The next morning he ran away, with the evil spirit woman in pursuit. A heron and a porcupine tried to protect the boy and killed the woman repeatedly, but she kept returning to life. Finally, an old man came to his rescue and ordered his dog to tear the evil woman to shreds. The old man then took the boy to the village where his father and mother lived. "And when the people saw that the boy who had been stolen was still alive, lo, there was great rejoicing and feasting." What happened in history, however, had a much different ending.[54]

Like the rabbit of this story, a Narraganset leader tried to warn his fellow Indians about the English invaders. "You know our fathers had plenty of deer and skins, our plains were full of deer, as also our woods, and of turkeys, and our coves full of fish and fowl," Miantonomo told the Montauks of Long Island in 1642. "But these English having gotten our land, they with scythes cut down the grass, and with axes fell the trees; their cows and horses eat the grass, and their hogs spoil our clam banks, and we shall all be starved." Miantonomo called for pan-Indian unity to resist the strangers: "For so are we all Indians as the English are, and say brother to one another; so must we be one as they are, otherwise we shall all be gone shortly." They should attack the colonists, and "kill men, women and children, but no cows." They should raise the cattle for food "till our deer be increased again."[55]

In 1735, twenty-seven Pequots complained to the governor of Connecticut that the English settlers had encroached on their lands, planting wheat fields and allowing their cattle to roam into Indian cornfields. The Pequots protested: "We see plainly that their chiefest desire is to deprive us of the privilege of our land, and drive us off to our utter ruin." The native people of America were finding that the white strangers from across the ocean were threatening their way of life. In a 1789 petition to the Assembly of Connecticut, the Mohegans lamented that "the times" had been "Exceedingly alter'd":

Yea the Times have turn'd everything Upside down, or rather we have Chang'd the good Times, Chiefly by the help of the White People. For in Times past our Fore-Fathers live in Peace, Love and great harmony, and had everything in Great plenty. When they Wanted meat they would just run into the Bush a little ways with their Weapons and would Soon bring home good venison, Racoon, Bear and Fowl. If they Choose to have Fish, they Wo'd only go to the River or along the Sea Shore and they wou'd presently fill their Cannous With Veriety of Fish, both Scaled and shell Fish, and they had abundance of Nuts, Wild Fruit, Ground Nuts and Ground Beans, and they planted but little Corn and Beans and they kept no Cattle or Horses for they needed none — And they had no Contention about their Lands, it lay in Common to them all, and they had but one large Dish and they Cou'd all eat together in Peace and Love — But alas, it is not so now, all our Fishing, Hunting and Fowling is entirely gone, And we have now begun to Work on our Land, keep Cattle, Horses and Hogs And We Build Houses and fence in Lots, And now we plainly See that one Dish and one Fire will not do any longer for us — Some few there are Stronger than others and they will keep off the poor, weak, the halt and the Blind, And Will take the Dish to themselves. Yea, they will rather Call White People and Molattoes to eat With them out of our Dish, and poor Widows and Orphans Must be pushed one side and there they Must Set a Crying, Starving and die.[56]

Aware of these changing times, Delaware leader Neolin warned Indians in the 1760s that they must either return to their original state before the arrival of white people or face slow extinction at the hands of the settlers.

What is to be done, and what remedy is to be applied? I will tell you, my friends. Hear what the Great Spirit has ordered me to tell you! You are to make sacrifices, in the manner that I shall direct; to put off entirely from yourselves the customs which you have adopted since the white people came among us; you are to return to that former happy state, in which we live in peace and plenty, before these strangers came to disturb us, and above all, you must abstain from drinking their deadly beson [liquor] which they have forced upon us for the sake of increasing their gains and diminishing our numbers. . . . Wherefore do you suffer the whites to dwell upon your lands? Drive them away; wage war against them.[57]

But by the 1760s, the strangers and their descendants had established colonies and had also begun a movement that would lead to the creation of a new nation. An emerging question was: What would be the Indians' future in the republic? One of the Founding Fathers who addressed this issue was a young lawyer and planter who would later become president of the United States. In 1781, as governor of Virginia, Thomas Jefferson declared to the Kaskaskias that whites and Indians were both "Americans, born in the same land," and that he hoped the two peoples would "long continue to smoke in friendship together." At the same time, Jefferson advocated the removal and even the destruction of hostile Indians. "Nothing will reduce those wretches so soon as pushing the war into the heart of their country," he wrote to a colleague in 1776. "But I would not stop there. I would never cease pursuing them while one of them remained on this side [of] the Mississippi. . . . We would never cease pursuing them with war while one remained on the face of the earth." In his view, Indians were to be civilized or exterminated.[58]

To civilize Indians meant, for Jefferson, to take them from their hunting way of life and convert them into farmers. President Jefferson explained to the Shawnees why they had no choice but to accept civilization: "When the white people first came to this land, they were few, and you were many; now we are many, and you few; and why? because, by cultivating the earth, we produce plenty to raise our children, while yours . . . suffer for want of food . . . are exposed to weather in your hunting camps, get diseases and die. Hence it is that your numbers lessen." They were, in other words, victims of their own culture, not the decimation of their game to satisfy the voracious fur trade, the introduction of unfamiliar diseases, the appropriation of their lands, and the brutal warfare waged against them.[59]

In blaming the Indians for their own decline, Jefferson insisted that the transfer of Indian lands to whites had been done fairly and legally. "That the lands of this country were taken from them by conquest," he argued in *Notes on the State of Virginia*, "is not so general a truth as is supposed. I find in our historians and records, repeated proofs of purchase. . . ." If Jefferson's denial of guilt contained a quality of defensiveness, there was a reason for it. In the original manuscript, he had written and then crossed out: "It is true that these purchases were sometimes made with the price in one hand and the sword in the other."[60]

In order to survive, Jefferson declared, Indians must adopt the culture of the white man. They must no longer live so boundlessly; instead, they must enclose farms as private property and learn arithmetic so they would be able to keep accounts of their production. "My children," Jefferson told the Cherokees, "I shall rejoice to see the day when the red man, our neighbors, become truly one people with us, enjoying all the rights and privileges we do, and living in peace and plenty as we do. . . . But are you prepared for this? Have you the resolution to leave off hunting for your living, to lay off a farm for each family to itself, to live by industry, the men working that farm with their hands . . . ?" "Indians must learn how," Jefferson explained, "a little land, well cultivated, was superior in value to a great deal, unimproved." He offered a grisly analogy to illustrate his point: "The wisdom of the animal which amputates and abandons to the hunter the parts for which he is pursued should be theirs, with this difference, that the former sacrifices what is useful, the latter what is not." Possibly Jefferson did not fully realize the implications of this metaphor. Likened to "animals," Indians could survive by "amputating" their lands and leaving them behind for whites, the "hunters."[61]

Jefferson, however, was actually more concerned about white expansion than Indian survival. Civilizing the Indians was a strategy designed to acquire land for white settlement. As president, he assured the Indians that whites would respect their territorial possessions. "We take from no nation what belongs to it," he told them. "Our growing numbers make us always willing to buy lands from our red brethren, when they are willing to sell." He elaborated: "Your lands are your own; your right to them shall never be violated by us; they are yours to keep or to sell as you please. . . . When a want of land in a particular place induces us to ask you to sell, still you are always free to say 'No'. . . ."[62]

However, while he offered these assurances, Jefferson worked to create conditions that would make Indians "willing to sell." In an 1803 "Confidential Message" to Congress, he explained how this could be done. First, encourage them to abandon hunting and turn to agriculture. "The extensive forests necessary in the hunting life will then become useless." Second, sell more manufactured goods to Indians by multiplying the trading houses and bring them into the market. This policy, Jefferson predicted, would lead the Indians to transfer their lands to whites. On February 27, 1803, in an "unofficial and private" letter to Indiana governor William Henry Harrison, Jefferson recommended: "To promote this disposition to exchange lands, which they have to spare and we want, we shall push our trading houses, and be glad to see the good and influential individuals among them run in debt, because we observe that when these debts get beyond what the individuals can pay, they become willing to lop them off by a cession of lands." To destroy Indians financially, Jefferson favored federal over private trading houses. While private business had to make profits, government enterprise could sell goods to Indians at prices "so low as merely to repay us cost and charges." By this process, he continued, white settlements would gradually "circumscribe" the Indians, and in time they would either "incorporate" with whites as "citizens" or retreat westward beyond civilization.[63]

All Indians, regardless of whether they were farmers or hunters, were subject to removal, even extermination, if they continued in their "barbarism." Should any tribe be foolhardy enough to take up the hatchet against the United States, the president wrote Governor Harrison, the federal government should seize the whole country of that tribe and drive them across the Mississippi as the only condition of peace. During a conflict between the United States and England in 1809, President Jefferson warned his Indian "children": "If you love the land in which you were born, if you wish to inhabit the earth which covers the bones of your fathers, take no part in the war between the English and us. . . . [T]he tribe which shall begin an unprovoked war against us, we will extirpate from the earth, or drive to such a distance as they shall never again be able to strike us."[64]

But Jefferson's feelings toward Indians were complex. In a letter to John Adams, he described childhood memories of Indian chiefs visiting his home. "They were in the habit of coming often. . . . I knew much the great Outasette, the warrior and orator of the Cherokees. He was always the guest of my father, on his journeys to and from Williamsburg. I was in camp when he made his great farewell oration to his people, the evening before his departure for England. . . . His sounding voice, distinct articulation, animated action, and the solemn silence of his people at their several fires, filled me with awe and veneration, altho' I did not understand a word he uttered." Jefferson explained to Adams that these early "impressions" had created "attachment and commiseration" for the Indians which had "never been obliterated."[65]

Jefferson's hope was to save the Indians. In this letter to Adams, he noted how the Cherokees had "enclosed fields" as well as livestock and had chosen to advance themselves "in civilization." But any Indians who rejected assimilation would face a different future. "These will relapse into barbarism and misery, lose numbers by war and want, and we shall be obliged to drive them, with the beasts of the forest into the Stony mountains." Ultimately, for Jefferson, Indians as Indians would not be allowed to remain within the borders of civilized society. A century or so earlier, Puritans had celebrated the disappearance of wolves and bears in "new" England; now Jefferson and men like him were clearing more wilderness for a new nation. The very transformation of the land emblematized progress, the distance whites in America had come from the time when barbarism had been dominant:

> Let a philosophic observer commence a journey from the savages of the Rocky Mountains, eastwardly towards our sea-coast. There he would observe in the earliest stage of association living under no law but that of nature, subsisting and covering themselves with flesh and skins of wild beasts. He would next find those on our frontiers in the pastoral state, raising domestic animals to supply the defects of hunting. Then succeed our own semi-barbarous citizens, the pioneers of the advance of civilization, and so in progress he would meet the gradual shades of improving man until he would reach his, as yet, most improved state in our seaport towns. This, in fact, is equivalent to a survey, in time, of the progress of man from infancy to the present day.[66]

Here was a vision of progress — a Jeffersonian version of John Winthrop's "city upon a hill" and Edward Johnson's New England of the "wonder-working Providence." The land was not to be allowed to "lie waste without any improvement," the early forefathers had commanded, and now the republican "errand into the wilderness" was requiring the citizens of the new nation to subdue the land and advance their frontier westward. Such a view carried dire consequences for the Calibans of America called Indians. Jefferson, like Prospero before him, saw the triumph over the continent and the Indians as the movement from "savagery" to "civilization."

3

THE "GIDDY MULTITUDE"

The Hidden Origins of Slavery

BUT CALIBAN COULD have been African. As they watched *The Tempest* in London, the theatergoers were aware of this possibility. Some might have seen Africans in England. In 1554, according to trader William Towrson, five "Negroes" were transported to England where they were "kept till they could speak the language," and then they were taken back to Africa as translators for English traders. Two decades later, in 1578, voyager George Best stated: "I myself have seen an Ethiopian as black as coal brought into England, who taking a faire English woman to wife, begat a son in all respects as black as the father was. . . ." Best speculated about the cause of the African's skin color: "It seemeth this blackness proceedeth rather of some natural infection of that man, which was so strong that neither the nature of the Clime, neither the good complexion of the mother concurring, could anything alter. . . ."[1]

"Freckled," dark in complexion, a "thing of darkness," Caliban was a "bastard": his father was a demon and his mother was Sycorax, a witch who had lived in Africa. As historian Winthrop Jordan noted, what struck the English most about Africans was their color. "These people are all blacke, and are called Negros, without any apparell, saving before their privities," wrote an English traveler during his visit to Cape Verde in the 1560s. In the English mind, the color black was freighted with an array of negative images: "deeply stained with dirt," "foul," "dark or deadly" in purpose, "malignant," "sinister," "wicked." The color white, on the other hand, signified purity, innocence, and goodness.[2]

To the English, Caliban seemed to personify what they considered African traits. "Brutish," he belonged to a "vile race"; he was sexually interested in Miranda, threatening to people the isle with little Calibans. In travel reports, the theatergoers could read about Africans as "a people of beastly living, without a God, law, religion." Their color allegedly made them "Devils incarnate." The Devil had "infused prodigious Idolatry into their hearts, enough to rellish his pallat and aggrandize their tortures" when he was ready to "fry their souls, as the raging Sun had already scorched their coal-black carcasses." Africans were also said to be cannibals: they allegedly ate human beings as the English would eat "befe or mutton."[3]

Described as a "monster," Caliban appeared onstage at a time when the English were reading about associations between apes and Africans. In his *Historie of Foure-Footed Beastes,* published in 1608, Edward Topsell reported that apes could be found in "all that desert Woods betwixt *Egypt, Æthiopia* and *Lybia,*" and offered the following comparison: the men with their "low and flat nostrils" were "Libidinous as Apes," and their thick lips were like the lips of apes. In one scene, Caliban appeared as a "strange beast"; hiding on his knees under a cover, he seemed to have "four legs."[4]

In 1611, when Shakespeare's play was first performed, there were no African Calibans in Virginia. Indeed, the introduction of Africans was something that had not even been considered at the time. As it turned out, the presence of Africans in America did become a reality. But how they came to be enslaved and numerous has been largely "hidden" from our understanding of the making of multicultural America.

A View from the Cabins: White and Black Laborers in Early Virginia

Caliban, as described in the list of actors, was not only a "savage" but also a "deformed slave." The audience heard Prospero refer to him as "Caliban, my slave." "We cannot miss him," declared the master. "He does make our fire, fetch our wood, and serves in offices that profit us." In history, Caliban turned out to be African. Some Indians were enslaved: captured in wars by the English colonists, they were shipped as slaves to the West Indies. Indian slavery, however, did not develop in the continental colonies. Indian slaves could escape and find refuge outside the settlements, and formidable Indian military power deterred the English from exploiting them as slaves.

Eight years after the first performance of *The Tempest,* a Virginia colonist recorded a significant moment in the history of the English New World. "About the last of August," wrote John Rolfe in his diary, "came in a dutch man of warre that sold us twenty Negars."[5]

These twenty Africans had probably been captured in wars or raids by enemy tribes before they were sold to the Dutch slaver. Their ordeal must have been similar to the experience of Olaudah Equiano. After he had been captured by members of another tribe, he was marched to the seacoast.

> The first object which saluted my eyes when I arrived [he recalled] was the sea, and a slaveship, which was then riding at anchor, and waiting for its cargo. These filled me with astonishment, which was soon converted into terror. . . . When I was carried on board I was immediately handled, and tossed up, to see if I were sound, by some of the crew; and I was now persuaded that I had got into a world of bad spirits, and that they were going to kill me. Their complexions too differing so much from ours, their long hair, and the language they spoke, which was very different from any I had ever heard, united to confirm me in this belief. . . . When I looked round the ship too, and saw a large furnace or copper boiling, and a multitude of black people of every description chained together, every one of their countenances expressing dejection and sorrow, I no longer doubted of my fate; and, quite overpowered with horror and anguish, I fell motionless on the deck and fainted. . . . I was soon put down under the decks, and there I received such a salutation in my nostrils as I had never experienced in my life; so that, with the loathsomeness of the stench, and crying together, I became so sick and low that I was not able to eat. . . . [After a long voyage, the slaves finally sighted land.] We thought . . . we should be eaten by these ugly men . . . and . . . there was much dread and trembling among us, and nothing but bitter cries to be heard all the night from these apprehensions, insomuch that at last the white people got some old slaves from the land to pacify us. They told us we were not to be eaten, but to work. . . .[6]

Though they had been "sold," the first twenty Africans might not have been slaves, persons reduced to property and required to work without wages for life. Like many English colonists who were also sold as indentured servants, many or possibly all of them were bound by contract to serve a master for four to seven years in order to repay the expense of their passage. While Africans continued to be transported to Virginia during the next several decades, they remained a very small population. But what happened to them paved the way for the establishment of slavery in Virginia as well as Maryland, the Carolinas, and Georgia, and would have consequences for all of America down the corridors of time.[7]

In the early days of the Virginia colony, most workers were white indentured servants. In fact, 75 percent of the colonists came as servants during the seventeenth century. In 1664, the Council of Foreign Plantations reported that the colony's population had been "increased principally by sending of Servants." Production and the improvement of property depended on these workers. Describing how one planter with six indentured servants had made a thousand pounds with one crop of tobacco, John Pory of Virginia observed: "Our principal wealth . . . consisteth in servants."[8]

Coming mainly from England but also from Germany and Ireland, these men and women were the outcasts of society. As described by historian Abbot Emerson Smith, they included convicts, "rogues, vagabonds, whores, cheats, and rabble of all descriptions, raked from the gutter," "decoyed, deceived, seduced, inveigled, or forcibly kidnapped and carried as servants to the plantations." They were regarded as the "surplus inhabitants" of England. Virtually all of these indentured servants came without families.[9]

Like the Africans, many white indentured servants came involuntarily, "spirited" here by unscrupulous recruiters. The "spirits," an Englishman reported, "take up all the idle, lazie, simple people they can entice, such as have professed idleness, and will rather beg than work. . . ." In an English court, Christian Chacrett was accused of being "a Spirit, one that [took] up men and women and children and [sold] them on a ship to be conveyed beyond the sea" to Virginia. Some of the servants were victims of the Irish "slave-trade." English poor laws for the correction and punishment of rogues and idle people were enforced in Ireland, and this led to the wholesale kidnapping of young Irish women and men to supply the labor needs of the colonies. One of them, John King, recalled how he and others were "stolen in Ireland" by English soldiers. Taken from their beds at night "against their Consents," they were put on a ship. "Weeping and Crying," the Irish captives were kept on board until "a Lord's day morning" when the ship set sail for America.[10]

Coming from different shores, white and black laborers in Virginia had very limited understanding as well as negative notions of each other, and mutual feelings of fear and hostility undoubtedly existed.

Still both groups occupied a common social space — a terrain of racial liminality that had not yet developed rigid caste lines. White and black, they shared a condition of class exploitation and abuse: they were all unfree laborers. Sometimes they had to wear iron collars around their necks. When they were recalcitrant, they were beaten and even tortured. They were required to have passes whenever they left their plantations. White and black, laborers experienced the day-to-day exhaustion and harshness of work. They had to cut trees and clear brush, plow the soil and prepare it for planting. In the hot and humid tobacco fields, they worked side by side — their backs bent over row after row of tobacco, their arms sore from topping young plants, their legs cramped from carrying heavy loads of tobacco leaves to the wagons, their nostrils filled with dust, and their ears stinging from the barking commands of their masters. Weary from work, they returned to their roughly built cabins and huts where they were fed a dreary mess made from ground Indian corn called "lob-lolly." A white servant in Virginia was undoubtedly expressing the anguish of many laborers, whether from Europe or Africa, when he wrote: "I thought no head had been able to hold so much water as hath and doth daily flow from mine eyes."[11]

Occasionally, perhaps often, whites and blacks ran away together. Court records indicated repeated instances of blacks and whites conspiring to escape together. In one case, the Virginia court declared: "Whereas [six English] . . . Servants . . . and Jno. a negro Servant . . . hath Run away and Absented themselves from their . . . masters Two months, It is ordered that the Sherriffe . . . take Care that all of them be whipped . . . and Each of them have thirty nine lashes well layed on. . . ." The problem of whites and blacks absconding together became so serious that the Virginia legislature complained about "English servants running away with Negroes."[12]

Some blacks and whites formed another kind of partnership. In 1630, the Virginia court decided that Hugh Davis was "to be soundly whipped before an assembly of negroes and others for abusing himself to the dishonor of God and the shame of Christianity by defiling his body in lying with a negro." The court again punished a white man and a black woman in 1640: "Whereas Robert Sweat hath begotten with child a negro woman servant belonging unto Lieutenant Sheppard, the court hath therefore ordered that the said negro woman shall be whipped at the whipping post and the said Sweat shall tomorrow in the forenoon do public pennance for his offence at James city church in the time of divine service." Similarly, William Watts, a white man, and Mary, a black servant, were punished for fornication in 1649. A year later, a white man and black woman, found guilty of having sexual relations, were required to stand clad in white sheets before a congregation. In 1667, the court convicted Irish servant John Dorman of getting a "Negro woman" with child. Between 1690 and 1698 in Westmoreland County, fourteen white women were punished for having illegitimate children; at least four of these nineteen children were mulatto.[13]

Increasingly, black servants were separated from white servants and singled out for special treatment. In 1640, for example, the Virginia legislature passed a law stating that masters should furnish arms to all men, "excepting negros." Blacks were also serving longer time periods for indenture as punishment for running away. In 1640, for example, three runaway servants — two white men and a black man — were captured and returned. They were each given thirty lashes. In addition, both white men were required to work for their masters for an additional year and for the colony for three more years. But the third runaway received the most severe punishment: "Being a Negro named *John Punch* shall serve his said master or his assigns for the time of his natural Life here or elsewhere." During the same year, six white men and a black man were arrested for running away. Communicating between two plantations, they had carefully planned their escape and gathered "corn powder and shot and guns"; after stealing a skiff and sailing down the Elizabeth River, they were apprehended. One of the white men, Christian Miller, received an especially harsh penalty — thirty lashes, an "R" (for Rogue) to be burned into his cheek, a shackle on his leg for at least a year, and seven years of service to the colony after he had completed his obligation to his master. The Negro Emanuel was given a similar punishment, except he was not ordered to serve additional time, implying he was required to labor for life. In other words, he was a slave.[14]

Some estate inventories showed that African laborers were more valuable than English indentured servants, indicating that the former had a longer period of bound service. For example, the inventory of the estate of William Burdett, dated November 13, 1643, included this list:

	lb tobacco
Sarah Hickman to serve one year at	0700
John Gibbs to serve one year at	0650

Nehemia Coventon Aged 12 years to serve
   8 years at   1000
Symon Caldron a boy very Lame and 14 years old
   to serve 7   0500
William Young another boy full of the scurvy
   to serve six years at   0600
Edward Southerne a little Boy very sick
   having seven years to serve at   0700
Michael Pacey a boy to serve six years at   1100
Caine the negro, very ancient at   3000
One negro girl about 8 years old at   2000
32 goats young and old at   2500
A parcel of hogs at   1800[15]

What was happening was evident: Africans, unlike whites, were being degraded into a condition of servitude for life and even the status of property. According to the Virginia court records of 1642, Thomas Jacob transferred a "negro Woman Susan" to Bridgett Seaverne and her son: "I do hereby declare that I have given the negro unto them and their heirs and Assigns Freely forever. . . ." Two years later, William Hawley borrowed money from William Stone and provided as collateral "my Negro Mingo." In 1646, Francis Pott sold a Negro woman and boy to Stephen Charlton "to the use of him . . . forever." Wills provided that white servants were to serve their "full term of time" and Negroes "forever." African slaves as well as their future children could be inherited. A 1648 deed included a provision for a "Negro woman and all her increase (which for future time shall be born of her body)." In 1652, a Negro girl was sold to H. Armsteadinger "and his heirs . . . forever with all her increase both male and female." A year later, William Whittington sold John Pott "one Negro girl named Jowan; aged about Ten years and with her Issue and produce during her (or either of them) for their Life time. And their Successors forever." In 1645, Ralph Wormeley presented in court a certificate of a gift to Agatha Stubbings in "Consideration of Matrimony" — "Four Negro men and Two women . . . Ten Cows, six Draft Oxen."[16]

Clearly, blacks were enslaved before 1660. Yet historian Oscar Handlin asserted: "The status of Negroes was that of indentured servants and so they were identified and treated down to the 1660s." What Handlin failed to recognize was de facto slavery — chattel bondage in practice if not in law. By the 1650s, according to Alden T. Vaughan's count, 70 percent of the blacks in Virginia were serving as slaves.[17]

In 1661, the Virginia Assembly began to institutionalize slavery, to make it *de jure*. A law regarding the punishment of servants referred to "those Negroes who are incapable of making satisfaction by addition of time." In other words, they were required to serve for life. Eight years later, the Virginia legislature defined a slave as property, a part of the owner's "estate."[18]

English colonists in Virginia did not develop the institution of slavery for Africans on their own: they knew of its existence elsewhere in the English New World. In the West Indies, Africans were slaves. In 1636, Governor Henry Hawley and the Council in Barbados resolved "that *Negroes* and *Indians*, that came here to be sold, should serve for Life, unless a Contract was before made to the contrary." In New England, the Puritans believed that captives of a "just war" could be enslaved; after their victory over the Pequots in 1637, they shipped Indian captives to the West Indies in exchange for African slaves. Eight years later, in a letter to his brother-in-law, John Winthrop, Emanuel Downing calculated the economic potential of such exchanges: "If upon a Just war [with the Narraganset Indians] the Lord should deliver them into our hands, we might easily have men and women and children enough to exchange for Moors [Africans], which will be more gainful pillage for us than we conceive, for I do not see how we can thrive until we get into a stock of slaves sufficient to do all our business." Twenty black slaves, Downing added, could be maintained cheaper than one English servant. A colonist in Massachusetts attempted to breed two of his African slaves. "*Mr. Maverick* was desirous to have a breed of Negroes," an English visitor reported in 1639, "and therefore seeing [that his Negro woman] would not yield by persuasions to [make] company with a Negro man he had in his house; he commanded him [to go to bed with her] which was no sooner done but she kicked him out again, this she took in high disdain beyond her slavery."[19]

Slavery did not develop in New England, however, for the region did not produce a staple crop and therefore did not have a significant need for labor, slave or indentured. In the 1650s, a contemporary observed that colonists in New England do their own work and "so have rarely above one Servant." But, he added, "Virginia thrives by keeping many servants."[20]

Indeed, Virginia was developing into a tobacco-producing colony, and the need for labor was expanding. Yet, the African population increased very slowly. In 1650, Africans constituted only 300 of Virginia's 15,000 inhabitants, or 2 percent. Twenty-five years later, of the colony's approximately 32,000 inhabitants, they totaled only 1,600, or 5 percent. The Barbados represented a striking contrast. By 1645, there were 5,000 blacks in the islands and 20,000 by 1660, constituting a majority of the total population.[21]

Why was it that English settlers in Virginia did not seek more "gainful pillage" by increasing their stock of African slaves?

Carrying to Virginia negative images of Africans, English settlers undoubtedly felt hesitant about peopling their colony with Calibans. Unlike their counterparts in the Barbados, they were not businessmen seeking to make money and return to England. Rather, the Virginians had brought their families with them and were planning to stay. They were making new homes for themselves and had to determine who should and should not settle in the colony. To them, religion and race mattered greatly.

Initially, religion served to identify different racial groups. The English colonists viewed themselves as Christians and the Africans as heathens. But this line was shortly ruptured by the conversion of Africans to Christianity. Hence, laws were passed that separated race from religion. In 1667, Virginia declared that "the conferring of baptism does not alter the condition of the person as to his bondage or freedom." Three years later, Virginia enacted a law declaring that "no negro or Indian," though baptized and free, should be allowed to purchase Christians. The distinction was no longer between Christianity and heathenism or freedom and slavery, but between white and black.[22]

This division based on race helped to delineate the border between savagery and civilization. In the wilderness, the English colonists felt a great urgency to destroy what historian Jordan described as "the living image of primitive aggressions which they said was the Negro but was really their own." Far away from the security and surveillance of society in England, the colonists feared the possibility of losing self-control over their passions. "Intermixture and insurrection, violent sex and sexual violence, creation and destruction, life and death — the stuff of animal existence was rumbling at the gates of rational and moral judgment." If the gates fell, the colonists feared, so would civilization. Thus, they projected their hidden and rejected instinctual parts of human nature onto blacks. Jordan imagined them insisting: "We, therefore, do not lust and destroy; it is someone else. We are not great black bucks of the fields. But a buck *is* loose, his great horns menacing to gore into us with life and destruction. Chain him, either chain him or expel his black shape from our midst, before we realize that he is ourselves." Internal boundaries of control were required, or else whites would be swept away by the boundlessness of the wilderness.[23]

The vision of Virginia as a colony for the settlement of English families, combined with the powerful negative feelings and fears that the English harbored toward Africans, generated pressures to minimize the number of blacks in the colony.

During the last quarter of the century, however, the black population of Virginia increased steeply to 9,000 and possibly even to 20,000 out of 63,000 for the entire colony. Their proportion was around 25 percent in 1715 and over 40 percent by 1750. "There were as many buyers as negros," Francis Nicholson commented on a sale of 230 slaves in Virginia in 1700, "and I think that, if 2000 were imported, there would be substantial buyers for them." "The negroes are brought annually in large numbers," a visitor to Virginia reported. "They can be selected according to pleasure, young and old, men and women. They are entirely naked when they arrive, having only corals of different colors around their neck and arms." Unlike the first "twenty Negars," these Africans arrived as slaves. A 1705 Virginia law provided that "all servants imported and brought into this country, by sea or land, who were not christians in their native country . . . shall be . . . slaves, and as such be here bought and sold notwithstanding a conversion to christianity afterwards."[24]

Why was there such a dramatic turn away from white indentured servants and toward enslaved blacks? According to Handlin, planters suddenly realized the advantages of having laborers bound for life. "By mid-century the servitude of Negroes seems generally lengthier than that of whites," he explained; "and thereafter the consciousness dawns that the blacks will toil for the whole of their lives, not through any particular concern with their status, but simply by contrast with those whose years of labor are limited by statute." Soon laws institutionalizing slavery for blacks were passed, and it became "obvious which was the cheapest, most available, most exploitable labor supply."[25]

But, as we have seen, such "consciousness" had "dawned" much earlier, at least in practice. Moreover, if the planters were aware of the advantage of slaves in the 1650s, why did they wait until after 1675 to change their labor force? Other factors must have come into play. First, as historian Russell Menard noted, there was a decrease in the number of indentured servants migrating to Virginia after the 1670s. This would have produced pressure to draw from an African labor supply. Despite this shortage, however, planters still did not seem to prefer African slaves to white servants. "It was not until at least a decade after the decline in the supply of servants," Menard observed, "that the number of blacks imported each year rose above a trickle. . . ." Second, as conditions in Virginia improved, both whites and blacks were living longer. Hence, where earlier it had been more expensive to invest in blacks as slaves than in whites as indentured servants, it became less of a risk as longevity increased for everyone. Lifetime servitude had become more profitable. But something else also happened after 1675 that opened the way for a switch from indentured white labor to black slave labor.[26]

"English and Negroes in Armes"

That "something" occurred within white society in Virginia. To understand race relations by focusing on race sometimes obscures; indeed, the "hidden" origins of slavery were rooted in class. Here again, *The Tempest* might be illuminating. The theatergoers were given a scenario that was uncanny in its anticipation of what would happen in Virginia. What they saw on the stage was an interracial class revolt to overthrow Prospero. When the jester Trinculo and the butler Stephano first encountered Caliban, they found him repulsive — a fishlike monster and a devil. They gave him wine, and the inebriated Caliban offered to show Trinculo every "fertile inch o' the island" and worship him as a god. Defying Prospero, Caliban chanted:

> 'Ban, 'Ban, Ca-Caliban
> Has a new master. Get a new man.

A fierce desire drove the subversive stance: "Freedom, highday! highday, freedom! freedom, highday, freedom!" Complaining about how Prospero had colonized his island, Caliban concocted a plot for rebellion. If Stephano would kill Prospero ("knock a nail into his head"), Caliban declared, the butler would become the lord of the island and husband of Miranda. Caliban promised Stephano: "She will become thy bed." Stirred by these promises, the butler exclaimed: "Lead, monster; we'll follow." Warned in advance about the "foul conspiracy of the beast Caliban and his confederates," Prospero unleashed his hunting dogs against the rebels: "Fury, Fury! There, Tyrant, there! Go, charge my goblins that they grind their joints. . . ." A victim, Caliban was also an actor, a participant in the making of events. What attracted Stephano and Trinculo to his revolutionary leadership was their shared "otherness" rooted in class.[27]

Like Prospero, the English settlers had brought to America not only racial prejudice but also a hierarchical class structure. While a few were from the aristocracy and many were from what could be called the middle class, most English colonists migrated to Virginia as indentured servants. They planned to complete their period of indenture and become landowners. According to Governor William Berkeley, white servants came with a "hope of bettering their condition in a Growing Country." They thought the American expanse offered the possibility of starting over, creating new selves and new lives. Land in Virginia, taken from the Indians, was available and cheap, and each freeman could claim title to fifty acres. Perhaps they could even become wealthy, for a new cash crop, tobacco, offered farmers the opportunity to enter the market. Like the butler Stephano and the jester Trinculo, they wanted to become "lords" of land in America.[28]

The very abundance of land and the profitability of tobacco production, however, unleashed a land boom and speculation. Colonists with financial advantage quickly scrambled to possess the best lands along the navigable rivers. Representing a landed elite, they dominated the Virginia Assembly and began to enact legislation to advance and protect their class interests. They passed laws that extended the time of indentured servitude for whites and increased the length of service for white runaways. In this way, they minimized competition for lands and at the same time maximized the supply of white laborers by keeping them in servitude for as long as possible.[29]

Consequently, white freemen increasingly found it difficult to become landowners. In 1663, the House of Burgesses turned down a proposal to levy taxes on land instead of polls. Such a basis for taxation, it was argued, would limit the suffrage to landholders, and such a restriction would be resented by "the other freemen" who were "the more in number." The majority of freemen, the burgesses were acknowledging, did not own land. Thirteen years later, two members of the Virginia council, Thomas Ludwell and Robert Smith, estimated that at least one-fourth of the population consisted of "merchants and single freemen and such others as have no land." A growing group of tenant farmers existed.[30]

Hopes of landownership became dreams deferred for many English colonists. Frustrated and angry, many white workers felt they had been duped into coming to America. In 1649, pamphleteer William Bullock warned planters about the men and women who, "not finding what was promised," had become "dejected" and recalcitrant workers. In England, they had been viewed as the "Surcharge of necessitous people, the matter or fuel of dangerous insurrections." In Virginia, they became an even greater threat to social order, forming what the planter elite fearfully called a "giddy multitude" — a discontented class of indentured servants, slaves, and landless freemen, both white and black, the Stephanos and Trinculos as well as the Calibans of Virginia. They constituted a volatile element. In the early 1660s, for example, indentured servant Isaac Friend led a conspiracy to band together forty servants and "get Arms." He issued the rebellious cry: "who would be for Liberty, and free from bondage." Others would join the revolt, Friend promised, and together they would "go through the Country and kill those that made any opposition," and would "either be free or die for it." The authorities were informed about Friend's plan and quickly suppressed the plot. Again, in 1663, a Gloucester court accused nine "Laborers" of conspiring to overthrow the Virginia government and sentenced several of them to be executed. This incident gave planters a frightening example of "the horror" in Virginia — the presence of "villains" engaged in a "barbarous design" to subvert "rights and privileges" in the colony.[31]

But unruliness and discontent continued to grow. Fearing this landless class, the Virginia legislature restricted the suffrage to landowners in 1670. Governor William Berkeley was worried about the explosive class conditions in his colony where "six parts of seven" of the people were "Poor Indebted Discontented and Armed." The ownership of guns was widespread among whites, for every white man had a right to bear arms and was required by law to have a gun in order to help defend the colony. The landed elite distrusted this armed lower class of whites so much that they were even afraid to organize them for military service. On one occasion, in 1673, Governor Berkeley raised troops to defend Virginia against Dutch warships, but he did so very reluctantly. Of the men he enlisted in his army, Berkeley apprehensively noted, at least one-third were freemen or debtors. They could not be trusted, he cautioned, for in battle, they might revolt and join the enemy "in hopes of bettering their Condition by Sharing the Plunder of the Country with them."[32]

Three years later, the very revolt Berkeley feared took place. One of the landholders in the upcountry was Nathaniel Bacon, a friend of Berkeley's and a member of the Virginia council. Seeking to protect settlers against the Indians, he helped raise a militia. Bacon recognized the danger of organizing armed men who came from the ranks of the "giddy multitude." But Bacon calculated that an expedition against the Indians would serve a dual purpose — eliminate a foe and redirect the white lower class's anger away from the white elite to the Indians. The unruly and armed poor would focus on the external red enemy, rather than on the legislature's high taxes and the governor's failure to provide for defense against the Indians. "Since my being with the volunteers," he wrote to Berkeley, "the Exclaiming concerning forts and Leavys has been suppressed and the discourse and earnestness of the people is against the Indians...."[33]

Bacon's actions shocked Berkeley and his council, who were more worried about armed white freemen than hostile Indians. In their view, Bacon's followers were a "Rabble Crew, only the Rascallity and meanest of the people ... there being hardly two amongst them that we have heard of who have Estates or are persons of Reputation and indeed very few who can either write or read." Ignoring their concerns, Bacon led a march against the Indians, killing Susquehannahs as well as friendly Occaneechees. He justified his expedition as a "Glorious" defense of the country. But the governor angrily declared Bacon a rebel and charged him with treason, an act punishable by death. Bacon retaliated by marching five hundred armed men to Jamestown.[34]

Blacks joined Bacon's army: they realized that they had a greater stake in the rebellion than their white brothers in arms, for many of them were bound servants for life. White and black, Bacon's soldiers formed what contemporaries described as "an incredible Number of the meanest People," "every where Armed." They were the "tag, rag, and bobtayle," the "Rabble" against "the better sort of people." A colonial official reported that Bacon had raised hundreds of soldiers "whose fortunes & Inclinations" were "desperate," and that almost all of them were either "Idle" and would not work, or in debt because of "Debaucherie or Ill Husbandry." Bacon had unleashed a radical class boundlessness that threatened the very foundations of order in Virginia.[35]

The rebels forced Berkeley to escape by ship and burned Jamestown to the ground. Shortly afterward, Bacon died, probably from dysentery; Berkeley then returned with armed ships. Like Prospero with his hunting dogs, the governor violently suppressed the rebellion. At one of the rebel fortifications, Captain Thomas Grantham encountered some four hundred "English and Negroes in Armes." Lying to them, Grantham said they had been "pardoned and freed from their Slavery." Most of them accepted his offer, but eighty black and twenty white rebels refused to surrender. Promised safe passage across the York River, the holdouts were captured when Grantham threatened to blow them out of the water. All of the captured "Negroes & Servants," Grantham reported, were returned "to their Masters."[36]

By force and deceit, the rebels of the "giddy multitude" had been defeated, but they had fought in what historian Edmund Morgan called "the largest rebellion known in any American colony before the [American] Revolution." Bacon's Rebellion had exposed the volatility of class tensions within white society in Virginia. During the conflict, the specter of class revolution had become a reality, and the scare shook the elite landholders: they were no longer confident they could control the "giddy multitude." Five years after the rebellion, planters continued to harbor fears of class disorder and urged the king to keep royal soldiers in Virginia to "prevent or suppress any Insurrection that may otherwise happen during the necessitous unsettled condition of the Colony." Large landowners could see that the social order would always be in danger so long as they had to depend on white labor. They had come to a crossing. They could open economic opportunities to white workers and extend political privileges to them. But this would erode their own economic advantage and potentially undermine their political hegemony. Or they could try to reorganize society on the basis of class *and* race. By importing and buying more slaves, they would decrease the proportion of white indentured servants. They would then be able to exploit a group of workers who had been enslaved and denied the right to bear arms because of their race. To increase the black population would mean to create a biracial society. However, such a development could help the planters control an armed white labor force and possibly solve the class problem within white society.[37]

While such a scenario of the "hidden" origins of slavery might not have been a deliberate strategy, what was so striking about the transition from white to black labor was its timing. The planter elite were becoming increasingly concerned about the growing discontent and rebelliousness among white servants during the 1660s — the very moment when the legislature made slavery *de jure*. During this time, the black population began to increase, an indication that planters had started shifting to this source of labor. But it was still not clear whether Africans would become the major work force and slavery would become the primary system of labor. After Bacon's Rebellion, however, the turn to slavery became sharp and significant. Even though the supply of white indentured servants seemed to have declined at this time, planters did not try to expand their recruitment efforts. Instead, they did something they had resisted until then — prefer black slaves over white indentured servants. In a letter to Ralph Wormely in 1681, William Fitzhugh noted that there were "some Negro Ships expected into York now every day." "If you intend to buy any for yours self, and it be not too much trouble," Fitzhugh added, ". . . secure me five or six." The growing dependency on slave laborers rather than white indentured servants can be measured decade by decade from the tax lists of Surry County. Slaves constituted 20 percent of households in 1674, 33 percent in 1686, and 48 percent in 1694. In other words, by the end of the century, nearly half the work force in Surry County was black and enslaved.[38]

Moreover, what the landed gentry systematically developed after the rebellion was a racially subordinated labor force. After 1680, they enacted laws that denied slaves freedom of assembly and movement. The "frequent meeting of considerable number of negroe slaves under pretense of feasts and burials" was "judged of dangerous consequence." Masters and overseers were prohibited from allowing "any Negro or Slave not properly belonging to him or them, to Remain or be upon his or their Plantation above the space of four hours." Militia patrollers were authorized to visit "negro quarters and other places suspected of entertaining unlawful assemblies," and to "take up" those assembling "or any other, strolling about from one plantation to another, without a pass from his or her master, mistress, or overseer." The gentry also disarmed blacks: in an act entitled "Preventing Negroes Insurrections," the legislature ordered that "it shall not be lawful for any negro or other slave to carry or arm himself with any club, staff, gun, sword or any other weapon." The planter class saw that black slaves could be more effectively controlled by state power than white servants, for they could be denied certain rights based on the color of their skin.[39]

Although the number of white indentured servants entering Virginia declined sharply after 1700, the white lower class did not disappear. In 1720, in Christ Church, Virginia, out of 146 householders, only 86 were landowners. The landed elite continued to view the white lower class as a bothersome problem. The planters offered a carrot: in 1705, the assembly provided that upon completion of their term, white servants would not only be entitled to fifty acres of land but would also be given ten bushels of Indian corn, thirty shillings, and a musket. The planters also wielded a stick: they petitioned the legislature in 1699 to pass a law punishing "Vagrant Vagabond and Idle Persons and to assess the Wages of Common Labourers." In 1723, the assembly enacted a poor law that empowered county courts to punish "vagrants" by giving them thirty-nine lashes or by binding them out as servants. The law complained that "diverse Idle and disorderly persons," who had "no visible Estates or Employments," frequently "strolled from One County to another" and would not labor or pay their taxes.[40]

By then, landless white Stephanos and Trinculos were less likely to join with enslaved black Calibans on a class basis. The cultural gap between white and black workers had widened in the late seventeenth century. Where the early black arrivals had been "seasoned" in the Barbados and were often able to speak some English, new blacks were transported directly from Africa. These Africans must have seemed especially strange to whites, even to those who occupied a common exploited class position.[41]

This cultural chasm between the whites and blacks of the "giddy multitude" was transformed into a political separation as the landed gentry instituted new borders between white and black laborers. Four years after Bacon's Rebellion, the Virginia Assembly repealed all penalties imposed on white servants for plundering during the revolt, but did not extend this pardon to black freemen and black indentured servants. Moreover, the gentry reinforced the separate labor status for each group: blacks were forced to occupy a racially subordinate and stigmatized status, one below all whites regardless of their class. Black was made to signify slave. In 1691, the assembly prohibited the manumission of slaves unless the master paid for transporting them out of the colony. New laws sharpened the lines of a caste system: who was "black" was given expanded definition. Earlier, in 1662, the legislature had declared that children born in Virginia should be slave or free according to the condition of the mother. In 1691, the Virginia Assembly passed a law that prohibited the "abominable mixture and spurious issue" of interracial unions and that provided for the banishment of white violators. The assembly took special aim at white women: the law specified that a free white mother of a racially mixed illegitimate child would be fined fifteen pounds and that the child would be required to be in servitude for thirty years. The effect of these laws was not only to make mulattoes slaves but also to stigmatize them as black. Moreover, the legislature also denied free blacks the right to vote, hold office, and testify in court.[42]

Meanwhile, the Virginia elite deliberately pitted white laborers and black slaves against each other. The legislature permitted whites to abuse blacks physically with impunity: in 1680, it prescribed thirty lashes on the bare back "if any negro or other slave shall presume to lift up his hand in opposition against any christian." Planters used landless whites to help put down slave revolts. In the early eighteenth century, Hugh Jones reported that each county had "a great number of disciplined and armed militia, ready in case of any sudden eruption of Indians or insurrection of Negroes." In 1705, Virginia legislated that "all horses, cattle, and hogs, now belonging, or that hereafter shall belong to any slave, or of any slaves mark . . . shall be seized and sold by the church-wardens of the parish . . . and the profit thereof applied to the use of the poor." Here was a policy to transfer farm animals and food from slaves to poor whites. Later, during the American Revolution, the Virginia Assembly went even farther: to recruit white men for the struggle for liberty, the legislature rewarded each soldier with a bounty of three hundred acres of land and a slave — "a healthy, sound Negro between ten and thirty years of age."[43]

The Wolf by the Ears

As the governor of Virginia during the Revolution, Thomas Jefferson supported the broadening of landownership, for he believed it provided the basis of social and political stability. Like the Virginia planters before him, Jefferson worried about class tensions and conflicts within white society. The New World, he saw, offered something Europe could not — an abundance of uncultivated land. Americans would remain virtuous as long as they were primarily involved in agriculture, and this would last as long as there were "vacant lands" in America. In his *Notes on the State of Virginia,* Jefferson observed: "Those who labor in the earth are the chosen people of God, if ever He had a chosen people, whose breasts He has made His peculiar deposit for substantial and genuine virtue. . . . [Let] our workshops remain in Europe. . . . The mobs of great cities add just so much to the support of pure government, as sores do to the strength of the human body."[44]

In Jefferson's judgment, the way to avoid class conflicts in American society was to open opportunities for white men to become farmers. As free individuals and owners of property, they would become responsible citizens. "Here every one, by his property, or by his satisfactory situation, is interested in the support of law and order," Jefferson observed. "And such men may safely and advantageously reserve to themselves a whole-some control over their public affairs, and a degree of freedom, which, in the hands of the canaille of the cities of Europe, would be instantly perverted to the demolition and destruction of everything public and private." Jefferson's was a vision of a republic of independent and vir-tuous yeoman farmers.[45]

Jefferson himself, however, was an elite planter. A beneficiary of the seventeenth-century turn to slavery, he was a slaveowner and actively participated in the buying and selling of slaves. "The value of our lands and slaves, taken conjunctly, doubles in about twenty years," he coolly calculated. "This arises from the multiplication of our slaves, from the extension of culture, and increased demands for lands." His observation was not merely theoretical: Jefferson's ownership of lands and slaves made him one of the wealthiest men in Virginia. Yet he continued to expand his slaveholdings. In 1805, he informed John Jordan that he was "endeavoring to purchase young and able negro men." In a letter to his manager regarding "a breeding woman," Jefferson referred to the "loss of 5 little ones in 4 years" and complained that the overseers had not permitted the slave women to devote as much time as was necessary to care for their children. "They view their labor as the 1st object and the raising of their children but as secondary," he continued. "I consider the labor of a breeding woman as no object, and that a child raised every 2 years is of more profit than the crop of the best laboring man." By 1822, Jefferson owned 267 slaves.[46]

Jefferson was capable of punishing his slaves with great cruelty. He used James Hubbard, a captured runaway slave, as a lesson to discipline the other slaves: "I had him severely flogged in the presence of his old companions." On another occasion, Jefferson punished a slave in order to make an example of him in "terrorem" to others and then sold him to a slave trader from Georgia. Jefferson wanted him to be sent to a place "so distant as never more to be heard among us," and make it seem to the other slaves on his plantation "as if he were put out of the way by death."[47]

Jefferson felt profoundly ambivalent toward slavery, however. He could see that the switch from white to black labor in the seventeenth century had been terribly unfortunate, for this had led to the expansion of an immoral institution. "The love of justice and the love of country plead equally the cause of these people [slaves]," Jefferson confessed, "and it is a moral reproach to us that they should have pleaded it so long in vain. . . ." As a member of the Virginia legislature, he supported an effort for the emancipation of slaves. In his *Notes on the State of Virginia,* he recommended the gradual abolition of slavery, and in a letter to a friend written in 1788, he wrote: "You know that nobody wishes more ardently to see an abolition not only of the [African slave] trade but of the condition of slavery: and certainly nobody will be more willing to encounter every sacrifice for that object."[48]

Jefferson personally felt guilty about his slave ownership. In a letter to his brother-in-law, Francis Eppes, on July 30, 1787, he made a revealing slip. Once "my debts" have been cleared off, he promised, "I shall try some plan of making their [his slaves'] situation happier, determined to content myself with a small portion of their liberty [crossed out] labour." He tried to excuse himself for appropriating only their "labour," not their "liberty." In a letter to a friend written only a day earlier, Jefferson exploded with guilt: "The torment of mind, I will endure till the moment shall arrive when I shall not owe a shilling on earth is such really as to render life of little value." Dependent on the labor of his slaves to pay off his debts, he hoped to be able to free them, which he promised he would do the moment "they" had paid off the estate's debts, two-thirds of which had been "contracted by purchasing them." Unfortunately for Jefferson, and especially for his slaves, he remained in debt until his death.[49]

In Jefferson's view, slavery did more than deprive blacks of their liberty. It also had a pernicious and "unhappy" influence on the masters and their children:

> The whole commerce between master and slave is a perpetual exercise of the most boisterous passions, the most unremitting despotism on the one part, and degrading submissions on the other. Our children see this, and learn to imitate it; for man is an imitative animal. This quality is the germ of all education in him. From his cradle to his grave he is learning to do what he sees others do. If a parent could find no motive either in his philanthropy or his self-love, for restraining the intemperance of passion toward his slave, it should always be a sufficient one that his child is present. But generally it is not sufficient. The parent storms, the child looks on, catches the lineaments of wrath, puts on the same airs in the circle of smaller slaves, gives a loose to his worst of passions, and thus nursed, educated, and daily exercised in tyranny, cannot but be stamped by it with odious peculiarities. The man must be a prodigy who can retain his manner and morals un-depraved by such circumstances.[50]

Slavery had to be abolished, Jefferson argued, but when freed, blacks would have to be removed from American society. This had to be done as soon as possible because slaves already composed nearly half of Virginia's population. "Under the mild treatment our slaves experience, and their wholesome, though coarse, food," Jefferson observed, "this blot in our country increases fast, or faster, than the whites." Delays for removal only meant the growth of the "blot." Jefferson impatiently insisted: "I can say, with conscious truth, that there is not a man on earth who would sacrifice more than I would to relieve us from this heavy reproach, in any practicable way. The cession of that kind of property . . . is a bagatelle which would not cost me a second thought, if, in that way, a general emancipation and expatriation could be effected."[51]

But how could a million and half slaves be expatriated? To send them away all at once, Jefferson answered, would not be "practicable." He estimated that such a removal would take twenty-five years, during which time the slave population would have doubled. Furthermore, the value of these slaves would amount to $600 million, and the cost of transportation and provisions an additional $300 million. "It cannot be done in this way," Jefferson decided. The only "practicable" plan, he thought, was to deport the future generation: black infants would be taken from their mothers and trained for occupations until they reached a proper age for deportation. Since an infant was worth only $22.50, Jefferson calculated, the loss of slave property would be reduced from $600 million to only $37.5 million. Jefferson suggested that slave children be shipped to the independent black nation of Santo Domingo. "Suppose the whole annual increase to be sixty thousand effective births, fifty vessels, of four hundred tons burthen each, constantly employed in that short run, would carry off the increase of every year, and the old stock would die off in the ordinary course of nature, lessening from the commencement until its final disappearance." He was confident the effects of his plan would be "blessed." As for taking children from their mothers, Jefferson remarked: "The separation of infants from mothers . . . would produce some scruples of humanity. But this would be straining at a gnat, and swallowing a camel."[52]

One of the reasons why colonization would have to be a condition for emancipation was clear to Jefferson: blacks and whites could never coexist in America because of "the real distinctions" which "nature" had made between the two races. "The first difference which strikes us is that of color," Jefferson explained. This difference, "fixed in nature," was of great importance. "Is it not the foundation of a greater or less share of beauty in the two races?" he asked rhetorically. "Are not the fine mixtures of red and white, the expressions of every passion by greater or less suffusions of color in the one, preferable to that eternal monotony, which reigns in the countenances, that immovable veil of black which covers the emotions of the other race?" The differences between the races, in Jefferson's view, also involved intelligence. He publicly stated his "opinion" that blacks were "inferior" in the faculty of reason. However, he conceded that such a claim had to be "hazarded with great diffidence" and that he would be willing to have it refuted.[53]

But Jefferson received challenges and evidence contradicting his claim with a closed mind. For example, he refused to consider seriously the poetry of Phillis Wheatley. In 1773, this young black writer published a book of *Poems on Various Subjects, Religious and Moral*. Her poems stirred interest and appreciation among many readers. Praising them, a French official living in America during the American Revolution wrote: "Phyllis is a negress, born in Africa, brought to Boston at the age of ten, and sold to a citizen of that city. She learned English with unusual ease, eagerly read and reread the Bible . . . became steeped in the poetic images of which it is full, and at the age of seventeen published a number of poems in which there is imagination, poetry, and zeal. . . ." In one of her poems, Wheatley insisted that Africans were just as capable of Christian virtue and salvation as whites:

> *'Twas mercy brought me from my* Pagan *land,*
> *Taught my benighted soul to understand*
> *That there's a God, that there's a* Saviour *too:*
> *Once I redemption neither sought nor knew.*
> *Some view our sable race with scornful eye,*
> *"Their colour is a diabolic die."*
> *Remember,* Christians, Negroes, *black as* Cain,
> *May be refin'd, and join th' angelic train.*

During the American Revolution, Wheatley proclaimed:

> *No more,* America, *in mournful strain*
> *Of wrongs, and grievance unredress'd complain,*
> *No longer shalt thou dread the iron chain,*
> *Which wanton* Tyranny *with lawless hand*
> *Had made, and with it meant t'enslave the land.*

> *Should you, my lord, while you peruse my song,*
> *Wonder from whence my love of* Freedom *sprung,*
> *Whence flow these wishes for the common good,*
> *By feeling hearts alone best understood,*
> *I, young in life, by seeming cruel fate*
> *Was snatch'd from* Afric's *fancy'd happy seat:*
> *What pangs excruciating must molest,*
> *What sorrows labour in my parent's breast?*
> *Steel'd was that soul and by no misery mov'd*
> *That from a father seiz'd his babe belov'd:*

Such, such my case. And can I then but pray
Others may never feel tyrannic sway?

Like Jefferson and many theoreticians of the American Revolution, Wheatley understood the meaning of the struggle for liberty. She, too, identified British tyranny as a form of slavery, but Wheatley reminded her readers that her understanding of freedom was not merely philosophical, for it tragically sprang from her black experience — the slave trade, forced separation from parents, and bondage in America.[54]

Whether Jefferson read her poems is not known, but he contemptuously dismissed her writing: "The compositions published under her name are below the dignity of criticism." Jefferson considered blacks incapable of writing poetry. "Misery is often the parent of the most affecting touches in poetry," he observed. "Among the blacks is misery enough, God knows, but no poetry. Love is the peculiar oestrum of the poet. Their love is ardent, but it kindles the sense only, not the imagination." Jefferson caustically commented: "Religion, indeed, has produced a Phyllis Whately [*sic*]; but it could not produce a poet." Significantly, Jefferson had misspelled her name.[55]

Like Phillis Wheatley, Benjamin Banneker challenged Jefferson's "opinion" of black intellectual inferiority. On August 19, 1791, the free black mathematician from Maryland sent Jefferson a copy of the almanac he had compiled. "I suppose it is a truth too well attested to you, to need a proof here," Banneker wrote in his cover letter, "that we are a race of beings, who have long labored under the abuse and censure of the world . . . that we have long been considered rather as brutish than human, and scarcely capable of mental endowments." Noting that the almanac would soon be published, Banneker explained that he was sending Jefferson the "manuscript" of the work so that it could be viewed in his "own hand writing."[56]

Seeking to do more than demonstrate and affirm the intelligence of blacks, Banneker also scolded the author of the Declaration of Independence for his hypocrisy on the subject of slavery.

Sir, suffer me to recall to your mind that time, in which the arms of the British crown were exerted, with every powerful effort, in order to reduce you to a state of servitude: look back, I entreat you . . . you were then impressed with proper ideas of the great violation of liberty, and the free possession of those blessings, to which you were entitled by nature; but, Sir, how pitiable is it to reflect that although you were so fully convinced of the benevolence of the Father of Mankind, and of his equal and impartial distribution of these rights and privileges which he hath conferred upon them, that you should at the same time counteract his mercies, in detaining by fraud and violence, so numerous a part of my brethren under groaning captivity and cruel oppression, that you should at the same time be found guilty of that most criminal act, which you professedly detested in others.

The American Revolution, in Banneker's mind, had unleashed a new idea — "liberty" as a natural right. Commitment to this principle demanded consistency. The overthrow of the British enslavement of the colonies required the abolition of slavery in the new republic.[57]

On August 30, 1791, Jefferson responded: "Nobody wishes more than I do to see such proofs as you exhibit, that nature has given to our black brethren, talent equal to those of the other colors of men; and that the appearance of a want of them is owing merely to the degraded condition of their existence. . . ." But actually Jefferson did not take Banneker seriously. In a letter to Joel Harlow, Jefferson claimed that the mathematician had "a mind of very common stature," and that the black scholar had aid from Andrew Ellicot, a white neighbor who "never missed an opportunity of puffing him."[58]

Parsimonious toward Wheatley as a poet and skeptical about Banneker as a mathematician, Jefferson was unable to free himself from his belief in black intellectual inferiority. Like Prospero, he insisted that, to borrow Shakespeare's poetic language, "nurture" could not improve the "nature" of blacks. Comparing Roman slavery and American black slavery, Jefferson pointed out: "Epictetus, Terence, and Phaedrus, were slaves. But they were of the race of whites. It is not their condition then, but nature, which has produced the distinction." Black slaves in America, on the other hand, were mentally inferior: "In general, their existence appears to participate more of sensation than reflection. . . . [I]t appears to me that in memory they are equal to the whites; in reason much inferior, as I think one could scarcely be found capable of tracing and comprehending the investigations of Euclid; and that in imagination they are dull, tasteless, and anomalous."[59]

In Jefferson's view, blacks were a libidinous race. "They [black men] are more ardent after their female," he claimed; "but love seems with them to be more an eager desire, than a tender delicate mixture of sentiment and sensation." The black man, he added, "preferred" the white woman with her "flowing hair" and "more elegant symmetry of form" as "uniformly" as the male "Oranootan for the black woman of those of his own species." Dominated by their passions, blacks threatened white racial purity, Jefferson believed. "This unfortunate difference in color, and perhaps of faculty," Jefferson argued, "is a powerful obstacle to the emancipation of these people. Many of their advocates, while they wish to vindicate the liberty of human nature, are anxious to preserve its dignity and beauty. . . . Among the Romans emancipation required but one effort. The slave, when made free, might mix with, without staining the blood of his master." For Jefferson, interracial sex and racially mixed offspring would rupture the borders of caste. Such crossings had to be tabooed, for racial liminality undermined social order. To be betwixt and between would dangerously blur the division between white and black.[60]

What worried Jefferson more than the threat of miscegenation was the danger of race war. "Deep-rooted prejudices entertained by the whites," he anxiously explained, "ten thousand recollections, by the blacks, of the injuries they have sustained; new provocations; the real distinctions which nature has made and many other circumstances, will divide us into parties, and produce convulsions, which will probably never end but in the extermination of one or the other race."[61]

Unless slavery were abolished, Jefferson feared, whites would continue to face the danger of servile insurrection. Commenting on the slave revolt in Santo Domingo, he wrote to James Monroe in 1793: "It is high time we should foresee the bloody scenes which our children certainly, and possibly ourselves (south of Potomac) have to wade through, and try to avert them." In 1797, referring to the need for a plan for emancipation and removal, Jefferson anxiously confessed to a friend: "If something is not done, and soon done, we shall be the murderers of our children." Three years later, an attempted slave revolt shook Jefferson like "a fire bell in the night." The Gabriel Prosser conspiracy was crushed, and twenty-five blacks were hanged. Though the insurrectionary spirit among the slaves had been quelled in this instance, Jefferson warned, it would become general and more formidable after every defeat, until whites would be forced "after dreadful scenes and sufferings to release them in their own way." He predicted that slavery would be abolished — "whether brought on by the generous energy of our own minds" or "by the bloody process of St. Domingo." In Jefferson's nightmare, slaves would seize their freedom with daggers.[62]

By Jefferson's time, it had become clear that the seventeenth-century planters had not fully considered the explosive consequences of changing from white indentured servants to black slave laborers. They wanted to diminish the presence and power of a white proletariat, armed and numerous. African slaves seemed to offer a solution to the problem of class conflict within white society. Slavery enabled planters to develop a disfranchised and disarmed black work force. Negative images of blacks that had predated the institutionalization of slavery in English America dynamically interacted with economic and political developments on the stage called Virginia.

Driven by immediate economic interests and blinded by a short time horizon, the planters had not carefully thought through what they were doing to black people as well as to American society and future generations. They had created an enslaved "giddy multitude" that constantly threatened social order. "As it is," Jefferson cried out, "we have the wolf by the ears, and we can neither hold him, nor safely let him go. Justice is in one scale, and self-preservation in the other." Jefferson had hoped America would be able to abolish slavery and remove the blacks. But, by then, it was too late. Like Caliban, blacks had been forced to become slaves and serve in "offices that profited" their masters, who, unlike Prospero, could not simply free them and leave the island. "All torment, trouble, wonder, and amazement inhabits here," the English theatergoers heard the old counselor Gonzalo pray. "Some heavenly power guide us out of this fearful country!"[63]

PART TWO

Borders

Prospero Unbound: The Market Revolution

L
IKE JOHN WINTHROP, Jefferson believed Americans had a special destiny and responsibility: "The eyes of the virtuous all over the earth are turned with anxiety upon us, as the only depositories of the sacred fire of liberty, and . . . our falling into anarchy would decide forever the destinies of mankind, and seal the political heresy that man is incapable of self-government." Here was a republican vision of "the city upon a hill." To be self-governing meant that men in America no longer needed a parent country, especially a king. Like Prospero, they would re-create themselves in the New World.[1]

If Americans were to be a virtuous people, would all of the people in the new nation be allowed to become Americans? Shortly before the beginning of the American Revolution, Benjamin Franklin noted that the number of "purely white People" in the world was proportionately very small. All Africa was black or tawny, Asian chiefly tawny, and "America (exclusive of the new comers) wholly so." The English were the "principle Body of white People," and Franklin wanted more of this type in America. "And while we are . . . *Scouring* our Planet, by clearing America of Woods, and so making this Side of our globe reflect a brighter Light to the Eyes of Inhabitants in Mars or Venus," he declared, "why should we in the Sight of Superior Beings, darken its People? Why increase the Sons of Africa, by Planting them in America, where we have so fair an opportunity, by excluding all Blacks and Tawnys, of increasing the lovely White. . . ?"[2]

Independence had given new importance to this question. The Founding Fathers needed to define political membership for the new republic. In Congress, they enacted the Naturalization Act of 1790. In supporting this law, they affirmed their commitment to the "pure principles of Republicanism" and their determination to develop a citizenry of good and "useful" men. Only the "worthy part of mankind" would be encouraged to settle in the new republic and be eligible for citizenship. Prospective citizens would be required to go through a probationary period so they would have time to understand republican principles and demonstrate "proper and decent behavior." Through this careful screening, the government would exclude "vagrants," "paupers," and "bad men." But the policymakers went further in their efforts to create a homogeneous society. Applicants for naturalized citizenship were required to reside in the United States for two years as well as provide "proof" of good character in court and document their republican fitness. They also had to be "white." This law reflected what Thomas Jefferson envisioned as a society composed of "a people speaking the same language, governed in similar forms, and by similar laws." The Naturalization Act excluded from citizenship not only nonwhite immigrants but also a group of people already here — Indians. Though they were born in the United States, they were regarded as members of tribes, or as domestic subjects; their status was considered analogous to children of foreign diplomats born here. As domestic "foreigners," Native Americans could not seek naturalized citizenship, for they were not "white."[3]

Republicanism provided a psychology that would fuel economic acquisition and expansion in America. In the act of independence, Americans had seized not only power from the king but also the freedom to create a vibrant economy. The Protestant ethic had defined work as virtuous, requiring the habits of self-control and the accumulation of wealth as a sign of salvation; republicanism was now proclaiming worldly goods as markers of virtue. The war for political independence had secured economic freedom for America: freedom to convert Indian lands west of the Appalachians into private property, to trade whenever and with whomever they wished, to import products like tea and molasses without paying taxes to an external authority, to issue their own currency, to develop their own manufacturing, and in general, to expand the market.[4]

This republican "errand into the wilderness" generated a frenetic pursuit for individual materialistic success. Visiting the United States in the 1830s, Alexis de Tocqueville noticed "an inordinate love of material gratification" among Americans. Democracy itself seemed to be its source. "When the reverence that belonged to what is old has vanished," he explained, "birth, cóndition, and profession no longer distinguish men . . . hardly anything but money remains to create strongly marked differences between them and to raise some of them above the common level." Money had become the nexus of social relations. "When all the members of the community are independent of or indifferent to each other, the co-operation of each of them can be obtained only by paying for it: This infinitely multiplies the purposes to which wealth may be applied and increases its value." Unbound, like Prospero, white men were no longer restrained by laws made in the old country as they ushered America into the era of the Market Revolution — the "take-off" years that transformed America into a highly complex industrial economy.[5]

In 1800, the United States had a population of six million, of which only 320,000 were listed as urban. A large percentage of the rural population was engaged in subsistence farming, growing food crops mainly for their own needs. Living in the interior regions, many of these farmers found that the transportation of surplus crops to the market was too expensive. The cost of carrying a ton of goods only thirty miles overland was as much as shipping it three thousand miles from America to Europe. Thus commercial activity was limited to the areas near the seaboard and navigable waterways.

By 1860, this static economy had been transformed. Advances in transportation such as the steamboat and the railroad now linked the three major regions — the East, West, and South. Each region represented a division of production. New England and the Middle Atlantic states concentrated on manufacturing and commerce and relied on the West for foodstuffs for its growing urban population and the South for raw cotton to supply its textile factories. In 1860, the total value of manufactured goods in the East was $1,270,937,679, compared to only $540,137,811 for the other two regions combined. The western states of Ohio, Indiana, and Illinois exported grain and livestock to the East and South while depending on the East for manufactured goods. In 1860, the West shipped a million barrels of flour and 31 million barrels of grain through Buffalo to the East, and $185,211,254 worth of produce through New Orleans to the South. The South, mainly Georgia, South Carolina, Alabama, Mississippi, and Louisiana, became the cotton kingdom, producing fiber for the textile mills of the East and purchasing foodstuffs from the West and manufactured goods from the East. Meanwhile, cotton had become the country's most important export product. Cotton constituted 39 percent of the total value of exports from 1816 to 1820 63 percent from 1836 to 1840, and over 50 percent from 1840 to 1860.

The causes of this tremendous economic transformation were multiple. The shipping boom of the early 1800s had enabled merchants like Francis Lowell to accumulate capital to invest in manufacturing ventures.

The proliferation of banks and the expansion of the credit system made it possible for farmers to borrow money and buy land for commercial agriculture. Technological progress introduced new machinery and paved the way for factory production. Government intervention in the form of protective tariffs and the development of transportation also contributed to the advance of the market. The transportation revolution laid vast networks of turnpikes, canals, and railroads across the country: between 1815 and 1860, freight charges for shipments overland had been reduced by 95 percent.[6]

But the most "decisive" impetus of the Market Revolution was cotton. "Cotton was strategic," observed economist Douglass C. North, "because it was the major independent variable in the interdependent structure of internal and international trade. The demands for western foodstuffs and northeastern services and manufactures were basically dependent upon the income received from the cotton trade." Dominant in the export trade, cotton was crucial in the development of interregional specialization. The income derived from the export of cotton helped to finance enterprises throughout the American economy.[7]

The development of the cotton export sector depended on the appropriation of Indian lands and the expansion of slavery. The major cotton-producing states — Alabama, Mississippi, and Louisiana — were carved out of Indian territory. Tribe after tribe in the South was forced to cede their lands to the federal government and move west of the Mississippi River. Eleven treaties of cession were negotiated with these tribes between 1814 and 1824; from these agreements the United States acquired millions of acres of lands, including one-fifth of Mississippi and three-quarters of Alabama. Sales of Indian lands were followed by increases in the slave population: between 1820 and 1850, the number of slaves jumped from 42,000 to 343,000 in Alabama, 33,000 to 310,000 in Mississippi, and 69,000 to 245,000 in Louisiana. Cotton production in Alabama, Arkansas, Florida, Louisiana, and Mississippi nearly doubled, from 559,000 bales in 1833 to 1,160,000 ten years later.

The Market Revolution opened the way to the making of an even more multicultural America, for it led to the massive influx of laborers from Ireland, the war against Mexico with its annexation of the Southwest territories, and eventually to American expansion into Asia and Chinese immigration to America. The inclusion of these new groups of Calibans created a greater "pluribus," a racially and culturally diverse "giddy multitude" that challenged the vision of Jefferson's "homogeneous" America and Franklin's society of "the lovely White." The economy fastened these different peoples to each other, their histories woven into the tapestry of a greater "unum" called America. Working in the textile mills of New England, Irish immigrant women manufactured fabric made from cotton grown on former Indian land and picked by enslaved blacks; meanwhile, Irish immigrant men labored in New England shoe factories, making shoes from hides shipped by Mexican workers in California. Chinese and Irish railroad workers laid the transcontinental tracks that closed the frontier and changed forever the lives of Indians in the West. America was becoming a nation of peoples from many different shores.

But as the Market Revolution buttressed the institution of slavery and the westward expansion into Indian territory, the very boundlessness of this racial and ethnic diversity generated a need to reinforce interior borders. This dilemma of preserving racial homogeneity while becoming a multicultural society perplexed the policymakers of the new nation. They were especially concerned about two of the groups. "Next to the case of the black race within our bosom," worried James Madison, "that of the red on our borders is the problem most baffling to the policy of our country."[8]

4

TOWARD THE STONY
MOUNTAINS

From Removal to Reservation

Andrew Jackson: Symbol for an Age

ON FEBRUARY 16, 1803, President Thomas Jefferson wrote a letter to a political leader in Tennessee regarding federal policies toward Indians. The government, he informed Andrew Jackson, must advise the Indians to sell their "useless" forests and become farmers. The Founding Father was confident that the young westerner would be able to advance the borders of a homogeneous America. Indeed, under Jackson's leadership, the United States achieved one of Jefferson's goals — the removal of the southern Indians toward the "Stony mountains."[1]

Jackson's fortunes, both economic and political, were tied to what happened to the Indians. In 1787, he moved from North Carolina to Nashville, where he practiced law, opened stores, and engaged in land speculation — lands that had originally belonged to Indians. Like Prospero, he had migrated west, seeking a new environment offering the possibility of re-creating himself. Jackson paid $100 for 2,500 acres at the Chickasaw bluffs on the Mississippi and immediately sold half of this property for $312. He kept the rest of the land until 1818, when he sold it for $5,000. Jackson had personally negotiated the Chickasaw treaty and opened the area to white settlement in 1814.

Meanwhile, Jackson had led American troops against the Creeks in Mississippi and conquered "the cream of the Creek country" for the expansion of the "republick." During the war against the Creeks, commander Jackson dehumanized his enemies as "savage bloodhounds" and "blood thirsty barbarians." When Jackson learned that hostile Creeks had killed more than two hundred whites at Fort Mims, he vowed revenge. "I know," he told his soldiers, "you will teach the cannibals who reveled in the carnage of our unoffending Citizens at Fort Meems that the thunder of our arms is more terrible than the Earth quakes of their Prophets, and that Heaven Dooms to inevitable destruction the wretch who Smiles at the torture he inflicts and who neither spares female innocence, declining age nor helpless infancy." Jackson furiously denounced the Indian capture of a white woman, who was confined to a post, "naked, lascerated," and urged the "brave sons of Tennessee" to wipe away this "blushing shame."[2]

Shortly before the Battle of Horse Shoe Bend in March 1814, Jackson raged in letters to Major General Thomas Pinckney. "I must distroy those deluded victims doomed to distruction by their own restless and savage conduct." Calling them "savage dogs," he wrote: "It is by the charge I distroy from eight to ten of them . . . I have on all occasions preserved the scalps of my killed." At the Battle of Horse Shoe Bend, Jackson and his troops surrounded eight hundred Creeks and killed almost all of them, including the women and children. Afterward, his soldiers made bridle reins from strips of skin taken from the corpses; they also cut off the tip of each dead Indian's nose for body count. Jackson sent clothing worn by the slain warriors to the ladies of Tennessee. In a letter to his wife, he wrote: "The *carnage* was *dreadful*. . . . I hope shortly to put an end to the war and return to your arms, kiss my little andrew for me, tell him I have a warriors bow and quiver for him." In a letter to Thomas Pinckney, Jackson boasted that he had conquered Indian lands, the "valuable country" west of the Cosee and north of the "allabama."[3]

But Jackson shrouded the destruction of Indians and the appropriation of their lands in a metaphysical mantle of moral justification. After the bloody victory, Jackson told his troops:

> The fiends of the Tallapoosa will no longer murder our women
> and children, or disturb the quiet of our borders. . . . They have

disappeared from the face of the Earth. In their places a new generation will arise who will know their duties better. The weapons of warfare will be exchanged for the utensils of husbandry; and the wilderness which now withers in sterility and seems to mourn the desolation which overspreads it, will blossom as the rose, and become the nursery of the arts. . . . How lamentable it is that the path to peace should lead through blood, and over the carcases of the slain!! But it is in the dispensation of that providence, which inflicts partial evil to produce general good.

His soldiers were advancing civilization, Jackson insisted. Their violence was an instrument of progress.[4]

Revered as a victorious hero of Indian wars, Jackson was elected to the presidency of the United States in 1828. As chief executive, Jackson supported the efforts of Mississippi and Georgia to abolish Indian tribal units and extend state authority over Indians. These states then opened Indian territory to settlement, even allowing whites to take improved or cultivated Indian tracts. As Jackson watched the states violate federal treaties with tribes, he pleaded presidential helplessness. "If the states chose to extend their laws over them," he told Congress, "it would not be in the power of the federal government to prevent it." Actually, treaties and federal laws had given authority over the Indians to Congress, not the states. The 1802 Indian Trade and Intercourse Act had provided that no land cessions could be made except by treaty with a tribe, and that federal rather than state law would operate in Indian territory. In 1832, after the Supreme Court ruled that states could not legally extend their jurisdiction into Indian territory, Jackson simply refused to enforce the court's decision.[5]

Jackson's claim of presidential powerlessness and his failure to uphold the law functioned as a facade for collaboration and conspiracy. Behind the scene, he actively worked for Indian removal. General John Coffee laid out the strategy. "Deprive the chiefs of the power they now possess," he wrote to the president, "take from them their own code of laws, and reduce them to plain citizenship . . . and they will soon determine to move, and then there will be no difficulty in getting the poor Indians to give their consent. All this will be done by the State of Georgia if the United States do not interfere with her law." All Jackson had to do was stay out of the way.[6]

In his support for the states, Jackson went beyond noninterference: he employed "confidential agents" to manipulate the chiefs. Their secret mission, as stated in a letter from Secretary of War John Eaton to General William Carroll, was to use bribery in order to persuade "the Chiefs and influential men." "Since no circumstance is too slight to excite their suspicion or awaken their jealousy, presents in your discretion to the amount of not more than $2000 might be made with effect, by attaching to you the poorer Indians, as you pass through their Country, given as their friend; and the same to the Children of the Chiefs, and the Chiefs themselves, in clothes, or otherwise."[7]

In his justification for Indian removal, President Jackson explained that efforts to civilize the Indians had failed. Whites had purchased their lands, thereby thrusting them farther into the wilderness, where they remained in a "wandering state." Some Indians had become civilized and agricultural, Jackson acknowledged, but they had set up "independent" nations within the states. Such "foreign" governments could not be tolerated, and the Indians would have to submit to state authority. But Jackson did not think that they could survive within white society. "The fate of the Mohigan, the Narragansett, and the Delaware is fast overtaking the Choctaw, the Cherokee, and the Creek. That this fate surely awaits them if they remain within the [states] does not admit of a doubt." Like the tribes before them, they would disappear. "Humanity and national honor demand that every effort be made to avert so great a calamity."[8]

Driven by "feelings of justice," Jackson declared that he wanted "to preserve this much-injured race." He proposed a solution — the setting aside of a district west of the Mississippi "to be guaranteed to the Indian tribes as long as they shall occupy it." Beyond the borders of white society, Indians would be free to live in peace and to have their own governments "as long as the grass grows, or water runs." Jackson advised Indians to seek new homes in the West and follow the example of whites: restless and boundless, whites were constantly seeking to improve themselves and settle in new places. "Doubtless it will be painful [for Indians] to leave the graves of their fathers," Jackson declared. "But what do they more than our ancestors did or than our children are now doing? To better their condition in an unknown land our forefathers left all that was dear in earthly objects."[9]

Insisting that he wanted to be "just" and "humane" toward the Indians, Jackson claimed his goal was to protect them from the "mercenary influence of white men." Seeking to exercise "parental" control over them, he regarded himself as a "father," concerned about the welfare of his Indian "children." But if these "children" refused to accept his advice, Jackson warned, they would be responsible for the consequences. "I feel conscious of having done my duty to my red children, and if any failure of my good intentions arises, it will be attributable to their want of duty to themselves, not to me."[10]

Like the early Puritans, Jackson affirmed the "errand into the wilderness" in his justification for Indian removal and destruction. What happened to the natives of America, he argued, was moral and inevitable. Indian graves, while stirring "melancholy reflections," represented progress — the extension of civilization across the expanse called America. Nothing, Jackson insisted, was to be "regretted." "Humanity has often wept over the fate of the aborigines of this country, and Philanthropy has been long busily employed in devising means to avert it," Jackson explained in a message to Congress, "but its progress has never for a moment been arrested, and one by one have many powerful tribes disappeared from the earth. To follow to the tomb the last of his race and tread on the graves of extinct nations excite melancholy reflections." But "philanthropy could not wish to see this continent restored to the condition in which it was found by our forefathers." The philosophical president then asked: "What good man would prefer a country covered with forests and ranged by a few thousand savages to our extensive Republic, studded with cities, towns, and prosperous farms ... filled with all the blessings of liberty, civilization, and religion?"[11]

Native Americans saw the chicanery of this metaphysics. Like Caliban cursing Prospero, Cherokee leader John Ross declared that "the perpetrator of a wrong" would never forgive "his victims." But President Jackson maintained a legal and moral posture. Acting under an 1830 law providing for Indian removal, Jackson uprooted some seventy thousand Indians from their homes and drove them west of the Mississippi River. Removal was carried out in two ways — indirectly through land allotment and directly through treaty.[12]

The Land-Allotment Strategy: The Choctaw Experience

Instituted by President Thomas Jefferson, the land-allotment program became the principal strategy for taking territory away from the Creeks, Chickasaws, and Choctaws. In the 1805 Choctaw Treaty, the federal government had reserved certain tracts of land for individual Choctaws. Jefferson told a delegation of chiefs: "Let me entreat you ... on the land now given to you, to begin to give every man a farm; let him enclose it, cultivate it, build a warm house on it, and when he dies, let it belong to his wife and children after him." The aim of Jefferson's policy was the transformation of the Choctaws into farmers.[13]

Actually, the Choctaws of Mississippi had been horticulturalists since long before the arrival of whites. They employed the slash and burn method to clear areas for planting corn, beans, squash, pumpkins, and watermelons. To prepare the ground, they used a digging stick, a short heavy pole of hard wood with a sharp point. Then, in the early summer, they celebrated the Green Corn Dance, a ceremony to bless the fields. After the harvest, they laid out the corn in small lots to dry, and then layered the corn between grass and clay mortar in little piles, "each covered and arranged side by side," looking "like a big mud dauber's nest." The Choctaws prepared the corn in various ways. "First they roast it in the fire and eat it so," a French traveler reported. "When it is very tender they pound it and make porridge of it, but the most esteemed among them is the cold meal."[14]

Before contact with the strangers from Europe, the Choctaws practiced communalism. Living in towns and organized in chiefdoms, they hunted in groups and distributed the deer among themselves; they also shared common grain reserves. After the harvest, the people erected a large granary. "To this each family carries and deposits a certain quantity, according to his ability or inclination, or none at all if he so chooses," reported a visitor. This "public treasury" supplied individual tribal members in need as well as neighboring towns suffering from crop failures. Reciprocity provided the basis of Choctaw community and social relations. Critical of European individualism and possessiveness, they condemned the English for allowing their poor to suffer from hunger. Trader James Adair reported that the Choctaws were "very kind and liberal to every one of their own tribe, even to the last morsel of food they enjoy."[15]

By the early nineteenth century, many Choctaws had turned to stock-raising. Domesticated cows, horses, and pigs on enclosed farms replaced wild deer in open hunting preserves. Chief Franchimastabe explained that Choctaws would now have to raise cattle and live like white men, for the time of "hunting and living by the Gun" was nearly over. Choctaws also cultivated cotton for the market. Some of them had extensive operations: Greenwood LeFlore had 250 acres of cotton fields worked by thirty-two slaves, and David Folsom had 150 acres with a labor force of seventeen slaves.[16]

Even after they had become property owners and producers for the market, the Choctaws were still not wanted in Mississippi, for they were the wrong color, unable to cross the racial border and blend into

Benjamin Franklin's society of "the lovely White." Agent Stephen Ward reported that the Choctaws were becoming civilized persons and land-owners, but none of this mattered to many white Mississippians. "I know an Indian will be an Indian," one of them declared in a local newspaper, "because we have had plenty of Indians in Natchez, and can you show me who has been civilized by being brought among us?"[17]

In January 1830, the Mississippi state government abolished the sovereignty of the Choctaw Nation. Any Choctaw who opposed state authority would be subjected to a thousand-dollar fine and a year in prison. In September, federal commissioners met with the Choctaws at Dancing Rabbit Creek to negotiate a treaty for acquiring their lands and removing them beyond the Mississippi. Robert H. Grant, a trader in the Choctaw Nation, reported that "there was a strong, and I believe universal feeling, in opposition to the sale of any portion of their remaining country in Mississippi." The Choctaw representatives turned down the offer: "It is the voice of a very large majority of the people here present not to sell the land of their forefathers." Thinking that the meeting was over, many Choctaws left. But the federal commissioners refused to accept no for an answer and bluntly told the remaining chiefs that the Choctaws must move or be governed by Mississippi state law. If they resisted, they would be destroyed by federal forces in a few weeks. A treaty was finally secured by intimidation.[18]

"We are exceedingly tired," wrote Chief David Folsom in a letter to Presbyterian missionaries. "We have just heard of the ratification of the Choctaw Treaty. Our doom is sealed. There is no other course for us but to turn our faces to our new homes toward the setting sun." Years later, Chief Cobb told Captain J. McRea, an officer in charge of removal: "Brother: Our hearts are full. Twelve winters ago our chiefs sold our country. Every warrior that you see here was opposed to the treaty. If the dead could have counted, it could never have been made, but alas! Though they stood around, they could not be seen or heard. Their tears came in the raindrops, and their voices in the wailing wind, but the pale faces knew it not, and our land was taken away."[19]

The Treaty of Dancing Rabbit Creek provided that the Choctaws cede all of their 10,423,130 acres to the federal government and migrate to lands west of the Mississippi River. Not all of the Choctaws were required to leave, however. Choctaw families and individuals were instructed to register with an Indian agent within six months after ratification of the treaty if they wished to remain in Mississippi and receive a land grant. Seemingly, the program gave Choctaws a fair chance to succeed in white society as individual landowners.[20]

Federal certifying agents, however, proceeded to collaborate with land speculators to transfer Indian lands from the tribes to individual Indians and then to whites. Speculators took Indians by groups from one agent to another and had them sign contracts for land grants. Often the speculators were the federal agents themselves. After they secured lands for individual Indians, speculators made loans to them in exchange for their titles as collateral, and then they took over the deeds when the Indians failed to repay their debts.

Meanwhile, many whites simply took possession of Indian lands. "Owing to the law of the State of Mississippi passed at the last session, granting permission to the whites to settle in the Choctaw Nation," a contemporary reported, "hundreds have come in and are squatting on the lands in all directions." Once they occupied Indian lands, they usually offered to pay for the property. "For the most part, every purchaser of cultivated reservations have made small advances to the Indians, with a promise to pay the balance when the Indians make a good title; which can hardly be effected, owing to the remote residence of the Indians when they remove to the west."[21]

The Treaty of Dancing Rabbit Creek and the land allotment program unleashed white expansion: speculators, farmers, and planters proceeded to take Indian lands "legally," while absolving themselves from responsibility for Indian removal. Whites could not be blamed if Indians got into debt, lost their lands, and had to move beyond the Mississippi. "Our citizens were disposed to buy and the Indians to sell," explained Secretary of War Cass. "The improvident habits of the Indians cannot be controlled by [federal] regulations. . . . If they waste it, as waste it they too often will, it is deeply to be regretted yet still it is only exercising a right conferred upon them by the treaty." Indians were responsible for their own ruin. Behind the blame, however, was a hidden agenda. In a letter to General John Coffee, April 7, 1832, President Jackson wrote: "The object of the government now is, to have all their reservations surveyed and laid off as early as we can." Once Indians had been granted their individual land allotments, he added, they would "sell and move to the West." Jackson reassured Coffee: "When the reserves are surveyed it will require but a short time to compleat the ballance and have it into markett. . . ."[22]

A year after the Treaty of Dancing Rabbit Creek, thousands of Choctaws began their trek to the new territory west of the Mississippi River. "The feeling which many of them evince in separating, never to return again, from their own long cherished hills, poor as they are in this section of country," wrote an army officer, "is truly painful to witness. . . ." But what was even more distressing to see was the suffering. While en route to their new homes, many Choctaws encountered terrible winter storms. One eyewitness recorded the experience of several hundred migrating Choctaws: "There are very aged persons and very young children in the company; many had nothing to shelter them from the storm by day or night. The weather was excessively cold, and yet . . . not one in ten of the women had even a moccasin on their feet and the great majority of them were walking. . . . One party came to us and begged for an ear of corn apiece [to relieve] their suffering." Not only the cold weather but also diseases like cholera stalked the migrants. "Not a family but more or less sick," reported Lieutenant Gabriel Rains to his general; "the Choctaws are dying to an alarming extent. . . . Near the agency there are 3,000 Indians and within the hearing of a gun from this spot 100 have died within five weeks. . . . The mortality among these people since the beginning of fall as far as ascertained, amounts to one-fifth of the whole number."[23]

A French visitor witnessed the Choctaws crossing the Mississippi River on their way to the West. "It was then the middle of winter," reported Alexis de Tocqueville, "and the cold was unusually severe; the snow had frozen hard upon the ground, and the river was drifting huge masses of ice. The Indians had their families with them, and they brought in their train the wounded and the sick, with children newly born and old men upon the verge of death." Before his eyes was a microcosm of the epic story of Indian retreat before white expansion. "Three or four thousand soldiers drive before them the wandering races of the aborigines; these are followed by the pioneers, who pierce the woods, scare off the beasts of prey, explore the courses of the inland streams, and make ready the triumphal march of civilization across the desert." What struck Tocqueville was how whites were able to deprive Indians of their rights and exterminate them "with singular felicity, tranquilly, legally, philanthropically, without shedding blood, and without violating a single great principle of morality in the eyes of the world." Indeed, he wryly remarked, it was impossible to destroy men with "more respect for the laws of humanity."[24]

Uprooted, many Choctaws felt bitter and angry. "The privations of a whole nation before setting out, their turmoil and losses on the road, and settling their homes in a wild world," one of them declared, "are all calculated to embitter the human heart." In a "Farewell Letter to the American People, 1832," George W. Harkins explained why his people had left their ancestral lands: "We were hedged in by two evils, and we chose that which we thought least." The Mississippi legislators, he insisted, were not qualified to become lawmakers for a people so dissimilar in culture as the Choctaws were to whites. A "mountain of prejudice" would continue to obstruct "the streams of justice." Thus the Choctaws chose to "suffer and be free" rather than live under the degrading influence of laws where their voices could not be heard. But they went unwillingly, for their attachment to their "native land" was strong. "That cord is now broken," Harkins cried out, "and we must now go forth as wanderers in a strange land!"[25]

The Choctaws denounced the president for betraying them. "The man [Andrew Jackson] who said that he would plant a stake and draw a line around us, that never should be passed," a Choctaw charged, "was the first to say he could not guard the lines, and drew up the stake and wiped out all traces of the line." The angry protester urged his compatriots to resist "the gloom and horrors of the present separation." They should establish themselves in their "destined home" so that they would never be uprooted by whites again and would be able to "live free" forever.[26]

The total cost of Choctaw removal, including salaries for the agents and land-fraud settlements, was $5,097,367.50. To pay for these expenses, the federal government sold the Choctaw lands to white settlers and received $8,095,614.89. In the Treaty of Dancing Rabbit Creek, the government had agreed that it would not make any profits from the sales of Choctaw lands. The Choctaws sued in federal court and won $2,981,247.39, but most of the awarded sum went to pay their lawyers.[27]

The Treaty Strategy: The Cherokees' Trail of Tears

In the beginning, according to Cherokee legend, water covered the entire earth and all of the animals lived in the sky. One day, a beaver dove into the ocean, and created land by bringing mud to the surface and fastening it to the sky with four cords. Then the Great Buzzard flew to earth. "When he reached the Cherokee country, he was very tired, and his wings began to flap and strike the ground, and wherever they struck the earth there was a valley, and where they turned up again there was a mountain." This beautiful land of valleys and mountains became the home of the Cherokees.[28]

But, like the Choctaws in Mississippi, the Cherokees in Georgia were dispossessed, their lands "legally" moved into the "markett." In 1829, the Georgia legislature had passed a law extending state authority over the territory of the Cherokee Nation. The law also provided that any member of the tribe who tried to influence a fellow Cherokee to remain in Georgia would be imprisoned, and that no Cherokee would "be deemed a competent witness in any court of this state to which a white person may be a party." They were given a choice — leave the state or be subjugated by white rule.[29]

In a message to the General Council of the Cherokee Nation in July 1830, Chief John Ross protested the new policy. He criticized President Andrew Jackson for refusing to protect the Cherokees against Georgia's illegal and unfair actions. Jackson's inaction had placed their relationship with the federal government in "a strange dilemma." Ross urged his fellow Cherokees to stand united against Georgia and Jackson. Again, on April 14, 1831, he warned: "The object of the President is . . . to create divisions among ourselves." Ross warned that Jackson's strategy was to divide and conquer: "Will you break sticks to put into the hands of the president to break your own heads with?"[30]

The Cherokees refused to abandon their homes and lands. The federal government, they insisted, was obligated to honor the treaties guaranteeing the sovereignty of the Cherokee Nation and the integrity of their territory. In a protest to Secretary of War Lewis Cass on February 6, 1834, Chief Ross condemned Georgia's lawlessness: "The right of property and even the life of the Cherokee is in jeopardy, and are at the mercy of the robber and the assasin. By these acts the citizen of Georgia is licensed to come into immediate collision with the Cherokee individual, by violence, if he chooses, for any and everything that is sacred to the existence of man upon earth. And the Cherokee is denied the right of appearing before the sanctuary of justice created by law for the redress of wrongs." A month later, Chief Ross wrote directly to President Jackson: "The relations of peace and friendship so happily and so long established between the white and the red man . . . induces us, as representatives of the Cherokee nation, to address you [as] Father. The appellation in its original sense carries with it simplicity, and the force of filial regard." By treaty, the Cherokee people had placed themselves under the protection of the federal government, which in turn had given "*assurances* of protection, good neighborhood and the solemn guarantee" for the territorial integrity of the Cherokee Nation. A good father, the Cherokee chief insisted, should honor his promises to his children.[31]

But the appeals fell on deaf ears in Washington. Instead, President Jackson instructed Commissioner J. F. Schermerhorn to negotiate a treaty for Cherokee removal. Schermerhorn secured an agreement from John

Ridge, the head of a small proremoval faction of Cherokees. According to the terms, the Cherokees would cede their land and be removed in exchange for a payment of $3,250,000. The treaty was signed in Washington on March 14, 1835, but it needed to be ratified by the tribe in full council to be valid.

Schermerhorn arranged to present the treaty to the Cherokee council at a meeting in New Echota, Georgia, to be held in December. To Secretary of War Lewis Cass, the commissioner wrote: "We shall make a treaty with those who attend, and rely upon it." What he meant was that only the proremoval faction would be permitted to attend. Before the meeting took place, the Georgia militia jailed Chief Ross and suppressed the Cherokee newspaper in order to restrict information about the meeting and to curb criticism. "The manner of seizure of the public press," Chief Ross protested in a letter to his people, "could not have been sanctioned for any other purpose than to stifle the voice of the Cherokee people, raised by their cries from the wounds inflicted upon them by the unsparing hand of their oppressors, and that the ear of humanity might thereby be prevented from hearing them." With the opposition to removal silenced, Schermerhorn proceeded to sign a treaty at New Echota.[32]

The treaty was a sham: only a tiny fraction of the entire Cherokee Nation attended, and none of the tribal officers was present. According to Schermerhorn's own report, only about three to five hundred Cherokees out of a population of over seventeen thousand were present. Chief Ross and the antiremoval Cherokee leaders tried to block the treaty's approval in Congress. "This instrument," they declared to the Senate, "purports to be a contract with the Cherokee people, when in fact it has been agreed upon, in direct violation of their will, wishes, and interest, by a few unauthorized individuals of the [Cherokee] Nation. . . ." Some government officials confirmed that the treaty was indeed a fraud. In a letter to Secretary Cass, Major W. M. Davis described what had actually happened at New Echota: "Sir, that paper . . . called a treaty, is no treaty at all." It was "not sanctioned by the great body of the Cherokee," and was made "without their participation or assent." Davis charged that "Mr. Schermerhorn's apparent design was to conceal the real number present. . . . The delegation taken to Washington by Mr. Schermerhorn had no more authority to make a treaty than any other dozen Cherokee accidentally picked up for the purpose." Clearly, the treaty was chicanery; yet President Jackson "relied upon it" and Congress ratified it.[33]

The treaty let loose thousands of white intruders, who seized the "ceded" lands, murdering many Cherokees and forcing others to abandon their farms. In a letter to President Jackson, proremoval leader Ridge complained about the atrocities:

> We come now to address you on the subject of our griefs and afflictions from the acts of the white people. They have got our lands and now they are preparing to fleece us of the money accruing from the treaty. We found our plantations taken either in whole or in part by the Georgians — suits instituted against us for back rents for our own farms. . . . Even the Georgia laws, which deny us our oaths, are thrown aside, and notwithstanding the cries of our people . . . the lowest classes of the white people are flogging the Cherokees with cowhides, hickories, and clubs.[34]

Most of the Cherokees refused to migrate. In the spring of 1838, Chief Ross again protested against the treaty by presenting Congress with a petition signed by 15, 665 Cherokees. But the federal government dismissed it and ordered the military to carry out an order for forced removal.[35]

In command of seven thousand soldiers, General Winfield Scott warned the Cherokees that they had to cooperate: "My troops already occupy many positions . . . and thousands and thousands are approaching from every quarter to render assistance and escape alike hopeless. Will you, then by resistance compel us to resort to arms . . . or will you by flight seek to hide yourself in mountains and forests and thus oblige us to hunt you down?" The soldiers first erected internment camps and then rounded up the Cherokees. "Families at dinner were startled by the sudden gleam of bayonets in the doorway and rose up to be driven with blows and oaths along the weary miles of trail that led to the stockade. Men were seized in their fields . . . women were taken from their wheels and children from their play." The process of dispossession was violent and cruel. "The Cherokees are nearly all prisoners," the Reverend Evan Jones protested. "They had been dragged from their houses . . . allowed no time to take any thing with them, except the clothes they had on. Well-furnished houses were left prey to plunderers, who, like hungry wolves, follow in the train of the captors. . . . The property of many have been taken, and sold before their eyes for almost nothing — the sellers and buyers, in many cases having combined to cheat the poor Indians."[36]

From the internment camps, the Cherokees were marched westward.

"We are now about to take our final leave and kind farewell to our native land the country that the Great Spirit gave our Fathers," a Cherokee informed Chief Ross. "We are on the eve of leaving that Country that gave us birth. . . . [I]t is with [sorrow] that we are forced by the authority of the white man to quit the scenes of our childhood."[37]

The march took place in the dead of winter. "We are still nearly three hundred miles short of our destination," wrote Reverend Evan Jones in Little Prairie, Missouri. "It has been exceedingly cold . . . those thinly clad very uncomfortable . . . we have, since the cold set in so severely, sent on a company every morning, to make fires along the road, at short intervals. . . . At the Mississippi river, we were stopped from crossing, by the ice running so that boats could not pass. . . ." The exiles were defenseless against the weather and disease. "Among the recent immigrants," wrote a witness near Little Rock, "there has been much sickness, and in some neighborhoods the mortality has been great. . . . Since last October about 2,000 immigrants have come. Twenty-five hundred more are on their way . . . much sickness and mortality among them." Quatie Ross, the wife of the chief, died of pneumonia at Little Rock. "Long time we travel on way to new land," one of the exiles recalled bitterly. "People feel bad when they leave Old Nation. Women cry and make sad wails. Children cry and many men cry, and all look sad when friends die, but they say nothing and just put heads down and keep on going towards West."[38]

Removal meant separation from a special and sacred place — their homeland created by the Great Buzzard. A Cherokee song acquired new and deeper meaning from the horror of removal:

> *Toward the black coffin of the upland in the Darkening Land*
> *   your paths shall stretch out.*
> *So shall it be for you. . . .*
> *Now your soul has faded away.*
> *It has become blue.*
> *When darkness comes your spirit shall grow less and dwindle*
> *   away, never to reappear.*

A Cherokee recalled how there were so many bodies to bury: "Looks like maybe all be dead before we get to new Indian country, but always we keep marching on." By the time they reached the new land west of the Mississippi, more than four thousand Cherokees — nearly one-fourth of this exiled Indian nation — died on what they have bitterly remembered as the "Trail of Tears."[39]

Where the Buffalo No Longer Roam

Beyond the Mississippi River lived the Plains Indians — the Cheyenne, Arapaho, Kiowa, Sioux, and Pawnee. Inhabiting central Nebraska and northern Kansas, the Pawnees depended on buffalo and corn for their sustenance. Both sources of life were celebrated in Pawnee legends. When the Pawnee people were placed on the earth a long time ago, they wandered from place to place and lived on roots and berries. But food became scarce, and they suffered from hunger. Then one day, a young man looked into a cave and saw an old woman; he followed her into the cave and found another country with game and fields. "My son," she told him, "the gods have given you the buffalo. The buffalo are to run out of this cave, and the first buffalo that shall go out shall be killed by your people. Its hide must be tanned, the head must be cut off, and the skull set up on this high hill. When the meat and everything has been cut off from the skull, it must be taken to the village and put in the lodge." Next, the old woman gave the young man four bundles of corn of different colors, braided together: "These are the seeds for the people. . . . Now you must go and give the seeds to the people, and let them put them in the ground." With their buffalo and corn, the Pawnees were self-sufficient.[40]

The buffalo hunt was a sacred activity, historian Richard White noted, and rituals guided the Pawnees in their migrations to the hunting grounds during the summers. Before the start of the hunt, they performed a ceremony. Pantomiming the buffalo, they chanted:

> Listen, he said, yonder the buffalo are coming,
> These are his sayings, yonder the buffalo are coming,
> They walk, they stand, they are coming,
> Yonder the buffalo are coming.
> Now you are going to trot
> Buffalo who are killed falling.

In another song, they described a herd of buffalo that had been sleeping on the plains. A calf, awakened by a frightening dream, warns grandfather buffalo:

> Grandfather, I had a dream.
> The people are gathering to surround us.

Truly they will surprise us. . . .
They drove you near the village,
And then the playful boys killed you.
Truly they will surprise us. . . .[41]

The hunt was highly organized. When the Pawnees located the buffalo, they would form a horseshoe with the open end facing the animals. At the two points, men on foot would begin the attack, shooting the buffalo at the edge of the herd. Then men on horses would charge. "When sufficient buffalo were killed for food and other needs, the butchering began," a Pawnee told his grandson years later. "This was neither a delicate or pleasant task." Skinning the buffalo in the winter was very difficult, for the "meat and skin would begin to freeze and the blood would cake and ice on the hands." In the summer, "the flies and gnats would become unbearable and it was then the young boys would offer to wave willow branches over the carcass, and at the same time drive away the dogs that would follow the hunters from the camp. . . ."[42]

Strict taboos limited the buffalo kill to what the Pawnees were able to consume, thus conserving this crucial food supply. Nothing was wasted — the hides became tepees and robes, the horns spoons, the bones tools, the meat food. "The flesh, vitals, and even the intestines, all had their place in the Pawnee cuisine," reported John B. Dunbar in 1880. "The small entrails were carefully separated, freed from their contents by being pressed rapidly between the fingers, then braided together and dried with the adhering fat, forming in this condition a favorite relish. The integument of the paunch was preserved and eaten. The liver was frequently eaten raw while retaining its natural warmth, and was deemed a delicacy."[43]

The Pawnees were also farmers. In the spring, the Pawnees planted corn. They knew the time had come, for they could smell "the different perfumes of the white weeds." "As soon as the frost was out of the ground, these patches were cleared up and planted," reported a witness. Planting corn was a sacred activity: during the ceremony, women pantomimed the breaking of the ground with decorative hoes made from the shoulder blades of buffalo. Songs thanking Mother Corn and celebrating the growth of the plant accompanied their motions:

The ground now she clears. . . .
My mother the earth comes sidewise. . . .
Now the earth is dug into my mother. . . .
Earth lively Mother Corn. . . .

It is budding. . . .
The sprouts are coming out. . . .
The earth they are tossing it about. . . .
Life movement.[44]

"The corn was hoed twice, the last time about the middle of June," a contemporary reported. "Immediately thereafter they started on the summer hunt and remained away till about the first of September, when the young corn had attained sufficient maturity for drying." In the fall, the Pawnees harvested their crops and prepared for winter.[45]

In their ceremonies for hunting buffalo and planting corn, the Pawnees brought out their tribal sacred bundles, containing the artifacts that symbolized the sources of sustenance and life. The Pawnees believed that the bundles had been given to them by gods. One of the bundles, for example, contained "a buffalo robe, fancifully dressed, skins of several fur bearing animals . . . the skull of a wild cat, stuffed skins of a sparrowhawk . . . and the swallow-tailed fly catcher, several bundles of scalps and broken arrows taken from enemies, a small bundle of Pawnee arrows, some ears of corn and a few wads of buffalo hair. . . ."[46]

During the early nineteenth century, the Pawnees began to participate in the fur trade. Although they were able to resist the introduction of liquor because the chiefs had banned alcohol in the villages, they found the market threatening them in other ways. "The foundations of Pawnee life were undermined in the course of the fur trade, generally imperceptibly, sometimes catastrophically," observed historian David J. Wishart. "Pre-contact conceptions of nature were gradually supplanted: commerical motivations intervened and hunting was secularized; the idea of reciprocity with the environment was slowly abandoned; wildlife overkill became more feasible and common." Contact due to the fur trade also led to the introduction of new diseases like smallpox, which reduced the Pawnee population from ten thousand in the 1830s to four thousand fifteen years later.[47]

By then, an even greater threat to the Pawnees had emerged — the railroad. In his 1831 annual message to Congress, President Andrew Jackson praised science for expanding man's power over nature by linking cities and extending trade over the mountains. The entire country had only 73 miles of railroad tracks in 1830. Ten years later, track mileage measured 3,328 miles, then stretched to 8,879 in 1850 and 30,636 in 1860 — more than in all of Europe.[48]

As its tracks traversed the continent, the railroad was ushering in a new era. In 1853, a newspaper editorial welcomed the ascendency of steam-driven transportation: "The human race very soon need not *toil*, but merely direct: hard work will be done by steam. Horses themselves are rapidly becoming obsolete. In a few years, like Indians, they will be merely traditional." Horses and also Indians would have no place in modern America. As the railroad crossed the plains and reached toward the Pacific coast, the iron horse was bringing the frontier to an end.[49]

"What shall we do with the Indians?" asked a writer for *The Nation* in 1867, as the Irish crews of the Union Pacific and the Chinese crews of the Central Pacific raced to complete the transcontinental railroad. The "highways to the Pacific" must not be obstructed. The Indians must either be "exterminated" or subjected to the "law and habits of industry." Civilizing the Indians, he suggested, would be "the easiest and cheapest as well as the only honorable way of securing peace." This would require the integration of Indians into white society. "We need only treat Indians like men, treat them as we do ourselves, putting on them the same responsibilities, letting them sue and be sued, and taxing them as fast as they settle down and have anything to tax."[50]

Two years later, in his annual message to Congress, President Ulysses S. Grant reflected on what the railroad portended for the Indians: "The building of railroads, and the access thereby given to all the agricultural and mineral regions of the country, is rapidly bringing civilized settlements into contact with all tribes of Indians. No matter what ought to be the relations between such settlements and the aborigines, the fact is they do not harmonize well, and one or the other has to give way in the end. A system which looks to the extinction of a race is too horrible for a nation to adopt without entailing upon itself the wrath of all Christendom and engendering in the citizen a disregard for human life and the rights of others, dangerous to society."[51]

That year, the transcontinental railroad was completed, and an iron line now adorned the face of America from coast to coast. Secretary of the Interior J. D. Cox boasted that the railroad had "totally changed" the nature of the westward migration. Previously, settlement had taken place gradually; but the railroad had "pierced" the "very center of the desert," and every station was becoming a "nucleus for a civilized settlement." Similarly, the editor of the *Cheyenne Leader* trumpeted the train as "the advance guard of empire": "The iron horse in his resistless 'march to the sea' surprises the aborigines upon their distant hunting grounds and frightens the buffalo from the plains where, for untold ages, his face has gazed in the eternal solitudes. The march of empire no longer proceeds with stately, measured strides, but has the wings of morning, and flies with the speed of lightning." As the railroad advanced to the Pacific, this mighty engine of technology was bespangling towns and cities across America, their lights glowing here and there on the horizon.[52]

Behind the "resistless" railroad were powerful corporate interests, deliberately planning the white settlement of the West and the extension of the market. Railroad companies saw the tribes as obstacles to track construction and actively lobbied the government to secure rights-of-way through Indian territory. They pushed for the passage of the 1871 Indian Appropriation Act, which declared that "hereafter no Indian nation or tribe within the territory of the United States shall be acknowledged or recognized as an independent nation, tribe, or power, with whom the United States may contract by treaty." Explaining the law's significance, an attorney for a railroad corporation stated: "It is not a mere prohibition of the making of future treaties with these tribes. It goes beyond this, and destroys the political existence of the tribes." Armed with the 1871 Indian Appropriation Act, railroad companies rapidly threw tracks across America and opened the West to new settlement.[53]

Rail lines through Indian territory suddenly recompositioned the population in terms of race. By the tens of thousands, whites were scurrying across the Mississippi. They were lining the Missouri border "impatiently awaiting the privilege of locating in the Territory," reported the *St. Joseph Gazette* in 1852. "There is no portion of the territory of the United States that is more desirable than this for agricultural and stock-raising purposes, or which would in a short period of time be filled with so large and prosperous population." Two years later, the white population numbered 2,732; by 1860, it had jumped to 28,826. Similarly, the Indian territory between Kansas and Texas had a white population of only 7,000 in 1880; by 1889, five years after the completion of the railroad in this region, the white population had exploded to 110,000. When President Benjamin Harrison announced the opening of the Oklahoma District to white settlement, sixteen trains carried thousands of whites over the line on the day of the great "run" — the dramatic race to stake out homesteads in what had been Indian territory. All of this was seen by whites as progress, the advance of civilization.[54]

Indians viewed the railroad very differently. They watched the iron horse transport white hunters to the plains, transforming the prairies into buffalo killing fields. They found carcasses littering and rotting along the railroad tracks, a trail of death for the buffalo, which were a main source of life for the Indians. Sioux chief Shakopee predicted ecological disaster and a grim future for his people: "The great herds that once covered the prairies are no more. The white men are like locusts when they fly so thick that the whole sky is like a snowstorm. You may kill one, two, ten; yes, as many as the leaves in the forest yonder, and their brothers will not miss them. Count your fingers all day long and white men with guns in their hands will come faster than you can count." The decimation of the buffalo signified the end of the Pawnee way of life.[55]

Along with the advance of the railroad and the increasing arrival of white settlers came a cry for Pawnee removal. "Pawnee Indians are in possession of some of the most valuable government land in the Territory," *The Nebraskian* editorialized. "The region of the country about the junction of Salt Creek and the Platte is very attractive and there would immediately grow up a thriving settlement were it not for the Pawnees. It is the duty of Uncle Sam to remove the Pawnee population."[56]

The Pawnees also found themselves under attack from the Sioux, who were moving south into their territory, also pushed by white settlers and driven by the decline of buffalo herds. Mainly a horticultural people, the Pawnees were militarily vulnerable. Women were murdered in the fields, earth lodges destroyed, corn crops burned, and food caches robbed. In 1873, a Pawnee hunting party was attacked by the Sioux at Massacre Canyon, and more than a hundred Pawnees were killed. Stunned by this tragedy, the Pawnees had to decide whether they should retreat to federal reservations for protection and survival. "I do not want to leave this place," Chief Terrecowah declared. "God gave us these lands." Lone Chief echoed: "I have made up my mind to stay here on my land. I am not going where I have nothing." But most Pawnees felt they had no choice, and followed the lead of Good Chief and migrated to a reservation in Kansas.[57]

On the reservation, one of their songs reminded them of their home in Nebraska:

> It is there that our hearts are set,
> In the expanse of the heavens.

The very identity and existence of the Pawnees had depended on the boundlessness of their sky and earth. But now railroad tracks cut across their land like long gashes, and fences enclosed their grasslands where buffalo once roamed freely. Indians had become a racial minority on lands they had occupied for thousands of years. "If the white man had stayed on the other side of the big water," Pawnee chief Likitaweelashar sadly reflected, "we Indians would have been better off for we are neither white men nor Indians now." Another Pawnee, Overtakes the Enemy, angrily exclaimed: "To do what they [whites] called civilizing us . . . was to destroy us. You know they thought that changing us, getting rid of our old ways and language and names would make us like white men. But why should we want to be like them, cheaters and greedy? Why should we change and abandon the ways that made us men and not the beggars we became?"[58]

The world as the Plains Indians had known it was coming to an end, and the Indians of many tribes felt bitter toward whites. An Arapaho song described the hardships and hunger:

> My children, I when at first I liked the whites
> My children, I when at first I liked the whites
> I gave them fruits.
> I gave them fruits.
>
> Father have pity on me
> Father have pity on me
> I am crying for thirst
> I am crying for thirst
> All is gone — I have nothing to eat.

Similarly, many Sioux denounced the whites for taking their lands. "The white men have surrounded me and have left me nothing but an island," protested Red Cloud. "When we first had this land we were strong. Now our nation is melting away like snow on the hillsides where the sun is warm; while the white prople grow like blades of grass when summer is coming." A song expressed a refusal to give up their Sioux culture:

> The great grandfather [The president]
> has said
> so they report
> "Dakotas
> be citizens,"
> he said . . .
> but

> *it will be impossible for me*
> *the Dakota ways*
> *Them*
> *I love. . . .*[59]

Their love for the land and for their traditional ways had inspired many Plains Indians to resist white westward expansion. Neither whites nor their goods were welcome in their country. A Pawnee chief told a white man who tried to offer gifts of blankets, guns, and knives: "You see, my brother, that the Ruler has given us all that we need; the buffalo for food and clothing; the corn to eat with our dried meat, or for cultivating the ground. Now go back to the country from whence you came. We do not want your presents, and we do not want you to come into our country." The Plains Indians had struggled to preserve the buffalo herds, a chief source of life and economic independence for them. Whites had no right to hunt buffalo, Pawnee chief Patalasharo complained, because "our fathers owned both the land and the animals feeding on it. We sold the land to the whites, but reserved the buffalo." As he watched engineers surveying for a railroad in Wyoming, Red Cloud told them: "We do not want you here. You are scaring away the buffalo."[60]

5

NO MORE PECK O' CORN
Slavery and Its Discontents

U NLIKE INDIANS, blacks were not outside white society's "borders"; rather they were within what James Madison called the "bosom" of the republic, living in northern ghettos and on southern plantations. David Walker lived in both of these worlds. Born in North Carolina in 1785, he was the son of a slave father and a free mother. Walker himself was free: according to southern law, children inherited the status of their mothers. Living below the Mason-Dixon Line was a painful contradiction for him: he saw people who shared his color defined as property. Somehow, Walker learned to read and write; he studied history and pondered why blacks in America were in such a wretched condition.[1]

Walker continued to reflect on this question after he moved to Boston, where he sold old clothes. Freedom in northern society, he realized, was only a facade for the reality of caste. Blacks were allowed to have only menial jobs. "Here we are — reduced to degradation," Walker observed. "Here we are cleaning the white man's shoes." Resentful of stereotypes of blacks as savages, Walker countered that whites were the true barbarians: the enslavement of blacks, the selling and whipping of slaves — such practices were signs of savagery, not civilization. Slavery, he believed, could be destroyed only through violence. "Masters want us for their slaves and think nothing of murdering us in order to subject us to that wretched condition — therefore, if there is an *attempt* made by us, kill or be killed."[2]

In 1829, Walker published his revolutionary thoughts in an *Appeal to the Colored Citizens of the World*. Southern legislators denounced the pamphlet as "seditious" and restricted its circulation; even northern white abolitionists like Benjamin Lundy and William Lloyd Garrison criticized it as "inflamatory" and "injudicious." A year later, Walker died, mysteriously. What he had presented was a candid, disturbing assessment of the condition of blacks: they had been reduced to slaves in the South and pariahs in the North.[3]

Racial Borders in the Free States

Very few blacks lived in the North. They were "free," for the northern states had abolished slavery after the American Revolution. In 1860, they represented 225,000, or a hardly noticeable one percent, of the total population. Their presence was far from pervasive, and blacks certainly did not threaten the racial homogeneity of white society. Yet they were the target of virulent racism. "The same schools do not receive the children of the black and European," Alexis de Tocqueville observed in the 1830s.

> In the theaters gold cannot procure a seat for the servile race beside their former masters; in the hospitals they lie apart; and although they are allowed to invoke the same God as the whites, it must be at a different altar and in their own churches, with their own clergy. The gates of heaven are not closed against them, but their inferiority is continued to the confines of the other world. When the Negro dies, his bones are caste aside, and the distinction of condition prevails even in the equality of death.[4]

Indeed, everywhere in the North, blacks experienced discrimination and segregation. "The colored people are . . . charged with want of desire for education and improvement," a black protested, "yet, if a colored man comes to the door of our institutions of learning, with desires ever so strong, the lords of these institutions rise up and shut the door; and then you say we have not the desire nor the ability to acquire education. Thus, while the white youths enjoy all these advantages, we are excluded and shut out, and must remain ignorant." Transportation facilities were often segregated. In Philadelphia, blacks were allowed to ride only on the front platforms of streetcars, and New York City had separate buses — one exclusively for blacks. Told their presence in white residential districts would depreciate property values, blacks found themselves trapped in squalid slums.[5]

Although they were free, blacks were restricted in their right to vote. Ironically, the political proscription of blacks often accompanied the advance of democracy for whites. In 1821, for example, the New York constitutional convention expanded suffrage for free "white" male citizens: they had to own property, or they could qualify in other ways such as paying taxes, serving in the militia, and working on the highways. On the other hand, blacks were required to be property owners in order to vote. The Pennsylvania constitutional convention of 1838 was more direct: it simply established universal "white" manhood suffrage and thus disfranchised blacks completely.

Blacks also suffered from attacks by white workers. Time and again in northern cities, white mobs invaded black communities, killing black people and destroying their homes and churches. Philadelphia, the "city of brotherly love," was the scene of several bloody antiblack riots. In 1834, rampaging whites forced blacks to flee the city. Seven years later, in Cincinnati, white workers used a cannon against blacks, who armed themselves to defend their families. The mayor then persuaded about three hundred black men to be jailed for their own security, assuring them that their wives and children would be protected. But the white rioters attacked again, and order was not restored until the governor sent troops.

Victims of discrimination, segregation, and violence, blacks in the North encountered a powerful cluster of negative racial images. These stereotypes contributed to the conditions of racial degradation and poverty, which, in turn, reinforced prejudice.

Blacks were denounced as "immature," "indolent," and "good-for-nothing." As one white Pennsylvanian charged, they were "simply unfit," "naturally lazy, childlike." Stereotypes of blacks as children were linked to notions of black intellectual inferiority. In his research on racial differences in intelligence, Dr. Samuel Morton of Philadelphia measured the cranial capacities of the skulls of whites and blacks. Finding that those of whites were larger, Dr. Morton concluded that whites were more intelligent. But the skulls of the whites that Morton examined belonged to men who had been hanged as criminals. Thus, as historian Thomas F. Gossett has remarked, it "would have been just as logical to conclude that a large head indicated criminal tendencies." This presumably "scientific evidence" of black mental inferiority, however, was used to support the notion of white supremacy and to justify racial segregation. An Indiana senator, for example, declared in 1850: "The same power that has given him a black skin, with less weight or volume of brain has given us a white skin, with greater volume of brain and intellect; and that we can never live together upon an equality is as certain as that no two antagonistic principles can exist together at the same time."[6]

While northern whites generally viewed blacks as childlike and mentally deficient, they also feared them as criminals. During the 1820s, Pennsylvania's governor expressed apprehension about the rising crime rate among blacks, and newspapers repeatedly reported Negro burglaries, Negro robberies, and Negro assaults against whites. The image of the black criminal led whites to restrict black migration into certain states. Ohio and Indiana required entering blacks to post a $500 bond as a guarantee against becoming a public charge and as a pledge of good behavior. The editor of an Indiana newspaper demanded the law be enforced in order to "drive away a gang of pilferers."[7]

Moreover, blacks were seen as threats to racial purity — what Benjamin Franklin had described as "the lovely White." In Pennsylvania, whites petitioned the legislature to enact an antimiscegenation law, and Indiana and Illinois prohibited interracial marriages. Everywhere, white social sentiment abhorred white and black relationships. "It is true," observed Tocqueville, "that in the North . . . marriages may be contracted between Negroes and whites; but public opinion would stigmatize as infamous a man who should connect himself with a Negress, and it would be difficult to cite a single instance of such a union." Fears of miscegenation triggered demands for exclusion and political proscription. In a petition to the Indiana legislature, whites called for the exclusion of blacks, warning that their wives and daughters would be "insulted and abused by those Africans." At the 1847 Illinois constitutional convention, a delegate explained that the failure to restrict black migration was tantamount to allowing blacks "to make proposals to marry our daughters." Efforts to disfranchise blacks were often accompanied by denunciations of interracial sex. A delegate to the 1821 New York constitutional convention advocated the denial of suffrage to blacks in order to avoid the time "when the colors shall intermarry." In Wisconsin, opponents of black suffrage warned that political rights granted to blacks would encourage them to "marry our sisters and daughters."[8]

Fears of interracial unions stirred demands for segregated schools. Whites petitioned the Indiana Senate to establish segregated schools. The committee on education agreed that the Negro race was inferior and that the admission of Negro children "into our public schools would ultimately tend to bring about that feeling which favour their amalgamation with our own people." When Massachusetts prohibited racial discrimination in the public schools, a northern newspaper cried: "Now the blood of the Winthrops, the Otises, the Lymans, the Endicotts, and the Eliots, is in a fair way to be amalgamated with the Sambos, the Catos, and the Pompeys. The North is to be Africanized."[9]

The North for blacks was not the promised land. Although they were not slaves, they were hardly free. Under slavery, they were forced to work; as wage-earners, they were excluded from many jobs. In New York, white dock workers attacked blacks seeking employment. In Cincinnati, white mechanics opposed the training of young blacks, and white cabinet shop workers demanded the dismissal of a recently hired black worker. Unable to find skilled jobs, many blacks were pushed into menial labor. In the 1850s, 87 percent of New York's gainfully employed blacks held menial jobs. Blacks were painfully aware of their grim prospects. "Why should I strive hard and acquire all the constituents of a man," a young man complained bitterly, "if the prevailing genius of the land admit me not as such, or but in an inferior degree! Pardon me if I feel insignificant and weak. . . . What are my prospects? To what shall I turn my hand? Shall I be a mechanic? No one will employ me; white boys won't work with me. . . . Drudgery and servitude, then, are my prospective portion."[10]

Was Sambo Real?

Meanwhile, in the South, four million blacks were slaves, representing 35 percent of the total population in 1860. Like Caliban, they served the Prosperos of the master class. They constituted the essential labor force in southern agriculture for tobacco, hemp, rice, sugar, and especially cotton cultivation. The majority of the slaves worked on plantations, agricultural production units with more than twenty slaves.

Work on the plantations, according to historian Kenneth Stampp, began early in the morning when a horn awakened the slaves an hour before daylight. "All work-hands are [then] required to rise and prepare their cooking, etc. for the day," a plantation manual stated. "The second horn is blown just at good day-light, when it is the duty of the driver to visit every house and see that all have left for the field." Work was highly regimented. A glimpse of plantation labor was captured by a traveler in Mississippi:

First came, led by an old driver carrying a whip, forty of the largest and strongest women I ever saw together; they were all in a simple uniform dress of a bluish check stuff, the skirts reaching little below the knee; their legs and feet were bare; they carried themselves loftily, each having a hoe over the shoulder, and walking with a free, powerful swing, like *chasseurs* on the march. Behind came the cavalry, thirty strong, mostly men, but a few of them women, two of whom rode astride on the plow mules. A lean and vigilant white overseer, on a brisk pony, brought up the rear.[11]

A slave described the routine of a workday: "The hands are required to be in the cotton field as soon as it is light in the morning, and, with the exception of ten or fifteen minutes, which is given to them at noon to swallow their allowance of cold bacon, they are not permitted to be a moment idle until it is too dark to see, and when the moon is full, they often times labor till the middle of the night." After they left the fields, they had more work to do. "Each one must attend to his respective chores. One feeds the mules, another the swine — another cuts the wood, and so forth; besides the packing [of cotton] is all done by candle light. Finally, at a late hour, they reach the quarters, sleepy and overcome with the long day's toil."[12]

To manage this enslaved labor force, masters used various methods of discipline and control. They sometimes used kindness. "Now I contend that the surest and best method of managing negroes, is to love them," a Georgia planter explained. "We know . . . that if we love our horse, we will treat him well, and if we treat him well, he will become gentle, docile and obedient . . . and if this treatment has this effect upon all the animal creation . . . why will it not have the same effect upon slaves?" But masters also believed that strict discipline was essential and that power had to be based on fear. South Carolina's Senator James Hammond, owner of more than three hundred slaves, fully understood the need for the absolute submission of a slave to his master: "We have to rely more and more on the power of fear. We are determined to continue masters, and to do so we have to draw the reign [*sic*] tighter and tighter day by day to be assured that we hold them in complete check." Employing psychological reins, masters tried to brainwash their slaves into believing they were racially inferior and racially suited for bondage. Kept illiterate and ignorant, they were told they were incapable of caring for themselves.[13]

To many white southerners, slaves were childlike, irresponsible, lazy, affectionate, and happy. Altogether, these alleged qualities represented a type of personality — the Sambo.

"Slaves never become men or women," a traveler in the South commented. Slavemasters frequently referred to adult blacks as "grown up children," or "boys" and "girls." Regarding themselves as guardians, they claimed their slaves had to be "governed as children." Unable to plan for their future, slaves would not "lay up in summer for the wants of winter" and "accumulate in youth for the exigencies of age."[14]

Slavemasters repeatedly complained about the problem of laziness, saying their black laborers had to be supervised or they would not work. If slaves were freed, they would become "an insufferable burden to society." Slavemasters insisted that blacks had to be kept in slavery; otherwise they would surely become "indolent lazy thievish drunken," working only when they could not steal.[15]

But slavemasters also cherished the bonds of affection they claimed existed between themselves and their childlike slaves. In his *Black Diamonds Gathered in the Darkey Homes of the South,* Edward Pollard exclaimed: "I love to study his affectionate heart; I love to mark that peculiarity in him, which beneath all his buffoonery exhibits him as a creature of the tenderest sensibilities, mingling his joys and his sorrows with those of his master's home." Slaveholders described their slaves as the happiest people in the world, working little and spending the rest of their time "singing, dancing, laughing, chattering, and bringing up pigs and chickens." "At present we have in South Carolina," one slaveholder boasted, "two hundred and fifty thousand civilized and peaceable slaves, happy and contented. . . ." In their private journals, masters recorded moments of closeness with their slaves. One of them scribbled into his diary on January 1, 1859: "The hands as usual came in to greet the New Year with their good wishes — the scene is well calculated to excite sympathies; notwithstanding bondage, affections find roots in the heart of the slave for the master."[16]

But the boast betrayed nervousness. The image of the slave as Sambo had special significance: the whole Western world was ideologically opposed to southern slavery, and therefore masters felt compelled to justify their peculiar institution as a "positive good." If they could show that their slaves were happy and satisfied with their condition, then perhaps they could defend themselves against their moral critics. They insisted that "ours is a patriarchal institution now, founded in pity and protection on the one side, and dependence and gratitude on the other."[17]

The planter class also had to persuade the white nonslaveholders of the South that slavery was right. In 1860, only 5.5 percent of the southern white population were slaveholders. In fact, the vast majority of whites had no vested economic interest in slavery. One of them, an Alabama farmer, was asked by a northern visitor what he thought about emancipating the slaves, and he replied:

Well, I'll tell you what I think on it; I'd like it if we could get rid on 'em to youst. I wouldn't like to hev 'em freed, if they was gwine to hang 'round. They ought to get some country and put 'em war they could be by themselves. It wouldn't do no good to free 'em, and let 'em hang 'round, because they is so monstrous lazy; if they hadn't got nobody to take keer on 'em, you see they wouldn't do nothin' but juss nat'rally laze 'round, and steal, and pilfer, and no man couldn't live, you see, war they was — if they was free, no man couldn't live — and this ere's the other. Now suppose they was free, you see they'd all think themselves just as good as we, of course they would, if they was free. Now, just suppose you had a family of children, how would you like to hev a niggar steppin' up to your darter? Of course you wouldn't, and that's the reason I wouldn't like to hev 'em free; but I tell you, I don't think it's right to hev 'em slaves so; that's the fac — taant right to keep 'em as they is.[18]

Thus, there were moral misgivings among white southerners themselves. "We must satisfy them that slavery is of itself right," the defenders of the institution declared, "that it is not a sin against God." Time and again they insisted that the slavemaster was "enlightened," "humane," and "Christian," and that the slave was "submissive," "docile," "happy," "conscious of his own inferiority and proud of being owned & governed by a superior."[19]

Many masters had doubts about the morality of the peculiar institution. "Slavery," admitted the governor of Mississippi, "is an evil at best." Similarly, a white Virginian anxiously confessed: "This, sir, is a Christian community. Southerners read in their Bibles, 'Do unto all men as you would have them do unto you'; and this golden rule and slavery are hard to reconcile." One slaveholder jotted in his diary: "Oh what trouble, — running sore, constant pressing weight, perpetual wearing, dripping, is this patriarchal institution! What miserable folly for men to cling to it as something heaven-descended. And here we and our children after us must groan under the burden — our hands tied from freeing ourselves." Few slaveholders could "openly and honestly look the thing [slavery] in the face," a European traveler in the South observed. "They wind and turn about in all sorts of ways, and make use of every argument . . . to convince me that the slaves are the happiest people in the world."[20]

While claims that slaves were Sambos helped to comfort anguished consciences, they also offered the masters psychological assurances that their slaves were under control. Surely happy slaves would not come at night and slit the throats of their masters. In reality, slaveholders were terrified by the specter of slave rebellion. Aware of the bloody slave revolts in Santo Domingo in the 1790s, they were warned by an American official in Haiti: "Negroes only cease to be *children* when they degenerate into *savages*." After the brutal suppression of the 1822 Denmark Vesey slave conspiracy in Charleston, a worried South Carolina slaveholder warned that blacks were "barbarians who would, IF THEY COULD, become the DESTROYERS of our race."[21]

Holding what Thomas Jefferson had called the "wolf by the ears," masters lived in constant dread of slave insurrection. Southern newspapers frequently reported news of slave unrest and "evidences of a very unsettled state of mind among the servile population." Married to a Georgia planter, Frances A. Kemble reported that slaves were "a threatening source of constant insecurity" and that "every southern *woman*" lived in terror of her slaves. A Louisiana slaveholder recalled tense times "when there was not a single planter who had a calm night's rest," and when every master went to bed with a gun at his side.[22]

Here was a society almost hysterically afraid of a black "giddy multitude." The master-slave relationship was dynamic, contradictory, and above all uncertain. Sambo existed and did not exist. What was the reality? How did the slaves themselves view their own behavior?

There were slaves who appeared to be Sambos. Asked about whether he desired freedom, a slave replied to a curious visitor: "No, massa, me no want to be free, have good massa, take care of me when I sick, never 'buse nigger; no, me no want to be free." In a letter to his master who was away on a trip, a slave ended his report on plantation operations: "The respects of your affec. Svt. unto D[eath] in hopes ever to merit your esteem. Your most dutiful servant. Harford."[23]

But slaves who behaved like Sambos might not have actually been Sambos: they might have been playing the role of loyal and congenial slaves in order to get favors or to survive, while keeping their inner selves hidden. Masters themselves sometimes had difficulty determining a slave's true personality. "So deceitful is the Negro," a master explained, "that as far as my own experience extends I could never in a single instance decipher his character. . . . We planters could never get at the truth." For many slaves, illusion protected them from their masters. "The only weapon of self defence that I could use successfully, was that of deception," explained fugitive slave Henry Bibb. Another former slave explained that one had to "know the *heart* of the poor slave — learn his secret thoughts — thoughts he dare not utter in the hearing of the white man."[24]

Indeed, many slaves wore masks of docility and deference in order to shroud subversive plans. Every year thousands of slaves became fugitives, making their way north to freedom, and many of these runaways had seemed passive and cheerful before they escaped.

> No more peck o' corn for me,
> No more, no more;
> No more peck o' corn for me,
> Many tousand go.
>
> No more driver's lash for me.
> No more pint o' salt for me.
> No more hundred lash for me.
> No more mistress call for me.[25]

After his flight north, fugitive J. W. Loguen received a letter from his former owner. "You know that we reared you as we reared our own children," wrote Mrs. Sarah Logue; "that you was never abused, and that shortly before you ran away, when your master asked you if you would like to be sold, you said you would not leave him to go with any body." In his reply, Loguen caustically remarked: "Woman, did you raise your *own children* for the market? Did you raise them for the whipping-post?" The ex-slave boldly proclaimed his love for liberty: "Wretched woman! Be it known to you that I value my freedom . . . more, indeed, than my own life; more than all the lives of all the slaveholders and tyrants under heaven."[26]

Sometimes a slave would play the role of Sambo and then strike directly at his tyrant. Slavemaster William Pearce told one of his erring slaves that he would be whipped after supper. When the slave was called out, he approached Pearce submissively. As soon as he was within striking distance, the slave pulled out a concealed ax and split his master's head. Nat Turner, according to historian Stampp, was "apparently as humble and docile as a slave was expected to be." In Virginia on August 22, 1831, he led seventy fellow slaves in a violent insurrection that lasted two days and left nearly sixty whites dead. After his arrest, Turner made a statement to the authorities. His master, he acknowledged, was "kind": "in fact, I had no cause to complain of his treatment to me." But Turner had had a religious experience: "I had a vision — and I saw white spirits and black spirits engaged in battle . . . and blood flowed in streams. . . ." A voice told him to wait for a sign from heaven: "And on the appearance of the sign, (the eclipse of the sun last February) I should arise and prepare myself, and slay my enemies with their own weapons." Turner carried out his mission, and a white Virginian nervously observed: "It will long be remembered in the annals of our country, and many a mother as she presses her infant darling to her bosom, will shudder at the recollection of Nat Turner." The slave rebel's action was a frightening revelation to white southerners: smiling and holding his hat in hand, Sambo could be planning their destruction.[27]

The reality for many slaves may have been even more complex and subtle than a duality of roles. Some Sambo-like behavior may have been not so much a veil to hide inner emotions of rage and discontent as a means of expressing them. Lying, stealing, laziness, immaturity, and ignorance all contained within them an aggressive quality: they constituted, in effect, resistance to efficiency, discipline, work, and productivity.

"Hands won't work unless I am in sight," a Virginia planter scribbled angrily in his diary. "I left the Field at 12 [with] all going on well, but very little done after [that]." Slaves occasionally destroyed tools and machinery and treated farm work animals so brutally that they frequently crippled them. "They can neither hoe, nor ditch, chop wood, nor perform any kind of labor with a white man's skill," complained a master. "They break and destroy more farming utensils, ruin more carts, break more gates, spoil more cattle and horses, and commit more waste than five times the number of white laborers do." A continual problem for masters was the stealing of chickens and pigs. But slaves often viewed the matter differently: they were simply "taking" property (pigs) for use by other property (themselves). In other words, the master's "meat" was taken out of "one tub" and put in "another." "When I tuk the turkey and eat it," a slave said, "it got to be a part of me." This appropriation seemed justified because their weekly food allowance was so meager, and their masters were profiting from their labor. Slaves saw themselves as exploited workers. Even as they shucked corn, they sang:

Massa in the great house, counting out his money,
Oh, shuck that corn and throw it in the barn.
Missis in the parlor, eating bread and honey,
Oh, shuck that corn and throw it in the barn.

Resenting the unfair appropriation of their labor, many slaves feigned illness and lied in order to avoid work. One planter complained that slaves were sick on workdays but not on Sundays. One slave managed to avoid work for many years by claiming he was nearly blind; after the Civil War, he was suddenly able to see again and became a successful farmer. Where masters perceived the destructiveness, lying, and laziness of their slaves as mischievous, childish, and irresponsible behavior, many slaves saw refusal to be exploited.[28]

Unlike slaves on the plantation, many slaves in the cities did not have to engage in such ambiguity. In 1860, there were 70,000 urban slaves. They labored in textile mills, iron furnaces, and tobacco factories. Many of them had been "hired out" and were working as wage-earners. The hiring-out system generally involved a contract that specified the wage, the length of service, some assurances concerning treatment, and the type of work to be performed. In a contract signed on January 1, 1832, for example, C. W. Thruston and his brother promised "to pay James Brown Ninety Dollars for the hire of Negro Phill until 25 Dec. next. And we agree to pay taxes & doctor bills. Clothe him during said time & return him . . . with good substantial cloth . . . shoes and socks and a blanket."[29]

In this case it appears that the master found the job for his slave, but this was not always the practice. Slavemasters would often simply let their slaves find their own jobs and require them to make weekly payments. In effect, slaves were renting their own labor from their masters. One Savannah slave used the hiring-out system imaginatively. First, he purchased his own time from his master at $250 a year, paying in monthly installments. Then he hired about seven or eight slaves to work for him.[30]

The hiring-out system ruptured the border between slavery and freedom because it gave slaves a certain amount of bargaining power. While traveling through Richmond, Virginia, an English visitor overheard a conversation between a slave and a prospective employer:

I was rather amused at the efforts of a market gardener to hire a young woman as a domestic servant. The price her owner put upon her services was not objected to by him, but they could not agree about other terms. The grand obstacle was that she would not consent to work in the garden, even when she had nothing else to do. After taking an hour's walk in another part of town I again met the two at the old bargain. Stepping towards them, I now learned that she was pleading for other privileges — her friends and favourites must be allowed to visit her. At length she agreed to go and visit her proposed home and see how things looked.

Unlike a plantation slave, this woman could negotiate her terms, insisting on certain work conditions almost as if she were a free laborer.[31]

Hiring out weakened the slave system. No longer directly under the supervision of their masters, slaves could feel the loosening of reins. They took care of themselves and had many of the privileges of free persons. In fact, they were sometimes called "free slaves." Many of them were even permitted to "live out" — to make their own housing arrangements by renting a room or a house. Living away from their masters' watchful eyes, they enjoyed a degree of independence. Though they were slaves, they were in contact with free laborers, black and white, and saw what it meant to be free. "Hundreds of slaves in New Orleans," Frederick Law Olmsted noted as he traveled in Louisiana, "must be constantly reflecting and saying to one another, 'I am as capable of taking care of myself as this Irish hod-carrier, or this German market-gardener; why can't I have the enjoyment of my labor as well as they? I am as capable of taking care of my own family as much as they of theirs; why should I be subject to have them taken from me by those men who call themselves our owners?' "[32]

No wonder one white southerner complained: "The cities is no place for niggers! They get strange notions into their heads and grow discontented. They ought, every one of them, be sent onto the plantations." A Louisville editor claimed that "negroes scarcely realize[d] the fact that they [were] slaves" in the city. They became "insolent, intractable, and in many cases wholly worthless." They made "free negroes their associates," "imbibing" their feelings and imitating their conduct. Another white southerner anxiously described the behavior of slaves in New Orleans: "It was not unusual for slaves to gather on street corners at night . . . where they challenged whites to attempt to pass, hurled taunts at white women, and kept whole neighborhoods disturbed by shouts and curses. Nor was it safe to accost them, as many went armed with knives and pistols in flagrant defiance of all the precautions of the Black Code." Urban slaves did not behave like Sambos.[33]

How did plantation slaves behave during the Civil War as federal troops destroyed the authority of the slave system? The war, as historian Eugene Genovese observed, was "the moment of truth." Everyone — white and black — understood the meaning of the conflict. "There is a war commenced between the North and the South," a planter told his slaves. "If the North whups, you will be as free a man as I is. If the South whups, you will be slaves all your days." Information about the war circulated through the slave quarters. Pretending indifference, house servants listened intently as their masters talked among themselves about the military and political events of the conflict. "We'se can't read, but we'se can listen," a South Carolina slave told Union soldiers.[34]

When slave Abram Harris heard that his master had been killed in the war, he felt loss and sorrow. "Us wus boys togedder, me en Marse Hampton, en wus jist er bout de same size," he said. "Hit so did hurt me when Marse Hampton got kilt kase I lubed dat white man." There were other instances of slave affection. "I shall never forget the feeling of sickness which swept over me," recalled a former slave. "I saw no reason for rejoicing as others were doing. It was my opinion that we were being driven from our homes and set adrift to wander, I knew not where. I did not relish the idea of parting with my young master who was as true a friend as I ever had." Occasionally, expressions of loyalty were accompanied by demands for respect. One slave told his master: "When you'all had de power you was good to me, and I'll protect you now. No nigger, nor Yankee, shall touch you. If you want anything, call for Sambo. I mean, call for Mr. Samuel — that's my name now."[35]

Slave Dora Franks felt very differently as she overheard her master and mistress discussing the war: "He say he feared all de slaves 'ud be took away. She say if dat was true she feel lak jumpin' in de well. I hate to hear her say dat, but from dat minute I started prayin' for freedom." What was most striking was the way the presence of federal troops in an area stimulated noticeable changes in slave behavior. A few days after Union soldiers camped near her plantation, a slaveholder wrote in her diary: "The Negroes are going off in great numbers and are beginning to be very independent and impudent." In *The War Time Journal of a Georgia Girl*, Eliza Andrews described the strange behavior of one of her slaves. Alfred, "one of the most peaceful and humble negroes on the plantation," was charged with attacking a white man. "I hope there is some mistake," she commented fearfully, "though the negroes are getting unruly since the Yankees are so near." Mrs. Mary Jones recorded similar disillusionment in her diary. "The people are all idle on the plantations, most of them seeking their own pleasure," she wrote on January 6, 1865.

"Susan, a Virginia Negro and nurse to my little Mary Ruth, went off with Mac, her husband, to Arcadia the night after the first day the Yankees appeared. . . . She has acted a faithless part as soon as she could." On January 21, she reported that her "faithful" cook, Kate, had suddenly left the plantation. Disappointed and angry, Jones concluded: "Their condition is one of perfect anarchy and rebellion."[36]

Indeed, during the war, plantation discipline generally disintegrated. "The wretches [are] trying all they can," complained a slaveholder in Texas, "it seems to me, to agrivate me, taking no interest, having no care about the future, neglecting their duty." Many slaves engaged in work slowdowns; others refused to work. Masters had difficulty extracting obedience. With the coercive power of the government focused on the battlefronts, many slaves became assertive, redefining their relationships with their masters.[37]

Slaves were impatient, ready to break for freedom. An old slave who had fled to the Union lines told the Yankees: "Ise eighty-eight year old. Too ole for come? Mas'r joking. Neber too ole for leave de land o' bondage." During the war, some half million slaves ran off to the federal lines. In 1863, a northern clergyman asked a Virginia slave whether she had heard of the Emancipation Proclamation. "Oh, yes, massa!" she responded, "we all knows about it; only we darsn't let on. We pretends not to know. I said to my ole massa, 'What's this Massa Lincoln is going to do to the poor nigger? I hear he is going to cut 'em up awful bad. How is it, massa?' I just pretended foolish, sort of." Shortly after this conversation, she ran off to the Union lines. Another slave remembered the day the Union troops arrived at his master's plantation located on the coast of South Carolina: "De people was all a hoein'. . . . Dey was a hoein' in de rice-field, when de gunboats come. Den ebry man drap dem hoe, and leff de rice. De mas'r he stand and call, 'Run to de wood for hide. Yankee come, sell you to Cuba! run for hide!' Ebry man he run, and my God! run all toder way! Mas'r stand in de wood. . . . He say 'Run to de wood!' an ebry man run by him, straight to de boat."[38]

Watching their once loyal slaves suddenly bolt for the Union lines, many white southerners jettisoned their opinions about their slaves as Sambos. Emily C. Douglas was shocked that her trusted slaves had deserted her: "They left without even a good-bye." Notions of slave docility were nullified. "You can form no idea of my situation and anxiety of mind," an overseer wrote to his employer in 1863. "All is anarchy and confusion here — everything going to destruction — and the negroes on the plantation insubordinate — My life has been several times in danger." In the minds of many whites, blacks had changed from children into savages. "The 'faithful slave' is about played out," a slave-holder observed bitterly. "They are the most treacherous, brutal, and ungrateful race on the globe." Similarly, a Georgia planter condemned the "ingratitude evinced by the African character." "This war has taught us the perfect impossibility of placing the least confidence in any Negro," he observed. "In too numerous instances, those we esteemed the most have been the first to desert us."[39]

Many of the deserters were women. For them, freedom had a par-ticular meaning, for they had experienced bondage in different ways than the men. Like the men, they worked in the fields and the factories. But, as women, they were also important for the reproduction of the slave population. The federal government had prohibited the African slave trade in 1808, and the South had depended on natural increase for its supply of bonded labor. Slave women were viewed as "breeders," and the laws allowed masters to separate slave children from their moth-ers and sell them. A South Carolina court, for example, ruled that "the young of slaves . . . stand on the same footing as animals." As mothers, enslaved women bore a peculiarly heavy burden under slavery. They knew their children were not even legally theirs and could be taken away from them. Mothers were especially distressed over the future of their daughters. One mother, Margaret Garner, tried to escape with her daugh-ter: as she was about to be apprehended near Cincinnati, she killed her own child. "Now she would never know," Garner exclaimed, "what a woman suffers as a slave." Hers were the anguish and rage of a slave mother — tormented feelings explored by novelist Toni Morrison in *Beloved*.[40]

As slaves, many women found that more than their labor and their children were appropriated: their bodies were regarded as property to be used to satisfy the erotic pleasures of their masters. "The punishment inflicted on women exceeded in intensity the punishment suffered by their men," Angela Davis argued, "for women were not only whipped and mutilated, they were also *raped*." A former female slave, Harriet Jacobs, had made a similar observation: "Slavery is terrible for men; but it is far more terrible for women. Superadded to the burden common to all, *they* have wrongs, and sufferings, and mortifications peculiarly their own." As a fifteen-year-old slave, Jacobs herself had been victimized by her master. "He peopled my young mind with unclean images, such as only a vile monster could think of," she recalled. "He told me I was his property; that I must be subject to his will in all things. . . . I shuddered to think of being the mother of children that should be owned by my . . . tyrant. I knew that as soon as a new fancy took him, his victims were sold far off to get rid of them; especially if they had children. I had seen several women sold, with his babies at the breast. He never allowed his offspring by slaves to remain long in sight of himself and his wife." Sexual exploitation of enslaved women was widespread in the South. The presence of a large mulatto population stood as vivid proof and a constant reminder of such sexual abuse. "Like the patriarchs of old," a southern white woman bitterly complained, "our men live all in one house with their wives and their concubines; and the mulattoes one sees in every family partly resemble the white children. Any lady is ready to tell you who is the father of all the mulatto children in everybody's household but her own. These, she seems to think, drop from the clouds."[41]

Slave Son, White Father

One of these mulatto slave children was Frederick Douglass. As a young slave child on a Maryland plantation, he had been sent by his master, Thomas Auld, to live with his grandparents, Betsey and Isaac Bailey. Grandmother Bailey was in charge of the children of the younger slave women. Her cabin was isolated, located twelve miles from the plantation and far away psychologically from the reality of slavery. "I had always lived with my grandmother on the outskirts of the plantation," Douglass later recalled. "I had therefore been . . . out of the way of the bloody scenes that often occurred on the plantation."[42]

Douglass's childhood years at Grandmother Bailey's home were happy and secure. Frederick was never hungry, for his grandmother was skillful at fishing and farming. "Living here, with my dear old grandmother and grandfather," he noted later, "it was a long time before I knew myself to be a *slave*. . . . Grandmother and grandfather were the greatest people in the world to me; and being with them so snugly in their own little cabin — I supposed it to be their own — knowing no higher authority over me . . . than the authority of grandmamma, for a time there was nothing to disturb me."[43]

But this period turned out to be somewhat short. As a young boy, Douglass was placed in the home of Hugh Auld, his master's brother who lived in Baltimore. Sophia Auld had not owned slaves before, and she initially regarded him as "a child, like any other." Her own son, Tommy, and Frederick "got on swimmingly together." She was like a mother to him, the slave thought. Under her care, he was "well-off": he had a straw bed with a cover, plenty of food, and clean clothes. "Why should I hang down my head, and speak with bated breath, when there was no pride to scorn me, no coldness to repel me, and no hatred to inspire me with fear?" Sophia seemed to say to him: "Look up, child; don't be afraid."[44]

But the slave system soon came down on both of them. Shortly after Frederick joined the Auld household, he developed a strong desire to learn to read, and Sophia gladly agreed to teach him. The boy was precocious and learned quickly. Sophia seemed almost as proud of his progress as if he had been "her own child" and told her husband about her new pupil. Hugh Auld scolded her severely, forbidding her to give the young slave any further lessons. "If you give a nigger an inch he will take an ell," he angrily lectured her. "Learning will spoil the best nigger in the world." Master Auld's fury had a damaging effect on Sophia. Her husband's "iron sentences, cold and harsh," disciplined her, and like "an obedient wife," she set herself like a "flint" against Frederick's education. "In ceasing to instruct me," he later wrote, "my mistress had to seek to justify herself to herself. . . . She finally became even more violent in her opposition to my learning to read than Mr. Auld himself." She spied on him and even interrogated him about his activities. Whenever she caught him reading a book, she would snatch it away.[45]

But Douglass's sense of selfhood had already been formed, and his experiences in Baltimore reinforced his inner urge for freedom. Urban slavery was not as closed and coercive as plantation slavery. Indeed, in Baltimore, which had a large population of free blacks, Douglass saw that not all blacks were slaves. "I was living among freemen, and was in all respects equal to them by nature and attainments. Why should I be a slave?" On the wharves, the young slave met two Irishmen who told him about the free society of the North, and he went home with thoughts of escape and freedom pounding in his head. The city also offered Douglass educational opportunities. Once he understood that knowledge could be a path to freedom, he was determined to educate himself. He carried a copy of *Webster's Spelling Book* in his pocket when he went outside to play and took spelling lessons from his white playmates. He bought an antislavery book, *The Columbian Orator,* with money he had earned from blackening boots. In the urban environment, he had greater freedom of movement and contact with a wider variety of people and ideas than slaves on the plantation. "It is quite probable," Douglass speculated, "that but for the mere circumstance of being thus removed [to Baltimore], before the rigors of slavery had been fully fastened upon me, before my young spirit had been crushed under the iron control of the slave driver, I might have continued in slavery until emancipated by the war."[46]

Master Thomas Auld realized he had made a mistake. He complained that "city life" had influenced Frederick "perniciously" and made him restless. Consequently, Auld placed the sixteen-year-old slave under the supervision of slave-breaker Edward Covey. His instructions were simple and clear: Frederick was "to be broken," transformed psychologically into an obedient slave. "To make a contented slave," Douglass later explained, "you must make a thoughtless one. . . . He must be able to detect no inconsistencies in slavery. The man who takes his earnings must be able to convince him that he has a perfect right to do so. It must not depend on mere force — the slave must know no higher law than his master's will. The whole relationship must not only demonstrate to his mind its necessity, but its absolute rightfulness."[47]

Reduced to a field hand for the first time in his life, Douglass was so cruelly whipped and overworked that he felt Covey had indeed succeeded in breaking his spirit. "My natural elasticity was crushed; my intellect languished; the disposition to read departed; the cheerful spark that lingered about my eye died out; the dark night of slavery closed in upon me, and behold a man transformed to a brute!" But the young man did not realize how greatly Grandmother Bailey, Sophia Auld, and Baltimore had unfitted him for slavery. Thus, though he found himself in a "sort of beast-like stupor between sleeping and waking," he still gazed at the sailboats skimming across Chesapeake Bay and exclaimed: "You are loosed from your moorings, and free. I am fast in my chains, and am a slave! . . . O, that I were free! . . . I will run away. . . . I had as well be killed running as die standing."[48]

Covey sensed the slave's discontent and was determined to stamp out any thoughts of freedom. While working in the treading yard one hot August day, Douglass collapsed from heat and exhaustion. Too ill to respond to Covey's order to get up and work, he was savagely kicked. Bleeding profusely, he crawled to Master Auld, pleading for protection from the inhuman slave-breaker. Instead, he was scolded and ordered to return to Covey. Douglass had not expected Auld to protect him "*as a man*," but he had hoped his master would at least protect him "*as his property*."[49]

Douglass knew he had to defend himself. Back at Covey's farm, he violently resisted the slave-breaker's efforts to tie and whip him. "The fighting madness had come upon me, and I found my strong fingers firmly attached to the throat of the tyrant, as heedless of consequences, at the moment, as if we stood as equals before the law. The very color of the man was forgotten. . . . I held him so firmly by the throat that his blood followed my nails." In this supreme moment of physical confrontation, Douglass felt something profound. "I was a changed being after that fight. I was nothing before — I was a man now. . . . I had reached the point at which I was *not afraid to die*. This spirit made me a freeman in *fact*, though I still remained a slave in form."[50]

The fight with Covey taught him a lesson he would always remember: "A man without force is without the essential dignity of humanity." Years later, after Douglass escaped from slavery and was active in the abolitionist movement in the North, he broke from the moral suasion approach of William Lloyd Garrison and moved toward the violent strategy of radical abolitionist John Brown. After his meeting with Brown in 1847, Douglass became less confident in the peaceful abolition of slavery. "My utterances became more and more tinged by the color of this man's strong impressions." Two years later, Douglass announced that he would welcome the news that the slaves had rebelled and were spreading "death and devastation" in the South. In 1859, he justified Brown's attack on Harpers Ferry — a bold attempt to seize arms from an arsenal and lead slaves in armed insurrection. "Capt. Brown has initiated a new mode of carrying on the crusade of freedom," Douglass declared, "and his blow has sent dread and terror throughout the entire ranks of the piratical army of slavery."[51]

Yet violence against the oppressor was not easy for Douglass to embrace. Slavery, as he had experienced it, was too complicated and too contradictory for him to have a single and clear set of attitudes toward white southerners. The raised knife of revolt would be aimed not only at people tragically ensnared in a vicious system, but also at people he cared about — Sophia Auld and perhaps even his own father.

Douglass was never certain about his paternity. "In regard to the *time* of my birth, I cannot be definite as I have been respecting the *place*. Nor, indeed, can I impart much knowledge concerning my parents." But he thought that his father might have been Master Thomas Auld. "I was given away by my father [Thomas Auld], or the man who was called my father, to his own brother [Hugh Auld]." Told his father was a white man and possibly his owner, Douglass bitterly condemned slavery as a system that cruelly forced slavemasters to reject their slave children. Years later, after the Civil War and emancipation, Douglass visited Thomas

Auld, and as he stood at the old man's bedside, he crossed a significant border separating them. Douglass insisted that Auld call him "Frederick," "as formerly," and asked his former master to satisfy an old, lingering, and anxious curiosity — his birthdate. The date of his birth and his paternity were puzzling questions Douglass had linked in his mind. Reminiscing about his escape, Douglass assured Auld that he had not run away from him but from slavery. The two men had a warm reunion. "He was to me no longer a slaveholder either in fact or in spirit, and I regarded him as I did myself, a victim of the circumstances of birth, education, and custom."[52]

Douglass was intensely aware of his biracial ancestry. Time and again in his antislavery lectures he described himself as "the child of a white man" and "the son of a slaveholder." During an antislavery tour abroad, Douglass described England as "the land of my paternal ancestors." After the death of his wife Anna, he married Helen Pits, a white woman. In defense of this marriage, he remarked that his first wife "was the color of my mother and the second, the color of my father," and that "no one ever complained of my marriage to my former wife, though contrast of color was more decided and pronounced than in the present instance. . . ." Angry over the racial exclusion of his daughter from a private school, Douglass told one of the parents responsible for the injustice: "We differ in color, it is true, (and not much in that respect). . . ."[53]

Descended from both white and black parents, Douglass hoped for an integrated and interracial America, a society without racial borders. In his opposition to black emigration and separatism, Douglass argued that blacks were Americans and did not wish to return to Africa or form "a separate union" in America. In his essay on "The Future of the Colored Race," Douglass predicted that blacks would be "absorbed, assimilated," and would "only appear as the Phoenicians now appear on the shores of the Shannon in the features of a blended race."[54]

Black Nationalism: Nostalgia in the Niger

Douglass viewed the future of blacks in America very differently than did Martin Delany, the leading black nationalist of the nineteenth century. "I thank God for making me a man simply," Douglass observed, "but Delany always thanks him for making him a *black* man." Delany's pride in his blackness was reflected in his passionate interest in Africa. "*Africa for the African race*," he declared, "*and black men to rule them.*

By black men, I mean, men of African descent who claim an identity with the race."[55]

Delany's African identity was inspired by his parentage. He was born in 1812 in Charles Town, (West) Virginia, the son of a slave father and a free mother — Samuel and Pati Delany. Samuel Delany, the son of a Golah chieftain, managed to purchase his freedom when Martin was about ten years old. Pati Delany's father was a Mandingo prince, Shango, who had been captured as a youth during intertribal hostilities and brought to America with his betrothed, Graci. Shango was given his freedom because of his noble birth and returned to Africa; Graci was also freed but remained in America with their daughter, Pati. During his childhood, Martin had an intimate source of contact with Africa — his Mandingo grandmother (who died at the age of 107).[56]

As a child, Martin learned that his membership in the black race made him the object of white scorn. Pati Delany's efforts to teach her children to read and write aroused angry opposition from white neighbors who were anxious to preserve their belief in black intellectual inferiority and were afraid of educated black rebels like Denmark Vesey. White resentment was so intense that she felt compelled to move her family across the border to Pennsylvania.

But even north of slavery, racism was prevalent. As a young man studying in Pittsburgh during the 1830s, Delany experienced the brutality of antiblack riots led by mobs composed of white workers.

As a journalist and as an antislavery lecturer during the 1840s, Delany traveled widely throughout the North and often encountered racial hostility and violence. On one occasion, a white mob in Marseilles, Ohio, threatened to tar and feather him and burn him alive. Delany found that white children, even while involved in play, were never too busy to notice a black passing by and scream "nigger." "As the deportment of individuals is a characteristic evidence of their breeding," he noted, "so is the conduct of children generally observed as an evidence of the character of their parents." Delany found the racial epithets not only "an abuse of the feelings," but also "a blasting outrage on humanity."[57]

His bitterness toward northern society was sharpened by an admissions controversy at Harvard Medical School. In 1850, Delany along with two other blacks had been admitted to the school. Their admission, however, was conditional: upon graduation, they would have to emigrate and practice medicine in Africa. Even so, their presence at Harvard provoked protests from white students. Demanding the dismissal of the blacks, they argued that integration would lower the "reputation" of

Harvard and "lessen the value" of their diploma. The whites refused to attend classes with the blacks. Racial integration at Harvard, they warned, was "but the beginning of an Evil, which, if not checked will increase, and that the number of respectable *white* students will, in future, be in an inverse ratio, to that of *blacks*." Finally, the angry students attached a threat to their protest: if the faculty did not heed their demand, they would transfer to another school.[58]

The faculty quickly capitulated, ignoring a student counterpetition favoring the admission of the blacks. Deeming it "inexpedient" to allow blacks to attend lectures, the faculty defended their decision based on their commitment to teaching and academic excellence. They explained that the presence of blacks was a "source of irritation and distraction," which interfered with the "success of their teaching." Furthermore, the "intermixing" of the white and black races was "distasteful" to a large portion of the class and therefore "injurious" to the interests of the school.[59]

The incident filled Delany with rage. He was fully qualified for admission to Harvard Medical School. His letters of recommendation from his private instructors, Dr. Joseph Gazzam and Dr. Julius Le Moyne, provided evidence of his competence to study medicine. Two years later, Delany issued his manifesto for black emigration — *The Condition, Elevation, Emigration and Destiny of the Colored People of the United States*. Emerging as a leading theoretician of black nationalism, he organized the National Emigration Convention; in 1859, Delany visited Africa to secure a land grant for the settlement of American blacks in the Niger Valley.

In his call for black emigration to Africa, Delany presented a detailed analysis of the degradation and despair blacks were experiencing in northern society. The inferior and dependent economic and social position blacks occupied in the North not only reinforced white prejudice, but also inculcated feelings of inferiority and self-hatred among blacks. "Caste our eyes about us and reflect for a moment," Delany sadly declared, "and what do we behold! every thing that presents to view gives evidence of the skill of the white man. Should we purchase a pound of groceries, a yard of linen, a vessel of crockeryware, a piece of furniture, the very provisions that we eat, — all, all are the products of the white man." Delany argued that this condition of dependency with its constant reminders of their subordinate status had an insidious influence on black self-esteem. Black children, born under oppression, could not "be raised in this country, without being stooped shouldered." Black men and women, moreover, appeared to be satisfied as menial workers, "accustomed" to being maids and cooks. They seemed to lack a sense of "self-respect." In Delany's judgment, blacks had been so broken by white oppression that they were actually helping to perpetuate their tragic condition.[60]

Blacks would never achieve acceptance and equality in America, Delany contended, unless they changed their condition and became self-reliant like whites — "a business, money-making people," educated for "the Store and Counting House." Black liberation, he believed, depended upon entrepreneurial success. They must strive to acquire what had enabled whites to succeed — "a knowledge of all the various business enterprises, trades, professions, and sciences," a "practical Education" in business rather than a "Classical" education. "What did John Jacob Astor, Stephen Girard, or do the millionaires and the greater part of the merchant princes, and mariners, know of Latin and Greek, and the Classics?"[61]

But Delany had no confidence that blacks would be able to change their condition in America. In his judgment, the oppression of blacks was essentially based on caste, not class. Although white laborers shared many class interests with blacks, the two groups would never join in common efforts to elevate themselves. The problem for blacks was "not a question of the rich against the poor" but of "white against black." Aware of antiblack hatred among white workers, Delany ruled out class struggle as a strategy for black liberation.[62]

Even if slavery were abolished, Delany believed, racism would persist as long as there were both whites and blacks living in America. The only way to rid society of race would be through amalgamation — for Americans to become a blended people. Delany believed this would never happen; moreover, he did not view racial mixture as desirable. Unlike Frederick Douglass, Delany did not want blacks to lose their "identity as a distinct race." "The truth is," he declared, "we are not identical with the Anglo-Saxon . . . and the sooner we know and acknowledge this truth, the better for ourselves and posterity." Blacks should be proud of themselves, for they possessed "the highest traits of civilization" and would someday instruct the world in the true principles of morals, religion, and law.[63]

To be redeemed, blacks had to emigrate to Africa in order to separate themselves from their white oppressors. "Were we content to remain as we are," Delany warned, "sparsely interspersed among our white fellow-countrymen, we might never be expected to equal them in any honorable or respectable competition for a livelihood." Therefore, the struggle had to focus on Africa. "No people can be free who themselves do not constitute an essential part of the *ruling element* of the country in which they live." If blacks were able to establish a proud and powerful black African nation, they would be able to win respect for blacks everywhere in the world and hasten the emancipation of slaves in America. "The claims of no people, according to established policy and usage," Delany insisted, "are respected by any nation, until they are presented in a national capacity."[64]

At the same time as Delany was celebrating Africa, he was also identifying with America. His book on emigration reflected this tension. It was "sincerely dedicated to the American people, North and South. By their most devout, and patriotic fellow-citizen, the author." Delany presented a strong case for black American citizenship by pointing to the immense contributions blacks had made to the American economy. Reminding readers about the black patriots of the American Revolution, he also argued: "Among the highest claims that an individual has upon his country, is that of serving in its cause, and assisting to fight its battles." America, for Delany, was home. "Here is our nativity," he observed, "and here have we the natural right to abide and be elevated through the measure of our own efforts. . . . Our common country is the United States. Here were we born, here raised and educated, here are the scenes of childhood . . . the sacred graves of our departed fathers and mothers." But here, too, Delany had experienced the abuse of white children, the violence of white mobs, and the scorn of the white students at Harvard. "We love our country, dearly love her," Delany cried, "but she [doesn't] love us — she despises us."[65]

This sense of agonizing ambivalence evoked complex and contradictory feelings within Delany during his visit to the Niger Valley in 1859. "The first sight and impressions of the coast of Africa are always inspiring, producing the most pleasant emotions," he scribbled in his diary. He was finally in the homeland described in his grandmother's Mandingo chants. During the first several days, Delany felt an "almost intense excitement," "a hilarity of feeling" approaching "intoxication." But then followed fatigue. This second "stage" of feeling, Delany thought, was "acclimation," often accompanied by nausea, chills, and violent headaches. During this period, he became homesick — *a feeling of regret that you [had] left your native country for a strange one; an almost frantic desire to see friends and nativity; a despondency and loss of the hope of ever seeing those you [loved] at home again.*" Then Delany added in his diary: "These feelings, of course, must be resisted, and *regarded as a mere morbid affection of the mind* at the time, arising from an approaching disease." When he recovered from his malady, Delany felt an "ardent and abiding" love for Africa. After he completed his negotiations for a land grant in the Niger Valley, Delany sailed for America, vowing he would return to Africa.[66]

"Tell Linkum Dat We Wants Land"

Deliverance from slavery, for both Douglass and Delany, was to come from the barrel of a gun. Black men in blue, Douglass pointed out, were "on the battlefield mingling their blood with that of white men in one common effort to save the country." Through their participation in the war to save the Union, they were earning their right to claim full citizenship. Abandoning his dreams of emigrating to Africa, Delany volunteered for the Union Army and received an appointment as a major in the 104th Regiment of United States Colored Troops. "It is the duty of every colored man to vindicate his manhood by becoming a soldier," Delany declared, "and with his own stout arm to battle for the emancipation of his race." Indeed, the federal occupation of the South as well as the Emancipation Proclamation and the Thirteenth Amendment liberated some four million blacks. But what were the hopes and dreams of these newly freed people?[67]

Blacks knew precisely what they needed to raise themselves from freedom to equality. Initially, many of them felt they needed to withdraw from their ex-masters and move their cabins away from the big house in order to separate themselves from white proximity and supervision. In 1865, General William Sherman asked twenty black leaders whether they preferred to live scattered among whites or in colonies by themselves. They replied that they would prefer to have their own separate communities because racial prejudice would take years to overcome. When the agents of the Freedmen's Aid Commission arrived in the South, they found blacks asking: "When will you open school?" In addition to education, blacks wanted political power through suffrage.[68]

What blacks wanted most of all, more than education and voting rights, was economic power:

> *Don't you see the lightning flashing in the cane*
> *brakes,*
> *Looks like we gonna have a storm*

Although you're mistaken it's the Yankee soldiers
Going to fight for Uncle Sam.
Old master was a colonel in the Rebel army
Just before he had to run away —
Look out the battle is a-falling
The darkies gonna occupy the land.[69]

Blacks viewed landownership as the basis of economic power. Their demand for land, they argued, was reasonable and just. For one thing, they had paid for it through their military participation in the war: 186,000 blacks, most of them recruited or conscripted in the slave states, had served in the Union Army, and one-third of them were listed as missing or dead. Black soldiers had fought bravely against their masters. "Now we sogers are men — men de first time in our lives," one of them stated proudly. "Now we can look our old masters in de face. They used to sell and whip us, and we did not dare say one word. Now we ain't afraid, if they meet us, to run the bayonet through them." Blacks as soldiers had helped to bring the war to an end, and they felt they were entitled to some land.[70]

Moreover, blacks had already paid for the land "through a life of tears and groans, under the lash and yoke of tyranny." When a freedman named Cyrus was questioned by his former owner about his absence from the fields, he explained the new situation: "Seems lak we'uns do all the wuck and gits a part. Der ain't goin' ter be no more Master and Mistress, Miss Emma. All is equal. I done hear it from de cotehouse steps. . . . All de land belongs to de Yankees now, and dey gwine to divide it out 'mong de colored people. Besides, de kitchen of de big house is my share. I help built hit." Another freedman, Uncle Smart, told a northern teacher: "Do, my missus, tell Linkum dat we wants land — dis bery land dat is rich wid de sweat ob we face and de blood ob we back."[71]

Some Radical Republicans including Charles Sumner, Thaddeus Stevens, and George W. Julian understood the need to grant land to the freed slaves. They argued that emancipation had to be accompanied by land confiscation from the planter class and land distribution to the newly freed blacks. The perpetuation of the large estates would mean the development of a semifeudal system based on the cheap labor of exploited and powerless blacks. But Congress was only willing to grant them civil and political rights through the Fourteenth and Fifteenth amendments. The lawmakers rejected legislation for land distribution —

known as the "40 acres and a mule" bill. Land should not be given to the freedmen, the *New York Times* argued, because they had to be taught the lessons of hard work, patience, and frugality. *The Nation* protested that land confiscation and distribution would violate the principle of property rights.[72]

During the war, however, forty thousand blacks had been granted land by military order. In 1864, after General Sherman completed his march to the sea, black leaders told him: "The way we can best take care of ourselves is to have land, and turn it and till it by our own labor." In response, General Sherman issued Special Field Order Number 15, which set aside large sections of South Carolina and Georgia for distribution to black people. They were given "possessory titles" to forty-acre lots until Congress could decide their final disposition. The blacks believed that they owned the lands. But after the planters were pardoned by President Andrew Johnson, they began to reclaim the lands and force their former slaves to work for them. The black landowners resisted: "To turn us off from the land that the Government has allowed us to occupy, is nothing less than returning us to involuntary servitude." "We own the land now. Put it out of your head that it will ever be yours again." In their protest to President Johnson, they pointed out how they had joined the Union Army and had fought to put down the southern rebellion: "Man that have stud upon the feal of battle & have shot there master and sons now going to ask ether one for bread or for shelter or comfortable for his wife & children sunch a thing the U S should not ought to expect a man [to do]." Some of them declared they were prepared to defend their property with guns. Federal troops quickly crushed the resistance: seizing the lands, they tore up the freedmen's title papers and restored the lands to the planter class.[73]

Thus ended the possibility of real freedom. A Union general explained to Congress: "I believe it is the policy of the majority of the farm owners to prevent negroes from becoming landholders. They desire to keep the negroes landless, and as nearly in a condition of slavery as it is possible for them to do." The newly freed blacks made this same point more directly and frankly: "Gib us our own land and we take care ourselves, but widout land, de ole massas can hire us or starve us, as dey please." Frederick Douglass explained the failure of Reconstruction: "Could the nation have been induced to listen to those Stalwart Republicans, Thaddeus Stevens and Charles Sumner, some of the evils which we now suffer would have been averted. The Negro would not today be on his knees, as he is, supplicating the old master class to give him leave to toil."[74]

Though the Civil War had led to the destruction of slavery, blacks in the South found themselves transformed from "property" to "freedmen," not "free" people. No longer slaves, they became wage-earners or sharecroppers, working the land of their former master in exchange for a part of the crop. Forced to buy goods from the planter's store, they were trapped in a vicious economic cycle, making barely enough to pay off their debts. For example, according to an account book, the following transactions occurred between Polly and landowner Presley George:

Due Presley George by Polly:

For 4¾ cuts wool @ 75 cents/cut	$ 3.50
22 yds. cloth @ 50 cents/yd.	$11.00
5 yds. thread @ 50 cents/yd.	2.50
Boarding one child (who didn't work) for 5 months	12.00
10 bushels corn @ $1.00/bushel	10.00
30 bushels corn @ $1.00/bushel	30.00
TOTAL	$69.00

Due Polly by Presley George:

For 3 months' work "by self" @ $4.00/month	$12.00
For 4 months' work by son Peter @ $8.00/month	32.00
For 4 months' work by son Burrel @ $4.00/month	16.00
For 4 months' work by daughter Siller @ $2.25/month	9.00
TOTAL	$69.00

Thus, the earnings of Polly and her family amounted to zero. All they had been able to do was to reimburse planter George for the debts they had incurred from their purchases.[75]

A black laborer described his condition of debt peonage: "I signed a contract — that is, I made my mark for one year. The Captain was to give me $3.50 a week, and furnish me a little house on the plantation. . . ." A year later, he found himself in debt to the planter, and so he signed another contract, this one for ten years. During this time, he was "compelled" to buy his food, clothing, and other supplies from the plantation store. "We never used any money in our dealings with the commissary, only tickets or orders, and we had a general settlement once each year, in October. In this store we were charged all sorts of high prices for goods, because we seldom had more than $5 or $10 coming to us — and that for a whole year's work." At the end of his contract, he tried to leave the plantation but was told he owed $165 and consequently found himself reduced to a "lifetime slave." A black folk song lamented:

> Slabery an' freedom
> Dey's mos' de same
> No difference hahdly
> Cep' in de name.[76]

Meanwhile, the era known as the "New South" was emerging. Four years after the withdrawal of federal troops from the South in 1877, the editor of the New Orleans Times-Democrat reported that a "magic transformation" had occurred below the Mason-Dixon Line. The "stagnation of despair" had given way to the "buoyance" of hope and courage, and the "silence of inertia" to the "thrilling uproar of action." Southerners were a "new people," and the region was experiencing a "new birth." The vision of the "New South" was the industrialization of the old Cotton Kingdom.[77]

The signs of "progress" were especially evident in the rise of cities and the proliferation of factories. Atlanta, which had only 14,000 residents when General Sherman marched his army to the sea, had a population close to 40,000 in 1880 and 90,000 two decades later. The pride of the New South's manufacturing was centered on its textile and iron production. The number of spindles had jumped from 600,000 in 1860 to 175,000,000 in 1890; the number of textile mills from 161 in 1880 to 400 in 1900. By the late 1880s, southern pig-iron production had surpassed the total output of the entire country in 1860. Jefferson County, the home of Birmingham, had only twenty-two factories in 1870; thirty years later it had five hundred plants.

During this economic boom, blacks were drawn into the factories and mills of the "New South." Although they were systematically excluded from certain industries such as textiles and continued to be employed primarily in agriculture, blacks became an important source of industrial labor. In 1890, 6 percent of the total black work force was employed in manufacturing, compared with 19 percent of the total native white work force. Between 1890 and 1910, the number of black male workers in nonagricultural occupations increased by two-thirds, or to 400,000, due mainly to the expansion in sawmills, coal mining, and railroad construction. in 1880, 41 percent of Birmingham's industrial workers were black; thirty years later, blacks made up 39 percent of all steelworkers in the South.

Southern industrialists were eager to employ blacks. Richard H. Edmunds, editor of the *Manufacturers' Record,* regarded blacks as "the most important working factor in the development of the great and varied resources of our country." The manager of Shelby Iron Works insisted he would not exchange his black workers "for any other people on earth." After white workers struck at Chattanooga and Knoxville iron companies in 1883, management turned to black laborers and found them to be "fully as good as" white labor. Praising his black workers, the superintendent of the Saluda Cotton Factory stated that they not only worked as well as whites, but were also less expensive and could be "easily controlled."[78]

One prominent symbol of the "New South" was the 1895 Atlanta Exposition. Thousands of visitors crowded into Atlanta to marvel at the industrial achievements of the postwar South. Included among the exhibits were the latest advances in technology, such as a battery of eight boilers and fourteen engines with a capacity of 2,250 horsepower. There was also a "Negro Building" designed and erected wholly by black mechanics and devoted to "showing the progress of the Negro since freedom." The main entrance of this building had relief work that depicted a "slave mammy" and a portrait of Frederick Douglass; inside was a steam engine built by students from the Tuskegee Normal and Industrial Institute.[79]

The most noted speaker at the opening of the exposition was Booker T. Washington, the thirty-nine-year-old principal of Tuskegee Institute. The invitation to give the address had greatly moved him. From slave to honored guest, he had been given the opportunity to speak to an audience composed of the wealth and culture of the South, the representatives of his former masters. The event was momentous: it was the first time in southern history that a black had been asked to speak at such an important occasion.

As Washington stood on the platform in Atlanta, he told his black and white listeners in the segregated auditorium to "cast down their buckets" where they were. To blacks, he declared: "It is at the bottom of life we must begin, and not at the top." The agitation for "social equality" was the "extremest folly." "The opportunity to earn a dollar in a factory just now is worth infinitely more than the opportunity to spend a dollar in an opera-house." To whites, Washington recommended: cast down your bucket "among eight millions of Negroes whose habits you know, whose fidelity and love you have tested in days when to have proved treacherous meant the ruin of your firesides. Cast down your bucket among these people who have, without strikes and labour wars, tilled your fields, cleared your forests, built your railroads and cities." To both races, Washington dramatically advised: "In all things that are purely social we can be as separate as the fingers, yet one as the hand in all things essential to mutual progress." Washington's speech "electrified" the audience, drawing a "delirium of applause." After his address, known as the "Atlanta Compromise," Washington suddenly found himself elevated by whites in power as the leader of his race.[80]

Although Washington had publicly offered black cooperation to the southern elite, he was actually not an accommodationist. In Chicago five years later, he gave a speech condemning racism in American society. Congratulating the country for its recent victory in the Spanish-American War, he declared that Americans had won every conflict in history, "except the effort to conquer ourselves in blotting out racial prejudice. . . . Until we thus conquer ourselves I make no empty statement when I say that we shall have a cancer gnawing at the heart of this republic that shall some day prove to be as dangerous as an attack from an army without or within." When Washington arrived to speak at a hall in Tampa, Florida, and found that the audience had been divided into blacks and whites with a line of sheets separating the two groups, he refused to speak until the sheets were taken down. Behind the scenes, Washington strenuously fought against discrimination and disfranchisement, covertly funding lawsuits against railroad segregation in Virginia and disfranchisement legislation in Louisiana and Alabama.[81]

Moreover, Washington had always felt a sense of race pride. "From any point of view," he acknowledged in his autobiography, "I had rather be what I am, a member of the Negro race, than be able to claim membership with the most favoured of any other race." Blacks, in Washington's view, should pursue a strategy of self-help, directing their own destiny, uplifting themselves, and establishing black institutions like Tuskegee and the Negro Business League. Like Delany, Washington urged blacks to pursue economic success. Before he sailed to Europe on a vacation in 1910, he resolved not to enter a single palace, gallery, cathedral, or museum. "I find markets more instructive than museums," he explained. As an educator, Washington had little respect for what he called "mere book education." He wanted his students to study "actual things," to acquire a practical education. For blacks, industrial training would be the path to economic independence and racial equality. "Let there be in a community," Washington predicted, "a Negro who by virtue of his superior knowledge of the chemistry of the soil, his acquaintance with the most improved tools and best breeds of stock, can raise fifty bushels of corn to the acre while his white neighbor only raises thirty, and the white man will come to the black man to learn. Further, they will sit down on the same train, in the same coach and on the same seat to talk about it."[82]

By the end of the nineteenth century, however, the possibility of progress for blacks was distressingly remote. Racial borders had been reinforced by class and caste. Most black farmers were sharecroppers or tenants, working a white man's land with a white man's plow and a white man's mule. "Every colored man will be a slave, & feel himself a slave," a black soldier had warned during the Civil War, "until he can raise him own bale of cotton & put him own mark upon it & say dis is mine!" By this measure of freedom, blacks were still "slaves." During the 1890s, new laws buttressed segregation by defining more precisely the "Negro's place" on trains and streetcars and in schools, parks, theaters, hotels, and hospitals. Proclaiming the doctrine of separate but equal in the 1896 ruling of *Plessy v. Ferguson*, the Supreme Court upheld the constitutionality of segregation. Poll taxes and literacy requirements for suffrage were effectively disfranchising blacks, and hundreds of blacks were annually being lynched. This era was brutally repressive — what historian Rayford Logan described as "the nadir."[83]

6

EMIGRANTS FROM ERIN
Ethnicity and Class within White America

T HE AGE OF Jackson witnessed not only Indian removal and the expansion of slavery, but also the massive influx of a new group of immigrants. Suddenly, blacks in the North were competing with Irish workers. "Every hour sees us elbowed out of some employment to make room perhaps for some newly arrived immigrants, whose hunger and color are thought to give them a title to special favor," Frederick Douglass complained. "White men are becoming house servants, cooks, stewards, common laborers and flunkeys to our gentry." Then he warned that Irish immigrants would soon find that in taking "our vocation" they had also assumed "our degradation." But Douglass also found himself empathizing with the Irish. During a visit to Ireland in the 1840s, he witnessed the terrible suffering inflicted by the potato famine and was "much affected" upon hearing the "wailing notes" of Irish ballads that reminded him of the "wild notes" of slave songs.[1]

The Irish Exodus

The Irish described their migration to America in Gaelic terms: *deorai* or "exiles," *dithreabhach* or "homeless," and *dibeartach* or "banished people." "*Dob eigean dom imeacht go Meirice,*" they explained, "I had to go to America," or "going to America was a necessity for me." As historian Kerby Miller pointed out, many did not want to leave Ireland.

"There's such a clinging to the country," a contemporary noted, "that they would rather live on anything rather than go." Their songs told mournful tales of exile in a foreign land:

> *Such troubles we know that have often*
> *Caused stout Irish hearts to roam . . .*
> *And . . . sons from their homes were drove. . . .*

> *The hills and the valleys so dear to my heart;*
> *It grieves me to think that from them I must part.*
> *Compelled to emigrate far, far o'er the sea. . . .*

Between 1815 and 1920, five and a half million Irish emigrated to America.[2]

Feeling like the "children of Israel," the Irish viewed themselves as a people driven from their beloved homeland by "English tyranny," the British "yoke" "enslaving" Ireland. The British were seen as "savage tyrants" and "cursed intruders." The movement to America was "artificial," explained one Irish migrant, because the poverty of Ireland had been created by English colonial policies. "Foul British laws," they declared, were the "whole cause" of their emigration. British oppression was defrauding them of the fruits of their hard labor. Time and again, migrants complained that they were being pushed out of their country by strangers from England:

> *I would not live in Ireland now, for she's a fallen land,*
> *And the tyrant's heel is on her neck, with her reeking*
> *   blood-stained hand.*
> *There's not a foot of Irish ground, but's trodden*
> *   down by slaves,*
> *Who die unwept, and then are flung, like dogs,*
> *   into their graves.*[3]

British oppression was rooted deeply in Irish history. Centuries earlier, in 1166, Norman armies had arrived to assist the king of Leinster in a struggle against Rory O'Connor, the high king of Ireland. During the next ten years, King Henry II of England also sent troops and was declared the ruler of Ireland by the Norman invaders. The English conquest led to the abolition of traditional Irish laws and obligations and the confiscation of Irish lands, which then became estates for resettled

English landlords. By 1700, the Irish owned only 14 percent of Ireland. Meanwhile, the English colonizers had forced the Irish to become Christian; but when the Church of England became Protestant in the sixteenth century, the Irish suddenly found themselves defending Catholicism.

> *Three centuries the foreign race*
> *has ground us 'neath the harrow;*
> *The sweat aye running down our face*
> *in travail and in sorrow;*
> *Our priests, proscribed, were forced to say*
> *their Mass in secret hollow....*[4]

As subsistence farmers, Irish peasants formed *clachans,* or "small communities of families," and worked the land collectively. Beginning in the late eighteenth century, however, Protestant landlords decided to make their estates more productive and profitable. Therefore, they initiated a campaign to commercialize the Irish economy and transform the island into a "cattle civilization." By enclosing their estates and evicting peasant families, landlords shifted agricultural production from tillage to pasture. Between 1820 and 1840, livestock increased at a faster rate than the population, and cattle exports more than quadrupled. The conversion of land from tillage to grazing meant that 90 percent of the laborers previously needed for planting and harvesting had become superfluous.[5]

The landlords sought to bring Ireland into the British market. Between 1750 and 1810, Irish exports increased from two million to six million pounds. During a visit to Ireland in 1771, Benjamin Franklin reported that British colonialism and its emphasis on exports had reduced the Irish people to "extremely poor" tenants, "living in the most sordid wretchedness, in dirty Hovels of Mud and Straw, and cloatheed only in Rags." The Irish had been forced to survive on "Potatoes and Buttermilk, without Shirts," so that the "Merchants" could export "Beef, Butter, and Linnen" to England.

> *... the Landlord calls for rent,*
> *The flood which over-spread the Land, has caused*
> *them to lament,*
> *And yet John Bull must have the Beef, let it be*
> *cooked or raw,*

We're told by each big English thief:
we darsen't break the law.

By the 1830s, according to an observer, Ireland had developed a profitable export economy. But, he added, this commercialization of agriculture was accompanied by a "visible deterioration" in the condition of the "labouring classes and of the small farmers." "Progress" for the landlords meant pauperization for the peasants.

Ireland's oppressors soon must know, they can't
for ever last,
Landlords [have] been cruel for generations
past,
What right have they to claim the soil which
never was their own,
When thousands now are starving and evicted
from their home?[6]

"Misery, naked and famishing," reported visitor Gustave de Beaumont in the 1830s, was "everywhere, and at every hour of the day." The typical single-room cabin of an Irish family consisted of four walls of dried mud with a straw roof and a hole cut in the roof for the chimney. Inside lived the father, mother, children, and sometimes a grandfather or grandmother. There was no furniture in this "wretched hovel"; a single bed of straw served the entire family. "Five or six half-naked children [could] be seen crouched near a miserable fire, the ashes of which [covered] a few potatoes, the sole nourishment of the family." The squalor was oppressive, stifling. "What a Country this [was] to live in," a farmer complained, where Catholics were "only breathing, afraid & scarce able to raise their heads."[7]

But there was an alternative. Rather than "toil and starve like slaves," they could emigrate to "the Land of Promise." A song explained:

My father holds 5 acres of land, it was not
enough to support us all,
Which banished me from my native land, to
old Ireland dear I bid farewell.
My holdings here I can't endure since here
no longer I can stay.
I take my lot and leave this spot and try the
land of liberty.

By the thousands, Irish were leaving for America where there was "room for all — employment for all and success for many." Letters from friends and family in the United States glowingly described riches "growing like grass," and the boundlessness of a country where there was no tyranny and oppression from landlords. Between 1815 and 1845, one million Irish came to America.[8]

During this period, however, most Irish endured their hardships at home. Rather than emigrate, many became *spalpeens,* or "migratory workers," leaving their cottages each spring for agricultural or construction labor within Ireland, then returning to their families in the fall with "the rent money sewn inside their clothes." Their earnings, while meager, enabled many families to farm small plots and grow potatoes. By the early 1840s, the rural poor existed mainly on potatoes; between late spring and the time of harvest, many ate only one meal a day. Sometimes they cooked their potatoes only partially, keeping the cores or "bones" of the potatoes raw in order to digest their food more slowly. These hardy peasants believed they could survive in their homeland forever, for a family could produce a year's supply of potatoes on one acre of land. "What did we eat?" said an Irish immigrant. "Well, just potatoes."[9]

Then, suddenly, a little-known fungus appeared and changed the course of Irish history. Although potato crops had been attacked by plant diseases in past years, a new blight destroyed about 40 percent of the crop in 1845. "Coming on the harvest time . . . the crops looked splendid," a farmer said as he recalled the beginning of the famine, "but one fine morning in July there was a cry around that some blight had struck the potato stalks." As the leaves blackened and crumbled, the air became "laden with a sickly odor of decay, as if the hand of death had stricken the potato field, and . . . everything growing in it was rotten." Returning annually, the deadly disease continued its relentless devastation. By 1855, some one million people had died from hunger and sickness.[10]

The Great Famine intensified the already terrible suffering. Unable to pay their rent, thousands of families were evicted. For many landlords, the famine offered an opportunity to convert more land into fields for grazing. The evicted peasants angrily denounced their oppressors:

> 'Twas famine's wasting breath,
> That winged the shaft of death,
> And the landlord, lost to feeling,
> Who drove us from our sheeling. . . .[11]

During the famine years, Ireland continued to export grain and cattle to British markets. Half the people of Ireland could have been fed with the livestock exported in 1846: 186,483 cattle, 6,363 calves, 259,257 sheep, and 180,827 swine. Throughout the country one could see "famished and ghastly skeletons," "cowering wretches almost naked in the savage weather," children with "their faces bloated yet wrinkled and of a pale greenish hue," and families eating seaweed and suffering from fevers and dysentery. According to an English visitor, the streets of one town were "crowded with gaunt wanderers, sauntering to and fro with hopeless air and hunger-struck look," while the poor-house was surrounded by "a mob of starved, almost naked, women," "clamoring for soup tickets." So many people died that corpses were placed in reusable "trap-coffins" with hinged bottoms. For the living, the choice became clear: emigrate or suffer destitution and death.

> *Desert a land of curse and slave,*
> *Of pauper woe . . .*
> *Poor Eire now is all a grave. . . .*[12]

In panic, one and a half million Irish fled to the United States during the Great Famine. More so than the earlier emigrants, these people were the "uprooted." The *Cork Examiner* reported that they were "running away from fever and disease and hunger, with money scarcely sufficient to pay passage for . . . the voyage." The potato blight reversed Irish attitudes toward emigration. What had earlier been viewed as banishment was now regarded as release. Their reason for coming to America was survival. It was not ambition, a ballad declared, but

> *the blackening of the potatoes*
> *That drove us over the sea*
> *To earn our pay in Baltimore.*[13]

Generally poor and unskilled, these immigrants were mostly laborers. They were young: in 1850, the median ages for both Irish immigrant men and women in Philadelphia were under thirty. More than the pre-famine immigrants, they included women, the elderly, and children, and many Irish emigrated as family groups. Overwhelmingly Catholic, they were also strongly Gaelic in culture and language.[14]

With bundles on their shoulders, the migrants were "laving dear old

Ireland without warnin' " to "shtart for Philadelphia in the mornin' " and cross the "briny ocean." But before they left, they attended an "American wake" — a party hosted by the families. Sharing food and music, they said their good-byes and mourned what everyone knew would be a permanent separation.

> Sad was the day we said farewell,
>   Dear native land, to thee;
> And wander'd forth to find a home,
>   Beyond the stormy sea.
> Hard then our fate; fast flow'd the tears,
>   We tried to hide in vain,
> At thought of those we left behind,
>   And might ne'er see again.[15]

After the "wake," they traveled to Dublin and then to Liverpool, where they boarded crowded ships bound for America. The crossing was traumatic. "The emigrant is shown a berth," *The Times* reported, "a shelf of coarse pinewood, situated in a noisome dungeon, airless and lightless, in which several hundred persons of both sexes and all ages are stowed away on shelves two feet one inch above the other, three feet wide and six feet long, still reeking from the ineradicable stench left by the emigrants of the last voyage." On one ship, according to a witness, hundreds of passengers lay together like sacks, motionless. Some were dead, while others were sick, feverish, and delirious, scarcely able to turn in their narrow berths. That year, 20 percent of the emigrants died during the passage or immediately after arrival.[16]

The terrible blights finally ended in 1854, but the commercialization of agriculture, the eviction of families from their lands, and the decline of Irish crafts due to the importation of British manufactured goods continued to pauperize the Irish peasantry and depopulate Ireland. A contemporary described his country's melancholy condition: "This grass grown road, over which seemingly little, if any, traffic passes, is a type of solitude everywhere found. Tillage there is none; but in its stead one vast expanse of pasture land extends. Human habitations are rarer than the bare walls of roofless cottages. Where once a population dwelt . . . see how lonely and untrodden are these roads." In the 1860s, an American consul reported that there were "many thousands of strong young men" who sighed for "food & employment in the US," "and would gladly embrace *any* opportunity of removal from the misery & starvation" in

Ireland. Between 1855 and 1920, three million more Irish came to America.[17]

An "Immortal Irish Brigade" of Workers

Pushed from Ireland by economic hardships and famine, the immigrants were pulled to America by the Market Revolution's demand for labor. Yankees regarded the Irishman "as one made to work," reported Reverend Michael Buckley, a visitor from Ireland. "Where they want labour they will engage Paddy as they would a drayhorse." An Irish worker recalled how he labored "so severely" digging cellars, "up before the Stars and working till darkness," "driven like horses" to be "a slave for the Americans." Working in the mines of Pennsylvania, Irish miners "sucked up" the black dust into their lungs as they dug the "bloody coal."[18]

Irish immigrants provided the labor for the construction of roads and canals for the Market Revolution. Watching them work on the National Road in Pennsylvania, a farmer described them as an "immortal Irish brigade, a thousand strong, with their carts, wheelbarrows, shovels and blasting tools, grading the commons, and climbing the mountainside . . . leaving behind them a roadway good enough for an emperor to travel over." Irish laborers helped to build waterways, including Connecticut's Enfield Canal, Rhode Island's Blackstone Canal, and, most important, New York's Erie Canal, described by Reverend Buckley as "one of the grandest pieces of engineering ever seen in the world" and "proof" of "Irish talent." Standing knee-deep in water while cursing swarms of mosquitoes, the workers dug and shoveled earth as they sang:

> When I came to this wonderful rampire, it filled me with
>   the greatest surprise,
> To see such a great undertaking, on the like I never
>   opened my eye.
> To see a full thousand brave fellows at work among
>   mountains so tall,
> To dig through the vallies so level, through rocks for
>   to cut a canal.[19]

Irish workers built thousands of miles of rail lines such as the Western and Atlantic Railroad from Atlanta to Chattanooga and the Union Pacific segment of the transcontinental railroad. All day they were ordered:

"Now Mick do this, and Mick do that." And they shouted back: "The devil take the railroad!" As they laid tracks, they tuned their bodies to the rhythms of a work song:

> *Then drill, my Paddies, drill —*
> *Drill, my heroes, drill,*
> *Drill all day, no sugar in your tay*
> *Workin' on the U. P. railway.*

At night, they continued to feel the vibrations of the sledgehammers in their hands and arms and to hear the pounding ringing in their heads. Exhausted, they tried to rest:

> *When I lay me down to sleep,*
> *The ugly bugs around me creep;*
> *Bad luck to the wink that I can sleep,*
> *While workin' on the railroad.*[20]

The pervasive presence of the Irish in railroad work produced the popular saying that there was "an Irishman buried under every tie." Indeed, the Irish had high accident rates, for they were frequently assigned to the hazardous jobs. A Connecticut ax manufacturer explained that he employed the Irish as grinders because the death rate due to accidents was so high he had difficulty finding "Yankees" to do this dangerous work. "My father carried the mark of the quarry to his grave," wrote Elizabeth Gurley Flynn. "When he was a boy, working in a quarry in Maine, carrying tools, the sight of one eye was destroyed by a flying chip of granite." Time and again, newspapers reported accidents — "an Irishman drowned — an Irishman crushed by a beam — an Irishman suffocated in a pit — an Irishman blown to atoms by a steam engine — ten, twenty Irishmen buried alive in the sinking of a bank. . . ."[21]

Irish laborers, an immigrant complained, were "thought nothing of more than *dogs . . .* despised & kicked about." They lived in "clumsy, rough and wretched hovels," made with "roofs of sod and grass" and "walls of mud," observed Charles Dickens during a visit to the United States. "Hideously ugly old women and very buxom young ones, pigs, dogs, men, children, babies, pots, kettles, dung hills, vile refuse, rank straw and standing water, all wallowing together in an inseparable heap, composed the furniture of every dark and dirty hut." America turned out to be a nightmare for many Irish immigrants. They had crossed the ocean in pursuit of riches, but they failed to find "gold on the street corners."[22]

Instead, Irish immigrants found themselves not only exploited as laborers but also pitted against workers of other races, including the Chinese. While competition between Irish and Chinese workers was extensive in California, it dramatically surfaced in New England. Workers in the shoemaking industry were struggling against low wages and the introduction of labor-eliminating machines; consequently, they organized the Secret Order of the Knights of St. Crispin. The Crispins quickly became the largest labor organization in the United States; in 1870, it had a membership of 50,000. Demanding higher wages and an eight-hour day, the Crispins went out on strike at a shoe factory in North Adams, Massachusetts. The owner, Calvin T. Sampson, fired the disgruntled workers and pursued a strategy of divide-and-control by driving a "wedge" between himself and the strikers.[23]

This "wedge" turned out to be a contingent of seventy-five Chinese workers from San Francisco. Brought to North Adams as scabs to break the Irish strike, they were housed in dormitories inside the locked and guarded gates of the factory yard. Sampson's experiment caught the attention of other capitalists as well as the national news media. Within three months after their arrival in North Adams, the Chinese workers were producing more shoes than the same number of white workers had been making before the strike. The success of Sampson's strategy was celebrated in the press. "The Chinese, and this especially annoys the Crispins," the editor of *The Nation* wrote, "show the usual quickness of their race in learning the process of their new business, and already do creditable hand and machine work."[24]

The Chinese were held up as a model for Irish laborers. Writing for *Scribner's Monthly,* William Shanks compared the Chinese to the Irish workers. The Chinese "labored regularly and constantly, losing no blue Mondays on account of Sunday's dissipations nor wasting hours on idle holidays," he reported. "The quality of the work was found to be fully equal to that of the Crispins." Through the use of Chinese labor, Sampson had widened his profit margin: the weekly saving in labor costs was $840, or $40,000 a year. These figures inspired Shanks to calculate: "There are 115 establishments in the State, employing 5,415 men . . . capable of producing 7,942 cases of shoes per week. Under the Chinese system of Mr. Sampson, a saving of $69,594 per week, or say $3,500,000 a year, would be effected, thus revolutionizing the trade."[25]

In their response to Sampson's "wedge," the Irish strikers tried to promote working-class solidarity by trying to organize a Chinese lodge of St. Crispin. Watching this initiative to build Irish-Chinese unity, the editor of *The Nation* commented: "Chinese lodges and strikes will come in time when enough Chinamen are collected together in any given place; but the prospect appears not immediately flattering at North Adams." Based on self-interest rather than an ideological commitment to class solidarity, this attempt to unionize the Chinese workers quickly collapsed. At a meeting in Boston, white workers turned against the Chinese laborers, condemning them for reducing "American labor" to "the Chinese standard of rice and rats."[26]

Sampson's daring action had a sobering effect on striking workers at nearby shoe factories. Ten days after the arrival of Sampson's "Mongolian battery," Parker Brothers, Cady Brothers, Millard and Whitman, and E. R. and N. L. Millard were able to force their laborers to return to work with a 10 percent wage cut. Commenting on the significance of Sampson's experiment of substituting Chinese for Irish laborers, a writer for *Scribner's Monthly* observed: "If for no other purpose than the breaking up of the incipient steps toward labor combinations and 'Trade Unions' . . . the advent of Chinese labor should be hailed with warm welcome." The "heathen Chinee," he concluded, could be the "final solution" to the labor problem in America.[27]

While they were contrasted with the Chinese, Irish immigrants found themselves compared to blacks. During the mid-nineteenth century, anti-Irish stereotypes emphasized nature over nurture and descent over consent. The Irish were imaged as apelike and "a race of savages," at the same level of intelligence as blacks. Pursuing the "lower" rather than the "higher" pleasures, seeking "vicious excitement" and "gratification merely animal," the Irish were said to be "slaves" of "passions." Since sexual restraint was the most widely used method of birth control, the large families of these immigrants seemed to indicate a lack of self-control: "Did wealth consist in children, it is well known, that the Irish would be rich people. . . ." In a sermon on "The Dangerous Classes," Reverend Theodore Parker of Boston identified the "inferior peoples in the world," claiming that some were "inferior in nature, some perhaps only behind us in development" on "a lower form in the great school of Providence — negroes, Indians, Mexicans, Irish, and the like." A southern planter stated that slaves were like the Irish in "their subserviency, their flattering, their lying, and their pilfering as traits common to the characters of both peoples." An English traveler reported that both the Irish and blacks were viewed as outcasts: "To be called an

'Irishman' is almost as great an insult as to be stigmatized as a 'nigger feller'. . . ." Sometimes the immigrants were described as "Irish niggers."[28]

Like blacks, Irish workers were condemned for lacking the habits of punctuality and industry. They were dismissed from their jobs for laziness, gambling, drinking, and "other debaucheries," as well as for "levity" and "impudence." A saying claimed: "It's as natural for a Hibernian to tipple as it is for a pig to grunt." Their "idleness" and "brutal leprosy of blue Monday habits," it was argued, rendered them unreliable as workers and kept them impoverished. Like the "giddy multitude" of seventeenth-century Virginia, the Irish were chastised as an unruly and disorderly laboring class. In Jersey City, Irish workers were denounced by a newspaper editor as "a mongrel mass of ignorance and crime and and superstition, as utterly unfit for its duties, as they [were] for the common courtesies and decencies of civilized life." Irish children, moreover, were seen as "undisciplined" and "uninstructed," "inheriting" the "stupidity of centuries of ignorant ancestors." At school, they allegedly emitted a "pungent odor" — the "fumes of New-England rum." The Massachusetts Board of State Charities calculated that it would take two or three generations to "correct the constitutional tendencies to disease and early decay." Worried about the alarming presence of a largely Irish working class, Horace Mann was determined to educate the children in order to save the masses from "falling back into the conditions of half-barbarous or of savage life."[29]

Many Irish saw parallels between themselves as a degraded people and blacks in bondage. In Ireland, they had identified themselves as the "slaves" of the British, and many supported the abolition of slavery in the United States. In 1842, thousands of them signed a petition that declared: "Irishmen and Irishwomen! treat the colored people as your equals, as brethren." But Irish sympathy for black slaves seemed to disappear with the Atlantic crossing. In America, many of them became antiblack. Frederick Douglass criticized the Irish immigrants for abandoning the idea of "liberty" they nurtured in their homeland by becoming "the oppressors of another race" in America. Irish freedom fighter Daniel O'Connell shared Douglass's disappointment. Chastising the immigrants for their racism, O'Connell declared: "It was not in Ireland you learned this cruelty."[30]

What the Irish had learned in America was actually a painful and complex lesson. Stereotyped as ignorant and inferior, they were forced to occupy the bottom rungs of employment. In the South, they were even made to do the dirty and hazardous jobs that masters did not want to assign to their slaves. A planter told a northern visitor that he had hired an Irish gang rather than use his own slaves to drain a flooded area. "It's dangerous work," he explained, "and a negro's life is too valuable to be risked at it. If a negro dies, it's a considerable loss, you know." In the North, Irish repeatedly fought blacks for jobs as waiters and longshoremen. During the 1830s, a Philadelphia newspaper reported that the immigrants were displacing blacks as hackney coachmen, draymen, and stevedores. Irish Stephanos and Trinculos were taking menial jobs away from black Calibans.[31]

As they competed against blacks for employment, many Irish immigrants promoted their whiteness. "In a country of the whites where [white workers] find it difficult to earn a subsistence," they asked, "what right has the negro either to preference or to equality, or to admission?" The Irish were insisting on what historian David Roediger perceptively termed "their own whiteness and on white supremacy." Targets of nativist hatred toward them as outsiders, or foreigners, they sought to become insiders, or Americans, by claiming their membership as whites. A powerful way to transform their own identity from "Irish" to "American" was to attack blacks. Thus, blacks as the "other" served to facilitate the assimilation of Irish foreigners.[32]

Victims of English prejudice and repression in Ireland, the Irish in America often redirected their rage in a pecking order. "They [the Irish] have been oppressed enough themselves to be oppressive whenever they have a chance," commented an observer, "and the despised and degraded condition of the blacks, presenting to them a very ugly resemblance of their own home circumstances, naturally excites in them the exercise of the disgust and contempt of which they themselves are very habitually the objects. . . ." Viewing blacks as "a soulless race," some Irish said they "would shoot a black man with as little regard to moral consequences as they would a wild hog." An Irish song warned:

> When the negroes shall be free
> To cut the throats of all they see,
> Then this dear land will come to be
> The den of foul rascality.

The Irish opposed suffrage for blacks, fearful this would set "the Niggers high." Complaining that blacks did not know their place, they shouted:

"Down with the Nagurs!" "Let them go back to Africa, where they belong."[33]

Irish antagonism toward blacks exploded during the Civil War. Many Irish were angry at President Abraham Lincoln for expanding the aims of the war to include emancipation. An Irish song declared:

> 'Twas not to subjugate the South, those Irish braves went
> forth,
> Nor emancipate their negroes to satisfy the North —
> But bring them back unto the laws, their noble sires had
> made,
> And place again, beneath our Flag, each Southern renegade.[34]

Condemning abolitionism as "Niggerology," many Irish immigrants were willing to support the war only to preserve the Union. They did not want to fight to free the slaves and thereby increase labor competition. "Let the niggers stay in the South!" Irish workers shouted. They had been warned by Democrats during the 1860 election: "Vote against Abraham Lincoln, or you will have negro labor dragging you from your free labor." "Let the four million of slaves in the South be set at liberty . . . and we should very soon have . . . a terrible conflict between white labor and black labor. . . . The unemployed slaves will be found among you in sufficient numbers to compete with you at your wharves and your docks, and in every branch of labor in which white people alone are now employed."[35]

During the Civil War, New York Democratic politicians warned that the Republicans were willing to "spend" Irish blood to win the abolitionist war, and that freed blacks would be transported north to "steal the work and the bread of the honest Irish." Similarly, an Irish newspaper, the Boston Pilot, aroused the fears of its readers: "We have already upon us bloody contention between white and black labor. . . . The North is becoming black with refugee Negroes from the South. These wretches crowd our cities, and by overstocking the market of labor, do incalculable injury to white hands."[36]

In July 1863, a mass meeting in New York City protested a new draft law that allowed a draftee to avoid military service by paying $300 or providing a substitute. This law clearly discriminated against the working class. Many of the first draftees were Irish, poor men unable to pay the $300. In protest, angry gangs composed mostly of Irish stormed and burned the draft office. Then the Irish turned on blacks. Hundreds of rioters destroyed an orphanage for black children and many homes of blacks. "Vengeance on every nigger in New York," the rioters screamed as they assaulted blacks in the streets. One of the victims, William Green, said later: "They stripped me naked . . . they had a rope to hang me, and a man saved me." General rampage exploded as mobs vandalized and pillaged stores. "I saw the rioters in the street — 100 or 150 of them," a passerby stated, describing the looting of a liquor store. "Some three or four stout boys with clubs attacked the windows and broke them in; they then smashed in the doors; then the crowd rushed in; they pitched out boxes of cigars and bottles, and in about 10 minutes the house was on fire."[37]

Led by Irish longshoremen, the rioters warned employers "not to put any niggers to work" and blacks to stay away from the docks. They insisted that all stevedore jobs belonged to white men. The riot continued for four days. Finally, an army regiment rushed to the city from Gettysburg and restored order. By then scores of people had been injured and 105 killed. Condemning the "revolting, fiendish, cowardly, cruel" treatment of "the poor unfortunate negroes," an Irish newspaper, the *Metropolitan Record,* declared that "a superior race should disdain to vent their passions on an inferior one."[38]

Reacting to Irish hostility, blacks called their tormentors "white niggers." They resented being told by immigrants to leave the country of their birth and "go back" to Africa, a place they had never been. On one plantation, slaves mocked their Irish overseer by saying that an Irishman was "only a Negro turned inside out." Blacks told anti-Irish stories about the alleged gullibility and stupidity of the newcomers:

Two Irishmen were walking along one day, and they came across a wagonload of watermelons. Neither one had ever seen a watermelon before, and they inquired of some negroes, who were working nearby, what they were, and what they were good for. The negroes answered their questions very politely, and then, as it was their dinner hour, sat down in the shade to eat. The Irishmen concluded to buy a melon and see how they liked it. They went a little distance and cut the melon, but, taking pity on the poor negroes, decided to share it with them. "Faith!" they said, "guts is good enough for naygurs." So they cut the heart out of the melon and gave it away, and ate the rind themselves.[39]

Blacks complained that the Irish were taking jobs from them. "These impoverished and destitute beings, transported from the trans-Atlantic shores," a black observed, "are crowding themselves into every place of business and labor, and driving the poor colored American citizen out. Along the wharves, where the colored man once done the whole business of shipping and unshipping — in stores where his services were once rendered, and in families where the chief places were filled by him, in all these situations there are substituted foreigners. . . ."[40]

As Americans, many blacks aimed nativist barbs against the Irish foreigners. "Pat O'Flannagan does not have the least thing in the world against Jim from Dixie," a black observed, "but it didn't take Pat long after passing the Statue of Liberty to learn that it is popular to give Jim a whack." Blacks scornfully described the Irish as "hyphenates," and mocked their accent as such "a heavy brogue that it sounded as if they had marbles in their mouths." "It is to be regretted," black journalist John E. Bruce observed, "that in [America] where the outcasts — the scum of European society — can come and enjoy the fullest social and political privileges, the Native Born American with wooly hair and dark complexion is made the Victim . . . of Social Ostracism."[41]

The Irish Maid in America

Labor competition between the Irish and blacks was fierce in the domestic services. According to an English visitor, employers were willing to "let negroes be servants, and if not negroes, let Irish fill their place." In 1830, the majority of the servants in New York City were black: twenty years later, they were Irish women. Daughters of farmers in Ireland, they had become maids in America.

More than half of the Irish immigrants were women, compared to only 21 percent for southern Italians and 4 percent for Greeks. In New York City in 1860, Irish women outnumbered Irish men — 117,000 to 87,000. This massive migration of women was saluted in a song:

> Oh brave, brave Irish girls,
> We well might call you brave
> Should the least of all your perils
> The Stormy ocean waves.[42]

In Ireland, the struggle for economic survival had a particular impact on women. Increasingly after 1815, farmers practiced impartible inheritance: their land was not divided among their sons but left to only one. Consequently, many sons had little choice but to emigrate. "If you divide a farm and give it to two sons, neither is going to have a heck of a lot," an Irish immigrant explained. "So I began to realize that [I] would have to go somewhere." Women, too, came to a similar realization. They found that many noninheriting sons lacked the resources to marry and that their own possibilities for marriage were extremely limited unless they had dowries. Marriage rates declined: by 1841, 44 percent of the men and 36 percent of the women aged twenty-six to thirty-five were single. Many young women felt gloomy about their futures in terms of marriage and family. "There is no fun in Ireland at all," lamented a young woman, "the times are very lonesome . . . there are no one getting married."[43]

The times were also hard on women economically. The commercialization of agriculture and the decline of Irish cottage manufacturing such as weaving left thousands of women excluded from the economy. "Laws made by men shut them out of all hope of inheritance in their native land," an observer noted. "Their male relatives exploited their labour and returned them never a penny as a reward, and finally, when at last their labour could not wring sufficient from the meagre soil to satisfy the exertions of all, these girls were incontinently packed across the ocean. . . ."[44]

To these daughters of Erin, possibilities for marriage and money were waiting for them across the ocean. "Every servant-maid thinks of [America as] the land of promise," the *Cork Examiner* announced, "where . . . husbands are thought more procurable than in Ireland." A dowry was not necessary there. "Over in Ireland people marry for riches," a woman wrote from Philadelphia, "but here in America we marry for love and work for riches." On this side of the Atlantic, women could find jobs, especially as maids. Guidebooks for prospective Irish immigrants announced that servant girls in America were paid from eight to sixteen dollars a month and offered enticing prospects: if a domestic worker saved half her wages and its accumulated interest, she would be rich within ten years. Indeed, many maids had "in the course of twenty or thirty years, by faithful industry and moderate economy become owners of from three to five thousand dollars."

> *She being inclined to Emigrate*
> *her wages did demand,*
> *To seek a situation in America's FREE LAND.*
> *This undaunted Female hearing that a ship*
> *at Dublin Quay,*

Had advertised for Servants to go to America,
She bid farewell to all her friends. . . .[45]

Irish immigrant women became ubiquitous as maids. In the 1850s, they represented 80 percent of all female household laborers in New York City. Irish women went west to San Francisco, where they, like many Chinese men, became servants. In California, Dennis Kearney led an anti-Chinese labor movement, charging that the Chinese threatened the employment of Irish women. "The Chinese Must Go!" shouted Kearney. "Our Women Are Degraded by Coolie Labor."[46]

Irish women entered domestic service in greater numbers and proportions than women of other immigrant groups. In 1900, 54 percent were classified as "servants and waitresses," compared to only 9 percent for Italian female workers. A Boston study reported that over two-fifths of the immigrant women who entered the city in 1905–06 became servants and that they were almost all Irish. Jewish and Italian women did not generally become domestic workers. Italian women found that their parents or husbands did not want them to work in other people's homes. "Italian women were more likely to take in boarders because the men rarely permitted their wives to work as maids, cleaning women, or factory hands," explained historian Virginia Yans-McLaughlin. "The Italian ideal was to keep women at home."[47]

Unlike Italian women, who came to America with their husbands or fathers, Irish immigrant women tended to be unmarried and unattached to families. Hence, they were attracted to work offering housing and meals as well as wages. Employment in homes rather than in factories offered a healthier environment and often paid more. In 1906, maids in Massachusetts earned an average of $9.08 weekly, while textile workers received only $7.15. "Single women can get along here better than men as they can get employment more readily than men," an Irish laborer in Philadelphia wrote home to his sisters in 1883. "For instance liveing out girls or as the[y] are called at home servant girls gets from eight to twelve shillings per week and keep, that is from two to three dollars of American money. . . . Labouring mens wages averages from six to nine dollars per week. . . . But their work is not near so steady as womens."[48]

For these women, service work offered more than shelter, sustenance, and money: some became attached to their employers and their families. "I got a place for general housework with Mrs. Carr," said an Irish woman. "I got $2 till I learned to cook good, and then $3 and then $4. I was in that house as cook and nurse for twenty-two years. . . . Mrs.

156

Carr's interests was my interests. I took better care of her things than she did herself, and I loved the children as if they was my own." Furthermore, domestic service provided an introduction to American culture. Irish women had come to settle permanently; knowing that they would never return home, they had to adapt to American society. "Certainly, they had to begin immediately the process of acculturation on their own terms," historian Hasia Diner noted, "and domestic service provided perhaps the most intimate glimpse of what middle-class America was really like."[49]

But, while they lived inside middle-class American homes, Irish maids were still outsiders, made conscious of the border within the household. Their relationship to the family was a hierarchical one of upstairs and downstairs, masters and servants. They were present but invisible in a very intimate setting. Far from their own parents in Ireland, many of them hungered to belong to the families of their employers. "Ladies wonder how their girls can complain of loneliness in a house full of people, but oh! it is the worst kind of loneliness — their share is but the work of the house," a domestic servant said. "They do not share in the pleasures and delights of a home. One must remember that there is a difference between a *house,* a place of shelter, and a *home,* a place where all your affections are centered." Another servant echoed: "What I minded . . . was the awful lonesomeness. I went for general housework, because I knew all about it, and there were only three in the family." But the family members, "except to give orders," had "nothing to do with me. It got to feel sort of crushing at least."[50]

Moreover, the work itself was demanding and often demeaning. Most worked as live-in servants, available on a beck-and-call schedule around the clock, usually for seven days a week. Their employers "bossed" them "everlastingly" and wanted them to be "on tap from six in the morning to 10 or 11 at night." One servant complained about her employer: "She had no more thought for me than if I had been a machine. She'd sit in her sitting-room on the second floor and ring for me twenty times a day to do little things, and she wanted me up till eleven to answer the bell, for she had a great deal of company." "A smart girl keeps on her feet all the time to prove she isn't lazy," a maid said, "for if the mistress finds her sitting down, she thinks there can't be much to do and that she doesn't earn her wages."[51]

As they cooked, cleaned, laundered, and took care of the children, servants were required to wear caps and aprons, badges of social inferiority. The servants felt like "prisoners," always "looked down upon."

The daughter of a maid protested: "I hate the word service. . . . We came to this country to better ourselves, and it's not bettering to have anybody ordering you around! . . . If there was such a thing as fixed hours and some certain time to yourself, it might be different, but now I tell every girl I know, 'Whatever you do, don't go into service.' "[52]

The nature of domestic service involved what sociologist Stephen Steinberg termed "the exploitation of the whole person." Where the factory operative had her labor appropriated at the workplace, the servant found that her employer demanded more of her than the execution of assigned tasks. "Though the textile worker might be reduced to a commodity, paradoxically, her inner self was left intact." On the other hand, the servant could not have such space and privacy, for she lived and worked in her employer's home. Her character and manners were scrutinized for approval. In this sense, it was not just her labor that was purchased, but the laborer herself. This lack of personal freedom was the reason why one Irish woman chose to work in a paper box factory rather than in "the service":

It's freedom that we want when the day's work is done. I know some nice girls . . . that make more money and dress better and everything for being in service. They're waitresses, and have Thursday afternoon out and part of every other Sunday. But they're never sure of one minute that's their own when they're in the house. Our day is ten hours long, but when it's done it's done, and we can do what we like with the evenings. That's what I've heard from every nice girl that ever tried service. You're never sure that your soul's your own except when you are out of the house, and I couldn't stand that a day.[53]

Factory work, however, was also difficult to "stand." Denouncing such labor as "especially fatal to women," Archbishop John Lancaster Spalding declared that there were "few sadder sights than the poor women of the cotton mills of New England," so many of them "Irish girls, whose cheeks once bloomed with health as fresh and fair as the purity of their hearts." Irish women were preponderant in the New England textile mills of Lawrence, Holyoke, Fall River, and other towns. In Lowell, the City of Spindles, they represented 58 percent of the total textile work force. "The gray mills in Manchester [New Hampshire]," remembered Elizabeth Gurley Flynn, "stretched like prisons along the banks of the Merrimac River. Fifty percent of the workers were women. . . . Many lived in the antiquated 'corporation boarding houses,' relics of when the mills were built. Our neighbors, men and women, rushed to the mills before the sun rose on cold winter days and returned after dark. They were poorly dressed and poverty stricken."[54]

In the dusty and noisy mills, the women felt their heads become "empty of sense and their ears . . . deaf." Constantly standing and tying knots, they suffered backaches "until they lost their minds and ran amuck." Far from the rural countryside of Ireland, they had become tenders of machines, their activities routinized and measured by the clock.

> *When I set out for Lowell,*
> *Some factory for to find,*
> *I left my native country*
> *And all my friends behind.*
>
> *But now I am in Lowell,*
> *And summon'd by the bell,*
> *I think less of the factory*
> *Than of my native dell.*
>
> *The factory bell begins to ring*
> *And we must all obey,*
> *And to our old employment go,*
> *Or else be turned away.*
>
> *Come all ye weary factory girls,*
> *I'll have your understand,*
> *I'm going to leave the factory*
> *And return to my native land.*

The "factory girls" also worked in dangerous conditions. On January 10, 1860, a terrible tragedy occurred at Lowell's Pemberton Mill. A building suddenly collapsed, trapping nine hundred workers, mostly Irish women; then a fire broke out, adding to the terror and destruction. One hundred and sixteen women were seriously hurt, while eighty-eight were killed. The list of victims included many daughters of Erin.[55]

Irish women were heavily employed in the sewing trades. "No female that can handle a needle need be idle," a young woman in Philadelphia wrote home. By 1900, a third of all seamstresses and dressmakers in the United States were Irish women. Work in the garment industry was repetitious and dirty, and the wages were pitifully low. "I am a good seamstress and work hard," one woman explained. "I try but I can not make over $1 per day. I pay rent for my machine, $2.50 per month. Am not able to afford to ride on street cars, therefore I have to walk, and if I happen to be one minute late, I have to walk up long flights of stairs and am not allowed to go on the elevator."[56]

Still, for many Irish women, America was a land of opportunity. "My dear Father," a daughter wrote from New York in 1850, "I must only say this is a good place and a good country. . . . [A]ny man or woman without a family are fools that would not venture and come to this plentyful Country where no man or woman ever hungered or ever will and where you will not be seen naked. . . ." Similarly, in the same year, Margaret McCarthy wrote home to her family: "Come you all Together Couragiously and bid adieu to that lovely land of our Birth" where there was so much misery, oppression, and degradation. She enclosed twenty dollars, urging her father to clear away from "that place all together and the Sooner the Better."[57]

For these women, America represented not only jobs and wages but also economic self-sufficiency — freedom from dependency on fathers or husbands. "I am getting along splendid and likes my work . . . it seems like a new life," one of them wrote to her younger sister in Ireland. "I will soon have a trade and be more independint. . . . You know it was always what I wanted so I have reached my highest ambition." Thomas McCann wrote home about his sister: "Maggie is well and likes this Country. She would not go back to old Ireland for any money." What Maggie especially valued was the "independence" she had found in America.[58]

The Irish "Ethnic" Strategy

These immigrant women, however, were mainly confined to domestic service and factory work. Significantly, their daughters did not follow in their occupational footsteps. In 1900, only 19 percent of the Irish women born in America worked as servants or laundresses, compared to 61 percent of the immigrant generation. An employment agent reported that most immigrant Irish women were illiterate: "In fact they are the only class I know of that cannot read or write." But their daughters, he added, were educated and shunned domestic service. Increasingly, young women were entering white-collar employment as secretaries, nurses, and teachers. By 1910, Irish-American women constituted one-fifth of all public school teachers in northern cities and one-third in Chicago alone.[59]

These advances for Irish women reflected a broader pattern of Irish success — a rise out of the ranks of the "giddy multitude." By 1900, two-thirds of the Irish were citizens by birth, and they were better educated and had greater occupational mobility than their parents. In Boston, for example, 40 percent of those born in America had white-collar jobs in 1890, compared to only 10 percent for the immigrants. The family of John Kearney of Poughkeepsie, New York, represented this pattern. After arriving in America, Kearney worked as an unskilled laborer and then became a junk dealer; one of his sons rose from post office clerk to superintendent of city streets, and another son from grocery clerk to inspector of the city's waterworks. "My children [are] doing first rate," an Irish immigrant proudly declared, but "if they were back there [in Ireland] what would they be?"[60]

By the early 1900s, Irish Americans were attending college in greater proportion than their Protestant counterparts. They had even begun to enter Harvard University in substantial numbers. Initially, the students at this elite school resented the Irish presence, but gradually they came to accept the newcomers. President Abbott Lawrence Lowell viewed the Irish favorably and highlighted Harvard's role in assimilating them into American society. "What we need," he had explained earlier, "is not to dominate the Irish but to absorb them." We want them to become "rich," he added, "send their sons to our colleges, to share our prosperity and our sentiments." In his opinion, such inclusionism should be reserved for certain groups. The "theory of universal political equality," he argued, should not be applied to "tribal Indians," "Chinese," or "negroes under all conditions, [but] only to our own race, and to those people whom we can assimilate rapidly." Lowell added that the Irish were unlike Jewish immigrants: they were Christian as well as culturally similar to Americans of English origin. The Irish could, therefore, become "so merged in the American people" that they would not be "distinguished as a class."[61]

The Irish were also able to make such great social and economic strides because they settled in the cities rather than in the country. A rural people in Ireland, they had become urban in America. In 1850, one in three Irish immigrants lived in fifteen cities, including 134,000 in New York City, 72,000 in Philadelphia, and 35,000 in Boston. Thirty years later, one-third of New York City's population was Irish. By 1885, Boston's Irish children outnumbered Protestant white children. This city was no longer the "Boston of the Endicotts and the Winthrops" but had become "the Boston of the Collinses and the O'Briens."[62]

This Irish concentration in certain cities provided the basis for the development of their political power. As "white" immigrants, they were eligible for naturalized citizenship. Their rates for becoming citizens and voters were the highest of all immigrant groups. They wanted to become Americans, for they had come here as settlers rather than sojourners: only 10 percent of them went back to Ireland, while Italians had a return rate ranging from 40 to 60 percent. "The outstanding fact" about the Irish "return tide was its minuteness," observed historian Arnold Schrier. "Compared with the vast numbers who left Ireland it was a mere trickle." The Irish entry into citizenship and politics was facilitated by their language skills. "The Irish had one advantage which other immigrants did not share — they did not have to learn to speak English," recalled Elizabeth Gurley Flynn. Thus "they more easily became citizens."[63]

Unlike the Chinese immigrants, who were barred from naturalized citizenship, and the blacks, who were largely disenfranchised, the Irish possessed suffrage. As voters, they consciously cultivated and promoted "Green Power." Led by politicians like John Kelly, New York's Tammany Hall helped elect the city's first Irish Catholic mayor, William R. Grace. By 1890, the Irish had captured most of the Democratic party organizations in northern cities. In New York, Boston, Chicago, and San Francisco, Irish political machines functioned like "Robin Hoods," taking taxes from the Yankee middle class and giving revenues to the Irish through the public payrolls. By 1900, the Irish represented 30 percent of the municipal employees in these cities. Through the political machines, the Irish were able to get jobs in the fire and police departments as well as municipally owned utilities, subways, street railways, waterworks, port facilities, and in city hall itself. The "Irish cop" and "Irish fireman" became ubiquitous at this time. The Irish political bosses also awarded public works projects to Irish building contractors.[64]

As early as 1870, Irish building contractors constituted a fifth of all contractors in the country. An "Irish ethic" led these contractors to give preferential treatment to compatriot subcontractors and workers. Meanwhile, ethnic associations like the Ancient Order of Hibernians and the Clan na Gael functioned as networks for employment, while unionized skilled Irish workers monopolized many trades and shared job opportunities only with their sons and compatriots. Emigration was no longer "like going into a City where you don't know anybody," a worker wrote to a relative in Ireland. "Should your Brother Paddy Come to America . . . he can rely on his Cousins to promote his interests in Procuring work."[65]

Heavily concentrated in the building trades, Irish workers became highly unionized. Many of the prominent leaders in the labor movement were Irish — Terence Powderly of the Knights of Labor, Mary Kenny O'Sullivan of the American Federation of Labor, and Cork-born Mary Harris, the legendary labor activist known as "Mother Jones." Through this leadership and the unions, many Irish were able to experience what historian David Montgomery described as "the much celebrated rise . . . from rags to riches." Thus what especially boosted the Irish as a class was their opportunity to participate in the higher-waged skilled and unionized trades.[66]

By 1900, the Irish occupied a significant niche in the skilled labor market: 1.2 million were employed in the blue-collar trades, representing 65 percent of all Irish workers. Most of these blue-collar laborers — 78 percent — were skilled. While the Irish composed only 7.5 percent of the entire male work force, they were disproportionately represented in the elite construction and industrial occupations — one-third of the plumbers and steamfitters, one-fifth of the stonecutters and brass workers, and one-sixth of the teamsters and steelworkers. This Irish dominance in the skilled and high-wage jobs represented what historian Roediger called "the wages of whiteness." Irish workers had successfully campaigned to make American labor equal "white" labor. Once they became members of the privileged stratum of the work force, they monopolized the better jobs. Their social and economic rise resulted, to a significant extent, from keeping down workers of other groups. Irish "ethnic solidarity" and influence in the unions enabled them to exclude the "others" such as the Chinese and blacks — the Calibans of color.[67]

Ironically, Irish entry into the economic mainstream threatened their ethnicity and sense of group unity. "How shall we preserve our identity?" asked an Irish immigrant in 1872. "How shall we preserve our faith and nationality, through our posterity, and leave our impress on the civilization of this country. . . ?"[68]

There were different views about whether the Irish should preserve their cultural identity or assimilate. The *Irish American* urged its readers to learn Gaelic so they could "feel more proud and manly as Irish, and be more respected as American citizens." But the Irish experienced intense pressure to assimilate in America's "melting pot." Earlier, they had been warned by John Quincy Adams: "[The Irish] come to . . . a life of labor — and, if they cannot accommodate themselves to the character, moral, political, and physical, of this country . . . the Atlantic is always open to them to return to the land of their fathers. . . . They must cast off their European skin, never to resume it. They must look forward to their posterity rather than backward to their ancestors; they must be sure that whatever their own feelings may be, those of their children will cling to the prejudices of this country." Similarly, in 1896, a writer for the *Atlantic Monthly* predicted: "The Irish will, before many years are past, be lost in the American [people] and . . . there will no longer be an 'Irish question' or an 'Irish vote,' but a people one in feelings, and practically one in race."[69]

Indeed, many Irish immigrants struggled to raise themselves from "greenhorns," speak with an "American accent," drink ice cream sodas, and feel like "real Yankees." Some of them even tried to separate themselves from their Irish past. "The second generation here are not interested in their ancestors," an immigrant admitted, because "we have never told them of the realities of life [in Ireland], and would not encourage any of them to visit. . . . When we left there, we left the old world behind, we are all American citizens and proud of it." For them, the ocean was a psychological border, protecting them from hidden injuries and bitter memories. Many immigrants wanted to focus on their future and America as their new homeland. "We have too many loved ones in the Cemetary here to leave them," an immigrant wrote to her brother in Ireland. "We have been here a long time — and it is home to us now."[70]

But even as the Irish immigrants took possession of America, many of them reaffirmed their Irish identity by telling and retelling stories about British oppression in the homeland. Elizabeth Gurley Flynn, for example, remembered how in the 1890s "the awareness of being Irish came to us as small children, through plaintive song and heroic story. The Irish people fought to wrest their native soil from foreign landlords, to speak their native Gaelic tongue, to worship in the church of their choice, to have their own schools, to be independent and self-governing. . . . We drew in a burning hatred of British rule with our mother's milk. Until my father died at over eighty, he never said *England* without adding, 'God damn her!' "[71]

Though they had planted new roots in America, many Irish found their minds wandering across the Atlantic to the hills of Ireland. Lying in bed at night, they could hear "a little voice" calling them back to their "far, far counthrie":

> My thoughts were on old Erin's isle,
> My own dear native land;

Altho' compelled to exile myself
To some far distant shore,
My heart is still on Erin's isle,
What Paddy can say more?

They missed the small farming communities where people engaged in conversation across hedges and stone walls, and neighbors "visited, talked, sang, and danced in each other's cottages" in the evenings. In America, gathering in their homes, church halls, and bars, they created a community of Irish memory through song:

Time may roll o'er me its circles uncheering,
Columbia's proud forests around me shall wave,
But the exile shall never forget thee, loved Eire,
Till, unmourned, he sleep in a far, foreign grave,
a far, foreign grave.[72]

FOREIGNERS IN THEIR
NATIVE LAND

Manifest Destiny in the Southwest

AS IRISH WOMEN worked in Lowell's mills manufacturing textiles and as Irish men helped to build a national system of transportation, America's frontier was advancing beyond what
Jefferson called the "Stony mountains." "Let our workshops remain in
Europe," Jefferson had warned. "The mobs of great cities add just so
much to the support of pure government, as sores do the strength of the
human body." By the 1840s, however, the workshops, or factories, had
come to America, and great cities had developed in the eastern section
of the country. But Jefferson's vision of an American continent covered
with "a people speaking the same language, governed in similar forms,
and by similar laws" was being realized. Indeed, the Market Revolution
had set in motion forces that were propelling American expansion toward the Pacific. Between our border and this western ocean in the
Southwest lay Mexico.[1]

"In the Hands of an Enterprising People"

During the war against Mexico in the 1840s, many Irish immigrants
served in the United States armed forces. Ironically, the Irish had been
pushed from their homeland by British colonialism, and here they found

themselves becoming Americans by participating in the conquest of the Southwest — an American expansionist thrust celebrated as "manifest destiny." In California, this conflict began in the small town of Sonoma. There, on June 6, 1846, General Mariano Vallejo was rudely wakened at his home by thirty armed Americans. They had arrived "before it was quite light," one of them recalled. "We knocked on the front of his dwelling and one of his servants came out. We was standing all a-horseback. . . ."[2]

So began the revolt to wrest California from Mexico and establish what would be called the "Bear Flag Republic." American westward expansion was reaching the Pacific, and Americans were entering California. The rebels were mostly uncouth frontiersmen, viewed by the Mexicans as "grimy adventurers" and "exiles from civilization." Some of them had crossed the border after the Mexican government had prohibited American immigration, and hence were illegal aliens. Most of the intruders had been in California for less than a year, and now they were claiming the territory as theirs. Their homemade flag displayed the image of a grizzly bear facing a lone star suggesting an analogy to the Texas Republic. To the Mexicans, the bear was a thief, a plunderer of their cattle; they would call the armed intruders *los Osos,* "the Bears."[3]

When she saw the rebels, Doña Francisca Vallejo urged her husband to escape through the back door, but the general refused. Commandante Vallejo represented Mexican authority in the region of California north of San Francisco, and the American rebels had come to "arrest" him. Actually, Vallejo was no longer on active duty, and there were no Mexican troops at the fort. The ragtag rebels entered the general's elegant home with its handsome mahogany chairs and fine piano; a gentleman always, Vallejo offered them a bottle of wine before returning to his bedroom to change his clothes. A striking contrast to the Americans, Vallejo was educated and cultured, the possessor of a vast library. The general and his brother Salvador as well as his brother-in-law Jacob Leese were then taken as prisoners to Fort Sutter near Sacramento. Salvador Vallejo bitterly recalled that his captors would check on them and comment: "Let me see if my Greasers are safe."[4]

Two months later, General Vallejo was freed and allowed to return home, only to find his rancho stripped. "I left Sacramento half dead, and arrived here [Sonoma] almost without life, but am now much better," Vallejo wrote to an American friend in San Francisco. "The political change has cost a great deal to my person and mind, and likewise to my property. I have lost more than one thousand live horned cattle, six hundred tame horses, and many other things of value. . . . All is lost."[5]

Unlike his immigrant captors, Don Vallejo was a Californian by birth. As the commander of the Sonoma fort, he represented a long history of Spanish and Mexican efforts to secure the California territory against American and Russian expansion. Three centuries earlier, believing that Asia was close to Mexico, Hernán Cortés had sent an expedition to California, and in 1542, Juan Rodríguez Cabrillo sailed along its coast. The Spanish colonization of this region began in 1769 when Father Junípero Serra founded the mission of San Diego de Alcala. The plan was to extend the Spanish frontier as the colonizers took Indian lands and converted the native peoples. During the next half century, twenty-one missions were established, stretching five hundred miles along the California coast northward to Los Angeles, Santa Barbara, Monterey, San Jose, San Francisco, and Sonoma.

While some of the settlers came from Spain, most were from Mexico, recruited from the ranks of the desperately poor. They were generally "mestizo": the forty-six settlers sent to Los Angeles, for example, were "a mixture of Indian and Negro with here and there a trace of Spanish." The government promised the colonists equipment and food, including herds of cattle. By 1781, however, there were only about six hundred settlers in Alta California. Trying to bolster immigration, Governor Diego de Borica reported: "This is a great country, the most peaceful and quiet country in the world . . . [with] good bread, excellent meat, tolerable fish." But California failed to attract settlers: by 1821, there were only three thousand Mexicans, most of them the offspring of the first colonists. Meanwhile, Spain had overextended its empire, and Mexico became an independent country.[6]

A member of the landed elite, Don Vallejo owned 175,000 acres. He and the other rancheros had been granted vast tracts of land by the Spanish and Mexican governments. Many of them had originally been soldiers and were given land for their service. In 1784, for example, Governor Pedro Fages wrote to his superiors requesting land grants: "The cattle are increasing in such manner, that it is necessary in the case of several owners to give them additional lands; they have asked me for some 'sitios' which I have granted provisionally, namely to Juan Jose Dominguez who was a soldier in the presidio of San Diego . . . to Manual Nieto for a similar reason that of la Zanja on the highway from said mission. . . ."[7]

Society in Don Vallejo's California was stratified. At the top were the *gente de razon*. The Spanish term for "people of reason" generally meant Spanish and Castilian-speaking, although it did come to include mestizos who were properly educated. Some of the Mexicans, Richard Henry Dana reported in his autobiographical *Two Years before the Mast,* were "even as fair" as the English: of "pure Spanish blood," they formed the upper class. Below them was the laboring class. Racially, the laborers "[went] down by regular shades," Dana noted, "growing more and more dark and muddy" with "pure" Indians at the bottom rung. "Throughout all California," John Marsh reported in 1836, "the Indians are the principal laborers; without them the business of the country could hardly be carried on." The laborers worked not only on the range but also in the hacienda. "Each one of my children, boys and girls, has a servant who has no other duty than to care for him or her," Doña Francisca Vallejo, the mother of sixteen children, told a visitor. "I have two for my own personal service. Four or five grind the corn for the tortillas; for here we entertain so many guests that three could not furnish enough meals to feed them all. About six or seven are set apart for service in the kitchen. Five or six are continually occupied in washing clothes of the children and the rest employed in the house; and finally, nearly a dozen are charged to attend the sewing and spinning." A traveler observed that the Indians herding the cattle were kept "poor" and "in debt," seldom paid more than "two or three bullock hides per month or six dollars in goods."[8]

Vallejo and his fellow rancheros practiced a patriarchical culture. "All our servants are very much attached to us," explained Doña Vallejo. "They do not ask for money, nor do they have a fixed wage; we give them all they need, and if they are ill we care for them like members of the family. If they have children we stand as godparents and see to their education. . . . [W]e treat our servants rather as friends than as servants." Wealth was important to these rancheros, not for capitalist accumulation and investment, but as a means to support a genteel lifestyle of "splendid idleness." Describing one of these Mexican gentlemen farmers, Dana wrote: Don Juan Bandini "had a slight and elegant figure, moved gracefully, danced and waltzed beautifully, spoke good Castilian, with a pleasant and refined voice and accent, and had, throughout, the bearing of a man of birth and figure."[9]

Men like Don Bandini cultivated a pastoral and aristocratic style. "We were the pioneers of the Pacific coast, building towns and Missions," remembered Guadalupe Vallejo, nephew of Mariano. "[A] few hundred large Spanish ranches and Mission tracts occupied the whole country from the Pacific to the San Joaquin [valley]." Though the rancheros lived on widely scattered estates, they frequently socialized at events like dances and weddings. Capturing one of these moments, Guadalupe Vallejo wrote:

> Nothing was more attractive than the wedding cavalcade on its way from the bride's house to the Mission church. The horses were more richly caparisoned than for any other ceremony, and the bride's nearest relative or family representative carried her before him, she sitting on the saddle with her white satin shoe in a loop of golden or silver braid, while he on the bear-skin covered anquera behind. The groom and his friends mingled with the bride's party, all on the best horses that could be obtained, and they rode gaily from the ranch house to the Mission, sometimes fifteen or twenty miles away.[10]

Initially, Mexicans in California, especially rancheros like Vallejo, welcomed foreigners from the United States. "The kindness and hospitality of the native Californians have not been overstated," observed John Bidwell, who arrived in 1841. "They had a custom of never charging for anything . . . for entertainment — food, use of horses, etc. . . . When you had eaten, the invariable custom was to rise, deliver to the woman or hostess the plate on which you had eaten the meat and beans . . . and say, 'Muchas gracias, Senora' ('Many thanks, madame'); and the hostess as invariably replied, 'Buen provecho' ('May it do you much good')." A visitor to the Vallejo home in 1839, William Heath Davis, described the hospitality of his host: "We were very cordially received, handsomely entertained at dinner, and invited to pass the night, which we did at Casa Grande of Mariano Vallejo. On retiring we were shown to our several apartments; I found an elegant bed with beautifully trimmed and embroidered sheets. . . ."[11]

Coming to California as individuals and few in number, the first Americans were generally accepted, even offered land grants by the Mexican government if they converted to Catholicism and became naturalized citizens. For example, Jacob Leese married Rosalia Vallejo, a sister of Mariano Vallejo. Don Abel Stearns of Massachusetts married into the wealthy Bandini family and became a large landowner and cattle rancher. These American men became "Dons," a title signifying high status and membership in the California landed elite. Learning Spanish and practicing the local customs, they became part of their adopted society. "While here [in San Gabriel]," an American visitor reported, "I met with a Yankee — Daniel A. Hill [from Santa Barbara] . . . who had been a resident in the country for many years, and who had become, in manner and appearance, a complete Californian."[12]

But the Mexican people found themselves and their world criticized by other Yankees. For example, Richard Henry Dana complained that the Mexicans were "an idle, thriftless people." He disdainfully noticed that many Americans were marrying "natives" and bringing up their children as Catholics and Mexicans. Perhaps he had in mind his uncle. After his arrival in Santa Barbara in 1826, William G. Dana of Boston converted to Catholicism and married sixteen-year-old Josefa Carillo after delaying the nuptial ceremony for two years in order to complete naturalization formalities. Don "Guillermo" and Doña Josefa had twenty-one children. Richard never visited his uncle during his stay in California. If the "California fever" (laziness) spared the first generation, the younger Dana warned, it was likely to "attack" the second, for Mexicans lacked the enterprise and calculating mentality that characterized Americans. Thus, although Mexicans grew an abundance of grapes, they bought "at a great price, bad wine made in Boston"; they also bartered the hides of cattle, valued at two dollars, for something worth only seventy-five cents in Boston. Inefficient in enterprise, they spent their time in pleasure-giving activities such as festive parties called fandangos. What distinguished Anglos from Mexicans, in Dana's opinion, was their Yankeeness — their industry, frugality, sobriety, and enterprise. Impressed with California's natural resources, its forests, grazing land, and harbors, Dana exclaimed: "In the hands of an enterprising people, what a country this might be!"[13]

By the 1840s, more Yankees were entering Vallejo's world, driven there by dreams of wealth and landownership generated by pamphlets and books about California. Determined to transform the territory into their own image, American foreigners were now coming in groups; many brought their families and saw themselves as Americans, not future Mexicans. They were a different sort than the first Americanos. "Many [of these early immigrants] settled among us and contributed with their intelligence and industry to the progress of my beloved country," Governor Juan Alvarado observed and then added unhappily: "Would that the foreigners that came to settle in Alta California after 1841 had been of the same quality as those who preceded them!" Mexicans complained about the new foreigners: "The idea these gentlemen have formed for themselves is, that God made the world and them also, therefore what there is in the world belongs to them as sons of God." "These Americans are so contriving that some day they will build ladders to touch the sky, and once in the heavens they will change the whole face of the universe and even the color of the stars."[14]

By 1846, there were several hundred American foreigners in this Mexican territory. "We find ourselves threatened by hordes of Yankee immigrants who have already begun to flock into our country and whose progress we cannot arrest," complained Governor Pío Pico nervously. Many of them had come west fully intending to take the territory from Mexico. The leader of Vallejo's captors, Benjamin Ide, told his men: "We must be conquerors . . . [or] we are robbers."[15]

Shortly after the rebels arrested General Vallejo and established the Bear Flag Republic, Commander John D. Sloat sailed his ship into Monterey Bay and declared California a possession of the United States. He had instructions to occupy ports in California and establish American authority in the event of war with Mexico.

A key American objective of the Mexican-American War was the annexation of California. This territory was an important source of raw material for the Market Revolution: it exported cattle hides to New England, where Irish factory laborers manufactured boots and shoes. California was also the site of strategic harbors. Sperm oil from whales was a crucial fuel and lubricant in the economy of the Market Revolution, and the American whaling industry was sending its ships to the Pacific Ocean. The ports of California were needed for repairs and supplies. Moreover, policymakers wanted to promote American trade with the Pacific rim. In a message to Congress, President James K. Polk explained that California's harbors "would afford shelter for our navy, for our numerous whale ships, and other merchant vessels employed in the Pacific ocean, and would in a short period become the marts of an extensive and profitable commerce with China, and other countries of the East."[16]

The Bear Flag rebellion coincided with the beginning of the war against Mexico. The rebels had insisted that they were defending the interests of American settlers against unfair and arbitrary Mexican rule. But the manager of Fort Sutter where Vallejo was imprisoned refuted this claim. "This was simply a pretense," John Bidwell charged, "to justify the premature beginning of the war [in California], which henceforth was to be carried in the name of the United States." What Vallejo's armed captors were doing, he added, was playing "the Texas game."[17]

The war itself began more than a thousand miles away — in Texas.

The Market Revolution had stimulated the expansion of the Cotton Kingdom toward Mexico. During the 1820s, Americans crossed the Mexican border, settling in a territory known as Texas. Many of them were slaveholders from the South in search of new lands for cotton cultivation. President John Quincy Adams tried to purchase Texas for a million dollars in 1826, but Mexico refused the offer.

A year later, worried about U.S. westward expansion, the Mexican government sent a commission to investigate the influx of Americans into Texas. In his diary, Lieutenant José María Sánchez described how the foreign intruders were growing in number and defying Mexican laws. "The Americans from the north have taken possession of practically all the eastern part of Texas, in most cases without the permission of the authorities. They immigrate constantly, finding no one to prevent them, and take possession of the sitio [location] that best suits them without either asking leave or going through any formality other than that of building their homes." While visiting the American settlement of San Felipe de Austin, Sánchez predicted: "In my judgment, the spark that will start the conflagration that will deprive us of Texas, will start from this colony." Similarly, Commissioner Manuel Mier y Terán reported: "The incoming stream of new settlers is unceasing. . . ." As the military commander of Mexico's eastern interior provinces in 1829, Mier y Terán again expressed apprehension: "The department of Texas is contiguous to the most avid nation in the world. The North Americans have conquered whatever territory adjoins them." Then he added ominously: "They incite uprisings in the territory in question."[18]

In 1830, the Mexican government outlawed the institution of slavery and prohibited further American immigration into Texas. The new policy, however, provoked opposition among some Mexicans in the territory. The *ayuntamiento* (council) of San Antonio, composed of members of the Mexican elite, favored keeping the border open to Americans. "The industrious, honest North American settlers have made great improvements in the past seven or eight years," the council declared. "They have raised cotton and cane and erected gins and sawmills."[19]

Meanwhile, American foreigners in Texas were furious at the new restrictions. As slaveholders, many of them were determined to defy the Mexican law abolishing slavery. Americans continued to cross the border as illegal aliens. By 1835, there were some twenty thousand Americans in Texas, greatly outnumbering the four thousand Mexicans. Tensions were escalating. Stephen Austin urged his countrymen to "Americanize" Texas and bring the territory under the U.S. flag. He stated that his "sole and only desire" since he first saw Texas was to "redeem it from the wilderness — to settle it with an intelligent honorable and interprising [sic] people." He invited compatriots to come to Texas, "each man with his rifle," "passports or no passports." Viewing the conflict as one between a "mongrel Spanish-Indian and negro race" and "civilization and the Anglo-American race," Austin declared that violence was inevitable: "War is our only recourse. There is no other remedy."[20]

The war came in 1836, when some Americans in Texas began an armed insurrection against Mexican authority. The center of the rebellion for independence was San Antonio, where a mission had been converted into a fort that would become the stuff of American legend. Barricading themselves in the Alamo, 175 Texas rebels initiated hostilities in a struggle for what would be called the Lone Star Republic. The Mexican government declared the action illegal and sent troops to suppress the rebellion. Surrounded by Mexican soldiers, the rebels refused to surrender. According to one story, their leader, William Barret Travis, dramatically drew "a line in the sand." All the men who crossed it, he declared, would fight to the death.[21]

Led by General Antonio López de Santa Anna, the Mexican soldiers stormed the Alamo and killed most of the rebels, including Jim Bowie and Davy Crockett. Among the men slain were a few Mexicans including Juan Abamillo, Carlos Espalier, and Antonio Fuentes who had decided to side with the Americans. The conflict even pitted brother against brother — Gregorio Esparza defended the fort while Francisco Esparza was one of the attacking soldiers. Santa Anna's army then captured the town of Goliad, where four hundred American prisoners were executed. Rallying around the cry "Remember the Alamo," Sam Houston organized a counterattack. Houston's troops surprised Santa Anna's forces at San Jacinto. According to historian Carlos Castañeda, they "clubbed and stabbed" Mexican soldiers seeking to surrender, "some on their knees." The slaughter became "methodical" as "the Texan riflemen knelt and poured a steady fire into the packed, jostling ranks." After the battle, two Americans and 630 Mexicans lay dead.[22]

Houston forced Santa Anna to cede Texas; Mexico repudiated the treaty, but Houston declared Texas an independent republic and was subsequently elected its president. In his inaugural address, Houston claimed that the Lone Star Republic reflected "glory on the Anglo-Saxon race." He insisted that theirs was a struggle against Mexican "tyranny" and for American "democracy": "With these principles we will march across the Rio Grande, and . . . ere the banner of Mexico shall triumphantly float upon the banks of the Sabine, the Texan standard of the single star, borne by the Anglo-Saxon race, shall display its bright folds in Liberty's triumph, on the isthmus of Darien."[23]

Immediately after the United States annexation of Texas in 1845, Mexico broke off diplomatic relations. Tensions between the two countries then focused on a border dispute: the United States claimed that the southern border of Texas was the Rio Grande, but Mexico insisted that it was 150 miles to the north at the Nueces River. In early January 1846, President James K. Polk ordered General Zachary Taylor to take his troops into the disputed territory. The American forces occupied an area near the mouth of the Rio Grande and blockaded the river — an act of war under international law. On May 11, an armed skirmish between American and Mexican forces occurred, providing the pretext for a declaration of war. In his war message, Polk declared that Mexican troops had "passed the boundary of the United States . . . invaded our territory and shed American blood upon American soil." He added: "War exists notwithstanding all our efforts to avoid it."[24]

What followed was a brutal, unrestrained military campaign. American soldiers themselves documented the actrocities committed against the Mexican civilian population. "Since we have been in Matamoros a great many murders have been committed," a young captain, Ulysses S. Grant, wrote in a private letter. "Some of the volunteers and about all the Texans seem to think it perfectly right to impose on the people of a conquered city to any extent, and even to murder them where the act can be covered by dark. And how much they seem to enjoy acts of violence too!" Another officer, George G. Meade, wrote in a letter: "They [the volunteers] have killed five or six innocent people walking in the street, for no other object than their own amusement. . . . They rob and steal the cattle and corn of the poor farmers. . . ." General Winfield Scott admitted that American soldiers had "committed atrocities to make Heaven weep and every American of Christian morals blush for his country. Murder, robbery and rape of mothers and daughters in the presence of tied-up males of the families have been common all along the Rio Grande." A Mexican newspaper denounced the outrages, describing the American invaders as "the horde of banditti, of drunkards, of fornicators . . . vandals vomited from hell, monsters who bid defiance to the laws of nature . . . shameless, daring, ignorant, ragged, bad-smelling, long-bearded men with hats turned up at the brim, thirsty with the desire to appropriate our riches and our beautiful damsels."[25]

The horror ended in early 1848, a few months after General Winfield Scott's army occupied Mexico City. In the Treaty of Guadalupe Hidalgo, Mexico accepted the Rio Grande as the Texas border and ceded the Southwest territories to the United States for $15 million. The acquisition included the present-day states of California, New Mexico, Nevada, and parts of Colorado, Arizona, and Utah, a total of over one million square miles. Together with Texas, the area amounted to one-half of Mexico.

To many Americans, the war and the conquest had extended the "errand into the wilderness" to the Pacific. In 1845, *Democratic Review* editor John L. O'Sullivan announced that "to overspread the continent allotted by Providence for the free development of our yearly multiplying millions" was America's "manifest destiny." Like John Winthrop's "city upon a hill," this vision depicted the national mission as divinely designed: the course of the country's past and future was something inexorable, destined.[26]

The doctrine of "manifest destiny" embraced a belief in American Anglo-Saxon superiority — the expansion of Jefferson's homogeneous republic and Franklin's America of "the lovely White." "This continent," a congressman declared, "was intended by Providence as a vast theatre on which to work out the grand experiment of Republican government, under the auspices of the Anglo-Saxon race." Former secretary of state of the Texas Republic Ashbel Smith confidently predicted: "The two races, the Americans distinctively so called, and the Spanish Americans or Mexicans, are now brought by the war into inseparable contact. No treaties can henceforth dissever them; and the inferior must give way before the superior race.... After the war, when the 40,000 soldiers now in Mexico shall be withdrawn, their places will be soon more than supplied by a still greater number of merchants, mechanics, physicians, lawyers, preachers, schoolmasters, and printers." As a soldier during the war, Colonel Thomas Jefferson Green described America's glowing future: "The Rio Grande ... is capable of maintaining many millions of population, with a variety of products which no river upon the north continent can boast. This river once settled with the enterprise and intelligence of the English race, will yearly send forth an export which it will require hundreds of steamers to transport to its delta...."[27]

The war also seemed to manifest a masculine destiny. American men bragged how they were displaying their prowess in the Southwest not only on the battlefield but also in bed. They claimed that their sexual attractiveness to Mexican women was God-given. A poem published during the war, entitled "They Wait for Us," boasted:

The Spanish maid, with eye of fire,
At balmy evening turns her lyre
And, looking to the Eastern sky,
Awaits our Yankee chivalry
Whose purer blood and valiant arms,
Are fit to clasp her budding charms.

The man, her mate, is sunk in sloth —
To love, his senseless heart is loth:
The pipe and glass and tinkling lute,
A sofa, and a dish of fruit;
A nap, some dozen times by day;
Sombre and sad, and never gay.[28]

In an essay on "The Conquest of California," the editor of the *Southern Quarterly Review* proudly explained the reason why the "senoritas of California . . . invariably preferred" the men of the Anglo-Saxon race. The conquest was inevitable, the editor insisted. "There are some nations that have a doom upon them. . . . The nation that makes no onward progress . . . that wastes its treasure wantonly — that cherishes not its resources — such a nation will burn out . . . will become the easy prey of the more adventurous enemy." Enterprising Americans, the editor reported, had already begun to "penetrate" the remote territory of California, extracting her vast and hidden riches, and would soon make her resources "useful" by opening her "swollen veins" of precious metals.[29]

"Occupied" Mexico

Mexicans viewed the conquest of their land very differently. Suddenly, they were "thrown among those who were strangers to their language, customs, laws, and habits." The border had been moved, and now thousands of Mexicans found themselves inside the United States. The treaty permitted them to remain in the United States or to move across the new southern border. If they stayed, they would be guaranteed "the enjoyment of all the rights of citizens of the United States according to the principles of the Constitution."[30]

Most remained, but they felt a peculiar alienation. "Our race, our unfortunate people will have to wander in search of hospitality in a strange land, only to be ejected later," Mexican diplomat Manuel Cresción Rejón predicted. "Descendents of the Indians that we are, the North

Americans hate us, their spokesmen depreciate us, even if they recognize the justice of our cause, and they consider us unworthy to form with them one nation and one society, they clearly manifest that their future expansion begins with the territory that they take from us and pushing aside our citizens who inhabit the land." A few years later, Pablo de la Guerra vented his frustrations before the California Senate. The "conquered" Mexicans, he complained, did not understand the new language, English, which was now "prevalent" on "their native soil." They had become "*foreigners in their own land.*"[31]

What this meant for many Mexicans was political vulnerability and powerlessness. In California, for example, while Mexicans were granted suffrage, they found that democracy was essentially for Anglos only. At first, they greatly outnumbered Anglos, by about ten to one. But the discovery of gold near John Sutter's mill led to a massive migration into California; by 1849, the Anglo population had reached 100,000, compared to only 13,000 Mexicans.

Dominant in the state legislature, Anglos enacted laws aimed at Mexicans. An antivagrancy act, described as the "Greaser Act," defined vagrants as "all persons who [were] commonly known as 'Greasers' or the issue of Spanish or Indian blood . . . and who [went] armed and [were] not peaceable and quiet persons." A foreign miners' tax of $20 monthly was in practice a "Mexican Miners' Tax." The tax collectors took fees mainly from Spanish-speaking miners, including American citizens of Mexican ancestry.[32]

Many of the miners had come from Mexico, where techniques for extracting gold had been developed. In California, they shared this knowledge with Anglo miners, introducing Spanish mining terms such as *bonanza* (rich ore) and *placer* (deposits containing gold particles). But Anglos resented the Mexicans as competitors, making no distinction between Mexicans and Mexican Americans. "The Yankee regarded every man but a native American as an interloper," observed a contemporary, "who had no right to come to California and pick up the gold of 'free and enlightened citizens.' " Anglo miners sometimes violently defended what they regarded as their "right" to the gold. In his memoir, Antonio Franco Coronel described one frightening experience: "I arrived at the Placer Seco [about March 1849] and began to work at a regular digging. . . . Presently news was circulated that it had been resolved to evict all those who were not American citizens from the placers because it was believed that the foreigners did not have the right to exploit the placers." Shortly afterward, a hundred Anglos invaded the diggings of

Coronel and some other Mexicans, forcing them to flee for their lives. "All of these men raised their pistols, their Bowie knives; some had rifles, others pickaxes and shovels."[33]

Though Mexicans were a minority of the state population, they continued to constitute a sizable presence in Southern California. In Santa Barbara, for example, Mexicans represented a majority of the voters and dominated local elections. "The Americans have very little influence in the elections," complained Charles Huse in the 1850s. The Mexicans possessed a majority of the votes. When they were united, they were able to elect whomever they wished. However, Huse predicted that Anglos would have "all the power" in a few years and would not consult the Mexicans about anything. Indeed, Mexicans soon became a minority as Anglos flocked to Santa Barbara. In 1873, Mexican voters were overwhelmed at the polls. Though they elected Nicolas Covarrubias as county sheriff, they lost the positions of county assessor, clerk, treasurer, and district attorney. Politically, the Anglos were now in command. "The native population wear a wondering, bewildered look at the sudden change of affairs," a visitor noted, "yet seem resigned to their unexpected situation, while the conquerors are proud and elated with their conquest." Mexican political participation declined precipitously in Santa Barbara — to only 15 percent of registered voters in 1904 and only 3 percent in 1920.[34]

Compared to California, the political proscription of Mexicans in Texas was more direct. There, Mexicans were granted suffrage, but only in principle. A merchant in Corpus Christi reported that the practice in several counties was to withhold the franchise from Mexicans. A traveler observed that the Mexicans in San Antonio could elect a government of their own if they voted but added: "Such a step would be followed, however, by a summary revolution." In 1863, after a closely contested election, the *Fort Brown Flag* editorialized: "We are opposed to allowing an ignorant crowd of Mexicans to determine the political questions in this country, where a man is supposed to vote knowingly and thoughtfully." During the 1890s, many counties established "white primaries" to disfranchise Mexicans as well as blacks, and the legislature instituted additional measures like the poll tax to reduce Mexican political participation.[35]

Political restrictions lessened the ability of Mexicans not only to claim their rights as citizens, but also to protect their rights as landowners. The original version of the Treaty of Guadalupe Hidalgo had contained a provision, Article X, which guaranteed protection of "all prior and pending titles to property of every description." In ratifying the treaty, however, the U.S. Senate omitted this article. Instead, American emissaries offered the Mexican government a "Statement of Protocol" to reassure Mexicans that "the American government by suppressing the Xth article . . . did not in any way intend to annul the grants of lands made by Mexico in the ceded territories." Grantees would be allowed to have their legitimate titles acknowledged in American courts.[36]

But whether the courts would in fact confirm their land titles was another matter. In New Mexico, the state surveyor general handled conflicts over land claims until 1891, when a Court of Private Land Claims was established. Dominated by Anglo legal officials, the court confirmed the grants of only 2,051,526 acres, turning down claims for 33,439,493 acres. The court's actions led to Anglo ownership of four-fifths of the Mexican land grants.[37]

Similarly, in California, Mexican land titles were contested. Three years after the Treaty of Guadalupe Hidalgo, Congress passed a land law establishing a commission to review the validity of some twenty land grants made under Spanish rule and another five hundred by the Mexican government. The boundaries for these land grants had been drawn without surveying instruments and were loosely marked on maps indicating a notched tree, a spot "between the hills at the head of a running water," a pile of stones, and the like. Frequently, land was measured with the expression *poco más o menos,* "a little more or less." The entire Pomona Valley, for example, was described as "the place being vacant which is known by the name of [Rancho] San Jose, distant some six leagues, more or less, from the Ex-Mission of San Gabriel. . . ." U.S. land law, however, required accurate boundaries and proof of legitimate titles.[38]

Such evidence, Mexican landholders discovered, was very difficult to provide. Unfamiliar with American law and lacking English language skills, they became prey to Anglo lawyers. If they were successfully able to prove their claim, they would often be required to pay their lawyers one-quarter of their land. Others borrowed money at high interest rates in order to pay legal fees; after they won their cases, many rancheros were forced to sell their land to pay off their debts. "The *average* length of time required to secure evidence of ownership," historian Walton Bean calculated, "was 17 *years* from the time of submitting a claim to the board." Furthermore, during this time, squatters often occupied the lands, and when the rancheros finally proved their ownership, they found it difficult and sometimes impossible to remove them. In the end, whether or not they won their claims, most of the great Mexican rancheros in northern California lost their lands.[39]

"When they [the rancheros] receive patent," *El Clamor Publico* of Los Angeles observed, "if they are not already ruined, they will be very close to it." In an 1859 petition to Congress, sixty rancheros protested that they had been forced to sell their lands to pay interests, taxes, and litigation expenses. "Some, who at one time had been the richest land-holders," they observed, "today find themselves without a foot of ground, living as objects of charity."[40]

After paying his lawyers $80,000, Salvador Vallejo managed to prove his land claim before the Land Commission; during his appeal in the district court, however, squatters settled on his rancho. They kept burning his crops, and he finally sold his property for $160,000 and moved to San Francisco. Although Mariano Vallejo lost his Soscol land claim, he won his Petaluma land claim in appeals to the United States Supreme Court. But squatters occupied his land and refused to move; they also ran off his Indian laborers and destroyed his crops. Vallejo was forced to sell parts of his vast estate, which had originally totaled more than 100,000 acres, until he was down to only 280 acres in Sonoma. Bitter over the loss of his lands, Vallejo cursed the new Anglo order: "The language now spoken in our country, the laws which govern us, the faces which we encounter daily are those of the masters of the land, and of course antagonistic to our interests and rights, but what does that matter to the conqueror? He wishes his own well-being and not ours!"[41]

Meanwhile, in Texas, many rancheros had also lost their lands in courts or to squatters. "The hacendado class, as a class," the historian T. R. Fehrenbach observed, "was stripped of property perfectly legally, according to the highest traditions of U.S. law." Mexican landowners had to defend their "ancient titles in court, and they lost either way, either to their own lawyers or to the claimants." In the Rio Grande Valley, for example, Anglo squatters occupied land known as the Espiritu Santo grant belonging to Francisco Cavazos and made claims based on their rights as squatters. Trading-post operator Charles Stillman then purchased the squatters' claims. The conflicting claims were then taken to court, which validated Cavazos's title to the land. Represented by the law firm of Basse and Horde, Stillman offered $33,000 for the grant, threatening to appeal the decision. The land itself was worth $214,000, but the Cavazos family accepted the offer because the legal costs to defend the grant would have been prohibitive. In the end, the Cavazos family received nothing: Stillman never paid the $33,000.[42]

Meanwhile, the "play of the market" contributed to the dispossession of the Mexican landed class. The cattle industry in California had begun to decline in the late 1850s; lacking the financial resources to convert their lands from grazing to agriculture, many Mexican ranchers were forced to sell their lands. In Texas, the cattle industry was extremely unstable and volatile. The periodic fall in the cattle market generated sales and transfers of lands from Mexican to Anglo ranchers. "During the ten-year boom of 1875–1885, the King ranch purchased nearly 58,000 acres of Mexican-owned land," historian David Montejano calculated, "but the ranch would acquire nearly as much, 54,000 acres, in the following five years, a time of market collapse (1886–1891)."[43]

The market also gave Anglo ranchers an edge over Mexican ranchers during periods of drought. For example, the drought of the 1890s financially devastated rancher Victoriano Chapa of Texas. In 1901, at the age of eighty-nine years, Chapa was persuaded to sell his stock and lease the land. The approaching transfer made him depressed. Chapa told historian J. Frank Dobie, whose family owned a nearby ranch: "Why have we been talked into this evil trade? We belong here. My roots go deeper than those of any mesquite growing up and down this long arroyo. We do not need money. When a man belongs to a place and lives there, all the money in the world cannot buy him anything else so good. *Valgame Dios*, why, why, why?" Chapa took his life two days before the transfer of his land. While drought was a tragedy for Mexican ranchers like Chapa, it opened the way for Anglo ranchers to acquire Mexican land. They, too, suffered losses of livestock during times of drought, but they were able to protect their ranches better than their Mexican competitors because they had greater access to bank credit and could obtain funds to develop deeper wells. After the drought, they were financially stronger and able to purchase lands from economically distressed Mexican ranchers.[44]

What made the market especially destructive for Mexican ranchers was the introduction of a new system of taxation. Previously, under Mexican rule, the products of the land were taxed. This policy made sense in a region where climatic conditions caused income from agriculture to fluxuate; ranchers and farmers paid taxes only when their cattle or crops yielded profits. Under the new order, however, the land itself was taxed. This hurt landholders during years of business losses and made them economically vulnerable: unable to pay their taxes, many lost title to their land.

While this tax system was color-blind and applied to all landowners, it assisted the dispossession of Mexican landowners. Anglos sometimes took over lands from Mexicans by paying the back taxes based on $1.50 an acre, and then they had Anglo tax assessors reduce the land tax to thirty or forty cents an acre. Many Mexicans borrowed money to pay their taxes only to be forced to sell their lands to pay off debts incurred by the interest. In Southern California, for example, Julio Verdugo mortgaged his Rancho San Rafael to Jacob Elias for $3,445 at 3 percent interest per month. After eight years, Verdugo owed $58,000 and had to sell his entire rancho to Alfred B. Chapman. Chapman, feeling sorry for Verdugo, gave the old ranchero some land for a residence. Suffering from plummeting profits in the cattle trade, Santa Barbara rancheros found it difficult to pay their taxes. "Everybody in this town is broke," one of them complained, and "cattle can be bought at any price." By 1865, their herds had been reduced from more than 300,000 head to only 7,000.[45]

As Mexican ranchers told and retold stories about the loss of their lands, they created a community of the dispossessed. They recalled how "the native Californians were an agricultural people" and had "wished to continue so." But then they "encountered the obstacle of the enterprising genius of the Americans, who . . . assumed possession of their lands, [took] their cattle, and destroyed their woods." In Santa Barbara, a Mexican old-timer recounted the decline of the rancheros who had fallen into debt to Anglo merchants and lost their lands: "The Spanish people had to live and as the dwindling herds would not pay their bills, they mortgaged their land to the Americanos." They bought supplies on credit from a store run by Americans, "two tall dark, gloomy men who dressed in black. The Spanish people called them 'Los Evangelistas' because they looked like the evangelists who preached the sorrowful Yankee religion in those days. They got much of our lands."[46]

In 1910, the Laredo *La Cronica* described the degradation of many Mexicans from landholders to laborers: "The Mexicans have sold the great share of their landholdings and some work as day laborers on what once belonged to them. How sad this truth!" A Mexican woman remembered her grandmother's bitterness: "Grandmother would not trust any gringo, because they did take their land grants away and it still was a memory to her. She always used to say, 'Stay with your race, stay with your own.' " A Mexican song poignantly expressed how it felt to be dispossessed and alienated on their native soil:

> *The Mexico-Texan, he's one fonny man*
> *Who lives in the region that's north of the Gran';*
> *Of Mexican father, he born in thees part.*

For the Mexico-Texan, he no gotta lan';
And sometimes he rues it, deep down in hees heart.
He stomped on da neck on both sides of the Gran';
The dam gringo lingo no cannot spick,
It twista da tong and it maka heem sik;
A cit'zen of Texas they say that he ees!
But then, — why they call heem da Mexican Grease?
Soft talk and hard action, he can't understan',
The Mexico-Texan, he no gotta lan'.[47]

The Making of a Mexican Proletariat

As the American market expanded into the Southwest, it appropriated not only Mexican land but also Mexican labor. They were now working for strangers who had come into their country. Mexicans were extensively used as workers in ranching and agriculture. In Texas, Mexican cowboys, "vaqueros," helped to drive the cattle herds on the Chisholm and Western trails to the railroad centers in Abilene and Dodge City. The original cowboys, the vaqueros taught the Anglos their time-tested techniques of roping, branding, and handling cattle. Rancher C. C. Cox described the work of the vaqueros at a roundup: "Once a week or oftener we would make a rodeo or round up the cattle. The plan is to have one herding ground on the Ranch — the cattle soon learn to run together at that place when they see the vacqueros on the wing — and when those on the outskirts of the range are started, the movement becomes general, and no prettier or more interesting sight can be imagined than a rodeo in full progress — every cow catches the alarm and starts off at a brisk trot headed for the herding ground. . . ."[48]

But the vaqueros soon began to vanish. The extension of rail lines into Texas eliminated the cattle drives, and agriculture in the state shifted from grazing to tillage. Mexican cowboys had looked down on farm laborers with "mingled contempt and pity," rancher J. Frank Dobie observed in the 1920s, but "more and more of the *vaqueros*" were turning to "cotton picking each fall."[49]

Mexican farm laborers had been in the cotton fields even before Texan independence. As cotton cultivation expanded during the second half of the nineteenth century, they became the mainstay of agricultural labor. "Soil and climate are suitable and cheap labor is at hand," announced the *Corpus Christi Weekly Caller* in 1885. "Mexican farm labor can be utilized in the culture of cotton as well during the picking season." These workers also cleared the lands for planting. "Grubbing brush," many Anglos said, "is a Mexican job." They also dug irrigation ditches, bringing water from rivers and streams to parched areas. Some of the irrigation methods had originally been developed by the Moors in Africa before the tenth century and had been brought to the Southwest by the Spanish. Other techniques had come from the Pueblo Indians, who had developed irrigation systems in the region long before the arrival of the first Spaniards. Mexican laborers would level the land, then divide the fields into squares with low embankments to hold the water. After soaking a block, they would make a hole in one of the walls, permitting the water to flow into the next square. This method of irrigation came to be known as "the Mexican system." Over the years, these laborers transformed the Texas terrain from scrub bushes to the green fields of the Lower Valley known as the "winter garden."[50]

Mexicans also served as an important work force in railroad construction. During the 1880s, they constituted a majority of the laborers laying tracks for the Texas and Mexican Railroad. An Arizona newspaper stated: "It is difficult to get white men to work, the wages being only $1.50 a day, and board $5 per week with some minor charges, which reduce a man's net earnings." When the first Mexican section crew began working in Santa Barbara in 1894, the *Morning Press* reported that the "Chinamen section hands" of the Southern Pacific had been replaced by "a gang of Mexicans." By 1900, the Southern Pacific Railroad had 4,500 Mexican employees in California.[51]

Railroad construction work was migratory. Railroad workers and their families literally lived in boxcars and were shunted to the places where they were needed. "Their abode," a manager said, "is where these cars are placed." In the torrid heat of summer and the freezing cold of winter, the workers laid tracks as they sang:

> *Some unloaded rails*
> *Others unloaded ties. . . .*

An army of bending backs and swinging arms, they connected the cities of the Southwest with ribbons of steel.

> *Those who knew the work*
> *Went repairing the jack*
> *With sledge hammers and shovels,*
> *Throwing earth up the track.*

They shoveled up not only dirt, but also complaints about the low wages and exhausting work.

> *And others of my companions*
> *Threw out thousands of curses.*[52]

Meanwhile, Mexicans were also working in the mining industries. In the New Almaden Quicksilver Mine in California, Mexican miners labored deep in the bowels of the earth. To bring the ore to the surface, each worker carried a two-hundred-pound pack strapped to his shoulders and forehead. Their nerves straining and muscles quivering, hundreds of these carriers ascended perpendicular steps, "winding through deep caverns" in darkness lit by candles on the walls. They wore pantaloons with the legs cut above the knees, calico shirts, and leather sandals fastened at their ankles. Emerging into the daylight at the entrance of the mine, they deposited their burdens into cars and then took time to smoke their cigarros before descending again. In the copper mines of Arizona, Mexicans extracted the "red metal" used to manufacture electrical wires. "One might say," observed historian Carey McWilliams, ". . . that Mexican miners in the copper mines of Arizona, Utah, and Nevada, have played an important role in making possible the illumination of America by electricity."[53]

Now "in the hands of an enterprising people," Mexican laborers found themselves in a caste labor system — a racially stratified occupational hierarchy. On the Anglo-owned cattle ranches in Texas, for example, the managers and foremen were Anglo, while the cowhands were Mexican. In the New Mexico mines, Anglo workers operated the machines, while Mexican miners did the manual and dangerous work. In Santa Barbara, building contractors hired Anglos as skilled carpenters and Mexicans as unskilled ditch diggers. Sixty-one percent of the Mexican laborers in San Antonio were unskilled in 1870, compared to only 24 percent of the Anglos. In Southern California cities like Santa Barbara and Los Angeles, 75 percent of the Mexican workers were crowded into low blue-collar occupations such as service and unskilled labor, compared to 30 percent of the Anglos. Less than 10 percent of the Mexican workers were employed in white-collar jobs, compared to over 40 percent of the Anglos. The situation for Mexicans actually deteriorated over time. In 1850, the rural Mexican population in Texas was evenly distributed into three strata — 34 percent ranch-farm owners, 29 percent skilled laborers, and 34 percent manual laborers. Fifty years later, the first tier had shrunk to only 16 percent and the second to 12 percent, while the lowest tier had ballooned to 67 percent.[54]

Even where Mexicans did the same work as Anglos, they were paid less than their counterparts. In the silver-mining industry of Arizona, for example, Mexican workers received between $12 and $30 a month plus a weekly ration of flour, while "American" miners got between $30 and $70 a month plus board. In the copper industry, companies listed their Mexican employees on their payrolls under the special heading of "Mexican labor," paying them at lower rates than Anglo laborers for the same job classifications. "The differences in the wages paid Mexicans and the native-born and north Europeans employed as general laborers," a congressional investigation reported, ". . . are largely accounted for by discrimination against the Mexicans in payment of wages." Trapped in this dual wage system, Mexican miners were especially vulnerable to debt peonage. Forced to live in company towns, they had no choice but to buy necessities from the company store, where they had to use their low wages to pay high prices for food and clothing. Allowed to make purchases on credit, these miners frequently found themselves financially chained to the company.[55]

Justifying this racial hierarchy, mine owner Sylvester Mowry invoked the images as well as language used earlier by slavemasters to describe the affection and loyalty of their slaves. "My own experience has taught me that the lower class of Mexicans . . . ," Mowry declared, "are docile, faithful, good servants, capable of strong attachments when firmly and kindly treated. They have been 'peons' for generations. They will always remain so, as it is their natural condition."[56]

But, like the enslaved blacks of the Old South, Mexican workers demonstrated that they were capable of defying these stereotypes of docility and submissiveness. They had a sense of self-respect and the worth of their work, and they repeatedly went out on strike. In 1901, two hundred Mexican construction workers of the El Paso Electric Street Car Company struck, demanding a wage increase and an end to management's practice of replacing them with lower-paid workers recruited from Juárez, Mexico. While they did not win a raise, they successfully protected their jobs against imported laborers. Two years later, Mexican members of the United Mine Workers won strike demands for a pay increase and an eight-hour day from the Texas and Pacific Coal Company in Thurber, Texas.[57]

Protesting wage cuts, two hundred Mexican farm workers joined hundreds of fellow Japanese laborers in a 1903 strike at Oxnard,

California. Together, the two groups organized the Japanese-Mexican Labor Association (JMLA). The strikers elected Kosaburo Baba as president, Y. Yamaguchi as secretary of the Japanese branch, and J. M. Lizarras as secretary of the Mexican branch. At their union meetings, discussions were conducted in both Japanese and Spanish, with English serving as a common language for both groups. For the first time in the history of California, two minority groups, feeling a solidarity based on class, had come together to form a union. Here was a West Coast version of the "giddy multitude."

In a statement written jointly by Yamaguchi and Lizarras, the union declared: "Many of us have family, were born in the country, and are lawfully seeking to protect the only property that we have — our labor. It is just as necessary for the welfare of the valley that we get a decent living wage, as it is that the machines in the great sugar factory be properly oiled — if the machines stop, the wealth of the valley stops, and likewise if the laborers are not given a decent wage, they too, must stop work and the whole people of this country suffer with them." The strikers successfully forced the farmers to pay union laborers a piecework rate of five dollars per acre for thinning beets. The JMLA had emerged as a victorious and powerful force for organizing farm laborers.[58]

Flushed with victory, the Mexican secretary of the JMLA, J. M. Lizarras, petitioned the American Federation of Labor to charter their organization as the Sugar Beet Farm Laborers' Union of Oxnard. Samuel Gompers, the president of the federation, agreed to issue a charter to Lizarras on one condition: "Your union will under no circumstances accept membership of any Chinese or Japanese." This requirement contradicted the very principles of the Oxnard strike. Refusing the charter, Lizarras protested:

> We beg to say in reply that our Japanese brothers here were the first to recognize the importance of cooperating and uniting in demanding a fair wage scale. . . . In the past we have counseled, fought and lived on very short rations with our Japanese brothers, and toiled with them in the fields, and they have been uniformly kind and considerate. We would be false to them and to ourselves and to the cause of unionism if we now accepted privileges for ourselves which are not accorded to them. . . . We will refuse any other kind of charter, except one which will wipe out race prejudice and recognize our fellow workers as being as good as ourselves. I am ordered by the Mexican union to write this letter to you and they fully approve its words.

Without the AFL charter and the general support of organized labor, the Japanese and Mexican union passed out of existence within a few years. Their strike, however, had demonstrated that Mexican laborers were ready to stand with fellow Japanese in a movement based on interethnic class unity.[59]

The most powerful Mexican workers' show of force occurred in Arizona. There, in 1903, the Clifton-Morenci mines were struck by some 3,500 miners, 80 percent of them Mexican. The strikers demanded an eight-hour day, free hospitalization, paid life insurance, fair prices at the company stores, and the abolition of the dual wage system. Italian and Slavonian workers joined them in demanding wages equal to those paid to Anglo Americans and northern Europeans. The strikers successfully shut down the mines, but they were forced to return to work after heavy rains and flooding destroyed many of their homes. Several strike leaders were convicted of inciting a riot and sent to prison. Twelve years later, however, the miners struck again. To thwart the actions of the 5,000 strikers, the company sealed the mine entrances with cement and told them "to go back to Mexico." Hundreds of strikers were arrested during the nineteen-week conflict. The national guard was ordered to break the strike, but in the end, the strikers managed to extract wage increases. "Everyone knows," commented the *Los Angeles Labor Press,* "that it was the Mexican miners that won the strike at Clifton and Morenci by standing like a stone wall until the bosses came to terms."[60]

These strikes reflected a feeling of Mexican ethnic solidarity. "*Abajo los gerentes,*" the workers chanted, "down with the bosses." Mexican musicians provided entertainment for the parades and meetings, while Mexican merchants, *comerciantes,* offered food and clothing to the strikers. More importantly, the *huelgas,* "strikes," were often supported by Mexican *mutualistas,* "benevolent associations." "The Mexicans belong to numerous societies and through these they can exert some sort of organizational stand together," reported a local newspaper during the 1903 strike at the Clifton-Morenci mines.[61]

The *mutualistas* reinforced this consciousness of being Mexican north of the border. Everywhere in the barrios of Arizona, Texas, New Mexico, and California, there were organizations like Sociedad Benevolencia, Miguel Hidalgo, Sociedad Mutualista, Sociedad Obreros, Los Caballeros del Progreso, and Sociedad Mutualista Mexicana. Members of the *mutualistas* were laborers as well as shopkeepers and professionals such as lawyers, newspaper editors, and doctors. These associations helped individual members cover hospitalization and funeral expenses, provide low-interest loans, and raise money for people in time of dire need. Taking some of their names from national heroes and conducting their meetings in Spanish, they reminded Mexicans of their common origins as children of "the same mother: Mexico."[62]

The *mutualistas* dispelled the myth of Mexicans as a quiet, siesta-loving, sombreroed people. Through these ethnic organizations, Mexicans resisted labor exploitation and racism. In 1911, several Texas *mutualistas* came together in a statewide convention, the Congreso Mexicanista. Concerned about anti-Mexican hostility and violence, the congress called for ethnic solidarity: "*Por la raza y para la raza,*" "All for one and one for all." One of the delegates, the Reverend Pedro Grado, defined their struggle as one of class and race: "The Mexican braceros who work in a mill, on a hacienda, or in a plantation would do well to establish *Ligas Mexicanistas,* and see that their neighbors form them." United, they would have the strength to "strike back at the hatred of some bad sons of Uncle Sam who believe themselves better than the Mexicans because of the magic that surrounds the word *white.*" The *mutualistas* reflected a dynamic Mexican-American identity — a proud attachment to the culture south of the border as well as a fierce determination to claim their rights and dignity in "occupied" Mexico.[63]

8

SEARCHING FOR GOLD
MOUNTAIN

Strangers from a Pacific Shore

B
UT CALIBAN COULD have been Asian. "Have we devils here?"
the theatergoers heard Stephano declare in *The Tempest*. "Do you
put tricks upon's with savages and men of Inde, ha?" The war
against Mexico reflected America's quest for a passage to India. During
the nineteenth century, this vision inspired Senator Thomas Hart Benton
of Missouri to proclaim the movement toward Asia as America's destiny.
The "White" race was obeying the "divine command, to subdue and
replenish the earth," as it searched for new and distant lands. As whites
migrated westward, Benton pointed out, they were destroying "savagery." As civilization advanced, the "Capitol" had replaced the "wig-
wam," "Christians" had replaced "savages," and "white matrons" had
replaced "red squaws." Under the "touch" of an "American road to
India," Benton exclaimed, the western wilderness would "start" into
life, creating a long line of cities across the continent. Crossing the Rocky
Mountains and reaching the Pacific, whites were finally circumnavigating
the earth to bring civilization to the "Yellow" race.[1]

The annexation of California led not only to American expansion
toward Asia, but also the migration of Asians to America. In a plan sent
to Congress in 1848 shortly after the Treaty of Guadalupe Hidalgo,

policymaker Aaron H. Palmer predicted that San Francisco, connected by railroad to the Atlantic states, would become the "great emporium of our commerce on the Pacific." Chinese laborers, he proposed, should be imported to build the transcontinental railroad as well as bring the fertile lands of California under cultivation. "No people in all the East are so well adapted for clearing wild lands and raising every species of agricultural product . . . as the Chinese."[2]

Pioneers from Asia

A year later, Chinese migrants began arriving in America, but they came for their own reasons. Many sought sanctuary from intense conflicts in China caused by the British Opium Wars. Significantly, while British colonialism in Ireland was creating conditions of push there, it was also generating pressures for emigration from China. Many migrants were also fleeing from the turmoil of peasant rebellions such as the Red Turban Rebellion and the bloody strife between the *Punti* (Local People) and the *Hakkas* (Guest People) over possession of the fertile delta lands. "Ever since the disturbances caused by the Red [Turban] bandits and the Kejia bandits," a Chinese government report noted, "dealings with foreigners have increased greatly. The able-bodied go abroad."[3]

Harsh economic conditions also drove Chinese migrants to seek survival in America. Forced to pay large indemnities to Western imperialist powers, the Qing government imposed high taxes on peasant farmers; unable to pay these taxes, many of them lost their lands. Floods intensified the suffering. "The rains have been falling for forty days," an 1847 report to the emperor stated, "until the rivers, and the sea, and the lakes, and the streams have joined in one sheet over the land [for miles]." Behind the emigrating spirit was starvation. "The population is extremely dense," an observer explained; "the means of subsistence, in ordinary times, are seldom above the demand, and consequently, the least failure of the rice crop produces wretchedness."[4]

Learning about *Gam Saan*, "Gold Mountain," many of the younger, more impatient, and more daring Chinese left their villages for America. The migrants were mostly men, planning to work away from home temporarily. They were illiterate or had very little schooling, but they dreamed of new possibilities inspired by stories of the "gold hills." To these hopeful migrants, America possessed an alluring boundlessness, promising not only gold but also opportunities for employment. In the port cities, circulars distributed by labor brokers announced: "Americans are very rich people. They want the Chinaman to come and make him very welcome. There you will have great pay, large houses, and food and clothing of the finest description. . . . It is a nice country, without mandarins or soldiers. . . . Money is in great plenty and to spare in America." Chinese who returned to their villages with money they had made in Hawaii and America reinforced the excitement of emigration. Sixteen-year-old Lee Chew recalled the triumphant return of a fellow villager from the "country of the American wizards." With the money he had earned overseas, he bought land as spacious as "four city blocks" and built a palace on it. Then he invited his family and friends to a grand party where they were served a hundred roasted pigs, chickens, ducks, geese, and an abundance of dainties. Young Lee was inspired, eager to leave for this fabulous country.[5]

America seemed so beckoning. "After leaving the village," an immigrant said, "I went to Hong Kong and stayed at a [firm] owned by people named Quan. I stayed there ten days to take care of the paper work for passage. At that time all I knew was that [travelers to the Golden Mountain] who came back were always rich." During the 1860s, a Chinese laborer might earn three to five dollars a month in China; in California, he could work for the railroad and make thirty dollars a month. A folk song expressed the emotions of many migrants:

> In the second reign year of Haamfung [1852], a trip
> to Gold Mountain was made.
> With a pillow on my shoulder, I began my perilous
> journey:
> Sailing a boat with bamboo poles across the sea,
> Leaving behind wife and sisters in search of money,
> No longer lingering with the woman in the bedroom,
> No longer paying respect to parents at home.[6]

Contrary to the popular stereotype and myth, these Chinese migrants were not "coolies" — unfree laborers who had been kidnapped or pressed into service by coercion and shipped to a foreign country. Actually, they had come to America voluntarily as free laborers: some of them paid their own way, and probably most of them borrowed the necessary funding through the credit-ticket system. Under this arrangement, an individual borrowed money from a broker to cover the cost of transportation and then paid off the loan plus interest out of his earnings in the new country. "The Chinese emigration to California," reported a British official stationed in Hong Kong in 1853, "was, by and large, free and voluntary. The Chinese emigration to California is now almost wholly confined to independent emigrants who pay their own passage money, and are in a condition to look to their arrangements." William Speer, who worked as a missionary in San Francisco's Chinatown for decades beginning in the 1850s, never found evidence that Chinese laborers had been "brought over by capitalists and worked as slaves . . . against their will." The claim that the Chinese were "coolies," Speer declared, was "fiction."[7]

The majority of the migrants were married. As they prepared to leave their farms and villages, they realized that they would probably not see their wives again for years. But they promised to return someday.

> *Right after we were wed, Husband, you set*
> *out on a journey.*
> *How was I to tell you how I felt?*
> *Wandering around a foreign country, when*
> *will you ever come home?*
> *I beg of you, after you depart, to come back soon,*
> *Our separation will be only a flash of time;*
> *I only wish that you would have good fortune,*
> *In three years you would be home again.*
> *Also, I beg of you that your heart won't change,*
> *That you keep your heart and mind on taking care*
> *of your family;*
> *Each month or half a month send a letter home,*
> *In two or three years my wish is to welcome*
> *you home.*[8]

And so they left China, by the hundreds of thousands. Three hundred and twenty-five Chinese migrants joined the "Forty-Niners" rushing to California. Like their counterparts from the eastern United States and elsewhere, they came to search for gold. A year later, 450 more Chinese arrived in California; then, suddenly, they came in greatly increasing numbers — 2,716 in 1851 and 20,026 in 1852. By 1870, there were 63,000 Chinese in the United States. Most of them — 77 percent — were living in California, but they were elsewhere in the West as well as in the Southwest, New England, and the South. The Chinese constituted a sizable proportion of the population in certain areas: 29 percent in Idaho, 10 percent in Montana, and 9 percent in California. By 1930, about 400,000 had made the Pacific crossing to America. Significantly, about half of them stayed and made the United States their permanent home.

At first, there were signs that the Chinese were welcome in California. "Quite a large number of the Celestials have arrived among us of late, enticed thither by the golden romance that has filled the world," the *Daily Alta California* reported in 1852. "Scarcely a ship arrives that does not bring an increase to this worthy integer of our population." The paper predicted that "the China boys will yet vote at the same polls, study at the same schools and bow at the same altar as our own countrymen." Three years later, merchant Lai Chun-Chuen of San Francisco sanguinely observed that "the people of the Flowery land [China] were received like guests," and "greeted with favor. Each treated the other with politeness. From far and near we came and were pleased."[9]

But Lai failed to notice the rapidly changing political climate that had begun to turn against his fellow immigrants. From the gold fields of the Sierras came the nativist cry: "California for Americans." In 1850, the legislature enacted a foreign miners' tax designed to eliminate Mexican miners. This law was soon repealed, but in 1852, the legislature enacted another foreign miners' tax. Aimed mainly at the Chinese, this tax required a monthly payment of three dollars from every foreign miner who did not desire to become a citizen. Even if they had wanted to, the Chinese could not have become citizens, for they had been rendered ineligible for citizenship by a 1790 federal law that reserved naturalized citizenship for "white" persons. The foreign miners' tax remained in force until it was voided by the 1870 Civil Rights Act. By then, California had collected five million dollars from the Chinese, a sum representing 25 to 50 percent of all state revenue.[10]

During the 1860s, twenty-four thousand Chinese, two-thirds of the Chinese population in America, were working in the California mines. Most of these miners were independent prospectors. Many organized themselves into small groups and formed their own companies. A newspaper correspondent described companies of twenty or thirty Chinese "inhabiting close cabins, so small that one . . . would not be of sufficient size to allow a couple of Americans to breathe in it. Chinamen, stools, tables, cooking utensils, bunks, etc., all huddled up together in indiscriminate confusion, and enwreathed with dense smoke, presented a spectacle." These miners worked mainly placer claims. To extract the gold, they shoveled sand from the stream into a pan or rocker and then washed away the sand and dirt until only the heavy particles of gold remained. Chinese miners became a common sight in the California foothills, especially along the Yuba River and its tributaries and in towns like Long Bar, North-east Bar, and Foster Bar. They wore blue cotton shirts, baggy pants, wooden shoes, and wide-brimmed hats and had queues hanging down their backs.[11]

Day-to-day life for these miners was competitive and anxious. Telegrams sent from Downieville in the mountains reflected their tense lives:

Quong Chung Shing & Co   Downieville, Cal.,
724 Com'cl St., San Francisco   March 2, 1874

Git Wo. I want you pay your cousin Ah Hoey expenses to come Downieville quick attend to claim. Am afraid there will be big fight. Answer.

Fong Sing
Kim Bayo

Ah Chu   Downieville, Cal.,
        March 4, 1874

Trouble about mining claims. I owe a share and all the company want you come. I want you come. Ans yes or no.

Fong Sing
Ah Jake

Yu Wo & Co   Downieville, Cal.,
717 Dupont St., San Francisco   March 28, 1874

What the price of opium. Answer.

Fong Wo & Co[12]

Mining profits had already begun to decrease, however, and the Chinese were leaving the gold fields. Thousands of them joined other Chinese migrants to work on the railroad. In February 1865, fifty Chinese workers were hired by the Central Pacific Railroad to help lay tracks for the transcontinental line leading east from Sacramento; shortly afterward, fifty more were hired. The immigrant laborers were praised by company president Leland Stanford as "quiet, peaceable, industrious, economical — ready and apt to learn all the different kinds of work" required in railroad building. "They prove nearly equal to white men in the amount of labor they perform, and are much more reliable," company superintendent Charles Crocker reported. "No danger of strikes among them. We are training them to do all kinds of labor: blasting, driving horses, handling rock as well as pick and shovel." When white workers demanded that the company stop hiring Chinese laborers, Crocker retorted: "We can't get enough white labor to build this railroad, and build it we must, so we're forced to hire them. If you can't get along with them, we have only one alternative. We'll let you go and hire nobody but them." Within two years, Crocker had hired twelve thousand Chinese, representing 90 percent of the entire work force. The savings derived from the employment of Chinese rather than white workers was enormous. The company paid the Chinese workers $31 a month; had management used white workers, they would have had to pay the same wages plus board and lodging, which would have increased labor costs by one-third.[13]

The construction of the Central Pacific Railroad line was a Chinese achievement. They performed the physical labor required to lay the tracks and provided important technical labor such as operating power drills and handling explosives for boring the tunnels through Donner Summit. The Chinese workers were, in one observer's description, "a great army laying siege to Nature in her strongest citadel. The rugged mountains looked like stupendous ant-hills. They swarmed with Celestials, shoveling, wheeling, carting, drilling and blasting rocks and earth." Time was critical to the company's interest, for the amount of payment it received in land and subsidy from the federal government was based on the miles of track it built. Determined to accelerate construction, the managers forced the Chinese laborers to work through the winter of 1866. Snow drifts, over sixty feet tall, covered construction operations. The workers lived and worked in tunnels under the snow, with shafts for air and lanterns for light. Work was dangerous, occasionally deadly. "The snow slides carried away our camps and we lost a good many men in those slides," a company official reported matter-of-factly; "many of them we did not find until the next season when the snow melted."[14]

The Chinese workers struck that spring. Demanding wages of $45 a month and an eight-hour day, five thousand laborers walked out "as one man." The company offered to raise their wages from $31 to $35 a month, but the strikers stood by their original demands. "Eight hours a day good for white men, all the same good for Chinamen," they declared. The *San Francisco Alta* condemned the strike as a conspiracy: "The foundation of this strike appears to have been a circular, printed in the Chinese language, sent among them by designing persons for the purpose of destroying their efficiency as laborers." The insinuation was transparent: the strikers' demands had been merely drummed up, with agents of the competing Union Pacific behind the Chinese protest. The intent was to nullify the possibility that the workers themselves had minds and wills and were capable of acting in their own interest. Meanwhile, the managers moved to break the strike. They wired New York to inquire about the feasibility of transporting ten thousand blacks to replace the striking Chinese. Superintendent Crocker isolated the strikers and cut off their food supply. "I stopped the provisions on them," he stated, "stopped the butchers from butchering, and used such coercive measures." Coercion worked. Virtually imprisoned in their camps in the Sierras and starving, the strikers surrendered within a week.[15]

Forced to return to work, the Chinese completed the railroad, the "new highway to the commerce of Asia." After they were released by the Central Pacific Railroad in 1869, thousands of them went to San Francisco, where their compatriots were already heavily involved in manufacturing. The formation of an urban Chinese community and the industrial development of the city paralleled each other. In 1860, only 2,719 Chinese resided in San Francisco, representing 7.8 percent of the Chinese population in California. Ten years later, the Chinese population in the city had zoomed to 12,022, a 343 percent increase. Meanwhile, San Francisco had begun to develop as a locus of industry: in 1860, it had about two hundred manufacturing firms employing some 1,500 workers. Ten years later, with nearly one-fourth of California's Chinese population living there, San Francisco had over 12,000 laborers employed in industrial production and was the ninth leading manufacturing city in the United States. Half of the labor force in the city's four key industries — boot and shoe, woolens, cigar and tobacco, and sewing — was Chinese.[16]

These laborers were concentrated in the low-wage jobs. Cigar workers, for example, received only $287 in annual wages, and 92 percent of them were Chinese. In contrast, tailors and seamsters earned $588 a year, and only 9 percent were Chinese. They were also segregated within individual industries and paid less than white workers. In factories where the labor force was racially mixed, whites were the skilled workers and Chinese the menial. Where they were assigned to the same tasks as whites, they were paid less than their white counterparts in a racially based differential wage system: the work was equal but the wages were unequal.[17]

Meanwhile, in the rural regions, the Chinese were helping to develop

California's agriculture. Between 1860 and 1880, as historian Sucheng Chan found, hundreds of Chinese were able to become farmers through tenancy, which offered a way to enter the business with minimum capital. In exchange for the use of the land, equipment, and the marketing of crops, tenant farmers raised fruit and vegetables and then divided the profits with the white landowners. Tenant farmers often organized themselves into companies. Collectively, the partners were responsible for the lease and the operation of the farm. "We found the broad fields apportioned off and rented to separate companies of Chinamen who were working them upon shares — each little company having its own cabin," an observer reported in 1869. "Teams being furnished them, they do all the work, preparing the ground, seeding, tending the crop, and gathering the fruit, leaving nothing for the proprietor to do but to attend to the marketing, and to put into his own pocket half of the proceeds."[18]

Most of the Chinese engaged in agriculture were workers, however. They helped to transform farming in California from wheat to fruit. "They were a vital factor," historian Carey McWilliams wrote, "one is inclined to state *the* vital factor, in making the transition possible." Experienced farmers in the Pearl River Delta before coming to America, the Chinese shared their agricultural knowledge with their white employers, teaching them how to plant, cultivate, and harvest orchard and garden crops.[19]

Indeed, the Chinese built the agricultural industry of California. In the San Joaquin and Sacramento River deltas, they constructed networks of irrigation canals and miles of dikes and ditches. Wielding shovels and working waist-deep in water, they drained the tule swamps and transformed the marshes into agricultural lands. In 1869, a writer for the *Overland Monthly* acknowledged the change in the landscape wrought by the Chinese: "The ditches and dykes which at present protect only a few little patches here and there of the most fruitful soil that the sun shines on, may be made to perform a like service all over the Tulare swamps; and the descendants of the people who drained those almost limitless marshes on either side of their own swiftly-flowing Yellow River, and turned them into luxuriant fields, are able to do the same thing on the banks of the Sacramento and the San Joaquin." In the Salinas Valley, Chinese laborers dug six miles of ditches to drain the land, cutting the peat soil "with huge knife-like spades and pitching it out with steel forks and hooks." Their work boosted the value of the land from $28 per acre in 1875 to $100 per acre two years later.[20]

Paid by the cubic yard of earth that was dug and used as filler for the levees, Chinese laborers sometimes resorted to tricks to increase their wages. To calculate how much his laborers should be paid, P. J. van Loben Sels would measure the size of the pit every four or five days. But it was difficult to make accurate measurements, because of the unevenness of the terrain. In order to calculate the depth of the hole, the Chinese workers would leave a column of dirt in the middle of each pit to serve as a ruler. They tended, van Loben Sels noticed, to use the highest point of ground for their column before digging. Occasionally, they gave their column an "operation" during the night, surgically cutting the column crosswise somewhere in the middle and then inserting a new layer of dirt. In the morning, the pit appeared deeper, and the laborers expected their boss to measure the hole and pay them accordingly. Whenever they were caught making these nocturnal adjustments, they were fined.[21]

In 1869, the *Overland Monthly* described the ubiquitous presence of Chinese laborers in California agriculture: "Visit a hop plantation in the picking season, and count its 50, 60, or 70 pickers in the garb of the eastern Asiatics, working steadily and noiselessly on from morning till night, gathering, curing and sacking the crop. . . . Go through the fields of strawberries . . . the vineyards and orchards, and you will learn that most of these fruits are gathered or boxed for market by this same people." In 1880, the Chinese represented 86 percent of the agricultural labor force in Sacramento County, 85 percent in Yuba, and 67 percent in Solano.[22]

Though they were paid low wages, Chinese farm laborers did not always passively accept what their employers offered them. In 1880, fruit pickers in Santa Clara County went out on strike for higher wages. After the 1882 Chinese Exclusion Act reduced the supply of farm labor, Chinese agricultural workers demanded higher rates for their wages. In 1900, the Bureau of Labor Statistics reported: "Relieved, by the operation of the Exclusion Acts, in great measure from the pressing competition of his fellow-countrymen, the Chinese worker was not slow to take advantage of circumstances and demand in exchange for his labor a higher price, and, as time went on, even becoming Americanized to the extent of enforcing such demands in some cases through the medium of labor organization."[23]

Meanwhile, Chinese workers became targets of white labor resentment, especially during hard times. "White men and women who desire to earn a living," the *Los Angeles Times* reported on August 14, 1893, "have for some time been entering quiet protests against vineyardists and packers employing Chinese in preference to whites." Their protests soon became violent as economic depression led to anti-Chinese riots by unemployed white workers throughout California. From Ukiah to the Napa Valley to Fresno to Redlands, Chinese were beaten and shot by white workers and often loaded onto trains and shipped out of town. These immigrants bitterly remember this violence and expulsion as the "driving out."[24]

"Ethnic antagonism" in the mines, factories, and fields forced thousands of Chinese into self-employment — stores, restaurants, and especially laundries. Chinese wash-houses were a common sight as early as the 1850s. By 1890, there were 6,400 Chinese laundry workers in California, representing 69 percent of all laundry workers. During this period, the ratio of Chinese laundry workers to all Chinese workers jumped from one out of every seventeen to one out of every twelve.[25]

The "Chinese laundryman" was an American phenomenon. "The Chinese laundryman does not learn his trade in China; there are no laundries in China," stated Lee Chew, who came to America in the early 1860s. "The women there do the washing in tubs and have no washboards or flat irons. All the Chinese laundrymen here were taught in the first place by American women just as I was taught." In China, observed Wong Chin Foo of New York, laundry work was a "woman's occupation," and men did not "step into it for fear of losing their social standing."[26]

Why did Chinese men in America enter this line of work? Unlike the retail or restaurant business, a laundry could be opened with a small capital outlay of from seventy-five to two hundred dollars. The requirements were minimal: a stove, trough, dry-room, sleeping apartment, and a sign. A Chinese laundryman did not need to speak much English to operate his business. "In this sort of menial labor," said one, "I can get along speaking only 'yes' and 'no.' " He could also manage without knowing numbers. "Being illiterate, he could not write the numbers," another laundryman said describing a fellow operator. "He had a way and what a way! See, he would draw a circle as big as a half dollar coin to represent a half dollar, and a circle as big as a dime for a dime, and so on. When the customers came in to call for their laundry, they would catch on to the meaning of the circles and pay accordingly."[27]

But "Chinese laundrymen" were also "pushed" into their occupation. Laundry work was one of the few opportunities that were open to Chinese. "Men of other nationalities who are jealous of the Chinese have raised such a great outcry about Chinese cheap labor that they have shut him out of working on farms or in factories or building railroads or making streets or digging sewers," explained Lee Chew. "So he opens a laundry." Thus the "Chinese laundry" represented a retreat into self-employment from a narrowly restricted labor market. "You couldn't work in the cigar factories or the jute or woolen mills any more — all the Chinese had been driven out," old Chinese men later sadly recalled. "About all they could be was laundrymen or vegetable peddlers then." In 1900, one out of four employed Chinese men worked in a laundry.[28]

While most Chinese lived in the West, they were present elsewhere in the United States, including the South. A year after the end of the Civil War, a planter declared: "We can drive the niggers out and import coolies that will work better at less expense, and relieve us from the cursed nigger impudence." The plan was to turn from black to Chinese labor. "Emancipation has spoiled the negro and carried him away from the fields of agriculture," the editor of the *Vicksburg Times* in Mississippi complained in 1869. "Our prosperity depends entirely upon the recovery of lost ground, and we therefore say let the Coolies come." That same year, the southern planters' convention in Memphis announced that it was "desirable and necessary to look to the teeming population of Asia for assistance in the cultivation of our soil and the development of our industrial interests." In his address to the convention, labor contractor Cornelius Koopmanshoop announced that his company had imported thirty thousand Chinese laborers into California and offered to make them available in the South.[29]

Planters soon saw that the Chinese could be employed as models for black workers: hardworking and frugal, the Chinese would be the "educators" of former slaves. During the 1870s, Louisiana and Mississippi planters imported several hundred Chinese laborers and pitted them against black workers. They praised the foreign workers for outproducing blacks and for "regulating" the "detestable system of black labor." A southern governor frankly explained: "Undoubtedly the underlying motive for this effort to bring in Chinese laborers was to punish the negro for having abandoned the control of his old master, and to regulate the conditions of his employment and the scale of wages to be paid him." An editor in Kentucky spoke even more bluntly when he predicted that the introduction of Chinese labor would change the "tune" from " 'forty acres and a mule' " to " 'work nigger or starve.' "[30]

Planters welcomed their new workers. "Messrs. Ferris and Estell, who are cultivating on the Hughs place, near Prentiss," a Mississippi newspaper reported in 1870, "recently imported direct from Hong Kong, a lot of Chinese, sixteen in number, with whom as laborers, they are well pleased." The owner of a plantation near New Orleans had a work force of 140 Chinese. A traveling correspondent offered this vivid account:

> Mounting horses and spreading our umbrellas, we rode out a mile or more through the fields, past countless negroes and mule-teams ploughing, to the spot off by themselves where the picturesque heathens were hoeing cane. . . . Apart, in the middle of the field stood the imperturbable sinecurist who made a faint show of overseeing his countrymen. . . . The Chinamen went on with their work, hoeing the young cane, and doing it very carefully and precisely. Occasionally they would look up at us, but in a very stolid, careless way. Ah Sing approached and greeted us with a polite, "Hallo, how do?" On learning that we were well, he observed . . . , "Belly hot to-day."

In a letter to her daughter, the wife of a Louisiana planter described some Chinese workers: "Yesterday was their Christmas day and they asked for half the day and had prepared themselves a good dinner." One of the "Chinamen" had come into the yard and asked for her. "I went to the porch to see what he wanted. He took off his hat, got down on his knees, and bowed himself his head touching the ground four times very stately then got up. I thought he was drunk but it was a mark of respect he was showing."[31]

The Chinese did not stay long on the plantations, however. As early as 1871, the *New Orleans Times* noted that the Chinese preferred to work in the city rather than do the "plodding work of the plantations." In 1880, about a hundred Chinese were living in New Orleans, where they worked as laundrymen, cigar makers, shoemakers, cooks, and woodcarvers. By then, the southern planters had overthrown Reconstruction; with their political power over blacks restored, they quickly lost interest in Chinese labor.[32]

The use of Chinese labor and its success raised two crucial questions. "What shall we do with them is not quite clear yet," remarked Samuel Bowles in 1869 in his book *Our New West*. "How they are to rank, socially, civilly, and politically, among us is one of the nuts for our social science students to crack, — if they can. . . ." And what would happen to white workers as America's industrial development depended more and more on Chinese labor?[33]

One answer to both questions was the concept of a yellow proletariat in America. According to this view, the Chinese would constitute a permanently degraded caste labor force. They would be, in effect, a unique "industrial reserve army" of migrant laborers forced to be foreigners forever. Thus, unlike European immigrant laborers, the Chinese would be a politically proscribed labor force. Serving the needs of American employers, they would be here only on a temporary basis. "I do not believe they are going to remain here long enough to become good citizens," Central Pacific manager Charles Crocker told a legislative committee, "and I would not admit them to citizenship." The employers of Chinese labor argued that they did not intend to allow the migrants to remain and become "thick" (to use Crocker's term) in American society.[34]

The advocates of Chinese labor offered assurances to white laborers. They explained that Chinese "cheap" labor would reduce production costs, and the resulting low prices for goods would be equivalent to a wage increase for white workers. They also argued that Chinese labor would upgrade white labor, for whites would be elevated to foremen and directors. "If society must have 'mudsills,' " they elaborated, "it is certainly better to take them from a race which would be benefited by even that position in a civilized community, than subject a portion of our own race to a position which they have outgrown." Charles Crocker explained:

> I believe that the effect of Chinese labor upon white labor has an elevating instead of degrading tendency. I think that every white man who is intelligent and able to work, who is more than a digger in a ditch . . . who has the capacity of being something else, can get to be something else by the presence of Chinese labor. . . . There is proof of that in the fact that after we got Chinamen to work, we took the more intelligent of the white laborers and made foremen of them. I know of several of them now who never expected, never had a dream that they were going to be anything but shovelers of dirt, hewers of wood and drawers of water, and they are now respectable farmers, owning farms. They got their start by controlling Chinese labor on our railroad.[35]

Chinese Calibans: The Borders of Exclusion

What enabled businessmen like Crocker to degrade the Chinese into a subservient laboring caste was the dominant ideology that defined America as a racially homogeneous society and Americans as white. The status of racial inferiority assigned to the Chinese had been prefigured in the black and Indian past.

Indeed, the newcomers from a Pacific shore found that racial qualities previously assigned to blacks had become "Chinese" characteristics. Calling for Chinese exclusion, the *San Francisco Alta* warned in 1853: "Every reason that exists against the toleration of free blacks in Illinois may be argued against that of the Chinese here." White workers referred to the Chinese as "nagurs," and a magazine cartoon in California depicted the Chinese as a bloodsucking vampire with slanted eyes, a pigtail, dark skin, and thick lips. Like blacks, the Chinese were described as heathen, morally inferior, savage, childlike, and lustful. Chinese women were condemned as a "depraved class," their immorality associated with a physical appearance "but a slight removal from the African race."[36]

Like blacks, Chinese men were viewed as threats to white racial purity. At the 1878 California Constitutional Convention, John F. Miller warned: "Were the Chinese to amalgamate at all with our people, it would be the lowest, most vile and degraded of our race, and the result of that amalgamation would be a hybrid of the most despicable, a mongrel of the most detestable that has ever afflicted the earth." Two years later, lawmakers prohibited marriage between a white person and a "negro, mulatto, or Mongolian."[37]

In the minds of many whites, the Chinese were also sometimes associated with Indians. The editor of the *California Marin Journal* declared that the winning of the West from the "red man" would be in vain if whites were now to surrender the conquered land to a "horde of Chinese." Policies toward Indians suggested a way to solve the "Chinese Problem." "We do not let the Indian stand in the way of civilization," stated former New York governor Horatio Seymour, "so why let the Chinese barbarian?" In a letter published in the *New York Times,* Seymour continued: "Today we are dividing the lands of the native Indians into states, counties, and townships. We are driving off from their property the game upon which they live, by railroads. We tell them plainly, they must give up their homes and property, and live upon corners of their own territories, because they are in the way of our civilization. If we can do this, then we can keep away another form of barbarism which has no right to be here." A United States senator from Alabama "likened" the Chinese to Indians, "inferior" socially and subject to federal government control. The government, he argued, should do to the Chinese what it had already done to the Indians — put them on reservations.[38]

All three groups — blacks, Indians, and Chinese — shared a common identity: they were all Calibans of color. This view was made explicit in the 1854 California Supreme Court decision of *People v. Hall.* A year before, George W. Hall and two others were tried for murdering Ling

Sing. During the trial, one Caucasian and three Chinese witnesses testified for the prosecution. After the jury returned a guilty verdict, the judge sentenced Hall to be hanged. Hall's lawyer then appealed the verdict, arguing that the Chinese witnesses should not have been permitted to testify against Hall. An existing California statute provided that "no black or mulatto person, or Indian, shall be permitted to give evidence in favor of, or against, any white person," and the question was whether this restriction included the Chinese. In its review, the California Supreme Court reversed Hall's conviction, declaring that the words "Indian, Negro, Black, and White" were "generic terms, designating races," and that therefore "Chinese and other people not white" could not testify against whites.[39]

This view of a shared racial status among all three groups led President Rutherford Hayes to warn Americans about the "Chinese Problem." The "present Chinese invasion," he argued in 1879, was "pernicious and should be discouraged. Our experience in dealing with the weaker races — the Negroes and Indians . . . — is not encouraging. . . . I would consider with favor any suitable measures to discourage the Chinese from coming to our shores."[40]

Three years later, Congress prohibited Chinese immigration, closing America's borders to these strangers from a different shore. Actually, there was very little objective basis for viewing Chinese immigrants as a threat to a homogeneous white society. The Chinese constituted a mere .002 percent of the United States population in 1880.

Behind the exclusion act were fears and forces that had little relationship to the Chinese. Something had gone wrong in America, and an age of economic opportunity seemed to be coming to an end. This country had been a place where an abundance of land and jobs had always been available. The problem for employers had always been the need for more labor. But suddenly, during the closing decades of the nineteenth century, society was experiencing what historian John A. Garraty called "the discovery of unemployment." This new reality plunged society into a national crisis. Enormous expansions of the economy had been followed by intense and painful contractions: tens of thousands of men and women were thrown out of work, and social convulsions such as the violent 1877 Railroad Strike rocked the nation.[41]

Within this context of economic crisis and social strife, Congress made it unlawful for Chinese laborers to enter the United States for the next ten years and denied naturalized citizenship to the Chinese already here. Support for exclusion was overwhelming. In the debate, lawmakers revealed fears that went much deeper than race. They warned that the presence of an "industrial army of Asiatic laborers" was exacerbating class conflict between labor and capital within white society. They claimed that white workers had been "forced to the wall" by corporations employing Chinese. The struggle between labor unions and the industrial "nabobs" and "grandees" was erupting into "disorder, strikes, riot and bloodshed." "The gate," nervous men in Congress declared, "must be closed." The specter of the "giddy multitude" was haunting American society again.[42]

Six years later, the prohibition was broadened to include "all persons of the Chinese race," although exemptions were provided for Chinese officials, teachers, students, tourists, and merchants. Renewed in 1892, the Chinese Exclusion Act was extended indefinitely in 1902.[43]

Meanwhile, contrary to the stereotype of Chinese passivity, the Chinese fought discrimination. Time and again, they took their struggle for civil rights to court. Believing that the Chinese should be entitled to citizenship, they challenged the 1790 Naturalization Law. In 1855, Chan Yong applied for citizenship in San Francisco's federal district court. The local newspapers noted that Chan Yong was more "white" in appearance than most Chinese. The court denied him citizenship, however, ruling that the 1790 law restricted citizenship to "whites" and that the Chinese were not "white." Seven years later, Ling Sing sued the San Francisco tax collector, challenging the $2.50 head tax levied on Chinese. In *Ling Sing v. Washburn,* the California Supreme Court ruled that while the Chinese could be taxed as other residents, they could not be set apart for special taxation. Significantly in this case, a state law was invalidated on the grounds that it violated the United States Constitution.[44]

The *Ling Sing* decision underscored the need for the federal protection of civil rights for the Chinese. During the negotiations between the United States and China regarding a treaty between the two countries in 1868, the Chinese Six Companies, the powerful organization of district associations, lobbied for the inclusion of provisions for the protection of Chinese. They contacted Daniel Cleveland, a San Francisco lawyer and adviser to the federal officials involved in the treaty negotiations, and explained to him that federal legislation was greatly needed to "free" the Chinese in the United States from "wrongs" and to protect Chinese lives and property. Federal protection of Chinese property would also encourage Chinese investments in this country as well as promote American trade with China. The outcome of the negotiations was a major victory for the Chinese Six Companies. The 1868 Burlingame Treaty recognized the "free migration and emigration" of the Chinese to the United States as visitors, traders, or "permanent residents," and the rights of Chinese in the United States to "enjoy the same privileges, immunities, and exemptions in respect to travel or residence, as may there be enjoyed as the citizens or subjects of the most favored nation."[45]

Buoyed by the Burlingame Treaty, Chinese merchants sought federal legislation to abolish discriminatory state laws. They successfully lobbied Congress to include protections for them in the 1870 Civil Rights Act, which declared that "all persons" within the jurisdiction of the United States shall have "the same right" to "make and enforce contracts, to sue, be parties, give evidence, and to the full and equal benefit of all laws and proceedings for the security of person and property as is enjoyed by white citizens." Furthermore "no tax" shall be imposed "by any State upon any person immigrating thereto from a foreign country which is not equally imposed and enforced upon every person emigrating to such State from any other foreign country, and any law of any State from any other foreign country is hereby declared null and void."[46]

But guarantees of equal protection by treaty and by federal law had little effect on what actually happened in society. The Chinese continued to be vulnerable, victims of racial violence. Blamed as "the source of the troubles" of white working men, the Chinese suffered from racial attacks. They had to flee from boys who threw rocks at them and screamed, "God Damn Chinamen." "When I first came," Andrew Kan recounted, "Chinese treated worse than dog. Oh, it was terrible, terrible. At that time all Chinese have queue and dress same as in China. The hoodlums, roughnecks and young boys pull your queue, slap your face, throw all kind of old vegetables and rotten eggs at you." "The Chinese were in a pitiable condition in those days," recalled Huie Kin in his account of San Francisco Chinatown during the 1870s. "We were simply terrified; we kept indoors after dark for fear of being shot in the back. Children spit upon us as we passed by and called us rats."[47]

The Chinese saw the source of their oppression as racism. "Up to 800,000 Europeans enter the United States per year, yet the labor unions hardly cared," the Chinese Six Companies noted. "A few thousands of the Chinese arrivals would irritate American workers . . . and European immigrants get citizenships and voting rights often immediately after their arrival in the United States." Similarly, a Chinese worker explained that what separated them from the other immigrant groups was race. "The cheap labor cry was always a falsehood," argued Lee Chew. Chinese labor was "never cheap" and "always commanded the highest market price." But "it was the jealousy of laboring men of other nationalities — especially the Irish — that raised all the outcry against the Chinese. No one would hire an Irishman, German, Englishman or Italian when he could get a Chinese, because our countrymen [were] so much more honest, industrious, steady, sober, and painstaking. The Chinese were persecuted, not for their vices, but for their virtues." Noting the flaws of other immigrant groups, Lee Chew continued: "Irish fill the almshouses and prisons and orphan asylums, Italians are among the most dangerous of men, Jews are unclean and ignorant. Yet they are all let in, while Chinese, who are sober, or duly law abiding, clean, educated and industrious, are shut out. . . . More than half the Chinese in this country would become citizens if allowed to do so, and would be patriotic Americans."[48]

But Chinese migrants were generally apprehensive about settling in America. They had been "warned" not to come to America, a Chinese merchant in San Francisco explained, and consequently they did not find "peace in their hearts in regard to bringing families."[49]

Twice a Minority: Chinese Women in America

The migrants lived in a virtually womanless world. Very few Chinese women came to Gold Mountain. In 1852, of the 11,794 Chinese in California, only seven were women. Eighteen years later, of 63,199 Chinese in the United States, 4,566 were female — a ratio of fourteen to one. In 1900, of the 89,863 Chinese on the United States mainland, only 4,522, or 5 percent, were female.

Chinese tradition and culture limited migration for women. Confucianism defined the place of a woman: she was instructed to obey her father as a daughter, her husband as a wife, and her eldest son as a widow. According to custom, the afterbirths of children were buried in different places, depending on the sex of the baby — in the floor by the bed for boys and outside the window for girls. This practice symbolized what was expected to happen to a woman: she would leave her home to join the family of her husband. As a daughter-in-law, she would take care of her husband's aging parents. A daughter's name was not recorded on her family tree; it was entered later next to her husband's name in his genealogy.[50]

Women of all classes were regarded as inferior to men and were expected to remain at home, attentive to family and domestic responsibilities. The "bound feet" of women of "gentle birth," while indicating social rank and considered "beautiful," symbolized their subordinate gender and served to prevent them from wandering. In 1855, a Chinese merchant of San Francisco explained why many men did not bring their wives: the women of the "better families" generally had "compressed feet" and were "unused to winds and waves." While peasant women did not have bound feet, they, too, were confined to a narrow world circumscribed by gender. Tied to family and home, they stayed within the walls of their villages. For the Chinese, family and home were synonymous: they even shared the same character in written Chinese.[51]

Women were also left behind because it would have been too expensive for them to accompany their husbands, and the men thought they would be gone only temporarily. Moreover, according to an explanation sometimes known as the "hostage theory," women were kept home in order to ensure that their absent husbands would not become prodigal sons in America. The Chinese system of patrilineal descent provided for the equal division of a family's land among all adult sons and the sharing of responsibility for their elderly parents. By keeping the wives and children of their sons at home, parents hoped they would be able to buttress family ties and filial obligations: their wandering sons would send money home and also return someday. "The mother wanted her son to come back," explained a Chinese woman. "If wife go to America, then son no go back home and no send money."[52]

There were also conditions in America that discouraged women from joining their husbands. In California, Chinese men entered a society of harsh frontier conditions and racial hostility. As railroad and farm workers, they were viewed by employers as temporary and migratory. The very nature of their work rendered it difficult to have families here. But even if they had wanted to bring their wives, the men discovered that many whites viewed America as a "white man's country" and perceived the entry of Chinese women and families as threatening to racial homogeneity. Federal immigration policies had been enacted to bar Chinese women. Passed in 1875 to prohibit the entry of prostitutes, the Page Law was enforced so strictly and broadly that it excluded not only Chinese prostitutes but also Chinese wives. The 1882 prohibition of "Chinese laborers" included women.[53]

Earlier, however, some Chinese men had been able to bring their wives to America or to have women sent here to become their wives. Ah Chew came to California in 1854 when he was fifteen years old. After he decided to settle down in the Sacramento Delta, his grandson explained, he went back to "China on a sailboat to marry, and then brought his wife over here." Similarly, in 1862, Chin Gee-Hee came to Washington Territory, where he worked in a lumber mill. Within a few years, he sent for a wife and got her a job as a cook in the mill's cookhouse. In 1875, Mrs. Chin gave birth to their son, Chin Lem, believed to be the first Chinese born in the Washington Territory. In 1869, A. W. Loomis reported the case of "a wife coming all the way alone across the stormy sea" to be with her husband. "Friends at home besought her not to do a thing so in conflict with Chinese custom; the husband and his relatives in this country, when they heard of her purpose, wrote entreating her not to expose herself to the hardships and perils on the sea, and to the trials which would be liable to befall her here; but she answered that where the husband was there she had a right to be." She came to California where she supported herself and her child by sewing garments and making cigarettes while her husband worked for a mining company in the Kern River area.[54]

In America, Chinese families were gradually forming as men began to leave mining and railroad construction and enter more stable pursuits like farming and shopkeeping. One area of enterprise that encouraged the formation of Chinese families was the fishing industry in Monterey. In the fishing village of Point Alones, for example, nearly half of the Chinese were female. According to a description published in the 1870s, the village was organized into "companies," but most of these companies were actually groups of families: "Man Lee Company, three men and three women; Sun Sing Lee Company, three men, two women and three children. . . ." As early as 1876, in its memorial to President Ulysses Grant, the Chinese Six Companies noted the presence of "a few hundred Chinese families" in the country, and added: "There are also among us a few hundred, perhaps a thousand, Chinese children born in America."[55]

During the early decades, most of the Chinese women came alone, often forcibly transported to America as prostitutes. In the 1870 census manuscripts, 61 percent of the 3,536 Chinese women in California listed their occupation as "prostitute."[56]

One prostitute, Lilac Chen, was only six years old when she was brought to San Francisco. Years later, at the age of eighty-four, she recalled the day her father said he was taking her to her grandmother's house: "And that worthless father, my own father, imagine . . . sold me on the ferry boat. Locked me in the cabin while he was negotiating my sale." Chen kicked and screamed; when she was finally let out, she could not find her father. "He had left me, you see, with a strange woman." Another prostitute, Wong Ah So, described her tragic experience: "I was nineteen when this man came to my mother and said that in America there was a great deal of gold. . . . He was a laundryman, but said he earned plenty of money. He was very nice to me, and my mother liked him, so my mother was glad to have me go with him as his wife. I thought that I was his wife, and was very grateful that he was taking me to such a grand, free country, where everyone was rich and happy." But two weeks after Wong Ah So arrived in San Francisco, she was shocked to learn that her companion had taken her to America as a "slave" and that she would be forced to work as a prostitute.[57]

Most of the Chinese prostitutes were in debt peonage, under contracts like this one signed by Xin Jin:

> The contractee Xin Jin became indebted to her master/mistress for food and passage from China to San Francisco. Since she is without funds, she will voluntarily work as a prostitute at Tan Fu's place for four and one-half years for an advance of 1,205 yuan (U.S. $524) to pay this debt. There shall be no interest on the money and Xin Jin shall receive no wages. At the expiration of the contract, Xin Jin shall be free to do as she pleases. Until then, she shall first secure the master/mistress's permission if a customer asks to take her out. If she has the four loathsome diseases she shall be returned within 100 days; beyond that time the procurer has no responsibility. Menstruation disorder is limited to one month's rest only. If Xin Jin becomes sick at any time for more than 15 days, she shall work one month extra; if she becomes pregnant, she shall work one year extra. Should Xin Jin run away before her term is out, she shall pay whatever expense is incurred in finding and returning her to the brothel. This is a contract to be retained by the master/mistress as evidence of the agreement. Receipt of 1205 yuan by Ah Yo. Thumb print of Xin Jin in the contractee. Eighth month 11th day of the 12th year of Guang-zu (1886).[58]

Called *lougeui* (always holding her legs up) and *baak haak chai* (hundred men's wife), Chinese prostitutes worked in the mining outposts, railroad camps, and agricultural villages and in the Chinatowns of Sacramento, Marysville, and San Francisco. Dressed in fancy clothes and jewelry, some prostitutes worked in high-class brothels. "And every night, seven o'clock, all these girls were dressed in silk and satin, and sat in front of a big window," recalled Lilac Chen, who had been brought to San Francisco in 1893 by a brothel owner, "and the men would look in and choose their girls who they'd want for the night." Most prostitutes worked in lower-grade brothels or in "cribs" — 4-by-6-foot street-level compartments with their windowed doors covered with bars or heavy screens. Dressed in cotton tunics and trousers, women peered from the windows, promising men pleasure for twenty-five or fifty cents: "Lookee two bits, feelee floor bits, doee six bits." They were fed two or three times a day, their dinner usually consisting of rice and a stew of pork, eggs, liver, and kidneys. These prostitutes were enormously profitable to their owners. "At an average of 38 cents per customer and seven customers per day," Lucie Cheng Hirata has calculated, "a lower-grade prostitute would earn about 850 dollars per year and 3,404 dollars after four years of servitude. Since women in the inferior dens were kept at the subsistence level, the cost of maintaining them must not have exceeded 8 dollars per month or 96 dollars per year per person." The average capital outlay, or purchase price, of a woman was usually about $530. "These calculations indicate that the owner would begin to make a profit from the prostitute's labor in the first year of her service!"[59]

Virtual slaves, many of the prostitutes became opium addicts, seeking a drug-induced psychic sanctuary from the daily abuse and degradation. "My owners were never satisfied, no matter how much money I made," a prostitute complained. Her owners would often beat her with wooden clubs, and once they threatened her with a pistol. "My last mistress was very cruel to me," another prostitute said; "she used to whip me, pull my hair, and pinch the inside of my cheeks." Disease was a constant threat: syphilis and gonorrhea were widespread. Life was dangerous and sometimes short. Occasionally, prostitutes were beaten to death by their customers or owners, and others committed suicide by taking an overdose of drugs or drowning themselves in the San Francisco Bay.[60]

Chinese prostitutes in California decreased in numbers significantly after 1870. By 1880, only 24 percent of the 3,171 Chinese women in the state were designated as "prostitute" in the census. The number of adult Chinese females listed as "housekeepers" (women who did household chores without pay) doubled from 21 percent in 1870 to 46 percent in 1880. Many prostitutes had been able to pay off their debts and free themselves. Others escaped from their bondage by fleeing to the Presbyterian Mission in San Francisco's Chinatown. Later known as Cameron House, this refuge for Chinese prostitutes was operated by white women. A Chinese folk song urged Chinese prostitutes to seek husbands and a safer life:

> *Prostitution ruins the body most harmfully.*
> *Come ashore, the sooner the better.*

My advice is to get hitched to a man, and don't
ever forget, dear young lass:
It's no shame to have a decent meal with plain tea.
All in all —
You'd also gain a husband.
We've all witnessed the frequent raids of brothels
in the Golden Gate;
You need not to worry about these roughnecks
once you live with a man.[61]

Perhaps one of these women was Min Que. She was living in Wadsworth, Nevada, in 1874, when Fook Sing of Downieville, California, was told about her and decided that he would like to marry her. On July 25, 1874, he sent a telegraph to Kaw Chung in Wadsworth, Nevada: "Don't you let her go. I will come tomorrow and see her. I want to bring her to Downieville to live with me. What time does the train start? Answer quick." The next day he sent another message to Chung: "I will start for Wadsworth today and meet her. . . . Tell her to wait for me to come and if she wants to go I will let her. Don't care. Answer." But she went off with or was taken by another man. On August 12, Ah Tom sent a telegram to Ting Yeu of Downieville: "Fook Sing's woman has gone to Marysville." The next day, the disappointed and anxious Fook Sing sent telegrams to Sing Lung in Marysville: "Bring woman up right away will pay three hundred dollars. Answer." "Is man who took woman there? Answer." At 11:05 A.M. the same day, Sing Lung wired Tie Yuen in Downieville: "Tell Fook Sing Min Que is here. What you going to do? Answer quick." Fook Sing had found the woman, but would Min Que agree to marry him? At 4:20 P.M. Sing Lung telegraphed Fook Sing: "She wants you to come right away and get warrant with officer, friends will help. You don't be afraid. We will get her sure." Fook Sing rushed to Marysville, and on August 15, he wired Tie Yuen: "I saw the woman but have not [taken her away from the other man]. Send marriage certificate." Immediately, Tie Yuen responded: "Will send the certificate next stage."[62]

While these telegrams contain a silence by leaving out the voice of Min Que, they tell the story of what appears to be Fook Sing's successful search for a wife. But he was one of the lucky few. "In all New York there are less than forty Chinese women," Lee Chew commented bitterly, "and it is impossible to get a Chinese woman out here [to the United States] unless one goes to China and marries her there, and then he must collect affidavits to prove that she is really his wife. That is in the case of a merchant. A laundryman can't bring his wife here under any circumstances." Protesting the legislation prohibiting the entry of Chinese women, a Chinese man asked: "What Chinese going do for wife?" For the overwhelming majority of Chinese men, their future would not include a family in their adopted country. "Pathetic the lonely bachelors stranded in a foreign land," reflected a Cantonese rhyme.[63]

A Colony of "Bachelors"

Though they generally considered themselves sojourners, the Chinese showed signs of settling down from the very beginning. During the 1850s, Chinatown in San Francisco was already a bustling colony of thirty-three general merchandise stores, fifteen apothecaries, five restaurants, five herb shops, three boardinghouses, five butcher stores, and three tailor shops. "The majority of the houses were of Chinese importation," observed a traveler, "and were stores, stocked with hams, tea, dried fish, dried ducks, and other Chinese eatables, besides copper pots and kettles, fans, shawls, chessmen, and all sorts of curiosities. Suspended over the doors were brilliantly-colored boards covered with Chinese writings, and with several yards of red ribbon streaming from them; while the streets thronged with Celestials, chattering vociferously as they rushed about from store to store." A Chinese immigrant, arriving in San Francisco in 1868, found a thriving and colorful Chinatown, "made up of stores catering to the Chinese only." The people were "all in their native costume, with queues down their backs," and the entire street fronts of the stores were open, with groceries and vegetables overflowing on the sidewalks. Every morning, vegetable peddlers could be seen in the streets, wearing "loose pajamalike" clothes and "carrying two deep baskets of greens, fruits, and melons, balanced on their shoulders with the help of a pole."[64]

Nine years later, the Chinese quarter of San Francisco was six blocks long, running from California Street to Broadway. All day long and often until late at night, the streets were crowded with people. According to Reverend Otis Gibson, they had shaven crowns and neatly braided queues, and they sauntered "lazily along, talking, visiting, trading, laughing, and scolding in the strangest, and, to an American, the most discordant jargon." Here and there, they gathered in groups on street corners. Frequently, "a group of these fellows" would amuse themselves for a long time at "the expense of some party of 'white people,' who, passing through 'Chinatown' to see the sights, all unconscious to themselves," presented to the Chinese "a show quite as novel as they themselves [could] boast of seeing."[65]

The stores and shops had signs with euphonious and poetic names. Adorning the entrances of wholesale houses were signs for "everlasting harmony, producing wealth," "unitedly prospering," "the flowery fountain," and "ten thousand profits." Apothecary shops offered assurances: "The hall of the approved medicines of every province and of every land." Restaurants described their culinary delights: "Fragrant almond chamber," "Chamber of the odors of distant lands," "Fragrant tea chamber." Fan-tan saloons enticed men with dreams of quick wealth: "Get rich, please come in," "Riches ever flowing." On the glass windows and doors of their stalls, opium dealers pasted red cards: "Opium dipped up in fractional quantities, Foreign smoke in broken parcels, No. 2 Opium to be sold at all times." Scrolls on the walls of stores announced: "Ten thousand customers constantly arriving, Let rich customers continually come."[66]

The immigrants also built Chinatowns in rural towns like Sacramento, Marysville, and Stockton, where these business communities served the needs of Chinese miners and farmers. By 1860, there were 121 Chinese merchants, storekeepers, and grocers in the three counties of Sacramento, Yuba, and San Joaquin. Twenty years later, their number had increased by 44 percent, to 174. In addition, there were 22 restaurant keepers, 54 butchers and fish sellers, and 564 laundrymen and laundresses.[67]

Organizations abounded in Chinatowns. Tongs were present almost from the very beginning: in 1852, the first secret society, the Kwangtek-tong, was founded in California. Originally underground antigovernment movements in the homeland, the tongs served a particular need in Chinese America. "We are strangers in a strange country," explained a tong member. "We must have an organization to control our country fellows and develop our friendship." Tongs also provided protection. "Occasionally members of the tongs use their organization to take advantage of non-members of tongs," said a Chinese. Meeting the needs of immigrants, tongs proliferated in the United States. Extending their activities beyond mutual assistance, they came to control the opium trade as well as gambling and prostitution in the Chinese communities.[68]

The immigrants also formed fongs, organizations composed of family and village members, and clans, larger groups of village associations. These associations maintained clubhouses, which functioned as residences and social centers. They established temples, transmitted letters to villages in China, and shipped home the bodies or bones of the deceased. In addition, district associations were responsible for receiving migrants, providing initial housing, and finding employment. They also administered the "credit-ticket" system, checking migrants to make certain all their debts had been paid before they returned to China. In San Francisco, the Chinese Six Companies helped settle interdistrict conflicts and provided educational and health services to the community. The leaders of the Chinese Six Companies were merchants who interacted with the city's white business community and had access to public officials.

Gradually, the Chinese were creating their own communities in America. They built altars to honor their gods and celebrated traditional holidays. During Chinese New Year in January or February, they first did their *Dah Faw Hom Muy,* or "housecleaning." The house could not be cleaned again until after the celebration, or else any good fortune arriving with the New Year would be swept away. "Oh yes — we cleaned the house upside down," an immigrant recalled. "You know it was good luck to have plenty at the start of the New Year. We couldn't buy too much, but a bit of everything. And then there would be oranges and lishee [gifts of money wrapped in red paper for good luck]. We didn't have money for the lishee — we used dried nuts for money." Then the people ushered in the New Year with lion dances and firecrackers. During the celebration, whites also joined the festive throngs in Chinatown. "The merchants," observed Reverend A. W. Loomis of San Francisco in 1869, "appear highly delighted to see and to welcome all of our citizens whom they can recognize as friends, and all with whom they have had any kind of business connections." As soon as the clock tolled off the last minute of the departing year, firecrackers exploded in a roaring, crackling din, filling entire streets with columns of smoke and sheets of fire to frighten away the evil spirits for the New Year.[69]

For recreation, many men attended the Chinese theater. The first Chinese play in America was presented in 1852 when 123 actors of the Hong Fook Tong performed at the American Theater in San Francisco. In 1879, a Chinese theater was erected, a three-story brick building with a seating capacity of twenty-five hundred people. The price of admission was thirty-five cents. During performances, the men — sometimes a few hundred, sometimes a thousand — sat on benches in the gallery. Smoking cigars and cigarettes and eating mandarin oranges and melon seeds, they listened to the Chinese orchestra and watched the drama.

On Sundays, most of the men had no families to take on outings.

They had "no *homes* in this country," observed Otis Gibson of San Francisco. They strolled the streets, he added, for they had "nothing to do, and nowhere else to go." When asked about what he did during his free time, a waiter at a restaurant replied: "Yes, go to theater. When I no work? I sleep. Sometimes gamble a little." At night and during the weekends, men played mah-jongg, fan-tan, and *baakgapbiu,* a game similar to keno. "Gambling is mostly fan tan," reported Lee Chew, "but there is a good deal of poker, which the Chinese have learned from Americans and can play very well. They also gamble with dominoes and dice." Tom Lee, a cook and houseboy, said: "No get lonely for home China, many China boys all same one family. Sometime have holiday. Put on Merican hat, shoe, tie, all same White man, walk to Stockton have good time."[70]

Mostly, the men spent their leisure hours in the backrooms of stores. There "all Chinese came," a migrant recalled. "Not just relatives. They all just like to get together. They talk together." Cut off from their wives, men spent endless hours talking about their lives. The future had seemed so promising when they had left their villages for Gold Mountain:

> *If you have a daughter, marry her quickly to a*
> *traveller to Gold Mountain,*
> *For when he gets off the boat, he will bring*
> *hundreds of pieces of silver.*

Sometimes "Letters for the colony" would arrive from China, directed in care of the store that served as a community post office. "Our village had something to do — they send a letter over here, we get together and talk it over — and send it back," a migrant stated. "We communicate, see, otherwise you're alone. You know nothing."[71]

One sojourner received a letter from his mother, a wailing reminder to fulfill his filial obligations:

> I hear that you,———, my son, are acting the prodigal. . . . For many months there has arrived no letter, nor money. My supplies are exhausted. I am old; too infirm to work; too lame to beg. Your father in the mines of the mountains suffers from a crushed foot. He is weak, and unable to accumulate money. Hereafter, my son, change your course; be industrious and frugal, and remit to me your earnings; and within the year let me welcome home both your father and yourself.[72]

Married men received letters from their "widows" in China. Stranded sojourners, they read "letters of love, soaked with tears" that complained about their long absence. Since most of the men were illiterate, they relied on the store proprietors to write letters for them. One migrant dictated a letter that began, "My Beloved Wife":

It has been several autumns now since your dull husband left you for a far remote alien land. Thanks to my hearty body I am all right. Therefore stop your embroidering worries about me.

Yesterday I received another of your letters. I could not keep tears from running down my cheeks when thinking about the miserable and needy circumstances of our home, and thinking back to the time of our separation.

Because of our destitution I went out, trying to make a living. Who could know that the Fate is always opposite to man's design? Because I can get no gold, I am detained in this secluded corner of a strange land. Furthermore, my beauty, you are implicated in an endless misfortune. I wish this paper would console you a little. This is all what I can do for now. . . .

This letter was never finished and never mailed, left in a desk drawer of the Kam Wah Chung Store in Oregon.[73] What happened to the nameless writer of this unmailed letter might have paralleled the life stories of the owners of the store where it was found. Lung On and Ing Hay had come to America as sojourners in the 1880s. At first, they worked as wage-earners and then opened their own general store. Gradually over the years, as they built their business and developed personal and social ties to their new community, they came to feel detached from their homeland and their families. In 1899, Lung's father commanded in a letter: "Come home as soon as you can. Don't say 'no' to me any more. . . . You are my only son. You have no brothers and your age is near forty. . . . You have been away from home for seventeen years, you know nothing about our domestic situation. . . . Come back, let our family be reunited and enjoy the rest of our lives." In a letter to "My Husband-lord," Lung's wife scolded her absent mate: "According to Mr. Wang, you are indulging in sensuality, and have no desire to return home. On hearing this I am shocked and pained. I have been expecting your return day after day. . . . But, alas, I don't know what kind of substance your heart is made of. . . . Your daughter is now at the age of betrothal and it is your responsibility to arrange her marriage." Her appeal must have moved her husband, for Lung wrote to his cousin Liang Kwang-jin on March 2, 1905: "We are fine here, thank you. Tell my family that I will go back as soon as I accumulate enough money to pay the fare." But a few weeks later, Lung learned from a letter written by his cousin, dated March 4, that certain family events had already passed him by: "Two years ago your mother died. Last year your daughter married. Your aged father is immobile. He will pass away any time now. Your wife feels left out and hurt. . . . Come back as soon as you receive this message." Meanwhile, Ing's father had also written to his son in 1903: "Men go abroad so that they might make money for support of their families, but you have sent neither money nor a letter since you left."[74]

Separated from their families in China, these two men missed the company of their own children — their sounds and laughter. Perhaps this was why Lung On and Ing Hay regularly cut pictures of children from calendars, advertisements, and newspapers, and placed them safely in a box. Discovered decades later in a desk drawer of the abandoned store, this box of pictures told a sad tale of Chinese immigrant fathers living far away from their children. The two shopkeepers also pampered the white children in the neighborhood. Years later, one of them, Mrs. John W. Murray, recalled: "Doc Hay always gave us children Chinese candy, oranges and other goodies."[75]

But returning home was not easy for many sojourners. Ing Weh-teh, for example, lost his hard-earned savings when a friend invested it without his consent. "Because you took away that money," he wrote to Ing Pang-chi, "I could not return home. I came to America — to labor, to suffer, floating from one place to another, persecuted by the whites, for more than twenty years. . . . Do you know that both the old and the young at my home are awaiting me to deliver them out of starvation and cold?" Liang Kau-tsi, who had also been in America for two decades, was scolded by his brother in a letter: "Because of our family's poverty, you went out of the country to make a living. You still haven't made any money during all of these twenty years? I am afraid that you are Americanized and totally forget about us."[76]

Ing Weh-teh and Liang Kau-tsi and thousands of their fellow Chinese had come to America in search of Gold Mountain, but many of them found themselves "eating bitterness." The venture had turned out to be a sad failure:

> *My life's half gone, but I'm still unsettled;*
> *I've erred, I'm an expert at whoring and*

> *gambling.*
> *Syphilis almost ended my life.*
> *I turned to friends for a loan, but no one took*
> *   pity on me.*
> *Ashamed, frightened —*
> *Now, I must wake up after this long nightmare. . . .*[77]

In America, the Chinese found their lives circumscribed in new and different ways. As strangers from a different shore, they had been denied equality of opportunity and were separated from their homeland by the "tyrannical laws" of exclusion. "They called us 'Chink,' " complained an old laundryman, cursing the "white demons." "They think we no good! America cut us off. No more come now, too bad!" Though they could not become citizens, they felt they had earned the right to claim their adopted country. "Since I have lived and made money in this country," Andrew Kan argued in 1924, after forty-four years of working in America, "I should be able to become an American citizen."[78]

PART THREE

Distances

The End of the Frontier

IN 1891, the Census Bureau announced that the frontier no longer existed. Americans had now reached beyond what Jefferson called the "Stony mountains" and were settling the entire continent from the Atlantic to the Pacific. This conquest over nature, conceived initially as an "errand into the wilderness," had led to the building of what Max Weber called "the tremendous cosmos of the modern economic order." What had happened was the explosive formation of an industrial economy. Between 1815 and 1860, the value of manufactured goods increased eightfold. By 1890, United States manufacturing production had surpassed the combined total of England and Germany. American labor patterns reflected these economic changes. In 1840, agricultural workers had constituted 70 percent of the labor force, while those in manufacturing, trades, and construction represented only 15 percent. Sixty years later, the number of workers in agriculture had decreased to 37 percent, while those in manufacturing and related areas such as transportation and public utilities had increased to 35 percent.[1]

What would the future hold for a frontierless America? This question, prompted by the Census Bureau's announcement, fascinated a young historian. At the 1893 American Historical Association meeting in Chicago, Frederick Jackson Turner presented a sweeping interpretation of "the significance of the frontier in American history." The end of the frontier, he observed, marked the close of a great historic movement. Westward expansion had eliminated "free land" and concentrated people in cities. Technological "progress," the "complexity of city life," and the "factory system" had become realities in the new industrial order. Would the new "age of machinery," asked Turner, represent an era of social disintegration and chaos?[2]

To find the answer, Turner turned to the past. He pointed out how the frontier had been the country's most crucial force. By providing "free land," it had created the American character with its "inventive turn of mind," "restless nervous energy," individualism, and democracy. In their history, Americans were continually beginning over again on the frontier — the "meeting point between savagery and civilization." They had experienced "perennial birth" as they moved west with its new opportunities and its continuous contact with the "simplicity of primitive society." Europeans originally, they had been "Americanized" by the wilderness.

> The frontier is the line of most rapid and effective Americanization. The wilderness masters the colonist. It finds him a European in dress, industries, tools, modes of travel, and thought. It takes him from the railroad car and puts him in the birch canoe. It strips off the garments of civilization, and arrays him in the hunting shirt and the moccasin. It puts him in the log cabin of the Cherokee and the Iroquois. . . . Before long he has gone to planting Indian corn and plowing with a sharp stick; he shouts the war cry and takes the scalp in orthodox Indian fashion. In short, at the frontier the environment is at first too strong for the man. He must accept the conditions which it furnishes, or perish, and so he fits himself into the Indian clearings and follows the Indian trails. Little by little he transforms the wilderness, but the outcome is not the Old Europe. . . . The fact is that here is a new product that is American.[3]

Turner viewed the future optimistically. "He would be a rash prophet," challenged the historian, "who should assert that the expansive character of American life has now entirely ceased. . . . Movement has been its dominant fact, and, unless this training has no effect upon a people, the American intellect will continually demand a wider field for its exercise." The frontier would have lasting significance, even though it was gone, Turner predicted, for Americans had been transformed into a new and virile people in their encounters with the wilderness and Indians.[4]

Still, there was a widely shared feeling within society that the seeming boundlessness of America was diminishing. Without the expanse of the West and without the country's source of liminality, modern America was now facing the fearful prospect of explosive class conflicts between the Calibans and Prosperos of an industrial society. More than ever before, there was a need for borders in order to maintain racial and class hierarchy. "Vacant" lands no longer existed, so now distances had to be redefined. The world that Turner inhabited was immensely different from the America that Thomas Jefferson had envisioned — a nation of a racially homogeneous people covering the entire continent. Here in the making was a multicultural America composed of an increasingly polymorphous "giddy multitude" — blacks, Indians, Irish, Mexicans, and Chinese as well as new groups, including Jews and Japanese. The end of the frontier was a significant crossing in American history: our society was entering a modern era of even greater multiethnicity.

9

THE "INDIAN QUESTION"
From Reservation to Reorganization

Wounded Knee:
The Significance of the Frontier in Indian History

I N 1890, three years before Frederick Jackson Turner presented his
seminal paper on the end of the frontier, a voice came from the shores
of Pyramid Lake in Nevada. Claiming he was the messiah, Wovoka
of the Paiutes called for Indians everywhere to dance the Ghost Dance,
for Christ had returned to earth as an Indian. As they danced, Wovoka's
followers wore muslin "ghost shirts," decorated with sacred symbols of
blue and yellow lines. They believed that the garments would protect
them against bullets. Wovoka's message promised the restoration of
Indian ways as well as their land and the buffalo:

> All Indians must dance, everywhere, keep on dancing. Pretty soon in
> next spring Big Man [Great Spirit] come. He bring back all game of
> every kind. The game be thick everywhere. All dead Indians come
> back and live again. . . . When Old Man [God] comes this way, then
> all the Indians go to mountains, high up away from whites. Whites
> can't hurt Indians then. Then while Indians way up high, big flood
> comes like water and all white people die, get drowned. After that
> water go away and then nobody but Indians everywhere and game
> all kinds thick.[1]

Wovoka's vision of a world without whites spread like prairie fire through Indian country. On Sioux reservations, Ghost Dancing became the rage, seizing Indian imaginations and mobilizing their frustrations. "Indians are dancing in the snow and are wild and crazy," a nervous agent at Pine Ridge Reservation in South Dakota reported in a telegram to Washington. "We need protection and we need it now. The leaders should be arrested and confined at some military post until the matter is quieted, and this should be done at once."[2]

The Indian Bureau in Washington quickly identified the Ghost Dance "fomenters of disturbances" and ordered the army to arrest them, including chiefs Sitting Bull and Big Foot. Sent to Pine Ridge to help resolve the crisis, former Indian agent Dr. Valentine McGillycuddy advised Washington to pull back the soldiers: "I should let the dance continue. The coming of the troops has frightened the Indians. If the Seventh-Day Adventists prepare their ascension robes for the second coming of the Savior, the United States Army is not put in motion to prevent them. Why should not the Indians have the same privilege? If the troops remain, trouble is sure to come."[3]

But Washington pursued the Ghost Dance leaders. Indian policemen were sent to Sitting Bull's cabin; after arresting him, they were confronted by angry and armed Sioux. During an exchange of gunfire, the police shot and killed the chief. The news of Sitting Bull's murder alarmed Big Foot, chief of another group of Sioux. While trying to escape, Big Foot and his people, mostly women and children, were intercepted by the cavalry. They surrendered and were escorted to a camp near a frozen creek called Wounded Knee.

As the Indians set up their tepees for the night, they saw two manned Hotchkiss guns on the ridge above them. "That evening I noticed that they were erecting cannons up [there]," Wasu Maza recalled, "also hauling up quite a lot of ammunition." The guns were trained on the Indian camps, and the scene seemed terribly ominous. In the morning, under a clear blue sky, the Indians heard a bugle call. Surrounded by mounted soldiers, they were told that all of their men should assemble at the center of camp. Suffering from pneumonia, Big Foot was carried to the meeting.[4]

The captives were ordered to turn over their weapons. "They called for guns and arms," White Lance recounted, "so all of us gave the guns and they were stacked up in the center." But the soldiers thought there were more arms hidden in the tepees and began a search. The situation became tense, volatile, and the Indians sensed the danger. Medicine man

Yellow Bird began dancing the Ghost Dance to reassure the worried Indians. He urged them to wear their sacred shirts: "The bullets will not hurt you." Suddenly, a shot rang out. Instantly, the troops began shooting indiscriminately at the Indians. "There were only about a hundred warriors and there were nearly five hundred soldiers," Black Elk reported. "The warriors rushed to where they had piled their guns and knives."[5]

The Indians tried to defend themselves, but then they heard an "awful roar," the death sounds of the Hotchkiss guns. Shells hailed down upon them, at the rate of fifty per minute, each missile carrying a two-pound charge that exploded into thousands of shrapnel. The smoke was so dense it was like fog, blinding the Indians. "My father ran and fell down and the blood came out of his mouth [he was shot through the head]," recalled Yellow Bird's son, who was four years old at the time. Blue Whirlwind received fourteen wounds, while her two children running at her sides were also shot. "We tried to run, but they shot us like we were buffalo," said Louise Weasel Bear. "I know there are some good white people, but the soldiers must be mean to shoot children and women."[6]

Fleeing the camp, the Indians were pursued by the soldiers. "I saw some of the other Indians running up the coulee so I ran with them, but the soldiers kept shooting at us and the bullets flew all around us," reported Mrs. Rough Feathers. "My father, my grandmother, my older brother and my younger brother were all killed. My son who was two years old was shot in the mouth that later caused his death." Trails marked by blood and bodies radiated outward from the camp. "Dead and wounded women and children and little babies were scattered all along there where they had been trying to run away," Black Elk reported. "The soldiers had followed them along the gulch, as they ran, and murdered them in there." There were also some dead soldiers, Black Elk noted. In one of the gulches, "two little boys" had guns, and "they had been killing soldiers all by themselves."[7]

When the Hotchkiss guns stopped spewing their deadly charges, a terrible silence descended on the bloody scene. Hundreds of Indians lay dead or wounded on the icy ground, along with scores of soldiers, most of them hit by their own fire. Shortly afterward, clouds rolled across the sky and "a heavy snow began to fall," covering the corpses like a white blanket as if Nature were trying to shroud or cleanse the gore and blood. After the storm passed, the soldiers threw the dead Indians into a long trench, their frozen bodies "piled one upon another like so much cordwood, until the pit was full." Many of the corpses were naked: the "ghost shirts" had been stripped from the dead as souvenirs. A photograph of Big Foot lying in the snow showed the contorted body of the chief, his hands still trying to shield himself and his face fixed in a grotesque grimace by the horror he had witnessed. For Indian America, Wounded Knee violently symbolized the end of the frontier.[8]

The Father of the Reservation System

As commissioner of Indian affairs during the 1870s, Francis Amasa Walker had tried to avoid the use of armed force against Indians. American soldiers, he recommended, should not surprise Indian "camps on winter nights" and shoot down "men, women, and children together in the snow." Instead, Walker believed the government should pursue a "Peace Policy" — buy off and feed the Indians in order to avoid violent conflict. Whites did not have to be concerned about maintaining their manhood in dealings with Indians, Walker explained. "There can be no question of national dignity involved in the treatment of savages by a civilized power. The proudest Anglo-Saxon will climb a tree with a bear behind him, and deem not his honor, but his safety, compromised by the situation. With wild men, as with wild beasts, the question whether to fight, coax, or run, is a question merely of what is easiest or safest in the situation given. Points of dignity only arise between those who are, or assume to be, equals."[9]

Though Walker was the commissioner of Indian affairs, he had very limited personal contact with Indians. He made only one visit of inquiry and inspection to the agencies of the Sioux in the Wyoming and Nebraska territories. During this tour, he had an unforgettable experience:

The day and the hour of the feast came. We met in a great tepee; and I sat, as was proper, on the right of Swift Bear. The chiefs and braves, with the agent and the interpreter, sat around in a circle. Soon some young men entered, bearing the steaming food. . . . Under my eyes, under my nose, was set down one of those bowls, which contained a quarter of puppy, with leg lifting itself towards me in a very tempting way. I think I could have stood even that, had it not been for the little velvet mats, where the claws were, or should have been. The Indian cook had been too realistic in his desire to give the fullest possible effect to nature. I looked down and felt myself growing white.

Except for this one visit, Walker learned about Indians from government reports and novels such as James Fenimore Cooper's *Last of the Mohicans*.[10]

But Walker did not allow his superficial knowledge of Indians to inhibit him from making policy for them. Like Prospero, he identified himself as mind, capable of caring for these Calibans called Indians. What gave Commissioner Walker such confidence was his belief in technology and the market as the great forces of civilization. Like Jefferson, Walker saw progress unfolding in America. "The labor that is made free by discoveries and inventions," he observed, "is applied to overcome the difficulties which withstand the gratification of newly-felt desires. The hut is pulled down to make room for the cottage; the cottage gives way to the mansion, the mansion to the palace. The rude covering of skins is replaced by the comely garment of woven stuffs; and these, in the progress of luxury, by the most splendid fabrics of human skill. In a thousand forms wealth is created by the whole energy of the community, quickened by a zeal greater than that which animated the exertions of their rude forefathers to obtain a scanty and squalid subsistence."[11]

This very progress was bringing an end to the frontier and the Indian way of life. The railroad — "the great plough of industrial civilization" — had drawn its "deep furrow" across America, Walker explained, and whites were now migrating west, "creeping along the course of every stream, seeking out every habitable valley, following up every indication of gold among the ravines and mountains . . . and even making lodgment at a hundred points on lands secured by treaty to the Indians." Indians faced a grim future in this rapidly changing world. Thus the "friends of humanity should exert themselves in this juncture, and lose not time" in order to save the Indians. For Walker, the "Indian Question" had become urgent: what should be done to ensure the survival of the Plains Indians?[12]

As the commissioner of Indian affairs, Walker believed in social engineering: government should scientifically manage the affairs and welfare of Indians. Since industrial "progress" had cut them off from their traditional means of livelihood, Indians should be given temporary support to help them make the necessary adjustment for entering civilization. To accomplish this transition, Walker decided, Indians should be located on reservations. During the colonial period, native peoples had been placed on specially designated reserved lands; in the 1850s, the federal government began establishing reservations for Plains Indians.

Now Commissioner Walker was actively promoting the relocation of tribes on reservations. A theoretician, he created a rationale for the reservation system. According to his plan, warlike tribes would be corraled onto reservations, and all Indian bands outside their boundaries would be "liable to be struck by the military at any time, without warning." Such areas would be, in effect, free fire zones. Indian tribes would be consolidated into one or two "grand reservations" with railroads cutting through them here and there, leaving the rest of the territory open for white settlement, free from Indian "obstruction or molestation."[13]

The ultimate goal, Walker explained, was the eventual assimilation of Indians. On the reservations, the government would subject them to "a rigid reformatory discipline." Not allowed to "escape work," they would be "required" to acquire industrial skills until at least one generation had been placed on a course of "self-improvement." This program was necessary because Indians were "unused to manual labor." Accustomed to "the habits of the chase," they lacked "forethought," "intellectual tastes," and self-discipline. They were unable to control their "strong animal appetites." Unless the government planned their education, Walker predicted, the "now roving Indians" would become "vagabonds" and "festering sores" upon civilization.[14]

Relocated within the borders of the reservations, Indians would not be permitted to leave, except by permission. "We mean by this," Walker stated, "something more than that a 'pass system' should be created for every tribe under the control of the government, to prevent individual Indians from straying away for an occasional debauch at the settlements." Authorities would have the power to confine Indians on the reservations and to "arrest" and return those who wandered away. Seclusion was necessary, Walker explained, because Indians were disposed toward the "lower and baser elements of civilization," and whenever they became "restive under compulsion to labor," they were inclined to break away and resume their "old roving spirit." Trained and reformed on the reservations, Indians were to be prepared to enter civilized society.[15]

What he hoped his reservation system would do, Walker insisted, was to help the Indians over the rough places on "the white man's road." He believed he knew, from his own experience, what was required. He once told a friend that Indians were like "children" who disliked school and preferred to "play truant at pleasure." Then he added: "I used to have to be whipped myself to get me to school and keep me there, yet

I always liked to study when once within the school-room walls." Grateful for the "whipping" he had received as a child and the self-discipline he had developed, Walker was certain "wild Indians" would become "industrious" and "frugal" through "a severe course of industrial instruction and exercise under restraint." Indian life must be regulated by the federal government. Indians should not be left alone, "letting such as will, go to the dogs, letting such as can, find a place for themselves in the social and industrial order." In Walker's view, Indians could not remain Indians. There was no longer a West, no longer the boundlessness of "vacant lands" on the other side of the frontier. Indians everywhere would eventually have to settle down to farming and urban labor.[16]

Allotment and Assimilation

Other white reformers had a different solution to the "Indian Question," however. Regarding themselves as "friends" of the Indians, they believed that the reservations only served to segregate native peoples from white society and postpone their assimilation. Their viewpoint became policy in 1887 when Congress passed the Dawes Act. Hailed by the reformers as the "Indian Emancipation Act," the law reversed Walker's strategy, seeking instead to break up the reservations and accelerate the transformation of Indians into property owners and U.S. citizens. Under the Dawes Act, the president was granted the power, at his discretion and without the Indians' consent, to allot reservation lands to individual heads of families in the amount of 160 acres. These lands would be ineligible for sale, or "inalienable," for twenty-five years. This would protect the Indians from land-grabbers and also give them time to become farmers. The federal government was authorized to sell "surplus" reservation land — land that remained after allotment — to white settlers in 160-acre tracts. Such transactions required tribal consent, and money derived from the sales would be held in trust for the Indians to be used for their "education and civilization." Citizenship would be conferred upon the allotees and any other Indians who agreed to abandon their tribal affiliation and adopt the "habits of civilized life."[17]

During the debate over the bill, a senator from Texas declared his opposition to Indian citizenship: "Look at your Chinamen, are they not specifically excepted from the naturalization laws?" But Indians, unlike the Chinese, were generally seen as capable of assimilation. "The new law," observed historian Frederick Hoxie, "was made possible by the belief that Indians did not have the 'deficiencies' of other groups: they were fewer in number, the beneficiaries of a public sympathy and pity, and capable of advancement."[18]

To advance and civilize the Indians, the white reformers argued, the tribal system had to be destroyed, for it was perpetuating "habits of nomadic barbarism" and "savagery." As long as Indians lived in tribes, they would continue to live in idleness, frivolity, and debauchery. The key to civilizing Indians was to convert them into individual landowners. As long as Indians owned their lands in common, Senator Henry Dawes contended, they would lack "selfishness," which was "at the bottom of civilization." Unless Indians divided the land among themselves as individuals, they would not make much progress. In her eloquent protest against "a century of dishonor," liberal reformer Helen Hunt Jackson urged the government to parcel out tribal lands: "Instead of a liberal and far-sighted policy looking to the education and civilization and possible citizenship of the Indian tribes, we have suffered these people to remain as savages. . . ." They should be "entirely changed," made to "feel both the incentives and the restraints" of private landownership.[19]

Repeatedly, these "friends" of the Indians declared that allotment was designed to make them more independent and self-reliant. With the breakup of the reservations and the sale of "surplus" lands to whites, they would learn the "habits of thrift and industry" from their white neighbors. "The aggressive and enterprising Anglo-Saxons" would set up their farms "side by side" with Indian farms, and "in a little while contact alone" would lead Indians to emulate the work ethic of their white neighbors. "With white settlers on every alternative section of Indian lands," allotment supporters predicted, "there will be a school-house built, with Indian children and white children together; there will be churches at which there will be an attendance of Indian and white people alike. They will readily learn the tongue of the white race. They will for a while speak their own language, but they will readily learn the ways of civilization."[20]

This conversion of Indians into individual landowners was ceremonialized at "last-arrow" pageants. On these occasions, the Indians were ordered by the government to attend a large assembly on the reservation. Dressed in traditional costume and carrying a bow and arrow, each Indian was individually summoned from a tepee and told to shoot an arrow. He then retreated to the tepee and reemerged wearing "civilized" clothing, symbolizing a crossing from the primitive to the modern world. Standing before a plow, the Indian was told: "Take the handle of this plow, this act means that you have chosen to live the life of the white man — and the white man lives by work." At the close of the ceremony, each allottee was given an American flag and a purse with the instruction: "This purse will always say to you that the money you gain from your labor must be wisely kept."[21]

While giving Indians what they already owned, their land, the Dawes Act also took lands away from them. White farmers and business interests were well aware of the economic advantages that the allotment program offered. In 1880, secretary of the interior Carl Schurz predicted that allotment would "eventually open to settlement by white men the large tracts of land now belonging to the reservations, but not used by the Indians." Shortly after Congress passed the bill, Senator Dawes recounted an experience he had had while traveling by train on a recently completed railroad track across five hundred miles of Indian territory. The potential of the terrain impressed Dawes. "The land I passed through was as fine a wheat-growing country as it could be. The railroad has gone through there, and it was black with emigrants ready to take advantage of it." In his recommendation for allotment on the White Earth Reservation in Minnesota, a government official pointed out that the present Chippewa lands were "valuable for the pine timber growing thereon, for which, if the Indian title should be extinguished, a ready sale could be found."[22]

Legislation which granted railroad corporations right-of-way through Indian lands coincided with the enactment of the Dawes law: in 1886–87, Congress made six land grants to railroad interests. "The past year," the Indian affairs commissioner observed that September, "has been one of unusual activity in the projection and building of numerous additional railroads through Indian lands." During the next two sessions, Congress enacted twenty-three laws granting railroad rights-of-way through Indian territories.[23]

Four years after the passage of the Dawes Act, Indian affairs commissioner Thomas Morgan calculated that Indian land reductions for the year 1891 alone totaled 17,400,000 acres, or one-seventh of all Indian lands. "This might seem like a somewhat rapid reduction of the land estate of the Indians," he noted. But the Indians were not "using" most of the relinquished land "for any purpose whatever" and had "scarcely any of it . . . in cultivation," and therefore they "did not need it." Moreover, they had been "reasonably well paid" for the land. "The sooner the tribal relations are broken up and the reservation system done away with," Morgan added, "the better it will be for all concerned. If there were no other reason for this change, the fact that individual ownership of property is the universal custom among civilized people of this country would be a sufficient reason for urging the handful of Indians to adopt it."[24]

In 1902, Congress accelerated the transfer of lands from Indians to whites: a new law required that all allotted lands, upon the death of the owners, be sold at public auctions by the heirs. Unless they were able to purchase their own family lands, Indians would lose what had been their property. "Under the present system," a government official informed President Theodore Roosevelt, "every Indian's land comes into the market at his death, so that it will be but a few years at most before all the Indians' land will have passed into the possession of the settlers." Four years later, Congress passed the Burke Act, which nullified the twenty-five-year trust provision in the Dawes Act and granted the secretary of the interior the power to issue fee-simple title to any allottee "competent and capable of managing his or her affairs." Thus, Indian allotments were no longer protected from white land purchasers.[25]

Native Americans resisted these efforts to usurp their lands. Chief Lone Wolf of the Kiowas, for example, insisted in court that the 1868 Treaty of Medicine Lodge Creek had provided for tribal approval of all land cessions. But in 1903, the Supreme Court decided that the federal government had the power to abrogate the provisions of an Indian treaty. An official of the Indian affairs bureau welcomed the *Lone Wolf* decision, for it allowed the government to dispose of Indian land without the consent of the Indians. If their consent were required, he asserted, it would take fifty years to eliminate the reservations. Now the government had the power to allot reservation lands and sell "the balance" of reservation lands in order to make "homes for white farmers."[26]

What would be the future for the Indians if they no longer had their lands? "When the last acre and last dollar are gone," Indian affairs commissioner Francis Leupp answered, "the Indians will be where the Negro freedmen started thirty-five years ago." Therefore, it was the government's duty to transform Indians into wage-earners. In order to train Indians to become agricultural workers, Leupp arranged for the leasing of tribal lands to sugar beet companies willing to employ Indians. As a field laborer, the commissioner explained, the Indian would acquire valuable work habits. "In this process the sensible course is to tempt him to the pursuit of a gainful occupation by choosing for him at the outset the sort of work which he finds the pleasantest; and the Indian takes to beet farming as naturally as the Italian takes to art or the German to science. . . . Even the little papoose can be taught to weed the rows just as the pickaninny in the South can be used as a cotton picker."[27]

But allotment led neither to self-sufficient Indian farmers nor to wage-earners. Most reservations were located in the Plains region where land could be effectively used only for ranching or large-scale farming. One-hundred-and-sixty-acre plots were hardly realistic. What happened to the Cheyennes and Arapahoes illustrated a general pattern of dispossession and pauperization. The reservation lands of both tribes had been allotted in 1891, and the "surplus" lands sold to whites. Sixteen years later, the combined income of the Cheyennes and Arapahoes totaled $217,312. About two-thirds of this revenue came from the sale of inherited lands and the remainder from leasing allotments; only $5,312 came from farming. Per capita tribal income for that year was only seventy-eight dollars.[28]

Forty years after the Dawes Act, the Brookings Institute reported that 55 percent of all Indians had a per capita annual income of less than two hundred dollars, and that only 2 percent had incomes of more than five hundred dollars per year. In 1933, the federal government found that almost half of the Indians living on reservations that had been subject to allotment were landless. By then, the Indians had lost about 60 percent of the 138,000,000-acre land base they had owned at the time of the Dawes Act. Allotment had been transforming Indians into a landless people.[29]

The Indian New Deal: The Remaking of Native America

But the allotment program was suddenly halted in 1934 by the Indian Reorganization Act, a policy devised by John Collier. As the Indian affairs commissioner appointed by President Franklin D. Roosevelt, he offered Indians a "New Deal."

A critic of individualism, Collier admired the sense of community he found among the Indians of New Mexico. "Only the Indians," he observed, ". . . were still the possessors and users of the fundamental secret of human life — the secret of building great personality through the instrumentality of social institutions." This valuable knowledge should be preserved. Defining "the individual and his society as wholly reciprocal," the Indian way of life had much to teach whites and should be appreciated "as a gift for us all." Allow Indians to remain Indians, Collier insisted. "*Assimilation,* not into our culture but into modern life, and *preservation and intensification of heritage* are not hostile choices, excluding one another, but are interdependent through and through." Collier's philosophy called for cultural pluralism: "Modernity and white Americanism are not identical. If the Indian life is a good life, then we should be proud and glad to have this different and native culture going on by the side of ours. . . . America is coming to understand this, and to know that in helping the Indian to save himself, we are helping to save something that is precious to us as well as to him."[30]

In Collier's view, allotment was destroying the Indian communal way of life. By breaking the tribal domain into individual holdings, allotment had been "much more than just a huge white land grab; it was a blow, meant to be fatal, at Indian tribal existence." The goal of government policy, Collier contended, should not be the absorption of Indians into the white population, but the maintenance of Indian cultures on their communally owned lands. Thus, as the architect of the Indian reorganization bill, Collier proposed the abolition of allotment and the establishment of Indian self-government as well as the preservation of "Indian civilization," including their arts, crafts, and traditions.[31]

After reading a draft of the bill, President Franklin D. Roosevelt noted on the margin: "Great stuff." On June 18, 1934, he signed the Indian Reorganization Act. While the final version of the law did not include a provision for the preservation of Indian culture, it abolished the allotment program and authorized funding for tribal land acquisition, reversing policy dating back not only to 1887 but to 1607. Indians on reservations would be allowed to establish local self-governments. Reorganization, however, would apply only to those tribes in which a majority of members had voted to accept it. "This was . . . a further means of throwing back upon the tribes the control over their own destinies — of placing Indian salvation firmly in Indian hands," Collier explained. "The role of government was to help, but not coerce, the tribal efforts." The following year, 172 tribes representing 132,426 people voted in favor of the law, while 73 tribes with a combined population of 63,467 chose to be excluded.[32]

One of the tribes that turned down the Indian Reorganization Act was the Navajos. The Navajos' negative vote reflected their opposition to Collier and the Indian New Deal. To them, Collier belonged to a tradition reaching back to Jefferson and Walker: though he was articulating a philosophy of Indian autonomy, Collier seemed to be telling the Navajos what was good for them.[33]

Navajos remembered how whites had been telling them what to do for a long time. Since the seventeenth century, when they acquired sheep from the Spanish, Navajos had been herders. After the war against

Mexico and the American annexation of the Southwest, they encountered white intruders. In 1863, they surrendered to Kit Carson after his troops destroyed their orchards and sheep herds. According to a Navajo account, "those who escaped were driven to the Grand Canyon and the Painted Desert, where they hid in the rocks like wild animals, but all except a few were rounded up and caught and taken away to Hwalte [Bosque Redondo]." The captives were instructed to migrate from their homeland to an area in southern New Mexico where they would be allowed to live in peace. Navajos have remembered this march as the "Long Walk."[34]

"A majority of the Navajos," according to a member of the tribe, "didn't know the reason why they were being rounded up and different stories went around among the people." Many feared that they "would be put to death eventually." When they arrived at Bosque Redondo, they were told by the government to irrigate the land and become farmers. The general in charge of removal explained that the Navajos had to be taken away from "the haunts and hills and hiding places of their country" in order to teach them "the art of peace" and "the truths of Christianity." On their new lands, they would acquire "new habits, new ideas, new modes of life" as they ceased to be "nomads" and became "an agricultural people." The experiment failed; in 1868, the government changed its policy and informed the Navajos that they were to be resettled on a reservation in their original homeland and issued sheep to replace the stock Kit Carson's forces had destroyed.[35]

Now in the 1930s, their instructions were coming, not from a conquering Kit Carson, but from a liberal government administrator. Although Collier was proposing to give Indians self-rule, he was also trying to socially engineer the Indian world — what he called an "ethnic laboratory." Collier's policy reflected the broad philosophy of the New Deal with its faith in government planning and participation in economic development. "To this extent," observed historian Graham D. Taylor, "it resembled earlier Indian policies in that it proposed to manipulate Indian behavior in ways which their white 'guardians' thought best for them."[36]

In 1933, Collier decided that it was best for the Navajos to reduce their stock. Government studies had determined that the Navajo reservation had half a million more livestock than their range could support, and that this excess had produced overgrazing and severe soil erosion. Unless the problem of erosion were controlled soon, Collier feared, the sheep-raising Navajos would experience great hardship and suffering.

The government had to intervene for the sake of the tribe's survival. "The future of the Navajo is in our hands," stated an official. "His very economy is dependent upon our successful solution of his land problems. . . . We believe that we have found that solution." Using a revealing metaphor to describe the relationship between the government and the Navajos, he explained: "When formerly the parents placated the children with a stick of candy when it cried, now the parents are attempting to find the cause of the tears and to take such corrective measures as are necessary. . . . The youngster will not always understand a dose of castor oil may sometimes be more efficacious than a stick of candy."[37]

While Collier was concerned about Navajo survival, he was also worried about white interests. He had received reports that silt from erosion on Navajo land was filling the Colorado River and threatening to clog Boulder Dam. Under construction during the early 1930s, the dam was designed to supply water to California's Imperial Valley and electricity to Los Angeles. The United States Geological Survey had studied the silt problem and located its origin on the Navajo reservation: "Briefly, in the main Colorado system, the Little Colorado and the San Juan are major silt problems, while within each of these basins the Navajo Reservation's tributaries are the major silt problem. The fact is the . . . Navajo Reservation is practically 'Public Enemy No. 1' in causing the Colorado Silt problem." Unless Navajo sheep overgrazing, and hence erosion, were controlled, the silt would block economic development in the Southwest. Collier told the Navajo council:

> Down there on the Colorado River is the biggest, most expensive dam in the world, the Boulder Dam now being built which will furnish all Southern California with water and with electric power, and the Boulder Dam will be filled up with your fine agricultural soil in no great number of years if we do not stop erosion on the Navajo reservation. This reservation, along with the other Indian reservations on the Colorado River, is supplying much more than half of all the silt that goes down the Colorado River, which will in the course of a comparatively few years render the Boulder Dam useless and thereby injure the population of all Southern California and a good deal of Arizona too.[38]

Driven by concerns for Navajo survival and the need to protect Boulder Dam, Collier initiated a stock reduction program on the Navajo reservation. The federal government would purchase 400,000 sheep and goats, and wages from employment on federal projects would compensate for any loss of income resulting from this stock reduction. Collier flew to the Navajo reservation seventeen times over the next five years to explain and promote the program. But the Navajos were not receptive. "The Council members, and hundreds, even thousands, of Navajos listened and answered back," Collier recalled. "In my long life of social effort and struggle, I have not experienced among any other Indian group, or any group whatsoever, an anxiety-ridden and anguished hostility even approaching that which the Navajos were undergoing."[39]

Determined to have his way, Collier brought in a federal government expert to explain to the Navajos how less was actually more, or how herd reduction would actually mean increased livelihood. Using a chart to present his ideas, A. C. Cooley showed a blue line for the number of stock, a yellow line for wages from federal projects, and a red line for income derived from stock. He then argued that as the blue and yellow lines fell over the next few years, the red line would rise with improved grazing conditions, livestock breeding, and management. The Navajos in the audience were not impressed. One of them asked Cooley why all three lines could not rise together.[40]

Collier kept pushing his agenda for stock reduction and finally managed to secure the support of the Navajo tribal council. But the Navajos themselves, Collier found, "resisted with a bitterness sometimes sad, sometimes wild, but always angry." Indeed, many Navajos felt Collier had manipulated the council. "We elected the council, but they couldn't do anything," a Navajo complained, "and we think they are just put in to try to get us to listen to Collier."[41]

What worried the Navajos was the fact that they depended on sheep for their livelihood. For them, sheep and survival were the same. "Remember what I've told you," a Navajo father instructed his son, "you must not lose, kill or give away young ewes, young mares and cows, because . . . there's a million in one of those." He warned: "So with anyone who comes to you and tells you to let the herd go. You mustn't let the herd go, because as soon as you do there'll be nothing left of them. . . . The herd is money. It gives you clothing and different kinds of food. . . . Everything comes from the sheep."[42]

Raising sheep was a way of life for the Navajos. The animals were a part of their world. "When the sheep are grazing," said Haske Chamiso, "I always walked right in the middle of the sheep. I didn't turn the sheep back. I just go along with the sheep. When I get tired, I just lay down in the middle of the sheep and go to sleep and finally my sister would find me." Navajo boys grew up caring for the flocks. "The only thing I did was herding sheep," recounted Yazi Begay. "When I was a little boy, I was herding sheep all of my life. I didn't like to herd sheep. I was really lazy. The way I think I don't see why I am herding sheep. Finally, I grew up to be a big tall boy, but at that time I was still herding sheep." Herding represented family and the teaching of values. "All I was doing was herding sheep all the time," explained Ted Chamiso. "I was raised right there at my home . . . with my mother and father all the time. . . . Then my father used to teach me once in a while. Told me never to steal anything. So I never steal horses, sheep, or goats that don't belong to me. So I never steal all my life since I know myself. I never do any of those bad things my father told me not to do. Not to laugh or make fun of people."[43]

Now the government was ordering the Navajos to reduce their stock. In a letter to Navajo minister Jacob C. Morgan, a group of Navajos denounced Collier and his administrative approach:

> He wanted to make us vote for the [Indian Reorganization] bill and govern ourselves, and when we refused . . . he got very angry at us. He started a lot of new things; and now, when we want to do something like handling our own affairs and advising him what we want, he said, "No; but you got to take my advice." If he thinks we can be our own boss, why does he tell us what to do.
>
> John Collier promised to help us more than any other white man, but before he made these promises he forced us to agree to some hard things that we didn't like. We tried it out, but Collier just fooled us. He only did some of the stock reduction. We know how many sheep we have now and how much our country will take care of, and we don't think we are overgrazed.

The disgruntled Navajos concluded critically: "We Indians don't think it is right for Collier to tell us we should govern ourselves, and then tell us how to do it. Why does he want to fool us that way and make us believe we are running our country, when he makes us do what he wants."[44] The Navajos tried to resist the stock reduction program, but Collier and his experts would not let them do much talking at the meetings and would not listen to them. Instead, the government proceeded to carry out the policy. "No Washington people came here to reduce the goats," a Navajo reported. "But policemen told us those were orders from Washington and we had to be rid of the goats. The poorest people were scared and they just reduced the goats and sheep."[45]

As they watched the agents take their animals, the Navajos anxiously wondered how they would live without their stock. They especially resented the loss of their goats. "The poorest people owned goats — the easiest people to take away from," a Navajo protested. "The pressure was so great the little fellow sold, everyone sold. A goat sold for one dollar. The money doesn't mean half so much to the family as having the goat to kill and eat for several days." One herder saw Collier's program as a "war" against the Navajos. "I sure don't understand why he wants us to be poor. They reduce all sheep. They say they only goin' to let Indians have five sheep, three goats, one cattle, and one horse." Another Navajo recalled bitterly: "A great number of the people's livestock was taken away. Although we were told that it was to restore the land, the fact remains that hunger and poverty stood with their mouths wide open to devour us." After his sheep had been taken away from him, a Navajo herder cursed the officials: "You people are indeed heartless. You have now killed me. You have cut off my arms. You have cut off my legs. You have taken my head off. There is nothing left for me. This is the end of the trail."[46]

By 1935, the stock had been reduced by 400,000 sheep and goats; still Collier was not satisfied. Noting that 1,269,910 animals were still grazing on land capable of supporting only 560,000, he impatiently stated: "This means that a further reduction of 56 percent would be necessary in order to reduce the stock to the carrying capacity of the range." A Navajo complained: "The sheep business . . . gives us the only decent living. When we have no more sheep then Mr. Collier will dance the jig and be happy." Meanwhile, Navajos found themselves becoming increasingly dependent on wage income: nearly 40 percent of their annual per capita income of $128 came from wage earnings, mostly from temporary government employment. The stock reduction program had reduced many Navajos to dependency on the federal government as employees in New Deal work programs. They denounced Collier's project as "the most devastating experience in Navaho history" since the imprisonment at Bosque Redondo in the 1860s.[47]

Tragically, the stock reduction program was unnecessary as an erosion control program. Actually, overgrazing proved to be a secondary cause of erosion. Scientists would do further research on silt settlement and determine that overgrazing was not the source of the problem. "By the 1950s, although 5 percent of the Lake Mead reservoir had already silted up," according to historian Richard White, "scientists were far more hesitant in attributing blame for the situation than their colleagues in the 1930s."[48]

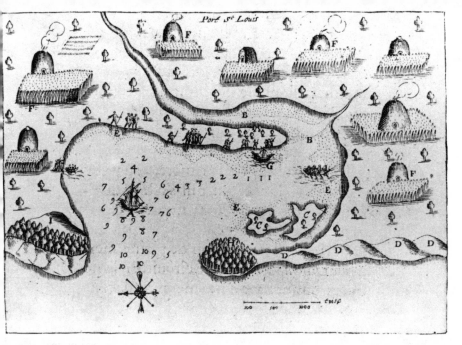

A map of Wampanoag villages and corn fields on Cape Cod drawn by Samuel de Champlain. (*Des Sauvages: ou Voyage de Samuel de Champlain de Brouage faict en la France Novelle [Paris, 1604]*)

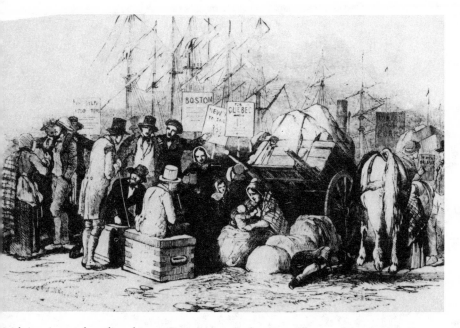

Irish immigrants boarding ships at Queenstown, Cork, 1851. (*Illustrated London News, May 10, 1851*)

Learning about "Gold Mountain," many of the younger, more impatient, and more daring Chinese left their villages for America. *(Asian American Studies Library, University of California, Berkeley)*

European immigrants packed on a ship bound for America. *(Library of Congress)*

Black Union soldiers, mustered out at Little Rock, Arkansas. (Harper's Weekly, *vol. 10* [*May 19, 1866*])

Arrival of Japanese immigrants. (*Hawaii State Archives*)

Left: Red Cloud, photograph by Charles M. Bell, 1880. *(Smithsonian Institution)*

Below: "Chinese Cheap Labor" in Louisiana. (Every Saturday, *vol. 3, no. 83 [July 29, 1871]*)

Facing page, right: Chinese railroad workers building the transcontinental railroad, circa 1866. *(Asian American Studies Library, University of California, Berkeley)*

Facing page, below: Irish railroad workers building the transcontinental railroad, circa 1866. *(Union Pacific Railroad Museum Collection, Omaha, Nebraska)*

Left: Big Foot lying in the snow after the massacre at Wounded Knee, 1890. *(Smithsonian Institution)*

Below: Many Chinese men spent their leisure hours in the backrooms of stores. *(Asian American Studies Library, University of California, Berkeley)*

Facing page: Hester Street, Lower East Side. Pushcarts lined the streets, and a cacophony of Yiddish voices rose from the crowds. *(Brown Brothers)*

Japanese immigrant women sewing clothing for laborers in a garment shop on a plantation in Hawaii. *(Hawaii State Archives) Below:* Jewish immigrant women working in a garment factory. "The machines were all in a row. And it was so hot, not even a fan. And you worked, and you sweated." *(Brown Brothers)*

Irish immigrant maids. As they cooked, laundered, and took care of the children, servants were required to wear aprons. *(State Historical Society of Wisconsin) Below:* Mexican workers in San Antonio, Texas, 1924. *(Goldbeck Collection, Humanities Research Center, University of Texas, Austin)*

The Triangle Shirtwaist Factory fire, 1911. "They hit the pavement just like hail," a fireman reported. *(Brown Brothers)*

Mexican miners in Arizona. *(Arizona Historical Society)*

Chicano laborers shelling pecans in San Antonio, Texas, in the 1930s. *(National Archives)*

Striking Jewish shirtwaist workers, 1909. (Munsey's Magazine, *1910*)

One of "MacArthur's boys," Marine Ira Hayes of the Pima tribe participated in the landing at Iwo Jima in 1945. *(U.S. Department of the Army)*

Mrs. Emily Lee Shek became the first Chinese woman to join the WAACS. She is pictured here with Eleanor Roosevelt. *(U.S. Department of the Army)*

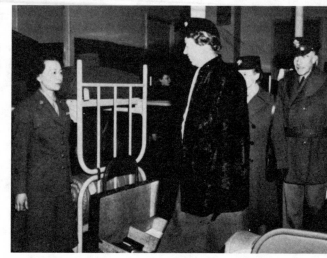

At Dachau, Jewish prisoners were liberated by U.S. troops, including Japanese-American soldiers. *(Photograph by Sus Ito. Courtesy of the Japanese American Resource Center and Rudy Tokiwa)*

Black female worker in a shipyard during World War II. (*National Archives*)

Chicana railroad workers during World War II. (*Library of Congress*)

Frederick Douglass. *(Reproduced in Frederick Douglass, My Bondage and My Freedom [New York, 1855])*

Martin Delany, Union Officer. *(Howard University Library. Reproduced in* Martin Robinson Delany *[New York: Doubleday, 1971])*

Marcus Garvey, 1922. *(United Press Photo)*

The three civil rights workers murdered in Mississippi — Michael Schwerner, James Chaney, and Andrew Goodman. *(AP/Wide World)*

Sit-in at the Greensboro Woolworth's lunch counter, February 2, 1960 — Joseph McNeil, Franklin McCain, Billy Smith, and Clarence Henderson. (Greensboro News & Record *Library*)

Martin Luther King, Jr., and Malcolm X. *(Library of Congress)*

But the Navajos had been telling this to the New Dealers all along. They argued that erosion had been reported as early as the 1890s and was related more to drought than to overgrazing. Trying to explain this cycle of dry weather and subsequent erosion to the government experts, Navajos had pointed out that the 1930s were also years with little rain and predicted that the range would recover when the drought ended. They reminded the government bureaucrats: "We know something about that by nature because we were born here and raised here and we knew about the processes of nature on our range." One of their ancient songs told them about their land's dependency on rain:

> *House made of dawn,*
> *House made of evening light,*
> *House made of the dark cloud . . .*
> *Dark cloud is at the house's door,*
> *The trail out of it is dark cloud,*
> *The zigzag lightning stands high upon it . . .*
> *Happily may I walk.*
> *Happily, with abundant showers, may I walk.*
> *Happily, with abundant plants, may I walk.*

Grass had always returned along with the rain, Navajos knew as they searched the skies for dark clouds in the dawn and evening, hopeful that showers would bless the land and their people.[49]

10

PACIFIC CROSSINGS

Seeking the Land of Money Trees

DURING THE 1890s, American society witnessed not only the Wounded Knee massacre and the end of the frontier, but also the arrival of a new group of immigrants. Unlike the Irish, the Japanese went east to America. But they, too, were pushed here by external influences. During the nineteenth century, America's expansionist thrust reached all the way across the Pacific Ocean. In 1853, Commodore Matthew C. Perry had sailed his armed naval ships into Tokyo Bay and forcefully opened Japan's doors to the West. As Japanese leaders watched Western powers colonizing China, they worried that their country would be the next victim. Thus, in 1868, they restored the Meiji emperor and established a strong centralized government. To defend Japan, they pursued a twin strategy of industrialization and militarization and levied heavy taxes to finance their program.

Bearing the burden of this taxation, farmers suffered severe economic hardships during the 1880s. "The distress among the agricultural class has reached a point never before attained," the *Japan Weekly Mail* reported. "Most of the farmers have been unable to pay their taxes, and hundreds of families in one village alone have been compelled to sell their property in order to liquidate their debts." Thousands of farmers lost their lands, and hunger stalked many parts of the country. "What strikes me most is the hardships paupers are having in surviving," reported a journalist. "Their regular fare consists of rice husk or buckwheat chaff ground into powder and the dregs of bean curd mixed with leaves and grass."[1]

Searching for a way out of this terrible plight, impoverished farmers were seized by an emigration *netsu,* or "fever." Fabulous stories of high wages stirred their imaginations. A plantation laborer in the Kingdom of Hawaii could earn six times more than in Japan; in three years, a worker might save four hundred yen — an amount equal to ten years of earnings in Japan. When the Japanese government first announced it would be filling six hundred emigrant slots for the first shipment of laborers to Hawaii, it received 28,000 applications. Stories about wages in the United States seemed even more fantastic — about a dollar a day, or more than two yen. This meant that in one year a worker could save about eight hundred yen — an amount almost equal to the income of a governor in Japan. No wonder a young man begged his parents: "By all means let me go to America." Between 1885 and 1924, 200,000 left for Hawaii and 180,000 for the United States mainland. In haiku, one Japanese migrant captured the feeling of expectation and excitement:

> *Huge dreams of fortune*
> *Go with me to foreign lands,*
> *Across the ocean.*

To prospective Japanese migrants, "money grew on trees" in America.[2]

Picture Brides in America

Initially, most of the migrants from Japan were men, but what became striking about the Japanese immigration was its eventual inclusion of a significant number of women. By 1920, women represented 46 percent of the Japanese population in Hawaii and 35 percent in California. Clearly, in terms of gender, the Japanese resembled the Irish and Jews rather than the Chinese. This difference had consequences for the two Asian groups in terms of the formation of families. In 1900, fifty years after the beginning of Chinese immigration, only 5 percent were women. In this community composed mostly of "bachelors," only 4 percent were American-born. "The greatest impression I have of my childhood in those days was that there were very few families in Chinatown," a resident recalled. "Babies were looked on with a kind of wonder." On the other hand, in 1930, 52 percent of the Japanese population had been born in America. But why did proportionately more women emigrate from Japan than China?[3]

Unlike China, Japan was ruled by a strong central government that was able to regulate emigration. Prospective immigrants were required to apply to the government for permission to leave for the United States and were screened by review boards to certify that they were healthy and literate and would creditably "maintain Japan's national honor." Japan had received reports about the Chinese in America and was determined to monitor the quality of its emigrants. Seeking to avoid the problems of prostitution, gambling, and drunkenness that reportedly plagued the predominantly male Chinese community in the United States, the Japanese government promoted female emigration. The 1882 Chinese Exclusion Act prohibited the entry of "laborers," both men and women, but militarily strong Japan was able to negotiate the 1908 Gentlemen's Agreement. While this treaty prohibited the entry of Japanese "laborers," it allowed Japanese women to emigrate to the United States as family members.[4]

Through this opening in immigration policy came over sixty thousand women, many as "picture brides." The picture bride system was based on the established custom of arranged marriage. In Japanese society, marriage was not an individual matter but rather a family concern, and parents consulted go-betweens to help them select partners for their sons and daughters. In situations involving families located far away, the prospective bride and groom would exchange photographs before the initial meeting. This traditional practice lent itself readily to the needs of Japanese migrants. "When I told my parents about my desire to go to a foreign land, the story spread throughout the town," picture bride Ai Miyasaki later recalled. "From here and there requests for marriage came pouring in just like rain!" Similarly, Riyo Orite had a "picture marriage." Her marriage to a Japanese man in America had been arranged through a relative. "All agreed to our marriage, but I didn't get married immediately," she recalled. "I was engaged at the age of sixteen and didn't meet Orite until I was almost eighteen. I had seen him only in a picture at first. . . . Being young, I was unromantic. I just believed that girls should get married. I felt he was a little old, about thirty, but the people around me praised the match. His brother in Tokyo sent me a lot of beautiful pictures [taken in the United States]. . . . My name was entered in the Orites' *koseki* [family register]. Thus we were married."[5]

The emigration of Japanese women occurred within the context of internal economic developments. While women in China were restricted to farm and home, Japanese women were increasingly entering the wage-earning work force. Thousands of them were employed in construction work as well as in the coal mines where they carried heavy loads on their backs out of the tunnels. Young women were leaving their family farms for employment in textile mills where they worked sixteen-hour shifts and lived in dormitories. By 1900, 60 percent of Japan's industrial laborers were women. While it is not known how many of the women who emigrated had been wage-earners, this proletarianization of women already well under way in Japan paved the way for such laborers to consider working in America.[6]

Japanese women were also more receptive to the idea of traveling overseas than Chinese women. The Meiji government required the education of female children, stipulating that "girls should be educated ... alongside boys." Emperor Meiji himself promoted female education. Japanese boys as well as girls, he declared, should learn about foreign countries and become enlightened about the world. Female education included reading and writing skills as well as general knowledge. Japanese women, unlike their Chinese counterparts, were more likely to be literate. "We studied English and Japanese, mathematics, literature, writing, and religion," recalled Michiko Tanaka. Under the reorganization of the school system in 1876, English was adopted as a major subject in middle school. This education exposed Japanese women to the outside world. They also heard stories describing America as "heavenly," and some of the picture brides were more eager to see the new land than to meet their husbands. "I wanted to see foreign countries and besides I had consented to marriage with Papa because I had the dream of seeing America," Michiko Tanaka revealed to her daughter years later. "I wanted to see America and Papa was a way to get there." "I was bubbling over with great expectations," said another picture bride. "My young heart, 19 years and 8 months old, burned, not so much with the prospects of reuniting with my new husband, but with the thought of the New World."[7]

The emigration of women was also influenced by Japanese views on gender. A folk saying popular among farmers recommended that a family should have three children: "One to sell, one to follow, and one in reserve." The "one to sell" was the daughter. Of course, this was meant only figuratively: she was expected to marry and enter her husband's family. "Once you become someone's wife you belong to his family," explained Tsuru Yamauchi. "My parents said once I went over to be married, I should treat his parents as my own and be good to them."

One day, Yamauchi was told that she would be going to Hawaii to join her future husband: "I learned about the marriage proposal when we had to exchange pictures." Emigration for her was not a choice but an obligation to her husband.[8]

Whether a Japanese woman went to America depended on which son she married — the son "to follow" or the son "in reserve." Unlike the Chinese, Japanese farmers had an inheritance system based on impartible inheritance and primogeniture. Only one of the sons in the family, usually the eldest, inherited the family's holdings: he was the son who was expected "to follow" his father. In the mountainous island nation of Japan, arable land was limited, and most of the farm holdings were small, less than two and a half acres. Division of a tiny family holding would mean disaster for the family. As the possessor of the family farm, the eldest son had the responsibility of caring for his aged parents and hence had to stay home. The second or noninheriting son — the one held "in reserve" in case something happened to the first son — had to leave the family farm and find employment in town. This practice of relocating within Japan could easily be applied to movement abroad. Thus, although the migrants included first sons, they tended to be the younger sons. Unlike Chinese sons who had to share responsibility for their parents, these Japanese men were not as tightly bound to their parents and were allowed to take their wives and children with them to distant lands.[9]

But whether or not women migrated was also influenced by the needs in the receiving countries. In Hawaii, the government initially stipulated that 40 percent of the Japanese contract labor emigrants — laborers under contract to work for three years — were to be women. During the government-sponsored contract labor period from 1885 to 1894, women constituted 20 percent of the emigrants. During the period from 1894 to 1908, thousands of additional women sailed to Hawaii as private contract laborers. Planters viewed Japanese women as workers and assigned 72 percent of them to field labor. Furthermore, they promoted the Japanese family as a mechanism of labor control. In 1886, Hawaii's inspector-general of immigration reported that Japanese men were better workers on plantations where they had their wives: "Several of the planters are desirous that each man should have his wife." After 1900, when Hawaii became a territory of the United States, planters became even more anxious to bring Japanese women to Hawaii. Since the American law prohibiting contract labor now applied to the islands, planters had to find ways to stabilize their labor force. Realizing that men with families were more likely to stay on the plantations, managers asked their business agents in Honolulu to send "men with families."[10]

Meanwhile, Japanese women were pulled to the United States mainland where they were needed as workers by their husbands. Shopkeepers and farmers sent for their wives, thinking they could assist as unpaid family labor. Wives were particularly useful on farms where production was labor intensive. "Nearly all of these tenant farmers are married and have their families with them," a researcher noted in 1915. "The wives do much work in the fields."[11]

As they prepared to leave their villages for Hawaii and America, many of these women felt separation anxieties. One woman remembered her husband's brother saying farewell: "Don't stay in the [United] States too long. Come back in five years and farm with us." But her father quickly remarked: "Are you kidding? They can't learn anything in five years. They'll even have a baby over there. . . . Be patient for twenty years." Her father's words shocked her so much that she could not control her tears: suddenly she realized how long the separation could be. Another woman recalled the painful moment she experienced when her parents came to see her off: "They did not join the crowd, but quietly stood in front of the wall. They didn't say 'good luck,' or 'take care,' or anything. . . . They couldn't say anything because they knew, as I did, that I would never return." As their ships sailed from the harbor, many women gazed at the diminishing shore:

> With tears in my eyes
> I turn back to my homeland,
> Taking one last look.[12]

Tears in the Canefields

"Get labor first," sugar planters in Hawaii declared, "and capital will follow." By pursuing this strategy, they successfully developed a profitable sugar export economy. Between 1875 and 1910, cultivated plantation lands multiplied nearly eighteen times, or from 12,000 to 214,000 acres. To achieve this triumph, planters had to find workers, and their chief source was Japan. To their labor suppliers, they sent requisitions for the commodities that their plantations needed. In a letter to a plantation manager, July 2, 1890, the Davies Company of Honolulu acknowledged receipt of an order for:

> *bonemeal*
> *canvas*
> *Japanese laborers*
> *macaroni*
> *Chinamen*

In another letter, January 3, 1898, the Davies Company confirmed a list of orders which included:

> DRIED BLOOD [fertilizer].
> LABORERS. We will book your order for 75 Japanese to
>   come as soon as possible.
> MULES & HORSES.[13]

Though they imported workers as supplies, planters were conscious of the nationalities of their laborers. The employers were systematically developing an ethnically diverse labor force in order to create divisions among their workers and reinforce management control. Complaining about the frequency of strikes on plantations where the workers were mostly from the same country, plantation managers recommended: "Keep a variety of laborers, that is different nationalities, and thus prevent any concerted action in case of strikes, for there are few, if any, cases of Japs, Chinese, and Portuguese entering into a strike as a unit." In a "confidential" letter to planter George Wilcox, a labor supply company wrote: "Regarding the proportion of Chinese and Japanese laborers we beg to advise, that the Hawaiian Sugar Planters' Association and the Bureau of Immigration have agreed upon 2/3rd of the former and 1/3 of the latter. For your *private* information we mention, that the reason for this increasing the percentage of the Chinese laborers is due to the desire of breaking up the preponderance of the Japanese element."[14]

Planters explained that they preferred to divide the work force "about equally between two Oriental nationalities." In 1903, they began importing Korean laborers in order to pit them against the Japanese. Aware of the antagonism between these two groups, planters believed that the Koreans were "not likely to combine with the Japanese at any attempt at strikes." After receiving a demand for higher wages from Japanese laborers, a planter asked a labor supplier to send a shipment of Korean laborers: "In our opinion, it would be advisable, as soon as circumstances permit, to get a large number of Koreans in the country . . . and drive the Japs out."[15]

But the Korean labor supply was cut off in 1905. Informed about abuses suffered by the Koreans on the plantations, the Korean government prohibited further emigration to Hawaii. A year later, planters began bringing laborers from the Philippines, a territory acquired after the Spanish-American War. Again the purpose was to diversify and discipline the labor force. On July 28, 1909, the Hawaiian Sugar Planters' Association reported that several hundred Filipino laborers were en route to Hawaii: "It may be too soon to say that the Jap is to be supplanted, but it is certainly in order to take steps to clip his wings," and to give "encouragement to a new class [Filipinos] . . . to keep the more belligerent element in its proper place." Planters anxiously asked the labor suppliers to hurry the delivery of the Filipino workers. On August 7, for example, one of them complained about the high wages demanded by the Japanese laborers on his plantation: "If possible for you to arrange it I should very much like to get say 25 new Filipinos to put into our day gang. . . . In this way perhaps we can stir the Japs a bit." Twenty days later, he wrote again, stating that he was very pleased to receive the shipment of thirty Filipinos, and that he planned to use them to bring the Japanese workers to "their senses."[16]

Planters cultivated nationalistic consciousness in order to stimulate competition between the different groups of workers. Appealing to Filipino "race pride," the bosses urged them to work as hard as the Japanese. "We are all Filipinos, brothers," a work-gang leader told his men. "We all know how to hoe. So, let's do a good job and show the people of other nations what we can do. Let us not shame our skin!" The planters' divide-and-control strategy promoted interethnic tensions that sometimes erupted into fistfights in the fields and riots in the camps. On a Maui plantation in 1898, three hundred Japanese used sticks and clubs to drive a hundred Chinese laborers from the camps.[17]

To strengthen their authority over their ethnically diverse work force, planters stratified occupations according to race: whites occupied the skilled and supervisory positions, while Asian immigrants were the unskilled field laborers. In 1904, the Hawaiian Sugar Planters' Association passed a resolution that restricted skilled positions to "American citizens, or those eligible for citizenship." Asian immigrants were excluded, for they were not "white" and therefore ineligible to become naturalized citizens according to federal law. In 1915, Japanese laborers were mostly field hands and mill laborers. Of forty-five mill engineers, forty-one were of European ancestry, three were Hawaiian or part-Hawaiian, and only one was Japanese. A racial division was particularly evident in supervisory positions: of the 377 overseers, only two were Chinese and seventeen Japanese, while 313 were white. A Japanese worker told an interviewer how he was frustrated by racial discrimination. "I haven't got a chance" to get ahead in employment, he explained, "You can't go very high up and get big money unless your skin is white. You can work here all your life and yet a *haole* [white] who doesn't know a thing about the work can be ahead of you in no time." Coming to Hawaii with extravagant dreams, Japanese immigrants experienced disillusionment.

> *Hawaii, Hawaii*
> *Like a dream*
> *So I came*
> *But my tears*
> *Are flowing now*
> *In the canefields.*[18]

Reduced to supplies along with fertilizer, pitted against workers of other nationalities, and excluded from skilled employment, Japanese workers found themselves in a world of regimented labor. Early in the morning, they were jarred from their sleep by the loud scream of the plantation siren. A work song captured the beginning of the workday:

> *"Awake! stir your bones! Rouse up!"*
> *Shrieks the Five o'Clock Whistle.*
> *"Don't dream you can nestle*
> *For one more sweet nap.*
> *Or your ear-drums I'll rap*
> *With my steam-hammer tap*
> *Till they burst.*
> *Br-r-row-aw-i-e-ur-ur-rup!*
> *Wake up! wake up! wake up! w-a-k-e-u-u-u-up!*
>
> *Filipino and Japanee;*
> *Porto Rican and Portugee;*
> *Korean, Kanaka and Chinese;*
> *Everybody whoever you be*
> *On the whole plantation —*
> *Wake up! wake up! wake up! w-a-k-e-u-u-u-up!*
> *Br-r-row-aw-i-e-ur-ur-rup!"*[19]

When the whistle stopped shrieking, *lunas,* or "foremen," strode through the camps. "Get up, get up," they shouted as they knocked on the doors of the cottages and barracks. "*Hana-hana, hana-hana,* work, work."[20]

"All the workers on a plantation in all their tongues and kindreds, 'rolled out' sometime in the early morn, before the break of day," reported a visitor. One by one and two by two, laborers appeared from "the shadows, like a brigade of ghosts." From the labor camps, they came by train, "car after car of silent figures," their cigarettes glowing in the darkness. In front of the mill, they lined up, shouldering their hoes. As the sun rose, its rays striking the tall mill stack, "quietly the word was passed from somewhere in the dimness. Suddenly and silently the gang started for its work, dividing themselves with one accord to the four quarters of the compass, each heading toward his daily task." The workers were grouped into gangs of twenty to thirty workers and marched to the fields. Each gang was supervised by an "overseer, almost always a white man." The ethnicity of the gangs varied: some were composed of one nationality, while others included Hawaiians, Filipinos, Puerto Ricans, Chinese, Japanese, Portuguese, and Koreans.[21]

There were gangs of women workers, too. In 1920, 14 percent of the plantation labor force was female, mostly Japanese. Women were concentrated in field operations such as hoeing, stripping leaves, and harvesting. Though they were given many of the same assignments as men, women were paid less than their male counterparts. Female field hands, for example, received an average wage of only fifty-five cents per day in 1915, compared to seventy-eight cents for male field hands.[22]

Field work was punishing and brutal. "We worked like machines," a laborer complained. "For 200 of us workers, there were seven or eight lunas and above them was a field boss on a horse. We were watched constantly." A Japanese woman recalled: "We had to work in the canefields, cutting cane, being afraid, not knowing the language. When any *haole* or Portuguese luna came, we got frightened and thought we had to work harder or get fired." "The *luna* carried a whip and rode a horse," another Japanese laborer recounted. "If we talked too much the man swung the whip. He did not actually whip us but just swung his whip so that we would work harder."[23]

The *lunas* "never called a man by his name," the workers grumbled. "Every worker was called by number," one of them complained. "Always by the bango, 7209 or 6508 in that manner. And that was the thing I objected to. I wanted my name, not the number." Carried on chains around their necks, the *bangos* were small brass disks with stamped identification. In the old country, workers had names that connected them to family and community; but in Hawaii, they had become numbers. They resented this new impersonal identity. Laborers were "treated no better than cows or horses," one of them recalled. The *bango* seemed to emblematize a distance between themselves and their humanity.[24]

The laborers cursed the *lunas*, "talking stink" about the driving pace of the work: "It burns us up to have an ignorant *luna* stand around and holler and swear at us all the time for not working fast enough. Every so often, just to show how good he is, he'll come up and grab a hoe and work like hell for about two minutes and then say sarcastically, 'Why you no work like that?' He knows and we know he couldn't work for ten minutes at that pace." The *lunas* were just plain mean.

> *Hawaii, Hawaii*
> *But when I came*
> *What I saw*
> *Was hell*
> *The boss was Satan*
> *The lunas*
> *His helpers.*[25]

Under the supervision of the *lunas*, workers hoed weeds, one of the most tedious and backbreaking tasks. They had to "hoe hoe hoe . . . for four hours in a straight line and no talking," said a worker. "Hoe every weed along the way to your three rows. Hoe — chop chop chop, one chop for one small weed, two for all big ones." When the cane was ripe, *lunas* on horseback led the workers into the fields to harvest the crop. The cutting of the cane caught the eye of a visitor: "Just beyond these Chinese huts were canefields, an intense yellow-green, the long, slender leaves tossing in the breeze like a maize-field before the harvest. There were great bands of Japanese at work in the field." They worked with "incredible rapidity, the line of men crossing a field, levelling the cane."[26]

Harvesting the cane was dirty and exhausting work. As the workers mechanically swung their machetes, they felt the pain of blistered hands and scratched arms. "When you cutting the cane and you pulling the cane back," a worker said, "sometimes you get scratched with the leaves from the cane because they have a little edge just like a saw blade." Their heavy arms and their bent backs begged for a break, a moment of rest.

> *Becoming weary*
> *I sit for a while to rest*
> *In the cane field,*
> *And whistle*
> *To call the breezes.*[27]

Sometimes the breezes failed to come. Twelve feet high, the cane enclosed and dwarfed the Japanese workers. As they cut the stalks, they sweated from the terrible heat and humidity. Surrounded by clouds of red dust, the laborers covered their faces with handkerchiefs. The mucus they cleared from their noses looked like blood.

> *My husband cuts the cane stalks*
> *And I trim their leaves*
> *With sweat and tears we both work*
> *For our means.*[28]

After collecting the cane stalks, the workers tied them into bundles and loaded them onto railway cars. A train then pulled the cane to the mill where engines, presses, furnaces, boilers, vacuum pans, and centrifugal drums crushed the cane and boiled its juices into molasses and sugar. Inside the mill, laborers felt as if they were in the "hold of a steamer." The constant loud clanking and whirring of the machinery were deafening. "It was so hot with steam in the mill," Bashiro Tamashiro recalled, "that I became just like *pupule* [crazy]."[29]

At four-thirty in the afternoon, the plantation whistle shrieked the signal to stop working. "*Pau hana,*" the laborers sighed, "finished working." Though they were too tired to hoe another row or carry another bundle of stalks, they felt a sudden final burst of energy and eagerly scrambled to their camps.

> *In the rush at pau hana*
> *I get caught in cane leaves,*
> *When I stumble and fall,*
> *They prickle, they jab.*[30]

Japanese workers were not passive victims of exploitation. Contrary to the stereotype of the Japanese immigrants as quiet and accommodating, they aggressively protested against the unfair labor conditions and often engaged in strikes. Divided by their diverse national identities, laborers of different groups initially tended to define their class interests in terms of their particular ethnicity. Thus, Japanese workers organized themselves into "blood unions" based on ethnic membership.

The most important manifestation of "blood unionism" was the Japanese strike of 1909. Protesting against a differential wage system based on ethnicity, the strikers demanded higher wages and equal pay for equal work. They angrily pointed out that Portuguese laborers were paid $22.50 per month, while Japanese laborers received only $18.00 for the same work. "The wage is a reward for services done," they argued, "and a just wage is that which compensates the laborer to the full value of the service rendered by him. . . . If a laborer comes from Japan and he performs the same quantity of work of the same quality within the same period of time as those who hail from the opposite side of the world, what good reason is there to discriminate one as against the other? It is not the color of skin that grows cane in the field. It is labor that grows cane."[31]

Seven thousand Japanese plantation laborers halted operations on Oahu, while their compatriots on the other islands provided support by sending money and food. Japanese business organizations such as the Honolulu Retail Merchants Association contributed to the strike fund, and the Japanese Physicians Association gave free medical service to the strikers and their families. A strong sense of ethnic solidarity inspired the strikers. Stridently shouting "*banzais*" at rallies, they declared their determination to "stick together" as Japanese.[32]

The strike reflected an awakening consciousness among the workers, a transformation from sojourners to settlers, from Japanese to Japanese Americans. In their demand for a higher wage, the strikers explained: "We have decided to permanently settle here, to incorporate ourselves with the body politique [*sic*] of Hawaii — to unite our destiny with that of Hawaii, sharing the prosperity and adversity of Hawaii with other citizens of Hawaii." Significantly, the Japanese were framing their demands in "American" terms. They argued that the deplorable conditions on the plantations perpetuated an "undemocratic and un-American" society of "plutocrats and coolies." Such a pattern of social inequality was injurious to Hawaii in general. Fair wages would encourage laborers to work more industriously and productively and enable society to enjoy "perpetual peace and prosperity." The goal of the strike was to create "a thriving and contented middle class — the realization of the high ideal of Americanism."[33]

The planters responded by pressuring the government to arrest the strike leaders for "conspiracy." Then they hired Koreans, Hawaiians, Chinese, Portuguese, and Filipinos as scabs. The strikers held out for four months before they were forced to return to work. But they had actually scored a victory, for shortly afterward, the planters eliminated the differential wage system and raised the wages of the Japanese workers.

A strike based on ethnicity seemed to make sense to Japanese plantation laborers in 1909, for they constituted about 70 percent of the work force, while Filipinos represented less than 1 percent. But this ethnic solidarity also made it possible for the planters to use laborers of other nationalities to break the "Japanese" strike. After the 1909 strike was broken, planters imported Filipino laborers in massive numbers. Eleven years later, Japanese workers represented only 44 percent of the labor force, while Filipino workers had risen to 30 percent. Organized into separate "blood" unions, workers of both nationalities began to realize that the labor movement in Hawaii would have to be based on interethnic working-class unity.

In December 1919, the Japanese Federation of Labor and the Filipino Federation of Labor submitted separate demands to the Hawaiian Sugar Planters' Association. The workers wanted higher wages, an eight-hour day, an insurance fund for retired employees, and paid maternity leaves. Their demands were promptly rejected by the planters. The Japanese union thought that both groups should plan for a long strike. Feeling that the time for action had arrived, however, the Filipino Federation of Labor unilaterally issued an order for the Filipinos to strike and urged the Japanese to join them. "This is the opportunity that the Japanese should grasp," declared the leader of the Filipino union, "to show that they are in harmony with and willing to cooperate with other nationalities in this territory, concerning the principles of organized labor. . . . We should work on this strike shoulder to shoulder."[34]

Three thousand Filipino workers went out on strike. They set up picket lines and called for labor solidarity. "What's the matter? Why you *hanahana* [work]?" the Filipino strikers asked their Japanese co-workers. Several Japanese newspapers urged the Japanese laborers to support the Filipinos. The *Hawaii Shimpo* scolded Japanese workers for their hesitation: "Our sincere and desperate voices are also their voices. Their righteous indignation is our righteous indignation. . . . Fellow Japanese laborers! Don't be a race of unreliable dishonest people! Their problem is your problem!" The *Hawaii Hochi* advised Japanese laborers to strike immediately: "Laborers from different countries" should take "action together." Between Filipinos and Japanese, the *Hawaii Choho* declared, there should be "no barriers of nationality, race, or color." Sensing the will of the community, the Japanese Federation of Labor ordered its members to join the strike. United in struggle, eight thousand Filipino and Japanese strikers — 77 percent of the entire plantation work force on Oahu — brought production to a sudden stop. Here was a Hawaiian version of the "giddy multitude." "*Pau hana*," they told each other, "no go work." "*Pau hana*," they declared defiantly, "we on strike."[35]

During the strike, the leaders of the Japanese Federation of Labor questioned the wisdom of having two separate unions and consequently formed the Hawaii Laborers' Association — a name that conveyed multiethnic class camaraderie. They insisted that all workers, regardless of ethnicity, should cooperate in safeguarding their standard of living. The fact that the "capitalists were *haoles* [Caucasians]" and the "laborers Japanese and Filipinos" was a "mere coincidence," explained Takashi Tsutsumi. The fundamental *distance* was class. Japanese and Filipinos were acting as "laborers" in "a solid body" during the 1920 strike. What the workers were learning from their struggle, Tsutsumi continued, was the need to build "a big, powerful and non-racial labor organization" which could "effectively cope with the capitalists." Such a union would bring together "laborers of all nationalities."[36]

The strikers were learning a valuable lesson. Filipinos and Japanese, joined by Spanish, Portuguese, and Chinese, had participated in the first major interethnic working-class struggle in Hawaii. They had all been awakened by the 5:00 A.M. whistle and had labored together in the fields and mills; now they were fighting for a common goal. As they walked the picket lines and protested at mass rallies, they understood more deeply the contributions they had made as workers to Hawaii's economic development. "When we first came to Hawaii," they proudly declared, "these islands were covered with ohia forests, guava fields and areas of wild grass. Day and night did we work, cutting trees and burning grass, clearing lands and cultivating fields until we made the plantations what they are today."[37]

Confronted by this interethnic challenge, the planters turned to their time-tested strategy of divide and control. The president of one sugar corporation explained: "We are inclined to think that the best prospect, in connection with this strike, is the fact that two organizations, not entirely in harmony with each other, are connected with it, and if either of them falls out of line, the end will be in sight." The planters fomented distrust between the two unions. They offered a bribe to Filipino union leader Pablo Manlapit. Suddenly, to the surprise of both the Filipino and Japanese strikers, Manlapit called off the strike, condemning it as a Japanese action to cripple the economy of Hawaii. But, at the rank-and-file level, many Filipinos continued to strike. Escalating their attack, the planters launched a "program of propaganda": they claimed that the Japanese strikers were puppets of Japan and were seeking to "Japanise" the islands.[38]

Meanwhile, the planters enlisted Hawaiians, Portuguese, and Koreans as strikebreakers. They also served forty-eight-hour eviction notices to the strikers, forcing them to leave their homes and find makeshift shelters in Honolulu's empty lots. Homeless during the height of an influenza epidemic, thousands of workers and their family members became sick, and one hundred and fifty died. "My brother and mother had a high fever," Tadao Okada recalled, "but all of us were kicked out of our home." Tired, hungry, and ill, the strikers gave up their struggle in July. The planters claimed a complete victory, but three months later, they discreetly increased wages by 50 percent.[39]

But the strikes represented only the surface of a contested terrain. Beneath the conflict over who would control labor and benefit from the wealth it created was a quiet struggle over the content of culture in Hawaii. Would the culture be dominated by the Anglo-American planter class, or would it be enriched with the traditions and customs of the Japanese as well as of the other nationalities in Hawaii? Culture was critical, for it had the power to give or deny people a way of affirming their individual self-esteem and positive group identity. The plantation camps were sites of day-to-day cultural resistance.

In the camps, Japanese workers were conscious of the racial and class hierarchy symbolized by the plantation housing pattern. According to the graphic description of Milton Murayama in his novel *All I Asking for Is My Body,* the manager's house was on the top of the hill. Below it were the nice-looking homes of the Portuguese and Japanese *lunas,* then the identical wooden frame houses of the Japanese camp, and finally the more run-down Filipino camp. This stratified system was laid out around its sewage system. The concrete ditches that serviced the toilets and outhouses ran from the manager's house on the highest slope down to the Filipino camp on the lowest perimeter of the plantation. The tiered housing pattern and sewage system seemed emblematic: "Shit too was organized according to the plantation pyramid."[40]

Workers of different nationalities were usually housed in separate camps. "There were the Japanese camps," recalled Richard Okawa describing the Hawi Plantation on the Big Island, "and the Chinese and Filipino camps, and one camp for the Puerto Ricans." The Puunene Plantation on Maui had sixteen camps, including many Japanese and Filipino camps. There were also "Young Hee Camp," "Ah Fong Camp," "Spanish A Camp," "Spanish B Camp," and "Alabama Camp." "Yeah," explained Minoru Takaki, formerly of "McGerrow Camp" (named after one of the *lunas*), "we used to have Negroes on the plantation."[41]

Generally, the camps were crowded and unsanitary. According to a contemporary observer, workers were housed in dwellings that resembled "pig sties," and several hundred laborers "swarmed together" in one-storied "tenements." A Japanese laborer recalled: "Fifty of us, both bachelors and married couples, lived together in a humble shed — a long ten-foot-wide hallway made of wattle and lined along the sides with a slightly raised floor covered with a grass rug, and two *tatami* mats to be shared among us." Another worker described the "large partitioned house" she inhabited: "The type of room for married people was small, no bed or anything. . . . It was just a space to lay the futon down and sleep. We didn't have any household things, only our one wicker trunk, not even a closet. We just pounded a nail by the place we slept, a hook where I hung my muumuu, the old kanaka [Hawaiian] style."[42]

As planters employed men with families rather than single men, they began replacing the barracks with cottages for families. Planters decided that "dependable married men" were "preferred" as workers and authorized the building of cottages for married laborers. In 1920, the Hawaiian Sugar Planters' Association promoted the development of family housing units: "Housing conditions on the plantations have changed greatly during the past few years, lately on account of the change in labor from single to married men." But planters also had self-interested reasons for improving the camps. They wanted to "stimulate" a "home feeling" in order to make their workers happier and more productive. "Pleasant surroundings, with some of the modern comforts and conveniences," explained a plantation official, "go a long way to make the worker healthier and more efficient in his work."[43]

The laborers had their own reasons for beautifying their camps. Seeking to add a reminder of their homeland, Japanese workers placed *bonsai* plants on the steps of their cottages. They also created artistic gardens; a mainland visitor observed that the flowers and "miniature gardens with little rocky pools and goldfish" suggested "a corner of Japan." Determined to have their traditional hot baths, Japanese workers also built *furos*. "The bath was communal," Tokusuke Oshiro said. "We all took a bath together. If, however, you got in last, it would be very dirty."[44]

Meanwhile, the workers were transforming their camps into ethnic communities. "There was another thing I'd come to like about the camp," remarked Kiyoshi in Milton Murayama's novel about plantation life. "The hundred Japanese families were like one big family. Everybody knew everybody else, everybody was friendly."[45]

On plantations, Japanese immigrants established Buddhist temples and Japanese-language schools for their children. The camps became the sites for their traditional celebrations. During the midsummer, Japanese held their traditional *obon,* or festival of souls. Dressed in kimonos, they danced in circles to the beat of *taiko* drums to honor the reunion of the living with the spirits of the dead. In early November, they observed the Mikado's birthday. Irritated by the interruption of the plantation production schedule, plantation managers found they had no choice but to let their Japanese workers have the day off. "There is an old custom here among the Japs of observing the 3rd of November as a holiday," a plantation manager complained. "The Emperor's Birthday was celebrated everywhere," Tokusuke Oshiro recalled. "Mainly there was *sumo.* . . . Several young men, usually the good ones, got together at a camp and had Japanese-style *sumo* matches."[46]

The Japanese immigrants also enjoyed their own foods and participated in interethnic sharing. The daughter of a Portuguese laborer remembered how her mother would make gifts of her bread and "little buns for the children in the camp. The Japanese families gave us sushis and the Hawaiians would give us fish." "Everybody took their own lunches" to school, Lucy Robello of the Waialua plantation said. "And like the Japanese used to take their little riceballs with an *ume* [pickled plum] inside and little *daikon* [radish]. . . . And us Portuguese, we used to take bread with butter and jelly or bread with cheese inside." Then, at noon, Japanese and Portuguese children would trade their *kaukaus* (lunches) with each other. Meanwhile, in the fields, their parents were also sharing their lunches. "We get in a group," William Rego recalled. "We pick from this guy's lunch and that guy'll pick from my lunch and so forth." Crossing ethnic lines, workers would taste each other's foods and exclaim in Hawaiian: "*Ono, ono!*" "Tasty, tasty!"[47]

Initially, the laborers of each ethnic group spoke only their native language. Language gave each group a sense of community within the plantation camps, enabling its members to maintain ties with each other as they shared memories of their distant homelands and stories of their experiences in the new country.

But soon workers of different nationalities began to acquire a common language. Planters wanted the immigrant laborers to be taught a functional spoken English so they could give commands to their multilingual work force. "By this," explained a planter, "we do not mean the English of Shakespeare but the terms used in everyday plantation life. A great many of the small troubles arise from the imperfect understanding between overseers and laborers." Over the years, a plantation dialect developed called "pidgin English" — a simple English that incorporated Hawaiian, Japanese, Portuguese, and Chinese phrases as well as their rhythms and intonations. Though it had begun as "the language of command," this hybrid language with its luxuriant cadences, lyrical sounds, and expressive hand gestures soon became the language of the community. "The language we used had to be either pidgin English or broken English," explained a Filipino laborer describing the communication of different ethnic groups on the plantation. "And when we don't understand each other, we had to add some other words that would help to explain ourselves. That's how this pidgin English comes out beautiful."[48]

As pidgin English became the common language of the camps, it enabled people from different countries to communicate with each other and thus helped them create a new identity associated with Hawaii. This acquisition of a new language reflected a deeper change in their outlook toward themselves and their new land. They had come to Hawaii intending to earn money and then return to Japan. Of the 200,000 Japanese who entered Hawaii between 1885 and 1924, 110,000, or 55 percent, went home. What is so striking and so significant is the fact that so many sojourners stayed.

Gradually, over the years, Japanese immigrant workers found themselves establishing families in the new land. By 1920, 45 percent of the Japanese in Hawaii were nineteen years old and younger. The immigrants were planting new roots in Hawaii through their children. In a letter to his brother, Asakichi Inouye explained why he had decided not to return to Japan: "My children are here, and my grandson [Daniel, who would later be elected to the U.S. Senate], and it is here that I have passed most of the days of my life. I do not believe that my wife and I, in our last years, could find contentment in Yokoyama, which has become for us a strange place." When Shokichi and Matsu Fukuda migrated to Maui in 1900, they were sojourners. Some twenty years later, they decided they would return to Japan and take their Hawaiian-born children with them. But their son, Minoru, was a teenager by then, and Hawaii was his home, the only world he knew. "He refused to go," remembered his niece Aiko Mifune. "Japan was a foreign country to him. He was very adamant that the family should stay in Hawaii." Mitsue Takaki also found herself planting new roots in Hawaii. She had come as a picture bride in 1920; eleven years later, her husband injured his knee on the plantation and returned to Japan for medical treatment. When he tried to reenter Hawaii, the immigration authorities refused to grant him permission. Mitsue chose to remain in the islands with her three small children — Minoru, Susumu, and Kimiyo. She went to night school to learn English and worked as a maid in the plantation clubhouse to support her children. She wanted them to be educated and have opportunities in the land of their birth.[49]

But the planters did not want the children of immigrant workers to have opportunities: they needed the second generation as plantation laborers and saw Japanese Americans as a colonized labor force. In their view, these children should not be educated beyond the sixth or eighth grade, and their education should be vocational training. A sugar corporation president declared that teachers should not keep "their students from working on the plantations." If the schools continued to encourage high career aspirations, he warned, "we had better change our educational system here as soon as possible." Pointing to the need for agricultural labor, a plantation manager complained that the school system was too expensive: "Why blindly continue a ruinous system that keeps a boy and girl in school at the taxpayers' expense long after they have mastered more than sufficient learning for all ordinary purposes?" A visitor from the mainland noticed the presence of Japanese children on the plantations and asked a manager whether he thought the coming generation of Japanese would make intelligent citizens. "Oh, yes," he replied, "they'll make intelligent citizens all right enough, but not plantation laborers — and that's what we want."[50]

Many schools, however, were not preparing these children to be plantation laborers. They were learning about freedom and equality and reciting the Gettysburg Address and the Declaration of Independence. "Here the children learned about democracy or at least the theory of it," said a University of Hawaii student. They were taught that honest labor, fair play, and industriousness were virtues. But they "saw that it wasn't so on the plantation." They saw whites on the top and Asians on the bottom. Returning from school to their camps, students noticed the wide "disparity between theory and practice." This contradiction was glaring. "The public school system perhaps without realizing it," the university student observed, "created unrest and disorganization."[51]

Seeing their parents suffer from drudgery, low wages, and discrimination, many second-generation Japanese Americans did not want to be tracked into plantation labor. Education, they believed, was the key to employment opportunity and freedom from the plantation. "Father made up his mind to send his children to school so far as he possibly could," said the daughter of a Japanese plantation worker. "Yet he had no idea of forcing us. Instead he employed different methods which made us want to go to school. We were made to work in the cane fields at a very early age. . . . After a day's work in the fields dad used to ask: 'Are you tired? Would you want to work in the fields when you are old enough to leave school?' . . . My father did everything in his power to make us realize that going to school would be to our advantage."[52]

Indeed, the immigrant parents believed their children were entitled to educational advantages. After all, they had transformed the islands through their labor: their sweat had watered the carpets of canefields. As they spoke pidgin English and as they watched their children grow up in the camps and attend American schools, they realized that they had become settlers and that Hawaii had become their home.

With one woven basket
Alone I came
Now I have children
And even grandchildren too.[53]

Transforming the Land: From Deserts to Farms

During a visit to California in the 1920s, a young Japanese man from Hawaii was shocked by the pervasiveness and intensity of anti-Japanese hostility. He had heard "various rumors" about the terrible ways whites treated the Japanese there. "But I didn't realize the true situation until I had a personal experience," he said. "In one instance, I went to a barber shop to get my hair trimmed. On entering the shop, one of the barbers approached me and asked for my nationality. I answered that I was Japanese, and as soon as he heard that I was of the yellow race, he drove me out of the place as if he were driving away a cat or a dog."[54]

This Japanese American had come from a vastly different society. In Hawaii, the Japanese were needed as laborers, and they had been incorporated by the planters into a paternalistic racial hierarchy. A large white working class did not exist in the islands. In fact, most of the people in the islands were Asian, and by 1920, the Japanese alone represented about 40 percent of the population. Their problems and difficulties were primarily related to their condition as workers. They were generally confined to the wage-earning plantation labor force. Possibilities for self-employment in shopkeeping and small farming were limited. The plantations operated retail stores for food, clothing, and other provisions, and most of the arable land in the islands was owned by the government and the sugar corporations. Aware of their extremely limited opportunities to advance themselves through individualism and small business, the Japanese in Hawaii tended to emphasize a class strategy of unionization.

On the mainland, however, the Japanese faced a fundamentally different situation: they were a racial minority, only 2 percent of the California population in 1920. They felt scorned by white society and had become the target of hostile and violent white workers. Denied access to employment in the industrial labor market, many Japanese entered entrepreneurial activity. "When I was in Japan, I was an apprentice to a carpenter," explained an immigrant, "but in America at that time the carpenters' union wouldn't admit me, so I became a farmer." Unlike their counterparts in the islands, the mainland Japanese were able to find economic niches in shopkeeping and farming. Consequently, theirs would be a different path — ethnic solidarity and ethnic enterprise.[55]

Initially, the Japanese were employed in agriculture, railroad construction, and the canneries. As migratory farm laborers, they constantly moved from field to field. Similarly, railroad workers were shuttled from one construction site to another. "We slept in the freight cars," one of them recalled, "suffering a lot from the troops of bedbugs." Cannery workers were shipped from the West Coast to Alaska and then back after the fishing season.[56]

Work was punishing. Railroad laborers gritted their teeth as they loaded the heavy ties onto the cars and grunted in pain as the square logs bit into their shoulders. Cannery workers had to race furiously against the machinery. After the boats brought in their catch, conveyor belts carried as many as two hundred salmon per minute up to the deck. The men, holding hooks in both hands, had to sort this charging multitude of huge fish without a single moment to relax. When they returned to the bunkhouses, they exuded the "Alaskan smell," "a nasal cocktail of rotten fish, salt, sweat and filth." Meanwhile, farm workers were in the fields from dawn to dusk, harvesting crops and hoeing weeds, row after row, their bodies constantly bent.[57]

The weather was a daily harsh reality. In the California valleys during the summer, workers felt the hot wind blowing against their perspiring bodies as temperatures soared to 120 degrees and the field became as "hot as though it were paved with hot iron boards." In the mountains during the winter, railroad workers were whipped by frigid winds. "In winter . . . the temperature went down to 20 degrees below freezing," they recalled. "Because of the severe cold, our excrement froze immediately when we went to the toilet outside the tent."[58]

Japanese immigrants wanted to escape from such exhausting work. Most had been farmers in Japan: for centuries, their families had cultivated small plots, irrigating the land and relying on intensive labor. To become a farmer in America was their dream. Within two decades after the first immigrants arrived, thousands of them were rising from the ranks of common laborers to become farmers.[59]

To obtain land, the Japanese used four methods — contract, share, lease, and ownership. The contract system was a simple arrangement: the farmer agreed to plant and harvest a crop for a set amount to be paid by the landowner when the crop was sold. The share system involved greater risks as well as the possibility of greater remuneration because the farmer received a certain percentage of the crop's profit. The contract and share systems enabled Japanese immigrants to raise themselves from field laborers to farmers without much capital. Under both arrangements, the landowner provided the tools, seed, fertilizer, and everything else necessary for the production of the crop; the Japanese farmer, in turn, was responsible for the labor. In order to feed himself and his workers, he purchased supplies on credit from storekeepers and merchants. After the crop was harvested and sold, he then paid his expenses — wages owed to his laborers and bills owed to his creditors. Under the lease arrangement, the Japanese farmer rented the land. He could obtain capital through loans from brokers and shippers. At the end of the season, if he harvested a bountiful crop and received a good price for it, he would pay his rent and clear his debts.[60]

What enabled the Japanese to become farmers so rapidly was their timely entry into agriculture. Beginning in the late nineteenth century, industrialization and urbanization had led to increased demands for fresh produce in the cities. The development of irrigation in California at this time opened the way for intensive agriculture and a shift from grain to fruit and vegetable production: between 1879 and 1909, the value of crops representing intensive agriculture skyrocketed from just 4 percent to 50 percent of all crops grown in California. This tremendous expansion occurred under a market stimulus created by two extremely important technological achievements — the completion of the national railroad lines and the invention of the refrigerated car. Now these farmers were able to ship their perishable fruits and vegetables to almost anywhere in the United States.[61]

As early as 1910, Japanese farmers produced 70 percent of California's strawberries, and by 1940 they grew 95 percent of the fresh snap beans, 67 percent of the fresh tomatoes, 95 percent of the celery, 44 percent of the onions, and 40 percent of the fresh green peas. In 1900, California's Japanese farmers owned or leased twenty-nine farms totaling 4,698 acres. Within five years, the acreage had jumped to 61,858 and increased again to 194,742 by 1910 and to 458,056 acres ten years later.

The workday on the farms was long and demanding. Stooped over the rows of plants, husbands and wives worked side by side, their hands in constant motion as they felt the hot sun on their backs.

> Both of my hands grimy,
> Unable to wipe away
> The sweat from my brow,
> Using one arm as towel —
> That I was . . . working . . . working.

Remembering the relentless pace of farm work, Yoshiko Ueda said: "I got up at 4:30 A.M. and after preparing breakfast I went to the fields. I went with my husband to do jobs such as picking potatoes and sacking onions. Since I worked apace with ruffians I was tired out and limp as a rag, and when I went to the toilet I couldn't stoop down. Coming back from the fields, the first thing I had to do was start the fire [to cook dinner]." Ueda worked so hard she became extremely thin. "At one time I got down to 85 pounds, though my normal weight had been 150."[62]

Women had double duty — field work and housework. "I got up before dawn with my husband and picked tomatoes in the greenhouse," Kimiko Ono recounted. "At around 6:30 A.M. I prepared breakfast, awakened the children, and all the family sat down at the breakfast table together. Then my husband took the tomatoes to Pike Market. I watered the plants in the greenhouses, taking the children along with me. . . . My husband came back at about 7 P.M. and I worked with him for a while, then we had dinner and put the children to bed. Then I sorted the tomatoes which I had picked in the morning and put them into boxes

When I was finally through with the boxing, it was midnight — if I finished early — or 1:30 A.M. if I did not."

> Face black from the sun
> Even though creamed and powdered,
> No lighter for that!

"We worked from morning till night, blackened by the sun. My husband was a Meiji man; he didn't even glance at the house work or child care. No matter now busy I was, he would never change a diaper." Another woman described how after a long day laboring in the greenhouse and taking care of the children, she had to work at night: "I did miscellaneous chores until about midnight. However tired I was, the 'Meiji man' wouldn't let me sleep before him."[63]

These pioneer men and women felt a certain boundlessness, driven by their dreams of making the land yield rich harvests. Over the years, they converted marginal lands like the hog wallow lands in the San Joaquin Valley, the dusty lands in the Sacramento Valley, and the desert lands in the Imperial Valley into lush and profitable agricultural fields and orchards. "Much of what you call willow forests then," farmer S. Nitta proudly told an interviewer in 1924, "Japanese took that land, cleared it and made it fine farming land." In 1920, the agricultural production of Japanese farms was valued at $67,000,000 — approximately 10 percent of the total value of California's crops.[64]

One of the most successful Japanese farmers was Kinji Ushijima, better known as George Shima. After arriving in 1887, he worked as a potato picker in the San Joaquin Valley and then became a labor contractor, supplying Japanese workers to white farmers. Shima wanted to become a farmer himself and began by leasing fifteen acres. To expand his operations, he leased and purchased undeveloped swamplands in the delta; diking and draining his lands, he converted them into fertile farmlands. A fleet of a dozen steamboats, barges, tugboats, and launches transported Shima's potatoes from Stockton to San Francisco. By 1912, Shima controlled ten thousand acres of potatoes valued at $500,000 and was regarded as a Japanese Horatio Alger. The *San Francisco Chronicle* praised Shima as a model: his success "pointed to the opportunities here to anybody with pluck and intelligence." Wealth did not immunize Shima from racism, however. When he purchased a house in an attractive residential section close to the university in Berkeley, he was told by protesters led by a classics professor to move to the "Oriental" neighborhood. The local newspapers announced: "Jap Invades Fashionable Quarters" and "Yellow Peril in College Town." But Shima refused to move. America was his home, he insisted; he had lived in this country so long that he felt "more at home here than in Japan." Widely known as "the Potato King," Shima had an estate worth $15 million when he died in 1926. His pallbearers included David Starr Jordan, the chancellor of Stanford University, and James Rolph, Jr., the mayor of San Francisco.[65]

Many Japanese immigrants believed that their success, especially in agriculture, would help them become accepted into American society. This was the vision of Abiko Kyutaro. His mother had died giving birth to him in 1865, and Abiko was raised by his grandparents. When he was fourteen years old, he ran away to Tokyo where he was converted to Christianity. Separated from his family, Abiko lacked the usual ties binding him to Japan. Feeling his "ambitions were stifled" there, Abiko departed for America. In 1885, he arrived in San Francisco, with only a dollar in his pocket. While doing menial jobs to make ends meet, he attended the University of California but did not complete his degree. By the early 1890s, Japanese immigrants were arriving in increasing numbers, and Abiko saw opportunities in the service business. During the 1890s, he operated several enterprises, including a restaurant and a laundry, and began publishing a newspaper, the *Nichibei Shimbun*. Fluent in English and familiar with business, Abiko became a labor contractor and one of the founders of the Japanese American Industrial Corporation. His company quickly became one of the largest labor contracting agencies in California, supplying Japanese labor to agriculture, mining, and the railroads.[66]

A thoughtful man, Abiko worried about the future of the Japanese in America. They were coming as sojourners, and he believed that this mentality was one source of their problems. They seemed to be driven by a single purpose — to make money and return to Japan as soon as possible. Thinking they would be here only temporarily, they did not seem to care about their shabby living conditions and indiscreet behavior such as drinking, gambling, and carousing with prostitutes. Neither did they feel a desire or a responsibility to contribute to American society. The sojourner identity, in turn, was contributing to an anti-Japanese exclusionist movement, for it seemed to confirm hostile claims that they were foreign and unassimilable.

In Abiko's view, the Japanese should bring their families and settle in America. Abiko personally set an example: in 1909, he returned to

Japan to marry Yonako and brought her back to his new homeland. But the Japanese immigrants had to do more than establish families here, Abiko argued. They had to establish themselves as farmers. A student of American history and culture, Abiko realized that farming had been the path for many European immigrants to become Americans. He was certain the Japanese were suited to become Americans through agriculture, for most of them had been farmers in the old country. The realization of a Japanese-American community rooted in agriculture became Abiko's crusade. The *Nichibei Shimbun* became the voice of his message: go into farming, own land, be productive, put down roots in America.[67]

An activist, Abiko took his crusade beyond words. He decided to create an actual model of his ideal Japanese farming community. In 1906, he founded the American Land and Produce Company, which purchased 3,200 acres of undeveloped desert land near Livingston in the San Joaquin Valley and parceled them into forty-acre lots for sale to Japanese farmers. "We believe that the Japanese must settle permanently with their countrymen on large pieces of land if they are to succeed in America," Abiko's company announced in an advertisement. "Those wishing to take advantage of this opportunity for success are welcome to visit one of our offices." The settlement was called the Yamato Colony. "Yamato," the ancient name for Japan, was to be a "new Japan," Abiko's "city upon a hill" in the San Joaquin Valley of California.[68]

A handful of Japanese pioneers responded to the invitation in 1907 and moved to this desolate site where they were greeted by clouds of fine sand blowing in the wind. The colonists settled as families and planted grapevines, which took four seasons to mature — a sign they were planning to stay. Significantly, the pioneers chose a site for a cemetery. "If there was to be a permanent colony," Seinosuke Okuye wrote in his diary in 1907, "the spot for the cemetery should be chosen from the beginning." Abiko's faithful followers had left the graves of their ancestors in Japan, and now they were preparing to become literally one with the soil of their adopted land.[69]

The nearby Merced River had been dammed, and the Yamato colonists constructed a system of irrigation canals and ditches to tap this life-giving supply of water. By 1910, they had planted 1,064 acres of grapes, 507 acres of fruit trees, 100 acres of alfalfa, and 500 acres of hay. "In the eleven years since the Japanese founded their colony," reported the *San Francisco Chronicle* in 1918, "fruit shipments from Livingston have increased from nothing in 1906 to 260 carloads in 1917." By then, the Yamato Colony was home for forty-two farmers, all with families. They were mixing their labor with the soil and becoming Americans.

> A wasted grassland
> Turned to fertile fields by sweat
> Of cultivation:
> But I, made dry and fallow
> By tolerating insults.

Fertile fields moistened by sweat, Abiko hoped, would bring respect to the Japanese and an end to the insults directed against them as "strangers."[70]

But this strategy of acceptance through agriculture failed to recognize the depth of racial exclusionism. Their very success provoked a backlash and the creation of new borders. In 1908, the federal government pressured Japan to prohibit the emigration of laborers to the United States. Shortly afterward, California and many other states enacted legislation to exclude Japanese immigrants from owning and leasing land. These restrictive alien land laws were based on the ineligibility of the Japanese for naturalized citizenship: a 1790 law had provided that only "white" persons could become citizens. In 1922, the United States Supreme Court affirmed that Takao Ozawa, a Japanese immigrant, was not entitled to naturalized citizenship because he "clearly" was "not Caucasian." Commenting on the Court's decision, a Japanese-language newspaper expressed the rage and disappointment of the Japanese community: "The slim hope that we had entertained . . . has been shattered completely." In 1924, an even more devastating development occurred. Congress enacted a general immigration law that included a provision prohibiting the entry of "aliens ineligible to citizenship," the code phrase for the Japanese.[71]

The immigrants had hoped that their lands, transformed from deserts to farmlands, would entitle them to settlement in America. But now the Issei, the first generation, feared they would have no future in their adopted land, except through their children — the Nisei, the second generation. Representing a rapidly growing group within the Japanese community, the Nisei constituted 27 percent of the mainland Japanese population in 1920 and 63 percent twenty years later, on the eve of World War II.[72]

Through the Nisei, the parents hoped, the Japanese would someday find tolerance in America. English speaking and educated in American schools, the second-generation Japanese would be the "ambassadors" for the first: they would teach white Americans about the culture of Japan and the hopes of the immigrant generation. As "intermediaries," they would "interpret" the East to the West and the West to the East. The Nisei would be the "bridge" to the larger society.[73]

Because their children were Americans by birth, the Issei hoped the Nisei would be able to secure the dignity and equality of opportunity denied to them. "You are American citizens," they reminded their children time and again like a litany. "You have an opportunity your parents never had. Go to school and study. Don't miss that opportunity when it comes." Education would give the second generation access to employment opportunities denied to the immigrants. The parents were willing to give up their own comforts, even necessities, for the education of their children.

> *Alien hardships*
> *Made bearable by the hope*
> *I hold for my children.*[74]

But citizenship and education, the second generation soon discovered, did not immunize them from racial discrimination. Even they, American citizens by birth, were told to "go back" to Japan and were called "Japs." Walking home from school, Japanese children were often attacked by white boys throwing stones at them. Nisei were often perceived as foreigners. They winced when they were asked: "You speak English well; how long have you been in this country?" As citizens, they were legally allowed to own land and homes, but they experienced widespread housing discrimination. When Togo Tanaka tried to purchase a home in Los Angeles, he made 119 inquiries about houses for sale, and in 114 instances he was told: "You cannot live here. Your money is not good enough. The deed has a racially restrictive covenant, and only members of the Caucasian race may reside here."[75]

The Nisei also experienced difficulty finding jobs in the mainstream economy. Generally, Japanese Americans graduated from high school with good grades, even honors, and many had completed college. The average educational level of the Nisei was two years of college, well above the national average. Still they found themselves denied employment opportunities in the larger economy. Many came of age during the depression — a time of massive unemployment in the country. But job possibilities were especially limited for them because of racial discrimination. A study of 161 Nisei who graduated from the University of California between 1925 and 1935 found that only 25 percent were employed in professional vocations for which they had been trained. Twenty-five percent worked in family businesses or trades that did not require a college education, and 40 percent had "blind alley" jobs.[76]

The Nisei were trapped in an ethnic labor market. Only a very tiny percentage of them worked for white employers. In Los Angeles, only 5 percent were employed in white-owned businesses in 1940. The vast majority worked in small Japanese shops, laundries, hotels, fruit stands, and produce stores. "I am a fruitstand worker," a Nisei explained. "It is not a very attractive nor distinguished occupation. I would much rather it were doctor or lawyer . . . but my aspirations of developing into such [were] frustrated long ago by circumstances [and] I am only what I am, a professional carrot washer." Some Nisei became doctors and dentists, but they served the Japanese community exclusively; many more became "Japanese gardeners." As a senior in college, a Nisei woman described her restricted career future: "After I graduate, what can I do here? No American firm will employ me. All I can hope to become here is a bookkeeper in one of the little Japanese dry goods stores in the Little Tokyo section of Los Angeles, or else be a stenographer to the Japanese lawyer here." Denied equal employment opportunities in the larger economy, the Nisei were confined to "the Japanese colony."[77]

But the problem for the Nisei went far beyond the mere matter of jobs. It was profoundly cultural, involving the very definition of who was an American. In his reflective essay "The Rising Son of the Rising Sun," Aiji Tashiro explained why Japanese Americans were viewed as strangers. "The Jablioskis, Idovitches, and Johannsmanns streaming over from Europe," he pointed out, "[were able] to slip unobtrusively into the clothes of 'dyed-in-the-wool' Americans by the simple expedient of dropping their guttural speech and changing their names to Jones, Brown or Smith." Tashiro knew it would make no difference for him if he changed his name to Taylor. He spoke English fluently and had even adopted American slang, dress, and mannerisms. But "outwardly" he "possessed the marked characteristics of the race." To be accepted as an American seemed hopeless. "The voice of the flute has long been the unfathomable voice of the East beating upon the West with futility."[78]

Many other Nisei, however, cultivated an American cultural outlook. In 1939, the San Francisco *Japanese American News* celebrated the Nisei's American consciousness: "Once upon a time, and surely it was a long time ago, someone had the magnificent idea of the Nisei bridging the Pacific" to establish an understanding between Japan and America. But the moment had arrived to "burn a few of our bridges behind us." The Nisei did not really have ties to "the homeland of their parents." Their true culture was not one of Japanese art and music and literature but instead was essentially "middle-class American." Young Nisei listened to Bob Hope and Fred Allen, sang songs popularized by Bing Crosby, and read *Collier's* and the *Saturday Evening Post* as well as the *American Magazine*. They enjoyed "swing, the Sunday funnies, and Myrna Loy."[79]

Actually, the editorial had simplified the feelings of the Nisei. Deep in their hearts, many Nisei did not wish to be completely assimilated, to become simply "American." They felt they were a complex combination of the two cultures, and they should be allowed to embrace their twoness. Everything they had learned at school about their country had taken "root," and they felt they were Americans. Nevertheless, many second-generation Japanese did not want to reject the culture of their parents, which had also become a part of themselves. James Sakamoto explained how the Nisei had a "natural love for the country of their birth" as well as for the land of their parents. In their view, Japan was "a nation, complete in itself, great, wonderful, with a glorious future." Deep within, the Nisei experienced "the clash and the adjustment and the synthesis of the East and the West." They stood on the "border line" that separated the "Orient" from the "Occident," the "streams of two great civilizations — the old Japanese culture with its formal traditions and the newer American civilization with its individual freedom."[80]

But their hope to be both Japanese and American would be violently shattered on a December morning in 1941.

11

BETWEEN
"TWO ENDLESS DAYS"

*The Continuous Journey to the
Promised Land*

Exodus from the Pale

T HEY LEFT THE world of the shtetl. Coming from a different shore than the Japanese, the Jews of Russia and eastern Europe also began their migration to America during the 1880s. A persecuted ethnic minority within Russia, they were forced to leave as settlers rather than sojourners. Unlike the Japanese immigrants, they felt they could not return to their homeland. In an important sense, they were political refugees. "The government itself had set off the pogroms in order to save the throne from a revolutionary upheaval," observed immigrant Abraham Cahan. "By making the Jews the scapegoats, it had confused the common people so that in the end the peasants were certain that the Jews and not the Czar were the cause of their troubles." Almost everywhere, government officials encouraged acts of violence against Jews.[1]

The repression in Russia was pervasive. Jews were required to live in the Pale of Settlement, a region stretching from the Baltic to the Black

Sea. "Within this area the Czar commanded me to stay, with my father and mother and friends, and all other people like us," recalled Mary Antin, who emigrated to America in the 1890s. "We must not be found outside the Pale, because we were Jews." Special borders contained them: like Caliban, they were "styed." Prohibited from owning land, most Jews were forced to live in the urban areas where they earned their livelihoods as merchants and artisans. In 1879, 38 percent of the Jews were employed in manufacturing or crafts, 32 percent in commerce, and only 3 percent in agriculture. Their concentration in crafts made many of them especially vulnerable. "It was not easy to live, with such bitter competition as the congestion of the population made inevitable," an immigrant explained. "There were ten times as many stores as there should have been, ten times as many tailors, cobblers, barbers, tinsmiths. A Gentile, if he failed in Polotzk, could go elsewhere, where there was less competition. A Jew could make the circle of the Pale, only to find the same conditions as at home."[2]

Life in the Jewish towns and villages was also intensely insecure, for anti-Semitic violence was a ubiquitous reality in the shtetl. Especially dreaded were the pogroms — massacres of Jews and the destruction of their shops and synagogues. "I feel that every cobblestone in Russia is filled with Jewish blood," an immigrant bitterly recalled. "Absolutely every year, there was a *pogrom* before *Pesach* [Passover]. In big cities during the *pogroms,* they used any reason to get rid of you. As many Jews as they could kill, they did; but there were some Gentiles who would save you. We survived because Pa was a *gildikupets* [merchant] and knew many wealthy Gentiles. But he was hurt many times." Golda Meir never forgot the persecution her family experienced: "We lived then on the first floor of a small house in Kiev, and I can still recall distinctly hearing about a pogrom that was to descend on us. I didn't know then, of course, what a pogrom was, but I knew it had something to do with being Jewish and with the rabble that used to surge through town, brandishing knives and huge sticks, screaming 'Christ killers' as they looked for the Jews, and who were now going to do terrible things to me and to my family." Similarly, Mollie Linker was only a child when her father left Russia: "I remember sitting by the window . . . and looking out. When it got dark, you closed the shutters, you were afraid. You were actually always in fear because of big *pogroms*. . . . I remember that scare . . . was in us all the time." After poet Chaim Nacham Bialik witnessed the terrible destruction of the Jews and their homes in Kishinev, he wrote:

Arise and go now to the city of slaughter,
    and go into the courtyards,
And with your eyes you will see and with your hands you
    will feel on the fences,
And on the trees, and on the stones, and on the plaster
    of the walls,
The splattered blood and the dried brains of the victims.

The pogroms, observed Abraham Cahan, forced Jews to realize that "Russia was not their homeland and that a true home must be found for Jews. But where?"[3]

Spreading from shtetl to shtetl across Russia, a song pointed the way to the Promised Land:

    As the Russians, mercilessly
    Took revenge on us.
    There is a land, America,
    Where everyone lives free....[4]

By the beginning of World War I, one-third of all Jews in Russia and eastern Europe had emigrated, most of them to the United States. America had caught their "fancy." Stories about freedom and a better life there were "buzzing" all around them. The distant land was viewed as a "Garden of Eden," "the golden land," where Jews would no longer be enslaved by "dead drudgery." The cry "To America!" roared like "wild-fire." "America was in everybody's mouth. Businessmen talked of it over their accounts; the market women made up their quarrels that they might discuss it from stall to stall; people who had relatives in the famous land went around reading their letters." At a sewing school in Minsk, Jewish girls received letters from America describing astonishingly high wages — the starting pay for a seamstress in New York was four dollars a week, a sum equal to a month's earnings in rubles. In Abraham Cahan's autobiographical novel, David Levinsky was seized by this emigration fever: "It was one of these letters from America, in fact, which put the notion of emigrating to the New World definitely in my mind. An illiterate woman brought it to the synagogue to have it read to her, and I happened to be the one to whom she addressed her request. The concrete details of that letter gave New York tangible form in my imagination. It haunted me ever after." While reading a letter from her father who had gone to America ahead of his family, Mary

Antin felt "a stirring, a straining." "It was there, even though my mother stumbled over strange words. . . . My father was inspired by a vision. He saw something — he promised us something. It was this 'America.' And 'America' became my dream."[5]

Hopeful possibilities exploded in their heads. "Many socialists were heading for America, where they planned to establish communist colonies," one of them recalled. Fannie Edelman wanted to escape to America where she could "fall in love and marry": "I was fourteen years old when I heard that people were leaving for the United States. I used to think of running away from our little town and from my severe father and coming to a free world called America." Another young woman, after deciding she wanted to emigrate, had difficulty eating and sleeping: "I was fighting to death for the money to go to America. I used to see the people going to the train to leave. I used to envy those people like anything. They said, 'You'll get married and then you'll go to America.' I says, 'I need a shlepper [a dragger] to America? I can shlep myself!' Who didn't want to go to America?" The country also offered educational opportunities. "I heard so much about America as a free country for the Jews," said Fannie Shapiro, "and you . . . didn't have to pay for schooling, so I came." Children "played at emigrating," and a mother's lullaby told children:

> Your daddy's in America
> Little son of mine
> But you are just a child now
> So hush and go to sleep.
> America is for everyone
> They say, it's the greatest piece of luck
> For Jews, it's a garden of Eden
> A rare and precious place.
> People there eat challah
> In the middle of the week.[6]

Their fears of persecution and their extravagant dreams gave them the courage to uproot themselves and leave their birthplace forever. On the streets of the shtetl, Jewish women sold their beds, chairs, kitchen tables, and other belongings in order to raise money for the cost of transportation to America. Taking only their personal possessions, Jews left familiar little towns with their cobbled streets and alleys, their smells and sounds of crowded and colorful marketplaces. "The last I saw of

Polotzk was an agitated mass of people, waving handkerchiefs and other frantic bits of calico, madly gesticulating, falling on each other's necks, gone wild altogether," recalled an immigrant. "Then the station became invisible." Another explained that when he left Velizh, he had not realized that he was starting such a long journey: "This was the point at which I was cutting myself off from my past, from those I loved. Would I ever see them again?"[7]

Such questions haunted the migrants when they arrived at the seaports. As they boarded the ships, they "were all herded together in a dark, filthy compartment in the steerage." "We learned that our vessel had formerly been a cattle ship and had just been converted into a passenger boat," Alexander Harkavy wrote. "Our compartment was enormously large, and wooden bunks had been put up in two tiers, one on top of the other." The passengers felt the engine's vibrations and smelled the "choking, salty odor." As often as possible, they went up on deck, especially to see the sunset. "But as the wonderful colors sank with the sun, [their] hearts would fill with a terrible longing for home. Then [they] would draw together and sing Russian folk songs filled with nostalgia and yearning." The sea was stormy and the ship rocked, remembered Samuel Cohen. "I kept tossing about. I stuck my head out of the bunk a little. A shower of vomit came down from the upper bunk on my face."[8]

At night, the passengers thought about the world that they had left behind and the new one that awaited them. Would America be as boundless as in their dreams? But this very vision of the new land provoked anxiety. "My future . . . where am I going? to whom? what will I do?" a young Jewish woman worried. "In Grodno I was at least someone in the store." Would she be "someone" in America, "without language, with only a bit of education"? She found herself swept into a tempest of doubts and misgivings. "Then a real storm broke out. The ship heaved and turned. People threw up, dishes fell, women screamed . . . but in my heart I didn't care what happened." Perhaps she felt the deeper purpose of the exodus. "Every emigrating Jew moving westward realized he was involved in something more than a personal expedition," said Abraham Cahan. "Every Jew . . . came to feel that he was part of a historic event in the life of the Jewish people." The Jews were a "countryless people." Their migration to America seemed to be a continuation of a journey that had begun thousands of years earlier in Egypt, for as historian Irving Howe explained, "the events of Jewish life were divided in two endless days, the Biblical yesterday and the exile of today."[9]

Finally, after a long Atlantic crossing, the passengers sighted land. The moment was a deeply moving experience for Cahan's fictional David Levinsky: "When the ship reached Sandy Hook [New Jersey] I was literally overcome with the beauty of the landscape. The immigrant's arrival in his new home is like a second birth to him." Levinsky stood breathless before "the magnificent verdure of Staten Island, the tender blue of sea and sky, the dignified bustle of passing craft." In a trance, he excitedly murmured: "This, then, is America!" "Everybody was on deck," recalled Emma Goldman who was only seventeen years old when she arrived. "[My sister] Helena and I stood pressed to each other, enraptured by the sight of the harbor and the Statue of Liberty suddenly emerging from the mist. Ah, there she was, the symbol of hope, of freedom, of opportunity!" After a long voyage in a packed steerage of seasick people, a Polish girl climbed to the deck and saw "the big beautiful bay and the big woman with the spikes on her head and the lamp that [was] lighted at night in her hand." Suddenly, the passengers began shouting, "Ellis Island." Their bodies leaned forward, and their hands gripped the railing of the ship as they saw the immigration station. But their excitement was interrupted by gruff voices. "We were surrounded by gesticulating people — angry men, hysterical women, screaming children," remembered Goldman. "Guards roughly pushed us hither and thither, shouted orders to get ready to be transferred to Castle Garden."[10]

Who were they, these newcomers searching for a door to America? "The immigrants who had been forced to abandon their homes in Eastern Europe were a hardy lot," declared Gilbert Klaperman in *The Story of Yeshiva*. "With rare exceptions, they arrived penniless and inadequately trained in a profession or handicraft. They did possess, however, indomitable faith in themselves and unflagging courage to face all difficulties. They dug their roots deep into the alien soil until it became home to them. They founded families and raised children and children's children who enriched America with invaluable contributions. This immigrant generation of the post-1881 decades may be called, indeed, the heroic generation."[11]

Actually, the Jewish immigrants were a highly select group. They were educated: 80 percent of the men and 63 percent of the women who came between 1908 and 1912 were literate. While most of them were poor, they were not "inadequately trained in a profession or handicraft." Two-thirds of the Jews specifying an occupation were skilled workers, compared to only 16 percent of the Italians. But, as Klaperman correctly noted, the Jews came to America as settlers. Unlike most other European immigrant groups, they planned to stay. Sixty percent of the southern Italian migrants returned to their homeland, whereas the return rate for Jews was only 3 percent. In gender composition, the Jewish immigrants resembled the Irish. Almost half of the Jews were women, compared to only about 20 percent for southern Italians. Children represented one out of every four Jews. These immigrants saw themselves as exiles, unable to return to Russia so long as religious persecution persisted. The Jews had to make America their new home.[12]

A Shtetl in America

From Castle Garden, most of the immigrants headed for New York City's Lower East Side. During the early nineteenth century, German Jews had settled in this area. A new Jewish community blossomed as massive waves of Russian Jews began arriving in the 1880s; by 1905, the Lower East Side had a population of a half-million Jews. Unlike the mostly "bachelor" community of nearby Chinatown, the Jewish colony had throngs of young people. An 1890 survey found that nearly half of its residents were children.

The laughter of children joined "a symphony of discordant noises" filling the air of the Lower East Side. Pushcarts lined the streets, and a cacophony of Yiddish voices, "a continual roar," rose from the crowds. "Here and there were heaps of rotting fruit." The signboards were in English and Yiddish, and sometimes in Russian. "Shopkeepers grabbed the arms of passersby and with torrents of cajolery endeavored to pull them inside their stores, cursing those who had escaped their clutching hands." In this colony, Jews seemed to be living just as they had in Russia: they resided and worked "within that small compass, meeting only people of their own nationality." Rose Cohen found that the Lower East Side meant living in "practically the same environment" as in the homeland. It was as though "we were still in our village in Russia."[13]

But the Lower East Side was also different in significant ways. There was an "American atmosphere of breathless enterprise and breakneck speed." Throngs of people were on "the streets, shouting, going in all directions." Life did not seem "normal," for "everybody was in a hurry and money was the main thing in life." The "scurry and hustle of the people" were "overwhelmingly greater, both in volume and intensity," than in their native towns. They seemed like "a new race in the world." Pent up in the old country, their energies were being unleashed in this new land of apparent boundlessness. The "swing and step of the pedestrians, the voices and manner of the street peddlers" seemed to testify to far "more self-confidence and energy, to larger ambitions and wider scopes, than did the appearance of the crowds" back home.[14]

At the turn of the century, the Lower East Side was the most densely populated section of the city. Walking the streets during warm evenings, pedestrians found all the windows open and were able to see "the life inside with all its filth and sadness. Bare, scarred tables. Countless beds, with tangled sheets and blankets. The yellow gaslight, and so many, many children, and nakedness and noise." The tenth ward, located in the Jewish colony, housed over 500 people per acre; on Rivington Street, a contemporary reported, "the architecture seemed to sweat humanity at every window and door."[15]

But the residents were just trying to find sunlight and fresh air, to escape from the dark and stifling interiors of the "dumbbell" tenements. Six to seven stories in height, this type of apartment resembled a dumb-bell: on every floor there were two apartments at each end connected by a hallway. A narrow, five-foot-wide air shaft separated the buildings. A window facing the street or a small backyard offered the only direct light for each apartment. Writing for the *American Magazine* in 1888, a journalist described these dumbbell tenements:

> They are great prison-like structures of brick, with narrow doors and windows, cramped passages and steep rickety stairs. They are built through from one street to the other with a somewhat narrower build-ing connecting them. . . . The narrow court-yard . . . in the middle is a damp foul-smelling place, supposed to do duty as an airshaft; had the foul fiend designed these great barracks they could not have been more villainously arranged to avoid any chance of ventilation. . . . In case of fire they would be perfect death-traps, for it would be im-possible for the occupants of the crowded rooms to escape by the narrow stairways, and the flimsy fire-escapes . . . are so laden with broken furniture, bales and boxes that they would be worse than useless. In the hot summer months . . . these fire-escape balconies are used as sleeping-rooms by the poor wretches who are fortunate enough to have windows opening upon them.[16]

Typically, each apartment was packed with people, family members and also boarders. "At the hour of retiring," a witness told the United States Immigration Commission, "cots or folded beds and in many in-stances simply mattresses are spread about the floor, resembling very much a lot of bunks in the steerage of an ocean steamer." A 1908 survey of 250 Lower East Side families found that about 50 percent slept three or four persons to a room, and nearly 25 percent had five or more persons. Most of the tenements did not have baths. "I cannot get along without a 'sweat' [Russian bath] at least once a week," an immigrant complained. Occupants competed to use the toilet: each tenement had only two facilities for each floor. "A five-story house of this character contain[ed] apartments for eighteen or twenty families," counted Jacob Riis in the 1890s, "a population frequently amounting to 100 people, and sometimes increased by boarders and lodgers to 150 or more."[17]

To escape from the confinement of the tenements, the immigrants would retreat to the park. "On hot summer nights [we would] seek relief from the heat in Jackson Street Park," one of them remembered. "The park, innocent of grass and trees, was a large area close to the East River, with many lanes of benches . . . and a stone pavilion like a Greek temple, where a small band occasionally played and milk was dispensed at a penny a glass. The park was always crowded. The men were in their undershirts. The women, more fully dressed, carried newspapers for fans. Hordes of barefoot children played games, weaving in and out of the always thick mass of promenaders."[18]

As they settled in the Lower East Side, the Jews began to establish organizations and create community. They formed "networks" or "lodges," *landsmanshafts,* composed of people from the same town or district in Russia, seeking the company of friends from *di alte heym,* "the old home." They also found community and conversation in the public bathhouses as well as in the neighborhood delicatessens and candy stores that had become gathering places. In cafés like Schreibers on Canal Street and Café Royale on Second Avenue, Jewish intellectuals drank tea as they debated great philosophical and political issues before rushing off to hear lectures regularly presented by the Educational Alliance and the People's Institute at Cooper Union. "There were scores of lectures every week," said Marcus Ravage. "One night it was Darwin and the next it might be the principle of air pressure. On a Saturday night there were sometimes two meetings so arranged that both could be attended by the same audience." Others preferred the movie theaters, where for five cents they would watch a half-hour film. "If it's not too busy, you can see it several times," an immigrant said. "They open at one in the afternoon, and customers, mostly women and children, gossip, eat fruit and nuts, and have a good time."[19]

Everywhere outside the cafés and theaters, there were peddlers.

Carrying packs or pushing carts, they knocked on doors and cajoled housewives to buy their goods. Shortly after Isaac Raboy arrived at Ellis Island, he found himself on Delancey Street, where peddlers were hawking their wares as they pushed their carts filled with "exotic" things. Streams of people flowed down the streets. "Suspenders, collah buttons, 'lastic, matches, hankeches — please, lady, buy," peddlers shouted. "Bandannas and tin cups at two cents, peaches at a cent a quart, damaged eggs for a song, hats for a quarter, and spectacles warranted to suit the eye . . . for thirty-five cents." A contemporary observed: "There are few more pathetic sights than an old man with a long beard, a little black cap on his head and a venerable face — a man who had been perhaps a Hebraic or Talmudic scholar in the old country . . . standing for sixteen hours a day by his push-cart in one of the dozen crowded streets of the Ghetto . . . selling . . . apples, garden stuff, fish and second-hand shirts. . . ."[20]

The Jewish peddler soon became a figure of Jewish-American folklore. In one of Anzia Yezierska's stories, Gedalyeh Mindel wrote to his family: "My sun is beginning to shine in America. I am becoming a person — a businessman. I have for myself a stand in the most crowded part of America, where . . . every day is like market day by a fair. My business is from bananas and apples. The day begins with my pushcart full of fruit, and the day never ends before I count up at least two dollars' profit — that means . . . four rubles a day, twenty-four rubles a week! . . . [W]hite bread and meat I eat every day just like the millionaires."[21]

Indeed, representing over 50 percent of all peddlers in New York City in 1906, the Jewish peddler seemed to personify the mystique of Jewish immigrant success, the triumph of imported entrepreneurial virtues and values celebrated by some scholars. The Jews had come to America, observed sociologist Milton Gordon, with the middle-class values of thrift, sobriety, ambition, desire for education, and the delay of immediate gratification for the sake of long-range goals. These cultural values, he claimed, accounted for their rapid rise in occupational status and economic affluence. Similarly, sociologist Nathan Glazer explained Jewish immigrant success in terms of middle-class values carried to America, particularly the emphasis on postponing pleasure. "Saving money is one such form of postponement," argued Glazer. "Perhaps the most significant findings of Alfred Kinsey's study of male sexual behavior was on this point: the person who postponed sexual pleasure . . . was already essentially middle class; for even if such a person was now working class, he was going to rise into the middle class." For both Gordon and Glazer, Jewish socioeconomic mobility was the result of a Jewish work ethic.[22]

But immigrant Jewish postponement of pleasure and sexual gratification would be difficult to measure and document, and many of the values they carried here actually clashed with the so-called middle-class values of material accumulation. Jewish culture in the Old World invested high status (*yikhes*) in religious learning; parents sacrificed to send their sons to yeshiva, a school of religion, and were proud to have their daughters marry scholars of the Talmud. "Learned people were more important than rich people," a Jewish woman from Russia explained, "and a girl would be happy to marry a boy that does nothing — that sits and studies." Abraham Cahan remembered how his scholarly grandfather was the "pride of our family and the people of Podberezy. Distant relatives spoke his name with reverence. . . . I began to feel my own importance as the great man's grandson." A Lithuanian immigrant, Eva Broido, described her father and his role in the family: "Our father, a kind and not unintelligent man, looked upon us children as something extraneous, with which he would not concern himself. He was an unworldly Talmudic scholar, who needed little for himself and knew nothing of our needs. . . . It was left to our mother to provide for us all." A Yiddish song from Russia echoed Broido's memory of her father:

> He runs to the synagogue
> And reads all the laws,
> He runs here and there
> Growling like a bear.
>
> To market she must hurry
> Wood to buy and worry
> Bread she must bake
> Kindling she must break. . . .[23]

What the Jewish peddler in America represented was not so much the transference of "middle-class" values from the Old World as Jewish adaptation to American culture. Historian Moses Rischin noted that "the peddler's pack . . . provided the most direct introduction to American ways, the most promising school for the study of the country's speech, tastes and economic needs, and the broadest field for the play of the aspiring tradesman's imagination." The peddler personified the transformation of the Jewish immigrant from scholar to salesman.[24]

This journey was described in Cahan's novel. An old man who had been a Talmudic scholar in Russia found that his wife was not willing to support him in America. Insisting that he go out to peddle, she snapped: "America is not Russia. A man must make a living here." The husband told David Levinsky: "America is a topsy-turvy country." A quick learner, Levinsky abandoned his dream of becoming a scholar and turned to peddling: "I rented a push-cart and tried to sell remnants of dress-goods, linen, and oil cloth. . . . I would announce to the passers-by the glad news that I had struck a miraculous bargain at a wholesale bankruptcy sale . . . and exhort them not to miss their golden opportunity." In this way, Levinsky began his "rise."[25]

But while Jewish peddlers appeared ubiquitous, they actually represented only a very small proportion of working Jews. A survey of gainfully employed Jews living in New York City in 1890 revealed that only 10 percent were peddlers. On the other hand, 60 percent worked in the garment industry.[26]

In the Sweatshops: An Army of Garment Workers

What probably mattered more than the values they might have carried to America was the fact that many Jewish immigrants brought something even more useful — their skills, especially in the sewing trades. "I am a tailor," recalled an immigrant years later at the age of eighty-two, "and I was working piecework on Russian officers' uniforms. I saved up a few dollars and figured the best thing was to go to the U.S.A. Those days everybody's dream in the old country was to go to America. We heard people were free and we heard about better living."[27]

The arrival of these skilled immigrants was timely, for they were needed in New York's expanding garment industry. In earlier times, clothes had been tailor-made, but the Civil War had transformed garment manufacturing. In order to meet the Union Army's demand for clothing, tailors established uniform standards and measurements. This innovation enabled them to mass-produce garments in factories, utilizing new inventions such as the Singer sewing machine, the electric cutting knife, and the buttonhole machine. Between 1880 and 1890, the number of men's clothing factories doubled from 736 to 1,554, and women's cloak factories tripled from 236 to 740. The center of this growing new industry was New York City. Between 1880 and 1910, the number of clothing factories jumped from 10 percent of the city's factories to 47 percent, and garment workers from 28 percent to almost half of its industrial workers.[28]

German Jews, called *Yahudim* by the Russian Jews, had initially dominated the garment industry. Having come to America earlier, many of them had established themselves economically and socially by the time of the great Jewish migration from Russia. German-Jewish firms like Blumenthal Brothers, Kuppenheimers, and Hart, Schaffner & Marx were prominent in clothing manufacturing. Gradually, many Jewish newcomers from Russia became contractors and manufacturers themselves. Together, the German and Russian Jewish garment makers revolutionized the way clothes were made and what Americans wore. In his novel, Cahan described this triumph: "Foreigners ourselves, and mostly unable to speak English, we had Americanized the system of providing clothes for the American woman of moderate or humble means." The Jewish garment makers had democratized dress in America, offering the masses machine-made classy clothes. They had done away with "prohibitive prices and greatly improved the popular taste. Indeed, the Russian Jew had made the average American girl 'a tailor-made' girl."[29]

To meet their labor needs, Jewish entrepreneurs formed a network to hire immigrant Jews — the "army of tailors." After leaving Castle Garden, David Levinsky and a fellow immigrant found themselves in "a great strange city," and as they walked toward State Street, a voice hailed them in Yiddish. A prosperous-looking gentleman asked: "You're a tailor, aren't you?" And Levinsky's companion nodded: "I'm a ladies' tailor, but I have worked on men's clothing, too." The gentleman said that he had work for him and that he should come along. "As I learned subsequently," Levinsky commented, "the man who accosted us on State Street was a cloak contractor, and his presence in the neighborhood of Castle Garden was anything but a matter of chance. He came there quite often, in fact, his purpose being to angle for cheap labor among the newly arrived immigrants."[30]

This cloak contractor represented a growing group of Jewish entrepreneurs in the booming garment industry. In 1914, about 60 percent of the businesses were small shops, employing fewer than thirty workers. Contractors did not need much capital, only about $50, to start shops with foot-powered machines. Once their workers and machines were in place, they could bid for contracts from the manufacturers. Competition was fierce: "Normally there was not enough work to go around, so each of the tailors would bid rock-bottom in order to get the work at all. In a number of cases, the bidding was done away with altogether. The employer simply offered the bundles and paid [the contractor] for them after they were completed, just as little as he saw fit." "The shop was not the manufacturer's," wrote Cahan, describing the place where Levinsky worked. "It belonged to one of his contractors, who received from him 'bundles' of material which his employees . . . made up into cloaks or jackets. The cheaper goods were made entirely by operators; the better grades partly by tailors, partly by operators, or wholly by tailors; but these were mostly made 'inside,' in the manufacturer's own establishment." The nature of the industry pushed both workers and contractors. The laborers dared not stop working, "knowing that there were plenty of other men ready instantly to take their places," journalist Ray Stannard Baker explained; "and the contractor, himself the victim of frightful competition and the tool of the manufacturer, always playing upon their ready fears, always demanding a swifter pace, forced the price constantly downward."[31]

To increase production, many contractors employed the task system, assigning a quota to a team of ten or twenty workers — family members, boarders, or *lanslite,* neighbors from the old country. They worked as a unit, with specific tasks assigned to a sewing-machine operator, a baster, a presser, and a finisher. A team received a group wage based on the number of garments produced, with each member paid a certain percentage. This system drove everyone on the team, for each worker wanted to increase the pace of production for the group. "The highest speed of one was in substance made the minimum speed of others," an immigrant worker explained, "since no man could get ahead in his work without his fellow workmen keeping the same speed in the productive formation." Larger shops employed the "section" system of production: work was subdivided into several steps, and workers performed one task repeatedly. This system reduced skilled tailors and seamstresses to assembly-line workers. "When I came here," complained Bella Feiner, "I knew more than I know now. I knew how to make a whole dress." But this fragmentization of production also opened employment to unskilled immigrants. "The foreman asked me what I could do," remembered Lottie Spitzer. "And I said, 'I don't know anything.' In fact, I couldn't even handle a needle. But he taught me and [soon] I was basting sleeve linings." The list of specialized jobs in the shirtwaist industry, according to historian Susan A. Glenn, was long:

> sleeve makers
> body makers
> closers (side seams and hems)
> sleeve setters
> shirt makers

> belt makers
> joiners (join skirt and waist)
> hemstitchers
> tuckers
> hemmers
> lace runners
> trimmers
> binders
> buttonhole makers
> buttonhole markers
> button setters
> collar makers
> cuff makers
> collar setters
> machine embroiderers[32]

Everywhere, clothing workers could be seen inside the factories that filled the Lower East Side, like a huge, spreading industrial beehive. On the Second Avenue elevated train, a passenger could ride half a mile through the garment district. "Every open window of the big tenements, that [stood] like a continuous brick wall on both sides of the way, [gave] you a glimpse of one of these shops. . . . Men and women bending over their machines or ironing clothes at the window, half-naked. . . . Morning, noon, or night, it [made] no difference." From block after block of sweatshops came the "whir of a thousand sewing-machines, worked at high pressure from the earliest dawn till mind and muscle [gave] out together." Family members, from the youngest to the oldest, labored in "qualmy rooms, where meals [were] cooked and clothing washed and dried besides, the livelong day."[33]

In the sweatshops, the work was physically punishing. The section system gave the bosses power to set the pace of their workers, who sat in long rows with their "bodies bent over the machines." Each person completed an assigned task and then passed her part of the garment to the next worker on the line, while the foreman nagged them to hurry. "Most of them smoke cigarettes while they work," observed a contemporary; "beer and cheap whiskey are brought in several times a day by a peddler. Some sing Yiddish songs — while they race. The women chat and laugh sometimes — while they race." But many women were forced to work silently. "We were like slaves. You couldn't pick your head up. You couldn't talk. We used to go to the bathroom. The forelady used to go after us, we shouldn't stay too long."[34]

"The machines were all in a row. And it was so hot, not even a decent fan. And you . . . worked, and you sweated. Windows were open, of course; flies too. You had a little half hour for lunch (we worked close to ten hours). And you talked. But you were kept so busy and the machines were roaring. . . . You had to be careful not to stitch your fingers in." Accidents did happen. "The machines go like mad all day, because the faster you work the more money you get. Sometimes in my haste, I get my finger caught and the needle goes right through it. It goes so quick, though, that it does not hurt much. I bind the finger up with a piece of cotton and go on working. . . . Where the needle goes through the nail it makes a sore finger, or where it splinters a bone it does much harm."[35]

The long hours and the repetitious stitching made workers feel like appendages of their sewing machines. "You don't have to think," said Mollie Wexler, who worked in a dress factory. All you have to do is "pin together and put together," "just sit and shoot like the machine itself." Anzia Yezierska related a story about a young Jewish woman who had "dreamed of free schools, free colleges" where she could learn to give out her "innermost thoughts and feelings" to the world. But no sooner had she come off the ship than hunger drove her to the sweatshop, "to become a 'hand' — not a brain — not a soul — not a spirit — but just a 'hand' — cramped, deadened into a part of the machine." A Yiddish poet described the numbness workers felt as they toiled, trapped in the sweatshops:

I work, and I work, without rhyme, without reason —
produce, and produce, and produce without end.
For what? and for whom? I don't know, I don't wonder
— since when can a whirling machine comprehend?

No feelings, no thoughts, not the least understanding;
this bitter, this murderous drudgery drains
the noblest, the finest, the best and the richest,
the deepest, the highest that living contains.

Away rush the seconds, the minutes and hours;
each day and each night like a wind-driven sail;
I drive the machine, as though eager to catch them,
I drive without reason — no hope, no avail.[36]

The workday was long, from eleven to fifteen hours. "My work was sewing on buttons. While the morning was still dark I walked into a dark basement. And darkness met me when I turned out of the basement." The workers had to wait until night to begin living. "At the end of the day one feels so weak that there is a great temptation to lie right down and sleep," said a seamstress. "But you must go out and get air, and have some pleasure. . . . Sometimes we go to Coney Island, where there are good dancing places, and sometimes we go to Ulmer Park to picnics. I am very fond of dancing, and, in fact, all sorts of pleasure."[37]

Daughters of the Colony

Thousands of these garment workers were young women. Many of them had come first, before their families. "In growing numbers," observed historian Susan A. Glenn, "Jewish families were willing and found it practicable to send one or more children including their working-age daughters, in advance." What made it "practicable" to send them ahead was the fact that many possessed sewing skills. In the Pale of Settlement in the 1890s, over fifty thousand Jewish women worked in the sewing trades, constituting 70 percent of all registered female artisans. The first sewing machines had been introduced in Russia two decades earlier, and the Singer sewing machine came to symbolize guarantee of a good livelihood. Fannie Shapiro recalled that in each small Russian town there were little shops where "two, three, four, or five girls in a house, [were] working, making dresses and things. And they had a Singer's, a sewing machine." Girls reaching the age of thirteen were usually apprenticed to a seamstress. One of them, Sarah Rozner, had to work hard to learn how to operate the sewing machine: "I finally got it, and believe me it helped a lot when I came to this country."[38]

In America, most of the young Jewish women working in the garment industry were single, planning to work for a few years before marriage. One of them told an interviewer: "Henry has seen me home every night for a long time and makes love to me. He wants me to marry him, but I am not seventeen yet, and I think that is too young. . . . Lately he has been urging me more and more to get married — but I think I'll wait." In 1910, over 70 percent of the Jewish daughters sixteen years old or over were working for wages. "Right after Passover, I entered school," remembered one of them. "When school was out in June, I knew I couldn't go back any more, so coming home I cried all the way. . . . My father had a job for me. I couldn't do any thing — at that age, you know, you couldn't work till you were sixteen, but kids worked at fourteen and thirteen."[39]

Constituting over one-third of the garment industry's work force in 1910, these young women labored in dangerous and cramped conditions. In these sweatshops, they were literally packed together. On floor after floor, they worked elbow to elbow at sewing machines on row after row of long tables. "We are so crowded together that there is not an inch of space," they complained. "The machines are so close together that there is no way to escape in case of immergansie [*sic*]."[40]

An emergency did happen on March 26, 1911, when a fire suddenly exploded at the Triangle Shirtwaist Company. Eight hundred workers, mostly young women, were trapped in the burning building. "A stream of fire tore up through the elevator shaft and stairways to the upper floors. Fire instantly appeared at all windows, and tongues of flames crept higher and higher along the walls to where little groups of terrified girls, workers, stood in confusion." Screaming, struggling, they jumped from windows, some from the ninth floor, their bodies smashing on the sidewalks. "One girl after another fell, like shot birds, from above, from the burning floors," wrote Morris Rosenfeld in his account based on eyewitness reports. "They hit the pavement just like hail," a fireman at the scene reported. "We could hear the thuds faster than we could [see] the bodies fall." Jumping from the higher floors, the girls came down with such force that they tore the nets from the grasps of firemen or snapped the cords. Unable to escape, 146 young workers — mostly Jewish and Italian — died in the smoke and heat of the inferno. There were so many bodies they could not be all taken away in ambulances and patrol wagons; grocers and peddlers offered their wagons and pushcarts.[41]

Mothers rushed to the scene where they saw the blackened bodies of their daughters laid out on the sidewalks. Tearing their hair, they screamed: *"Oy vey, kindenyu!"* "Oy vey, my child!" "For a piece of bread, a terrible death, robbed me of my only child." "My little girl lies dead, shrouds instead of a wedding gown." The tragedy stunned the colony: fifty thousand people marched silently in a mass memorial parade to grieve for their dead daughters. The charred bodies were buried together in the Workmen's Circle Cemetery.

> *Over whom shall we weep first?*
> *Over the burned ones?*
> *Over those beyond recognition?*

Over those who have been crippled?
Or driven senseless?
Or smashed? . . .
This is our funeral,
These our graves,
Our children. . . .[42]

News of the horror rapidly spread to the shtetls of Russia. "I still remember what a panic that news caused in our town when it first came," said Elizabeth Hasanovitz. "Many a family had their young daughters in all parts of the United States who worked in shops. And as most of these old parents had an idea of America as one big town, each of them was almost sure that their daughter was a victim of that terrible catastrophe." In his description of the grisly scene, a reporter wrote: "I looked upon the dead bodies and I remembered these girls were the shirtwaist makers. I remembered their great strike of last year in which the same girls had demanded more sanitary conditions and more safety precautions in the shops. Their dead bodies were the answer."[43]

Indeed, many of the dead women had gone out on strike in 1909–10, participating in the famous "uprising of twenty thousand." In July, a spontaneous strike had erupted at Rosen Brothers, and then in September at Leiserson's and the Triangle Shirtwaist Factory. The striking women asked for assistance from the Ladies' Waist Makers Union Local 25. With only a hundred dues-paying members and four dollars in its treasury, Local 25 appealed to the International Ladies' Garment Workers' Union, requesting a call for a general strike in the shirtwaist industry. But the ILGWU, founded in 1900, had only a few thousand members and lacked the resources to mobilize such a massive action.

The power to do so had to come from the people themselves. On the night of November 22, thousands of workers crowded into Cooper Union to attend a mass meeting organized by the striking women. They had come to demonstrate their support for the strikers and to denounce the intransigence of the bosses and the brutality inflicted against the picketers by hired thugs and the police. In the packed hall, their bodies restless and taut with anger, they heard speaker after speaker advise them to be patient and act cautiously. Frustrated by the urgings of restraint, a fragile-looking teenager suddenly rushed to the platform. "I am a working girl," Clara Lemlich declared in Yiddish, "one of those striking against intolerable conditions." The charismatic leader passionately articulated the pent-up feelings of the audience. She compared the abuse of the garment workers to the experience of blacks: "[The bosses] yell at the girls and 'call them down' even worse than I imagine the Negro slaves were in the South." She urged action: "I am tired of listening to speakers who talk in generalities. What we are here for is to decide whether or not to strike. I offer a resolution that a general strike be declared — now." Her brave words and her call to action touched off a thunderous applause in Cooper Union. Meeting chairman Benjamin Feigenbaum jumped to the platform and joined hands with Lemlich. Their arms held high together, he asked the crowd in Yiddish to support her call for a general strike, framing it as a Jewish struggle: "Do you mean faith? Will you take the old Jewish Oath?" Aroused, the people raised their right hands and pledged: "If I turn traitor to the cause I now pledge, may this hand wither from the arm I now raise." The next morning, fifteen thousand shirtwaist workers were on strike.[44]

"The East Side was a seething mass of excited women, girls, and men." Strikers attending packed meeting halls spilled out into the streets. "All over the East Side a sea of excited faces, a mass of gesticulating women and men, blocked the streets." "Vast crowds" were "wildly demonstrative," marching through the streets and breaking into "storms of applause as the word that another boss had settled with the strikers was passed along." The strikers swelled in numbers, to over twenty thousand: they were overwhelmingly Jewish, with Italian women constituting about 6 percent. The demands of the strikers included a fifty-two-hour week, overtime pay, and union recognition.[45]

As they picketed, the strikers were arrested by the police and beaten by thugs. Still, according to one contemporary, "neither the police, nor the hooligan hirelings of the bosses nor the biting frost and chilling snow of December and January damped their willingness to picket the shops from early morn till late at night."

In the black winter of 1909
When we froze and bled on the picket line
We showed the world that women could fight
And we rose and we won with women's might.

Hail the waist makers of 1909
Making their stand on the picket line
Breaking the power of those who reign
Pointing the way and smashing the chain.

The courageous strikers impressed the community: they were proudly described as *"unzere vunderbare farbrente meydlekh,"* "our wonderful fervent girls." The strike was powerful, intimidating, and by February, more than 300 of the some 450 firms in the New York industry had been forced to make some kind of settlement.[46]

Several months later, another strike exploded as fifty thousand cloak and suit workers walked off their jobs. The strikers wanted higher wages, a forty-nine-hour week, and a "closed shop," or the hiring of union members only. Both sides reached agreement in September with the signing of a "Protocol of Peace." Among the gains the workers received were a fifty-hour week, wage increases, and preferential hiring for union members.[47]

These labor struggles represented a watershed in Jewish-American history. They initiated "a decade of labor unrest in the garment trades," noted historian Susan A. Glenn. "Between 1909 and 1920 a wave of strikes and mass organizational campaigns swept through the garment trades, changing a largely unorganized industry into a union stronghold. . . . [B]y the end of World War I clothing workers were among the best-organized members of the American labor force." The International Ladies' Garment Workers' Union had 100,000 dues-paying members in 1920, and 170,000 workers belonged to the Amalgamated Clothing Workers of America, a union for semiskilled laborers.[48]

These labor triumphs had ethnic as well as class significance. In their struggles, the workers had created a broadly based radical Jewish consciousness. "Until now there had been no more than a large scattering of Jewish immigrant workers who would sometimes cohere for a fierce outbreak and then crumble into isolated persons," Irving Howe noted. "The Jewish community in the United States was not really a Jewish community," remarked leftist Paul Novick, "it was just something in fermentation until the labor movement came along." Like the Japanese strikes in Hawaii and the Mexican strikes in Arizona, these strikes in New York were ethnic strikes: Jewish workers received support and sustenance from the Jewish community. Jewish neighborhood organizations donated food and clothing, and Jewish shopkeepers allowed striking workers and families to purchase goods on credit. Family members and boarders were all Jewish, involved in a common struggle, sharing news about the exploitative labor conditions and the strikes. "All the boarders were *landsleit*," an immigrant remembered. "The major topics most frequently bantered about concerned the union meetings and sometimes . . . strikes in the needle trades in which everyone worked." The "uprisings" of this era sharpened a shared sense of ethnicity, an immigrant Jewish identity in America.[49]

Up from Greenhorns: Crossing Delancey Street

The Jews had come to make new homes in America, and their strikes had given them a sense of belonging to the new land. They were making a claim on their adopted country and demanding wages that would allow them to enjoy the bounties of America. Their labor struggles, while springing from ethnic solidarity, were also transforming them from "greenhorns" into Americans.

"*Oysgrinen zikh,*" Jewish immigrants said to themselves, "Don't be a greenhorn." When they arrived in America, they were foreigners in their dress, language, and thinking. "I just didn't know how to cope with it all," a Jewish immigrant recalled. "I was unhappy because I didn't know anything, and I was frightened. . . . When they used to call me names like 'greenhorn,' I felt that I would rather die than hear it again."[50]

The passion to become American was reflected in one of the most frequently asked questions in the Lower East Side: "How long have you been in America?" "How long" was measured by their degree of assimilation. The Jewish immigrants began learning American ways in a process they called "purification." To become American meant to acquire "civility" — a quality of middle-class refinement in behavior and tastes. According to scholar John Cuddihy, they had been driven by the pogroms in Russia "out of their Middle Ages into the Anglo-American world of the *goyim* 'beyond the pale.' " In America, they were swept into a process of modernization, civilization, and assimilation.[51]

This process required what Cuddihy termed the "price of admission": they had to give up certain customs and cultural traits that had been tied to their ethnicity. Wearing the proper clothing was crucial in acquiring the appearance of civility. "I was such a greenhorn, you wouldn't believe," said Sophie Abrams. "My first day in America I went with my aunt to buy some American clothes. She bought me a shirtwaist . . . a blue print with red buttons and a hat, such a hat I had never seen. I took my old brown dress and shawl and threw them away! . . . When I looked in the mirror, I couldn't get over it. I said, boy, Sophie, look at you now. Just like an American." Immediately after arriving in the Lower East Side, Cahan's Levinsky noticed that the people were better dressed than people back home. "The poorest-looking man wore a hat (instead of a cap), a stiff collar and a necktie, and the poorest woman wore a hat or bonnet." Passersby looked at Levinsky and exclaimed: "There goes a green one!" The remark stung him, for he understood what they were implying: "We are not, of course. We are Americanized." Shortly afterward, a friend bought Levinsky a suit, hat, handkerchiefs, collars, shoes, and a necktie. "That will make you look American," said his benefactor. Levinsky gazed at himself in the mirror, "bewildered," scarcely recognizing himself in his "modern" makeup.[52]

Language was also an indicator of assimilation. In Russia, most Jews had made no effort to learn the dominant language, but as immigrants in America they were eager to learn English. "Today," observed a resident of New York's Jewish community in 1905, "English is more and more the language spoken on the East Side, whereas eight years ago it was rare to hear that tongue. . . ." In a letter to the *Jewish Daily Forward*, a mother complained about her daughter who had preceded her family to America: "During the few years she was here without us she became a regular Yankee and forgot how to talk Yiddish. . . . She says it is not nice to talk Yiddish and that I am a greenhorn." As a student at a public evening school, Levinsky was impressed by his teacher's facility in English: "I would hang on his lips, striving to memorize every English word I could catch and watching intently, not only his enunciation, but also his gestures, manners, and mannerisms, and accepting it all as part and parcel of the American way of speaking." More than dress, Levinsky believed, good English was a requirement for assimilation: "People who were born to speak English were superior beings. Even among the fallen women I would seek those who were real Americans." The acquisition of English was a way for the immigrants to become "regular Yankees" and lessen the ethnic distance between themselves and native-born Americans.[53]

Dress and language were part of the presentation of civility that seemed to allow Jews to be seen as Americans. On one occasion, in a fancy restaurant, Levinsky noticed a Jewish gentleman sitting at a nearby table. Actually, he was a butcher, yet he was "refined-looking," with matching vocabulary and manners. "He fascinated me," Levinsky said. "His cultured English and ways conflicted in my mind with the character of his business. I could not help thinking of raw beef, bones, and congealed blood. I said to myself, 'It takes a country like America to produce butchers who look and speak like noblemen.' "[54]

The quest to become American also led to the changing of names. "They [immigrant Jews] themselves seemed ready to accept the idea that they were nobodies," recalled the son of an immigrant. "They were so scared that they even dropped the pride of a family name." Russian -*ski*s and -*vitch*es were dropped, and names like Levinsky became Levin.

But names were also anglicized: from Bochlowitz to Buckley, Jacobson to Jackson, and Stepinsky to Stevens. Many young people happily adopted "American" first names in school: Dvoirah became Dora; Hyman, Howard; Moishe, Morris; Breina, Beatrice; and Rivka, Ruth. "My Hebrew name being Maryashe in full, Mashke for short, Russianized in Marya (*Mary-ya*)," said Mary Antin, "my friends said that it would hold good in English as *Mary;* which was very disappointing, as I longed to possess a strange-sounding American name. . . ."[55]

American holidays and consumerism became popular in the Jewish colony. The Yiddish daily *Forward* noted that Jews enjoyed giving presents at Christmastime and that this practice was "the first thing" that demonstrated one was not a "greenhorn." For many newcomers, the goal was to become an "allrightnik," "the successful Jewish immigrant who adopted American habits, particularly habits of consumption, so thoroughly as to blend into the group of cosmopolitan Jews who had attained a high degree of cultural assimilation." Many Jewish immigrants, historian Andrew R. Heinze observed, felt a special, somewhat unique intensity in their urge to become assimilated. One way was to possess American consumer goods — to display a piano in the parlor and to dress fashionably. "Some of the women blame me very much because I spend so much money on clothes," said a garment worker. "But a girl must have clothes if she is to go into good society at Ulmer Park or Coney Island or the theater. Those who blame me are the old country people who have old-fashioned notions, but people who have been here a long time know better. A girl who does not dress well is stuck in a corner, even if she is pretty." Ownership of luxury goods "proclaimed silently that the newcomer was a prospective citizen, and not 'the wretched refuse' of Europe's 'teeming shore.' " By adapting to abundance, the immigrants were adopting America.[56]

Not to be a "greenhorn" also meant to take summer vacations at resorts, especially in the Catskill Mountains. Vacationing in this resort region had been popular among wealthy families, and some seventy thousand people retreated there in 1883. As Jewish immigrants settled in America, they began flocking to cottages and hotels in small towns like Tannersville and Hunter. "One of the latest fashions among the poor people of the East Side," the *Commercial Advertiser* reported in 1899, "is for the father of a family to send his wife and children to the mountains for the summer. Not that East Side prosperity has placed some of the luxuries within reach of the poor. On the contrary, board in the Catskills has come down to a point where the 'keep' of a workingman's family in a boardinghouse is almost as cheap as it is at home in the city." The resorts also offered opportunities to flaunt newly acquired accoutrements that trumpeted their success. "The only good thing about the Catskills is the fresh air," observed the *Forward* wryly, "but instead of taking advantage of it, the women sit on the porch like a fashion show, each one showing off her clothes and jewelry."

> *And here in the Catskills what do Jews believe?*
> *In* kosher, *certainly; in* Shabbes, *less,*
> *(But somewhat, for they smoke in secret then.)*
> *In* Rosh Hashanah *and in* Yom Kippur,
> *In charity and in America;*
> *But most of all in pinochle and poker,*
> *In dancing and in jazz, in risqué stories,*
> *And everything that's smart and up-to-date.*

As Jewish businessmen, wives, garment workers, teachers, shopkeepers, and children spent their summers in the Catskills, they participated in "a distinctly Jewish version of the American vacation," an extravagant custom "fulfilling the vision of the earthly paradise" that the immigrants had carried to America.[57]

One of the "allrightniks" who vacationed in the Catskills was David Levinsky. He had gone there like the others — the "cloak-manufacturers, shirt-manufacturers, ladies'-waist-manufacturers, cigar-manufacturers, clothiers, furriers, jewelers, leather-goods men, real-estate men, physicians, dentists, lawyers" and their families. In most cases, these vacationers were "people who had blossomed out into nabobs in the course of the last few years," Levinsky reported. "The crowd was ablaze with diamonds, painted cheeks, and bright-colored silks," "a babel of self-consciousness," a miniature of "parvenu smugness."[58]

To be American, Levinsky thought he had to become economically successful — like the well-bred American merchants. As he "rose" in class, becoming a wealthy garment manufacturer, Levinsky "paraded" his newly acquired manners, his neckties, and his English vocabulary. He projected his image of America onto his business, especially his advertising. His models were "all American girls of Anglo-Saxon origin." A young woman of the "other stock," Levinsky said, was "not likely to be built on American lines," with the exception of Scandinavian and Irish girls, who had "the American figure." But, for Levinsky, figure alone was not enough. "In selecting my model-girls, I preferred a good-looking face and good manners, and . . . good grammar."[59]

Still, Levinsky always felt insecure, uncertain about his own American identity. The Promised Land still seemed culturally far away, in the distance. For example, he had difficulty with American slang. This limitation was a source of frustration: "The Americans I met were so quick to discern and adopt these phrases it seemed as if they were born with a special slang sense which I, poor foreigner that I was, lacked. That I was not born in America was something like a physical defect that asserted itself in many disagreeable ways — a physical defect which, alas! no surgeon in the world was capable of removing." Levinsky also viewed his "Talmud gesticulations" as an ethnic habit that worried him like a "physical defect." He resented stories of the gesticulating Russian Jew — "the man who never opened his mouth when he was out of doors and it was too cold for him to expose his hands," or the "man who never spoke when it was too dark that his hands could not be seen." Levinsky tried to train himself to speak with his hands in his pockets.[60]

For Jewish men to be "American" meant to participate in the world of business. But for married Jewish immigrant women, it meant to stay at home. A government study conducted in 1907–08 found that only 8 percent of Russian-Jewish wives were wage-earners, compared with 17 percent for southern Italians. Actually, many Jewish wives had incomes — the rent from their boarders: 56 percent of Jewish immigrant households in 1911 had boarders. Wives could also work in family businesses, and many of them could be seen and heard hawking from pushcarts. "At the time when girls were married it was terrible [for them] to go to work. . . . [T]hat was forbidden," recalled an immigrant woman. "[But] if they worked in their own business, they could have worked day and night. . . ."[61]

Not encouraged, perhaps not even permitted to be wage-earning workers, the Jewish wife was expected to be a *baleboste,* an "owner of the home," taking care of domestic responsibilities such as preparing meals and paying the bills. "We were high class with low-class means," an immigrant daughter recalled. "We just didn't let a woman like my mother go to work, even if she wanted to." Marriage meant the end of working outside the home. "When I came here I was thirteen and a half," said Mollie Linker. At the age of fifteen years, she was working and took "almost three hundred people [out] on strike." "I got married at eighteen. . . . Then the babies came." Mollie Linker's father-in-law told her that as a mother it was "a shame to go to work." Similarly,

Ruth Katz recalled: "At the time I came [to America], the woman was home cooking and cleaning and raising the children. Women weren't supposed to go out and work. . . . That I think we brought from Europe, that a Jewish wife should not go to work."[62]

While the role of the *baleboste* was imported, staying home for Jewish wives and mothers represented an American adaptation. In Russia, it had reflected the traditional notion of the husband's economic importance; here it acquired a new veneer. An Old World tradition had become a signature of bourgeois success in the New World. Jewish wives were reluctant to work for wages partly because of "a breadwinner ethic," wrote historian Glenn. "Over time Jewish immigrants became increasingly sensitive to bourgeois notions of respectability." Seeking to identify themselves with "upwardly mobile, assimilated Americans," many insisted that a wife should "devote herself exclusively to her domestic obligations and leave the task of breadwinning to the husband." To have the luxury of not working meant that Jewish wives and their families were no longer "greenhorns" and that they had "made it" socially and economically. They had entered the world of "civility."[63]

But perhaps staying home for wives was not a sign, but a means of success for the next generation. Jewish women, sociologist Barry Chiswick argued, contributed to Jewish-American success through their role as mothers. They had lower rates of fertility as well as labor force participation than Protestant and Catholic women. Thus, by staying at home and caring for a smaller number of children, a Jewish mother was able to cultivate "higher child quality" and thus raise high achievers — successful students who qualified for elite universities like Harvard and Columbia. Though "much ridiculed by Jewish writers and entertainers," Chiswick concluded, Jewish mothers were instrumental in "the economic success of their children, in large measure, by making rational choices in favor of quality of child rather than quantity of children."[64]

Chiswick's homage was overly generous. The achievement of the Jewish mother, while it certainly existed, was more mystique than reality. Actually, the fertility rate for married Jewish women was not low: between 1880 and 1905, according to a survey, Italian families averaged 2.62 children per family, while Jewish families averaged 3.21. Furthermore, higher rather than lower child "quality" would be difficult, even problematic, to measure. Many Jewish women helped young Jewish men advance educationally, but they did so not as mothers but as wage-working sisters. After the Triangle Shirtwaist Factory fire, Elizabeth Dutcher of the Women's Trade Union League spoke to the families of the victims and was surprised to learn how much these young women had been contributing to family budgets. They had been "supporting old fathers and mothers, both in this country and abroad; mothering and supporting younger brothers and sisters, sending brothers to high school, to art school, to dental college, to engineering courses." In 1910, the income of working daughters amounted to nearly 40 percent of the family's yearly earnings.[65]

What was probably more important than mothers staying at home was the determination of both parents to have their children become professionals rather than peddlers, merchants, and garment factory workers. Jewish parents wanted their children to get out of blue-collar jobs and into white-collar employment, to have occupations "higher than the dirty work in a factory." Describing the Jewish commitment to education, the *Jewish Daily Forward* editorialized: "The Jew undergoes privation, spills blood, to educate his child. In [this] is reflected one of the finest qualities of the Jewish people. It shows our capacity to make sacrifices for our children . . . as well as our love for education, for intellectual efforts."[66]

Moreover, Jewish "success" was already underway *before* the education of the second generation. "Most New York City Jews did not make the leap from poverty to the middle class by going to college," historian Selma C. Berrol found. "Rather, widespread utilization of secondary and higher education *followed* improvements in economic status and was as much a result as a cause of upward mobility." As skilled workers, as unionized laborers, and as businessmen, many Jewish immigrants had already begun their "rise" and had the economic means to support the education of their children.[67]

The education of the second generation was another way for Jewish immigrants to make their claim on America. In her autobiography, Mary Antin sketched a moving portrait of her father as he took his children to school and handed the admission papers directly to their teacher. In the classroom, he stood "tall, straight . . . with his earnest face and fine forehead, nervous hands eloquent in gesture, and a voice full of feeling." He had brought his children to school "as if it were an act of consecration," and he regarded the teacher with reverence. "I think Miss Nixon guessed what my father's best English could not convey," Antin commented. "She divined that by the simple act of delivering our school certificates to her he took possession of America."[68]

The second generation took "possession" with a passion. All children in New York were required to attend school until the age of fourteen, but many Jewish students continued their education beyond this point. A 1910 survey of the working-class sections of New York City found that there were more Jews above the age of sixteen still in school than any other ethnic group. Soon Jewish students began crowding into the colleges and universities in New York and elsewhere on the East Coast. "The thirst for knowledge," the *New York Evening Post* reported in 1905, "... fills our city colleges and Columbia's halls with the sons of Hebrews who came over in steerage. . . ." By 1916, Jewish students were ubiquitous on college campuses in the city — 44 percent of the enrollment at Hunter College and 73 percent at City College. A government report noted how City College was "practically filled with Jewish pupils, a considerable proportion of them children of Russian or Polish immigrants on the East Side." Jewish students had also begun to enter Harvard, and by 1920 this elite school's population was 20 percent Jewish. To be at Harvard was certainly a sign they had arrived at the gates of civility and were no longer "greenhorns."[69]

But the increasing presence of Jewish students at Harvard provoked a backlash. In 1923, a writer for *The Nation* complained that the upwardly mobile Jew sent "his children to college a generation or two sooner than other stocks," and that consequently there were "in fact more dirty Jews and tactless Jews in college than dirty and tactless Italians, Armenians, or Slovaks."[70]

On campus, anti-Semitic murmurs and complaints swept across the yard. A dormitory at Harvard was called "Little Jerusalem" because of its large number of Jewish students. Expressions of resentment and ethnic epithets began to circulate: "Jews are an unassimilable race, as dangerous to a college as indigestible food to man." "They are governed by selfishness." "They do not mix. They destroy the unity of the college." "They memorize their books! Thus they keep the average of scholarship so high that others with a degree of common sense, but less parrot-knowledge, are prevented from attaining a representative grade."[71]

President Abbott Lawrence Lowell announced that the college had a "Jewish problem" and led efforts to curb their enrollment. "It is the duty of Harvard," he wrote privately in a letter to a member of the Board of Overseers on March 29, 1922, "to receive just as many boys who have come, or whose parents have come, to this country without our background as we can effectively educate; including in education the imparting, not only of book knowledge, but of ideas and traditions of our people. Experience seems to place that proportion at about 15%." In his view, Harvard College should be primarily a school for the native elite. Two months later, President Lowell expressed concern that what had happened to resort hotels could happen to Harvard: "The summer hotel that is ruined by admitting Jews meets its fate, not because the Jews it admits are of bad character, but because they drive away the Gentiles. . . . This happened to a friend of mine with a school in New York, who thought, on principle, that he ought to admit Jews, but discovered in a few years that he had no school at all. A similar thing has happened in the case of Columbia College. . . ."[72]

In a letter to the *New York Times* published in June, Lowell offered another reason why he felt it was important for Harvard to keep Jewish enrollment stable: "There is perhaps no body of men in the United States . . . with so little anti-Semitic feeling as the instructing staff of Harvard University. There is, most unfortunately, a rapidly growing anti-Semitic feeling in this country . . . fraught with very great evils for the Jews. . . ." Arguing that quotas would help reduce anti-Semitism on campus, Lowell continued: "The anti-Semitic feeling among students is increasing, and it grows in proportion to the increase in the number of Jews."[73]

Meanwhile, Harvard had instituted new admissions criteria and procedures. Reflecting a stereotype of Jewish students as overly studious and an awareness that most of them were from New York City, the new policies respectively stressed the need for well-rounded students and "regional balance" in order to "raise the proportion of country boys and students from the interior." In addition, for the first time in Harvard's history, applicants were required to submit a passport-sized photograph "for purposes of identification and for later use by the Dean's office." What was meant by "identification" and what that "use" would be were not explained. But it was known that some Jews had changed their family names, and it was thought that Jews could be identified by their "Semitic" facial features. After the establishment of these new policies, Jewish admissions to Harvard declined, fluctuating between 10 and 16 percent of each freshman class during the 1920s and 1930s.[74]

Not everyone agreed with President Lowell. At a banquet of the Bunker Hill Knights of Columbus, Boston's mayor James Curley criticized Harvard for seeking to bar students because of "an accident of birth." An Irish American, he denounced discrimination against the Jews: "God gave them their parents and their race, as he has given me mine. All of us under the Constitution are guaranteed equality, without regard to race, creed, or color." Then Mayor Curley warned: "If the Jew is barred today, the Italian will be to-morrow, then the Spaniard and Pole, and at some future date the Irish."[75]

Mayor Curley could see that the restrictions at Harvard were part of a larger nativist movement. In 1924, Congress passed a severely restrictionist immigration act. Among the bill's supporters was Harvard's President Lowell. The law established immigration quotas designed to reduce immigration from southern and eastern Europe. These quotas were based on 2 percent of the number of foreign-born persons of each nationality in the United States in 1890 — before the height of Jewish immigration. The principle of restricting immigration according to nationality, first introduced with the 1882 Chinese Exclusion Act, was now given broader application, and Jewish immigration sharply declined after 1924.

What made Jews seem threatening to American society was the integration of a culturally different group that was growing in numbers. "As the Jewish population increases," observed Abraham Cahan, "animosity grows with it. Nations love only themselves, not strangers. If we get too close to the Americans with our language and customs, they will be annoyed. . . . [T]he chasm between *shtetl* Jews and Yankees — it's like two different worlds. When there are only a few Jews, gentiles go slumming to inspect the novelty. When the Jews fill up the streetcars and parks, we are resented."[76]

Earlier, representing a small group, immigrant German Jews had been welcomed in American society. "Wherever there is a chance for enterprise and energy the Jew is to be found," declared the *Philadelphia Evening Telegraph* appreciatively in 1872. "He brings into every community wealth and qualities which materially assist to strengthen and consolidate its polity. . . . No other element in the community is so orderly."[77]

But as Russian-Jewish immigrants began arriving in massive waves, this favorable view quickly faded. "Numerous complaints have been made in regard to the Hebrew immigrants who lounge about Battery Park, obstructing the walks and sitting on the chairs," the *New York Tribune* reported in 1882. "Their filthy condition has caused many of the people who are accustomed to go to the park to seek a little recreation and fresh air to give up this practice." Because many of the new immigrants had become peddlers and businessmen, they were seen as Shylocks. In "a society of Jews and brokers," lamented Henry Adams in 1893, "I have no place." In *The Passing of the Great Race,* published in 1916, Madison Grant warned that the Jewish "dwarf stature, peculiar mentality, and ruthless concentration on self-interest" were being "engrafted upon the stock of the nation." During the 1920s, Henry Ford led an anti-Semitic campaign against "international Jews," whose loyalties were allegedly not to America but only to their greedy interests.

"Jewish financiers" were not building "anything," Ford argued, and Jewish labor leaders were organizing unions in order "to interrupt work." Anti-Semitism also surfaced among workers. "The Russian Jews and the other Jews will completely control the finances and Government of this country in ten years, or they will all be dead," a workingman declared in a letter to the *New York Sun* in 1895. "The hatred with which they are regarded . . . ought to be a warning to them. The people of this country . . . won't be starved and driven to the wall by Jews who are guilty of all the crimes, tricks, and wiles that have hitherto been unknown and unthought of by civilized humanity." At the street level, "Jew-baiting" frequently occurred as rowdies taunted, stoned, and pulled the beards of Jewish peddlers. Fourteen Jewish societies in Brooklyn protested in 1899: "No Jew here can go on the street without exposing himself to the danger of being pitilessly beaten."[78]

Ironically, the very success of Jews in America seemed to fuel anti-Semitism. The Jews "reaped more and more dislike as they bettered themselves," noted historian John Higham. "The more avidly they reached out for acceptance and participation in American life, the more their reputation seemed to suffer." "It is not the failure of Jews to be assimilated into undergraduate society which troubles them [President Lowell and the supporters of quotas]," observed Horace Kallen in 1923. "They do not want Jews to be assimilated into undergraduate society. What troubles them is the completeness with which the Jews want to and have been assimilated." Indeed, as second-generation Jews became educated and began seeking white-collar employment in gentile companies, they often encountered discrimination. Classified job listings sometimes specified "Christians only." Quality hospitals turned away Jewish doctors for internships, and prestigious law firms refused to hire Jewish lawyers. The doors to university faculty appointments were often closed to Jews. A young professor of literature at Columbia University, Lionel Trilling, was told by his chairman in 1936 that his department was not prepared to keep "a Freudian, a Marxist, and a Jew . . . at our kind of institution."[79]

Antagonism against Jews sharpened as they began moving out of the Lower East Side, closing the distances between them and gentile America. Seeking new homes in more middle-class areas, they often encountered restrictive covenants. Around the turn of the century, Jews began moving uptown to Harlem. "For rent" signs warned that they were not welcome: *"Keine Juden, und keine Hunde"* ("No Jews, and no Dogs"). But the Jews kept settling in Harlem, and one of its sections eventually came to be known as "Little Russia." "Calvary Presbyterian Church," the *New York Times* reported, "is now one of the prettiest little Jewish synagogues in . . . New York."[80]

During the 1920s, over 100,000 Jews left the Lower East Side, crossing Delancey Street and the other borders of the colony as they spread into the Bronx and Brooklyn. There, in "the wilds of the Bronx," the "country" at the end of a long subway ride, they could live on tree-lined streets still bordered by open fields and vacant lots. As a young boy, Michael Gold accompanied his father to see a house for sale in Brooklyn. "The suburb was a place of half-finished skeleton houses and piles of lumber and brick," he later wrote. "Paved streets ran in rows between empty fields where only the weeds rattled. Real estate signs were stuck everywhere. In the midst of some rusty cans and muck would be a sign shouting, 'This Wonderful Apartment House Site for Sale!' In a muddy pool where ducks paddled, another sign read: 'Why Pay Rent? Build Your House in God's Country.'" Similarly, Zalman Yoffeh recalled: "When I was nine years old, my mother heard of a wonderful bargain in the then sparsely-populated Brownsville [in Brooklyn] — four rooms with a private bathroom. We moved there."[81]

While it was not like the movement out of Egypt or Russia, another exodus had begun. "The young married people are going to the outlying districts of the Bronx and Brooklyn," observed a settlement house worker in 1925. "Their standards of living are higher than those of their parents. They seek better homes . . . for the price they can afford to pay." They wanted to leave the dingy and dirty alleys of the Lower East Side where some "greenhorns" still lived and to reside in "American" neighborhoods. "The immigrant ghetto from the beginning was entered into only to be abandoned," wrote historian Ben Halpern. "The generation that entered the immigrant ghetto was confronted by one overwhelming task: to get out, or to enable the next generation to get out."[82]

Many Jews managed to get out of the colony, but their migrations led to "concentrated dispersal." They settled together in the newer neighborhoods and suburbs of New York. During the 1920s, the percentage of New York's Jews living in neighborhoods that were at least 40 percent Jewish increased from 54 to 72 percent. This new residential pattern was shaped not only by anti-Semitic housing discrimination, but also by Jewish networks of friends and family who shared information about available housing in Jewish neighborhoods. Also assisting them in their quest for new homes were Jewish real estate brokers and Jewish builders. Russian-Jewish contractors, "with hosts of carpenters, bricklayers, plumbers," observed Abraham Cahan, built housing in the Bronx and Brooklyn. "Vast areas of meadowland and rock were turned by them, as by a magic wand, into densely populated avenues and streets of brick and mortar. Under the spell of their activity cities larger than Odessa sprang up within the confines of Greater New York in the course of three or four years."[83]

They were migrating again, this time from the Lower East Side. Years earlier, the Jewish immigrants had left the shtetls of Russia. They eagerly embraced the liminality of their adopted land, striving to become full individuals and a people free from persecution. But, as they made their place in the Promised Land called America, they fearfully watched the rise of an evil empire in Europe that would lead to a defining moment in Jewish history. A horror awaited their brethren, and the "discovery" of the Holocaust would never allow Jews in America or anywhere else to forget who they were. Their Jewish identity would be seared in their hearts.[84]

12

EL NORTE

The Borderland of Chicano America

T O THE JEWISH exiles, America was the Promised Land, and to the immigrants from Mexico, it was "El Norte." A land across the river, this country became the stuff of boundless dreams for Mexican migrants. In growing numbers during the early twentieth century, they began to cross their northern border. Like the Japanese immigrants who were arriving about the same time, many of them came with extravagant hopes. In their villages and towns where they had been born and expected to live out their lives, they welcomed their brothers and friends returning from the United States. Look, they exclaimed, at their "shoes and good suits of clothes." A song filled their imaginations with vivid images of success:

> *If only you could see how nice*
> *the United States is;*
> *that is why the Mexicans*
> *are crazy about it.*

> *Your watch is on its chain*
> *and your scarf-pin in your tie*
> *and your pockets always filled*
> *with plenty of silver.*[1]

In Santa Barbara, California, a Mexican recounted the immigration fever that had swept through entire villages. People wrote to friends and relatives back home: "Come! come! come over it is good here." The news set off a chain reaction that brought "others and others." In this way, just one person had led to the migration of twenty-eight families from his village. A land of promise in the north was beckoning. "Since I was very small I had the idea of going out to know the world, to go about a lot in every direction," Jesus Garza recalled. "As I had heard a lot about the United States it was my dream to come here."[2]

The Crossing

Such dreams created a tremendous pull to the north. "If anyone has any doubt about the volume of this class of immigrant," an American reporter wrote in 1914, "a visit to South Texas would reveal the situation. In a day's journey by automobile through that region one passes hundreds of Mexicans, all journeying northward on foot, on burroback and in primitive two-wheel carts. They are so numerous as to almost fill the highways and byways. When questioned many of them will tell you that they fled from Mexico to escape starvation. In a great number of instances the refugees have friends or relatives in this country who have told them of the wealth and prosperity of the wonderful ESTADOS UNIDOS."[3]

Unlike the immigrants from Asia and Europe, Mexicans could enter and leave without passports whenever they wished. "All you had to do coming from Mexico, if you were a Mexican citizen," recalled Cleofas Calleros, who came with his family in the early 1900s, "was to report at the immigration office on the American side . . . give your name, the place of your birth, and where you were going to." Actually, entry was even easier. Mexicans could simply walk across the shallow Rio Grande. A federal official observed: "These immigrants appear at the border in sombrero, sarape, and sandals, which, before crossing the river, they usually exchange for a suit of 'American' clothing, shoes, and a less conspicuous hat."[4]

This great migration to El Norte after 1900 was an extension of population movements already under way within Mexico. Rural workers and their families had begun migrating to urban centers. A contemporary noted that "a constantly increasing number of the peon class [were] moving to the industrial centers." But once in the cities, these workers found themselves trapped in a condition of cyclical unemployment as industries expanded and contracted. "The Mexican people, with industries dying and the land not being cultivated," Marcelo Villegas observed, "are crushed, starved, and driven out of their country."[5]

Meanwhile, in the late nineteenth century, large landholders and speculators were expropriating small farms and uprooting rural families. An 1883 land law allowed private land-development companies to receive up to one-third of any land they surveyed and subdivided. By the 1890s, about one-fifth of Mexico's entire land area had been transferred to these companies. "In almost every state of the central plateau," wrote historian Lawrence Cardoso, "not one acre of land remained for the rural peasantry." Forced to become tenant farmers and sharecroppers, the peasants became especially vulnerable to exploitation. "The owners gave us the seeds, the animals, and the land," recalled Elias Garza after he had moved to Los Angeles, "but it turned out that when the crop was harvested there wasn't anything left for us even if we had worked very hard. That was terrible. Those land owners were robbers." Class divisions sharpened and social discontent deepened. A peasant song protested:

> Our homes and humble dwellings
> always full of sadness
> living like animals
> in the midst of riches.
> On the other hand, the haciendados,
> owners of lives and lands,
> appear disinterested
> and don't listen to our complaints.[6]

In 1910, this frustration and anger exploded in the Mexican Revolution. In the struggle against the Porfirio Díaz regime, Francisco Madero sparked optimism for reform and improved economic conditions. A *corrido* celebrated the rebellion:

> Mexico is very happy, people by the thousands are
> giving thanks;
> I will begin with Durango then Torreón and Ciudad Juárez;
> where the blood of government soldiers was seen to
> flow.
> Girls of Ciudad Juárez, you were greatly startled

313

> *to find yourselves in so many skirmishes, in so many*
> *battles,*
>> *to see the 'maderistas' setting up their machine guns.*[7]

After toppling the Díaz government in 1911, Madero was overthrown by General Victoriano Huerta. Then Huerta was forced into exile, and warring factions plunged the country into chaos and violence. General Alvaro Obregón and Venustiano Carranza were now pitted against Pancho Villa and Emiliano Zapata. Civil war spread across Mexico. After Tijuana was captured by rebel forces, a witness described a refugee camp: "Often whole families [were] herded under one bit of canvas stretched out to shelter them. . . . Many poor women walked all the eighteen miles into San Diego, carrying babies in their arms." Military clashes were fierce and bloody. "There was real fighting and we kept fighting until we got to the capital when the wide-trousered bandit Emiliano Zapata finally entered," Luis Murillo recalled. "We were then completely defeated and were disbanded." Civilians and soldiers were killed by the hundreds of thousands. A song cried out for peace:

> *We understand that*
> *the war is among brothers;*
> *although we are of different political beliefs,*
> *we are all Mexicans. . . .*
> *Let's try to end the war.*[8]

But the civil war seemed endless, forcing tens of thousands of refugees to flee northward in search of safety. "We were running away from the rebellion," said Jesus Moreno, who arrived in Los Angeles with his family in 1915. "There were a lot of people coming to that city [El Paso] because of the Revolution. . . . We came to the United States to wait out the conclusion of the Revolution. We thought it would be over in a few months." Pablo Mares of Jalisco recounted how he was almost shot: "He [a soldier] just missed killing me and that was because another soldier hit his arm and the bullet lodged in the roof of the house. . . . The Villistas pressed me into the service then, and took me with them as a soldier. But I didn't like that, because I never liked to go about fighting, especially about things that don't make any difference to one. So when we got to Torreon I ran away just as soon as I could." Mares escaped across the border. "I had to come to the United States, because it was impossible to live down there with so many revolutions."[9]

These political refugees had planned to return to Mexico. "I would rather cut my throat before changing my Mexican nationality," explained Carlos Ibáñez. "I am only waiting until conditions get better, until there is absolute peace before I go back." But the waiting stretched into years and years. "Of course I have never thought of changing my citizenship," sighed Fernando Sánchez in the 1920s, "but the truth is that I don't know when I will go back to Mexico for things are getting worse there day by day on account of the revolutions."[10]

Meanwhile, the civil war was devastating the economy. All over Mexico, mines and factories were being shut down. One man recalled how he "looked for work for a long time but everything had stopped, factories, mills, everybody was without work. With the farms burned there weren't even any tortillas to eat. . . ." Inflation, a constant problem, had worsened during the revolution. Between July 1914 and July 1915, the price of corn and beans jumped 2,000 percent. A song complained about the soaring cost of food:

> Now what the people ask . . .
> Is that prices are lowered in
> Every part of the nation.
> Earnings are not enough to live on
> Because everything is so expensive.[11]

Pushed from Mexico by poverty and the horror of war, migrants were pulled to El Norte. Essentially, they were searching for work and following wages. "We left Durango because work was very scarce," Pedro Villamil recalled, "and we were told that one could get good money in the United States and there was work for whoever wanted it." An immigrant construction worker in Santa Barbara explained: "Where I came from I used to work ten hours for $1.25. . . . Then I came here and they paid $1.25 for eight hours — it was good." "It is only natural," *El Paso del Norte* commented, "that the 'Supreme Law of Necessity' obliges all these people to emigrate to a foreign land in search of higher wages. . . ." A contemporary reported that there was a "steady drift of labor from south to north," drawn by American wages two to three times higher than wages in Mexico. Carlos Ibáñez explained he was paid so little for his labor in Zacatecas that he did not "even remember how much it was." So he decided to leave America "in search of fortune" in California.[12]

What accelerated the movement of Mexicans to the United States was the development of transportation: in 1895, the Mexican International Railroad had extended a line 900 miles into Mexico, linking the Texas border town of Eagle Pass with Durango. The railroad triggered a mass migration. "There is not a day in which passenger trains do not leave for the border, full of Mexican men who are going in gangs to work on railroad lines in the United States," reported a Mexican newspaper in 1904. An American visitor observed that railroad cars containing as many as two hundred Mexican laborers each were transporting men who were "leaving the country against the will of the government and the desire of the landowners." "Each week five or six trains are run from Laredo," the *Los Angeles Times* reported in 1916, "carrying Mexicans who have been employed by labor agents, and similar shipments are being made from other border points."[13]

The train became the means and the metaphor of the migration. Traveling by rail overnight, the migrants traversed great geographical as well as cultural distances:

> *The fleeting engine*
> *Can't do anything good*
> *Because at dusk it is at home*
> *And at dawn in a strange country.*

When they woke up, they found themselves far from familiar sights and sounds:

> *Oh! What sadness!*
> *The Mexicans will have to see*
> *The railroad train*
> *That the Americans bring. . . .*

A somberness swept over them as they wondered where they were going and what the crossing of the border would mean:

> *Listen, listen,*
> *To the train puffing;*
> *The train which carries men away*
> *And never brings them back again.*[14]

The trains carried tens of thousands of Mexicans to El Norte. Most of them were from the agricultural labor class, and they were predominantly young — between the ages of fifteen and forty-four. They included women: either a man brought his family with him, or he migrated first to find a job and a place to live and then sent for his family. Between 1900 and 1930, the Mexican population in the Southwest grew from an estimated 375,000 to 1,160,000; the majority of them had been born in Mexico. About 25,000 crossed the border during the first decade; then another 170,000 between 1910 and 1920. The greatest surge occurred during the 1920s, when nearly half a million Mexicans arrived. Altogether one-tenth of Mexico's population migrated to El Norte. They settled in Texas, Arizona, New Mexico, and California, and spread as far away as Michigan and Illinois.[15]

Driven north by economic desperation, they had been painfully separated from their homeland:

> *Don't condemn me*
> *For leaving my country,*
> *Poverty and necessity*
> *Are at fault.*
> *Good-bye, pretty Guanajuato*
> *The state in which I was born.*
> *I'm going to the United States*
> *Far away from you.*

Affirming their attachment and love for Mexico, they vowed:

> *Good-bye, my beloved country,*
> *now I am going away. . . .*
> *I go to the United States*
> *to seek to earn a living.*
> *Good-bye, my beloved land;*
> *I bear you in my heart.*[16]

A Reserve Army of Chicano Labor

During the early twentieth century, Mexicans were encouraged to cross the border because their labor was needed. "I have had to work very hard where I have found work," said a Chicano, "whether it was on the railroad, in the cotton fields or beet fields, in the hotels as a waiter, as an elevator man, or in the asphalt." Indeed, Chicanos worked in a wide range of jobs.[17]

A rural people in Mexico, many of them became urban industrial workers in America. They were the primary manual work force in the construction industry. "In southern California and in Texas," a researcher found in 1908, "Mexicans do most of the excavating and road building, and are otherwise employed on public works." In 1928, a Texas official estimated that Mexicans represented about 75 percent of all construction labor in the state. Chicanos were hired mainly as manual laborers. White labor unions jealously protected the skilled jobs by creating a two-tiered labor market that reflected a racial division. "I have gone from one place to another working as a laborer," Policarpo Castro said in the 1920s, "for I haven't found anything else because the masons' union don't want to admit Mexicans. . . . But although I have worked as a laborer I have always tried to learn everything that I could. I have worked in cement, in a brick-yard, laying pipes . . . and have learned all that sort of work, even how to make entrances and walks for a garage with an incline. All that will do me some good in Mexico. . . . I know that if I want to amount to something in any work I will have to do it there in Mexico, because the Americans only despise us." A Chicano bluntly explained why he was not able to be a carpenter: "They [whites] wouldn't let me on account of my race — discrimination."[18]

In Los Angeles, 70 percent of the Chicanos were unskilled blue-collar workers in 1918, compared to only 6 percent for Anglos. "In . . . many communities," a journalist observed in 1929, "it is the Mexicans who do the common labor. In fact, we have imported them for that very purpose." In El Paso, only 5 percent of the Chicanos were in professional and managerial occupations in 1920, compared to 30 percent of the Anglos. "There were no Mexican men or women, boys or girls, working in the banks," Cleofas Calleros recalled. "American offices, like insurances offices . . . they never hired Mexicans." Most Chicano workers were "locked" into low blue-collar occupations. Mexican heads of households living in Santa Barbara in 1900, for example, were still employed in the same jobs thirty years later.[19]

The urban Chicano work force included women. Employed in garment factories, food-processing plants, and canneries, many of them were members of a family wage economy, pooling resources in order to put food on the table. "My father was a busboy," a Chicana cannery worker recalled, "and to keep the family going . . . in order to bring in a little more money . . . my mother, my grandmother, my mother's brother, my sister, and I all worked together at Cal San." But working together in El Norte was very different from what it had been in Mexico.

Here a "harsh cannery whistle" shattered the "air at midnight" or the "frozen black hours of the near dawn" to rouse the workers from their beds. Then they rushed to the cannery as they buttoned their clothes, their "teeth chattering all the way." Inside the cannery, they felt the cold of the salt wind as they cut the heads and guts from the sardines. The fish kept coming down the chute, and they had to work faster and faster. Finally, the "silver stream" stopped flowing, and they went home tired, splattered with fish blood. But they had some money to buy food and pay the rent.[20]

Chicanas were usually assigned to the worst jobs and received the lowest wages. Even where Mexican and Anglo women did the same work, they received different wages. In the Los Angeles garment factories, Chicana seamstresses were paid only $3 a day, compared to $4 for their Anglo counterparts. In laundries, Mexican women did the unskilled labor, while Anglo women were given the skilled and supervisory positions. A laundry worker, Guadalupe Espejo, explained to a labor commission in 1919: "I am getting $7 a week in collar machine. I have one dependent. My room rent is $5 a month; groceries cost $5.50 a week and I cannot buy a coat a year or one in two years. My clothing costs $10 to $12 a year and two pairs of shoes a year cost $4.50 a pair. . . . I think $15 a week would be needed to live on comfortably." Most Chicanas worked as servants, waitresses, cooks, and maids. Elizabeth Rae Tyson remembered the ubiquitous presence of Chicana maids in El Paso: "Owing to the large Mexican majority, almost every Anglo-American family had at least one, sometimes two or three servants. . . . The maid came in after breakfast and cleaned up the breakfast dishes, and very likely last night's supper dishes as well; did the routine cleaning, washing and ironing, and after the family dinner in the middle of the day, washed dishes again, and then went home to perform similar service in her own home." Unlike Irish domestic servants, Chicana maids did not generally work on a live-in basis.[21]

Chicanos migrated to midwestern and eastern cities where managers of factories and steel mills recruited them as a strategy to prevent strikes. "If there are a couple of thousand waiting for a job, those who are working won't strike." Low-paid Chicano labor also helped to drive wages down generally. More than nine hundred Chicanos worked in the steel mills of Bethlehem, Pennsylvania. "We encouraged some families to come," said an executive. "We thought if there were families the Mexicans would be happier. . . . We wanted the Mexicans to feel that they had a good community." Thousands of others went to Chicago, where they constituted 35 percent of the workers at Inland Steel and 6 percent of the packing-house laborers at Armour and Swift Company. These laborers were also on the automobile assembly lines of plants in Detroit, Flint, and Saginaw.[22]

Chicanos were also heavily employed by the railroad companies. "[They] are not subject to agitators," a labor supplier stated. "They're not organized. They're peaceable . . . and will work on the desert or anywhere the Santa Fe wants to put them." The chief engineer of the Santa Fe Railroad commented: "The Mexican cannot be driven like the Negro, but anyone who knows how to manage the Mexicans can get more work out of them than any other class." A federal official listed the reasons why Mexicans made good railroad workers: "As a laborer the Mexican immigrant is said to be unambitious, physically not strong, and somewhat [indigent] and irregular, but against this is put the fact that he is docile, patient, orderly in camp, fairly intelligent under competent supervision, obedient, and cheap. His strongest point with the employers is his willingness to work for a low wage."[23]

Actually, many Chicanos found they had no choice but to work on the railroads. "When I arrived there [San Antonio]," recalled Jesus Garza, "I looked for work but couldn't find any so I went to the agency of *renganches* and contracted to work. They said that I was to go and work on the *traque*. I didn't know what that was but I contracted to work because my money was giving out. I only had three dollars left. I gave one to the *renganchista*, and he then took me with a lot of Mexicans to a railroad camp." Laying railroad tracks was physically punishing work. "We worked on the tracks, taking up and laying down the rails, removing the old ties and putting in new, and doing all kinds of hard work," said Elias Garza. "They paid us $1.50 and exploited us without mercy in the Commissary camp, for they sold us everything very high." Chicano laborers became a common sight on the railroads of the Southwest. When Ernesto Galarza arrived in Sacramento, he noticed them on the tracks. "Our train began to make a great circle, slowing down," he remembered. "The roadbed carried the train higher than the roof tops, giving us a panorama of the city. Track crews standing by with the familiar brown faces of Mexicans waved to us."[24]

Most Chicanos, however, worked in agriculture. In California, farmers turned increasingly to Mexican labor as immigration laws such as the 1908 Gentlemen's Agreement and the 1924 Immigration Act excluded Asian labor. An official for the California Fruit Growers' Association praised the Mexican workers: unlike the Chinese and Japanese, they were "not aggressive." Instead, they were "amenable to suggestions" and did their work obediently. The Mexican, claimed Dr. George Clements of the Los Angeles Chamber of Commerce's Agricultural Department, "supplied all the qualities of the Chinaman and endeared himself to the heart of the agricultural people." "Due to their crouching and bending habits," the "oriental and Mexican" were suited to tasks in the fields, added Dr. Clements, while whites were "physically unable to adapt" themselves to such work. A cotton grower in California's Imperial Valley declared that the farmers needed Mexicans as stoop laborers: "We mean to get Mexicans for the work and get all we need." By the 1920s, at least three-fourths of California's 200,000 farm laborers were Mexican.[25]

Mexican agricultural labor also became indispensable in Texas. The state employment service estimated that of the 200,000 to 300,000 full-time migrant workers in the state, 10 percent were Anglo, 5 percent black, and 85 percent Mexican. "We couldn't do it if we didn't have the labor," an official of the San Antonio Chamber of Commerce announced. "Yes, sir, we are dependent on the Mexican farm-labor supply, and we know it. Mexican farm-labor is rapidly proving the making of this State." A newspaper described the widespread employment of Mexicans in agricultural work: "To meet the demand agents have been sent across the border into Mexico. . . . Many of those [recruited workers] going into the cotton fields of Texas are accompanied by their entire families. This is to the liking of the planters, for it is maintained that children as a rule will pick as much cotton as the grown-ups." Texas farmers repeatedly offered similar explanations for the widespread employment of Mexicans: "The white people won't do the work and they won't live as the Mexicans do on beans and tortillas and in one room shacks." "Whites cannot be as easily domineered, led, or directed as the Mexicans." "I prefer Mexican labor to other classes of labor. It is more humble and you get more for your money." "No other class we could bring to Texas could take his place. He's a natural farm laborer."[26]

Mexican agricultural workers were not being exploited, white farmers argued: they were being treated fairly and were choosing to do this work. One grower claimed that the Mexican was "free as a bird of the air. . . . There never lived a person in such freedom." "All his work is by contract," he added, "no one drives him, he can stop any time and roll his shuck cigarette and Lobo tobacco, and his pay is by the weight at the scales. There's . . . no oppression."[27]

But, in fact, Chicano workers were not so free. They found themselves in a labor market that had been deliberately oversupplied in order to force them to work from contract to contract for low wages. Most of them were also unable to travel from farm to farm in search of higher wages. Growers discouraged Mexicans from owning cars. "If they have their own cars," a Texas farmer stated, "they travel every week to see where the cotton is. If they have no way to move about, it is better." Chicanos with cars were regularly pulled over by the highway patrol and cited for motor vehicle violations. But, as historian David Montejano noted, the growers and police were often frustrated by "Mexican truck drivers, loaded with their cargo of Mexican laborers," usually driving at night, "through back roads, following a zig-zag course to the beet fields of Michigan." As they made their escape, they sang:

> Goodbye State of Texas
> with all your fields,
> I leave your land
> so I won't have to pick cotton.[28]

Mexican laborers often discovered they could not leave their employers because they had been driven into debt. "Some of the farmers here advance from $250 to $500 a year to Mexican families," a United States Employment Service official in San Antonio reported. "They use the debt as a club to keep them on the place. They bluff the Mexicans through fear of the law and personal violence." Mexican laborers occasionally found themselves facing the barrel of a gun. In 1915, Emilio Flores of the Mexican Protective Association testified before the Federal Commission on Industrial Relations: "When they [the Mexican laborers] sometimes refuse to comply, because of the promises of the employment agency at the border or at San Antonio, they are guarded until they work out what they owe. I have known a number of Mexicans to be chained in Gonzales County and guarded by armed men with shotguns and made to work these moneys out."[29]

Mexican laborers under contract were required to stay on the farm until they completed their work. If they broke their labor contracts, they were often arrested and jailed. Elias Garza told sociologist Manuel Gamio what had happened to him in 1912:

> In San Antonio, we were under contract to go and pick cotton in a camp in the Valley of the Rio Grande. A group of countrymen and my wife and I went to pick. When we arrived at the camp the planter

gave us an old hovel which had been used as a chicken house before, to live in, out in the open. I didn't want to live there and told him that if he didn't give us a little house which was a little better we would go. He told us to go, and my wife and I and my children were leaving when the sheriff fell upon us. He took me to jail and there the planter told them that I wanted to leave without paying him for my passage. He charged me twice the cost of transportation, and though I tried first not to pay him, and then to pay him what it cost, I couldn't do anything. The authorities would only pay attention to him, and as they were in league with him they told me that if I didn't pay they would take my wife and my children to work. Then I paid them.[30]

In the Southwest, agricultural labor became virtually synonymous with Mexican labor, and Mexican wages with "cheap" wages. Chicano laborers in the Imperial Valley of California, for example, were paid 50 cents to $1 less per day than their white counterparts. Similarly, in Texas, Chicano laborers were paid lower wages than white workers for the same type and amount of work. Chicanos were also shut out of the more skilled jobs such as machine operators. Farmers in California told Taylor that "only a small minority of Mexicans" were "fitted for these types of labor at the present time."[31]

Chicanos were confined to the routine and backbreaking jobs in the field. Rosaura Valdez described how much work it took to pick a hundred pounds of cotton: "I'd have a twelve foot sack, about this wide. I'd tie the sack around my waist and the sack would go between my legs and I'd go on the cotton row, picking cotton and just putting it in there. . . . So when we finally got it filled real good then we would pick up the sack, toss it up on our shoulders, and then I would walk, put it up there on the scale and have it weighed, put it back on my shoulder, climb up a ladder on a wagon and empty that sack in." Like the men, women worked in the fields, but they also had to raise the children and do the household chores. "I am an agricultural working woman," one of them explained. "I came to this camp with my husband and baby. . . . I have to go out to work with the men . . . , taking my baby with me. When we finish work at suppertime, I have to do the cooking and wash the dishes. . . . Really I am suffering doubly. There must be several thousand women like me in the fields."[32]

Farm work was seasonal and migratory, with Chicanos following the crops. "Each family traveling on its own, they came in trucks piled with household goods or packed in the secondhand *fotingos* [travel-worn Fords] and *chevees*. The trucks and cars were ancient models, fresh out of a used-car lot, with license tags of many states." Where they would be living at any given time was determined by where the jobs were. "We went to Calipatria [California] and the whole family of us engaged in cotton picking," said Anastacio Torres. "They paid very well at the time. They paid us $2.00 or $1.75 for every 100 pounds of cotton which we picked and as all of the family picked we managed to make a good amount every day. When the cotton crop of 1919 was finished we went to Los Angeles and then I got a job as a laborer with a paper manufacturing company. They paid me $3.40 a day for eight hours work. I was at that work for some time and then returned to the Imperial Valley for lemon picking."[33]

From California, many of the Chicano field hands went to Ohio, Indiana, Minnesota, Iowa, the Dakotas, and Michigan:

> In the year 1923
> Of the present era
> The beet-field workers went
> To that Michigan, to their grief,
> Because all the bosses
> Began to scold. . . .

They found sugar beet hand work to be "one of the most arduous and disagreeable of all agricultural occupations," for it was monotonous drudgery, "frequently performed in inclement weather, combined with the long hours of work and low earnings."[34]

Conditions in the migrant labor camps were squalid and degrading. "Shelters were made of almost every conceivable thing — burlap, canvas, palm branches," reported a minister describing a camp in the Imperial Valley. There were no wooden floors, and chicken yards adjoined the shelters. Next to the houses was a huge pile of manure with children tumbling in it as though it were a haystack. "There were flies everywhere. . . . We found one woman carrying water in large milk pails from the irrigation ditch. The water was brown with mud, but we were assured that after it had been allowed to settle that it would be clear and pure. . . . There were no baths." The growers felt no responsibility for the housing conditions or the welfare of their workers. They thought of Mexicans as "here today and elsewhere tomorrow." Commenting on the Mexican laborers, a farmer bluntly stated: "[When] they have finished harvesting my crops, I will kick them out on the country road. My obligation is ended."[35]

Feeling they were entitled to dignity as well as better working conditions and higher wages, Chicanos actively participated in labor struggles, especially during the Great Depression. Between 1928 and 1933, Mexican farm laborers in California had their wages cut from 35 cents to 14 cents an hour. In response, they supported strikes led by trade unions such as the Confederación de Uniones de Obreras Mexicanas (Confederation of Mexican Labor Unions) and La Union de Trabajadores del Valle Imperial (the Imperial Valley Workers' Union). Their labor militancy contradicted and challenged stereotypes of Mexican passivity. "The growers became genuinely alarmed," reported an investigator for the California Department of Industrial Relations during one of the strikes. "Heretofore they have been accustomed to considering the Mexican workers as bovine and tractable individuals, best adapted to the climatic conditions in the Imperial Valley and therefore the most desirable workers in the valley. The organization of a union of Mexican laborers seems to have evoked in the growers an ardent wish for its earliest demise."[36]

One of the most powerful Mexican strikes occurred in 1933 when twelve thousand laborers in the San Joaquin Valley resisted wage reductions. The mostly Mexican work force turned down the growers' wage rate of 60 cents per hundredweight of picked cotton and struck for a rate of $1. To break the strike, employers evicted the strikers from their camps and dumped their belongings on the highway; they also used the local police to arrest the strike leaders and disrupt the picket lines. "We protect our farmers here in Kern County," a deputy sheriff told an interviewer. "They are our best people. They are always with us. They keep the country going. They put us here and they can put us out again, so we serve them. But the Mexicans are trash. They have no standard of living. We herd them like pigs." The local media also joined the attack on the strikers. "If the strike continues, it is more than likely that every last one of you will be gathered into one huge bull pen," a newspaper threatened. "Many of you don't know how the United States government can run a concentration camp. . . . Do you want to face the bull pen? Do you want to be deported to Mexico?"[37]

Mexican strikers refused to be intimidated. Striking women were particularly active: they posted picket lines daily, the older women in rebozos and the younger women wearing flapper styles. They urged the strikebreakers to support their struggle. Don't be "sellouts!" they shouted. "Join the strike. We also have to eat and we also have family." One of those who joined the strikers, Lydia Ramos, described the tremendous sense of solidarity she felt: "We didn't know what union it was or who was organizing or nothing. We just knew that there was a strike and that WE were not going to break a strike." Asked why not, she answered: "Well, we believe in justice. So I want everything that's good for me and I want everything that's good for somebody else. Not just for them . . . but equality and justice. If you're going to break somebody's strike, that's just going against your beliefs." In the end, the strikers won a compromise wage rate of 75 cents per hundredweight.[38]

The strikes reflected a deep discontent and disappointment Chicanos felt in El Norte. Many felt they had been driven "crazy from working so much" and "squeezed" by their bosses until they had been left "useless." Juan Berzunzolo, for example, had come here in 1908 and worked on the tracks of the Southern Pacific and in the beet fields of Colorado. "I have left the best of my life and my strength here," he said, "sprinkling with the sweat of my brow the fields and factories of these gringos, who only know how to make one sweat and don't even pay attention to one when they see that one is old."[39]

The Internal Borders of Exclusion

Included as laborers, Mexicans found themselves excluded socially, kept at a distance from Anglo society. Like Caliban, they were isolated by the borders of racial segregation. Their world was one of Anglo over Mexican. Even on the large cattle ranches of Texas where Mexicans and Anglos lived together and formed loyalties and sometimes even friendships, integration did not mean equality. J. Frank Dobie, for example, described one of the workers on his family's ranch. This "old, faithful Mexican" had been employed on the ranch for over twenty years and he was "almost the best friend" Dobie had. "Many a time 'out in the pasture' I have put my lips to the same water jug that he had drunk from," he remembered fondly. But Dobie added: "At the same time neither he nor I would think of his eating at the dining table with me."[40]

Racial etiquette defined proper demeanor and behavior for Mexicans. In the presence of Anglos, they were expected to assume "a deferential body posture and respectful voice tone." They knew that public buildings were considered "Anglo territory," and that they were permitted to shop in the Anglo business section of town only on Saturdays. They could patronize Anglo cafés, but only the counter and carry-out service. "A group of us Mexicans who were well dressed once went to a restaurant in Amarillo," complained Wenceslao Iglesias in the 1920s, "and they told us that if we wanted to eat we should go to the special department where it said 'For Colored People.' I told my friend that I would rather die from starvation than to humiliate myself before the Americans by eating with the Negroes." At sunset, Mexicans had to retreat to their barrios.[41]

In the morning, Mexican parents sent their children to segregated schools. "There would be a revolution in the community if the Mexicans wanted to come to the white schools," an educator said. "Sentiment is bitterly against it. It is based on racial inferiority. . . ." The wife of an Anglo ranch manager in Texas put it this way: "Let him [the Mexican] have as good an education but still let him know he is not as good as a white man. God did not intend him to be; He would have made them white if He had." For many Anglos, Mexicans also represented a threat to their daughters. "Why don't we let the Mexicans come to the white school?" an Anglo sharecropper angrily declared. "Because a damned greaser is not fit to sit side of a white girl."[42]

In the segregated schools, Mexican children were trained to become obedient workers. Like the sugar planters in Hawaii who wanted to keep the American-born generation of Japanese on the plantations, Anglo farmers in Texas wanted the schools to help reproduce the labor force. "If every [Mexican] child has a high school education," sugar beet growers asked, "who will labor?" A farmer in Texas explained: "If I wanted a man I would want one of the more ignorant ones. . . . Educated Mexicans are the hardest to handle. . . . It is all right to educate them no higher than we educate them here in these little towns. I will be frank. They would make more desirable citizens if they would stop about the seventh grade."[43]

Serving the interests of the growers, Anglo educators prepared Mexican children to take the place of their parents. "It isn't a matter of what is the best way to handle the education here to make citizens of them," a school trustee in Texas stated frankly. "It is politics." School policy was influenced by the needs of the local growers, he elaborated. "We don't need skilled or white-collared Mexicans. . . . The farmers are not interested in educating Mexicans. They know that then they can get better wages and conditions." A Texas school superintendent explained that not all school boards wanted him to enforce compulsory attendance: "When I come to a new school I always ask the board if they want the Mexicans in school. Here they told me to leave them alone. If I tried to enforce the compulsory attendance law here the board would get sore at me and maybe cause us to lose our places, so I don't say anything. If I got 150 Mexicans ready for school I would be out of a job." Another Texas superintendent explained why schools should not educate Mexican children: "You have doubtless heard that ignorance is bliss; it seems that it is so when one has to transplant onions. . . . If a man has very much sense or education either, he is not going to stick to this kind of work. So you see it is up to the white population to keep the Mexican on his knees in an onion patch. . . ."[44]

Consequently, the curriculum for Mexican students emphasized domestic science and manual training. In Los Angeles, they were taught not only manual-labor skills, but also the appropriate attitudes of hard work and disciplined behavior. "Before sending [Mexican] boys and girls out to accept positions," a Los Angeles teacher explained, "they must be taught that, technically expert though they may be, they must keep in mind that their employers carry the responsibility of the business and outline the work, and that the employees must be pliant, obedient, courteous, and willing to help the enterprise."[45]

There were educators who saw that Mexican children were capable of learning. "The Mexicans have good minds and are earnest students," a teacher stated. "The Mexican children generally are as capable intellectually as the Americans, but the Mexicans are poorer than the whites, so the comparison of their present progress in school isn't fair." Some teachers tried to give Mexican children a sense of dignity and self-respect. Ernesto Galarza recalled how his school principal "Miss Hopley and her teachers never let us forget why we were at Lincoln; for those who were alien, to become good Americans; for those who were so born, to accept the rest of us." Galarza and his fellow students discovered "the secrets of the English language" and grieved over the "tragedies of Bo-Peep." Every morning, the students stood and recited the pledge of allegiance to the flag of the United States. In his school, Americanization did not mean "scrubbing away" what made them Mexican. "No one was ever scolded or punished for speaking in his native tongue on the playground." The teachers tried to pronounce their Spanish names. "Becoming a proud American," Galarza said, "did not mean feeling ashamed of being a Mexican."[46]

Galarza's experience in school was exceptional, for Mexican children were not usually encouraged to develop self-esteem. "The Mexican children almost don't receive any education," Alonso Galvan complained to an interviewer in the 1920s. "They are taught hardly anything at the schools to which the Mexican children go, and I have heard many teachers, farmers and members of a School Board say, 'What do the Mexicans want to study for when they won't be needed as lawyers? They should be taught to be good; they are needed for cotton picking and work on the railroads.' " A Chicano remembered his sixth grade teacher advising him not to continue his education and attend high school. "Your people are here to dig ditches," the teacher said, "to do pick and shovel work. . . . I don't think any of you should plan to go to high school."[47]

But Mexican parents did not want their children to become ditch diggers. Isidro Osorio, who had worked on the railroad and in agriculture, described his hope for his children's future: "What I know is that I have worked very hard to earn my $4.00 a day, and that I am an ignorant laborer, but that is why I want to give a little schooling to my children so that they won't stay like I am and can earn more so that they won't have to kill themselves working." Similarly, Jesus Mendizabal told sociologist Gamio in the 1920s: "I have three children now; they are quite large and they are all going to school. One of them helps me a little now working during vacations and at times when he doesn't go to school. I pray to God that He may give me life to go on working, for I would rather die than take them out of school. I want them to amount to something, to learn all that they can, since I didn't learn anything." A boy explained why his parents emphasized the importance of education: "They want me to go to school so that I won't have to work beets." However, many parents also saw how schooling was creating cultural distances between themselves and their children. "The freedom and independence in this country bring the children into conflict with their parents," explained a mother. "They learn nicer ways, learn about the outside world, learn how to speak English, and then they become ashamed of their parents who brought them up there that they might have better advantages."[48]

As Mexicans migrated to El Norte and began attending American schools, they were increasingly viewed as threatening to Anglo racial and cultural homogeneity. In 1924, legally admitted Mexicans totaled 87,648 — equal to 45 percent of the immigrants from southern and eastern Europe. This large share of the immigration reflected the fact that the National Origins Act did not apply to nations in the Western Hemisphere. Consequently, Mexicans continued to come north to meet the demand for labor. To many Anglos, however, this influx represented an invasion, its magnitude so large "as to almost reverse the essential consequences of the Mexican War," making "a reconquest of the

Southwest more certain ... than America made the conquest" of the war itself.[49]

This dramatic change in the racial composition of immigration set off nativist alarms. In an obvious reference to Mexicans as a racially mixed group, Madison Grant warned: "From the racial point of view, it is not logical to limit the number of Europeans while we throw the country open without limitation to Negroes, Indians, and half-breeds." Mexicans were not only entering the country in great numbers, but they were also increasing rapidly because of their birthrate. The danger was Mexican fecundity, C. M. Goethe declared. "The average American family has three children," he calculated. "Mexican laborers average between nine and ten children to the family. At the three-child rate a couple would have twenty-seven great-grandchildren. At the nine-child rate 729 would be produced. Twenty-seven American children and 729 hybrids or Amerinds!" Another nativist charged that Mexican men constituted a miscegenationist threat to white racial purity: "If the time ever comes when men with a small fraction of colored blood can readily find mates among white women, the gates would be thrown open to a final radical race mixture of the whole population." In a petition to Congress sent in 1927, thirty-four prominent educators demanded the preservation of the nation's genetic purity by including Mexico in the national origins quota system. One of the signatories was A. Lawrence Lowell, president of Harvard University.[50]

Mexican immigration seemed to threaten not only the genetic makeup of Anglo America but also its cultural identity. Vanderbilt University economics professor Roy Garis urged white Americans to guard against the "Mexicanization" of the Southwest. The region should be the "future home for millions of the white race" rather than the "dumping ground for the human hordes of poverty stricken peon Indians of Mexico." The benefits derived from the "restriction of European and the exclusion of Oriental immigration" should not be nullified by allowing Mexican immigration to create a "race problem" that would "dwarf the negro problem of the South," destroying all that was "worthwhile" in "our white civilization."[51]

Mainstream magazines and newspapers joined the hysterical denunciation of racial and ethnic diversity, aiming barbs at Mexican immigrants. "The simple truth is that the dilution of the people and the institutions of this country has already gone too far," the *Saturday Evening Post* editorialized in March 1930. "The country is groping, must grope, toward more rather than less homogeneity. We may be obliged to absorb great numbers of Porto Ricans, Hawaiians and Filipinos; indeed, the Philippine problem has already reared its head in California. With the Mexicans already here, with the as yet unassimilated immigrants from certain European countries, and finally with the vast and growing negro population, we already have an almost superhuman task to bring about requisite national unity. We are under no obligation to continue to make this country an asylum for the Mexican peon, and we should not do so." Two months later, the *New York Times* echoed this call for the restriction of Mexican immigration: "It is folly to pretend that the more recently arrived Mexicans, who are largely of Indian blood, can be absorbed and incorporated into the American race."[52]

The demand for Mexican exclusion resonated among Anglo workers. Viewing Chicanos as a competitive labor force, they clamored for the closing of the border. "I wish the Mexicans could be put back in their country," a white worker declared. "It is economically better for the white man for the races to keep in their own countries." In 1910, the American Federation of Labor's *Advocate* asked: "Is it a pretty sight to see men, brawny American men with callouses on their hands and empty stomachs — sitting idly on benches in the plaza, while slim-legged peons with tortillas in their stomachs, work in the tall building across the way? Do you prefer the name Fernandez, alien, to the name, James, citizen, on your payroll?" Five years later, the *Advocate* again denounced the employment of Mexicans at low wages:

> Cheap labor, yes, at the sacrifice of manhood and homes and all that go to build up and sustain a community.
>
> Cheap labor — at the cost of every ideal cherished in the heart of every member of the white race, utterly destroyed and buried beneath the greedy ambitions of a few grasping money gluttons, who would not hesitate to sink the balance of society to the lowest levels of animalism, if by so doing they can increase their own bank account.
>
> True Americans do not want or advocate the importation of any people who cannot be absorbed into full citizenship, who cannot eventually be raised to our highest social standard. . . .[53]

Clearly, race was being used as a weapon by the American Federation of Labor: Mexicans not only constituted "cheap labor" but were regarded as incapable of becoming fully American. During the 1920s, the American Federation of Labor pressed for the restriction of Mexican immigrants. Samuel Gompers condemned their employment in industry as "this great evil," and urged Congress to apply the national origins quota system to nations in the Western Hemisphere. Based on 2 percent of the Mexican-born persons residing in the United States in 1890, a quota would have allowed only 1,500 Mexicans to enter the country annually. In 1928, the vice president of the California State Federation of Labor told the Senate Immigration Committee: "We have a great virgin country, and if we do not remain on guard it is not going to be our country. . . . Do you want a mongrel population consisting largely of Mexicans and Orientals?"[54]

But the employers of Mexican labor needed them as a source of cheap labor. "We have no Chinamen; we have not the Japs," they argued. "The Hindu is worthless; the Filipino is nothing, and the white man will not do the work." Anglo growers appealed to white workers, promising to elevate them as managers over Mexican laborers. Describing a racial hierarchy of white brains over Mexican brawn, a spokesman for the beet-growers declared that whites should not have to do the dirty and degrading work:

> I do not want to see the condition arise again when white men who are reared and educated in our schools have got to bend their backs and skin their fingers to pull those little beets. . . . You can let us have the only class of labor that will do the work, or close the beet factories, because our people will not do it, and I will say frankly I do not want them to do it. . . .
>
> If you are going to make the young men of America do this back-breaking work, shoveling manure to fertilize the ground, and shoveling beets, you are going to drive them away from agriculture. . . . You have got to give us a class of labor that will do this back-breaking work, and we have the brains and ability to supervise and handle the business part of it.

Here was an echo of Charles Crocker's declaration that whites should be elevated into the foremen of Chinese laborers.[55]

While employers insisted on maintaining their access to Mexican labor, they shared the exclusionists' disdain for racial diversity: they, too, did not want the Mexicans to stay permanently. "While the Mexicans are not easily assimilated," an immigration commission stated, "this is not of very great importance as long as most of them return to their native land after a short time." The strategy was to bring Mexicans here so long as their labor was needed and then return them to Mexico as soon as the demand diminished.[56]

The Great Depression drastically reduced the need for labor. Already on the economic edge of survival, Chicanos experienced massive layoffs and deepening poverty. Hunger haunted their homes, and starving children could be heard crying for food:

> *In these unhappy times*
> *depression still pursues us;*
> *lots of prickly pear is eaten*
> *for lack of other food.*

Utilities were cut off:

> *No light is seen in the houses*
> *nor does water flow from the tap;*
> *the people are in tatters*
> *and in a deplorable state.*[57]

Rendered superfluous as laborers and blamed for white unemployment, Mexicans became the targets of repatriation programs. "If we were rid of the aliens who have entered this country illegally since 1931," a Los Angeles County supervisor declared, "our present unemployment problem would shrink to the proportions of a relatively unimportant flat spot in business." Hungry Mexicans were sometimes granted temporary relief by welfare agencies only if they promised to return to Mexico at public expense. "Many Mexican immigrants are returning to Mexico under a sense of pressure," reported sociologist Emory Bogardus in 1933. "They fear that all welfare aid will be withdrawn if they do not accept the offer to take them out of our country." Forced to leave, many Mexicans crossed the border with a bitter song on their lips:

> *And so I take my leave,*
> *may you be happy.*
> *Here ends the song,*
> *but the depression goes on forever.*[58]

Employers pushed repatriation efforts as private charities and government agencies provided railroad transportation for tens of thousands of Mexicans to their "homeland." In Santa Barbara, Mexicans were literally shipped out from the Southern Pacific depot. "They [the immigration officials] put all the people . . . in boxcars instead of inside the trains," a witness recalled. "They sent a lot of people from around here too. . . . A big exodus. . . . They were in here illegally but the moral part of it, like separation and putting them in boxcars. . . . I'll never forget as long as I live." Many of the "repatriates" were children who had been born in the United States. The Los Angeles Chamber of Commerce estimated that 60 percent of the "repatriated" children were American citizens "without very much hope of ever coming back into the United States."[59]

Repatriation was an employment program for whites — a way to remove a surplus Mexican laboring population and preserve the few remaining jobs for white workers during the Great Depression. Altogether, about 400,000 Mexicans were "repatriated." Even as they supported repatriation, however, employers viewed the action as temporary. "The Los Angeles industrialists confidently predict that the Mexican can be lured back, whenever we need him," observed Carey McWilliams. Indeed, the distance between Mexico and the United States depended on whether there was a demand for labor. In 1926, a representative for the farmers had stated: "We, in California, would greatly prefer some set up in which our peak labor demands might be met and upon the completion of our harvest these laborers returned to their country." The border existed only when Mexican labor was not needed.[60]

The Barrio: Community in the Colony

For many Mexicans, the border was only an imaginary line — one that could be crossed and recrossed at will. Unlike the migrants from Europe, Africa, and Asia, they came from a country touching the United States. Standing on the border, migrants had difficulty knowing where one country began and the other ended. Mexicans had been in the Southwest long before the Anglos, and they would continue to emigrate despite repatriation programs. In El Norte, there were jobs and also communities.

Indeed, over the years, Chicanos had been creating a Mexican-American world in the barrios of El Norte. In their communities, they did not feel like aliens in a foreign land as they did whenever they crossed the railroad tracks and ventured uptown into the Anglo world. Though their neighborhood was a slum, a concentration of shacks and dilapidated houses, without sidewalks or even paved streets, the barrio was home to its residents. The people were all compatriots. They had come from different places in Mexico and had been here for different lengths of time, but together they formed "the *colonia mexicana*." "We came to know families from Chihuahua, Sonora, Jalisco, and Durango," remembered one of them. "Some had come to the United States even before the revolution, living in Texas before migrating to California. Like ourselves, our Mexican neighbors had come this far moving step by step, working and waiting. . . ."[61]

In El Norte, Chicanos were recreating a Mexican community and culture. They celebrated national holidays like the Sixteenth of September, Mexican Independence Day. "We are Mexicans," declared a speaker at one of the celebrations, "almost all of us here . . . by our fathers or ancestors, although we are now under a neighboring nation's flag to which we owe respect. Notwithstanding, this respect does not prevent us from remembering our Mexican anniversary." The celebrations, Ernesto Galarza recalled, "stirred everyone in the *barrio*" and gave them the feeling that they were "still Mexicans." At these festive occasions, there were parades in the plazas attended by city and county officials as well as Mexican consuls. The entire town became a *fandango*. Colorful musicians strolled, and people danced in the streets. Excited crowds shouted, "*Viva* Mexico!" and sang Mexican songs as fireworks exploded and *muchachos* (kids) listened to stories about Mexico told by the *viejitos* (old ones). Bands played the national anthems of both countries. The flags and the colors of the United States and Mexico were displayed together — red, white, and blue as well as red, white, and green.[62]

The religion of the Chicanos was a uniquely Mexican version of Catholicism, a blending of a faith brought from the Old World and beliefs that had been in the New World for thousands of years before Columbus. For the Mexicans, God was deeply personal, caring for each of them through their saints. In their homes, they decorated their altars with *santitos*, images of saints dear to them. They had a special relationship with the Virgen de Guadalupe: according to their account, she had visited a poor Indian and felt a particular concern for the people of Mexico. "I have with me an amulet which my mother gave to me before dying," a Mexican told an interviewer. "This amulet has the Virgin of Guadalupe on it and it is she who always protects me." Their Virgin Mary was Mexican: many paintings and statues represented her as dark in complexion.[63]

What bound the people together was not only ethnicity but also class. "We were all poor," a Mexican said, "we were all in the same situation."

The barrio was a "grapevine of job information." A frequently heard word was *trabajo* (work), and "the community was divided in two — the many who were looking for it and the few who had it to offer." Field hands, railroad workers, cannery workers, construction laborers, and maids came back to the barrio after work to tell one another where the jobs were and how much they paid and what the food and living quarters were like.[64]

In the colony, unskilled workers from Mexico were welcomed, for they had come from the homeland. "These Mexicans are hired on this side of the Rio Grande by agents of the larger farms, and are shipped in car load lots, with windows and doors locked, to their destination," a local newspaper reported. "After the cotton season the majority will work their way back to the border and into Mexico." But the barrio offered these migrant workers a place to stay north of the border. "Beds and meals, if the newcomers had no money at all, were provided — in one way or another — on trust, until the new *chicano* found a job." Aid was given freely, for everyone knew what it meant to be in need. "It was not charity or social welfare," Ernesto Galarza explained, "but something my mother called *asistencia*, a helping given and received on trust, to be repaid because those who had given it were themselves in need of what they had given. *Chicanos* who had found work on farms or in railroad camps came back to pay us a few dollars for *asistencia* we had provided weeks or months before."[65]

In the barrio, people helped each other, for survival depended on solidarity and mutual assistance. For example, Bonifacio Ortega had dislocated his arm while working in Los Angeles. "I was laid up and had to be in the hospital about three months," he recalled. "Fortunately my countrymen helped me a lot, for those who were working got something together every Saturday and took it to me at the hospital for whatever I needed. They also visited me and made me presents." Ortega's arm healed, and he returned to work at a brickyard. "We help one another, we fellow countrymen. We are almost all from the same town or from the nearby farms. The wife of one of the countrymen died the other day and we got enough money together to buy a coffin and enough so that he could go and take the body to Jalisco."[66]

Moreover, the barrio was a place where Mexicans could feel at home in simple, day-to-day ways. Women wearing rebozos, or traditional shawls, were seen everywhere, just as in Mexico. There were Mexican plays and *carpas* — acrobats and traveling sideshows. Stands and cafés offered tamales and other favorites such as frijoles, tortillas, *menudo* (tripe stew), and *dulces* made with *piloncillo* (Mexican sugar). Cantinas and bars were places to hang out and drink beer. *Mercados* stocked Mexican foods like *chorizo* (sausage), while *panderias* baked fresh bread. Shopping in the *tiendas* was familiar. "In the secondhand shops, where the *barrio* people sold and bought furniture and clothing, there were Mexican clerks who knew the Mexican ways of making a sale."[67]

In the early evenings, as the sun began to set, the people sat outside their homes, as they had on the other side of the border in their Mexican villages. The air still carried the smells of suppertime — "tortillas baking, beans boiling, chile roasting, coffee steaming, and kerosene stenching." The men "squatted on the ground, hunched against the wall of the house and smoked. The women and the girls . . . put away the kitchen things, the *candiles* turned down to save kerosene. They listened to the tales of the day if the men were in a talking mood." They spoke in two languages — "Spanish and with gestures." An old man talked about a time called "Before the Conquest." The Indian tribes had their "own kings and emperors," he said. "Then the Spaniards [came], killing the Indians and running them down with hunting dogs. The conquerors took the land along the rivers where there was water and rich soil, flat and easy to farm. On these lands the Spaniards set up their haciendas, where the Indians were forced to labor for nothing or were paid only a few centavos for a hard day's work."[68]

Feeling homesick, the people sometimes took out their cedar boxes to display memorabilia from Mexico — a butterfly serape worn to celebrate the Battle of Puebla, tin pictures of grandparents, and "bits of embroidery and lace" made by aunts still in the homeland. They "took deep breaths of the aroma of *puro cedro,* pure Jalcocotan mixed with camphor." A song in Spanish floated in the air:

> *I loved a little country girl*
> *She was so shy*
> *She couldn't even talk to me*
> *I would take her hand*
> *And she would sadly cry*
> *Now go away*
> *My mother will be scolding me.*[69]

As darkness descended, the people complained about how they were not allowed to feel at home north of the border: "They [Anglos] would rant at public meetings and declare that this was an American country and the Mexicans ought to be run out." "You can't forget those things. You try to forget because . . . you should forgive and forget, but there is still a pain in there that another human being could do that to you." Someone argued: "I haven't wanted to, nor do I want to learn English, for I am not thinking of living in this country all my life. I don't even like it here." A voice agreed: "They talk to us about becoming citizens, but if we become citizens we are still Mexicans. They look at our hair, and listen to our speech and call us Mexicans." Rejection in the new country reinforced a return mentality.[70]

An old man insisted on keeping his Mexican ties: "I have always had and now have my home in El Paso, but I shall never change my [Mexican] citizenship in spite of the fact that [here] I have greater opportunities and protection." Another admitted ambivalence: "I want to go back to Leon because it is my country and I love Mexico. But I like it better here for one can work more satisfactory. No one interferes with one and one doesn't have to fear that there will be or won't be revolutions."[71]

As the night air became chilly, the barrio people pulled their serapes and rebozos around their shoulders. They talked about this land as "occupied" Mexico and the nearness of the border. After arriving in Nogales, Arizona, a young Mexican boy was happy to be finally in the United States. "Look at the American flag," his mother said. As he watched it flying over a building near them, he noticed a Mexican flag on a staff beyond the depot down the street. "We are in the United States," his mother explained. "Mexico is over there." But no matter where they were in the United States, the border was always close to their hearts. Mexican Americans who were citizens by birth were often reminded that they were still Mexicans. By "nationality" my son is "American," a father explained, but he is "Mexicano" "by blood." A local Mexican newspaper criticized some Mexican Americans for not celebrating the Sixteenth of September: "To these 'Agringados' [Americanized Mexicans] who negate that they are Mexicans because they were born in the United States, we ask: what blood runs through their veins? Do they think they are members of the Anglo-Saxon race who only happen to have dark skins because they were born on the border! What nonsense! (Que barbaridad!)" A song chimed:

> . . . he who denies his race
> Is the most miserable creature. . . .
> A good Mexican
> Never disowns

338

The dear fatherland
Of his affections.[72]

Soon night fell, and the hunched figures blended into the darkness. But no one was sleepy yet, so the people continued to sit in front of their homes. The stars were brighter above Mexico, someone commented, and there were more of them. *Sí,* yes, another added, and there were coyotes howling nearby. Much was different in El Norte. But as in their old villages, the streets in the barrio had no lights, and now only their voices could be heard. "When they pulled on their cigarettes, they made ruby dots in the dark, as if they were putting periods in the low-toned conversation. The talk just faded away, the men went indoors, the doors were shut . . . there was nothing on the street but the dark. . . ."[73]

13

TO THE PROMISED LAND
Blacks in the Urban North

L IKE THE MEXICANS trekking to El Norte, southern blacks were migrating northward by the tens of thousands during the early twentieth century. They went to the cities of the Midwest and the Northeast, where they joined European immigrants, including the Irish and Jews. Describing the powerful spirit behind this great black migration, the daughter of a sharecropper wrote: "And Black men's feet learned roads. Some said good bye cheerfully . . . others fearfully, with terrors of unknown dangers in their mouths . . . others in their eagerness for distance said nothing. The daybreak found them gone. The wind said North. Trains said North. The tides and tongues said North, and men moved like the great herds before the glaciers." Blacks listened and heard the message:

> *Some are coming on the passenger,*
> *Some are coming on the freight,*
> *Others will be found walking,*
> *For none have time to wait.*[1]

An exodus was under way. "The Afro-American population of the large cities of the North and West," the *New York Age* reported in 1907, "is being constantly fed by a steady stream of new people from the Southern States." Between 1910 and 1920, the black population jumped

340

from 5,000 to 40,800 in Detroit, 8,400 to 34,400 in Cleveland, 44,000 to 109,400 in Chicago, and 91,700 to 152,400 in New York. "There can be no doubt of the drift of the black South northward," W. E. B. DuBois noted. They were making a crossing, pulled by a powerful liminality called the North.[2]

The Black Exodus

All over the South, blacks found themselves swept up in the migration "fever." "Everybody seems to be asleep about what is going on right under their noses," a Georgia newspaper stated. "That is, everybody but those farmers who have awakened up of mornings recently to find every male Negro over 21 . . . gone — to Cleveland, to Pittsburgh, to Chicago. . . ." After half the black population left her little town in Mississippi, a black woman said: "If I stay here any longer, I'll go wild. Every time I go home I have to pass house after house of all my friends who are in the North and prospering. I've been trying to hold on here and keep my property. There ain't enough people here I now know to give me a decent burial." To be left behind was to feel a sudden loneliness:

> I've watched the trains as they disappeared
> Behind the clouds of smoke,
> Carrying the crowds of working men
> To the land of hope. . . .[3]

On one Georgia plantation, a landlord was surprised to find all of his tenants gone, except two old men. Uncle Ben and Uncle Joe were too poor to purchase train tickets. But they sorrowfully told their landlord that everyone else had abandoned him and that they had loyally remained behind on the plantation. The landlord gave the two men some money because they promised to work the crops. Immediately after he left, the old-timers took the money and boarded the train to join their companions in the North.[4]

Like the immigrants from Asia, Mexico, and Europe, southern blacks were driven by particular "pushes." After emancipation, most blacks had been forced to become sharecroppers and tenant farmers. Dependent on white landlords and enslaved by debts, they complained:

> Working hard on southern
>   soil,
> Someone softly spoke;

"Toil and toil and toil and toil,
And yet I'm always broke."

The ordeal of sharecropping was crushing: at the end of the harvest, tenant farmers were often disappointed to find themselves only deeper in debt. Though they were free, many were in economic bondage. "There was," they had painfully come to realize, "no rise to the thing."

Where I come from
folks work hard
all their lives
until they die
and never own no part
of earth nor sky.

Their economic situation became dire as floods destroyed their farms and insects ravaged their cotton crops.

Boll-weevil in de cotton
Cut worm in de cotton,
Debil in de white man,
Wah's goin' on.[5]

Meanwhile, there were "pulls" from the North. World War I had virtually cut off the flow of European immigrants, reducing their numbers from 1,200,000 in 1914 to only 110,000 in 1918. Facing tremendous labor shortages, factory managers dispatched labor recruiters to the South. "These same factories, mills and workshops that have been closed to us, through necessity are being opened to us," a black newspaper in Chicago reported. "We are to be given a chance, not through choice but because it is expedient. Prejudice vanishes when the almighty dollar is on the wrong side of the balance sheet." Traveling in the South, journalist Ray Stannard Baker reported: "Trains were backed into several Southern cities and hundreds of Negroes were gathered up in a day, loaded into the cars, and whirled away to the North. I was told of instances in which Negro teamsters left their horses standing in the streets, or deserted their jobs and went to the trains without notifying their employers or even going home." A black worker told Baker: "The best wages I could make [in Georgia] was $1.25 or $1.50 a day. I went to work at a dye house at Newark, N.J., at $2.75 a day, with a rent-free room to live in. . . . The company paid my fare North."[6]

Like most Mexicans, blacks were following the jobs. "More positions open than men for them," announced the headlines of the *Chicago Defender*, which was owned by black editor Robert Abbott. Article after article described the great labor shortage and the willingness of employers to "give men a chance to learn the trade at $2.25 a day." Classified job listings beckoned:

Wanted — 10 molders. Must be experienced. $4.50 to $5.50 per day.

Men wanted at once. Good steady employment for colored. Thirty and 39½ cents per hour. Weekly payments. Good warm sanitary quarters free. . . . Towns of Newark and Jersey City.

Laborers wanted for foundry, warehouse and yard work. Excellent opportunity to learn trades, paying good money. Start $2.50–$2.75 per day. Extra for overtime.

$3.60 per day can be made in steel foundry in Minnesota, by strong, healthy, steady men.[7]

A young black woman asked the *Defender* to send her information about employment in the North:

Dear Sirs: I am writeing to you all asking a favor of you all. I am a girl of seventeen. . . . I now feel like I aught to go to work. And I would like very very well for you all to please forward me to a good job. . . . I am tired of down hear in this ———— / I am afraid to say.[8]

Meanwhile, blacks who had left for the Promised Land sent home glowing reports about their jobs in the North. "M ————, old boy," one of them wrote, "I was promoted on the first of the month I was made first assistant to the head carpenter . . . and was raised to $95 a month. . . . What's the news generally around H'burg [Hattiesburg]? I should have been here 20 years ago. I just begin to feel like a man. It's a great deal of pleasure in knowing that you have got some privilege. My children are going to the same school with the whites and I dont have to umble to no one. I have registered — Will vote the next election and there isnt any 'yes sir' and 'no sir' — its all yes and no and Sam and

Bill." "I am well and thankful to say I am doing well," wrote a black woman who had recently arrived in Chicago. "I work in Swifts packing Co., in the sausage department. . . . We get $1.50 a day. . . . Tell your husband work is plentiful here and he wont have to loaf if he want to work." A South Carolina newspaper described the good fortune of a Greenwood County farm boy who had gone north to work for twenty-five dollars a week. "He came home last week to assist his people on the farm and brought more than one hundred dollars and plenty of nice clothes. He gave his mother fifty dollars, and put fifty dollars in the Greenwood bank and had some pocket change left."[9]

But there was something more, something deeper than economics: a new generation of blacks was coming of age. "I have men," a white plantation owner stated, "who were slaves on the place. . . . They have always lived there and will probably die there, right on the plantation where they were born." The old former slaves were passing away, however, and so was the racial etiquette of deference and subordination they seemed to represent. "The South," W. E. B. DuBois observed, "laments today the slow, steady disappearance of a certain type of Negro — the faithful, courteous slave of other days, with his dignified . . . humility."[10]

In the place of such old-time Negroes, there were younger blacks, born after the Civil War and after slavery, an institution and way of life that seemed to them in the far distant past. To them, accounts of slavery "were but childhood tales." Slavery was not something they had experienced, something they could remember. They did not feel, as did the older generation, the lingering vividness and sedimentary power of the peculiar institution. White southerners frequently complained that this new generation of blacks was "worthless." Lacking the habits of "diligence, order, faithfulness" of those who had been born in slavery, they "rarely remain[ed] long enough under the supervision of any planter to allow him sufficient time to teach them." These young people were different from the "good old negroes . . . negroes about grown before the war": they were unwilling to stay on the plantations as servile laborers. Compared to the "older class of colored labor," men who were "pretty well up in years" and who constituted a "first rate class of labor," the blacks of the "younger class" were "discontented and wanted to be roaming."[11]

Most of the blacks who were moving north belonged to this post–Civil War generation, restless, dissatisfied, unwilling to mask their true selves and accommodate to traditional subservient roles. In a statement to a Labor Department investigator in 1916, a black man explained this generational difference:

My father was born and brought up as a slave. He never knew anything else until after I was born. He was taught his place and was content to keep it. But when he brought me up he let some of the old customs slip by. But I know there are certain things that I must do and I do them, and it doesn't worry me; yet in bringing up my own son, I let some more of the old customs slip by. For a year I have been keeping him from going to Chicago; but he tells me this is his last crop; that in the fall he's going. He says, "When a young white man talks rough to me, I can't talk rough to him. You can stand that; I can't. I have some education, and inside I has the feelings of a white man. I'm going."[12]

"Tired of the South," these young blacks "wanted to make a change." A migrant from North Carolina declared that he "couldn't live there and be a man and be treated like a man." A black in Mississippi told Ray Stannard Baker that he was planning to move to Indiana: "They're Jim Crowin' us down here too much; there's no chance for a coloured man who has any self-respect." "The exodus . . . of colored people from the sunny South to the colder states of the North," the *Richmond Reformer* explained, "has its very birth out of the 'Jim Crow' and 'Segregation' conditions which now exist in the cities of the South and which have crowded colored people into narrow unsanitary or unhealthy quarters . . . segregating them like cattle, hogs or sheep." More intolerable than segregation was racial violence. "For every lynching that takes place," noted Booker T. Washington in 1903, ". . . a score of colored people leave . . . for the city."

> *Yes, we are going to the north!*
> *I don't care to what state,*
> *Just so I cross the Dixon Line,*
> *From this southern land of hate,*
> *Lynched and burned and shot and hung,*
> *And not a word is said.*[13]

Young blacks spoke loudly with their feet: they left the South in search of what DuBois called "the possibility of escaping caste at least in its most aggravating personal features." Possessing "a certain sort of soul, a certain kind of spirit," they found the "narrow repression and provincialism of the South simply unbearable." Why stay in the South, asked the *Chicago Defender*, "where your mother, sister and daughter are raped and burned at the stake; where your father, brother and sons are treated with contempt and hung to a pole, riddled with bullets at the least mention that he does not like the way he is treated"? In letters to the *Defender,* blacks described their flight from southern racism:

> *Dear Sir Bro. . . .* I seen in the Defender where you was helping us a long in securing a posission as brickmason plaster cementers stone mason. I am writing to you for advice about comeing north. . . . We expect to do whatever you says. There is nothing here for the colored man but a hard time wich these southern crackers gives us.

They refused to be victimized by southern police abuse:

> *Dear Sir:* I am writing you for information to come north [and] to see if there is any way that you can help me by giving me the names of some of the firms that will send me a transportation as we are down here where we have to be shot down lik rabbits for every little orfence as I seen an orcurince hapen down here this after noon when three depties from the shrief office . . . come out and found some of our raice mens in a crap game and it makes me want to leave the south worse than I ever did. . . .

And they demanded their dignity:

> *Dear Sir:* wanted to leave the South and Go and Place where a man will Be any thing Except A Ker I thought would write you for Advise As where would be a Good Place for a Comperedly young man That want to Better his Standing who has a very Promising young Family. I am 30 years old and have Good Experience in Freight Handler and Can fill Position from Truck to Agt. would like Chicago or Philadelphia. But I dont Care where so long as I Go where a man is a man.[14]

Free from the shadow of slavery, these young people were able to imagine new possibilities for themselves in the North. "[I] didn't want to remain in one little place all my days," one of them stated. "I wanted to get out and see something of the world." Hoping to become a writer, a young black man went north during the 1920s. "I went to Chicago as a migrant from Mississippi," Richard Wright recalled. "And there in that great iron city, that impersonal, mechanical city, amid the steam, the smoke . . . there in that self-conscious city, that city so deadly dramatic and stimulating, we caught whispers of the meanings that life could have. . . ." Like novelist Toni Morrison's Joe and Violet in *Jazz*, country people who moved from Virginia to New York City, these migrants were responding to the inner urges of "their stronger, riskier selves." Arriving in the northern cities, they shouted: "At last, at last, everything's ahead."[15]

By 1930, some two million blacks had migrated to the cities of the North and changed the course of history. "The migration is probably, next to emancipation, the most noteworthy event which has ever happened to the Negro in America," observed Ray Stannard Baker in 1917. "Negroes are acting for themselves, self-consciously, almost for the first time in their history. They did not win their freedom: it was a gift thrust upon them by the North. But in the present migration . . . they are moving of their own accord. . . ."[16]

As they traveled to the North, they gave their migration religious meaning. They spoke excitedly about the "Flight out of Egypt," "Bound for the Promised Land," and "Going into Canaan." Jeremiah Taylor of Mississippi had been resigned to remain on his farm until his son returned from town one day and told him that folks were leaving "like Judgment day." After a group of migrants crossed the Ohio River, they knelt down in prayer and then sang: "I Done Come out of the Land of Egypt with the Good News." "The cry of "Goin' Nawth' hung over the land like the wail over Egypt at the death of the first-born," reported a sharecropper's daughter. "Railroads, hardroads, dirt roads, side roads, roads were in the minds of the black South and all roads led North."[17]

The Urban Crucible

But, as they journeyed to their Promised Land, the migrants carried not only hope but also uncertainties. Richard Wright recalled how he had left the South to fling himself into the "unknown." The *Defender* described the migrants' feelings of "trembling and fear": "They were going — they didn't know where — among strange people, strange customs." A song captured their mood of ambivalence:

> *I'm a poor boy and I'm a stranger blowed in your town,*
> *Yes I am,*
> *I'm a poor boy and I'm a stranger blowed in your town,*
> *I'm a poor boy and I'm a stranger blowed in your town,*
> *I'm goin' where a friend can be found.*

But their expectations of freedom exceeded their uneasiness about becoming strangers. And so they went to northern cities, especially to Chicago and New York.[18]

Chicago was "the mouth of the stream of Negroes from the South." Emmett J. Scott's metaphor aptly described this brawling midwestern city — the home of the *Defender,* which had been urging young blacks to come north. Chicago was also the terminus of the Illinois Central Railroad, with its rail lines connected to the small towns of Mississippi, Arkansas, and Louisiana. Chicago was a dynamic industrial center, spawning jobs and inspiring dreams.[19]

In 1900, Chicago had a black population of only thirty thousand. "I lived on Lincoln Street — there were foreigners there," a black resident remembered, describing the integrated neighborhoods of the time. "My children used to go to white kids' parties, for where we lived there was nothing much but foreigners. There was only one other colored family in that block." Only one ward in the entire city was 25 percent black, while 19 out of 35 wards were about 0.5 percent black. Twenty years later, however, the black population had jumped to 109,000, concentrated in the predominantly black neighborhoods of the South Side.[20]

The black migration to Chicago sparked an explosion of white resistance. "A new problem, demanding early solution, is facing Chicago," the *Tribune* warned. "It pertains to the sudden and unprecedented influx of southern Negro laborers." The newspaper depicted the newcomers as carefree and lazy: "In a house at Thirty-second and Wabash eight or ten Negroes were lying about on the floor, and one was picking a banjo and singing a song the chorus of which ended 'Mo' rain, mo' rest, / Mo' niggers sleep in de nest.' " Determined to repel this Negro "invasion," several hundred white residents organized the Hyde Park Improvement Protective Club, which announced that blacks must live in the "so-called Districts" and that real estate agents must not sell homes to blacks in white blocks. "The districts which are now white," a leader of the organization declared, "must remain white. There will be no compromise."[21]

The conflict over housing intensified during World War I as blacks responded to the labor needs of Chicago's war-related industries. In 1917, the Chicago Real Estate Board pointed out that southern blacks were "pouring into Chicago at the rate of ten thousand a month," and warned that this influx would precipitate a decline in property values. A year later, the Kenwood and Hyde Park Property Owners' Association urged whites not to sell or rent to blacks. Whites "won't be driven out," the association vowed; they would prevent a Negro "take-over" and keep their neighborhood "clear of undesirables . . . at all cost." "The depreciation of our property in this district has been two hundred and fifty millions since the invasion," the association's leaders argued. "If someone told you that there was to be an invasion that would injure your homes to that extent, wouldn't you rise up as one man and one woman, and say, as General Foch said: 'They shall not pass'?"[22]

Meanwhile, the schools had become racial battlegrounds. "I remember how I used to fight with the white children, especially the Dago children," said one black. "They would call out to us colored children, 'Nigger, nigger, never die, black face and China eye,' and when I catch one and get through with him he would think *he* was black." Another recalled: "The Italian boys were so low morally. They made several attempts to rape some of the girls . . . used to gang us. . . . We were always able to have a good fight and have some blood shed."[23]

Similarly, the workplace became a terrain of competition and conflict. Before the war, blacks were largely restricted to employment as servants. In 1910, over 60 percent of the women were domestic servants or laundresses; close to half of all the employed men worked as porters, servants, waiters, and janitors. Though generally excluded from industrial employment, blacks were allowed to cross caste labor lines occasionally as strikebreakers. Managers used them as scabs during the 1904 stockyards strike and the teamsters strike a year later. The *Broad Ax,* a black weekly, criticized employers for "bringing hundreds and hundreds of colored men here from the remote parts of the South . . . to temporarily serve as strikebreakers for such Negro-hating concerns as Marshall Field and Company, Mandel Brothers and Montgomery Ward and Company, who [had] no use for Negroes in general except to use them as brutish clubs to beat their white help over the head. . . ." After the settlement of both strikes, the black workers were discharged.[24]

The war, however, generated a sharp demand for labor and opened unusual opportunities for blacks in industries. By 1920, the majority of black men were employed in factories rather than domestic and personal services. Black women made similar, although smaller, inroads — 15 percent of them had become factory operatives. Blacks had been eager to get out of domestic work. Employers "almost make you a slave," complained a black woman who had quit her job as a maid to work in a mail-order house. Personal service reminded blacks of the South, where they had been dependent on whites and closely supervised. Like the Irish maids who left the "service" for factory work, many black women wanted more autonomy. "I'll never work in nobody's kitchen but my own any more," exclaimed one of them who was employed in a box factory. "No indeed! That's the one thing that makes me stick to this job. You do have some time to call your own." For the first time in their lives, thousands of black men and women were working in industries, making what they considered good wages — 42 cents an hour in the packing houses and even higher rates in manufacturing.[25]

In the stockyards and packing houses, managers deliberately employed blacks in order to subvert the union activities of white workers. Seeking to keep the work force racially divided, they hired a black promoter to set up a black company union, the American Unity Labor Union. Richard Parker served as a front man for the interests of management, playing on black suspicions of the white labor movement and pitting the company union blacks against the white workers. Parker distributed twenty thousand handbills warning blacks not to join the "white man's union." One of his advertisements published in a black newspaper declared:

GET A SQUARE DEAL WITH YOUR OWN RACE

Time has come for Negroes to do now or never. Get together and stick together is the call of the Negro. Like all other races, make your own way; other races have made their unions for themselves. They are not going to give it to you just because you join his union. Make a union of your own race; union is strength. . . .

This union does not *believe in strikes*. We believe all differences between laborers and capitalists can be arbitrated. Strike is our last motive if any at all.[26]

The Stockyards Labor Council tried to counter management's divide-and-conquer campaign by organizing an all-black local and launching its own recruitment drive among black workers. It issued appeals for interracial working-class unity: "The bosses think that because we are of different color and different nationalities we should fight each other. We're going to fool them and fight for a common cause — a square deal for all." At a union rally of black and white workers, a council leader declared: "It does me good to see such a checkerboard crowd — by that I mean all of the workers here are not standing apart in groups, one race huddled in one bunch, one nationality in another. You are all standing shoulder to shoulder as men, regardless of whether your face is white or black."[27]

But the council failed to organize the black laborers. "To be frank," an official conceded, "we have not had the support from the colored workers which we expected. Our method of propaganda may have been weak somewhere; probably we do not understand the colored workers as we do ourselves. . . . Be that as it may, the colored worker has not responded to the call of unionism." Actually, blacks did not respond because they lacked familiarity with unions, and many saw the union's all-black local as segregationist.[28]

Racial competition in the workplace added fuel to social antagonisms in the neighborhoods, where tensions were literally beginning to explode. In 1917, bombs destroyed the homes of several black families; a year later, a letter warned black tenants on Vincennes Avenue: "We are going to BLOW these FLATS TO HELL and if you don't want to go with them you had better move at once." Shortly after, three bombs went off in the neighborhood. Blacks complained that the police had failed to provide adequate protection for black families and to apprehend the bombers. In 1919, several bombings were aimed at the offices of real estate agents who had sold homes to blacks in white neighborhoods. Altogether scores of bombings resulted in two deaths and many injuries as well as the destruction of property worth thousands of dollars.[29]

To add to the terror, white gangs like Ragan's Colts attacked blacks in the streets and parks, especially Washington Park, which separated the black neighborhoods from Hyde Park. On June 21, 1919, white hoodlums killed two black men, reportedly because they wanted to "get a nigger." White gangs posted notices on the boundaries between white and black neighborhoods, threatening to "get all the niggers on the Fourth of July." Afraid and angry, blacks prepared to defend themselves. Black lawyer Beauregard Moseley warned that blacks had been pushed to the limit by racial violence and were "resolved to meet force with force."[30]

The Fourth of July passed, apparently without incident, but then the tinderbox of race hatred exploded on July 27. On that Sunday afternoon, Eugene Williams had been swimming at the segregated Twenty-ninth Street beach. Williams, who was clinging to a floating railroad tie, had drifted over to the white side of the beach. Somehow he drowned. Blacks at the scene claimed that Williams went down after he had been hit by stones thrown by whites. The charge swept across the beach: "White people have killed a Negro." Frustrated because the police refused to make any arrests, some blacks attacked several white men. Hours later, in retaliation, white gangs beat some blacks who had wandered into white neighborhoods. General rioting broke out, leaving two people dead and over fifty injured. The next day, violence flared up again. As blacks tried to return home from work at the stockyards, they were dragged from streetcars and assaulted by white mobs; armed whites in cars invaded black neighborhoods, shooting indiscriminately at homes. Innocent whites who worked at businesses located in the black areas were beaten by blacks seeking revenge. The rioting continued throughout the week until the militia was finally able to restore order. The casualty figures were horrendous — twenty-three blacks and fifteen whites were killed, while 342 blacks and 178 whites were injured.[31]

The deaths of blacks at the hands of white mobs provoked an angry call for violent revenge:

> If we must die — let it not be like hogs
>   Hunted and penned in an inglorious spot,
> While round us bark the mad and hungry dogs,
>   Making their mock at our accursed lot.
>
> If we must die — oh, let us nobly die,
>   So that our precious blood may not be shed
> In vain; then even the monsters we defy
>   Shall be constrained to honor us though dead!
>
> Oh, kinsmen! We must meet the common foe;
>   Though far outnumbered, let us still be brave,
> And for their thousand blows deal one death-blow!
>   What though before us lies the open grave?
> Like men we'll face the murderous, cowardly pack
> Pressed to the wall, dying, but — fighting back![32]

Another way to fight back was through black solidarity and ethnic enterprise. "We should hasten to build up our own marts and trades," a black minister told his congregation, "so we can give employment and help to provide against such a day as we are now experiencing." Many black political and business leaders advised blacks to turn inward and develop their own communities with their earnings from the steel mills, stockyards, and factories: "Why should these dollars be spent with white men . . . ? If white men are so determined that Negroes must live separate and apart, why not beat them at their own game?" Blacks were encouraged to establish their own banks, insurance companies, stores, churches, and communities.[33]

Chicago was the "Black Metropolis," but New York City was the home of Harlem, "the Negro Capital of the World." Blacks had been there since the seventeenth century: as slaves, they had constructed the original wagon road on Manhattan and also worked on farms and estates in New Amsterdam. Their presence continued after the transfer of the Dutch colony to England and after the American Revolution. In 1790, blacks constituted nearly a third of the population living in a section known as Harlem. But their presence gradually decreased over the years, and by 1890, Harlem had become predominantly white and wealthy. The community was soon to be rapidly transformed. Just as the black exodus from the South was beginning, a housing boom in Harlem collapsed.

The glut of vacant apartments attracted the attention of black real estate agents, especially Philip A. Payton, Jr. His strategy was simple: lease apartment houses from white landlords and then rent them to blacks at a profit. One of his advertisements in a real estate journal announced:

Colored Tenements Wanted
Colored man makes a speciality of managing colored tenements; references; bond. Philip A. Payton, Jr., agent and broker, 67 West 134th.

Payton explained: "By opening for colored tenants first a house on one block and then a house in another I have finally succeeded in securing over two hundred and fifty first class flats and private dwellings."[34]

But Payton's penetration encountered resistance from white residents. "Harlem has been devastated as a result of the steady influx of Negroes," a long-time resident complained in 1913. Some white homeowners organized to counter the black "invasion" and the "black hordes." They signed restrictive covenants which stated that their buildings should not be leased or sold to "colored" persons. The president of the Harlem Property Owners' Improvement Corporation declared: "It is the question of whether the white man will rule Harlem or the negro." He urged whites to drive the blacks out of Harlem "send them to the slums where they belonged." But white property owners often found that their choice was to rent to blacks or not rent at all. In order to make their own loan payments, many of them had to yield; reluctantly, they posted notices on their buildings:

NOTICE

We have endeavored for some time to avoid turning over this house to colored tenants, but as a result of . . . rapid changes in conditions . . . this issue has been forced upon us.[35]

"The 'border line' which separated whites and Negroes 'rapidly receded' each year," observed historian Gilbert Osofsky, "and by 1914 some 50,000 Negroes lived in the neighborhood." The border kept moving: between 1920 and 1930, 118,792 whites left the neighborhood, while 87,417 blacks arrived. Symbolically, Temple Israel of Harlem became Mount Olivet Baptist Church. Harlem became the home of more than two-thirds of all the blacks living in Manhattan — the "largest colony of colored people, in similar limits, in the world."[36]

Soon living conditions in Harlem became congested. In 1925, the population density was 336 persons per acre compared to only 223 for Manhattan as a whole. Meanwhile, landlords allowed their apartments to deteriorate, and tenants complained about broken pipes, leaking roofs, unsanitary conditions, and rats. Unable to move to other areas of the city because of discrimination, blacks were forced to pay higher rents, spending approximately 33 percent of their income on rent, compared to 20 percent for working-class whites. Housing costs were especially burdensome, for Harlem blacks were confined to low-wage employment. According to sociologist E. Franklin Frazier, New York had two types of businesses — those that employed "Negroes in menial positions" and those that employed "no Negroes at all." While some black women worked in the garment industry, most of them were domestic servants. Black men generally worked as longshoremen and teamsters or as elevator operators, janitors, porters, chauffeurs, and waiters.[37]

Though blacks were employed in the low-wage jobs, they felt a surge of power and a sense of pride. Coming to Harlem in search of the Promised Land, they had broken the chains of racial subordination forged by centuries of slavery. Harlem seemed liminal, a place where black people could begin anew in America. "I sit on my stoop on Seventh Avenue," one migrant declared, "and gaze at the sunkissed folk strolling up and down and think that surely Mississippi is here in New York, in Harlem, yes. . . ." This feeling of freedom inspired them to create a community that represented more than just a place where blacks lived. Restless and hopeful, they were ready, eager to listen to a charismatic leader articulate what was on fire within them — fierce dreams of dignity refusing to be deferred. Suddenly, in 1916, Marcus Garvey arrived in

Harlem. "Up, you mighty race," he declared, "you can accomplish what you will."[38]

Yearning for Blackness in Urban America

Garvey personified a new stirring, a vision of black pride sweeping through Harlem like a fresh breeze blowing north from Jamaica. In his autobiography, he recalled how he was unaware of race as a young child on the Caribbean island: "To me, at home in my early days, there was no difference between white and black." One of his friends was a "little white girl." "We were two innocent fools who never dreamed of a race feeling and problem. As a child, I went to school with white boys and girls, like all other negroes. We were not called negroes then." But at the age of fourteen, Garvey was told by his friend that her parents had decided to send her away to school and that she was not to write to him because he was a "nigger." The incident shook Garvey: "It was then that I found for the first time that there was some difference in humanity, and that there were different races, each having its own separate and distinct social life."[39]

A few years later, during a trip to Europe, Garvey began to formulate his ideology of black nationalism. "You are black," meaning inferior, he had been told. The insult led Garvey to ask: "Where is the black man's Government? Where is his King and his kingdom? Where is his President, his country, and his ambassador, his army, his navy, his men of big affairs?" Unable to find these institutions of power, Garvey declared: "I will help to make them." His imagination began to soar as he envisioned "a new world of black men, not peons, serfs, dogs and slaves, but a nation of sturdy men making their impress upon civilization and causing a new light to dawn upon the human race." In 1914, Garvey returned to Jamaica, where he founded the Universal Negro Improvement Association (UNIA) to unite all the "Negro peoples of the world" and establish a black nation in Africa.[40]

In order to expand his movement to the United States, Garvey contacted Booker T. Washington, whose book *Up from Slavery* had been a source of inspiration for him. In 1916, a year after Washington's death, Garvey visited Tuskegee to pay his "respects to the dead hero"; then he went to New York City to establish a division of the UNIA. When Garvey saw the thousands of blacks flocking to join his organization, he decided to stay and build the base for his movement in Harlem. The UNIA exploded with activity — colorful parades in Harlem led by Garvey dressed in military uniform, the publication of *The Negro World,* the establishment of small-business enterprises like grocery stores and laundries in the community, and the launching of the Black Star Line. During the 1920s, Garvey's organization had 9,000 members in Chicago, 6,000 in Philadelphia and Cincinnati, 4,000 in Detroit, and over 30,000 in New York.[41]

Garvey offered a message that electrified many blacks in Harlem and many other ghettos of urban America: the color of their skin was beautiful, and Africa had a glorious past. "When Europe was inhabited by a race of cannibals, a race of savages, naked men, heathens and pagans, Africa was peopled with a race of cultured black men, who were masters in art, science, and literature. . . ." Many Harlemites found their voices in their new leader. "Now we have started to speak," Garvey declared, "and I am only the forerunner of an awakened Africa that shall never go back to sleep." Garvey depicted a glorious future for blacks: "We are the descendants of a suffering people; we are the descendants of a people determined to suffer no more." To overthrow oppression, they must reclaim their continent: "If Europe is for the Europeans, then Africa shall be for the black peoples of the world. We say it; we mean it. . . . The other races have countries of their own and it is time for the 400,000,000 Negroes to claim Africa for themselves." A song of the Garvey movement urged:

> *Advance, advance to victory,*
> *Let Africa be free;*
> *Advance to meet the foe*
> *With the might*
> *Of the red, the black, and the green.*

Red symbolized the blood of the race, black their color, and green the greatness of Africa's future.[42]

Influenced by Washington's philosophy of black self-help and independence, Garvey promoted black capitalism and called upon his followers to invest in his shipping company: "The Black Star Line Corporation presents to every Black Man, Woman, and Child the opportunity to climb the great ladder of industrial and commercial progress. If you have ten dollars, one hundred dollars, or one or five thousand dollars to invest for profit, then take out shares in the Black Star Line, Inc. This corporation is chartered to trade on every sea and all waters. The Black Star Line will turn over large profits and dividends to stockholders, and operate to their interest even whilst they will be asleep." Some 40,000 blacks bought 155,510 shares amounting to three-quarters of a million dollars.[43]

The most prominent symbol of the UNIA, the Black Star Line became a slippery slope for Garvey. In 1922, the leader was arrested, charged with using the mails to defraud by advertising and selling stock for a nonexistent ship. According to Garvey, "a sum of $25,000 was paid by one of the officers of the corporation to a man to purchase a ship, but the ship was never obtained and the money was never returned." Garvey's managers had also made mistakes in their purchase of ships that required very costly repairs, and the corporation became mired in debt. The government's case was weak, for it could not prove intent to commit fraud. But Garvey was found guilty and sentenced to five years in prison. From the Atlanta penitentiary, Garvey sent a message: "My work is just begun. Be assured that I planted well the seed of Negro or black nationalism which cannot be destroyed even by the foul play that has been meted out to me." Released two years later by a presidential pardon, Garvey was deported to Jamaica as an undesirable alien.[44]

Garvey was gone, but the powerful dreams he represented remained in the hearts of Harlemites. The *New York News* declared that Garvey had "awakened the race consciousness and race pride of the masses of Africans everywhere as no man ever did . . . save Booker T. Washington." The *Spokesman,* a black publication, echoed: "Garvey made thousands think, who had never thought before. Thousands who merely dreamed dreams, now see visions."[45]

Actually, the visions were already there, carried to Harlem by the black migrants from the South. Many had been driven there by a sense of destiny. "If my race can make Harlem," exclaimed a proud resident, "good lord, what can't it do?" The Reverend Adam Clayton Powell of the Abyssinian Baptist Church declared: "Harlem became the symbol of liberty and the Promised Land to Negroes everywhere."[46]

For black intellectuals, Harlem was what Langston Hughes called the center of the "New Negro Renaissance," "a great magnet" pulling them from everywhere. "More than Paris, or the Shakespeare country, or Berlin, or the Alps," Hughes said, "I wanted to see Harlem, the greatest Negro city in the world." Hughes would remember forever the "thrill of the underground ride to Harlem": "I went up the steps and out into the bright September sunlight. Harlem! I stood there, dropped my bags, took a deep breath and felt happy again."[47]

The Harlem of the black literary renaissance was a place of the mind.

During the 1920s, in their flight from the Protestant ethic and materialism, white liberal intellectuals embraced Harlem and the "New Negro" as counterpoints to the bourgeois America of Babbitry. At night, they streamed to this black community to experience what they felt mainstream society was not — colorful, exotic, spontaneous, sensuous, and lively. "White people began to come to Harlem in droves," reported Hughes. Night after night, thousands of whites flooded the little cabarets and bars, "believing that all Harlemites left their houses at sundown to sing and dance in the cabarets."[48]

Black intellectuals were also gathering in Harlem and sitting in the cabarets. Drawing their inspiration and materials from black folk culture, they created a literature that rebelled against Middletown America. Actually, many of them had come from the black middle class. In his sociological profile of these writers, Robert Bone found that "the parents of the Renaissance novelists were 55 percent professional and 45 percent white collar." Hughes complained that his father, a wealthy rancher, was "interested only in making money." Many of the writers had attended college, and they felt especially hurt by the stings of discrimination and inequality. Educational and economic success, they had come to realize, did not mean social acceptance.[49]

To these middle-class black intellectuals, Harlem held out the promise of what Alain Locke called the "New Negro." The "mass movement of the urban immigration of Negroes" was "projected on the plane of an increasingly articulate elite." In the "largest Negro community in the world," "the peasant, the student, the business man, the professional man, artist, poet, musician, adventurer and worker, preacher and criminal, exploiter and social outcast" were coming together. They were forming a new community based on a vision of black pride. "In Harlem," Locke announced, "Negro life is seizing upon its first chances for group expression and self-determination. It is — or promises at least to be — a race capital."[50]

The "New Negro" would be "a collaborator and participant in American civilization," and black intellectuals would be in the forefront of this great movement. They would see the future in a different mirror. Hughes described the black tomorrow in song:

> I am the darker brother.
> They send me to sit in the kitchen
> When company comes,
> But I laugh,

And eat well,
And grow strong.

Tomorrow,
I'll sit at the table
When company comes.
Nobody'll dare
Say to me,
"Eat in the kitchen,"
Then.

Besides,
They'll see how beautiful I am
And be ashamed.[51]

But first blacks had to learn how to accept themselves. In his essay "The Negro Artist and the Racial Mountain," Hughes explained that the tragic problem of black intellectuals was denial: they did not want to be black or write about black life. A promising young Negro poet told Hughes: "I want to be a poet — not a Negro poet." What he meant, Hughes commented, was: " 'I want to write like a white poet'; meaning subconsciously, 'I would like to be a white poet'; meaning behind that, 'I would like to be white.' " But such a flight from black identity was bound to undermine his artistic creativity. "I was sorry the young man said that," Hughes continued, "for no great poet has ever been afraid of being himself. And I doubted then that, with his desire to run away spiritually from his race, this boy would ever be a great poet." Hughes understood this denial, for he knew that there was a "mountain standing in the way of any true Negro art in America — this urge within the race toward whiteness, this desire to pour racial identity into the mold of American standardization, and to be as little Negro and as much American as possible."[52]

To overcome the "racial mountain," Hughes insisted, black writers had to declare boldly: "I am a Negro — and beautiful!" The lives of common blacks had to be celebrated, for theirs was a counterculture affirming the joy of life rather than the fear of spontaneity. Simple people, they had their songs and a "nip of gin" on Saturday nights, Hughes stated; they were not obsessed with work and materialistic success. They furnished a "wealth of colorful, distinctive material for any artist" because they had been able to preserve their "own individuality in the face of American standardizations." "Perhaps these common people will give to the world its truly great Negro artist," Hughes declared, "the one who is not afraid to be himself."[53]

In his own poems, Hughes described his own search for identity. Was he African? he had wondered. "So long, so far away" was Africa; "not even memories" were "alive." "I did not feel the rhythms of the primitive surging through me," he explained apologetically. "I was only an American Negro — who had loved the surface of Africa and the rhythms of Africa — but I was not Africa. I was Chicago and Kansas City and Broadway and Harlem." Still, though the drums were "subdued and time-lost," Hughes felt he could hear a song of Africa through "some vast mist of race."[54]

Hughes was struggling to create an identity that was both African and American, a racial self symbolized by the rivers of both continents.

> *I've known rivers:*
> *I've known rivers ancient as the world and older than the*
> *   flow of human blood in human veins.*
> *My soul has grown deep like the rivers.*
>
> *I bathed in the Euphrates when dawns were young.*
> *I built my hut near the Congo and it lulled me to sleep.*
> *I looked upon the Nile and raised pyramids above it.*
> *I heard the singing of the Mississippi when Abe Lincoln went*
> *   down to New Orleans, and I've seen its muddy bosom*
> *   turn all golden in the sunset.*
>
> *I've known rivers:*
> *Ancient, dusky rivers.*
>
> *My soul has grown deep like the rivers.*[55]

But, in the struggle against the "racial mountain," could the black artist create an African-American sensibility? This was the question that pulled an aspiring young writer, Claude McKay, to Harlem. McKay had come from Jamaica as a student in 1912, but after two years at the Tuskegee Institute and then Kansas State College, he joined the exodus to Harlem, where he hoped to become a poet and novelist. Educated, he was essentially a middle-class intellectual trying to find his roots in black folk culture. In *Home to Harlem,* McKay searched for his black identity through his characters.

In this novel, Jake personifies spontaneity and a repudiation of the

Protestant ethic. He has been away from the United States, traveling around the world, but now he has come home — to Harlem. The community's lustiness, freedom, and vibrancy electrify him. Harlem offers a place where he can luxuriate in a "primitive passion for going against regulation." Carefree, joyous, and proud of his race, Jake is "no lineal descendant of Uncle Tom." Soon after his arrival, Jake meets a prostitute. He has $59 — all the money he possesses — and he spends $9 for drinks with her. On their way to her apartment, he asks her how much it will cost for sex, and she says $50. "Fine," Jake exclaims. Giving her all of his money, he boasts in soliloquy: "I ain't got a cent to my name, but ahm as happy as a prince, all the same. Yes, I is." Jake does not calculate, does not worry about money, and he finds black women tantalizing. "Sometimes there were two or three white women, who attracted attention because they were white and strange to Harlem, but they appeared like faded carnations among those burning orchids of a tropical race." In contrast to Jake, the chef in McKay's story has a regular job on a train and likes its routine. He does not eat watermelons or even pork chops — foods he associates with blacks. "I don't eat no poke chops, nigger," he tells a black waiter. "I cooks the stuff, but I don't eat it nevah." The chef hates his past, his folk culture: he "grimly . . . exists."[56]

Unlike both Jake and the chef is Ray: college-educated and a reader of books written by Fyodor Dostoyevski and Sherwood Anderson, he is filled with a yearning for the primitive. He feels that his education has shackled rather than freed him. His greatest contentment would be to lose himself "in some savage culture in the jungles of Africa." Ray would like to be spontaneous and uninhibited like Jake. "If he could have felt about things as Jake," McKay observed, "how different his life might have been! Just to hitch up for a short while and be irresponsible!" But Ray is trapped, a "slave of the civilized tradition."[57]

What McKay was describing in Ray was the dilemma many black writers experienced as they tried to celebrate the very folk culture that also challenged their identity as middle-class, educated intellectuals. But where could black writers truly learn about this folk culture? One of them decided he had to go home, not to Harlem, but to the rural South.

As a young writer searching for his roots, Jean Toomer wandered from university to university — Wisconsin, Chicago, New York University, City College of New York. He was the son of a white father and a mulatto mother. His father, a planter, had abandoned the family shortly after Toomer was born, and Jean and his mother lived in Washington,

D.C. In 1921, he left New York to teach in a black school in rural Georgia. In the South, black folk culture beckoned, and Toomer felt something irresistible surge within him. In a letter to Claude McKay in 1922, Toomer described the epiphany he had experienced: "Within the last two or three years . . . my growing need for artistic expression has pulled me deeper and deeper into the Negro group. . . . It has stimulated and fertilized whatever creative talent I may contain within me. A visit to Georgia last fall was the starting point of almost everything of worth that I have done. I heard folksongs come from the lips of Negro peasants. I saw the rich dusky beauty that I had heard many false accounts about, and of which till then, I was somewhat skeptical. And a deep part of my nature, a part that I had repressed, sprang suddenly to life and responded to them."[58]

What came out of this powerful encounter was the lyrical novel *Cane*. The story opens in rural Georgia, where the soil is a rich red, and the black people strong and beautiful. A girl is singing: "her voice is loud," and the echoes of her song, "like rain, sweep the valley." The roots of black culture reach all the way back to a continent across the Atlantic. The Dixie Pike is described as a road that "has grown from a goat path in Africa." The land is nurturing:

> *O land and soil, red soil and sweet-gum tree,*
> *So scant of grass, so profligate of pines,*
> *Now just before an epoch's sun declines*
> *Thy son, in time, I have returned to thee,*
> *Thy son, I have in time returned to thee.*
>
> *In time, for though the sun is setting on*
> *A song-lit race of slaves, it has not set;*
> *Though late, O soil, it is not too late yet*
> *To catch the plaintive soul, leaving, soon gone,*
> *Leaving, to catch thy plaintive soul soon gone.*[59]

But something tragic and evil haunts the land. The people are trapped in a cage of racism conditioned by slavery. In one story, a white woman, Becky, has two mulatto sons; they are ostracized by both whites and blacks. The sons build a cabin and hide their mother; the isolation becomes overwhelming. Goddamn everybody, the sons scream as they leave town. The cabin collapses, killing Becky. People come by to see the ruins, and someone throws a Bible on the pile of bricks and splintered lumber. But guilt cannot be so easily absolved. Racial hatred deforms lives, black and white. In another incident, Tom kills a white man in a fight over a black woman; caught and tied to a stake, Tom is drenched with kerosene. A match is thrown, and the white mob yells, then becomes silent as the air stinks of burning flesh and Tom's eyes pop. Rural Georgia, as it turns out, is a place of both beauty and brutality.[60]

In contrast, Washington, D.C., represents the city: its alleys, theaters, pool halls, and apartments symbolize a confinement stifling the souls of blacks from the rural South. Their culture has been carried to urban America, but here it struggles to survive: "A crude-boned, soft-skinned wedge of nigger life breathing its loafer air, jazz songs and love, thrusting unconscious rhythms, black reddish blood into the white and white-washed wood of Washington. Stale soggy wood of Washington. Wedges rust in soggy wood."[61]

Like a wedge, Dan Moore enters Washington. A young black man from rural Georgia, he has come to visit Muriel, a schoolteacher. When Dan arrives at her apartment, he encounters an iron gate and becomes confused because he cannot find the bell button. Frustrated, he wants to get an ax and smash the barrier. Proud of his rural roots, he declares to himself: "I am Dan Moore. I was born in a canefield." Finally, Muriel opens the door. Her hair is processed, her manner formal, her conversation mechanical. Muriel asks Dan what he is doing now. "Same old thing, Muriel," he replies. "Nothing, as the world would have it. Living, as I look at things. Living as much as I can without — ." "But you can't live without money, Dan," she interrupts. "Why don't you get a good job and settle down?" Dan rejects her lecture about conforming to middle-class standards and walks out of her apartment.[62]

Dan can always return home to the rural South, but such a journey can be difficult for college-educated blacks. Kabnis moves from the North to Georgia. The hills, valleys, folk songs, and red soil surround him, but he is unable to appreciate this beauty. Middle class and mulatto, he has become separated from blacks and their folk culture. He wants to connect himself to them but cannot come to terms with that part of his own black past symbolized by the old ex-slave Father John. When Kabnis sees Father John, he recoils, insisting: "An besides, he aint my past. My ancestors were Southern blue-bloods." His denial keeps him "suspended a few feet above the soil whose touch would resurrect him." To recover his wholeness would require his acknowledgment of slavery as well as his black ancestry.[63]

Toomer painfully understood this truth. Like Kabnis, he was never able to resolve the dilemma of his identity — the liminality of being biracial. In 1924, the same year as the publication of *Cane*, he went to France to study at the Georges Gurdjieff Institute, seeking to develop a cosmic consciousness. "I am," he told friends. "What I am and what I may become I am trying to find out." According to Darwin Turner, he looked like "an Indian or a dark-skinned European." Toomer had difficulty forming an identity that would reflect his racial duality. "What was I?" Toomer asked. "I thought about it independently, and, on the basis of fact, concluded I was neither white nor black, but simply an American." In 1930, James Weldon Johnson requested Toomer's permission to publish some of his poems in a book entitled *American Negro Poetry*. Toomer refused, explaining: "My poems are not Negro poems. My prose likewise. They are, first, mine. And, second, in so far as general race or stock is concerned, they spring from the result of racial blending here in America which has produced a new race or stock. We may call this stock . . . American. . . ." Toomer's decision to identify himself as "American" rather than Negro prompted Langston Hughes to remark: "Why should Mr. Toomer live in Harlem if he doesn't care to? Democracy is democracy, isn't it?" But Toomer realized that his reality was much more complicated than the "racial mountain" as Hughes had defined it.[64]

Like Toomer, Zora Neale Hurston felt compelled to touch the "soil" of black folk culture in the South. Born and raised in the all-black town of Eatonville, Florida, she initially attended Howard University, where she began writing and publishing short stories. As a young writer, she realized that Harlem was the place to be: "So, beginning to feel the urge to write, I wanted to be in New York." There she could set her hat "at a certain angle and saunter down Seventh Avenue, Harlem City, feeling as snooty as the lions in front of the Forty-Second Street Library." During the 1920s, Hurston studied anthropology with Franz Boas at Barnard College and Columbia University. But Harlem was not home for her, and in 1927, she returned to the South to do research on rural blacks and write about them, especially in *Their Eyes Were Watching God*.[65]

In this novel published in 1937, Hurston's main character, Janie, has been raised by her grandmother. As a slave, Nanny had been forced to have sexual relations with her master. After Nanny gave birth to a child "wid gray eyes and yaller hair," she was scolded by her master's wife and whipped. Nanny insisted it was not her fault: "Ah don't know nothin' but what Ah'm told tuh do, 'cause Ah ain't nothin' but uh nigger and uh slave." After emancipation, Nanny's daughter attended school, but she was raped by her teacher and then gave birth to Janie.[66]

Nanny's hope for Janie is to fulfill her own dream of "whut a woman oughta be and to do." She explains to her teenage granddaughter what she sees as the problem of race and gender: "Honey, de white man is de ruler of everything as fur as Ah been able tuh find out. . . . So de white man throw down de load and tell de nigger man tuh pick it up. He pick it up because he have to, but he don't tote it. He hand it to his women-folks. De nigger woman is de mule uh de world so fur as Ah can see." Nanny does not want the "menfolks white or black" making "a spit cup" out of Janie; so she arranges for Janie to marry an old man, Logan Killicks. Janie is told she must marry him because he owns sixty acres and can support her. Love, she hopes, will come after their marriage.[67]

But love fails to develop, and Janie runs off with a young man. She finds Joe Starks exciting, for he is ambitious and has a dream of building an all-black town. "De man dat built things oughta boss it," he declares. "Let colored folks build things too if dey wants to crow over somethin'." Starks has his own idea of what Janie should be: "A pretty doll-baby lak you is made to sit on de front porch and rock and fan yo'self and eat p'taters dat other folks plant just special for you." Janie discovers she has become "Mrs. Mayor Starks," a possession for "*him* to look at." She tries to rebel: "You sho loves to tell me whut to do, but Ah can't tell you nothin' Ah see!" And Starks retorts: "Dat's 'cause you need tellin'. It would be pitiful if Ah didn't. Somebody got to think for women and chillun and chickens and cows. I god, they sho don't think none themselves." Forced into submission, Janie learns to hush, but the "spirit of the marriage" leaves the bedroom.[68]

Several years later, Stark dies from an illness, and Janie meets and falls in love with Tea Cake. He teaches her how to play checkers. She feels a glow inside, generated by the invitation to play and by the acknowledgment that she is intelligent. Janie decides to marry and go off with him. "Dis is uh love game," she tells a friend. "Ah done lived Grandma's way, now Ah means tuh live mine." Nanny's dream had been for a black woman to live like a white woman. "She was borned in slavery time when folks, dat is black folks, didn't sit down anytime dey felt lak it. So sittin' on porches lak de white madam looked lak uh mighty find thing tuh her. Dat's whut she wanted for me — don't keer whut it cost. Git up on uh high chair and sit dere. She didn't have time tuh think what tuh do after you got up on de stool uh do nothin'." But to sit high on a stool seemed like death to Janie.[69]

Janie and Tea Cake move to "de muck," the Everglades, to "make money and fun and foolishness." The marriage has its stormy moments.

Tea Cake, too, feels a need to show Janie that he is the "boss" and slaps her around a bit. But as they work together, they come to share love and mutual respect based on equality. During a destructive hurricane, they face the prospect of violent death. Janie tells Tea Cake that she is not afraid to die: "We been tuhgether round two years. If you kin see de light at daybreak, you don't keer if you die at dusk." A rabid dog tries to attack Janie, and Tea Cake is badly bitten fending off the beast. He becomes raving mad, and Janie has to shoot her husband to save her own life. The tragedy leaves Janie with an understanding of the love they had shared. "Love ain't somethin' lak un grindstone dat's de same thing everywhere and do de same thing tuh everything it touch," Janie explains to a friend. "Love is lak de sea. It's uh movin' thing, but still and all, it takes its shape from de shore it meets, and it's different with every shore."[70]

Like Toomer, Hurston found Hughes's concept of the "racial mountain" too simplistic, too one-dimensional. What rendered race especially complex for her was gender. The "Negro Renaissance" seemed stifling to Hurston as an artist and as a woman. "From what I had read and heard," she complained, "Negroes were supposed to write about the Race Problem. I was and am thoroughly sick of the subject. My interest lies in what makes a man or a woman do such-and-so, regardless of . . . color." Indeed, within the world of blacks and whites, as she saw it, there was a gender mountain.[71]

"But a Few Pegs to Fall": The Great Depression

By the 1920s, Harlem had become a slum, the home of poor people desperately clinging to deferred dreams. The Harlem Renaissance, with its cabarets and literary lights, hid much of the ghetto's squalor. Then came the Great Crash of 1929 and the shattering of the economy, unshrouding the grim reality behind this veil of glamour. "The depression brought everybody down a peg or two," Langston Hughes observed. "And the Negroes had but a few pegs to fall."[72]

Blacks fell into deeper poverty everywhere, in the South as well as the North. In 1930, the majority of blacks still lived below the Mason-Dixon Line, growing cotton as sharecroppers and tenant farmers. Their livelihoods crumpled along with the stockmarket: cotton prices had dropped sharply from 18 cents per pound in 1929 to 6 cents in 1933. That year, two-thirds of the blacks cultivating cotton only broke even or went deeper into debt. Moving to southern cities in search of work, blacks encountered angry unemployed whites, shouting: "No Jobs for

Niggers Until Every White Man Has a Job!" "Niggers, back to the cotton fields — city jobs are for white folks." By 1932, more than 50 percent of blacks living in southern cities were unemployed.[73]

In northern cities, unemployment rates among blacks soared to similar levels. In 1932, sociologist Kelley Miller described the black worker as "the surplus man, the last to be hired and the first to be fired." In Harlem, according to social worker Anna Arnold Hedgeman, blacks were "faced with the reality of starvation and they turned sadly to public relief. . . . Meanwhile, men, women, and children combed the streets and searched in garbage cans for food, foraging with dogs and cats. . . . Many families had been reduced to living below street level. It was estimated that more than ten thousand Negroes lived in cellars and basements which had been converted into makeshift flats. Packed in damp, ratridden dungeons, they existed in squalor not too different from that of Arkansas sharecroppers."[74]

The statistics told the story of hardship and hunger for blacks. In its survey of 106 cities, the Urban League found that "with a few notable exceptions . . . the proportion of Negroes unemployed was from 30 to 60 percent greater than for whites." Similarly, government reports showed that blacks joined the relief rolls two times more frequently than whites due to unemployment. In October 1933, 18 percent of the black population was on relief, compared to 10 percent for whites. "Heretofore [the black's] employment problem has been chiefly one of advancement to positions commensurate with his ability," an Urban League leader explained. "Today he is endeavoring to hold the line against advancing armies of white workers intent upon gaining and content to accept occupations which were once thought too menial for white hands."[75]

The New Deal seemed to offer little relief to blacks. Federal programs designed to provide a safety net for people in distress forced blacks to take a back seat. The Agricultural Adjustment Administration offered white farmers and workers higher rates of support than their black counterparts. "The AAA was no new deal for blacks," wrote historian Harvard Sitkoff; "it was a continuation of the same old raw deal." Similarly, the National Recovery Administration failed to protect black workers from discrimination in employment and wages. Blacks denounced the NRA as "Negroes Ruined Again" and "Negro Removal Act." In 1935, at a conference on "The Position of the Negro in the Present Economic Crisis," black leaders and intellectuals grimly assessed the Roosevelt administration: "The Negro worker has good reason to feel that his government has betrayed him under the New Deal."[76]

The economic crisis and the failure of the New Deal generated strategy debates among blacks, especially within the NAACP. Feeling that blacks had been battered economically and politically, W. E. B. DuBois decided that they should consider "voluntary segregation." As a leader of the NAACP and the editor of *The Crisis,* DuBois had long been a fighter for integration. But the Great Depression led him to urge blacks to "herd together" and "segregate" themselves, at least on an interim basis, in order to survive. They should view themselves as black consumers and producers, committed to working together to build a black "economic nation within a nation." They should create a "closed economic circle" — shop at Negro-owned stores stocked with Negro-grown food, transported by Negro shippers, and processed by Negroes. What DuBois had in mind was not capitalism but a "cooperative and socialistic state" within the black community, "a collective system on a non-profit basis" with the consumers at "the center and the beginning of the organization."[77]

DuBois argued that such a separatist strategy was only "common sense." Blacks should "face the fact quite calmly that most white Americans [did] not like them." Criticized harshly by the NAACP for his segregationist proposal, DuBois resigned as editor. Declaring that segregation was an evil, the NAACP called for "the building of a labor movement, industrial in character, which will unite all labor, white and black, skilled and unskilled, agricultural and industrial."[78]

Indeed, blacks had begun to enter industrial employment and the labor movement. The economic crisis had underscored the power of management to use blacks as strikebreakers and the need for labor unions to combat this tactic by including black workers and by promoting unity among the Stephanos, Trinculos, and Calibans of depression America. Therefore, in 1933, the United Mine Workers led by John L. Lewis launched a campaign to bring black workers into the union by employing black organizers and demanding equal pay, regardless of race. Known as "the U.M.W. Formula," this strategy was adopted by the Committee for Industrial Organization (CIO), which initiated massive organizing drives across the country. Led by Philip Murray, the Steel Workers Organizing Committee announced that its policy was "one of absolute racial equality in Union membership." In St. Louis in 1937, an Urban League official reported: "The S.W.O.C. organizers are making it a point to have a Negro officer in each lodge, composed from a plant in which there are Negro workers." Practicing an early version of affirmative action, the Packinghouse Workers Organizing Committee successfully demanded that Swift and Company hire blacks in proportion to their percentage of the Chicago population. In the auto industry, the United Auto Workers urged blacks to join, pledging its opposition to racial discrimination. In 1941, after it enrolled black workers, who constituted 12 percent of Ford Motor Company's labor force, the UAW won union recognition and wage increases. While these achievements did not mean the end of racism among white workers, they demonstrated that interracial labor solidarity was essential, especially in the struggle against management during a time of economic crisis. Like the "giddy multitude" of Bacon's Rebellion, these black and white workers understood their common class interests.[79]

Meanwhile, seeking to attract black voters, New Deal policymakers were beginning to address the needs of blacks. The Public Works Administration, for example, mandated the proviso "There shall be no discrimination on account of race, creed or color." Blacks praised the WPA for prohibiting racial discrimination and for giving them a chance to participate in the program. "In the northern communities, particularly the urban centers," a black journal editorialized, "the Negro has been afforded his first real opportunity for employment in white-color occupations." The Democratic strategy of appealing to blacks, according to Sitkoff, paid off "handsomely." The massive migration of blacks to northern cities had led to a national political realignment; increasingly, they became an important force in the northern states that possessed a large number of electoral votes. A contemporary political analyst calculated that black voters held the power to control elections in northern states totaling 157 electoral votes, 31 more than the southern states. During the depression, disillusioned with Herbert Hoover and the Republicans, blacks were starting to abandon the party of Lincoln. In the 1936 presidential election, according to George Gallup, over three-fourths of northern blacks voted for Franklin D. Roosevelt, who had been promoted among them as the second "Emancipator."[80]

Blacks were becoming players in a newly emerging Democratic coalition, but their advances in labor and politics would soon be swept into the powerful international currents of World War II.

PART FOUR

Crossings

The Ashes at Dachau

LIKE BACON'S REBELLION and the emancipation of blacks during the Civil War, World War II represented a crossing in the making of multicultural America. German nazism with its ideology of Aryan racial supremacy forced Americans to look critically at the racism within their own society. Social scientists took the lead in this crucial self-examination. In *Man's Most Dangerous Myth: The Fallacy of Race*, published in 1942, Ashley Montagu framed the war as a conflict between the "spirit of the Nazi racist" and the "spirit of democracy." Nazism reflected the wrongheaded and dangerous thinking that "the shape of the nose or the color of skin" had something "to do with human values and culture." A year later, in *The Races of Mankind*, Ruth Benedict denounced racism as unscientific and urged the United States to "clean its own house" and "stand unashamed before the Nazis and condemn, without confusion, their doctrines of a Master Race."[1]

During the war, the most eloquent call for American society to confront its own racism appeared in Gunnar Myrdal's *American Dilemma: The Negro Problem and Modern Democracy*. In fighting this "ideological war," he argued, Americans must apply the principle of democracy more explicitly to race. "Fascism and nazism are based on a racial superiority dogma — not unlike the old hackneyed American caste theory — and they came to power by means of racial persecution and oppression." Therefore, Americans must stand before the whole world in support of racial tolerance and equality. "When in this crucial time the international leadership passes to America," Myrdal observed, "the great reason for hope is that this country has a national experience of uniting racial and cultural diversities and a national theory, if not a consistent practice, of freedom and equality for all. . . . The main trend in [this country's] history is the gradual realization of the American Creed."[2]

Similarly, pundits and policymakers depicted the war as a defense of democracy and a campaign against racism. "By making this a 'people's' war for freedom," it was argued, "we can help clear up the alien problem, the negro problem, the anti-Semitic problem." Republican leader Wendell Willkie echoed: "Today it is becoming increasingly apparent to thoughtful Americans that we cannot fight the forces of imperialism abroad and maintain a form of imperialism at home. . . . Our very proclamations of what we are fighting for have rendered our own inequities self-evident. When we talk of freedom of opportunity for all nations, the mocking paradoxes in our own society become so clear that they can no longer be ignored." "We are behind the times I admit," Frank Dixon, a former governor of Alabama, confessed to a friend. "The Huns have wrecked the theories of the master race with which we were so contented so long." The *New York Times* editorialized in May 1941: "A nation making an all-out effort cannot neglect any element in its population. If it is engaged on the side of democracy it must leave open the doors of opportunity to all, regardless of race."[3]

As president, Franklin D. Roosevelt framed the ideology of America's war purpose: the United States was the "arsenal of democracy." This country stood for the "four freedoms" — freedom of speech, freedom of worship, freedom from want, and freedom from fear. Our commitment to these freedoms, the president explained, buttressed America's condemnation of racism. "The principle on which this country was founded and by which it has always been governed is that Americanism is a matter of mind and heart," Roosevelt declared; "Americanism is not, and never was, a matter of race or ancestry."[4]

This was a lesson that had been forged in the crucible of America's multicultural history. Asians and Mexicans had emigrated to America searching for such freedoms, but they found themselves facing barriers because of race. On the eve of World War II, Asian immigrants were still excluded from citizenship; in many states, they were not allowed to own land. Mexican immigrants found themselves being pushed from welfare rolls and targeted for deportation. Indians were confined to reservations where they were governed by federal regulations and bureaucrats. In the North, African Americans were restricted to reservations called ghettos, and in the South, they were trapped in a system of peonage, euphemistically called sharecropping. But in their struggle for freedom — their resistance against racial borders and distances — all of these groups had been appropriating America's principle that "all men are created equal," endowed with "unalienable Rights" of life and liberty. Frederick Douglass had pointed out that the Constitution stated, "We the People," not "we the white people." As people, blacks should be "included in the benefits for which the Constitution of America was ordained and established." In this struggle for equality, racial minorities had been advancing a more inclusive definition of who was and could be American. Takao Ozawa had insisted on his entitlement to become a citizen of the United States even though he was not white.[5]

During World War II, America's "errand into the wilderness" was redefined as a democratic and antiracist mission, especially as Americans learned about Hitler's demonic program of Jewish genocide. In 1938, the frightening sound and fury of *Kristallnacht*'s shattering glass in Germany had echoed through the shtetls of America, evoking memories of an earlier terror. Also that year, when Germany incorporated Austria, the Hitler regime began terrorizing Austrian Jews. Tens of thousands of them were forced to flee for their lives. Although President Franklin Roosevelt ordered the State Department to raise the quotas for German and Austrian immigration to 26,000, he was unwilling to lift the ceiling any higher. Worried about a possible nativist backlash, he urged other countries to offer sanctuary. An international conference was held, but nothing was accomplished.

Meanwhile, Hitler was carrying out the systematic genocide of Jews as his "Final Solution." During the war, eyewitness accounts from the Polish underground were reporting gas chambers in the concentration camps for Jews. As information about the death camps reached America, a rage swept through the Lower East Side and other Jewish communities across America. Twenty thousand people gathered at Madison Square Garden on July 21, 1942, to demonstrate against Hitler's racist atrocities. "Citizens, regardless of religious allegiance," President Roosevelt assured them, "will share in the sorrow of our Jewish fellow-citizens over the savagery of the Nazis against their helpless victims. . . . The American people not only sympathize with all victims of Nazi crimes but will hold the perpetrators of these crimes to strict accountability in a day of reckoning which will surely come." On October 6, 1943, four hundred rabbis marched from the Capitol to the White House "to protest the silence of the world when an entire people [were] being murdered."[6]

At the time, however, Americans were unaware of the magnitude of the Holocaust — the destruction of six million Jews. This shocking revelation moved a Yiddish poet to weep: "Even an outcry is now a lie, even tears are mere literature, even prayers are false." The horror seemed inexplicable, beyond belief, sometimes even shattering a belief in God:

> Can I then choose not to believe
> in that living God whose purposes

when He destroys, seeming to forsake me,
I cannot conceive;
choose not to believe in Him
who having turned my body to fine ash
begins once more to wake me?[7]

Among the U.S. troops who liberated the Jewish prisoners at the Dachau concentration camp were some black soldiers. One of them recalled the sickening sensation he experienced as he scanned the horror — the survivors looking like ghosts, the ovens still warm. "Why Jews?" Paul Parks asked. "It doesn't make sense. Why were they killed?" A prisoner explained: "They were killed because they were Jews." Parks commented: "I understand that." Then he added: "I understand that because I've seen people lynched just because they were black." Parks compared the experiences of the two groups: "There's one other great incident of humanity that I'm very familiar with, the three hundred years of slavery in my own country, where people for generations were not allowed to be free, subject to the dictates of another race. Held in bondage, forced to work, and forced to do what another person wanted you to do. And if you didn't obey, there were no laws against killing you and destroying your family. So I said, 'As you talk, I see there's a close parallel between the history of my people in America and what's happened to the Jews in Europe.' "[8]

There were other soldiers at Dachau who also understood what it meant to be victimized because of their group membership. Shortly after Japan's attack on Pearl Harbor, the federal government forcibly interned 110,000 Japanese Americans, most of them citizens by birth. Their constitutional rights of due process had been denied solely because of their race — they were considered disloyal and judged to be an internal military security threat. Many of these Japanese-American soldiers had left their families in the internment camps at home in order to prove their loyalty by serving in the U.S. Army, and now, after fighting their way through Italy and France, they had reached Dachau. Surveying the gruesome scene, the Japanese-American soldiers were stunned by the demonic dimension of racism that had been unshrouded in the Nazi death camps. In his diary, Ichiro Imamura described the Holocaust's manifestation at Dachau:

When the gates swung open, we got our first good look at the prisoners. Many of them were Jews. They were wearing black and white striped prison suits and round caps. A few had shredded blanket rags draped over their shoulders. . . . The prisoners struggled to their feet [and] shuffled weakly out of the compound. They were like skeletons — all skin and bones. . . .

We had been ordered not to give out rations to the Dachau prisoners because the war was still on and such supplies were needed to keep our own fighting strength up, but we gave them food, clothing and medical supplies anyway. The officers looked the other way. These prisoners really needed help and they needed it right away. They were sick, starving and dying.

I saw one GI throw some orange peelings into a garbage can. One of the prisoners grabbed the peelings, tore them into small pieces and shared them with the others. They hadn't had any fruit or vegetables in months. They had scurvy. Their teeth were falling out of their gums.

We stayed near Dachau for several days and then got orders to move on. During this time, I found some large chalk-like bars, sort of oval-shaped, with numbers shaped on them. I was about to "liberate" a couple of them as souvenirs when an MP told me they were the remains of prisoners. The numbers were for identification. I put the bars back.[9]

Initially, the Jewish prisoners were surprised and confused to see soldiers of Japanese ancestry. "When they first came in, we thought they were allies of the Germans," a prisoner stated years later. "We believed they were there to torture us." Some of the Jewish prisoners thought that their liberators did not look like "Americans." "I am an American soldier," a Nisei soldier reassured them, "and you are free." A Jewish prisoner recalled that he was too weak to walk out of the camp, and a Japanese-American soldier picked him up and carried him to freedom. For these American soldiers of Japanese ancestry, Dachau served as a ghastly lesson of how an ideology of racial superiority could ultimately lead to genocide.[10]

14

THROUGH A GLASS
DARKLY

Toward the Twenty-first Century

A War for Democracy: Fighting as One People

AT DACHAU, Ichiro Imamura and his fellow Japanese-American soldiers understood more profoundly than ever before the importance of World War II as a struggle for democracy — democracy as a principle as well as a process to protect the rights of racial minorities. But they also knew that democracy in America had failed them: their own government had unjustly interned 110,000 Japanese Americans living on the West Coast. This action had been justified by policymakers as a "military necessity." But, if this were the case, why were the 150,000 Japanese Americans in Hawaii, where American armed forces had actually engaged the enemy and where concerns for internal security were real, not sent to internment camps?

Two days after the Japanese attack on Pearl Harbor, the military governor of Hawaii called for calm. "There is no intention or desire on the part of the federal authorities to operate mass concentration camps," declared General Delos Emmons. "No person, be he citizen or alien, need worry, provided he is not connected with subversive elements. . . . While we have been subjected to a serious attack by a ruthless and treacherous enemy, we must remember that this is America and we must do things the American Way. We must distinguish between loyalty and disloyalty among our people."[1]

But the War Department in Washington viewed the matter very differently and called for the mass evacuation of the Japanese from Hawaii. General Emmons countered that such a program would severely disrupt both the economy and defense of Oahu, for the Japanese represented over 90 percent of the carpenters, nearly all of the transportation workers, and a significant proportion of the agricultural laborers. Japanese labor, he argued, was "absolutely essential" for rebuilding the defenses destroyed at Pearl Harbor. Commenting on charges of Japanese-American fifth-column activities, General Emmons declared: "There have been no known acts of sabotage committed in Hawaii." In the end, he ordered the internment of only 1,444 Japanese.[2]

Emmons's resistance to mass evacuation had the support of Hawaii's business community. Most of the leading businessmen opposed mass internment. The president of the Honolulu Chamber of Commerce called for just treatment of the Japanese in Hawaii: "These people . . . want to live here because they like the country and like the American way of life. . . . The citizens of Japanese blood would fight as loyally for America as any other citizen. I have read or heard nothing in statements given out by the military, local police or FBI since December 7 to change my opinion. And I have gone out of my way to ask for the facts." Possessing a sense of genteel paternalism and a long history of interaction with the Japanese in the islands, the white business establishment was against the mass uprooting of Japanese Americans. Moreover, it was aware that the evacuation of over one-third of Hawaii's population would decimate the labor force and destroy the economy of the islands.[3]

Meanwhile, politicians and public officials also urged restraint and reason. Hawaii's congressional delegate, Sam King, advised the military to do nothing beyond apprehending known spies. When schools were reopened in January 1942, the superintendent of public instruction sent a directive to all teachers: "Let us be perfectly frank in recognizing the fact that the most helpless victims, emotionally and psychologically, of the present situation in Hawaii will be children of Japanese ancestry and their parents. . . . Let us keep constantly in mind that America is not making war on citizens of the United States or on law-abiding aliens within America."[4]

The press in Hawaii also behaved responsibly. Newspapers cautioned their readers not to spread or be influenced by rumors generated by the war situation. Within days after the attack on Pearl Habor, the *Honolulu Star Bulletin* dismissed reports of Japanese subversion in the islands as "weird, amazing, and damaging untruths." "Beware of rumors always," urged the *Paradise of the Pacific* magazine in February 1942, "avoid them like a plague and, when possible, kill them as you would a reptile. Don't repeat for a fact anything you do not know is a fact."[5]

Meanwhile, however, the Japanese on the West Coast found themselves facing a very different situation. Unlike General Emmons, Lieutenant General John L. DeWitt of the Western Defense Command pushed for the mass removal of Japanese Americans. DeWitt ignored or dismissed government reports that had confirmed Japanese-American loyalty. Lieutenant Commander K. D. Ringle of the Office of Naval Intelligence had determined that the large majority of Japanese Americans were at least passively loyal to the United States. Estimating that only about 3,500 of them could potentially be dangerous, he concluded that there was no need for mass action against the Japanese. Similarly, in his report to the attorney general submitted in early February 1942, FBI Director J. Edgar Hoover had insisted that mass evacuation of the Japanese could not be justified for security reasons. When Hoover learned that DeWitt had decided to go ahead with his plan, he bluntly remarked that DeWitt's intelligence information reflected "hysteria and lack of judgment." The claim of military necessity for mass evacuation, Hoover argued, was based "primarily upon public and political pressure rather than on factual data."[6]

Indeed, unlike the newspapers in Hawaii, the media in California helped to fuel the agitation for removal. Initially, after the attack on Pearl Harbor, West Coast newspapers tended to be restrained, advising readers to be considerate toward the Japanese. But the sentiments of the press suddenly began to shift. On January 5, John B. Hughes of the Mutal Broadcasting Company opened an attack on the Japanese in California. The Japanese were engaged in espionage, he charged, and their dominance in produce production and their control of the food supply were part of a master war plan. The *Los Angeles Times* questioned the loyalty of American-born Japanese, graphically suggesting that their affiliation with Japan was an inherited racial trait: "A viper is nonetheless a viper wherever the egg is hatched — so a Japanese American, born of Japanese parents — grows up to be a Japanese, not an American."[7]

As the press mounted its campaign against Japanese Americans, it was joined by patriotic organizations. The American Legion of California demanded that all Japanese known to possess dual citizenship be placed in "concentration camps," while American Legion posts in Washington and Oregon passed resolutions urging the evacuation of all Japanese. In the January issue of their publication, *The Grizzly Bear,* the Native Sons and Daughters of the Golden West admonished fellow Californians: "We told you so. Had the warnings been heeded — had the federal and state authorities been 'on the alert,' and rigidly enforced the Exclusion Law and the Alien Land Law . . . had the legislation been enacted denying citizenship to offspring of all aliens ineligible to citizenship . . . — the treacherous Japs probably would not have attacked Pearl Harbor . . . and this country would not today be at war with Japan."[8]

The anti-Japanese chorus included voices from farming interests such as the Grower-Shipper Vegetable Association, the Western Growers Protective Association, and the California Farm Bureau Federation. "We've been charged with wanting to get rid of the Japs for selfish reasons," the Grower-Shipper Vegetable Association stated in the *Saturday Evening Post.* "We might as well be honest. We do. It's a question of whether the white man lives on the Pacific Coast or the brown man. They came into this valley to work, and they stayed to take over. . . . If all the Japs were removed tomorrow, we'd never miss them in two weeks, because the white farmers can take over and produce everything the Jap grows."[9]

Meanwhile, local and state politicians were clamoring for Japanese removal. California Attorney General Earl Warren pressed federal authorities to remove the Japanese from sensitive areas on the West Coast. The Japanese in California, he warned, "may well be the Achilles heel of the entire civilian defense effort. Unless something is done it may bring about a repetition of Pearl Harbor."[10]

The Western Defense Command, headed by General DeWitt, operated within this context of racism and war hysteria. The Japanese Americans on the West Coast were extremely vulnerable. They were not needed as laborers in the mainstream economy, and many white farmers viewed Japanese farmers as competitors. The Japanese in California represented a small population. Isolated in their own communities and their own ethnic economy, they lacked the broad support that their counterparts in Hawaii had. In early February, General DeWitt sent Washington a written recommendation for mass evacuation. When Attorney General Francis Biddle received the recommendation, he told President Roosevelt that there were "no reasons" for such action. In his diary on February 10, Secretary of War Henry L. Stimson commented: "The second generation Japanese can only be evacuated either as part of a total evacuation . . . or by frankly trying to put them out on the ground that their racial characteristics are such that we cannot understand or trust even the citizen Japanese. This latter is the fact but I am afraid it will make a tremendous hole in our constitutional system to apply it." But in the end, President Roosevelt decided to violate the Constitution. On February 19, by executive order, he authorized General DeWitt to remove Japanese Americans from the West Coast and place them in internment camps.[11]

Under General DeWitt's command, the military ordered a curfew for all "enemy aliens" and all persons of Japanese ancestry and posted orders for evacuation. Years later, Congressman Robert Matsui, who was a baby in 1942, asked: "How could I as a 6-month-old child born in this country be declared by my own Government to be an enemy alien?" But the order applied to everyone, including children. An American birthright made absolutely no difference. "Doesn't my citizenship," protested a Nisei, "mean a single blessed thing to anyone?"[12]

When they arrived at the assembly centers, the evacuees were shocked to discover that they were to be housed in stockyards, fairgrounds, and racetracks. "The assembly center was filthy, smelly, and dirty. There were roughly two thousand people packed in one large building. No beds were provided, so they gave us gunny sacks to fill with straw, that was our bed." Stables served as housing. "Suddenly you realized that human beings were being put behind fences just like on the farm where we had horses and pigs in corrals." Conditions were crowded and noisy. "There was a constant buzzing — conversations, talk. Then, as the evening wore on, during the still of the night, things would get quiet, except for the occasional coughing, snoring, giggles. Then someone would get up to go to the bathroom. It was like a family of three thousand people camped out in a barn." There were curfews and roll calls, and "day and night camp police walked their beats within the center."[13]

After a brief stay in the assembly centers, the evacuees were herded into one hundred and seventy-one trains and transported to ten internment camps — Topaz in Utah, Poston and Gila River in Arizona, Amache in Colorado, Jerome and Rohwer in Arkansas, Minidoka in Idaho, Manzanar and Tule Lake in California, and Heart Mountain in Wyoming. Most of the camps were located in remote desert areas. "We did not know where we were," remembered an internee. "No houses were in sight, no trees or anything green — only scrubby sagebrush and an occasional low cactus, and mostly dry, baked earth."[14]

Housed in barracks, each family was assigned one room, 20 by

20 feet. The room had "a pot bellied stove, a single electric light hanging from the ceiling, an Army cot for each person and a blanket for the bed." The facility resembled both a military base and a prison. "Camp life was highly regimented and it was rushing to the wash basin to beat the other groups, rushing to the mess hall for breakfast, lunch, and dinner." The internees ate at long tables, and parents often sat at separate tables from their children. People were "crowded in a long line just like a snake," waiting "for a meal in the dust and wind." At school, the children began the day by saluting the flag of the United States and then singing, "My country, 'tis of thee, sweet land of liberty." Looking beyond the flagpole, they could see the barbed wire and the armed guards. "I was too young to understand," recalled George Takei, "but I remember soldiers carrying rifles, and I remember being afraid." Young married couples worried about having children born in the camps. "When I was pregnant with my second child, that's when I flipped," said a Nisei woman. "I guess that's when the reality really hit me. I thought to myself, gosh, what am I doing getting pregnant. I told my husband, 'This is crazy. You realize there's no future for us and what are we having kids for?' "[15]

But many young Japanese Americans were determined to create a better future for themselves as well as their parents, and they believed that one way to accomplish this was to serve in the American armed forces. By defending their country, they would be able to demonstrate the loyalty of Japanese Americans as well as claim their American birthright. During the war, 33,000 Japanese Americans were in uniform. Several thousand of them were members of the Military Intelligence Service, functioning as interpreters and translators on the Pacific front. Armed with Japanese-language skills, they provided an invaluable service by translating captured Japanese documents including battle plans and secret codes. Richard Sakakida's translation of Japanese plans for the landing on Bataan made it possible for American tanks to ambush the invaders as they landed. Japanese-American soldiers volunteered for service with Merrill's Marauders in Burma. Describing their heroic work, an officer reported: "During battles they crawled up close enough to be able to hear Jap officers' commands and to make verbal translations to our soldiers. They tapped lines, listened in on radios, translated documents and papers, made spot translations of messages and field orders. . . ." General Charles Willoughby, chief of intelligence in the Pacific, estimated that Japanese-American military contributions shortened the war by two years.[16]

Japanese-American soldiers also helped to win the war in Europe. As members of Hawaii's 100th Battalion, they participated in military campaigns in North Africa and Italy. So many of them were wounded or killed that the 100th was called the "Purple Heart Battalion." Japanese Americans of the 442nd Regiment fought at Luciana, Livorno, and the Arno River, where casualties totaled 1,272 men — more than one-fourth of the regiment. Then they were sent to France, where they captured the town of Bruyeres in heavy house-to-house fighting. After this battle, they were ordered to rescue the Texan "Lost Battalion," 211 men who were surrounded by German troops in the Vosges Mountains. "If we advanced a hundred yards, that was a good day's job," recalled a Japanese-American soldier. "We'd dig in again, move up another hundred yards, and dig in. That's how we went. It took us a whole week to get to the Lost Battalion. It was just a tree-to-tree fight." At the end of a week of intense fighting, the 442nd had suffered 800 casualties. When the trapped Texans finally saw their rescuers, some broke into sobs. One of the Texans remembered the moment: "[The Germans] would hit us from one flank and then the other, then from the front and the rear . . . we were never so glad to see anyone as those fighting Japanese Americans."[17]

When the war ended in May 1945, the soldiers of the 442nd Regiment had suffered 9,486 casualties, including 600 killed. "Just think of all those people — of the 990 that went over [with me], not more than 200 of them came back without getting hit," veteran Shig Doi sadly remarked. "If you look at the 442nd boys, don't look at their faces, look at their bodies. They got hit hard, some lost their limbs." The 442nd, military observers agreed, was "probably the most decorated unit in United States military history." They had earned 18,143 individual decorations — including a Congressional Medal of Honor, 47 Distinguished Service Crosses, 350 Silver Stars, 810 Bronze Stars, and more than 3,600 Purple Hearts. "They bought an awful hunk of America with their blood," declared General Joseph Stilwell. "You're damn right those Nisei boys have a place in the American heart, now and forever." In 1946, President Harry Truman welcomed home the 442nd Regiment: "You fought for the free nations of the world . . . you fought not only the enemy, you fought prejudice — and you won."[18]

Indeed, many Japanese-American soldiers had gone to war to fight racism at home. In a letter from the European battlefront, a Japanese-American soldier explained the purpose of his sacrifice:

> My friends and my family — they mean everything to me. They are the most important reason why I am giving up my education and

my happiness to go to fight a war that we never asked for. But our Country is involved in it. Not only that. By virtue of the Japanese attack on our nation, we as American citizens of Japanese ancestry have been mercilessly flogged with criticism and accusations. But I'm not going to take it sitting down! I may not be able to come back. But that matters little. My family and friends — they are the ones who will be able to back their arguments with facts. They are the ones who will be proud. In fact, it is better that we are sent to the front and that a few of us do not return, for the testimony will be stronger in favor of the folks back home.[19]

Many Japanese-American soldiers gave testimony on the battlefronts. Their parents had crossed an ocean to America, where they worked in the canefields of Hawaii and transformed the valleys of California from deserts to farmlands. But they had been forced to remain strangers in their adopted country. Now their sons were proving with their blood, their limbs, and their bodies that they were truly Americans.

THE day after the attack on Pearl Harbor, the United States and the Republic of China declared war on Japan, and the two countries became allies. America's entry into the war ignited patriotic explosions in Chinatowns across the country. In "A Memo to Mr. Hitler, Hirohito & Co.," the San Francisco Chinese community warned:

Have you heard the bad news? America is out to get you. America has a grim, but enthusiastic bombing party started, and you're the target in the parlor game.

San Francisco Chinatown, U.S.A., is joining the party. Chinatown will have fun blasting you to hell. Chinatown is proud to be a part of Freedom's legion in freeing all the decent people of the world from your spectacle.

Chinatown's part of the party will cost $500,000. Admission price to the fun is the purchase of a U.S. War Bond. We're all going to buy a War Bond for Victory.

P.S. More bad news. Everyone in Chinatown is going to this party. We're NOT missing this one.[20]

Young Chinese Americans were eager to fight in the war. Mrs. Emily Lee Shek became the first Chinese woman to join the WAACS. "She tried to join up right in the beginning [of the war]," the *Chinese Press* reported in September 1942, "but the 105-pound weight minimum barred her. When the requirement was dropped five pounds, she drank two gallons of water and lived on a special Chinese diet, and made it — yes, with one pound to spare." In New York's Chinatown, excited crowds cheered themselves hoarse when the first draft numbers drawn were for Chinese Americans. "To men of my generation," explained Charlie Leong of San Francisco's Chinatown, "World War II was the most important historic event of our times. For the first time we felt we could make it in American society." The war had given them the opportunity to leave Chinatown, don army uniforms, and be sent overseas, where they felt "they were part of the great patriotic United States war machine out to do battle with the enemy." Similarly, Harold Liu of New York's Chinatown recalled: "In the 1940s for the first time Chinese were accepted by Americans as being friends because at that time, Chinese and Americans were fighting against the Japanese and the Germans and the Nazis. Therefore, all of a sudden, we became part of an American dream. We had heroes with Chiang Kai-shek and Madame Chiang Kai-shek and so on. It was just a whole different era and in the community we began to feel very good about ourselves. . . . My own brother went into the service. We were so proud that they were in uniform." Altogether, 13,499 Chinese were drafted or enlisted in the United States armed forces — 22 percent of Chinese adult males.[21]

Confined for decades to the Chinese ethnic economy of restaurants and laundries, Chinese workers suddenly found the doors of employment opportunities opening to them, especially in the defense industries where labor shortages were acute. "At Douglas, home of the A-20 attack planes and dive bombers," the *Chinese Press* noted in 1943, "there are approximately 100 Chinese working." Chinese workers constituted 15 percent of the shipyard workers in the San Francisco Bay Area in 1943. They found employment in the defense industries at the Seattle-Tacoma Shipbuilding Corporation, the shipyards of Delaware and Mississippi, and the airplane factories on Long Island. The war also benefited Chinese women. Several hundred "alert young Chinese-American girls," the *Chinese Press* reported in 1942, "have gone to the defense industries as office workers. . . . They're part of the millions who stand behind the man behind the gun." A year later, in an article on "Women in the War," this newspaper congratulated Helen Young, Lucy Young, and Hilda Lee — "the first Chinese women aircraft workers in California" — for helping build B-24 bombers in San Diego.[22]

Writing for *Survey Graphic* in 1942, sociologist Rose Hum Lee recorded the positive ways the war was changing the lives of Chinese on the home front: "They have gone in the army and navy, into shipbuilding and aircraft plants. Even the girls are getting jobs." But while the Chinese were participating in the war effort as Americans, Lee pointed out, they lacked full equality. The Chinese should be accorded the same treatment as European immigrants, she argued, and should be allowed to enter the United States as well as to become naturalized citizens. Lee then exposed America's hypocrisy: "Surely racial discrimination should not be directed against those who are America's Allies in the Far East and are helping her in every way to win the war. . . . To be fighting for freedom and democracy in the Far East, at the cost of seven million lives in five years of hard, long, bitter warfare, and to be denied equal opportunity in the greatest of democracies, seems the height of irony."[23]

Many Americans agreed with Lee: the war abroad required reform at home. In 1943, Congress repealed the Chinese exclusion laws and allowed a quota for Chinese immigration. "China is our ally," President Franklin Roosevelt wrote in support of the bill. "For many long years she stood alone in the fight against aggression. Today we fight at her side. She has continued her gallant struggle against very great odds." Aware America needed to reinforce China's effort in the war, the president urged Congress to "be big enough" to acknowledge an error of the past: "By the repeal of the Chinese exclusion laws, we can correct a historic mistake and silence the distorted Japanese propaganda."[24]

Actually, this new policy permitted just a tiny trickle of Chinese immigrants, only 105 annually. The law also extended the right of naturalized citizenship to Chinese immigrants. But it required applicants to present documentation of their legal entry into the United States as well as pass tests for English competency and knowledge of American history and the Constitution. Between 1944 and 1952, only 1,428 Chinese were naturalized. Nevertheless, at last after almost one hundred years in America, Chinese immigrants could seek political membership in their adopted country. They had been among the original "Forty-Niners." They had helped to build America — its irrigation systems in California and its transcontinental railroad. "Gold Mountain" finally seemed to be a dream coming true.

SHOULD Indians fight for America? On one reservation, an agency superintendent observed: "There may be some justice in the Indians' opposition to registration. They feel that this country was taken away from them by white men and for that reason they should not now be required to help in case of invasion or attack." But, as Indian Affairs Commissioner John Collier explained, many Indians wanted to join the war effort because they felt the conflict was "more than just another war." Rather it was a "life-and-death struggle for the survival of those things for which they [had] been unceasingly waging an uphill fight for many generations" — their cultural independence, the right to their native religions, and the right to democracy. "Perhaps their experiences of the last ten years," he added, "in which there has been a rebirth of spirit, a reviving of the smoldering fires of local democracy, and a step toward economic rehabilitation, have helped them to see the possibilities in a world of the Four Freedoms."[25]

Though Indians had been treated badly by the United States, one of them explained, they would suffer much worse under Hitler. "We know that under Nazism we should have no rights at all; we should be used as slaves." In their declaration of war against Germany, Japan, and Italy, the Iroquois League announced: "It is the unanimous sentiment among the Indian people that the atrocities of the Axis nations are violently repulsive to all sense of righteousness of our people. This merciless slaughter of mankind upon the part of those enemies of free peoples can no longer be tolerated." The Cheyennes condemned the Axis nations as an "unholy triangle" seeking to "conquer and enslave the bodies, minds and souls of all free people."[26]

Altogether, 25,000 Indians served in the United States armed forces, including 800 Indian women. A year after the attack on Pearl Harbor, the *New York Times* reported that 8,800 of the 60,000 Indian males between the ages of twenty-one and forty-four were in military uniform, a higher rate than for the general population. They included volunteers from the Fort Peck Sioux-Assiniboine reservation in northern Montana. "The Sioux who left this reservation," John Collier noted, "were descendants of the band which whipped Custer." Collier described the enthusiastic Indian response to the war: "More than once an Indian or a group of Indians has shown up at agency headquarters, each man with his gun ready to register for Selective Service and to proceed immediately to the scene of the fighting." The Indian readiness to serve in the military prompted the *Saturday Evening Post* to editorialize: "We would not need the Selective Service if all volunteered like Indians."[27]

Praise for Indian patriotism and fighting prowess sometimes reflected stereotypical images from the frontier days. "The red soldier is tough," the *American Legion Magazine* declared. "Usually he has lived outdoors all his life, and lived by his senses; he is a natural Ranger. He takes to commando fighting with gusto. Why not? His ancestors invented it. . . . At ambushing, scouting, signaling, sniping, they're peerless. Some can smell a snake yards away and hear the faintest movement; all endure thirst and lack of food better than average." Similarly, Secretary of the Interior Harold Ickes noted how the "inherited talents of the Indian" made him "uniquely valuable — endurance, rhythm, time, coordination, sense perception, an uncanny ability to get over any sort of terrain at night, and . . . an enthusiasm for fighting."[28]

Indians contributed to the military campaign in unique ways. In the Philippines, a Choctaw scout, who had escaped from the Japanese at the battle of Corregidor, led underground guerrilla forces until the war ended. Indians such as the Oneidas, Chippewas, and Comanches were able to block the Japanese decoding of American military information by dispatching messages in their tribal languages. The Marine Corps organized a special all-Navajo signal unit, known as the Code Talkers. "When we were recruited," a Navajo recalled, "we knew only that we were to be specialists of some kind, but did not know we would have anything to do with the setting up of codes." In the codes, many Navajo words were given military meaning: "chicken hawk" for dive bomber, "hummingbird" for fighter plane, and "iron fish" for submarine. The Navajo Code Talkers participated in the landing at Guadalcanal, where they sent and received reports from the field commanders. Working behind enemy lines, Navajo communications teams sometimes found themselves mistaken for the Japanese enemy by other American soldiers.[29]

Indians also served in the Army Air Corps. More than thirty of them were awarded the Distinguished Flying Cross, while another seventy received the Air Medal. Indians tried to play down the importance of their awards. "Indians should not be considered apart from other Americans," one Cherokee pilot remarked in 1943. "We are just doing our job." Constituting 20 percent of the Forty-fifth Army Infantry Division, known as the "Thunderbird," Indian soldiers fought in North Africa, Italy, and France. The casualties for this division were extremely high — 3,747 dead, 4,403 missing, and 19,403 wounded.[30]

As Indian and white soldiers fought together against a common enemy, many of them came to know one another. Navajo Charlie Miguel recalled how he had learned to drill and handle a rifle in a Virginia bootcamp where he found himself among whites for the first time in his life: "Every evening we drank beer, ten cents a bottle, and had nice chow. I got along all right with the white boys. I didn't know much about

389

English, but I got along all right." In a poem, a Chippewa soldier described the feeling of unity that had been forged in the heat of battle:

> We bind each other's wounds and eat the same ration.
> We dream of our loved ones in the same nation.[31]

Scorned as the enemy during the frontier wars, Indians were now proudly fighting as American soldiers. In 1943, a Navajo soldier wrote to his tribal council: "I don't know anything about the white man's way. I never went outside the reservation. . . . I am proud to be in a suit like this now. It is to protect my country, my people, the head men, the chiefs of my people. . . ." "One time there were these Indians, see," explained an Indian in a novel written by the daughter of a Pueblo veteran. "They put on uniforms, cut their hair. They went off to a big war." Now "they were MacArthur's boys [and] got treated the same as everyone: Wake Island, Iwo Jima. They got the same medals for bravery, the same flag over the coffin. . . . This was the land of the free just like the teachers said in school. They had the uniform and they didn't look different no more. They got respect."[32]

One Indian soldier who gained respect and also fame was Ira Hayes of the Pima tribe. One of "MacArthur's boys," he participated in the marines' landing at Iwo Jima in 1945. During an advance against fierce enemy fire, Hayes and five fellow marines reached the summit of Mount Suribachi, where they raised the American flag. An Associated Press photograph inscribed this heroic moment in the minds of proud Americans across the country. After returning from the battlefront, Hayes became an honored celebrity: his face was featured on millions of posters for a war bond drive and also on a postage stamp.[33]

Meanwhile, on the home front, Indians supported the war financially. By April 1943, they had purchased $13 million in war bonds, which, according to Secretary Ickes, "equaled the per capita contribution of any racial group including the whites." Indians also contributed to the war effort by working in defense plants. "By war's end," reported historian Alison Bernstein, "40,000 persons — one-half of the able-bodied men who had not entered the military and one-fifth of the women — had left Indian lands for war-related work." Their participation in the war economy was reflected in their places of residence: in 1940, less than 5 percent of the entire Indian population lived in cities; ten years later, this figure had jumped to 20 percent. Trained in sheet metal and mechanics by reservation schools, Indians were applying their skills in shipyards, airplane plants, and tank factories. "The Indians are playing an important role in the agricultural and industrial production program of the war," Collier noted. "Skilled Indian workers are to be found scattered throughout important war industries in almost every section of the country. They are doing highly technical jobs in aircraft industries on the west coast, in Kansas, and in New York state. . . . More than two thousand Navahos were employed in the construction of a large ordnance depot in New Mexico. On this particular project it was most interesting to see long-haired, fullblood Indians tying steel, operating jack hammer, doing welding, and handling some of the most difficult machine operations."[34]

Transformed into modern construction workers, Indians seemed to have come a long way. In the nineteenth century, they had been what James Madison called "the red race on our border": they had been viewed as "savages" on the "frontier" — to be removed toward the "Stony mountains" and corralled on reservations. The war offered opportunities for Indian participation in the defense of America. Winning the war meant more than just defeating Hitler. "We want to win the war," an Indian explained, "because victory will mean new hope for men and women who have no hope."[35]

SHORTLY after Raul Morin heard the news of Japan's attack on Pearl Harbor, he rushed to find his friends on Olvera Street in Los Angeles. As they talked about the crisis, the young men nervously sought to reassure themselves by engaging in *vacilada,* or "humor." "*Ya estuvo* [This is it]," one of them said. "Now we can look for the authorities to round up all the Mexicans and deport them to Mexico — bad security risks." Another answered: "They don't have to deport me! I'm going on my own; you're not going to catch me fighting a war for somebody else. I belong to Mexico. *Soy puro mexicano!*"[36]

But the war led not to the deportation of Mexican Americans but to the importation of laborers from Mexico. To meet new demands for agricultural production, the federal government established the "bracero" program (from the Spanish word *brazos,* or "arms"). Under the supervision of the federal government, the braceros were to be imported as contract laborers who would be returned to Mexico at the end of their term. On September 29, 1942, the first 1,500 braceros were transported to California by train; on their passenger cars, someone had scribbled: "*De Las Democracias Sera La Victoria*" ("There will be victory of the democracies"). During the war years, the federal government appropriated over $100,000,000 for the labor importation program and recruited workers by the thousands: 4,000 in 1942, 52,000 in 1943, 62,000 in 1944, and 120,000 a year later.[37]

Like their brethren of earlier times, these Mexicans came to El Norte, blown this way by their hopeful dreams:

> From Morelia I came as a bracero,
> To earn dollars was my illusion.
> I bought shoes, I bought a sombrero,
> And even put on new pants.

They also experienced disappointment as they found themselves exploited as "arms":

> And now I find myself
> Breathless,
> I'm a shoemaker by profession
> But here they say I'm a camel
> And I work just with a shovel and a hoe.

But still they continued to migrate here, anxious for work:

> Braceros cross and cross
> During summer and spring. . . .
> I go and come, come and go
> Looking for bread for my children. . . .
> Braceros cross and cross.[38]

The braceros assisted the war effort by helping to grow and harvest sugar beets, tomatoes, peaches, plums, and cotton. They worked in twenty-one states, where in 1944 alone, they harvested crops worth $432,000,000. They also worked on the railroads as section hands and maintenance laborers, helping to transport military freight and personnel.

Meanwhile, Mexican Americans were directly involved in the defense of America. As members of the 200th and 515th Coast Artillery units of the New Mexico National Guard, Chicanos were already in the Philippines before the attack on Pearl Harbor. They had been sent to this American outpost because they spoke Spanish, and many of them were killed or captured at the battle of Bataan. The Congreso del Pueblo de

Habla Española (the Spanish-Speaking Congress) urged Mexican Americans to join their Anglo compatriots in arms: "Our liberties, our homes, and our lives directly threatened by Fascism demand our greatest unity. . . . We as Latinos have had centuries of gloriously fighting for freedom; we shall not abandon this historic tradition in these days of crisis." The Congreso affirmed their American identity: "We are also children of the United States. We will defend her."[39]

Altogether, half a million Mexican Americans served in the U.S. armed forces. California Congressman Jerry Voorhis congratulated them for their contributions to the defense of their country: "As I read the casualty lists from my state, I find anywhere from one-fourth to one-third of those names are names such as Gonzales or Sanchez, names indicating that the very lifeblood of our citizens of Latin-American descent in the uniform of the armed forces of the United States is being poured out to win victory in the war. We ought not to forget that. We ought to resolve that in the future every single one of these citizens shall have the fullest and freest opportunity which this country is capable of giving him, to advance to such positions of influence and eminence as their own personal capacities make possible." Although Mexican Americans comprised only one-tenth of the Los Angeles population, they represented one-fifth of the casualties.[40]

One of the Chicano slogans of World War II was "Americans All." On his way to the European front, a Mexican-American soldier reflected on the possibility of dying and the meaning of such a sacrifice: "What if I were killed? . . . What would happen to my wife, my three children? My mother? . . . All the horrible thoughts imaginable would grip me, and before I could find the answers, other thoughts would begin to swirl in. I remembered about us, the Mexican-Americans . . . how the Anglo had pushed and held back our people in the Southwest. . . . Why fight for America when you have not been treated as an American?" But he was overwhelmed by "the feeling" he had for his "home" in America, the country where he had been born. "All we wanted," he decided, "was a chance to prove how loyal and American we were." As they went off to fight for America, Chicano soldiers sang "Soldado Razo":

> *I leave as a common soldier,*
> *I'm going to join the ranks.*
> *I will be among the brave boys*
> *who leave their beloved mothers*
> *and sweethearts in tears,*

crying for their departure.
I'm leaving for the war, contented.
I'll have my rifle and gun ready.
When the shooting is over,
I will return as a Sergeant.
The only one thing I regret,
Is leaving my poor Mother alone.
Oh brunette Virgin, please take care of her.
Watch over her, she is a wonderful person.
Please take care of her till I return.
I will depart at early morn tomorrow,
right at the break of day.
And so . . . hereforth goes another Mexican
who is willing to gamble his life.
I say goodbye with this song . . .
Long live this Country of mine.[41]

But while Mexican Americans were defending American democracy abroad, they sometimes had to defend themselves against racial violence at home. In 1943, antagonism against Mexicans exploded in the Los Angeles "Zoot-Suit" riots when hundreds of Anglo servicemen went on a rampage, beating up scores of young Mexican Americans who were despised for their sharp dress and stereotyped as gang members. Meanwhile, in Texas, the Mexican foreign minister blasted the treatment of Mexicans: "In many parts of Texas, Mexicans cannot attend public gatherings without being subject to vexations, complaints and protests. There are towns where my fellow countrymen are forced to live in separate districts." In its condemnation of racism, the Mexican weekly *Mañana* editorialized: "The Nazis of Texas are not political partners of the Fuhrer of Germany but indeed they are slaves to the same prejudices. . . ."[42]

Chicanos believed they were entitled to equality and respect. They had been in the Southwest before the arrival of the Anglos, and many of them still viewed the territory as "occupied Mexico." During the early twentieth century, Mexican immigrants had crossed the border to El Norte searching for opportunity, only to find their dreams denied in the Promised Land. Now, through military sacrifice, Chicanos felt they had earned their right to full citizenship. "Mexican-American soldiers," declared Marine Corps veteran Balton Llanes, "shed at least a quarter of the blood spilled at Bataan. . . . What they want now is a decent job, a decent home, and a chance to live peacefully in the community." Through their military involvement and bravery, Chicano soldiers had bound their people to America. "The services have helped our Mexican-American," declared Manuel De La Raza in 1942. "It has dressed all alike and given opportunities for advancement on merit and work. . . . This war . . . is doing what we in our Mexican-American movement had planned to do in one generation. . . . It has shown those 'across the tracks' that we all share the same problems. It has shown them what the Mexican Americans will do, what responsibility he will take and what leadership qualities he will demonstrate. After this struggle, the status of the Mexican Americans will be different."[43]

SIMILARLY, African Americans hoped that World War II would lead to an improvement of their status. The war was challenging Americans of all races to come together in the fight for a "double victory" against fascism abroad and racism at home. "There should be no illusions about the nature of this struggle," declared black leader Ralph Bunche. "The fight now is not to save democracy, for that which does not exist cannot be saved. But the fight is to maintain those conditions under which people may continue to strive for realization of the democratic ideals. This is the inexorable logic of the nation's position as dictated by the world anti-democratic revolution and Hitler's projected new world order." There should be a price, the *Chicago Defender* declared, for black participation in the war: "We are not exaggerating when we say that the American Negro is damned tired of spilling his blood for empty promises of better days." The black newspaper asked: "Why die for democracy for some foreign country when we don't even have it here?" In order to unite the country and win the conflict, the *Defender* urged Americans to "bomb the color line."[44]

But what most Americans wanted was for blacks to bomb the enemy in Europe and Asia. Before the war, in 1940, there were only 5,000 blacks in an army of 230,000. By 1944, this figure had risen sharply to 700,000, while some 165,000 served in the Navy, 5,000 in the Coast Guard, and 17,000 in the Marine Corps. Four thousand black women served in the Women's Army Corps. On the European front alone, twenty-two black combat units fought in ground operations. The 761st Tank Battalion participated in the Battle of the Bulge; the heroic contributions of black infantrymen in the racially integrated units led the War Department to declare that they had "established themselves as fighting men no less courageous or aggressive than their white comrades."[45]

Though blacks fought bravely in the Pacific and Europe, they were defending a democracy that for them still represented a dream deferred. While serving the cause of the "Four Freedoms," blacks in uniform were generally assigned to segregated units. The War Department defended its segregationist policy, claiming that it could not ignore the "social relationships between Negroes and whites" that had been "established by the American people through custom and habit." In protest, the NAACP replied: "Declarations of war do not lessen the obligation to preserve and extend civil liberties here while the fight is being made to restore freedom from dictatorship abroad. . . . A Jim Crow army cannot fight for a free world."[46]

"Prove to us," blacks challenged whites, "that you are not hypocrites when you say this is a war for freedom." Blacks reminded America that there was a war for freedom to be fought in America's backyard. "The Army jim-crows us," complained a black student. "The Navy lets us serve only as messmen. . . . Employers and labor unions shut us out. Lynchings continue. We are disfranchised . . . spat upon. What more can Hitler do than that." Scheduled to be drafted into the army, a youth declared: "Just carve on my tombstone, 'Here lies a black man killed fighting a yellow man for the protection of a white man.' " Blues singer Lonnie Johnson expressed his resentment this way:

> And you can tell the world that I'm fightin'
> For what really belongs to me.[47]

Black columnist George Schuyler explained how African Americans saw the war: "Our war is not against Hitler in Europe, but against Hitler in America. Our war is not to defend democracy, but to get a democracy we have never had." The black *Amsterdam News* condemned "race discrimination and segregation, mob brutality — the entire Nazi pattern of U.S. racial conditions." A poem published in a black newspaper asked:

> Dear Lord, today
> I go to war:
> To fight, to die,
> Tell me what for?
>
> Dear Lord, I'll fight,
> I do not fear,

Germans or Japs;
My fears are here.
America![48]

Although they were allowed to fight and die for democracy, blacks were excluded from the defense industry. In 1940, they constituted only 0.2 percent of the workers in aircraft production. On the cover of its July issue, *The Crisis* featured a photograph of an airplane factory with the caption: "For Whites Only." The NAACP denounced discrimination in the defense industry: "Warplanes — Negro Americans may not build them, repair them, or fly them, but they must help pay for them."[49]

Before the war, blacks had generally been confined to the unskilled and the service occupations, and now they wanted the better and higher-paying factory jobs generated by the war. The political iron was hot, ready to be struck. Unwilling to wait for employers to open employment to them voluntarily, blacks demanded action from the federal government. At a meeting of frustrated blacks in Chicago in 1941, a black woman called for a mass demonstration in Washington: "We ought to throw 50,000 Negroes around the White House, bring them from all over the country, in jalopies, in trains and any way they can get there, and throw them around the White House and keep them there until we can get some action from the White House." The idea of a march on Washington seized A. Philip Randolph, the head of the Brotherhood of Sleeping Car Porters. He urged blacks across America to gather in the nation's capital to rally under the banner: "We Loyal Colored Americans Demand the Right to Work and Fight for Our Country." The march would pressure Congress and the president to translate pronouncements of democratic ideals into practice. Policymakers had to be pushed to do the right thing. "No one," explained a black woman supporting the march, "does anything — you never get anything — out of the goodness of people's hearts."[50]

The organizers of the march on Washington warned President Roosevelt to issue an executive order abolishing discrimination in the military and the defense industry, or else the country would face "the greatest demonstration of Negro mass power." The threat alarmed Washington officials. "What will they think in Berlin?" they anxiously asked. Blacks replied: "Oh, perhaps no more than they already think of America's racial policy." The pressure worked, and on June 25, 1941, President Roosevelt signed Executive Order 8802, establishing the Committee on Fair Employment Practices. "There shall be," he ordered, "no discrimination in the employment of workers in defense industries or Government because of race, creed, color, or national origin. . . . Again it is the duty of employers and of labor organizations . . . to provide for the full and equitable participation of all workers in defense industries. . . ."[51]

The new policy opened employment for tens of thousands of blacks in shipyards and factories geared for the nation's defense. This tide of black workers included women. "The women are working on that defense," observed black singer Huddie Ledbetter, "and they's making lots of money. . . ." In "National Defense Blues," he sang:

> *Just because she was working*
> *Making so much dough*
> *That woman got displaced*
> *Did not love me no more.*[52]

Almost one million blacks entered the industrial labor force during the war years; by 1945, they constituted more than 8 percent of all defense workers. Pulled by these employment opportunities, over half a million blacks left the South between 1940 and 1945; in Los Angeles, the black population nearly doubled from 75,000 to 135,000. This influx of blacks provoked violent white blacklashes, exploding in race riots in Detroit, Harlem, and many cities across the country. Still, World War II was a crossing, constituting what Robert C. Weaver called "more industrial and occupational diversification for Negroes than had occurred in the seventy-five preceding years."[53]

Three centuries earlier, the first Africans had been landed at a tiny English outpost called Jamestown. Since then African Americans had been contributing to the building of America. They had labored in the South's cotton economy, which was a vital basis of the Market Revolution; now they were defending their country against Nazi tyranny. They had participated militarily before — in Bacon's Rebellion, the American Revolution, the Civil War, and World War I. But this time, it was different, blacks thought, for they were fighting for America as a democracy. Surely, there would be a more enlightened, egalitarian America after the war.

But when peace came in 1945, Maya Angelou noticed black soldiers returning home only to hang out "on the ghetto corners like forgotten laundry left on a back yard fence." Their futures, brightened by the war, had suddenly clouded over again. "Thus we lived through a major war," Angelou commented. "The question in the ghettos was, Can we make it through a minor peace?" Domestic worker Ruth Shays was not hopeful blacks would hold on to even the small gains they had made. During the war, her white employer suddenly began using the word "colored" rather than "nigger" in her presence. "You see," she commented, "these Japanese and Germans was threatening to cut their toenails too short to walk, so she called herself friendly by not using that word 'nigger' because she knows I hate and despise it." Shays added: "Whenever they [whites] get a little scared they try to act like they might be decent, but when that war was over you didn't hear much about freedom and equal rights. . . ."⁵⁴

There would be no turning back to the old racial order, however. Something significant had occurred in the crucible of World War II. Before the war, the many different racial and ethnic groups of American society had felt little in common, and they lacked a shared sense of national purpose. Then the war came, and Americans of all races found themselves fighting as one people against nazism, bound by what Abraham Lincoln had described as the "mystic chords of memory" stretching from every battlefield and patriot grave to every "living heart and hearthstone" all over America. Indian Affairs Commissioner John Collier explained how the conflict had united Americans, forging an *unum* out of our *pluribus:* "Now a single ideal moves our entire nation, North and South, Indian and Black and White. That ideal is the preservation of democracy." W. E. B. DuBois defined World War II as a "War for Racial Equality" and a struggle for "democracy not only for white folks but for yellow, brown, and black."⁵⁵

America's Dilemma

World War II was the transition to the Civil Rights Revolution. The defense of democracy abroad stirred demands for racial justice at home; with peace came new challenges against discrimination and inequality. The winds of democracy began sweeping through American political institutions, especially the courts. In California, the Japanese challenged the Alien Land Law. In the Kajiro Oyama case of 1948, the United States Supreme Court ruled that the law prohibiting Japanese from owning and leasing land was "nothing more than outright racial discrimination" and therefore "unconstitutional." The Fourteenth Amendment, the Court argued, was "designed to bar States from denying to some groups, on account of race or color, any rights, privileges, and opportunities accorded to other groups." Significantly, the Court referred to the United

Nations Charter as well as the struggle against the racial ideology of the Third Reich. How could this nation be "faithful" to the United Nations Charter of human rights and freedom, the Court asked, if America had state laws that barred land ownership on account of race? Moreover, the Alien Land Law was "an unhappy facsimile, a disheartening reminder, of the racial policy pursued by those forces of evil whose destruction recently necessitated a devastating war." In haiku, a Japanese immigrant welcomed the Court's decision:

> Land laws faded out,
> It is comfortable now —
> This America.[56]

Racial discrimination was becoming un-American in the post–World War II years. In 1948, President Harry Truman desegregated the armed forces, mandating that the military would no longer have racially separate facilities and training programs. Truman also issued an executive order for a policy of "fair employment throughout the Federal establishment, without discrimination because of race, color, religion or national origin." Four years later, in the McCarran-Walter Act, Congress nullified the racial restriction of the 1790 Naturalization Law. Winning citizenship for the immigrant generation "was the culmination of our dreams," exclaimed Harry Takagi. "The bill established our parents as the legal equal of other Americans; it gave the Japanese equality with all other immigrants."[57]

Although they were now in their twilight years, many Japanese immigrants were eager to bridge past distances, become citizens of their adopted country.

> Going steadily to study English,
> Even through the rain at night,
> I thus attain,
> Late in life,
> American citizenship.[58]

But immigrants from Asia were still barred or severely restricted from entering the United States. Moral consistency compelled lawmakers to remove the barriers to Asian immigration, and in 1965, Congress enacted a new immigration law. "Just as we sought to eliminate discrimination in our land through the Civil Rights act [of 1964]," declared a congressman, "today we seek by phasing out the national origins quota system to eliminate discrimination in immigration to this nation composed of the descendants of immigrants." All groups should have equal opportunity to enter America. "Everywhere else in our national life, we have eliminated discrimination based on national origins," Attorney General Robert Kennedy told Congress. "Yet, this system is still the foundation of our immigration law." By abolishing discrimination against Asian immigrants, this new law represented a sharp ideological departure from the traditional view of America as a homogeneous white society — a perspective carried to the New World by the English colonists and reaffirmed in pronouncements by leaders such as Benjamin Franklin and Thomas Jefferson. The time had come for a redefinition of who could become an American.[59]

But there was still another ghost from the past that needed to be exorcised — the mass internment of Japanese Americans during World War II. "Stigmatized," the ex-internees had been silently carrying a "burden of shame." During the 1970s, however, many third-generation Japanese Americans were feeling a need to break the silence. Inspired by the Black Power movement and a growing sense of ethnic pride, they were searching for their roots. They learned that their immigrant grandparents had helped to transform California's valleys from deserts to rich farmlands while struggling against racial intolerance. Though these young people had educational and employment opportunities that had been denied to their parents and grandparents, they knew that Japanese Americans would continue to be viewed with suspicion unless they directly confronted the scurrilous charges of disloyalty aimed at Japanese Americans during World War II. Now they wanted their elders to tell them about the internment experience. "Why? Why!" their parents would ask defensively. "Why would you want to know about it? It's not important, we don't need to talk about it." Young Japanese Americans replied, "We need to tell the world what happened during those years of infamy," and urged their parents to join pilgrimages to the camps at Manzanar and Tule Lake.[60]

The questions and the pilgrimages inspired a demand for redress and reparations. In 1988, Congress passed a bill providing for an apology and a payment of $20,000 to each of the survivors of the internment camps. When President Ronald Reagan signed the bill, he admitted that the United States had committed "a grave wrong." During World War II, Japanese Americans had remained "utterly loyal" to this country, ·he pointed out. "Indeed, scores of Japanese Americans volunteered for our Armed Forces — many stepping forward in the internment camps themselves. The 442nd Regimental Combat Team, made up entirely of Japanese Americans, served with immense distinction — to defend this nation, their nation. Yet, back at home, the soldiers' families were being denied the very freedom for which so many of the soldiers themselves were laying down their lives." The nation needed, the president acknowledged, to end "a sad chapter in American history."[61]

Meanwhile, the grave wrong that blacks were seeking to have addressed was segregation. Blacks had defended democracy during World War II, but would they be allowed to participate in the American Dream as full citizens? In 1954, the question focused on equality of educational opportunity. In the *Brown v. Board of Education* decision, the United States Supreme Court declared that segregated schools were unconstitutional. Nullifying the "separate but equal" doctrine of *Plessy v. Ferguson,* the Court argued that separate educational facilities were "inherently unequal" and that school segregation was "a denial of the equal protection of the laws." The decision was hailed as a significant assault on the barriers of racial segregation and a powerful affirmation of America's principle of freedom. "We look upon this memorable decision not as a victory for Negroes alone," the NAACP announced, "but for the whole American people and as a vindication of America's leadership in the free world." Many blacks compared the decision to an earlier historic event. "My inner emotions must have been approximate to the Negro slaves' when they first heard about the Emancipation Proclamation," Robert Williams recalled. "Elation took hold of me so strongly that I found it very difficult to refrain from yielding to an urge of jubilation. . . . On this momentous night of May 17, 1954, I felt that at last the government was willing to assert itself on behalf of first-class citizenship, even for Negroes. I experienced a sense of loyalty that I had never felt before. I was sure that this was the beginning of a new era of American democracy." A year later, the Supreme Court delivered a supplementary ruling, instructing the lower courts to implement the *Brown* decision "with all deliberate speed."[62]

But integration remained largely a court ruling on paper, while segregation persisted as a reality in society. Pressure for change would have to come not from judicial pronouncements, but from a people's movement for civil rights. A year after the *Brown* decision, blacks shifted the focus of their struggle from the courts to the community. What would turn out to be a momentous stirring for racial justice began on December 1, 1955, when a forty-two-year-old black seamstress boarded a bus in Montgomery, Alabama. Tired from working all day at a department store, Rosa Parks sat down in the first seat behind the section reserved for whites. City law stipulated that the first four rows were reserved for whites, and that if whites filled up their section, blacks would have to move to make room for them. The bus became full, and the driver ordered Parks to stand up so that a white man could sit down. "Are you going to stand up?" he asked. "No," she replied. "Go on and have me arrested." Her arrest led to an explosive protest — the Montgomery bus boycott. Although blacks were dependent on the buses to get to and from work, thousands of them refused to take the bus.

> *Ain't gonna ride them buses no more*
> *Ain't gonna ride no more*
> *Why in the hell don't the white folk know*
> *That I ain't gonna ride no more.*

Instead, they shared rides, rode in black-owned taxis, and walked. "My feets is tired," a woman said, "but my soul is rested." Another walker, an elderly woman, explained: "I'm not walking for myself. I'm walking for my children and my grandchildren." This dramatic protest ushered in the Civil Rights Movement.[63]

Within this crucible, a young black minister found himself suddenly catapulted into the leadership of the struggle. When he arrived in Montgomery a year earlier to become the pastor of the Dexter Avenue Baptist Church, Martin Luther King, Jr., noticed that blacks represented almost half of the city's population. Confined to domestic service and common labor, they were surrounded by the walls of segregation. "The schools of course were segregated," King noted; "and the United States Supreme Court decision on school integration, handed down in May 1954, appeared to have no effect on Montgomery's determination to keep them that way." But, more than the schools, the buses had become an especially disliked symbol of segregation. King personally knew what it meant to be humiliated by discrimination on a bus. When he was in the eleventh grade, he had traveled with a teacher to a distant town in Georgia to give a speech at a contest. After winning a prize for his presentation on "The Negro and the Constitution," he and his teacher boarded the bus for Atlanta. When the bus filled up, the white driver told them to give up their seats for some white passengers. At first, King refused and was called "a black son-of-a-bitch." Advised by his teacher to avoid a confrontation, King reluctantly surrendered his seat. "That night will never leave my mind," King recalled. "It was the angriest I have ever been in my life."[64]

As the leader of the Montgomery bus boycott, King gave voice to black frustration. In his first speech to the boycotters, he declared: "There comes a time when people get tired. We are here this evening to say to those who have mistreated us so long that we are tired — tired of being segregated and humiliated; tired of being kicked about by the brutal feet of oppression." What should be the course of resistance? "Our actions must be guided by the deepest principles of our Christian faith," King declared. "Love must be our regulating ideal. Once again we must hear the words of Jesus echoing across the centuries: 'Love your enemies, bless them that curse you, and pray for them that despitefully use you.' " In the struggle for freedom, King fused together this Christian doctrine and Mahatma Gandhi's tactic of nonviolence. The boycott ended more than a year later when the court ordered the desegregation of the bus system. The victory affirmed the power of blacks to transform the conditions of their lives through a grass-roots movement. Their courageous action inspired an inner transformation — a hard-won sense of self-esteem. "We got our heads up now," exclaimed a black janitor proudly, "and we won't ever bow down again — no, sir — except before God."[65]

After the Montgomery protest came other crossings. First, there were the sit-ins of black students at the Woolworth's lunch counter in Greensboro, North Carolina, in 1960. "We're trying to eradicate the whole stigma of being inferior," the students explained. "We do not picket just because we want to eat. We do picket to protest the lack of dignity and respect shown us as human beings." One of the students, Franklin McCain, recalled: "I probably felt better that day than I've ever felt in my life. I felt as though I had gained my manhood, so to speak, and not only gained it, but had developed quite a lot of respect for it." Out of the lunch counter sit-ins emerged the Student Non-Violent Coordinating Committee (SNCC). The student sit-ins spread across the South. "I myself desegregated a lunch counter, not somebody else, not some big man, some powerful man, but me, little me," a black student boasted. "I walked the picket line and I sat in and the walls of segregation toppled. Now all people can eat there." The students were standing tall against humiliating racial borders. "A generation of young people," King observed, "has come out of decades of shadows to face naked state power; it has lost its fears, and experienced the majestic dignity of a direct struggle for its own liberation. These young people have connected up with their own history — the slave revolts, the incomplete revolution of the Civil War, the brotherhood of colonial colored men in Africa and Asia. They are an integral part of the history which is reshaping the world, replacing a dying order with a modern democracy." In their songs, the students expressed their determination to break the chains of discrimination:

> Ain't gonna let nobody turn me 'round
> turn me 'round, turn me 'round,
> Ain't gonna let nobody turn me 'round,
> I'm gonna keep on walkin', keep on a-talkin'
> Marching up to freedom land.[66]

A year after the Greensboro sit-ins came the "freedom rides" — acts of civil disobedience to integrate the interstate buses and bus terminals of the South. Led by the Congress of Racial Equality (CORE), black and white civil rights supporters defiantly and bravely rode together in buses, singing:

> Hallelujah, I'm traveling
> Hallelujah, ain't it fine,
> Hallelujah, I'm traveling
> Down Freedom's main line.

In the South, the freedom riders were yanked from the buses and brutally beaten by racist white mobs before television cameras. "Every Freedom Rider on that bus was beaten pretty bad," recalled Isaac Reynolds. "I'm still feeling the effect. I received a damaged ear." They faced injury and even death, but they knew they could not allow violence to turn them back. "I was afraid *not* to continue the Freedom Ride," explained Diane Nash. "If the signal was given to the opposition that violence could stop us . . . if we let the Freedom Ride stop then, whenever we tried to do anything in the Movement in the future, we were going to meet with a lot of violence. And we would probably have to get a number of people killed before we could reverse that message."[67]

Then, in 1963, came the famous March on Washington. The conscience of the nation was galvanized when marchers by the hundreds of thousands gathered in front of the Lincoln Memorial. "Five score years ago, a great American, in whose symbolic shadow we stand, signed the Emancipation Proclamation," King reminded them and millions of others watching the event broadcast on television. Now, a hundred years later, blacks were still not free. Like Frederick Douglass, King had a vision of blacks and whites living together in an America of equality: "I say to you today, my friends, that in spite of the difficulties and frustrations of the moment I still have a dream. It is a dream deeply rooted in the American dream. I have a dream that one day this nation will rise up and live out the true meaning of its creed: 'We hold these truths to be self-evident; that all men are created equal.' "[68]

"Black and white together," the marchers sang, "we shall overcome someday." Whites were also involved in the Civil Rights Movement, and many of them were Jews. Over half of the white students who went south to organize voter-registration drives during the Freedom Summer of 1964 were Jewish. The two white civil rights workers who were murdered with James Chaney in Mississippi that summer were Jewish — Andrew Goodman and Michael Schwerner. Jewish supporters wrote many of the checks that financed Martin Luther King's Southern Christian Leadership Conference as well as SNCC and CORE.[69]

Jewish involvement in the movement for black freedom had deep roots in American history. During the 1850s, three Jewish immigrants joined John Brown's armed struggle against slavery in "Bloody Kansas." Remembering the pogroms in Russia, Jewish immigrants identified with the victims of antiblack race riots in urban America. After the killing of thirty-eight blacks during the 1917 East St. Louis riot, the Jewish newspaper *Forward* compared this violence to a 1903 pogrom in Russia: "Kishinev and St. Louis — the same soil, the same people. It is a distance of four and a half thousand miles between these two cities and yet they are so close and so similar to each other. . . . Actually twin sisters, which could easily be mistaken for each other." Jews contributed leadership to the NAACP: its chairman for most of the years between 1914 and 1939 was Joel E. Spingarn. Jewish participation in the Civil Rights Movement was intensely active. One of Martin Luther King's closest personal advisers was Stanley Levison. Howard Zinn, a professor at Spellman College, was a counselor to SNCC. Over half of the white lawyers who went south to defend the civil rights protesters were Jewish. The head of the NAACP Legal Defense and Education Fund was Jack Greenberg, and the NAACP's fiery labor director was Herbert Hill, a graduate of an orthodox yeshiva.[70]

Why was there such significant Jewish involvement? One reason was what historian Jonathan Kaufman described as "Jewish self-interest." Jews remembered the persecution and violence they had experienced in Russia, and they knew that the border between racism and anti-Semitism often blurred. A society that opposed discrimination, they realized, would also allow Jews equality of opportunity. Even as a ten-year-old kid cheering for Jackie Robinson when he broke into major league baseball in 1947, Jack Greenberg understood what this victory meant for Jews. Robinson was "adopted as the surrogate hero by many of us growing up at the time," the civil rights lawyer recalled. "He was the way we saw ourselves triumphing against the forces of bigotry and ignorance." Those forces had curbed Jewish admissions at Harvard and were continuing to discriminate against the appointment of Jews to the faculties of elite universities. The frontline of the battle for equality for everyone, including Jews, was the civil rights struggle for blacks. Indeed, as Kaufman noted in hindsight, "Jews benefited enormously from the terrain shaped by the civil rights movement. Jews were the first to use antidiscrimination laws to gain access to restricted apartment buildings in large cities. The growing tide of tolerance left by the civil rights movement opened opportunities for Jews as well as for blacks in law firms, corporations, and universities."[71]

Jewish self-interest was only part of the story. "The civil rights movement spoke to the Jewish head," Kaufman pointed out, "but it also spoke to Jewish hearts." Though many Jews had left the Lower East Side for the suburbs and had entered the mainstream of the Promised Land, they carried in their hearts a religion that compelled them to be concerned about oppression. The American Dream had worked for them; now they felt a duty as well as a memory of their own hardships to help make this ideal work for blacks. Jewish civil rights workers often referred to "that quote" — the ancient pronouncement by Rabbi Hillel: "If I am not for myself, who will be for me? But if I am only for myself, what am I? And if not now, when?" Nazi genocide had unshrouded the horrible inhumanity of racism. As Jews, they nurtured a special understanding of what it meant to be victimized as a people.[72]

This black-Jewish "alliance," however, was soon "broken." As the focus of the struggle for black equality moved to the North, the relationship between blacks and Jews became increasingly strained. The Civil Rights Movement was shifting from demands for political rights to demands for economic equality. Until then, Kaufman noted, "the price of racial change had been taken out of the hide of the South. Northerners, including northern Jews, did not have to deal with consequences directly." In the North, the racial terrain was different: Jews owned about 30 percent of the stores in Harlem and other black communities. During the 1964 Harlem riot, blacks looted many Jewish-owned stores. A class divide separated the two groups. Ghetto blacks were also noticing that many of their landlords were Jewish. At a school integration meeting in Boston, a young black questioned whether blacks could work with Jews when Jewish landlords were exploiting them. According to Kaufman, a popular saying in the 1960s went: "Of the five people that a black meets in the course of the day — his landlord, the storeowner, the social worker, the teacher, the cop — one, the cop, is Irish. The other four are Jews." Blacks were now demanding their own representation. Meanwhile, developments in the Middle East aggravated tensions between black and Jewish civil rights workers: after the 1967 Arab-Israeli Six-Day War, SNCC denounced Israel for conquering "Arab homes and land through terror, force, and massacres." Many Jewish liberals like Nathan Glazer and Martin Peretz began to turn away from the Civil Rights Movement.[73]

At a deeper level, the split between Jews and blacks reflected a larger ideological divide, as conflicting visions of equality emerged. The Civil Rights Movement had begun as a struggle for equality for blacks through integration, which was often defined as a condition of equality. To "overcome" meant to integrate the schools, buses, lunch counters, and other public facilities; this goal was expanded to include equality of opportunity for voting and employment. But in 1966, like earlier black nationalists such as Martin Delany and Marcus Garvey, Stokely Carmichael and other young militant blacks issued a clarion for Black Power. Increasingly, they viewed racial oppression in America as "internal colonialism." Identifying themselves with the Third World, they saw themselves as members of Frantz Fanon's "wretched of the earth," the subjugated peoples of Africa, Latin America, and Asia engaged in struggles for liberation against white colonial domination. Equality, for many black militants, meant self-determination for blacks as a colonized people in America. This black nationalism sent a message: separatism rather than integration was to be the goal, and there was no place for whites, including Jews, in the movement for black liberation.[74]

Ironically, racial progress contributed to black-Jewish tensions. As tenants, servants, customers, and employees, African Americans had been confronting Jews; but in the early 1960s they began to enter the ranks of teachers, social workers, and civil service workers. This very rise led to a confrontation between the newly arrived middle-class blacks and an established Jewish professional class. "Once again, the accidents of history have put the Jew just ahead of the Negro, and just above him," observed Nathan Glazer in 1964. "Now the Negro teacher works under a Jewish principal, the Negro social worker under a Jewish supervisor." Moreover, the split between the two groups widened as the government began to act affirmatively to open educational and employment opportunities for blacks. Believing they had made it through meritocracy, many Jews defended individualism and color-blind criteria against the new affirmative action policies and the principle of group rights. They joined a growing backlash against the preferential treatment of racial minorities; leading the attack, Jewish intellectuals like Glazer denounced affirmative action as "reverse discrimination."[75]

But the Civil Rights Movement, composed of blacks and whites fighting together against discrimination, had led to successes. In 1964, Congress prohibited discrimination in public accommodations and employment and established the Fair Employment Opportunity Commission. A year later, lawmakers authorized federal examiners to register qualified voters and abolished devices like literacy tests designed to deny voting rights to blacks. These major laws, it was hoped, would help blacks overcome discrimination.

The Civil Rights Revolution, however, was unable to correct the structural economic foundations of racial inequality. While the laws and court orders prohibited discrimination, they failed to abolish poverty among blacks. African Americans had won the right to sit at a lunch counter and order a hamburger, but many of them did not have the money to pay for their meal. Blacks were told that the law now prohibited discrimination in employment, but they also saw that jobs for them were scarce. The desperation was especially acute in the inner cities of the North. "You know the average young person out here don't have a job, man, they don't have anything to do," a black in Harlem explained angrily in the early 1960s. "You go down to the employment agency and you can't get a job. They have you waiting all day, but you can't get a job." Young blacks of the inner cities knew the playing field was not level. "Those who are required to live in congested and rat-infested homes," scholar Kenneth Clark noted in *Dark Ghetto*, "are aware that others are not so dehumanized. Young people in the ghetto are aware that other young people have been taught to read, that they have been prepared for college, and can compete successfully for white-collar, managerial, and executive jobs." One of these alienated blacks predicted in 1962: "When the time comes, it is going to be too late. Everything will explode because the people they live under tension now; they going to a point where they can't stand it no more." This point was dramatically reached in Los Angeles during the long hot summer of 1965.[76]

"The fire bombs of Watts blasted the civil rights movement into a new phase," declared Martin Luther King. Ultimately, the struggle to realize the American Dream had to advance beyond antidiscrimination laws and confront what King called the "airtight cage of poverty." The underlying economic basis of racial inequality was a far more elusive and formidable foe than the lynch mobs and police attack dogs. "Jobs are harder and costlier to create than voting rolls," King explained. "The eradication of slums housing millions is complex far beyond integrating buses and lunch counters." This harsh reality of urban squalor and despair was reflected in the jagged mirrors of every northern ghetto. "I see a young Negro boy," King wrote in 1963. "He is sitting on a stoop in front of a vermin-infested apartment house in Harlem. The stench of garbage is in the halls. The drunks, the jobless, the junkies are shadow figures of his everyday world."[77]

This impoverished and depressing world was familiar to Malcolm X. "I don't see any American dream," he declared in 1964; "I see an American nightmare." Growing up in the ghettos of the North, Malcolm Little had pursued a life of drugs and crime. Arrested and found guilty of burglary, he was given an eight-year sentence. As Malcolm X later explained, his "high school" had been the "black ghetto of Roxbury" in Boston, his "college" the "streets of Harlem," and his graduate school the "prison." While serving time, he was converted to Elijah Muhammad's Nation of Islam. As a leader of the Black Muslims, Malcolm X advocated a separatist ideology and mocked King for his belief in integration as well as his strategy of nonviolence. Like David Walker, who had issued his revolutionary appeal in the early nineteenth century, Malcolm X advised blacks to use violence to defend their rights. As the struggle for racial justice shifted from the South to the urban North, Malcolm X's message exposed the failure of the Civil Rights Movement to address the problems of joblessness and poverty. Even Martin Luther King began to feel the despair. Four years after the March on Washington where he had passionately described his "dream," he confessed: "I watched that dream turn into a nightmare as I moved through the ghettos of the nation and saw black brothers and sisters perishing on a lonely island of poverty in the midst of a vast ocean of material prosperity, and saw the nation doing nothing to grapple with the Negroes' problem of poverty." After the Watts riot and his encounter with the "other America" of the ghetto, as historian James H. Cone noted, King more clearly and painfully understood "something of the world that created Malcolm X."[78]

The Civil Rights Movement was hitting the walls of inequality based on class as well as race — what King called the "inseparable twins" of economic injustice and racial injustice. Beginning in the 1960s, black America became deeply splintered into two classes. On the one hand, the black middle class experienced gains: the percentage of families earning $25,000 or more (in 1982 dollars) increased from 10 percent in 1960 to 25 percent in 1982, and the number of blacks in college nearly doubled between 1970 and 1980 (from 522,000 to over a million). On the other hand, there emerged what has been called a "black underclass." The distressing situation of this group can be measured by the persistence of intergenerational poverty, the increasing unemployment rates for young blacks, and the dramatic rise of black female-headed families. Between 1960 and 1980, the percentage of such families doubled, reaching 40 percent, compared to an increase from 8 to 12 percent for white families. While blacks composed only 12 percent of the American population in 1980, they constituted 43 percent of all welfare families.[79]

The context for this deteriorating condition for African Americans extended far beyond the borders of the ghetto. Between 1960 and 1980, the baby boomers of post–World War II entered young adulthood. During these years, the country's total population increased by a quarter, but the eighteen- to twenty-four-year-old group had nearly doubled. There were simply more workers entering the labor force: between 1970 and 1980, the labor force grew by 24 million, compared to only 13 million for the previous decade. The sudden entry of this age cohort into the labor market was accompanied by a sharp rise in unemployment — from 2.8 million in 1968 to 7.6 million in 1980. Meanwhile, families supported by Aid to Families with Dependent Children (AFDC) grew from 1.4 million to 3.5 million. Significantly, unemployment rose faster and in greater numbers than AFDC families. Thus, contrary to the claims of pundits like Charles Murray as well as politicians like Ronald Reagan, families were being pushed onto welfare rolls by unemployment, not simply pulled there by welfare benefits. The push was especially felt by young workers: for the age group twenty- to twenty-four-year-olds, unemployment jumped from 8 to 11 percent for white men and from 13 to 22 percent for black men. "By now my wife was pregnant," said John Godfrey. "And I was unemployed. . . . So push came to shove. We went down to welfare. I needed medical protection for her and the baby. It was a sobering experience. I felt — I don't know how to put it into words — I was totally disgusted with myself. I felt I had failed myself, because I was unable to take care of myself and my family."[80]

Soaring unemployment for black men was accompanied by rising welfare enrollments for black women with children. The majority of black mothers on AFDC were young — under thirty years old. They had extremely limited possibilities of finding black men with incomes capable of supporting families. According to sociologist William Julius Wilson's "male marriageable pool index," 72 percent of the black men between ages twenty and twenty-four in 1980 were either unemployed, employed only part-time, or working full-time but earning below poverty wages. For white men in the same age cohort, the rate was only 36 percent. Wilson's model was based on the assumption that the family would be a two-parent unit and that wives would be financially dependent on their husbands. But for black women, the problem of welfare dependency also resulted from gender inequality in the labor market. Like women in general, they found themselves crowded into so-called female-dominated occupations such as low-wage clerical and sales jobs. Some of these occupations, such as secretarial work, required training, but they did not pay "comparable worth" — what male-dominated jobs with similar requirements paid. Consequently, women with children to support often discovered that working did not pay enough to cover child care and living expenses. Therefore, they had no choice but to depend on AFDC in order to make ends meet. Black women were especially disadvantaged in the labor market and more dependent on welfare because of their lower levels of education and job skills.[81]

Survival for many black women, even for those with husbands, has been difficult on welfare. They have been trapped in a "catch-22" situation. They would like to get off welfare but find themselves forced by low wages to remain dependent on government subsidy. "None of my jobs ever paid more than minimum wage," said Alice Grady. "As soon as I can get a babysitter, I intend to go back to work. But it won't be easy. There is a bus stop right out front, but according to where your job is, you'd probably need two or three buses to get to work. You'd have to leave early in the morning, and you'd be leaving your children because they're not supposed to be at school until eight or nine o'clock. Then you'd have to find a babysitter for them in the evening until you got home. . . . But I'm hoping to get off welfare and get me a good job. Right now they're helping me, but it's just making ends meet. You don't have anything left. . . . Right now my husband is looking for a job. . . . We vote. This year we couldn't because we were homeless. You know, the homeless can't vote. You have to have an address. It's just rough on welfare. It's just not enough. What can I do for school clothes for the kids? When my husband gets a job, we'll be cut back on welfare."

A world of barriers surrounds women like Alice Grady, keeping them impoverished and blocking their avenues of exit. At several different points, they have been frustrated by a cycle of poverty generated by low wages and reinforced by inadequate childcare, poor public transportation, lack of affordable housing, and political disfranchisement.[82]

Moreover, the employment situation of both black women and men has been devastated by recent major changes in the economy. The movement of plants and offices to the suburbs during the last three decades has isolated urban blacks from many places of employment: in 1980, 71 percent of them lived in central cities, whereas 66 percent of whites resided in suburbs. Illustrating the dynamic interaction of the suburbanization of production, unemployment, and welfare, Chicago lost 229,000 jobs and enrolled 290,000 new welfare recipients in the sixties, while its suburbs gained 500,000 jobs. Meanwhile, blacks have also been suffering from the effects of the "deindustrialization of America." Due to the relocation of production in low-wage countries like South Korea and Mexico, some 22 million American workers lost their jobs between 1969 and 1976. "The decline in blue-collar employment hit black men especially hard," sociologist Andrew Hacker reported. "Blacks have been severely hurt by deindustrialization," William Julius Wilson explained, "because of their heavy concentration in the automobile, rubber, steel, and other smokestack industries."[83]

During the two world wars and the labor-organizing drives of the 1930s, blacks were able to find higher-paying jobs in the industrial sector. Opportunities continued after World War II. "I remember when you could quit one job one day and go out the next day and get a better job making more money," said Lawrence Hunter, referring to the bountiful employment situation in Milwaukee in the 1950s. The forty-eight-year-old machinery operator added: "You could go to a foundry and get a job any day. It was hard-bull work, but if push came to shove there was a job for you."[84]

But suddenly, beginning in the late 1960s, push came to shove, and many blacks found themselves out of work. One of these black workers was Jimmy Morse. After working for US Steel in Gary, Indiana, for thirty years, he voluntarily retired in 1983 rather than wait for the imminent layoff. His monthly retirement pay totaled $552.63, which did not pay all his bills. "Now, you get the light bill outta there," he explained in 1986. "You get the water bill outta there. Buy some food outta that plus $131 we get in food stamps. You're about $40 short." Asked about looking for other work, he replied that he was fifty-one years old and was unwilling to commute to Chicago for $3.75 an hour. During the 1970s, the region around Gary had lost 65,000 manufacturing jobs, including 12,000 at US Steel. "Foreign steel was takin' our man-hours away from us," Morse said. "And it ain't no racial thing either. That blue-eyed soul brother is catchin' jes' as much hell as I'm catching." Actually, black workers were catching more than their share of hell. In the ranks of this new army of displaced workers was a disproportionately large number of blacks. A study of 2,380 firms which were shut down in Illinois between 1975 and 1978 found that while blacks constituted only 14 percent of the state's work force, they totaled 20 percent of the laid-off laborers. Of the black workers displaced between 1979 and 1984, only 42 percent were able to secure new employment. The macroeconomic developments of plant shutdowns and economic relocations rather than the growth of the welfare state help explain why blacks have been "losing ground" and why many of them have become "truly disadvantaged."[85]

Staring at the boarded-up factories, many young blacks have been unable to get even their first jobs — work experience essential for acquiring skills as well as self-esteem. One of them, Darryl Swafford, grew up around Gary. Unemployed and dependent on food stamps, he had the same dream as most Americans: "I always had that goal, working in the mill. Have a home, a big car. But now there's no mill and I'm down. Just trying to make it, trying to survive." Many of the jobs available to young blacks have been in the fast-food services like Burger King and McDonald's. But these jobs pay very low wages and lead nowhere. "They treat you like a child on those minimum-wage jobs," complained Danny Coleman, who had worked in a fast-food restaurant. "And there is no way you can make it on that kind of salary. It is just a dead end." Young workers like Coleman have been facing an economy that says: Let them flip hamburgers.[86]

Meanwhile, African-American "failure" has been contrasted with Asian-American "success." In 1984, William Raspberry of the *Washington Post* noted that Asian Americans on the West Coast had "in fact" "outstripped" whites in income. Blacks should stop blaming racism for their plight, he argued, and follow the example of the self-reliant Asian Americans. In 1986, NBC *Nightly News* and *McNeil/Lehrer Report* aired special news segments on Asian Americans and their achievements. *U.S. News & World Report* featured Asian-American advances in a cover story, and *Newsweek* focused a lead article on "Asian Americans: A 'Model Minority,' " while *Fortune* applauded them as "America's Super Minority."[87]

But in their celebration of this "model minority," these media pundits have exaggerated Asian-American "success." Their comparisons of incomes between Asians and whites fail to recognize the regional locations of the Asian-American population. Concentrated in California, Hawaii, and New York, most Asian Americans reside in states with higher incomes but also higher costs of living than the national average: in 1980, 59 percent of all Asian Americans lived in these three states, compared to only 19 percent for the general population. The use of "family incomes" has been very misleading, for Asian-American families have more persons working per family than white families. Thus, the family incomes of Asian Americans indicate the presence of more workers in each family rather than higher individual incomes. Actually, in terms of personal incomes, Asian Americans have not reached equality.[88]

While many Asian Americans are doing well, others find themselves mired in poverty: they include Southeast-Asian refugees such as the Hmong and Mien as well as immigrant workers trapped in Chinatowns. Eighty percent of the people of New York Chinatown, 74 percent of San Francisco Chinatown, and 88 percent of Los Angeles Chinatown are foreign-born. Like the nineteenth-century Chinese immigrants in search of Gold Mountain, they came here to seek a better life. But what they found instead was work in Chinatown's low-wage service and garment industries: 40 to 50 percent of the workers in the Chinatowns of San Francisco and Los Angeles and almost 70 percent of the New York Chinatown laborers are crowded into such occupations.[89]

Most of these workers do not have a high school degree and lack English-language skills. Fifty-five percent of the residents of New York Chinatown do not speak English well or at all. "This does not mean that they are not trying to learn," explained Peter Kwong, who has worked as a community organizer for fifteen years. "In fact, there are at least two dozen English-language schools in the community. . . . Thousands of working people squeeze time out from their busy schedules to attend classes. However, the real problem is that they do not have the opportunity to use English on the job or with other Chinese immigrants. They soon forget the scant English they have learned."[90]

Unable to speak English, many Chinese immigrant women have no choice but to work as seamstresses. They have become a major source of labor for New York's garment industry, which had earlier employed Jewish immigrants. "These factories are one of New York City's unknown industrial success stories," said Harry Schwartz, president of the Garment Industry Development Corporation. "You walk around the Garment District and ask, 'Where have the production shops gone?'

Well, they've gone to Chinatown." In San Francisco, Chinese women produce almost half of the total volume of manufactured apparel, usually working for minimum wage in a sweatshop environment. "The conditions in the factories are terrible," reported a Chinatown resident. "Dirty air, long hours, from eight in the morning to eight at night, six days! They are paid by the piece and only a few can make good money. They don't protest because they don't know how to talk back and they don't know the law."[91]

While the women in Chinatown are located largely in the garment industry, the men are employed mainly in the restaurants. S. L. Wong, the director of an English-language school in San Francisco Chinatown, explained that recent immigrants find themselves locked in a low-wage restaurant-labor market: "Most immigrants coming into Chinatown with a language barrier cannot go outside this confined area into the mainstream of American industry." Danny Lowe described his predicament: "Before I was a painter in Hong Kong, but I can't do it here. I got no license, no education. . . . I want a living, so it's dishwasher, janitor or cook."[92]

The myth of the Asian-American "model minority" has been challenged, yet it continues to be widely believed. One reason for this is its instructional value. For whom are Asian Americans supposed to be a "model"? Shortly after the Civil War, southern planters recruited Chinese immigrants in order to pit them against the newly freed blacks as "examples" of laborers willing to work hard for low wages. Today, Asian Americans are again being used to discipline blacks. If the failure of blacks on welfare warns Americans in general how they should not behave, the triumph of Asian Americans affirms the deeply rooted values of the Protestant ethic and self-reliance. Our society needs an Asian-American "model minority" in an era anxious about a growing black underclass. Asian-American "success" has been used to explain the phenomenon of "losing ground" — why the situation of the poor has deteriorated during the last two decades while government social services have expanded. If Asian Americans can make it on their own, conservative pundits like Charles Murray are asking, why can't other groups? Many liberals have joined this chorus. In 1987, CBS's *60 Minutes* presented a glowing report on the stunning achievements of Asian Americans in the academy. "Why are Asian Americans doing so exceptionally well in school?" Mike Wallace asked and quickly added, "They must be doing something right. Let's bottle it." Wallace then suggested that failing black students should try to pursue the Asian-American formula for academic success.[93]

Betraying a nervousness over the seeming end of the American Dream's boundlessness, praise for this "super minority" has become society's most recent jeremiad — a call for a renewed commitment to the traditional virtues of hard work, thrift, and industry. After all, it has been argued, the war on poverty and affirmative action were not really necessary. Look at the Asian Americans! They did it by pulling themselves up by their bootstraps. For blacks shut out of the labor market, the Asian-American model provides the standards of acceptable behavior: blacks should not depend on welfare or affirmative action. While congratulating Asian Americans for their family values, hard work, and high incomes, President Ronald Reagan chastised blacks for their dependency on the "spider's web of welfare" and their failure to recognize that the "only barrier" to success was "within" them.[94]

But comparisons of Asian-American "success" and black "dependency" have shrouded the impact of the Cold War economy on the problems of unemployment and poverty. The strategic nuclear weapons program under the Reagan presidency was financed by enormous deficits. Defense expenditures under the Reagan administration more than doubled from $134 billion in 1980 to $282 billion in 1987. In that year, defense spending amounted to 60 cents out of every dollar received by the federal government in income tax. Meanwhile, resources were diverted from our social needs: defense spending was $35 billion greater in 1985 than in 1981, while funds for entitlement programs such as food stamps and welfare were cut by $30 billion. Moreover, the focus of our research and development on strategic nuclear weapons has greatly harmed our general economy. Since 1955, the federal government has spent more than $1 trillion on nuclear arms and other weaponry for the Cold War — a sum representing 62 percent of all federal research expenditures. This concentration on the military needs of the U.S.-Soviet rivalry drained our national resources and at the same time undermined our ability to produce competitive consumer goods, which in turn, generated trade imbalances and contributed to a decline in commercial manufacturing, especially for those sectors of the industrial economy where many blacks had been employed.[95]

These macrocosmic political and economic realities have even reached remote Indian reservations. During the nineteenth century, as white settlement expanded westward toward the "Stony mountains," policymakers like Francis Amasa Walker had moved Indian tribes onto reservations. Many of these reservations later became valuable sites for resources vital to the Cold War's nuclear weapons program as well as our energy-consuming economy. Fifty-five percent of our uranium deposits are located on Indian-owned lands, and nearly 100 percent of current mining occurs in Indian territory. In the Southwest, this industry employs 20 percent of working Laguna Pueblo Indians. The United Mine Workers Union estimated that approximately 80 percent of the workers in the uranium shaft mines will die of lung cancer.

Native Americans living near the shafts are also in danger, for they have been exposed to air and drinking water contaminated by radiation from the tailings generated by the mining and milling of uranium. In Edgemount, South Dakota, three million pounds of tailings were dumped near the Cheyenne River, and cancer rates for people drinking that water have been 50 percent higher than in any other county in the state. In 1978, the Department of Energy released a report stating that the risk of lung cancer for persons living near the tailings piles was twice that of the general population. Involved in the extract of uranium have been powerful corporations — Kerr-McGee, Exxon, Atlantic Richfield, Mobil Oil, and United Nuclear.[96]

By 1980, 740,000 Indians — more than half of the total Native American population — no longer lived on reservations. Instead, they resided in cities such as New York, San Francisco, Oakland, Seattle, Tulsa, Minneapolis–St. Paul, Chicago, and Los Angeles. In 1940, only 24,000 Native Americans, or 13 percent of the group's national population, lived in urban areas. World War II had attracted thousands of them to work in urban war-related industries. The major migration, however, occurred between 1953 and 1972: under the Bureau of Indian Affairs relocation program, 100,000 Indians left the reservations for the cities. One of the movers and shakers behind this new policy was Dillon S. Meyer. Appointed Commissioner of Indian Affairs in 1950, he had been the director of the War Relocation Authority, responsible for administering the Japanese-American internment camps during World War II. Meyer's goal had been to assimilate Japanese Americans by resettling them across the country. This idea of incorporation through dispersal became the basis of the Voluntary Relocation Program, which provided job training and transportation to cities where Indians would be given assistance in finding employment and housing. Like Commissioner Francis Amasa Walker, Meyer hoped to integrate Native Americans into modern urban society.[97]

The global context of the Cold War has also conditioned immigration from what had been the Soviet Union. Refugees fleeing from religious oppression, Jews have been arriving in America again. The collapse of communism in Eastern Europe and Russia has unleashed a new wave of anti-Semitism, and many Jews have been afraid of what will happen to them. "Anti-Semitism and all the other old national hatreds were never really extinguished by Communism, merely frozen in time," James E. Young noted in his review of Charles Hoffman's recently published study of the Jews of Eastern Europe in the post-Communist era. "When the thaw came, the traditional conflicts bloomed with a vengeance, picking up exactly where they left off 45 years ago." The unraveling of Communist controls has given freedom to old, pent-up nativist passions. "The country is experiencing a process of 'decivilization,'" explained a Moscow lawyer in 1990. "The layers of civilization are being peeled off, and underneath there is this ugliness, including fascism and anti-Semitic hatred. Jews are trying to get out of Russia as fast as they can." An old Jewish man in a village near Minsk told two American visitors: "It's time now. We have to go. It wouldn't be safe for us to stay." Ironically, he was not religiously Jewish. For lunch he served ham. Prohibited from practicing their religion, many Jews are Jewish mainly in terms of their ethnic origins. "The last of the [Jewish] culture-bearers were executed 40 years ago," explained Aleksandr Z. Burakovsky, chair of the Kiev Sholom Aleichem Society. "Schools, synagogues, libraries were all abolished." Aleksandr A. Shlayen, director of the Babi Yar Center, added: "They started to beat the Jewishness out of Jews a long time ago, under the czars."[98]

But, though many Jews in what had been the Soviet Union might not feel a strong identity as Jews, they have encountered hatred from neighbors and fellow citizens. In schools, Jewish children have been beaten and called names. Resentment has spread to the workplace: professional Jews have been experiencing discrimination in employment. Graffiti on walls have warned: "Jews get out." "My husband wanted to emigrate, but I didn't want to leave," recounted a young Jewish woman. "My parents are old and need to be cared for. I also thought of myself as a Soviet citizen." But many people saw her as a "Jew," and the harassment became "awful." Seeking sanctuary, half a million Jews have fled to Israel and also to America.[99]

Recently, 40,000 Soviet Jews have been entering the United States annually, and altogether they total over 200,000. Like the Jewish immigrants of the late nineteenth century, they have been selling their houses and furniture, giving away almost everything, and leaving with only what they can carry wrapped in bedspreads or packed in suitcases. After their arrival, they have had to start all over again. Describing the plight of a Jewish refugee family, Barbara Budnitz of Berkeley, California, explained: "These people have nothing. I offered them an old desk. They said they wanted it, but what they really needed was a bed." Many of these refugees had been engineers in the old country, but here they have been suffering from unemployment. Lacking English language skills and possessing technical knowledge that has limited transferability, many have been forced to find jobs as apartment managers, janitors, or even as helpers at McDonald's. According to Barbara Nelson of the Jewish Family Services in Oakland, California, about 80 percent of the Jewish refugee families have been compelled to seek welfare support.[100]

Still the Jews are glad to be in America where there is religious freedom. "My five-year-old daughter is attending school at the synagogue — something she could not do in the Ukraine," explained Sofiya Shapiro, who came with her family in 1991. "I am glad she can get to know Jewish tradition." Indeed, many of the refugees are learning about Judaism for the first time in their lives. But like the Jewish immigrants of earlier times, the recent refugees are hopeful this country will offer them an opportunity to begin again. "That's what America is," commented Budnitz. "We need to keep it that way."[101]

America's continuing allure has also been as a place for a fresh economic start. This has been particularly true for the recent arrivals from Ireland. Like the nineteenth-century Irish immigrants fleeing hunger and the ravages of the potato famine, these recent newcomers have been pushed by grim economic conditions at home: in 1990, unemployment in Ireland was a staggering 18 percent. Seeking work in America, many have entered illegally in the past decade. Undocumented Irish workers have been estimated to total as many as 120,000. "It's an anonymous floating population," stated Lena Deevy, director of the Irish Immigration Reform Movement office in Boston. "It's like counting the homeless." These illegal aliens constitute what one of them described as "an underclass," forced to take "the crummiest jobs at the lowest wages." The 1987 Immigration Reform Act, which made it unlawful for employers to hire undocumented workers, has created economic and social borders for many Irish. "You can't apply for a job," explained an Irish waitress who came to Boston in 1986. "You can't answer a want ad [because of the 1987 law]. It's all word of mouth." Undocumented Irish workers have to keep a low profile, she added: "My social life is limited to the Irish sector. I can't talk to Americans — you just have to tell too many lies." Director Deevy described their nervousness: "It's like living on the edge. There's a lot of fear" that someone "will squeal to the INS [Immigration and Naturalization Service]." In 1990, a new immigration law provided for the distribution of 40,000 green cards to be awarded by lottery, with 16,000 of them reserved for Irish. "I plan to fill out at least a thousand applications," said Joanne O'Connell of Queens, New York, as she looked forward to this "Irish Sweepstakes."[102]

Most of today's immigrants, however, come from Asia and Latin America. Over 80 percent of all immigrants have been arriving from these two regions, adding to America's racial diversity — a reality charged with consequences for our nation's work force. By the year 2000, there will be more than 21 million new workers. They will be 44 percent white, 16 percent black, 11 percent Asian and other groups, and 29 percent Hispanic. A preview of the significance of this racial diversity in the twenty-first century can be seen in California. There, Hispanics, composed mostly of Mexican Americans, number 4.5 million, or approximately 20 percent of the state's population. Many of them are recent newcomers, pulled here again by dreams of El Norte. Compared to the Anglos, the Hispanics are young. In 1985, they represented 32 percent of the youth (aged birth to fifteen years) and only 8 percent of the elderly (sixty-five years and over), compared to 52 percent and 83 percent for Anglos. The number of Hispanics entering the work force will increase, while Anglos will continue to constitute a large majority of the elderly.[103]

"What does all this portend for the future work force?" asked David Hayes-Bautista and his co-authors in their seminal study *The Burden of Support: Young Latinos in an Aging Society*. They noted that in 1980, working-age Anglos had an educational level of 13.5 years, while laborers in general had 12.9 years. But Hispanics, with a high school dropout rate of 60 percent, lagged behind with only 10.4 years. Hayes-Bautista calculated that if the 1980 differentials remained the same, the increase of Hispanics in the work force would decrease the overall educational level of the working population to only 12.1 years. "That the labor force of 2030 would actually be less educated than in 1980 is bad enough," he observed; "it would be particularly serious if, as seems certain, a more-educated, better-prepared labor force will be required for a high-tech future."[104]

Clearly, the educational level of Hispanics should be raised to meet the needs of the future California economy. But in 1983, California was forty-fifth of all states in per capita spending on education. Is the largely Anglo population of today, Hayes-Bautista asked, willing to commit a sufficient portion of its economic pie to an investment in Hispanic youth?[105]

The need to educate minority youth and prepare them to enter the work force suddenly became an urgent issue during the 1992 racial explosion in Los Angeles. "It took a brutal beating, an unexpected jury verdict, and the sudden rampage of rioting, looting, and indiscriminate violence to bring this crisis [of urban America] back to the forefront," *Business Week* reported. "Racism surely explains some of the carnage in Los Angeles. But the day-to-day living conditions with which many of America's urban poor must contend is an equally compelling story — a tale of economic injustice." This usually conservative magazine pointed out that "the poverty rate, which fell as low as 11% in the 1970s, moved higher in the Reagan years and jumped during the last couple of years. Last year, an estimated 36 million people — or about 14.7% of the total population — were living in poverty."[106]

South Central Los Angeles has come to symbolize the plight of poor blacks trapped in inner cities. "South Central Los Angeles is a Third World country," declared Krashaun Scott, a former member of the Los Angeles Crips gang. "There's a South Central in every city, in every state." Describing the desperate conditions in his community, he continued: "What we got is inadequate housing and inferior education. I wish someone would tell me the difference between Guatemala and South Central." This comparison graphically illustrates the squalor and poverty present within one of America's wealthiest and most modern cities. Like a Third World country, South Central Los Angeles is also extremely volatile. A gang member known as Bone explained that the recent violence was "not a riot — it was a class struggle. When Rodney King asked, 'Can we get along?' it ain't just about Rodney King. He was the lighter and it blew up."[107]

What exploded was anguish born of despair. "What happens to a dream deferred?" asked Langston Hughes in Harlem during the 1920s.

> *Does it dry up*
> *Like a raisin in the sun?*
> *. . . Or does it explode?*

But what happens when there are no dreams? Plants have been moving out of central Los Angeles into the suburbs as well as across the border into Mexico and even overseas to countries like South Korea. Abandoned inner-city factories, which had employed many of the parents of these young blacks, are now boarded up, like tombs. In terms of manufacturing jobs, South Central Los Angeles has become a wasteland. Many young black men and women nervously peer down the corridor of their futures and see no possibility of full-time employment paying above minimum wage, or any jobs at all. The unemployment rate in this area is 50 percent — higher than the national rate during the Great Depression.[108]

"Once again, young blacks are taking to the streets to express their outrage at perceived injustice," *Newsweek* reported, "and once again, whites are fearful that The Fire Next Time will consume them." But this time, the magazine noticed, the situation was different from the earlier riot: the recent conflict was not just between blacks and whites. "The nation is rapidly moving toward a multiethnic future," *Newsweek* reported, "in which Asians, Hispanics, Caribbean islanders, and many other immigrant groups compose a diverse and changing social mosaic that cannot be described by the old vocabulary of race relations in America." The terms "black" and "white," *Newsweek* concluded, no longer "depict the American social reality."[109]

At the street level, black community organizer Ted Watkins observed: "This riot was deeper, and more dangerous [than the 1965 uprising]. More ethnic groups were involved." Watkins had witnessed the Watts rebellion, an expression of black fury; since then, he had watched the influx of Hispanics and Koreans into South Central Los Angeles. Shortly after the 1992 explosion, social critic Richard Rodriguez reflected on the significance of these changes: "The Rodney King riots were appropriately multiracial in this multicultural capital of America. We cannot settle for black and white conclusions when one of the most important conflicts the riots revealed was the tension between Koreans and African Americans." He also noted that "the majority of looters who were arrested . . . turned out to be Hispanic." Out of the Los Angeles conflict came a sense of connectedness. "Here was a race riot that had no border," Rodriguez wrote, "a race riot without nationality. And, for the first time, everyone in the city realized — if only in fear — that they were related to one another."[110]

Beyond this awareness was another lesson: the need for all of us to become listeners. "A riot," Martin Luther King asserted, "is the language of the unheard." As Americans watched the live television coverage of the violence and destruction in Los Angeles, the cry of the ghetto could be heard everywhere. "I think good will come of [the riot]," stated Janet Harris, a chaplain at Central Juvenile Hall. "People need to take off their rose-colored glasses," she added, "and take a hard look at what they've been doing. They've been living in invisible cages. And they've shut out that world. And maybe the world came crashing in on them and now people will be moved to do something."[111]

The racial conflagration in Los Angeles violently highlighted America's economic problems. Racial antagonisms in Los Angeles and cities across the country are being fueled by a declining economy and rising general unemployment. One of the major causes for our economic downturn has been the recent deescalation of the U.S.-Soviet conflict: our economy has become so dependent on federal military spending that budget cuts for defense contractors have led to massive layoffs, especially in the weapons-producing states such as Massachusetts, Texas, and California. This economic crisis has been fanning the fires of racism in American society: Asian Americans have been bashed for the "invasion" of Japanese cars, Hispanics accused of taking jobs away from "Americans," and blacks attacked for their dependency on welfare and the special privileges of affirmative action.

Still, there are new prospects for change and progress. The end of the Cold War has given us the opportunity to shift our resources from nuclear weapons development to the production of consumer goods, which could help revitalize the American economy, making it more competitive with Japan and Germany. "It's as though America just won the lottery," the *New York Times* editorialized exuberantly in March 1990. "With Communism collapsing, the United States, having defended the free world for half a century, now stands to save a fortune. Defense spending could drop by $20 billion next year and $150 billion a year before the decade ends." This tremendous resource can now be directed into the consumer goods economy. What is needed, proposed Ann Markusen of Rutgers University, is "an independent Office of Economic Conversion, designed to be self-liquidating by the year 2000 and accountable to the President."[112]

In the wake of the Cold War, the United States is perched on the threshold of a new era of economic expansion. To meet the research needs of the military over the last half century, the government has educated and supported an impressive array of brilliant engineers and scientists. "These wizards of the cold war comprise the greatest force of scientific and engineering talent ever assembled," observed journalist William J. Broad in 1992. "Over the decades this army of government, academic and industry experts made the breakthroughs that gave the West its dazzling military edge." Released from military R&D, they now have the opportunity to give the United States an economic edge in the consumer goods market. Under the guidance of a comprehensive national industrial strategy, giant American corporations like Rockwell International, Grumman, Northrup, Martin Marietta, and Lockheed could now start designing and producing "smart" consumer goods rather than "smart" bombs. A growing demand for labor in a revitalized economy, combined with the rebuilding of the manufacturing base in inner cities as well as education and job training programs funded by the "peace dividend," could help to bring minority workers into the mainstream economy without making white laborers feel threatened. These needed economic changes face formidable difficulties, however. The tremendous federal debt incurred under President Reagan could dissipate the dividend generated by military budget reductions. Automation and the suburbanization of production could continue to shut out workers, especially minority laborers. The labor market has been internationalized, and American corporations could continue to relocate their production facilities in low-wage countries like Indonesia and Mexico, rendering millions of American workers superfluous. Nonetheless, the decomposition of the Soviet Union and the end of its military threat have given us new options for economic development.[113]

Moreover, American society in the 1990s has the opportunity to redefine the "errand into the wilderness" — to write our own ending to Shakespeare's play about America. The bard need not be prophetic, for we have the advantage of hindsight: we know what happened not only to Prospero but also to Caliban in America. "O brave new world that has such people in't," the London audience heard Miranda exclaim on the eve of English colonization in the New World. As it turned out in history, all of us are "such people," from the "giddy multitude" of colonial Virginia to the many ethnic groups of South Central Los Angeles. "Let America be America again," sang the poet Langston Hughes. "Let America be the dream the dreamers dreamed."

> Say who are you that mumbles in the dark?
> *I am the poor white, fooled and pushed apart,*
> *I am the Negro bearing slavery's scars.*
> *I am the red man driven from the land,*
> *I am the immigrant clutching the hope I seek.*[114]

Like the crew of the *Pequod* in Herman Melville's epic story, Americans represent the races and cultures of the world. On deck, Captain Ahab and his officers were all white men. Below deck, there were European Americans like Ishmael, Africans like Daggoo, Pacific Islanders like Queequeg, American Indians like Tashtego, and Asians like Fedallah. There was a noble class unity among the crew of the *Pequod*: they possessed "democratic dignity," and an "ethereal light" shone on the "workman's arm." On their voyage through history, Americans have found themselves bound to each other, especially as workers. Time and again, the paths of different ethnic groups have crisscrossed in this "brave new world" — Bacon's Rebellion, the Market Revolution, westward expansion, the strike at North Adams, World War II. Below deck, they have found their lives and cultures swirling together in the settling and building of America from the first meeting of the Powhatans and English on the Virginia shore to the last arrival of boatpeople from war-torn Vietnam.[115]

Together, we have created what Gloria Anzaldúa celebrated as a "borderland" — a place where "two or more cultures edge each other, where people of different races occupy the same territory." How can all of us meet on communal ground? "The struggle," Anzaldúa responded, "is inner: Chicano, *indio,* American Indian, *mojado, mexicano,* immigrant Latino, Anglo in power, working class Anglo, Black, Asian — our psyches resemble the bordertowns and are populated by the same people. . . . Awareness of our situation must come before inner changes, which in turn come before changes in society."[116]

Such awareness, in turn, must come from a "re-visioned" history. What Gloria Steinem termed "revolution from within" must ultimately be grounded in "unlearning" much of what we have been told about America's past and substituting a more inclusive and accurate history of all the peoples of America. "To finally recognize our own invisibility," declared Mitsuye Yamada, "is to finally be on the path toward visibility." To become visible is to see ourselves and each other in a different mirror of history. As Audre Lorde pointed out,

> It is a waste of time hating a mirror
> or its reflection
> instead of stopping the hand
> that makes glass with distortions.[117]

By viewing ourselves in a mirror which reflects reality, we can see our past as undistorted and no longer have to peer into our future as through a glass darkly. The face of our cultural future can be found on the western edge of the continent. "California, and especially Los Angeles, a gateway to both Asia and Latin America," Carlos Fuentes observed, "poses the universal question of the coming century: how do we deal with the Other?" Asked whether California, especially with its multiethnic society, represented the America of the twenty-first century,

Alice Walker replied: "If that's not the future reality of the United States, there won't be any United States, because that's who we are." Walker's own ancestry is a combination of Native American, African American, and European American. Paula Gunn Allen also has diverse ethnic roots — American Indian, Scotch, Jewish, and Lebanese. "Just people from everywhere are related to me by blood," she explained, "and so that's why I say I'm a multicultural event. . . . It's beautiful, it's a rainbow. . . . It reflects light, and I think that's what a person like me can do." Imagine what "light" a "multicultural event" called America can reflect. America has been settled by "the people of all nations," Herman Melville observed over a century ago, "all nations may claim her for their own. You can not spill a drop of American blood, without spilling the blood of the whole world." Americans are not "a narrow tribe"; they are not a nation, "so much as a world." In this new society, Melville optimistically declared, the "prejudices of national dislikes" could be "forever extinguish[ed]."[118]

But, as it has turned out, Melville was too sanguine. As our diversity is increasingly recognized today, it is accompanied by even more defensive denial, grim jeremiads of the Allan Blooms about the "closing of the American mind," and demagogic urgings of the Patrick Buchanans to take back "our cities, our culture, and our country." But who, in this case, are "we"? Such a backlash is defining our diversity as a "cultural war," a conflict between "us" and "them." Reflecting a traditional Eurocentrism that remains culturally hegemonic, this resistance is what is really driving the "disuniting of America."[119]

America's dilemma has been our resistance to ourselves — our denial of our immensely varied selves. But we have nothing to fear but our fear of our own diversity. "We can get along," Rodney King reassured us during an agonizing moment of racial hate and violence. To get along with each other, however, requires self-recognition as well as self-acceptance. Asked whether she had a specific proposal for improving the current racial climate in America, Toni Morrison answered: "Everybody remembers the first time they were taught that part of the human race was Other. That's a trauma. It's as though I told you that your left hand is not part of your body." In his vision of the "whole hoop of the world," Black Elk of the Sioux saw "in a sacred manner the shapes of all things in the spirit, and the shape of all shapes as they must live together like one being." And he saw that the "sacred hoop" of his people was "one of many hoops that made one circle, wide as daylight and as starlight, and in the center grew one mighty flowering tree to shelter all the children of one mother and one father." Today, what we need to do is to stop denying our wholeness as members of humanity as well as one nation.[120]

As Americans, we originally came from many different shores, and our diversity has been at the center of the making of America. While our stories contain the memories of different communities, together they inscribe a larger narrative. Filled with what Walt Whitman celebrated as the "varied carols" of America, our history generously gives all of us our "mystic chords of memory." Throughout our past of oppressions and struggles for equality, Americans of different races and ethnicities have been "singing with open mouths their strong melodious songs" in the textile mills of Lowell, the cotton fields of Mississippi, on the Indian reservations of South Dakota, the railroad tracks high in the Sierras of California, in the garment factories of the Lower East Side, the canefields of Hawaii, and a thousand other places across the country. Our denied history "bursts with telling." As we hear America singing, we find ourselves invited to bring our rich cultural diversity on deck, to accept ourselves. "Of every hue and caste am I," sang Whitman. "I resist any thing better than my own diversity."[121]

A NOTE OF APPRECIATION

M Y THANKS to Lawrence Friedman, Robert Blauner, William Simmons, Terry Wilson, Frederick Hoxie, David Thelen, and Mario Barrera for reading parts of the manuscript and giving me critical comments. A group of scholars gathered by the *Journal of American History* for a special issue on the meaning of "Discovery" in the New World helped me to think through issues about race and ethnicity. They included David Thelen, Frederick Hoxie, Francis Jennings, Richard White, Kenneth Cmiel, James R. Grossman, and Susan Armeny. James Kettner, William Simmons, and Terry Wilson generously gave me bibliographical help and even loaned me books from their personal libraries, a sign of trust and friendship. Robert Schwendinger suggested sources for Jewish-American poetry; Clara Sue Kidwell and Kurt Peters led me to some Native-American voices. Barbara Budnitz volunteered to do research on the recent Jewish refugees from what was the Soviet Union. Jack Cullen, Kirby Miller, Marion Casey, and Angela Carter of Irish Books and Graphics in New York City assisted in the search for photographs of Irish immigrants. Roberto Haro gave advice and encouragement along the way. Richard Balkin forced me to give conciseness to what had begun as a somewhat unwieldy conceptual framework for the book. Jennifer Josephy inspired me to expand a modest idea I originally had for a study of multicultural America. My deepest appreciation goes to Carol Rankin Takaki: she edited the entire work, and her valuable and at times insistent editorial criticisms helped immensely in the transformation of this study from the drafts to the polished, final version for publication. Finally, thanks to my Berkeley colleagues and students, who helped to envision and establish our university's American Cultures Requirement — a "different mirror" in the curriculum.

NOTES

Chapter 1. A Different Mirror

1. Toni Morrison, *Playing in the Dark: Whiteness in the Literary Imagination* (Cambridge, Mass., 1992), p. 47.

2. William A. Henry III, "Beyond the Melting Pot," in "America's Changing Colors," *Time*, vol. 135, no. 15 (April 9, 1990), pp. 28–31.

3. Allan Bloom, *The Closing of the American Mind: How Higher Education Has Failed Democracy and Impoverished the Souls of Today's Students* (New York, 1987), pp. 19, 91–93, 340–341, 344.

4. E. D. Hirsch, Jr., *Cultural Literacy: What Every American Needs to Know* (Boston, 1987), pp. xiii, xvii, 2, 18, 96. See also "The List," pp. 152–215.

5. Edward Fiske, "Lessons," *New York Times*, February 7, 1990; "University of Wisconsin-Madison: The Madison Plan," February 9, 1988; interview with Dean Fred Lukermann, University of Minnesota, 1987.

6. "A Conflict of the Have-Nots," *Newsweek*, December 12, 1988, pp. 28–29.

7. Rodney King's statement to the press, *New York Times*, May 2, 1992, p. 6.

8. Tim Rutten, "A New Kind of Riot," *New York Review of Books*, June 11, 1992, pp. 52–53; Maria Newman, "Riots Bring Attention to Growing Hispanic Presence in South-Central Area," *New York Times*, May 11, 1992, p. A10; Mike Davis, "In L.A. Burning All Illusions," *The Nation*, June 1, 1992, pp. 744–745; Jack Viets and Peter Fimrite, "S.F. Mayor Visits Riot-Torn Area to Buoy Businesses," *San Francisco Chronicle*, May 6, 1992, p. A6.

9. Rick DelVecchio, Suzanne Espinosa, and Carl Nolte, "Bradley Ready to Lift Curfew," *San Francisco Chronicle*, May 4, 1992, p. A1.

10. Oscar Handlin, *The Uprooted: The Epic Story of the Great Migrations That Made the American People* (New York, 1951); Arthur M. Schlesinger, Jr., *The Age of Jackson* (Boston, 1945).

11. Handlin, *The Uprooted*, p. 3; Irving Howe, *World of Our Fathers: The*

Journey of the East European Jews to America and the Life They Found and Made (New York, 1983); Dee Brown, *Bury My Heart at Wounded Knee: An Indian History of the American West* (New York, 1970); Albert Camarillo, *Chicanos in a Changing Society: From Mexican Pueblos to American Barrios in Santa Barbara and Southern California, 1848–1930* (Cambridge, Mass., 1979); Lawrence W. Levine, *Black Culture and Black Consciousness: Afro-American Folk Thought from Slavery to Freedom* (New York, 1977); Yuji Ichioka, *The Issei: The World of the First Generation Japanese Immigrants* (New York, 1988); Kerby A. Miller, *Emigrants and Exiles: Ireland and the Irish Exodus to North America* (New York, 1985).

12. Abraham Lincoln, "The Gettysburg Address," in *The Annals of America,* vol. 9, *1863–1865: The Crisis of the Union* (Chicago, 1968), pp. 462–463; Martin Luther King, *Why We Can't Wait* (New York, 1964), pp. 92–93.

13. Interview with old laundryman, in "Interviews with Two Chinese," circa 1924, Box 326, folder 325, Survey of Race Relations, Stanford University, Hoover Institution Archives; Congressman Robert Matsui, speech in the House of Representatives on the 442 bill for redress and reparations, September 17, 1987, *Congressional Record* (Washington, D.C., 1987), p. 7584.

14. Camarillo, *Chicanos in a Changing Society,* p. 2; Juan Nepomuceno Seguín, in David J. Weber (ed.), *Foreigners in Their Native Land: Historical Roots of the Mexican Americans* (Albuquerque, N. Mex., 1973), p. vi; Jesus Garza, in Manuel Gamio, *The Mexican Immigrant: His Life Story* (Chicago, 1931), p. 15; Ernesto Galarza, *Barrio Boy: The Story of a Boy's Acculturation* (Notre Dame, Ind., 1986), p. 200.

15. Lawrence J. McCaffrey, *The Irish Diaspora in America* (Washington, D.C., 1984), pp. 6, 62.

16. John Murray Cuddihy, *The Ordeal of Civility: Freud, Marx, Levi Strauss, and the Jewish Struggle with Modernity* (Boston, 1987), p. 165; Jonathan Kaufman, *Broken Alliance: The Turbulent Times between Blacks and Jews in America* (New York, 1989), pp. 28, 82, 83–84, 91, 93, 106.

17. Andrew Jackson, First Annual Message to Congress, December 8, 1829, in James D. Richardson (ed.), *A Compilation of the Messages and Papers of the Presidents, 1789–1897* (Washington, D.C., 1897), vol. 2, p. 457; Frederick Jackson Turner, "The Significance of the Frontier in American History," in *The Early Writings of Frederick Jackson Turner* (Madison, Wis., 1938), pp. 185ff.; Luther Standing Bear, "What the Indian Means to America," in Wayne Moquin (ed.), *Great Documents in American Indian History* (New York, 1973), p. 307; Vine Deloria, Jr., *Custer Died for Your Sins: An Indian Manifesto* (New York, 1969).

18. Nathan Glazer, *Affirmative Discrimination: Ethnic Inequality and Public Policy* (New York, 1978); Thomas Sowell, *Ethnic America: A History* (New York, 1981); David R. Roediger, *The Wages of Whiteness: Race and the Making of the American Working Class* (London, 1991), pp. 134–136; Dan Caldwell, "The Negroization of the Chinese Stereotype in California," *Southern California Quarterly,* vol. 33 (June 1971), pp. 123–131.

19. Tomas Almaguer, "Racial Domination and Class Conflict in Capitalist Agriculture: The Oxnard Sugar Beet Workers' Strike of 1903," *Labor History*, vol. 25, no. 3 (summer 1984), p. 347; Howard M. Sachar, *A History of the Jews in America* (New York, 1992), p. 183.

20. For the concept of liminality, see Victor Turner, *Dramas, Fields, and Metaphors: Symbolic Action in Human Society* (Ithaca, N.Y., 1974), pp. 232, 237; and Arnold Van Gennep, *The Rites of Passage* (Chicago, 1960). What I try to do is to apply liminality to the land called America.

21. Kazuo Ito, *Issei: A History of Japanese Immigrants in North America* (Seattle, 1973), p. 33; Arnold Schrier, *Ireland and the American Emigration, 1850–1900* (New York, 1970), p. 24; Abraham Cahan, *The Rise of David Levinsky* (New York, 1960; originally published in 1917), pp. 59–61; Mary Antin, quoted in Howe, *World of Our Fathers*, p. 27; Lawrence A. Cardoso, *Mexican Emigration to the United States, 1897–1931* (Tucson, Ariz., 1981), p. 80.

22. Ronald Takaki, *Strangers from a Different Shore: A History of Asian Americans* (Boston, 1989), pp. 88–89; Jack Weatherford, *Native Roots: How the Indians Enriched America* (New York, 1991), pp. 210, 212; Carey McWilliams, *North from Mexico: The Spanish-Speaking People of the United States* (New York, 1968), p. 154; Stephan Thernstrom (ed.), *Harvard Encyclopedia of American Ethnic Groups* (Cambridge, Mass., 1980), p. 22; Sachar, *A History of the Jews in America*, p. 367.

23. Walt Whitman, *Leaves of Grass* (New York, 1958), p. 284; Mathilde Bunton, "Negro Work Songs" (1940), 1 typescript in Box 91 ("Music"), Illinois Writers Project, U.S.W.P.A., in James R. Grossman, *Land of Hope: Chicago, Black Southerners, and the Great Migration* (Chicago, 1989), p. 192; Carl Wittke, *The Irish in America* (Baton Rouge, La., 1956), p. 39; Ito, *Issei, p.* 343; Manuel Gamio, *Mexican Immigration to the United States* (Chicago, 1930), pp. 84–85.

24. Abraham Lincoln, "First Inaugural Address," in *The Annals of America*, vol. 9, *1863–1865: The Crisis of the Union* (Chicago, 1968), p. 255; Lincoln, "The Gettysburg Address," pp. 462–463; Abraham Lincoln, letter to James C. Conkling, August 26, 1863, in *Annals of America*, p. 439; Frederick Douglass, in Herbert Aptheker (ed.), *A Documentary History of the Negro People in the United States* (New York, 1951), vol. 1, p. 496.

25. Weber (ed.), *Foreigners in Their Native Land*, p. vi; Hamilton Holt (ed.), *The Life Stories of Undistinguished Americans as Told by Themselves* (New York, 1906), p. 143.

26. "Social Document of Pany Lowe, interviewed by C. H. Burnett, Seattle, July 5, 1924," p. 6, Survey of Race Relations, Stanford University, Hoover Institution Archives; Minnie Miller, "Autobiography," private manuscript, copy from Richard Balkin; Tomo Shoji, presentation, Ohana Cultural Center, Oakland, California, March 4, 1988.

27. Sandra Cisneros, *The House on Mango Street* (New York, 1991), pp. 109–110; Leslie Marmon Silko, *Ceremony* (New York, 1978), p. 2; Harriet A. Jacobs,

Incidents in the Life of a Slave Girl, written by herself (Cambridge, Mass., 1987; originally published in 1857), p. xiii.

28. Carlos Fuentes, *The Buried Mirror: Reflections on Spain and the New World* (Boston, 1992), pp. 10, 11, 109; Barbara W. Tuchman, *A Distant Mirror: The Calamitous 14th Century* (New York, 1978), pp. xiii, xiv.

29. Adrienne Rich, *Blood, Bread, and Poetry: Selected Prose, 1979–1985* (New York, 1986), pp. 199.

30. Ishmael Reed, "America: The Multinational Society," in Rick Simonson and Scott Walker (eds.), *Multi-cultural Literacy* (St. Paul, 1988), p. 160; Ito, *Issei*, p. 497.

31. Arthur M. Schlesinger, Jr., *The Disuniting of America: Reflections on a Multicultural Society* (Knoxville, Tenn., 1991); Carlos Bulosan, *America Is in the Heart: A Personal History* (Seattle, 1981), pp. 188–189.

Part I: Before Columbus

1. "The Saga of the Greenlanders: Eirik the Red Takes Land in Iceland" and "The Saga of Eirik the Red: Leif Eiriksson Discovers Vinland," in *Vinland the Good: The Saga of Leif Eiriksson and the Viking Discovery of America, with a Preface by Helge Ingstad* (Oslo, 1986). The Greenland saga was written down in the fourteenth century and the saga of Eirik in the fifteenth century.

2. *Vinland the Good*, pp. 20, 26, 28.

3. *Vinland the Good*, pp. 65–66, 34, 71–72. The name "Skraelings" was applied by the Norsemen to Indians in Vinland and may be related to the modern Norwegian term *skraela*, or "scream." See Gwyn Jones, *The Norse Atlantic Saga: Being the Norse Voyages of Discovery and Settlement to Iceland, Greenland, America* (New York, 1964), pp. 59–60.

4. *Vinland the Good*, pp. 66, 68, 36, 69.

5. Christopher Columbus, Journal, October 21 and 23, 1492, in Samuel Eliot Morison (ed.), *Journals and Other Documents on the Life and Voyages of Christopher Columbus* (New York, 1963), pp. 78, 79.

Chapter 2. The "Tempest" in the Wilderness

1. Frank G. Speck, "Penobscot Tales and Religious Beliefs," *Journal of American Folklore*, vol. 48, no. 187 (January–March 1915), p. 19; William Wood, quoted in William S. Simmons, *Spirit of New England Tribes: Indian History and Folklore, 1620–1984* (Hanover, N.H., 1986), p. 66; Edward Johnson, *Wonder-working Providence, 1628–1651*, edited by F. Franklin Jameson (New York, 1910; originally published in 1654), p. 39; Colin G. Calloway (ed.), *Dawnland Encounters: Indians and Europeans in Northern New England* (Hanover, N.H., 1991), pp. 30, 50; Roger Williams, *A Key into the Language of America* (Detroit, 1973), p. 191. See also

James Axtell, "Through Another Glass Darkly: Early Indian Views of Europeans," in Axtell, *After Columbus: Essays in the Ethnohistory of Colonial North America* (New York, 1988), pp. 125–143.

2. Simmons, *Spirit of New England Tribes*, pp. 71, 72; Axtell, *After Columbus*, p. 129; James Axtell, *The Invasion Within: The Contest of Cultures in Colonial North America* (New York, 1985), p. 8.

3. William Shakespeare, *The Tempest* (New York, 1904), Act V, sc. i, 184–185. *The Tempest* has recently been swept into the storm over "political correctness." In 1991, George Will issued a scathing attack on "left" scholars and their "perverse" "liberation" of literature, especially their interpretation of this play as a reflection of "the imperialist rape of the Third World." Shakespeare specialist Stephen Greenblatt responded: "This is a curious example — since it is very difficult to argue that *The Tempest* is *not* about imperialism." Such an authoritative counterstatement clears the way for a study of this story in relationship to its historical setting. See George Will, "Literary Politics: 'The Tempest'? It's 'really' about imperialism. Emily Dickinson's poetry? Masturbation," *Newsweek*, April 22, 1991, p. 72; and Stephen Greenblatt, "The Best Way to Kill Our Literary Inheritance Is to Turn It into a Decorous Celebration of the New World Order," *Chronicle of Higher Education*, vol. 37, no. 39 (June 12, 1991), pp. B1, 3. As Adam Begley has recently noted, literary critic Stanley Fish reminds us that "the circumstances of an utterance determine its meaning." See Begley, "Souped-up Scholar," *New York Times Magazine*, May 3, 1992, p. 52. My appreciation to Frederick E. Hoxie and David Thelen for helping me develop the critical contours of my analysis.

4. Winthrop Jordan, *White Over Black: American Attitudes toward the Negro, 1550–1812* (Chapel Hill, N.C., 1968), pp. 37–40. *Othello* was first performed in 1604, before the founding of Jamestown. Jordan overlooked the rich possibility of studying *The Tempest*.

5. Nicholas P. Canny, "The Ideology of English Colonization: From Ireland to America," *William and Mary Quarterly*, 3rd series, vol. 30, no. 4 (October 1973), p. 585; David B. Quinn, *The Elizabethans and the Irish* (Ithaca, N.Y., 1966), p. 161; Francis Jennings, *The Invasion of America: Indians, Colonialism, and the Cant of Conquest* (New York, 1976), p. 7. In *White Supremacy: A Comparative Study in American & South African History* (New York, 1971), George Frederickson describes the conquest of Ireland as a "rehearsal" (p. 13).

6. Canny, "Ideology," pp. 585, 588; Howard Mumford Jones, *O Strange New World: American Culture, the Formative Years* (New York, 1965), p. 169; Keith Thomas, *Man and the Natural World: A History of the Modern Sensibility* (New York, 1983), p. 42; Jennings, *Invasion of America*, pp. 46, 49; James Muldoon, "The Indian as Irishman," *Essex Institute Historical Collections*, vol. 111 (October 1975, 269; Quinn, *Elizabethans and Irish*, p. 76.

7. Muldoon, "Indian as Irishman," p. 284; Quinn, *Elizabethans and Irish*, p. 108.

8. Canny, "Ideology," pp. 593, 582; Jennings, *Invasion of America*, p. 153;

Frederickson, *White Supremacy*, p. 15; Quinn, *Elizabethans and Irish*, pp. 132–133.

9. Canny, "Ideology," p. 582; Jennings, *Invasion of America*, p. 168; Douglas Hyde, *Literary History of Ireland* (London, 1894), p. 473.

10. Canny, "Ideology," p. 588; Jennings, *Invasion of America*, pp. 46, 49; Quinn, *Elizabethans and Irish*, p. 76; Shakespeare, *Tempest*, Act IV, sc. i, 188–189.

11. Quinn, *Elizabethans and Irish*, p. 121; William Christie MacLeod, "Celt and Indian: Britain's Old World Frontier in Relation to the New," in Paul Bohannan and Fred Plog (eds.), *Beyond the Frontier: Social Process and Cultural Change* (Garden City, N.Y., 1967), pp. 38–39; Jennings, *Invasion of America*, p. 312.

12. Quinn, *Elizabethans and Irish*, p. 121; Muldoon, "Indian as Irishman," p. 270; MacLeod, "Celt and Indian," p. 26; see also Canny, "Ideology," p. 576.

13. Shakespeare, *Tempest*, Act I, sc. ii, 229; Frank Kermode, "Introduction," *The Tempest*, The Arden Edition of the Works of William Shakespeare (London, 1969), p. xxvii; Robert R. Cawley, "Shakespeare's Use of the Voyagers in *The Tempest*," *Publications of the Modern Language Association of America*, vol. 41, no. 3 (September 1926), pp. 699–700, 689; Frederickson, *White Supremacy*, p. 22. See also Leo Marx, *The Machine in the Garden: Technology and the Pastoral Ideal in America* (New York, 1964), pp. 34–75.

14. Shakespeare, *Tempest*, Act II, sc. i, 45–53, 148–153; Cawley, "Shakespeare's Use," pp. 702, 703, 704; Kirkpatrick Sale, *The Conquest of Paradise: Christopher Columbus and the Columbian Legacy* (New York, 1990), p. 102. For analysis of America imaged as a woman, see Carolyn Merchant, *Ecological Revolutions: Nature, Gender, and Science in New England* (Chapel Hill, N.C., 1989), p. 101; Annette Kolodny, *The Lay of the Land: Metaphor as Experience and History in American Life and Letters* (Chapel Hill, N.C., 1975).

15. Kermode (ed.), introduction, *Tempest*, p. xxiv. For anagram of Hamlet, see dedication to William Shakespeare at Kronborg Castle, Denmark.

16. Christopher Columbus, Journal, November 12, 1492, in Samuel Eliot Morison (ed.), *Journals and Other Documents on the Life and Voyages of Christopher Columbus* (New York, 1963), p. 126; Sale, *Conquest of Paradise*, p. 126; Guillermo Coma to the Duke of Milan, December 13, 1494, in Morison (ed.), *Journals of Columbus*, p. 238; Cuneo to Lord Hieronymo Annari, October 15, 1495, in Morison (ed.), *Journals of Columbus*, pp. 226–227.

17. Kenneth M. Morrison, *The Embattled Northeast: The Elusive Ideal of Alliance in Abenaki-Euramerican Relations* (Berkeley, Calif., 1984), pp. 22–23; Leonard A. Adolf, "Squanto's Role in Pilgrim Diplomacy," *Ethnohistory*, vol. 11, no. 4 (fall 1964), pp. 247–248; Cawley, "Shakespeare's Use," pp. 720, 721; Shakespeare, *Tempest*, Act II, sc. ii, 70–72; Kermode (ed.), text explanation, *Tempest*, p. 62.

18. William Bradford, *Of Plymouth Plantation: 1620–1647* (New York, 1967), p. 26; Frederickson, *White Supremacy*, p. 11; Roy Harvey Pearce, *Savagism and Civilization: A Study of the Indian and the American Mind* (Baltimore, 1967), p. 12; Calloway (ed.), *Dawnland Encounters*, p. 33.

19. Wilcomb Washburn (ed.), *Indian and White Man* (New York, 1964), pp. 4–5; Morrison, *Embattled Northeast*, pp. 22–23; see Riane Eisler, *The Chalice and the Blade: Our History, Our Future* (New York, 1988) for the significance of "the sword."

20. Shakespeare, *Tempest*, Act IV, sc. i, 16–17; Act I, sc. ii, 345–352; Washburn (ed.), *Indian and White Man*, pp. 4, 5, 7.

21. Frederickson, *White Supremacy*, p. 9; the terms "descent" and "consent" are from Werner Sollors, *Beyond Ethnicity: Consent and Descent in American Culture* (New York, 1986), p. 6. Sollors minimizes the significance of race, arguing that it is "merely one aspect of ethnicity" (p. 36). I take the opposite position here as well as in Takaki, "Reflections on Racial Patterns in America," in Takaki (ed.), *From Different Shores: Perspectives on Race and Ethnicity in America* (New York, 1987), pp. 26–38; and Takaki, *Iron Cages: Race and Culture in Nineteenth-Century America* (New York, 1979).

22. Sollors, *Beyond Ethnicity*, pp. 36–37; Frederickson, *White Supremacy*, p. 8; Columbus, Journal, November 12 and December 25, 1492, in Morison (ed.), *Journals of Columbus*, pp. 92, 136; Shakespeare, *Tempest*, Act III, sc. iii, 29–31.

23. Shakespeare, *Tempest*, Act I, sc. ii, 352–360; Cawley, "Shakespeare's Use," p. 715; Frederickson, *White Supremacy*, p. 12; Pearce, *Savagism and Civilization*, pp. 9, 10. Aimé Césaire also recognized this angry and articulate Caliban and moved him from margin to center. See his *Tempest* (New York, 1969).

24. Axtell, *After Columbus*, p. 190; Helen C. Rountree, *The Powhatan Indians of Virginia: Their Traditional Culture* (Norman, Okla., 1990), pp. 44, 45, 46, 49, 60, 63.

25. Mortimer J. Adler (ed.), *The Annals of America*, vol. 1, *Discovering a New World* (Chicago, 1968), pp. 21, 26, 22.

26. Gary Nash, *Red, White, and Black: The Peoples of Early America* (Englewood Cliffs, N.J., 1974), p. 58; Adler (ed.), *Annals of America*, vol. 1, p. 26.

27. Cotton Mather, *Magnalia Christi Americana*, books 1 and 2 (Cambridge, Mass., 1977), p. 116; Frederickson, *White Supremacy*, p. 24; Sale, *Conquest of Paradise*, p. 277.

28. Jennings, *Invasion of America*, p. 66; Nash, *Red, White, and Black*, p. 57.

29. Merchant, *Ecological Revolutions*, p. 22; Shakespeare, *Tempest*, Act II, sc. i, 90–91; Act IV, sc. i, 160; Act III, sc. ii, 48–49; Thomas More, *Utopia* (New Haven, Conn., 1964), p. 76; Thomas, *Man and the Natural World*, p. 42; Cawley, "Shakespeare's Use," p. 715.

30. Jennings, *Invasion of America*, pp. 78, 80; Sale, *Conquest of Paradise*, p. 295.

31. Nash, *Red, White, and Black*, pp. 62, 63; Sale, *Conquest of Paradise*, pp. 293, 294; Jennings, *Invasion of America*, p. 153.

32. Sollors, *Beyond Ethnicity*, pp. 6, 36, 37.

33. Shakespeare, *Tempest*, Act IV, sc. i, 188–189; Act I, sc. ii, 255–260, 342–344, 350–365; Kermode (ed.), text explanation, *Tempest*, p. 63.

34. Howard S. Russell, *Indian New England Before the Mayflower* (Hanover, N.H., 1980), p. 11; John Smith, "A Description of New England," in Adler (ed.), *Annals of America*, vol. 1, p. 39.

35. Eva L. Butler, "Algonkian Culture and the Use of Maize in Southern New England," *Bulletin of the Archeological Society of Connecticut*, no. 22 (December 1948), p. 6; Speck, "Penobscot Tales," p. 75; Merchant, *Ecological Revolutions*, p. 72.

36. Russell, *Indian New England*, pp. 10, 11, 166; Merchant, *Ecological Revolutions*, p. 80; Peter A. Thomas, "Contrastive Subsistence Strategies and Land Use as Factors for Understanding Indian-White Relations in New England," *Ethnohistory*, vol. 23, no. 1 (winter 1976), p. 10; Williams, *A Key into the Language of America*, p. 170; Butler, "Algonkian Culture," pp. 15, 17. For a study of the Abenakis as hunters, see Merchant, *Ecological Revolutions*, pp. 29–68.

37. Johnson, *Wonder-working Providence*, p. 262; William Cronon, *Changes in the Land: Indians, Colonists, and the Ecology of New England* (New York, 1983), pp. 55, 56; William Wood, *New England's Prospect*, edited by Alden T. Vaughn (Amherst, Mass., 1977), p. 96.

38. Alfred W. Crosby, "Virgin Soil Epidemics as a Factor in the Aboriginal Depopulation in America," *William and Mary Quarterly*, vol. 33, no. 2 (April 1976), p. 289; Dean R. Snow, "Abenaki Fur Trade in the Sixteenth Century," *Western Canadian Journal of Anthropology*, vol. 6, no. 1 (1976), p. 8; Merchant, *Ecological Revolutions*, p. 90.

39. Bradford, *Of Plymouth Plantation*, pp. 270–271.

40. Roy Harvey Pearce, "The 'Ruines of Mankind': The Indian and Puritan Mind," *Journal of the History of Ideas*, vol. 13 (1952), p. 201; Peter Carroll, *Puritanism and the Wilderness: The Intellectual Significance of the Frontier, 1629–1700* (New York, 1969), p. 13; Johnson, *Wonder-working Providence*, p. 40.

41. Cronon, *Changes in the Land*, p. 90; Alfred W. Crosby, "God . . . Would Destroy Them, and Give Their Country to Another People," *American Heritage*, vol. 29, no. 6 (October/November 1978), p. 40; Bradford, *Of Plymouth Plantation*, pp. 65–66.

42. William S. Simmons, "Cultural Bias in the New England Puritans' Perception of Indians," *William and Mary Quarterly*, 3rd series, vol. 38 (January 1981), pp. 70, 62.

43. Kai Erikson, *Wayward Puritans: A Study in the Sociology of Deviance* (New York, 1966), pp. 13, 64; see also Pearce, *Savagism and Civilization*, p. 8.

44. Cotton Mather, *On Witchcraft: Being, The Wonders of the Invisible World* (New York, n.d.; originally published in 1692), p. 53; Simmons, "Cultural Bias," p. 71.

45. Richard Slotkin, *Regeneration through Violence: The Mythology of the American Frontier, 1600–1860* (Middetown, Conn., 1973), pp. 132, 142, 65.

46. Johnson, *Wonder-working Providence*, p. 263; Bradford, *Of Plymouth Plantation*, p. 205.

47. John Winthrop, *Winthrop Papers,* vol. 2 (1623–1630), Massachusetts Historical Society (1931), p. 139.

48. Thomas, "Contrastive Subsistence Strategies and Land Use," p. 4.

49. Charles M. Segal and David C. Stineback (eds.), *Puritans, Indians & Manifest Destiny* (New York, 1977), pp. 136–137, 111; Sherburne F. Cook, "Interracial Warfare and Population Decline among the New England Indians," *Ethnohistory,* vol. 20 (winter 1973), pp. 19–21; Simmons, "Cultural Bias," p. 67; Segal and Stineback (eds.), *Puritans, Indians & Manifest Destiny,* p. 182.

50. Johnson, *Wonder-working Providence,* pp. 71, 168, 211, 247–248; see Cronon, *Changes in the Land,* pp. 166–167.

51. Shakespeare, *Tempest,* Act III, sc. ii, 62.

52. Shakespeare, *Tempest,* Act IV, sc. i, 188–189; Sollors, *Beyond Ethnicity,* pp. 6–7, 36–37.

53. Perry Miller, "Errand into the Wilderness," in Miller, *Errand into the Wilderness* (New York, 1964), pp. 1–15; Miller's metaphor and theme originally came from Samuel Danforth's sermon, delivered on May 11, 1670, entitled "A Brief Recognition of New England's Errand into the Wilderness"; John Winthrop, "A Model of Christian Charity," in Perry Miller (ed.), *The American Puritans: Their Prose and Poetry* (New York, 1956), pp. 79–84; Simmons, "Cultural Bias," p. 67.

54. Speck, "Penobscot Tales," pp. 66–70.

55. Cronon, *Changes in the Land,* pp. 162–163.

56. Merchant, *Ecological Revolutions,* p. 93; Axtell, *Invasion Within,* p. 167.

57. Nash, *Red, White, and Black,* pp. 302–303.

58. Thomas Jefferson to Brother John Baptist de Coigne, chief of Kaskaskia, June 1781, and to John Page, August 5, 1776, in Andrew A. Lipscomb and Albert E. Bergh (eds.), *Writings of Thomas Jefferson,* 20 vols. (Washington, D.C., 1904), vol. 16, p. 372; vol. 4, pp. 270–271.

59. Jefferson to chiefs of the Shawnee Nation, February 19, 1807, in Lipscomb and Bergh (eds.), *Writings of Jefferson,* vol. 16, p. 424.

60. Thomas Jefferson, *Notes on the State of Virginia* (New York, 1861), p. 91.

61. Jefferson to chiefs of the Upper Cherokees, May 4, 1808, in Lipscomb and Bergh (eds.), *Writings of Jefferson,* vol. 16, p. 434; Jefferson to John Baptist de Coigne, June 1781, in Julian Boyd (ed.), *The Papers of Thomas Jefferson,* 18 vols. (Princeton, N.J., 1950–1965), vol. 6, pp. 60–63; Jefferson to Delawares, Mohicans, and Munries, December 21, 1808, in Lipscomb and Bergh (eds.), *Writings of Jefferson,* vol. 16, p. 452.

62. Jefferson to Choctaw Nation, December 17, 1803, and to chiefs of the Ottawas, Chippewas, Powtewatamies, Wyandots, and Senecas of Sandusky, April 22, 1808, in Lipscomb and Bergh (eds.), *Writings of Jefferson,* vol. 16, pp. 401, 429.

63. Jefferson, "Confidential Message Recommending a Western Exploring Expedition," January 18, 1803, in Lipscomb and Bergh (eds.), *Writings of Jefferson,* vol. 3, pp. 489–490; Jefferson to Governor William H. Harrison, February 27,

1803, in Lipscomb and Bergh (eds.), *Writings of Jefferson*, vol. 10, pp. 370–373; Jefferson to Horatio Gates, July 11, 1803, in Paul L. Ford (ed.), *The Works of Thomas Jefferson*, 20 vols. (New York, 1892–1899), vol. 10, p. 13; Jefferson, draft of an amendment to the Constitution, July 1803, in Ford (ed.), *Works of Jefferson*, vol. 8, pp. 241–248; Jefferson to Cherokees, January 9, 1809, in Lipscomb and Bergh (ed.), *Writings of Jefferson*, vol. 16, pp. 458–459.

64. Jefferson to John Adams, June 11, 1812, in Lester J. Cappon (ed.), *The Adams-Jefferson Letters*, 2 vols. (Chapel Hill, N.C., 1959), vol. 2, pp. 307–308; Jefferson to Governor William H. Harrison, February 27, 1803; to chiefs of the Ottawas, Chippewas, Powtewatamies, and Senecas, April 22, 1808; and to chiefs of the Wyandots, Ottawas, Chippewas, Powtewatamies, and Shawnees, January 10, 1809, in Lipscomb and Bergh (eds.), *Writings of Thomas Jefferson*, vol. 10, pp. 370–373; vol. 16, pp. 431–432, 463.

65. Jefferson to John Adams, June 11, 1812, in Cappon (ed.), *The Adams-Jefferson Letters*, vol. 2, pp. 307–308.

66. Jefferson to Adams, June 11, 1812, in Cappon (ed.), *The Adams-Jefferson Letters*, vol. 2, pp. 307–308; Jefferson to William Ludlow, September 6, 1824, in Lipscomb and Bergh (eds.), *Writings of Jefferson*, vol. 16, pp. 74–75.

Chapter 3. The "Giddy Multitude"

1. Winthrop Jordan, *White Over Black: American Attitudes toward the Negro, 1550–1812* (Chapel Hill, N.C., 1968), pp. 6, 15.

2. William Shakespeare, *The Tempest* (New York, 1904), Act I, sc. ii, 269–270; Jordan, *White Over Black*, pp. 4–5, 7.

3. Shakespeare, *Tempest*, Act I, sc. ii, 350–360; Jordan, *White Over Black*, pp. 24, 25.

4. Jordan, *White Over Black*, pp. 29–30; Shakespeare, *Tempest*, Act II, sc. ii, 20–30.

5. Shakespeare, *Tempest*, Act II, sc. ii, 310–311; Jordan, *White Over Black*, p. 73.

6. Olaudah Equiano, "Early Travels of Olaudah Equiano," in Philip D. Curtain, *Africa Remembered: Narratives by West Africans from the Era of the Slave Trade* (Madison, Wis., 1968), pp. 92–97.

7. Edmund Morgan, *American Slavery — American Freedom: The Ordeal of Colonial Virginia* (New York, 1975), p. 154. This is the most important study of class and race relations in early Virginia.

8. T. H. Breen and Stephen Innes, *"Myne Owne Grounde": Race and Freedom on Virginia's Eastern Shore, 1640–1676* (New York, 1980), p. 59; Abbot Emerson Smith, *Colonists in Bondage: White Servitude and Convict Labor in America, 1607–1776* (Gloucester, Mass., 1965), pp. 4, 13.

9. Smith, *Colonists in Bondage*, pp. 3, 45.

10. Smith, *Colonists in Bondage*, pp. 68–69, 163, 166–167; Marcus W.

Jernegan, *Laboring and Dependent Classes in Colonial America, 1607–1783* (New York, 1960), p. 50.

11. Smith, *Colonists in Bondage*, pp. 256, 253.

12. William W. Hening, *The Statutes at Large; Being a Collection of All the Laws of Virginia*, 13 vols. (Richmond, 1809–1823), vol. 2, p. 26; Helen Catterall (ed.), *Judicial Cases Concerning American Slavery and the Negro*, vol. 1, *Cases from the Courts of England, Virginia, West Virginia, and Kentucky* (New York, 1968), p. 80.

13. Catterall, *Judicial Cases*, pp. 77, 78; Morgan, *American Slavery — American Freedom*, pp. 155, 336; Winthrop Jordan, "Modern Tensions and the Origins of American Slavery," *Journal of Southern History*, vol. 28, no. 1 (February 1962), p. 28; Breen and Innes, *"Myne Owne Grounde,"* p. 96.

14. Hening, *Statutes*, vol. 1, p. 226; Breen and Innes, *"Myne Owne Grounde,"* pp. 25, 29; Catterall, *Judicial Cases*, p. 77.

15. "Inventory of the goods Cattle and Chattles of and belonging unto the estate of Mr. William Burdett," November 13, 1643, reprinted in Susie M. Ames (ed.), *County Court Records of Accomack-Northampton, Virginia, 1640–1645* (Charlottesville, Va., 1973), pp. 419–425.

16. Ames (ed.), *Court Records*, pp. 324, 255, 433–434; Jordan, *White Over Black*, p. 75; Morgan, *American Slavery — American Freedom*, p. 154; Carl Degler, *Out of Our Past: The Forces That Shaped Modern America* (New York, 1962), p. 34.

17. Oscar Handlin, *Race and Nationality in American Life* (New York, 1957), p. 7; Alden T. Vaughan, "The Origins Debate: Slavery and Racism in Seventeenth-Century Virginia," *Virginia Magazine of History and Biography*, vol. 97, no. 3 (July 1989), p. 354. See Degler, *Out of Our Past*, pp. 26–39, for a refutation of the Handlin thesis as presented in Handlin, *Race and Nationality*, pp. 3–22.

18. Hening, *Statutes*, vol. 2, pp. 26, 270.

19. Jordan, *White Over Black*, pp. 64, 69, 71; Mortimer J. Adler (ed.), *The Annals of America*, vol. 1, *Discovering a New World* (Chicago, 1968), p. 167.

20. Morgan, *American Slavery — American Freedom*, pp. 404, 422, 298; T. H. Breen, "A Changing Labor Force and Race Relations in Virginia, 1660–1710," *Journal of Social History*, vol. 7 (fall 1973), p. 8. Breen's essay is heuristic.

21. Smith, *Colonists in Bondage*, p. 29.

22. Hening, *Statutes*, vol. 2, pp. 260, 281. See Ann Stoler, "Sexual Affronts and Racial Frontiers: National Identity, 'Mixed Bloods,' and the Cultural Genealogies of Europeans in Colonial Southeast Asia," paper presented at the conference on "The Decolonization of Imagination: The New Europe and Its Others," Amsterdam, May 1991.

23. Jordan, *White Over Black*, p. 579.

24. Breen, "Changing Labor Force," pp. 16, 17; Morgan, *American Slavery — American Freedom*, pp. 404, 423; Degler, *Out of Our Past*, p. 27; Russell Menard, "From Servants to Slaves: The Transformation of the Chesapeake Labor System,"

Southern Studies, vol. 5 (winter 1977), p. 370; Hening, *Statutes,* vol. 3, pp. 447–448.

25. Handlin, *Race and Nationality,* pp. 13, 19.

26. Menard, "From Servants to Slaves," p. 363; Morgan, *American Slavery — American Freedom,* p. 299.

27. Shakespeare, *Tempest,* Act II, sc. ii, 180–190; Act II, sc. ii, 60–70; Act III, sc. ii, 110–140; Act IV, sc. i, 250–260.

28. Breen, "Changing Labor Force," p. 4.

29. Morgan, *American Slavery — American Freedom,* pp. 215–220.

30. Morgan, *American Slavery — American Freedom,* p. 221.

31. Breen, "Changing Labor Force," pp. 3, 8, 9; Breen and Innes, *"Myne Owne Grounde,"* p. 60; Smith, *Colonists in Bondage,* p. 138.

32. Breen, "Changing Labor Force," pp. 3–4; Morgan, *American Slavery — American Freedom,* pp. 241–242.

33. Morgan, *American Slavery — American Freedom,* p. 257. The House of Burgesses used the term "giddy multitude" to describe the followers of Nathaniel Bacon. H. R. McIlwaine (ed.), *Journals of the House of Burgesses of Virginia, 1659/60–1693* (Richmond, 1914). See Breen, "Changing Labor Force," p. 18.

34. Morgan, *American Slavery — American Freedom,* pp. 258, 260.

35. Breen, "Changing Labor Force," p. 10.

36. Breen, "Changing Labor Force," p. 11.

37. Morgan, *American Slavery — American Freedom,* p. 308; Breen, "Changing Labor Force," p. 12. Morgan is reluctant to press his analysis as far as I do. "The substitution of slaves for servants gradually eased and eventually ended the threat that the freedmen posed," he wrote. "As the annual number of imported servants dropped, so did the number of men turning free.... Planters who bought slaves instead of servants did not do so with any apparent consciousness of the social stability to be gained thereby." Perhaps not, but perhaps they did, though not apparently. See Theodore Allen, " '. . . They Would Have Destroyed Me': Slavery and the Origins of Racism," *Radical America,* vol. 9, no. 3 (May–June 1975), pp. 41–63, which I read after completing my analysis of Bacon's Rebellion, for an argument that the planters acted deliberately and consciously.

38. Darrett B. and Anita H. Rutman, *A Place in Time: Middlesex County, Virginia, 1650–1750* (New York, 1984), p. 165; Morgan, *American Slavery — American Freedom,* p. 306.

39. Hening, *Statutes,* vol. 2, pp. 481, 493.

40. Morgan, *American Slavery — American Freedom,* pp. 222, 339; Hening, *Statutes,* vol. 3, p. 451.

41. Breen and Innes, *"Mine Owne Grounde,"* p. 108.

42. Allen, " 'They Would Have Destroyed Me,' " p. 55; Hening, *Statutes,* vol. 3, pp. 86–87; Morgan, *American Slavery — American Freedom,* pp. 333, 335–337.

43. Hening, *Statutes,* vol. 2, p. 481; vol. 3, pp. 459–460; vol. 10, p. 331; Breen,

"Changing Labor Force," p. 17; Benjamin Quarles, *The Negro in the American Revolution* (Chapel Hill, N.C., 1961), p. 108.

44. Thomas Jefferson, *Notes on the State of Virginia* (New York, 1861), pp. 157–158.

45. Jefferson to John Adams, October 28, 1813, in Adrienne Koch and William Peden (eds.), *The Life and Selected Writings of Thomas Jefferson* (New York, 1944), p. 633.

46. Jefferson, *Notes*, p. 167; Jefferson to John Jordan, December 21, 1805, and to W. Eppes, June 30, 1830, in Edwin M. Betts (ed.), *Thomas Jefferson's Farm Book* (Princeton, N.J., 1953), pp. 21, 43.

47. Jefferson to Daniel Bradley, October 6, 1805, and to Thomas M. Randolph, June 8, 1803, in Betts (ed.), *Jefferson's Farm Book*, pp. 21, 19.

48. Jefferson to Edward Coles, August 25, 1814, in Paul L. Ford (ed.), *The Works of Thomas Jefferson*, 20 vols. (New York, 1892–1899), vol. 11, p. 416; Jefferson, *Notes*, p. 132; Jefferson to Brissot de Warville, February 11, 1788, in Julian Boyd (ed.), *The Papers of Thomas Jefferson*, 18 vols. (Princeton, N.J., 1950–1965), vol. 12, pp. 577–578.

49. Jefferson to Francis Eppes, July 30, 1787, in Boyd (ed.), *Papers*, vol. 10, p. 653; Jefferson to Nicholas Lewis, July 29, 1787, in Boyd (ed.), *Papers*, vol. 10, p. 640.

50. Jefferson, *Notes*, p. 155.

51. Jefferson, *Notes*, pp. 85–86; Jefferson to John Holmes, April 22, 1820, in Ford (ed.), *Works*, vol. 12, pp. 334.

52. Jefferson to Jared Sparks, February 4, 1824, in Ford (ed.), *Works*, vol. 13, p. 159.

53. Jefferson, *Notes*, pp. 127, 138.

54. Jordan, *White Over Black*, pp. 283–284; Phillis Wheatley, *The Poems of Phillis Wheatley*, edited by Julian Mason (Chapel Hill, N.C., 1966), pp. 7, 34.

55. Jordan, *White Over Black*, p. 437; Jefferson, *Notes*, p. 135.

56. Banneker to Jefferson, August 19, 1791, reprinted in George Ducas, with Charles Van Doren (eds.), *Great Documents in Black American History* (New York, 1970), pp. 23–26.

57. *Ibid.*

58. Jefferson to Banneker, August 30, 1791, in Ford (ed.), *Works*, vol. 6, pp. 309–310; Jefferson to Joel Harlow, October 8, 1809, in Ford (ed.), *Works*, vol. 11, p. 121.

59. Shakespeare, *Tempest*, Act IV, sc. i, 188–189; Jefferson, *Notes*, pp. 137–141.

60. Jefferson, *Notes*, pp. 138–139, 127.

61. Jefferson, *Notes*, pp. 132–133.

62. Jefferson to James Monroe, July 14, 1793, in Ford (ed.), *Works*, vol. 7, pp. 449–459; Jefferson to St. George Tucker, August 28, 1797, in Ford (ed.), *Works*, vol. 8, p. 335; Jefferson to James Monroe, September 20, 1800, in Ford (ed.), *Works*,

vol. 9, p. 147; Jefferson to William Burwell, January 28, 1805, in Betts (ed.), *Jefferson's Farm Book*, p. 20.

63. Jefferson to John Holmes, April 22, 1820, in Ford (ed.), *Works*, vol. 13, p. 159; Shakespeare, *Tempest*, Act I, sc. ii, 310–314; Act V, sc. i, 100–110.

Part II: Prospero Unbound

1. Jefferson to John Hollins, May 5, 1811, in Andrew A. Lipscomb and Albert E. Bergh (eds.), *Writings of Thomas Jefferson*, 20 vols. (Washington, D.C., 1904), vol. 13, p. 58. For the definitive study of the economy and society of the first half of the nineteenth century, see Charles Sellers, *The Market Revolution: Jacksonian America, 1815–1846* (New York, 1991). My appreciation to Professor Sellers for his inspiration and teaching.

2. Benjamin Franklin, *Observations Concerning the Increase of Mankind,* in Leonard W. Labaree (ed.), *The Papers of Benjamin Franklin* (New Haven, Conn., 1959–), vol. 4, p. 234.

3. *Debates and Proceedings in the Congress of the United States, 1789–1791,* 2 vols. (Washington, D.C.), vol. 1, pp. 998, 1284; vol. 2, pp. 1148–1156, 1162, 2264; Thomas Jefferson to James Monroe, November 24, 1801, in Paul L. Ford (ed.), *The Works of Thomas Jefferson,* 20 vols. (New York, 1892–1899), vol. 9, p. 317; Felix S. Cohen, *Handbook of Federal Indian Law* (Albuquerque, N. Mex., 1958), pp. 153–159.

4. Max Weber, *The Protestant Ethic and the Spirit of Capitalism* (New York, 1958; originally published in 1930).

5. Alexis de Tocqueville, *Democracy in America,* 2 vols. (New York, 1945; originally published in 1835), vol. 2, pp. 23, 239, 137. See also Douglass C. North, *The Economic Growth of the United States, 1790–1860* (New York, 1966).

6. See George R. Taylor, *The Transportation Revolution, 1815–1860* (New York, 1962).

7. North, *Economic Growth,* p. 129.

8. James Madison, quoted in Michael Paul Rogin, *Fathers and Children: Andrew Jackson and the Subjugation of the American Indian* (New York, 1975), p. 319.

Chapter 4. Toward the Stony Mountains

1. Jefferson to Andrew Jackson, February 16, 1803, in Andrew A. Lipscomb and Albert E. Bergh (eds.), *Writings of Thomas Jefferson,* 20 vols. (Washington, D.C., 1904), vol. 10, pp. 357–359. While the title for this subsection comes from John William Ward, *Andrew Jackson: Symbol for an Age* (New York, 1955), it suggests here that Jackson was also another kind of symbol. Richard White's *Roots of Dependency: Subsistence, Environment, and Social Change among the Choctaws, Pawnees, and Navajos* (Lincoln, Nebr., 1983) is pathbreaking in its comparative focus

on specific tribes. I have followed his lead in examining the Pawnees here and the Navajos in a later chapter.

2. Michael Paul Rogin, *Fathers and Children: Andrew Jackson and the Subjugation of the American Indian* (New York, 1975), pp. 140–141; Jackson to Willie Blount, July 10, 1812, in John Spencer Bassett (ed.), *Correspondence of Andrew Jackson*, 6 vols. (Washington, D.C., 1926), vol. 1, pp. 231–232; Jackson, General Order, September 19, 1813, and General Order, December 15, 1813, in Bassett (ed.), *Correspondence*, vol. 1, pp. 319–320, 429–430.

3. Jackson to Thomas Pinckney, February 16 and 17, 1814, and May 18, 1814, in Bassett (ed.), *Correspondence*, vol. 1, pp. 463–465; vol. 2, pp. 2–3; Jackson to Mrs. Jackson, April 1, 1814, in Bassett (ed.), *Correspondence*, vol. 1, p. 493.

4. Jackson, Proclamation, April 2, 1814, Fort Williams, in Bassett (ed.), *Correspondence*, vol. 1, p. 494. See Riane Eisler, *The Chalice and the Blade: Our History, Our Future* (New York, 1988).

5. Jackson, Special Message to the Senate, February 22, 1831, in James D. Richardson (ed.), *A Compilation of the Messages and Papers of the Presidents, 1789–1897* (Washington, D.C., 1897), vol. 2, p. 541; Rogin, *Fathers and Children*, p. 213.

6. Mary E. Young, "Indian Removal and Land Allotment: The Civilized Tribes and Jacksonian Justice," *American Historical Review*, vol. 64 (October 1958), p. 36.

7. John Eaton to William Carroll, May 30, 1829, reprinted in Annie Heloise Abel, *The History of Events Resulting in Indian Consolidation West of the Mississippi* (Washington, D.C., 1906), p. 371.

8. Jackson, speech to the Chickasaws, First Annual Message to Congress, in Richardson (ed.), *Papers of the Presidents*, vol. 2, pp. 241, 456–458.

9. Jackson, First Annual Message to Congress, in Richardson (ed.), *Papers of the Presidents*, vol. 2, pp. 456–458.

10. Jackson to Captain James Gadsden, October 12, 1829, in Bassett (ed.), *Correspondence*, vol. 4, p. 81; Jackson to Major David Haley, October 15, 1829, quoted in Abel, *Indian Consolidation*, p. 373; Jackson, speech to Chickasaws, Special Message to the Senate, in Richardson (ed.), *Papers of the Presidents*, vol. 2, pp. 241, 541.

11. Jackson, Proclamation, April 2, 1814, Fort Williams, in Bassett (ed.), *Correspondence*, vol. 1, p. 494; Jackson, Second Annual Message, in Richardson (ed.), *Papers of the Presidents*, vol. 2, pp. 520–522.

12. Rogin, *Fathers and Children*, p. 231.

13. F. P. Prucha, "Introduction," in D. S. Otis, *The Dawes Act and the Allotment of Indian Lands* (Norman, Okla., 1973), p. ix.

14. T. N. Campbell, "Choctaw Subsistence: Ethnographic Notes from the Lincecum Manuscript," *Florida Anthropologist*, vol. 12 (1959), pp. 16–19; John R. Swanton (ed.), "An Early Account of the Choctaw Indians," *Memoirs of the American Anthropological Association*, vol. 5 (April–June 1918), pp. 58–59.

15. White, *Roots of Dependency,* pp. 41, 42.

16. White, *Roots of Dependency,* pp. 102, 133–135.

17. Arthur H. DeRosier, Jr., *The Removal of the Choctaw Indians* (New York, 1972), p. 108.

18. DeRosier, *Removal of the Choctaw Indians,* pp. 104, 126, 122; White, *Roots of Dependency,* p. 143.

19. DeRosier, *Removal of the Choctaw Indians,* p. 128; Angie Debo, *The Rise and Fall of the Choctaw Republic* (Norman, Okla., 1934), p. 70.

20. DeRosier, *Removal of the Choctaw Indians,* p. 124.

21. Grant Foreman, *Indian Removal: The Emigration of the Five Civilized Tribes of Indians* (Norman, Okla., 1972), p. 73.

22. Rogin, *Fathers and Children,* p. 230; Jackson to General John Coffee, April 7, 1832, in Bassett (ed.), *Correspondence,* vol. 4, p. 430.

23. Foreman, *Indian Removal,* pp. 56, 64, 98.

24. Alexis de Tocqueville, *Democracy in America,* 2 vols. (New York, 1945; originally published in 1835), vol. 1, pp. 352–353, 364.

25. Debo, *Choctaw Republic,* p. 56; Wayne Moquin (ed.), *Great Documents in American Indian History* (New York, 1973), pp. 151–153.

26. Debo, *Choctaw Republic,* p. 56.

27. DeRosier, *Removal of the Choctaw Indians,* p. 163.

28. James Mooney, *Myths of the Cherokee,* published in United States Bureau of Ethnology, *Nineteenth Annual Report, 1897–1898* (Washington, D.C., 1900), pp. 239–240.

29. Foreman, *Indian Removal,* p. 229.

30. John Ross to General Council, July 10–16, 1830, in Gary E. Moulton (ed.), *The Papers of Chief John Ross,* 2 vols. (Norman, Okla., 1985), vol. 1, p. 190; Ross, "To the Cherokees," April 14, 1831, in Moulton (ed.), *Papers of Ross,* vol. 1, p. 218.

31. Ross to Cass, February 6, 1834, in Moulton (ed.), *Papers of Ross,* vol. 1, p. 275; Ross to Jackson, March 12, 1834, in Moulton (ed.), *Papers of Ross,* vol. 1, p. 277.

32. Rogin, *Fathers and Children,* p. 227; Ross, "Annual Message," October 12, 1835, in Moulton (ed)., *Papers of Ross,* vol. 1, p. 358.

33. Ross, "To the Senate," March 8, 1836, in Moulton (ed.), *Papers of Ross,* vol. 1, p. 394; Mooney, *Myths of the Cherokee,* pp. 126–127.

34. Mooney, *Myths of the Cherokee,* p. 127.

35. Foreman, *Indian Removal,* p. 283.

36. Foreman, *Indian Removal,* pp. 286–288.

37. George Hicks to John Ross, November 4, 1838, in Moulton (ed.), *Papers of Ross,* vol. 1, p. 687.

38. Foreman, *Indian Removal,* pp. 309, 296; Thurman Wilkins, *Cherokee Tragedy: The Story of the Ridge Family and of the Decimation of a People* (New York, 1970), p. 314.

39. Gloria Levitas, Frank Vivelo, and Jacquelien Vivelo (eds.), *American Indian Prose and Poetry* (New York, 1974), p. 180; Wilkins, *Cherokee Tragedy*, p. 314.

40. George A. Dorsey, *The Pawnee Mythology* (Washington, D.C., 1906), pp. 21–28.

41. White, *Roots of Dependency*, pp. 172–173; Frances Densmore, *Pawnee Music*, in Smithsonian Institution, *Bureau of Ethnology*, Bulletin 93 (Washington, D.C., 1929), p. 32; Gene Weltfish, *The Lost Universe* (New York, 1965), p. 203; Dorsey, *Pawnee Mythology*, p. 213.

42. Martha Royce Blaine, *Pawnee Passage: 1870–1875* (Norman, Okla., 1990), p. 81.

43. David J. Wishart, "The Dispossession of the Pawnee," in *Annals of the Association of American Geographers*, vol. 69, no. 3 (September 1979), p. 386; John B. Dunbar, "The Pawnee Indians: Their Habits and Customs," *Magazine of American History*, vol. 5, no. 5 (November 1880), pp. 327–328, 331; White, *Roots of Dependency*, p. 188.

44. Levitas *et al.* (eds.), *American Indian Prose and Poetry*, p. 41; John B. Dunbar, "The Pawnee Indians: Their History and Ethnology," *Magazine of American History*, vol. 4, no. 4 (April 1880), p. 275; James R. Murie, *Ceremonies of the Pawnee*, in Douglas R. Parks (ed.), *Smithsonian Contributions to Anthropology*, no. 27 (Washington, D.C., 1981), pp. 80–82.

45. Dunbar, "Pawnee . . . History," p. 276.

46. White, *Roots of Dependency*, p. 172; Densmore, *Pawnee Music*, p. 5.

47. White, *Roots of Dependency*, pp. 191–192; Wishart, "Dispossession of the Pawnee," p. 387.

48. Jackson, Third Annual Message to Congress, 1831, in Richardson (ed.), *Papers of the Presidents*, vol. 2, p. 545.

49. "The Spirit of the Times; or the Fast Age," *Democratic Review*, vol. 33 (September 1853), pp. 260–261.

50. Alfred L. Riggs, "What Shall We Do with the Indians?" *The Nation*, vol. 67 (October 31, 1867), p. 356.

51. Ulysses S. Grant, First Annual Message, 1869, in Richardson (ed.), *Papers of the Presidents*, vol. 9, p. 3993.

52. Robert G. Athearn, *William Tecumseh Sherman and the Settlement of the West* (Norman, Okla., 1956), pp. 324–325.

53. Francis Amasa Walker, *The Indian Question* (Boston, 1874), p. 5; Ira G. Clark, *Then Came the Railroads: The Century from Steam to Diesel in the Southwest* (Norman, Okla., 1958), pp. 121, 128.

54. Wishart, "Dispossession of the Pawnee," p. 390.

55. Levitas *et al.* (eds.), *American Indian Prose and Poetry*, p. 229.

56. Wishart, "Dispossession of the Pawnee," p. 392.

57. White, *Roots of Dependency*, p. 201; Blaine, *Pawnee Passage*, p. 215; Dunbar, "Pawnee . . . History," p. 251; Weltfish, *Lost Universe*, p. 4.

58. Densmore, *Pawnee Music*, p. 90; White, *Roots of Dependency*, p. 210; Blaine, *Pawnee Passage*, p. 143.

59. Levitas *et al.* (eds.), *American Indian Prose and Poetry*, pp. 210, 224, 222.

60. Peter Nabokov (ed.), *Native American Testimony: A Chronicle of Indian-White Relations from Prophecy to the Present, 1492–1992* (New York, 1991), p. 40; White, *Roots of Dependency*, p. 201; E. L. Sabin, *Building the Pacific Railway* (Philadelphia, 1919), p. 233.

Chapter 5. No More Peck o' Corn

1. James Madison, quoted in Michael Paul Rogin, *Fathers and Children: Andrew Jackson and the Subjugation of the American Indian* (New York, 1975), p. 319.

2. David Walker, *Appeal to the Colored Citizens of the World* (New York, 1965; originally published in 1829), pp. 72, 93, 34.

3. Leon Litwack, *North of Slavery: The Negro in the Free States, 1790–1860* (Chicago, 1965), p. 234; William Chambers, *Things as They Are in America* (Philadelphia, 1854), p. 354. Litwack's study is the standard work on this subject.

4. Alexis de Tocqueville, *Democracy in America*, 2 vols. (New York, 1945; originally published in 1835), vol. 1, pp. 373–374.

5. Litwack, *North of Slavery*, p. 120.

6. Robert A. Warner, *New Haven Negroes: A Social History* (New Haven, Conn., 1940), p. 34; Tocqueville, *Democracy in America*, vol. 1, p. 373; Litwack, *North of Slavery*, pp. 66, 98, 155–156; Frank U. Quillan, *The Color Line in Ohio: A History of Race Prejudice in a Typical Northern State* (Ann Arbor, Mich., 1913), p. 55; Thomas F. Gossett, *Race: The History of an Idea in America* (Dallas, 1963), p. 74.

7. Litwack, *North of Slavery*, p. 164; *Richmond Jeffersonian*, in Emma Lou Thornbrough, *The Negro in Indiana: A Study of a Minority* (n.p., 1957), p. 62.

8. Tocqueville, *Democracy in America*, vol. 1, p. 373; Eugene H. Berwanger, *The Frontier against Slavery: Western Anti-Negro Prejudice and the Slavery Extension Controversy* (Urbana, Ill., 1967), pp. 20, 36; Litwack, *North of Slavery*, p. 77.

9. Thornbrough, *Negro in Indiana*, p. 163; Litwack, *North of Slavery*, pp. 149–150.

10. Litwack, *North of Slavery*, pp. 153–154.

11. Kenneth Stampp, *The Peculiar Institution: Slavery in the Antebellum South* (New York, 1956), p. 44; Frederick Law Olmsted, *The Slave States* (New York, 1959; originally published as *A Journey in the Back Country* in 1860), pp. 176–177. Stampp's study is essential for an understanding of the institution of slavery.

12. Solomon Northrup, *Twelve Years a Slave* (Buffalo, 1853), pp. 166–168.

13. Stampp, *Peculiar Institution*, pp. 163, 146.

14. George Fitzhugh, "Sociology for the South," in Harvey Wish (ed.), *Antebellum: Writings of George Fitzhugh and Hinton Rowan Helper on Slavery* (New

York, 1960), pp. 88, 89; Bertram W. Doyle, *Etiquette of Race Relations in the South* (Chicago, 1931), p. 54.

15. John Hope Franklin, "The Enslavement of Free Negroes in North Carolina," *Journal of Negro History*, vol. 29 (October 1944), p. 405.

16. Edward Pollard, *Black Diamonds Gathered in the Darkey Homes of the South* (New York, 1859), pp. 57–58; Benjamin F. Perry, in Lillian Kibler, *Benjamin F. Perry: South Carolina Unionist* (Durham, N.C., 1946), p. 282; *Natchez Free Trader*, September 20, 1858; Gustave A. Breaux, Diary, January 1, 1859, Breaux Papers, Tulane University Library, New Orleans, Louisiana.

17. J. J. Pettigrew, in *De Bow's Review*, vol. 25 (September 1858), p. 293; Roger Pryor, in *De Bow's Review*, vol. 24 (June 1858), p. 582.

18. Frederick Law Olmsted, *A Journey in the Seaboard Slave States in the Years 1853–1854 with Remarks on Their Economy*, 2 vols. (New York, 1904), vol. 2, pp. 218–219.

19. *Galveston News*, December 6, 1856; *Charleston Mercury*, October 20, 1858; J. G. M. Ramsey to L. W. Spratt, April 23, 1858, Ramsey Papers, University of North Carolina Library, Chapel Hill, North Carolina.

20. Percy Lee Rainwater, *Mississippi, Storm Center of Secession, 1856–1861* (Baton Rouge, La., 1938), p. 12; Charles G. Sellers, Jr., *The Southerner as American* (Chapel Hill, N.C., 1960), p. 48; Ernest T. Thompson, *Presbyterians in the South, 1607–1861* (Richmond, 1963), p. 533; *Galveston News*, December 5, 1856.

21. *De Bow's Review*, vol. 14 (1853), p. 276, italics added; William W. Freehling, *Prelude to Civil War: The Nullification Controversy in South Carolina, 1816–1832* (New York, 1966), p. 59.

22. Fredericka Bremer, *The Homes of the New World: Impressions of America*, 3 vols. (London, 1853), vol. 2, p. 451; Frances A. Kemble, *Journal of a Residence on a Georgia Plantation in 1838–1839* (New York, 1961; originally published in 1863), p. 342; *New Orleans Picayune*, December 24, 1856.

23. Stampp, *Peculiar Institution*, p. 87; U. B. Phillips, *Life and Labor in the Old South* (Boston, 1929), p. 276.

24. Raymond and Alice H. Bauer, "Day to Day Resistance to Slavery," *Journal of Negro History*, vol. 27 (1942), pp. 388–419; Stampp, *Peculiar Institution*, pp. 88, 90; John Dollard, *Caste and Class in a Southern Town* (New York, 1949), p. 390; Leon Litwack, *Been in the Storm So Long: The Aftermath of Slavery* (New York, 1979), p. 221.

25. William Francis Allen et al., *Slave Songs of the United States* (New York, 1867), p. 48.

26. Sarah Logue to "Jarm," February 20, 1860, and J. W. Loguen to Mrs. Sarah Logue, reprinted in *Boston Liberator*, April 27, 1860.

27. Stampp, *Peculiar Institution*, p. 132; Phillips, *Life and Labor in the South*, p. 209; Nat Turner and T. R. Gray, *The Confessions of Nat Turner*, in Herbert Aptheker, *Nat Turner's Rebellion* (New York, 1968), appendix, pp. 136, 138, 130–131.

28. Quoted in Stampp, *Peculiar Institution*, pp. 100, 127; Eugene Genovese, *Roll, Jordan, Roll: The World the Slaves Made* (New York, 1974), pp. 300, 318, 602. Genovese's study offers an understanding of slavery from the viewpoint of the slaves as men and women.

29. Richard Wade, *Slavery in the Cities: The South, 1820–1860* (New York, 1964), p. 39.

30. Wade, *Slavery in the Cities*, p. 49.

31. U. B. Phillips, *American Negro Slavery* (New York, 1918), p. 408.

32. Wade, *Slavery in the Cities*, p. 279.

33. Wade, *Slavery in the Cities*, pp. 245–246; Eugene Genovese, *The Political Economy of Slavery* (New York, 1965), p. 226.

34. Genovese, *Roll, Jordan, Roll*, p. 97; Litwack, *Been in the Storm So Long*, pp. 6, 21. This is the best book on what it felt like to be suddenly free.

35. Litwack, *Been in the Storm So Long*, p. 7; E. Franklin Frazier, *The Negro Family in the United States* (Chicago, 1939), p. 79; Genovese, *Roll, Jordan, Roll*, p. 133.

36. Litwack, *Been in the Storm So Long*, p. 21; Bell Wiley, *Southern Negroes, 1861–1865* (New Haven, Conn., 1938), pp. 72, 70.

37. Litwack, *Been in the Storm So Long*, p. 12; Genovese, *Roll, Jordan, Roll*, pp. 105, 581.

38. Litwack, *Been in the Storm So Long*, pp. 19, 59; Edwin D. Hoffman, "From Slavery to Self-Reliance," *Journal of Negro History*, vol. 41 (January 1956), pp. 13–14.

39. Litwack, *Been in the Storm So Long*, pp. 144, 135; Wiley, *Southern Negroes*, p. 83; Genovese, *Roll, Jordan, Roll*, p. 101.

40. Angela Y. Davis, *Women, Race & Class* (New York, 1981), pp. 6, 7, 21; Toni Morrison, *Beloved: A Novel* (New York, 1987).

41. Davis, *Women, Race & Class*, p. 23; Harriet A. Jacobs, *Incidents in the Life of a Slave Girl, written by herself* (Cambridge, Mass., 1987; originally published in 1857), pp. 77, 27, 55; Mary B. Chesnut, *A Diary from Dixie* (Cambridge, Mass., 1961), pp. 21–22.

42. Frederick Douglass, *Narrative of the Life of Frederick Douglass* (New York, 1968; originally published in 1845), p. 26.

43. Frederick Douglass, *Life and Times of Frederick Douglass* (New York, 1889), pp. 27–30.

44. Douglass, *Life and Times*, pp. 76–78.

45. Douglass, *Life and Times*, pp. 78–82.

46. Douglass, *Life and Times*, pp. 75–94.

47. Douglass, *Life and Times*, pp. 112, 186.

48. Douglass, *Life and Times*, pp. 124–125.

49. Douglass, *Life and Times*, pp. 125–134.

50. Douglass, *Life and Times*, pp. 140, 142–143.

51. Douglass, *Life and Times*, pp. 271–275; Douglass, in *Boston Liberator*,

June 8, 1849; *Douglass's Monthly*, November 1859; Douglass, letter to John Brown, in *Boston Liberator*, November 11, 1859.

52. Douglass, *Life and Times*, pp. 440–452.

53. Douglass, letter to H. G. Warner, in *Boston Liberator*, October 6, 1848; Douglass, in Philip S. Foner (ed.), *The Life and Writings of Frederick Douglass*, 4 vols. (New York, 1950), vol. 1, p. 423; vol. 2, p. 421; vol. 4, pp. 116, 427; *Rochester North Star*, September 15, 1848; Douglass, quoted in Benjamin Quarles, *Frederick Douglass* (New York, 1968), p. 35; Douglass, *Life and Times*, p. 534; Douglass to Francis Jackson, January 29, 1846, Anti-Slavery Collection, Boston Public Library.

54. Douglass, *Life and Times*, pp. 284–290; Douglass, "The Future of the Colored Race," *The North American Review*, in Foner (ed.), *Life and Writings*, vol. 4, pp. 193–196.

55. Douglass, quoted in Frank A. Rollin, *Life and Public Services of Martin R. Delany* (Boston, 1883), p. 19; Martin Delany, *Official Report of the Niger Valley Exploring Party*, reprinted in Howard H. Bell, *Search for a Place: Black Separatism and Africa, 1860* (Ann Arbor, Mich., 1969), p. 121.

56. Bell, *Search for a Place*, p. 121.

57. Martin Delany, "American Civilization — Treatment of the Colored People in the United States," *Rochester North Star*, March 30, 1849.

58. Student petition to the faculty, December 10, 1850, Countway Library, Harvard Medical School.

59. Records of the Medical Faculty, Vol. 2: Minutes for December 16, 1859; drafts of letters to the Massachusetts Colonization Society and to Abraham R. Thompson, Countway Library.

60. Martin Delany, *The Condition, Elevation, Emigration and Destiny of the Colored People of the United States* (New York, 1969; originally published in 1852), pp. 42, 47–48, 190, 197–198; Delany, "Political Destiny," in Rollin, *Delany*, p. 358.

61. Delany, "Domestic Economy," *Rochester North Star*, March 23, 1849; Delany, in *Rochester North Star*, April 28, 1848; Delany, *Condition, Elevation, Emigration*, pp. 44–46, 192–195.

62. Delany, "Political Destiny," pp. 330–335, 355.

63. Delany, *Condition, Elevation, Emigration*, p. 44.

64. Delany, *Condition, Elevation, Emigration*, pp. 329–334, 183, 191, 205, 210.

65. Delany, *Condition, Elevation, Emigration*, pp. 48, 49, 67–84, 109, 203; "Platform: or Declaration of Sentiments of the Cleveland Convention," in Herbert Aptheker (ed.), *A Documentary History of the Negro People in the United States*, 2 vols. (New York, 1967), vol. 1, p. 365; Delany, *Official Report*, p. 32.

66. Delany, *Official Report*, p. 64.

67. Douglass, *Life and Times*, pp. 335–336, 365; Delany, in Victor Ullman, *Martin R. Delany: The Beginnings of Black Nationalism* (Boston, 1971), p. 312.

68. Herbert Aptheker (ed.), *A Documentary History of the Negro People in the*

United States, 2 vols. (New York, 1951), vol. 1, p. 496; James McPherson (ed.), *The Negro's Civil War: How American Negroes Felt and Acted during the War for the Union* (New York, 1965), p. 14.

69. Litwack, *Been in the Storm So Long,* p. 117.

70. Litwack, *Been in the Storm So Long,* p. 64.

71. Litwack, *Been in the Storm So Long,* p. 399; McPherson (ed.), *Negro's Civil War,* pp. 294, 298.

72. Litwack, *Been in the Storm So Long,* pp. 401–402.

73. La Wanda Cox, "The Promise of Land for the Freedmen," *Mississippi Valley Historical Review,* vol. 45 (December 1958), p. 429; James McPherson, *The Struggle for Equality: Abolitionists and the Negro in the Civil War and Reconstruction* (Princeton, N.J., 1964), p. 409; Hoffman, "From Slavery to Self-Reliance," pp. 22, 27.

74. Joel Williamson, *After Slavery: The Negro in South Carolina during Reconstruction, 1861–1877* (Chapel Hill, N.C., 1965), p. 54; McPherson, *Struggle for Equality,* p. 416; Ullman, *Delany,* p. 342.

75. Jacqueline Jones, *Labor of Love, Labor of Sorrow: Black Women, Work, and the Family from Slavery to the Present* (New York, 1985), p. 54.

76. "The Life Story of a Negro Peon," in Hamilton Holt (ed.), *The Life Stories of Undistinguished Americans as Told by Themselves* (New York, 1906), pp. 183–199; Negro folk song, in Edmund David Cronon, *Black Moses: The Story of Marcus Garvey and the Universal Improvement Association* (Madison, Wis., 1966), p. 21.

77. C. Vann Woodward, *Origins of the New South, 1877–1913* (Baton Rouge, La., 1951), p. 112.

78. Paul M. Gaston, *The New South Creed: A Study in Southern Mythmaking* (New York, 1970), p. 147; Broadus Mitchell, *The Rise of Cotton Mills in the South* (Baltimore, 1921), p. 214; Sterling D. Spero and Abram L. Harris, *The Black Worker: The Negro and the Labor Movement* (Port Washington, N.Y., 1966), p. 246; Woodward, *Origins of the New South,* p. 360; Paul B. Worthman, "Working Class Mobility in Birmingham, Alabama, 1880–1914," in Tamara K. Hareven (ed.), *Anonymous Americans: Explorations in Nineteenth-Century Social History* (Englewood Cliffs, N.J., 1971), p. 175.

79. James Creelman, in *New York World,* September 18, 1895, reprinted in Louis R. Harlan (ed.), *The Booker T. Washington Papers,* 4 vols. (Urbana, Ill., 1975), vol. 4, pp. 13, 14.

80. Booker T. Washington, "Atlanta Address," in *Up from Slavery* (New York, 1963; originally published in 1901), pp. 153–158; Creelman, in Harlan (ed.), *Booker T. Washington Papers,* vol. 4, p. 3.

81. August Meier, *Negro Thought in America, 1880–1915* (Ann Arbor, Mich., 1966), p. 107.

82. Washington, *Up from Slavery,* pp. 27, 83, 146; Booker T. Washington, "The Educational Outlook in the South," *Journal of the Proceedings and Addresses of*

the National Educational Association, Session of the Year 1884, at Madison, Wis. (Boston, 1885), pp. 125–130.

83. Litwack, *Been in the Storm So Long*, p. 399; Rayford Logan, *The Negro in American Life and Thought: The Nadir, 1877–1901* (New York, 1954).

Chapter 6. Emigrants from Erin

1. Leon Litwack, *North of Slavery: The Negro in the Free States, 1790–1860* (Chicago, 1965), p. 163; David R. Roediger, *The Wages of Whiteness: Race and the Making of the American Working Class* (London, 1991), p. 134.

2. Kerby A. Miller, *Emigrants and Exiles: Ireland and the Irish Exodus to North America* (New York, 1985), p. 105; Kerby Miller, Bruce Boling, and David Doyle, "Emigrants and Exiles: Irish Cultures and Irish Emigration to North America, 1790–1922," *Irish Historical Studies*, vol. 40 (1980), p. 112; Oliver MacDonagh, "The Irish Famine Emigration to the United States," *Perspectives in American History*, vol. 10 (1976), p. 358; Robert L. Wright (ed.), *Irish Emigrant Ballads and Songs* (Bowling Green, Ohio, 1975), pp. 35, 37. Miller's book is filled with archivally based information. Miller has done for the Irish immigrants what Irving Howe has done for the Jewish immigrants in *World of Our Fathers* (New York, 1976). The theme of "exile" is emphasized in Miller's study.

3. Miller *et al.*, "Emigrants and Exiles," pp. 100, 99; Wright (ed.), *Irish Emigrant Ballads*, pp. 592, 165, 129.

4. James N. Healy, *Irish Ballads and Songs of the Sea* (Cork, 1967), p. 96; Lawrence J. McCaffrey, *The Irish Diaspora in America* (Washington, D.C., 1984), pp. 17–18; Wright (ed.), *Irish Emigrant Ballads*, p. 70.

5. Arnold Schrier, *Ireland and the American Emigration, 1850–1900* (New York, 1970), p. 45.

6. Owen Dudley Edwards, "The American Image of Ireland: A Study of Its Early Phases," *Perspectives in American History*, vol. 4 (1970), p. 236; Miller, *Emigrants and Exiles*, p. 32; Wright (ed.), *Irish Emigrant Ballads*, pp. 96, 50.

7. MacDonagh, "Irish Famine Emigration," p. 366; Miller, *Emigrants and Exiles*, p. 241.

8. Miller, *Emigrants and Exiles*, pp. 139, 197, 202; Schrier, *Ireland and American Emigration*, p. 95.

9. Miller, *Emigrants and Exiles*, pp. 34, 53; Hamilton Holt, "Life Story of an Irish Cook," in Holt (ed.), *Life Stories of Undistinguished Americans as Told by Themselves* (New York, 1906), p. 144.

10. Miller, *Emigrants and Exiles*, p. 281.

11. Wright (ed.), *Irish Emigrant Ballads*, p. 46.

12. Miller, *Emigrants and Exiles*, pp. 285–287; Michael Kraus, *Immigration, The American Mosaic* (New York, 1966), p. 130; Schrier, *Ireland and American Emigration*, p. 42; Wright (ed.), *Irish Emigrant Ballads*, p. 3.

13. Oscar Handlin, *Boston's Immigrants: A Study in Acculturation* (New York,

1968), p. 51; MacDonagh, "Irish Famine Emigration," pp. 431, 407; Miller, *Emigrants and Exiles*, p. 298.

14. Dale B. Light, Jr., "The Role of Irish-American Organizations in Assimilation and Community Formation," in P. J. Drudy (ed.), *The Irish in America: Emigration, Assimilation and Impact* (New York, 1985), p. 117.

15. McCaffrey, *Irish Diaspora*, pp. 71, 72; Wright (ed.), *Irish Emigrant Ballads*, p. 126.

16. MacDonagh, "Irish Famine Emigration," pp. 403, 410–411.

17. Hasia R. Diner, *Erin's Daughters in America: Irish Immigrant Women in the Nineteenth Century* (Baltimore, 1983); Miller, *Emigrants and Exiles*, p. 360. Diner's study is an excellent example of the ways women's history can illuminate general understanding of immigration.

18. Stephan Thernstrom, *Poverty and Progress: Social Mobility in a Nineteenth Century City* (Cambridge, Mass., 1964), p. 27; Michael B. Buckley, *Diary of a Tour in America* (Dublin, 1886), p. 142; Miller, *Emigrants and Exiles*, p. 318; McCaffrey, *Irish Diaspora*, p. 71.

19. Carl Wittke, *The Irish in America* (Baton Rouge, La., 1956), pp. 32–33; Buckley, *Tour in America*, p. 164; Wright (ed.), *Irish Emigrant Ballads*, p. 533.

20. Wright (ed.), *Irish Emigrant Ballads*, p. 539; Wittke, *Irish in America*, p. 3.

21. Wittke, *Irish in America*, p. 37; Diner, *Erin's Daughters*, p. 60; Elizabeth Gurley Flynn, *I Speak My Own Piece* (New York, 1955), p. 20; Miller, *Emigrants and Exiles*, p. 267.

22. Miller, *Emigrants and Exiles*, p. 318; Anne Halley, "Afterword," in Mary Doyle Curran, *The Parish and the Hill* (New York, 1986), pp. 230–231; Kerby Miller, "Assimilation and Alienation: Irish Emigrants' Responses to Industrial America, 1871–1921," in Drudy (ed.), *Irish in America*, p. 105.

23. Frederick Rudolph, "Chinamen in Yankeedom: Anti-Unionism in Massachusetts in 1870," *American Historical Review*, vol. 53, no. 1 (October 1947), p. 10.

24. *The Nation*, vol. 10 (June 23, 1870), p. 397.

25. William Shanks, "Chinese Skilled Labor," *Scribner's Monthly*, vol. 2 (September 1871), pp. 495–496.

26. *The Nation*, vol. 10 (June 30, 1870), p. 412; Rudolph, "Chinamen in Yankeedom," p. 23.

27. Frank Norton, "Our Labor System and the Chinese," *Scribner's Monthly*, vol. 2 (May 1871), p. 70.

28. Roediger, *Wages of Whiteness*, pp. 133, 146; Michael B. Katz, *The Irony of School Reform: Educational Innovation in Mid-Nineteenth Century Massachusetts* (Boston, 1972), pp. 124, 120–121, 123, 41–43, 172, 88; Herbert G. Gutman, *Work, Culture & Society in Industrializing America* (New York, 1977), pp. 1–27, 71; Stanley K. Schultz, *The Culture Factory: Boston Public Schools, 1789–1860* (New York, 1973), p. 243; Herbert G. Gutman, *The Black Family in Slavery and Freedom, 1750–1925* (New York, 1976), p. 299; Litwack, *North of Slavery*, p. 163.

29. Halley, "Afterword," p. 27; Thernstrom, *Poverty and Progress*, p. 27; Schultz, *Culture Factory*, p. 289; Katz, *Irony of School Reform*, pp. 182–183, 43.

30. Roediger, *Wages of Whiteness*, pp. 136–137.

31. Frederick Law Olmsted, *The Slave States before the Civil War* (New York, 1859), p. 76; Litwack, *North of Slavery*, p. 166.

32. Roediger, *Wages of Whiteness*, p. 137.

33. Schultz, *Culture Factory*, p. 193; Eugene Genovese, *Roll, Jordan, Roll: The World the Slaves Made* (New York, 1974), p. 24; Litwack, *North of Slavery*, p. 163; Handlin, *Boston's Immigrants*, p. 133.

34. Wright (ed.), *Irish Emigrant Ballads*, p. 44.

35. Schultz, *Culture Factory*, p. 193; Wittke, *Irish in America*, p. 143; Albon P. Man, Jr., "Labor Competition and the New York Draft Riots of 1863," *Journal of Negro History*, vol. 36, no. 4 (October 1951), pp. 386, 377, 378.

36. Adrian Cook, *Armies of the Streets: The New York City Draft Riots of 1863* (Lexington, Ky., 1974), p. 205; Stephen Steinberg, *The Ethnic Myth: Race, Ethnicity, and Class in America* (New York, 1981), p. 177.

37. Cook, *Armies of the Streets*, pp. 80, 123; Iver Bernstein, *The New York City Draft Riots: Their Significance for American Society and Politics in the Age of the Civil War* (New York, 1990), pp. 17–42.

38. Cook, *Armies of the Streets*, p. 97; Man, "Labor Competition," p. 401; Bernstein, *New York City Draft Riots*, p. 27; Wittke, *Irish in America*, p. 146.

39. Litwack, *North of Slavery*, p. 163; Gutman, *Black Family*, p. 301; "Folk-Lore Scrap-Book," *Journal of American Folklore*, vol. 12, no. 46 (July–September 1899), p. 227.

40. Litwack, *North of Slavery*, p. 163; Roediger, *Wages of Whiteness*, p. 137.

41. Gilbert Osofsky, *Harlem: The Making of a Ghetto, Negro New York, 1890–1930* (New York, 1966), p. 45.

42. Litwack, *North of Slavery*, pp. 158–159; Steinberg, *Ethnic Myth*, p. 162; Diner, *Erin's Daughters*, pp. 31, 30.

43. Janet A. Nolan, *Ourselves Alone: Women's Emigration from Ireland, 1885–1920* (Lexington, Ky., 1989), pp. 23, 22; Diner, *Erin's Daughters*, p. 10; Lynn H. Lees and John Model, "The Irish Countryman Urbanized: A Comparative Perspective on the Famine Migration," *Journal of Urban History*, vol. 3, no. 4 (August 1977), p. 392; Miller, *Emigrants and Exiles*, p. 408.

44. Miller, *Emigrants and Exiles*, p. 407.

45. Miller, *Emigrants and Exiles*, p. 408; Schrier, *Ireland and American Emigration*, p. 26; Diner, *Erin's Daughters*, p. 90; Wright (ed.), *Irish Emigrant Ballads*, p. 100.

46. Diner, *Erin's Daughters*, p. 92.

47. Steinberg, *Ethnic Myth*, pp. 154, 155; Lucy Maynard Salmon, *Domestic Service* (New York, 1897), p. 79; Diner, *Erin's Daughters*, p. 83.

48. Diner, *Erin's Daughters*, p. 90; Schrier, *Ireland and American Emigration*, p. 29.

49. Holt, "Life Story of an Irish Cook," p. 146; Diner, *Erin's Daughters*, p. 94.

50. Lucy Maynard Salmon, *Domestic Service* (New York, 1897), p. 151; Helen

Campbell, *Prisoners of Poverty: Women Wage-Workers, Their Trades and Their Lives* (Boston, 1900), p. 226.

51. Campbell, *Prisoners of Poverty*, pp. 227, 229.

52. Campbell, *Prisoners of Poverty*, pp. 226, 15–16.

53. Steinberg, *Ethnic Myth*, p. 157; Campbell, *Prisoners of Poverty*, p. 224.

54. Diner, *Erin's Daughters*, p. 75; Flynn, *I Speak My Own Piece*, p. 24.

55. Miller, *Emigrants and Exiles*, p. 505; Philip S. Foner (ed.), *The Factory Girls* (Urbana, Ill., 1977), pp. 6–7; Diner, *Erin's Daughters*, p. 75.

56. Schrier, *Ireland and American Emigration*, p. 28; Diner, *Erin's Daughters*, pp. 77, 78.

57. Schrier, *Ireland and American Emigration*, p. 24; Carol Groneman, "Working-Class Immigrant Women in Mid-Nineteenth-Century New York: The Irish Woman's Experience," *Journal of Urban History*, vol. 4, no. 3 (May 1978), p. 269.

58. Schrier, *Ireland and American Emigration*, p. 38; Miller, "Assimilation and Alienation," p. 97.

59. David M. Katzman, *Seven Days A Week: Women and Domestic Service in Industrializing America* (New York, 1978), pp. 70, 231.

60. Thernstrom, *Poverty and Progress*, pp. 132–133; Miller, *Emigrants and Exiles*, pp. 496, 508.

61. Marcia Graham Synnott, *The Half-Opened Door: Discrimination and Admissions at Harvard, Yale, and Princeton, 1900–1970* (Westport, Conn., 1979), pp. 40–44, 245.

62. Wittke, *Irish in America*, p. 26.

63. Steven P. Erie, *Rainbow's End: Irish-Americans and the Dilemmas of Urban Machine Politics, 1840–1985* (Berkeley, Calif., 1988), p. 28; David M. Emmons, *The Butte Irish: Class and Ethnicity in an American Mining Town, 1875–1925* (Urbana, Ill., 1989), p. 6; Schrier, *Ireland and American Emigration*, p. 130; Flynn, *I Speak My Own Piece*, p. 19.

64. Erie, *Rainbow's End*, pp. 248, 2, 5, 8, 87; Nathan Glazer and Daniel P. Moynihan, *Beyond the Melting Pot* (Cambridge, Mass., 1963), pp. 218, 223–230.

65. Miller, *Emigrants and Exiles*, p. 500.

66. David Montgomery, "The Irish and the American Labor Movement," in David N. Doyle and Owen D. Edwards (eds.), *America and Ireland, 1776–1976* (Westport, Conn., 1980), pp. 211–212.

67. Roediger, *Wages of Whiteness*, pp. 133–166.

68. Douglas V. Shaw, *The Making of an Immigrant City: Ethnic and Cultural Conflict in Jersey City, New Jersey, 1850–1877* (New York, 1976), p. 2.

69. Shaw, *Making of an Immigrant City*, p. 2; Schultz, *Culture Factory*, p. 230; Kathleen Donovan, "Good Old Pat: An Irish-American Stereotype in Decline," *Eire-Ireland: A Journal of Irish Studies*, vol. 15, no. 2 (fall 1980), p. 9.

70. Miller, *Emigrants and Exiles*, pp. 508, 511, 512.

71. Flynn, *I Speak My Own Piece*, p. 13.

72. Wright (ed.), *Irish Emigrant Ballads*, pp. 495, 300, 144; McCaffrey, *Irish Diaspora*, p. 65.

Chapter 7. Foreigners in Their Native Land

1. Thomas Jefferson to John Adams, June 11, 1812, in Lester J. Cappon (ed.), *The Adams-Jefferson Letters*, 2 vols. (Chapel Hill, N.C., 1959), vol. 2, pp. 307–308; Jefferson to James Monroe, November 24, 1801, in Paul L. Ford (ed.), *The Works of Thomas Jefferson*, 20 vols. (New York, 1892–1899), vol. 9, p. 317. For the title of this chapter, see Juan Nepomuceno Seguín, who described himself as "*a foreigner in my native land*," in David J. Weber (ed.), *Foreigners in Their Native Land: Historical Roots of the Mexican Americans* (Albuquerque, N. Mex. 1973), p. 178.

2. Ben Kelsey, in exhibit on the Bear Flag Republic, Sonoma Mission Museum, Sonoma, California.

3. Leonard Pitt, *The Decline of the Californios: A Social History of the Spanish-Speaking Californians, 1846–1890* (Berkeley, Calif.,1970), p. 29.

4. Pitt, *Decline of the Californios*, p. 27.

5. Vallejo to Thomas Larkin, September 15, 1846, in Myrtle McKittrick, *Vallejo: Son of California* (Portland, Oreg., 1944), pp. 275–276.

6. Walton Bean, *California: An Interpretive History* (New York, 1978), pp. 32, 36, 40, 38.

7. Douglas Monroy, *Thrown among Strangers: The Making of Mexican Culture in Frontier California* (Berkeley, Calif., 1990), p. 113. This fine study presents the Indians and Mexicans humanistically.

8. Monroy, *Thrown among Strangers*, pp. 101–102, 22, 151, 153; exhibit on the Californios, Sonoma Mission Museum, Sonoma, California; Richard Henry Dana, *Two Years before the Mast* (New York, 1963; originally published in 1840), pp. 39, 60–61.

9. Monroy, *Thrown among Strangers*, p. 153; exhibit on the Californios, Sonoma Mission Museum, Sonoma, California; Dana, *Two Years before the Mast*, pp. 187–188.

10. Guadalupe Vallejo, in Weber (ed.), *Foreigners in Their Native Land*, pp. 46–47.

11. John Bidwell, "Life in California before the Gold Discovery," *Century Magazine*, vol. 41, no. 2 (December 1890), p. 170; exhibit on the Californios, Sonoma Mission Museum, Sonoma, California.

12. Bean, *California*, pp. 65–66; Pitt, *Decline of the Californios*, p. 19; Monroy, *Thrown among Strangers*, p. 161.

13. Bean, *California*, p. 65; Dana, *Two Years before the Mast*, pp. 136–137, 60–61, 188.

14. Monroy, *Thrown among Strangers*, pp. 163, 164.

15. Monroy, *Thrown among Strangers*, p. 163; Pitt, *Decline of the Californios*, p. 29.

16. James K. Polk, quoted in Norman Graebner, *Empire on the Pacific: A Study in American Continental Expansion* (New York, 1955), pp. 48–50.

17. John Bidwell, "Fremont in the Conquest of California," *Century Magazine*, reprinted by the California Department of Parks and Recreation (Sacramento, 1987), p. 522; Pitt, *Decline of the Californios*, p. 29.

18. Weber (ed.), *Foreigners in Their Native Land*, pp. 30, 102, 104–105.

19. Weber (ed.), *Foreigners in Their Native Land*, p. 84.

20. Weber (ed.), *Foreigners in Their Native Land*, p. 89; Arnold De Leon, *They Called Them Greasers: Anglo Attitudes toward Mexicans in Texas, 1821–1900* (Austin, Tex., 1983), pp. 3, 12; Rodolfo Acuña, *Occupied America: A History of Chicanos* (New York, 1981), pp. 6–7, 8.

21. Acuña, *Occupied America*, p. 9.

22. Weber (ed.), *Foreigners in Their Native Land*, p. 92; Acuña, *Occupied America*, p. 10.

23. Reginald Horsman, *Race and Manifest Destiny: The Origins of American Racial Anglo-Saxonism* (Cambridge, Mass., 1981), pp. 213–214.

24. Weber (ed.), *Foreigners in Their Native Land*, p. 95.

25. Acuña, *Occupied America*, p. 15; Carey McWilliams, *North from Mexico: The Spanish-Speaking People of the United States* (New York, 1968), pp. 102–103. McWilliams's study is a classic.

26. Albert K. Weinberg, *Manifest Destiny: A Study of Nationalist Expansionism in American History* (Chicago, 1963), p. 112.

27. Weinberg, *Manifest Destiny*, p. 111; David Montejano, *Anglos and Mexicans in the Making of Texas, 1836–1986* (Austin, Tex., 1987), pp. 14, 18. Montejano's work is an excellent and nuanced study based on original research.

28. William M'Carty (comp.), *National Songs, Ballads, and Other Patriotic Poetry* (Philadelphia, 1846), p. 45; see also Horsman, *Race and Manifest Destiny*, p. 233.

29. "The Conquest of California," *Southern Quarterly Review*, vol. 15 (July 1849), pp. 411–415.

30. Weber (ed.), *Foreigners in Their Native Land*, p. 199; Acuña, *Occupied America*, p. 19. The Treaty of Guadalupe Hidalgo described the newly acquired territory as places "occupied" by U.S. forces. See the terms of the treaty in Wayne Moquin (ed.), *A Documentary History of the Mexican Americans* (New York, 1972), pp. 182–187.

31. Acuña, *Occupied America*, p. 20; Weber (ed.), *Foreigners in Their Native Land*, p. 176.

32. Robert F. Heizer and Alan F. Almquist, *The Other Californians: Prejudice and Discrimination under Spain, Mexico, and the United States to 1920* (Berkeley, Calif., 1971), p. 151.

33. Heizer and Almquist, *Other Californians*, p. 143; Weber (ed.), *Foreigners in Their Native Land*, pp. 171–173.

34. Albert Camarillo, *Chicanos in a Changing Society: From Mexican Pueblos to American Barrios in Santa Barbara and Southern California, 1848–1930*

(Cambridge, Mass., 1979), pp. 23, 46, 41, 187. This is an important community study that provides insights into larger patterns of Chicano experiences.

35. Montejano, *Anglos and Mexicans*, pp. 39, 143; Weber (ed.), *Foreigners in Their Native Land*, pp. 146, 147.

36. Acuña, *Occupied America*, p. 19.

37. Mario Barrera, *Race and Class in the Southwest: A Theory of Racial Inequality* (Notre Dame, Ind., 1979), pp. 26–27. This is a very useful integration of theories of race and class and the history of Chicanos.

38. Monroy, *Thrown among Strangers*, p. 114; Bean, *California*, pp. 132–133.

39. Barrera, *Race and Class*, pp. 20, 19; Bean, *California*, p. 135; Heizer and Almquist, *Other Californians*, p. 150.

40. Pitt, *Decline of the Californios*, p. 118; Weber (ed.), *Foreigners in Their Native Land*, pp. 197–199.

41. Pitt, *Decline of the Californios*, pp. 96–97; McKittrick, *Vallejo*, pp. 316, 318, 322, 324, 347; M. G. Vallejo, "What the Gold Rush Brought to California," in Valeska Bari (ed.), *The Course of Empire: First Hand Accounts of California in the Days of the Gold Rush of '49* (New York, 1931), p. 53.

42. Barrera, *Race and Class*, p. 31; Acuña, *Occupied America*, pp. 29–30.

43. Montejano, *Anglos and Mexicans*, p. 68.

44. Montejano, *Anglos and Mexicans*, pp. 61, 62.

45. McWilliams, *North from Mexico*, p. 77; Camarillo, *Chicanos in a Changing Society*, pp. 45–46, 34, 35–36.

46. Weber (ed.), *Foreigners in Their Native Land*, p. 199; Camarillo, *Chicanos in a Changing Society*, p. 36.

47. Montejano, *Anglos and Mexicans*, pp. 113, 158; Camarillo, *Chicanos in a Changing Society*, p. 191.

48. McWilliams, *North from Mexico*, p. 154; Arnold De Leon, *The Tejano Community, 1836–1900* (Albuquerque, N. Mex., 1982), pp. 55–56.

49. Montejano, *Anglos and Mexicans*, p. 114.

50. De Leon, *Greasers*, p. 62; McWilliams, *North from Mexico*, pp. 176, 158.

51. Mario T. García, *Desert Immigrants: The Mexicans of El Paso, 1880–1920* (New Haven, Conn., 1981), p. 37; Camarillo, *Chicanos in a Changing Society*, p. 97. García's work is an excellent study based on primary sources, showing the ways the immigrants continued to think of themselves as Mexicans.

52. McWilliams, *North from Mexico*, p. 167; "Los Enganchados — the Hooked Ones," in Manuel Gamio, *Mexican Immigration to the United States* (Chicago, 1930), pp. 84–85.

53. Moquin (ed.), *A Documentary History of the Mexican Americans*, p. 212; McWilliams, *North from Mexico*, p. 144.

54. Barrera, *Race and Class*, pp. 45, 46; Camarillo, *Chicanos in a Changing Society*, p. 139; Montejano, *Anglos and Mexicans*, p. 73.

55. García, *Desert Immigrants*, p. 90; Barrera, *Race and Class*, p. 41.

56. Andres E. Jimenez Montoya, "Political Domination in the Labor Market:

Racial Division in the Arizona Copper Industry," Working Paper 103, Institute for the Study of Social Change, University of California, Berkeley (1977), p. 20.

57. De Leon, *Tejano Community*, p. 202.

58. Tomas Almaguer, "Racial Domination and Class Conflict in Capitalist Agriculture: The Oxnard Sugar Beet Workers' Strike of 1903," *Labor History*, vol. 25, no. 3 (summer 1984), p. 334.

59. Almaguer, "Racial Domination," pp. 346, 347.

60. McWilliams, *North from Mexico*, p. 197; Weber (ed.), *Foreigners in Their Native Land*, p. 219.

61. Acuña, *Occupied America*, p. 88.

62. De Leon, *Tejano Community*, pp. 194–196; García, *Desert Immigrants*, p. 224.

63. Weber (ed.), *Foreigners in Their Native Land*, pp. 248–250.

Chapter 8. Searching for Gold Mountain

1. William Shakespeare, *The Tempest* (New York, 1904), Act II, sc. ii, 60–63; Thomas Hart Benton, *Selections of Editorial Articles from the St. Louis Enquirer, on the Subject of Oregon and Texas, as Originally Published in That Paper in the Years 1818–1819* (St. Louis, 1844), pp. 5, 23; Thomas Hart Benton, Speech on the Oregon Question, May 28, 1846, U.S. Congress, Senate, *Congressional Globe*, 29th Cong., 1st sess. (Washington, D.C., 1846), pp. 915–917; Thomas Hart Benton, Speech on railroad bill, U.S. Congress, Senate, *Congressional Globe*, 30th Cong., 2nd sess. (Washington, D.C., 1849), pp. 473–474.

2. Aaron H. Palmer, *Memoir, geographical, political, and commercial, on the present state, productive resources, and capabilities for commerce, of Siberia, Manchuria, and the Asiatic Islands of the Northern Pacific Ocean; and on the importance of opening commercial intercourse with those countries, March 8, 1848*. U.S. Congress, Senate, 30th Cong., 1st sess., Senate misc. no. 80, pp. 1, 52, 60, 61.

3. June Mei, "Socioeconomic Origins of Emigration: Guandong to California, 1850–1882," in Lucie Cheng and Edna Bonacich (eds.), *Labor Immigration under Capitalism: Asian Workers in the United States before World War II* (Berkeley, Calif., 1984), p. 232.

4. Kil Young Zo, *Chinese Emigration into the United States, 1850–1880* (New York, 1971), p. 62; "The Celestials at Home and Abroad," *Littel's Living Age*, August 14, 1852, p. 294; Clarence E. Glick, *Sojourners and Settlers: Chinese Migrants in Hawaii* (Honolulu, 1980).

5. Circular, translation, in Diane Mei Lin Mark and Ginger Chih, *A Place Called Chinese America* (Dubuque, Iowa, 1982), p. 5; Lee Chew, interview, "Life Story of a Chinaman," in Hamilton Holt (ed.), *The Life Stories of Undistinguished Americans as Told by Themselves* (New York, 1906), pp. 287–288.

6. Mr. Quan, interview, in Him Mark Lai, Genny Lim, and Judy Yung, *Island: Poetry and History of Chinese Immigrants on Angel Island, 1910–1940* (San

Francisco, 1980), p. 48; popular saying, in Mark and Chih, *A Place Called Chinese America,* p. 6; Chinese sojourner to Henryk Sienkiewicz, in Sienkiewicz, "The Chinese in California," translated by Charles Morley, reprinted in *California Historical Quarterly,* vol. 34 (December 1955), p. 309; folk song, translation, in Marlon Hom, *Songs of Gold Mountain: Cantonese Rhymes from San Francisco Chinatown* (Berkeley, Calif., 1987), p. 39.

7. "Letter of the Chinamen to His Excellency, Gov. Bigler," San Francisco, April 28, 1852, reprinted in *Littel's Living Age,* July 3, 1852, pp. 32–34; message from Dr. Bowring to Lord Malmesbury, January 5, 1853, in Zo, *Chinese Emigration,* p. 86; William Speer, *The Oldest and the Newest Empire: China and the United States* (Hartford, 1870), pp. 475–478.

8. Folk song, in Hom, *Songs of Gold Mountain,* p. 146; Hakka folk song, in Tin-Yuke Char, *The Sandalwood Mountains: Readings and Stories of the Early Chinese in Hawaii* (Honolulu, 1957), p. 67.

9. *Daily Alta California,* May 12, 1852; Lai Chun-Chuen, *Remarks of the Chinese Merchants of San Francisco, upon Governor Bigler's Message* (San Francisco, 1855), p. 4.

10. Charles J. McClain, Jr., "The Chinese Struggle for Civil Rights in Nineteenth Century America: The First Phase, 1850–1870," *California Law Review,* vol. 72 (1984), pp. 544, 555.

11. Sucheng Chan, "Chinese Livelihood in Rural California: The Impact of Economic Change, 1860–1880," *Pacific Historical Review,* vol. 53, no. 3 (1984), pp. 281–282; Gunther Barth, *Bitter Strength: A History of the Chinese in the United States, 1850–1870* (Cambridge, Mass., 1964), pp. 114, 115; Otis Gibson, *The Chinese in America* (Cincinnati, 1877), p. 234.

12. Telegrams reprinted in Albert Dressler (ed.), *California Chinese Chatter* (San Francisco, 1927), pp. 2, 3, 9.

13. E. L. Sabin, *Building the Pacific Railway* (Philadelphia, 1919), p. 111; Corinne K. Hoexter, *From Canton to California: The Epic of Chinese Immigration* (New York, 1976), p. 73; Jack Chen, *The Chinese in America* (New York, 1981), p. 67.

14. Thomas Chinn, H. M. Lai, and Philip Choy, *A History of the Chinese in California* (San Francisco, 1969), p. 45; Albert P. Richardson, *Beyond the Mississippi* (Hartford, 1867), p. 462; Alexander Saxton, *The Indispensable Enemy: Labor and the Anti-Chinese Movement in California* (Berkeley, Calif., 1971), p. 65.

15. Thomas M. Chinn, ed., *A History of the Chinese in California* (San Francisco, 1969), p. 46; *San Francisco Alta,* July 1 and 3, 1867; Sabin, *Building the Pacific Railway,* p. 111.

16. Paul M. Ong, "Chinese Labor in Early San Francisco: Racial Segmentation and Industrial Expansion," *Amerasia,* vol. 8, no. 1 (1981), pp. 70–75.

17. Ong, "Chinese Labor in Early San Francisco," pp. 75–77.

18. Chan, "Chinese Livelihood in Rural California," pp. 288–289, 296, 300–307; A. W. Loomis, "How Our Chinamen Are Employed," *Overland Monthly,* March 1869, p. 234.

19. Carey McWilliams, *Factories in the Field: The Story of Migratory Farm Labor in California* (Santa Barbara, Calif., 1971), pp. 67, 71.

20. Loomis, "How Our Chinamen Are Employed," p. 237; Sandy Lydon, *Chinese Gold: The Chinese in the Monterey Bay Region* (Capitola, Calif., 1985), p. 286.

21. Sucheng Chan, *This Bitter-sweet Soil: The Chinese in California Agriculture, 1860–1910* (Berkeley, Calif., 1986), p. 176. This is a solid and definitive study of the subject.

22. Loomis, "How Our Chinamen Are Employed," pp. 233–234; calculations in Chan, *Bitter-sweet Soil*, pp. 305, 306, 307, 316, 317.

23. Chan, *Bitter-sweet Soil*, pp. 332–333.

24. McWilliams, *Factories in the Field*, p. 74.

25. Paul Ong, "Chinese Laundries as an Urban Occupation in Nineteenth Century California," in Douglas W. Lee (ed.), *The Annals of the Chinese Historical Society of the Pacific Northwest* (Seattle, 1983), p. 72.

26. Lee Chew, "Life Story of a Chinaman," pp. 289–290; Wong Chin Foo, "The Chinese in New York," *The Cosmopolitan*, vol. 5, no. 4 (June 1888), p. 298.

27. Paul Siu, *The Chinese Laundryman: A Study of Social Isolation* (New York, 1987), pp. 52, 119–123.

28. Lee Chew, "Life Story of a Chinaman," p. 296; Ong, "Chinese Laundries as an Urban Occupation," pp. 69, 70, 74; Victor and Brett de Bary Nee, *Longtime Californ': A Documentary Study of an American Chinatown* (New York, 1972), p. 22; Ng Poon Chew, "The Chinaman in America," *Chautauquan*, vol. 9. no. 4 (January 1889), p. 802.

29. Dan Caldwell, "The Negroization of the Chinese Stereotype in California," *Southern California Quarterly*, vol. 53 (June 1971), pp. 123–131; planter, quoted in Stephen Steinberg, *The Ethnic Myth: Race, Ethnicity, and Class in America* (New York, 1981), p. 184; *Vicksburg Times*, June 30, 1869, in James W. Loewen, *The Mississippi Chinese: Between Black and White* (Cambridge, Mass., 1971), p. 22; planters' convention report, reprinted in John R. Commons *et al.* (eds.), *A Documentary History of American Industrial Society* (Cleveland, 1910/11), vol. 9, p. 81.

30. John Todd, *The Sunset Land* (Boston, 1870), pp. 284–285; Lucy M. Cohen, *Chinese in the Post–Civil War South: A People without a History* (Baton Rouge, La., 1984), p. 109; Loewen, *The Mississippi Chinese*, p. 23; Barth, *Bitter Strength*, p. 189.

31. Loewen, *The Mississippi Chinese*, p. 24; Ralph Keeler, "The 'Heathen Chinee' in the South," *Every Saturday*, vol. 3, no. 83 (July 29, 1871), p. 117; Cohen, *Chinese in the Post–Civil War South*, pp. 123–124.

32. Cohen, *Chinese in the Post–Civil War South*, p. 136.

33. Samuel Bowles, *Our New West* (Hartford, 1869), p. 414.

34. *Report of the Joint Special Committee to Investigate Chinese Immigration*, Senate Report No. 689, 44th Cong., 2nd sess., 1876/7, pp. 679, 680.

35. Henry Robinson, "Our Manufacturing Era," *Overland Monthly*, vol. 2

(March 1869), p. 282; *Report of the Committee to Investigate Chinese Immigration,* p. 667.

36. *San Francisco Alta,* June 4, 1853; *Hutching's California Magazine,* vol. 1 (March 1857), p. 387; *New York Times,* December 26, 1873; *The Wasp Magazine,* vol. 30 (January–June 1893), pp. 10–11; *Report of the Committee to Investigate Chinese Immigration,* p. vi; Caldwell, "The Negroization of the Chinese Stereotype," pp. 123–131.

37. Megumi Dick Osumi, "Asians and California's Anti-Miscegenation Laws," in Nobuya Tsuchida (ed.), *Asian and Pacific American Experiences: Women's Perspectives* (Minneapolis, 1982), pp. 2, 6.

38. *California Marin Journal,* April 13, 1876; Seymour, in *New York Times,* August 6, 1870; *The Nation,* vol. 9 (July 15, 1869), p. 445; *Congressional Record,* 47th Cong., 1st sess., p. 3267.

39. California Supreme Court, *The People v. Hall,* October 1, 1854, in Robert F. Heizer and Alan F. Almquist, *The Other Californians: Prejudice and Discrimination under Spain, Mexico, and the United States to 1920* (Berkeley, Calif., 1971), p. 229.

40. Stuart C. Miller, *The Unwelcome Immigrant: The American Image of the Chinese, 1752–1882* (Berkeley, Calif., 1969), p. 190.

41. John A. Garraty, *Unemployment in History: Economic Thought and Public Policy* (New York, 1978), pp. 103–109.

42. *The Nation* (March 16, 1882), p. 222; *Congressional Record,* 47th Cong., 1st sess., pp. 2973–2974, 2033, 3310, 3265, 3268; appendix, pp. 48, 89, 21.

43. Chinese Exclusion Act of 1888, reprinted in Cheng-Tsu Wu, *"Chink!": A Documentary History of Anti-Chinese Prejudice in America* (New York, 1972), pp. 82–83.

44. Hoexter, *From Canton to California,* p. 44; McClain, "Chinese Struggle for Civil Rights," pp. 555–557.

45. McClain, "Chinese Struggle for Civil Rights," pp. 561–563.

46. Fung Tang, "Address to the Committee by the Chinese Merchants," *Daily Alta California,* June 26, 1869; McClain, "Chinese Struggle for Civil Rights," pp. 564–567.

47. Kwang Chang Ling, *Why Should the Chinese Go? A Pertinent Inquiry from a Mandarin High in Authority* (San Francisco, 1878), p. 16; "Life History as a Social Document of Mr. J. S. Look," August 13, 1924, p. 1, Survey of Race Relations, Stanford University, Hoover Institution Archives; "Life History as Social Document of Law Yow," August 12, 1924, p. 3, Survey of Race Relations; "Life History and Social Document of Andrew Kan," August 22, 1924, p. 2, Survey of Race Relations; Huie Kin, *Reminiscences* (Peiping, 1932), p. 27.

48. Zo, *Chinese Emigration,* p. 181; Lee Chew, "Life Story of a Chinaman," pp. 298–299.

49. Lai Chun-Chuen, *Remarks of the Chinese Merchants,* pp. 3, 6.

50. For a study of gender and race discrimination related to Chicanas, see Mar-

garita Melville (ed.), *Twice a Minority: Mexican American Women* (St. Louis, 1980), which inspired the title of this section.

51. Judy Yung, *Chinese Women of America: A Pictorial History* (Seattle, 1986), p. 11; Lai Chun-Chuen, *Remarks of the Chinese Merchants*, p. 3.

52. Victor Nee and Herbert Y. Wong, "Asian American Socioeconomic Achievement: The Strength of the Family Bond," *Sociological Perspectives,* vol. 28, no. 3 (July 1985), pp. 288–289; Len Mau Yun, interview, July 13, 1988.

53. *The Friend,* January 1880, p. 6; *In Re Ah Moy, on Habeas Corpus,* Circuit Court, District of California, in Robert Desty (ed.), *Federal Reporter: Circuit and District Courts of the United States, August–November, 1884* (St. Paul, 1884), pp. 785–789. On the exclusion of Chinese wives, see Osumi, "Asians and California's Anti-Miscegenation Laws," p. 7; the 1882 and 1888 acts are reprinted in Cheng-Tsu Wu, *"Chink!": A Documentary History,* pp. 70–75, 80–85.

54. Jack Chew, interview, in appendix of Peter C. Y. Leung, *One Day, One Dollar: Locke, California and the Chinese Farming Experience in the Sacramento Delta* (El Cerrito, Calif., 1984), p. 68; Willard G. Jue, "Chin Gee-Hee, Chinese Pioneer Entrepreneur in Seattle and Toishan," in Douglas W. Lee (ed.), *The Annals of the Chinese Historical Society of the Pacific Northwest* (Seattle, 1983), p. 32; A. W. Loomis, "Chinese Women in California," *Overland Monthly* (April 1869), pp. 349–350.

55. Lydon, *Chinese Gold,* pp. 156–158; "Memorial of the Chinese Six Companies," 1876, reprinted in Gibson, *Chinese in America,* p. 318.

56. Lucie Cheng Hirata, "Chinese Immigrant Women in Nineteenth-Century California," in Carol Berkin and Mary Norton (eds.), *Women of America* (Boston, 1979), pp. 243–244.

57. Lilac Chen, interview, in Nee, *Longtime Californ',* p. 84; "Story of Wong Ah So," in Social Science Institute, Fiske University, "Orientals and Their Cultural Adjustment" (Nashville, 1946), pp. 31–33.

58. Hirata, "Chinese Immigrant Women," pp. 243–244.

59. Hom, *Songs of Gold Mountain,* p. 309; Lilac Chen, in Nee, *Longtime Californ',* p. 85; Yung, *Chinese Women of America,* p. 23; Hirata, "Chinese Immigrant Women," p. 234.

60. Perrin, *Coming to America,* p. 19; Sing Kum, "Letter by a Chinese Girl," reprinted in Gibson, *Chinese in America,* pp. 220–221; "Story of Wong Ah So," pp. 31–32; "Story of Exslave, and Slave Owner," in "Two Schools for Chinese" by Mrs. Park, August 1924, pp. 3–4, Survey of Race Relations, Stanford University, Hoover Institution Archives.

61. Folk song, translation, in Hom, *Songs of Gold Mountain,* p. 321.

62. Telegrams reprinted in Dressler (ed.), *California Chinese Chatter,* pp. 12–22.

63. Lee Chew, "Life Story of a Chinaman," p. 295; "Life History of Mr. Woo Gen," July 29, 1924, p. 16, Survey of Race Relations, Stanford University, Hoover Institution Archives; "Conversation with waiter, International Chop Suey," February 2, 1924, Survey of Race Relations.

64. Chinn *et al., Chinese in California,* p. 10; Huie Kin, *Reminiscences,* pp. 25, 28; A. W. Loomis, "The Old East in the New West," *Overland Monthly* (October 1868), p. 364.

65. Gibson, *Chinese in America,* p. 14.

66. A. W. Loomis, "Chinese in California: Their Sign-Board Literature," *Overland Monthly* (August 1868), pp. 152–155.

67. Based on tables in appendix of Chan, "Chinese Livelihood in Rural California," pp. 300–307.

68. "Interview with Chinese Tong Members in Chicago, January 1925," Survey of Race Relations, Stanford University, Hoover Institution Archives; interview by C. H. Burnett, August 9, 1924, p. 5, Survey of Race Relations.

69. A. W. Loomis, "Holiday in the Chinese Quarter," *Overland Monthly* (February 1869), pp. 148, 149, 151.

70. Gibson, *Chinese in America,* pp. 15–16; A. W. Loomis, "The Old East in the New West," p. 364; Lee Chew, "Life Story of a Chinaman," p. 294; "Conversation with waiter, International Chop Suey"; "Interview with Tom Lee, Cook for Dr. N. C. Peterson," circa 1924, p. 2, Survey of Race Relations, Stanford University, Hoover Institution Archives.

71. Mark and Chih, *A Place Called Chinese America,* p. 52; Robert Stewart Culin, in Stanford M. Lyman, *Chinatown and Little Tokyo* (Millwood, N.Y., 1986), p. 123; Robert Culin, "Customs of the Chinese in America," *Journal of American Folklore* (July–September 1890), pp. 191, 193; Pardee Lowe, *Father and Glorious Descendant* (Boston, 1943), p. 98; Wong Chin Foo, "Chinese in New York," p. 301; folk song, in Him Mark Lai, Joe Huang, and Don Wong, *The Chinese of America, 1785–1980* (San Francisco, 1980), p. 51.

72. Translated and reprinted in Loomis, "The Old East in the New West," p. 362.

73. Letter by unknown Chinese migrant, in the Kam Wah Chung Company, John Day, Oregon, Papers.

74. Chu-chia to Lung On, July 1899; wife to Lung On, undated; Lung On to Liang Kwang-jin, March 2, 1905; Liang Kwang-jin to Lung On, March 4, 1905; Ing Du-hsio to Ing Hay, April 9, no year, translations by Chia-Lin Chen, Kam Wah Chung Company Papers.

75. Mrs. John W. Murray to Chia-Lin Chen, October 30, 1971, reprinted in Chen, "A Gold Dream in the Blue Mountains: A Study of the Chinese Immigrants in the John Day Area, Oregon, 1870–1910," M.A. thesis, Portland State University, 1972, pp. 123–124.

76. Personal letter in Chinese collected by Paul C. P. Siu, in Siu, "The Sojourner," *American Journal of Sociology,* vol. 58 (July 1952), pp. 35–36; Ing Wen-teh to Ing Pang-chi, June 16, 1897, and Liang Zu-teh to Liang Kau-tsi, November 28, 1902, Kam Wah Chung Company Papers.

77. Hom, *Songs of Gold Mountain,* p. 294.

78. Rose Hum Lee, "Chinese Dilemma," *Phylon* (1949), p. 139; Lai, Lim, and

Yung, *Island*, p. 12; interview with old laundryman, in "Interviews with Two Chinese," circa 1924, Box 326, folder 325, Survey of Race Relations, Stanford University, Hoover Institution Archives; "Life History and Social Document of Andrew Kan," p. 11, Survey of Race Relations.

Part III: The End of the Frontier

1. Max Weber, *The Protestant Ethic and the Spirit of Capitalism* (New York, 1958), pp. 181–182. For the industrial revolution, see George R. Taylor, *The Transportation Revolution, 1800–1860* (New York, 1962), pp. 63–64, 207, 212, 228, 249; Marvin M. Fisher, *Workshops in the Wilderness: The European Response to American Industrialism, 1830–1860* (New York, 1967), pp. 5, 12; Edward Kirkland, *Industry Comes of Age: Business, Labor, and Public Policy, 1860–1897* (New York, 1961), p. 46; Robert Higgs, *The Transformation of the American Economy, 1865–1914: An Essay in Interpretation* (New York, 1971), pp. 47, 59; Peter Temin, *Iron and Steel in Nineteenth-Century America: An Economic Inquiry* (Cambridge, Mass., 1964), pp. 166–167, 274.

2. Frederick Jackson Turner, "The Significance of the Frontier in American History," in *The Early Writings of Frederick Jackson Turner* (Madison, Wis., 1938), p. 198.

3. Turner, "Significance of the Frontier," pp. 185–186.

4. Turner, "Significance of the Frontier," pp. 202, 228.

Chapter 9. The "Indian Question"

1. James Mooney, *The Ghost-Dance Religion and the Sioux Outbreak of 1890*, Fourteenth Annual Report of the Bureau of Ethnology, 1892/93, Part 2 (Washington, D.C., 1896), p. 26.

2. Dee Brown, *Bury My Heart at Wounded Knee: An Indian History of the American West* (New York, 1970), p. 436.

3. Brown, *Bury My Heart*, p. 437.

4. James H. McGregor, *The Wounded Knee Massacre from the Viewpoint of the Sioux* (Minneapolis, 1950), p. 105.

5. McGregor, *Wounded Knee Massacre*, p. 118; Brown, *Bury My Heart*, p. 42; Black Elk, *Black Elk Speaks: Being the Life Story of a Holy Man of the Oglala Sioux*, as told to John G. Neihardt (Lincoln, Nebr., 1988), pp. 261–262.

6. McGregor, *Wounded Knee Massacre*, pp. 128, 111; Mooney, *Ghost-Dance Religion*, pp. 132, 118.

7. McGregor, *Wounded Knee Massacre*, p. 128; Black Elk, *Black Elk Speaks*, p. 259.

8. Black Elk, *Black Elk Speaks*, p. 262; Mooney, *Ghost-Dance Religion*, p. 130.

9. Francis Amasa Walker, *The Indian Question* (Boston, 1874), pp. 34–35, 99.

10. James P. Munroe, *A Life of Francis Amasa Walker* (New York, 1923), pp. 131–132; Francis Amasa Walker, "The Indian Problem, review of De B. R. Keim's *Sheridan's Troopers on the Borders*," *The Nation*, vol. 10 (June 16, 1870), pp. 822–829.

11. Francis Amasa Walker, *Political Economy* (New York, 1988), p. 9.

12. Walker, *Indian Question*, pp. 113–114, 38, 91–92.

13. Francis Amasa Walker, "Our Indians and Mr. Wells," *The Nation*, vol. 15 (August 1, 1872), p. 73; Walker, *Indian Question*, pp. 10, 62–63, 64–67; Robert F. Berkhofer, Jr., *The White Man's Indian: Images of the American Indian from Columbus to the Present* (New York, 1979), p. 168.

14. Francis Amasa Walker, *Annual Report of the Commissioner of Indian Affairs to the Secretary of the Interior for the Year 1872* (Washington, D.C., 1872), pp. 11, 63, 64.

15. Walker, *Annual Report*, pp. 77–79, 94–95.

16. Munroe, *Walker*, pp. 135, 25; Walker, *Annual Report*, p. 11; Walker, *Indian Question*, pp. 79–80.

17. D. S. Otis, *The Dawes Act and the Allotment of Indian Lands* (Norman, Okla., 1973), pp. x, 57; *U.S. Statutes at Large*, vol. 24, pp. 388–391.

18. Frederick E. Hoxie, *A Final Promise: The Campaign to Assimilate the Indians, 1880–1920* (Lincoln, Nebr., 1984), pp. 76, 77. This is an important and useful study of the decades following the Dawes Act: it fills a gap.

19. Otis, *Dawes Act*, pp. 4, 5, 9, 10, 38, 55; Robert W. Mardock, *The Reformers and the American Indian* (Columbia, Mo., 1971), p. 212; Helen Hunt Jackson, *A Century of Dishonor: A Sketch of the United States Government's Dealings with Some of the Indian Tribes* (Boston, 1886), pp. 1–4.

20. *Congressional Record*, 49th Cong., 2nd sess. (1887), vol. 18, pp. 189–192, 224–226, 973–974; *Congressional Record*, 49th Cong., 1st sess. (1887), vol. 17, p. 1634.

21. Hoxie, *Final Promise*, p. 180.

22. Francis Prucha, *Americanizing the American Indians: Writings by the "Friends of the Indian": 1800–1900* (Cambridge, Mass., 1973), pp. 108–109.

23. Otis, *Dawes Act*, pp. 17, 18, 86, 87; Loring Benson Priest, *Uncle Sam's Stepchildren: The Reformation of United States Indian Policy, 1865–1887* (New York, 1972), p. 223.

24. Leonard A. Carlson, *Indians, Bureaucrats, and Land: The Dawes Act and the Decline of Indian Farming* (Westport, Conn., 1981), pp. 11–12.

25. Hoxie, *Final Promise*, pp. 160, 165.

26. Hoxie, *Final Promise*, pp. 155, 158.

27. Hoxie, *Final Promise*, pp. 163, 168.

28. James S. Olson and Raymond Wilson, *Native Americans in the Twentieth Century* (Urbana, Ill., 1986), p. 86.

29. Graham D. Taylor, *The New Deal and American Indian Tribalism: The Administration of the Indian Reorganization Act, 1934–45* (Lincoln, Nebr., 1980),

p. 6; Michael T. Smith, "The Wheeler-Howard Act of 1934: The Indian New Deal," *Journal of the West,* vol. 10, no. 3 (July 1971), p. 521; Clayton R. Koppes, "From New Deal to Termination: Liberalism and Indian Policy, 1933–1953," *Pacific Historial Review,* vol. 46, no. 4 (November 1977), p. 546.

30. John Collier, *From Every Zenith: A Memoir and Some Essays on Life and Thought* (Denver, 1963), pp. 126, 203; Taylor, *New Deal and American Indian Tribalism,* p. x; see also Lawrence C. Kelley, *The Navajo Indians and Federal Indian Policy, 1900–1935* (Tucson, Ariz., 1968), p. 150; Donald L. Parman, *The Navajos and the New Deal* (New Haven, Conn., 1976), pp. 30–31.

31. Collier, *From Every Zenith,* pp. 129–130; Kelley, *Navajo Indians,* p. 157; Smith, "Wheeler-Howard Act," p. 525.

32. Koppes, "From New Deal to Termination," p. 551; Smith, "Wheeler-Howard Act," pp. 526, 531; Kelley, *Navajo Indians,* p. 298; Collier, *From Every Zenith,* p. 176.

33. Olson and Wilson, *Native Americans,* p. 123.

34. Peter Nabokov (ed.), *Native American Testimony* (New York, 1978), p. 203; Richard White, *The Roots of Dependency: Subsistence, Environment, and Social Change among the Choctaws, Pawnees, and Navajos* (Lincoln, Nebr., 1983), pp. 212–215.

35. Peter Iverson, *The Navajo Nation* (Westport, Conn., 1981), p. 9.

36. John Collier, *The Indians of the Americas* (New York, 1947), p. 280; Taylor, *New Deal and American Indian Tribalism,* p. 32.

37. Phelps-Stokes Fund, *The Navajo Indian Problem* (New York, 1939), pp. 8–9; David F. Aberle, *The Peyote Religion among the Navaho* (Chicago, 1966), pp. 55–64; Collier, *Indians of the Americas,* p. 276; Iverson, *Navajo Nation,* pp. 27, 28.

38. White, *Roots of Dependency,* pp. 251, 258; Edward H. Spicer, "Sheepmen and Technicians: A Program of Soil Conservation on the Navajo Indian Reservation," in Edward H. Spicer (ed.), *Human Problems in Technological Change* (New York, 1952), p. 185.

39. Collier, *From Every Zenith,* p. 252.

40. Parman, *Navajos and New Deal,* p. 44.

41. Collier, *From Every Zenith,* p. 252; Taylor, *New Deal and American Indian Tribalism,* p. 130.

42. Walker Dyk (ed.), *Son of Old Man Hat: A Navajo Autobiography* (New York, 1938), pp. 78, 103.

43. Evon Z. Vogt, *Navaho Veterans: A Study of Changing Values* (Cambridge, Mass., 1951), pp. 71, 156, 79.

44. Aberle, *Peyote Religion Among the Navaho,* pp. 63–64.

45. Spicer, "Sheepmen and Technicians," p. 194.

46. White, *Roots of Dependency,* pp. 265, 313; Spicer, "Sheepmen and Technicians," p. 193; Peter Nabokov, *Native American Testimony* (New York, 1991), p. 330.

47. White, *Roots of Dependency*, pp. 272, 282; Aberle, *Peyote Religion Among the Navaho*, p. 64; Iverson, *Navajo Nation*, p. 23.

48. White, *Roots of Dependency*, pp. 229, 313.

49. Parman, *Navajos and New Deal*, p. 45; White, *Roots of Dependency*, p. 260; "Night Chant," in John Collier, *On the Gleaming Way* (Chicago, 1962), p. 45.

Chapter 10. Pacific Crossings

1. *Japan Weekly Mail*, December 20, 1884, reprinted in Nippu Jiji, *Golden Jubilee of the Japanese in Hawaii, 1885–1935* (Honolulu, 1935), n.p.; Yuji Ichioka, *The Issei: The World of the First Generation Japanese Immigrants, 1885–1924* (New York, 1988), p. 45. Ichioka's is the best book on the subject.

2. Kazuo Ito, *Issei: A History of the Japanese Immigrants in North America* (Seattle, 1973), pp. 27, 38, 29. Ito's study is a massive and wonderful compilation of stories, oral histories, and poems. It is indispensable.

3. Victor and Brett de Bary Nee, *Longtime Californ': A Documentary Study of an American Chinatown* (New York, 1972), p. 148.

4. Robert Wilson and Bill Hosokawa, *East to America: A History of the Japanese in the United States* (New York, 1980), pp. 47, 113–114.

5. Eileen Sunada Sarasohn (ed.), *The Issei: Portrait of a Pioneer, An Oral History* (Palo Alto, Calif., 1983), pp. 44, 31–32.

6. Thomas C. Smith, *Nakahara: Family Farming and Population in a Japanese Village, 1717–1830* (Stanford, Calif., 1977), pp. 134, 152, 153; Sheila Matsumoto, "Women in Factories," in Joyce Lebra *et al.* (eds.), *Women in Changing Japan* (Boulder, Colo., 1976), pp. 51–53; Sharon L. Sievers, *Flowers in Salt: The Beginnings of Feminist Consciousness in Modern Japan* (Stanford, Calif., 1983), pp. 55, 62, 66, 84; Yukiko Hanawa, "The Several Worlds of Issei Women," unpublished M.A. thesis, California State University, Long Beach, 1982, pp. 31–34; Yasuo Wakatsuki, "Japanese Emigration to the United States, 1866–1924," *Perspectives in American History*, vol. 12 (1979), pp. 401, 404; Wilson and Hosokawa, *East to America*, p. 42.

7. Hanawa, "Several Worlds," pp. 13–16; Susan McCoin Kataoka, "Issei Women: A Study in Subordinate Status," unpublished Ph.D. thesis, University of California, Los Angeles, 1977, p. 6; Akemi Kikumura, *Through Harsh Winters: The Life of a Japanese Immigrant Woman* (Novato, Calif., 1981), pp. 18, 25; Emma Gee, "Issei: The First Women," in Emma Gee (ed.), *Asian Women* (Berkeley, Calif., 1971), p. 11.

8. Tsuru Yamauchi is quoted in Ethnic Studies Oral History Project (ed.), *Uchinanchu: A History of Okinawans in Hawaii* (Honolulu, 1981), pp. 490, 491; the folk saying can be found in Tadashi Fukutake, *Japanese Rural Society* (Ithaca, N.Y., 1967), p. 47.

9. Fukutake, *Japanese Rural Society*, pp. 6, 7, 39, 40, 42; Victor Nee and Herbert Y. Wong, "Asian American Socioeconomic Achievement: The Strength of the Family Bond," *Sociological Perspectives*, vol. 28, no. 3 (July 1985), p. 292.

10. Katherine Coman, *The History of Contract Labor in the Hawaiian Islands* (New York, 1903), p. 42; Alan Moriyama, "Causes of Emigration: The Background of Japanese Emigration to Hawaii, 1885–1894," in Edna Bonacich and Lucie Cheng (eds.), *Labor Immigration under Capitalism: Asian Workers in the United States before World War II* (Berkeley, Calif., 1984), p. 273; Republic of Hawaii, Bureau of Immigration, *Report* (Honolulu, 1886), p. 256; manager of the Hutchinson Sugar Company to W. G. Irwin and Company, February 5, 1902, and January 25, 1905, Hutchinson Plantation Records; for terms of the Gentlemen's Agreement, see Frank Chuman, *The Bamboo People: The Law and Japanese-Americans* (Del Mar, Calif., 1976), pp. 35–36.

11. H. A. Millis, *The Japanese Problem in the United States* (New York, 1915), p. 86.

12. Sarasohn (ed.), *Issei, p.* 34; Yuriko Sato, "Emigration of Issei Women" (Berkeley, 1982), in the Asian American Studies Library, University of California, Berkeley; Ito, *Issei*, p. 34.

13. *Pacific Commercial Advertiser,* April 25, 1874; Theo. H. Davies and Company to C. McLennan, July 2, 1890, and January 3, 1898, Laupahoehoe Plantation Records, microfilm, University of Hawaii Library; William G. Irwin and Company to George D. Hewitt, October 12, 1894, Hutchinson Plantation Records, microfilm, University of Hawaii Library; vice-president of H. Hackfield and Company to G. N. Wilcox, May 5, 1908, Grove Farm Plantation Records, Grove Farm Plantation, Kauai.

14. G. C. Hewitt to W. G. Irwin and Company, March 16, 1896, Hutchinson Plantation Records; Robert Hall, George F. Renton, and George H. Fairfield, in Republic of Hawaii, *Report of the Labor Commission on Strikes and Arbitration* (Honolulu, 1895), pp. 23–24, 28, 36, respectively; H. Hackfield and Company to George Wilcox, September 26, 1896, Grove Farm Plantation Records.

15. *Report of the Commission of Labor,* in *Planters' Monthly,* vol. 22, no. 7 (July 1903), p. 296; Walter Giffard to manager of the Hutchinson Sugar Plantation, October 3, 1898, in Wayne K. Patterson, *The Korean Frontier in America: Immigration to Hawaii, 1896–1910* (Honolulu, 1988), pp. 70–71, 84–87; manager of the Hutchinson Sugar Plantation to W. G. Irwin and Company, April 11, 1905, Hutchinson Plantation Records.

16. Labor committee of the Hawaiian Sugar Planters' Association to the trustees, July 28, 1909, Grove Farm Plantation Records; manager of the Hawaiian Agricultural Company to C. Brewer and Company, August 7 and 27, 1913, Hawaiian Agricultural Company Records, microfilm, University of Hawaii Library.

17. Hawaiian Sugar Planters' Association, circular, "The Labor Question," May 7, 1917, Grove Farm Plantation Records; Virgilio Felipe, "Hawaii: A Pilipino Dream," unpublished M.A. thesis, University of Hawaii, 1972, p. 177.

18. Hawaiian Sugar Planters' Association, resolution of trustees, November 18, 1904, Grove Farm Plantation Records; *Planters' Monthly,* vol. 1, no. 7 (October 1882), p. 242; Bureau of Labor Statistics, *Report of the Commissioner of Labor on*

Hawaii (Washington, D.C., 1916), pp. 120–153; Machiyo Mitamura, "Life on a Hawaiian Plantation: An Interview," *Social Process in Hawaii*, vol. 6 (1940), p. 51; song, in *Hawaii Herald*, October 26, 1973.

19. "The Five O'Clock Whistle," *Kohala Midget*, April 27, 1910.

20. Ethnic Studies Oral History Project, *The 1924 Filipino Strike on Kauai* (Honolulu, 1979), vol. 2, p. 662.

21. "Plantation Work Begins, Silently, in Early Morn," *Honolulu Star Bulletin*, January 13, 1934; Minnie Caroline Grant, *Scenes in Hawaii* (Toronto, 1888), pp. 140–142.

22. Lillian Ota Takaki, daughter of Yukino Takaki, letter to the author, August 10, 1985.

23. Ethnic Studies Oral History Project, *Uchinanchu*, pp. 360, 520, 513.

24. Ethnic Studies Oral History Project, *Waialua and Haleiwa: The People Tell Their Story* (Honolulu, 1977), vol. 8, p. 149.

25. Ethnic Studies Oral History Project, *Uchinanchu*, p. 488; Andrew Lind, *An Island Community* (Chicago, 1938), pp. 240–241; song, in *Hawaii Herald*, February 2, 1973.

26. H. Brett Melendy, *Asians in America* (Boston, 1977), pp. 86–87; Mary H. Drout, *Hawaii and a Revolution* (New York, 1898), pp. 237–238.

27. Ethnic Studies Oral History Project, *Waialua and Haleiwa*, vol. 8, p. 167; Yako Morishita, poem, in Jiro Nakano, "History of Japanese Short Poems (Tanka, Haiku and Senryu) in Hawaii," unpublished manuscript, 1986, p. 46.

28. Song, in Yukuo Uyehara, "The Horehore-Bushi: A Type of Japanese Folksong Developed and Sung among the Early Immigrants in Hawaii," *Social Process in Hawaii*, vol. 28 (1980–1981), p. 114.

29. Ethnic Studies Oral History Project, *Uchinanchu*, p. 369.

30. Song, in Uyehara, "The Horehore-Bushi," p. 114.

31. *The Higher Wage Question*, excerpts reprinted in Bureau of Labor Statistics, *Report of the Commissioner of Labor on Hawaii* (Washington, D.C., 1910), p. 76.

32. Yasutaro Soga, in *Honolulu Record*, July 7, 1949; Allan Beekman, "Hawaii's Great Japanese Strike," reprinted in Dennis Ogawa (ed.), *Kodomo no tame ni: For the sake of the children* (Honolulu, 1978), p. 158.

33. Letter to plantation manager E. K. Bull, signed by ninety-two strikers, May 19, 1909, reprinted in Bureau of Labor Statistics, *Report*, p. 80; Higher Wage Association, statement, in Bureau of Labor Statistics, *Report*, p. 68; *Higher Wage Question*, in Bureau of Labor Statistics, *Report*, pp. 77–78.

34. Takashi Tsutsumi, *History of Hawaii Laborers' Movement* (Honolulu, 1922), p. 175.

35. Tsutsumi, *Hawaii Laborers' Movement*, pp. 217, 224, 238, 240, 241, 242, 243.

36. Tsutsumi, *Hawaii Laborers' Movement*, pp. 12, 44, 17, 13, 22.

37. Hawaii Laborers' Association, *Facts About the Strike on Sugar Plantations in Hawaii* (Honolulu, 1920), p. 1.

38. President of C. Brewer and Company to James Campsie, manager of the Hawaiian Agricultural Company, February 3, 1920, Hawaiian Agricultural Company Records; R. D. Mead, director of the Labor Bureau, to manager of Grove Farm Plantation, February 13, 1920, Grove Farm Plantation Records.

39. Tadao Okada, interview, July 1980.

40. Milton Murayama, *All I Asking for Is My Body* (San Francisco, 1975), pp. 28, 96.

41. Richard Okawa, interviews, February 1978 and July 1980; Minoru Takaki, interview, July 1985.

42. Yasutaro Soga, "Looking Backward 50 Years in Hawaii," reprinted in *Honolulu Record,* March 31, 1949; Ethnic Studies Oral History Project, *Uchinanchu,* pp. 363, 489.

43. C. Brewer and Company to W. G. Ogg, August 2, 1916, Hawaiian Agricultural Company Records; Donald S. Bowman to Grove Farm Plantation, September 15, 1920, Grove Farm Plantation Records; W. Pfotenhauser, "President's Address," *The Hawaiian Planters' Record,* vol. 4, no. 1 (January 1911), p. 4; Donald S. Bowman, "Housing the Plantation Worker," *The Hawaiian Planters' Record,* vol. 22, no. 4 (April 1920), pp. 202–203.

44. Ethnic Studies Oral History Project, *Uchinanchu,* p. 382; Ito, *Issei,* p. 21.

45. Murayama, *All I Asking for Is My Body,* p. 45.

46. Manager of the Hawaiian Agricultural Company to C. Brewer and Company, October 17 and November 2, 1911, Hawaiian Agricultural Company Records; H. Hackfield and Company to George Wilcox, April 25, 1900, Grove Farm Plantation Records.

47. Ethnic Studies Oral History Project, *Uchinanchu,* p. 387; Mrs. Joe Rapozo, in *Honolulu Advertiser,* July 6, 1973; Ethnic Studies Oral History Project, *Waialua and Haleiwa,* vol. 8, p. 64, and vol. 9, p. 223.

48. Manager of the Hawaiian Agricultural Company to Bureau of Labor, Hawaiian Sugar Planters' Association, April 5, 1919, Hawaiian Agricultural Company Records; interviews, in Ethnic Studies Oral History Project, *Uchinanchu,* pp. 415, 470; William C. Smith, "Pidgin English in Hawaii," *American Speech,* vol. 8–9 (February 1933), pp. 15–19; Ethnic Studies Oral History Project, *Waialua and Haleiwa,* vol. 3, p. 11.

49. Daniel K. Inouye, *Journey to Washington* (Englewood Cliffs, N.J., 1967), pp. 24–25; Aiko Mifune, interview, February 18, 1988; Minoru Takaki and Susumu Takaki, interview on the Puunene Plantation, July 1985; Jeanette Takaki Watanabe, interview, March 14, 1987.

50. Ray Stannard Baker, "Human Nature in Hawaii: How the Few Want the Many to Work for Them — Perpetually, and at Low Wages," *American Magazine,* vol. 73 (January 1912), p. 330.

51. Curtis Aller, "The Evolution of Hawaiian Labor Relations: From Benevolent Paternalism to Mature Collective Bargaining," unpublished Ph.D. thesis, Harvard University, 1958, p. 39.

52. William C. Smith, *Americans in Process: A Study of Our Citizens of Oriental Ancestry* (Ann Arbor, Mich., 1937), p. 52.

53. Song, in *Hawaii Herald*, February 2, 1973.

54. William C. Smith, *The Second Generation Oriental in America* (Honolulu, 1927), p. 21.

55. Ito, *Issei*, p. 446.

56. Ito, *Issei*, p. 317.

57. Ito, *Issei*, pp. 335, 409; Ichioka, *Issei*, pp. 72–73.

58. Ito, *Issei*, pp. 435, 312.

59. Immigration Commission, *Japanese and Other Immigrant Races* (Washington, D.C., 1911), vol. 1, p. 80.

60. Ichioka, *Issei*, p. 121.

61. Paul S. Taylor and Tom Vasey, "Historical Background of California Farm Labor," *Rural Sociology*, vol. 1 (September 1936), p. 286; Gerald D. Nash, "Stages of California's Economic Growth, 1870–1970: An Interpretation," *California Historical Quarterly* (winter 1972), pp. 318–319.

62. Ito, *Issei*, pp. 250, 280.

63. Ito, *Issei*, pp. 251, 442, 255; Hanawa, "Several Worlds," p. 86.

64. "Interview with Mr. S. Nitta," 1924, p. 2, Survey of Race Relations, Stanford University, Hoover Institution Library; Bill Hosokawa, *Nisei: The Quiet Americans* (New York, 1969), p. 61.

65. Kiyoshi K. Kawakami, *Asia at the Door: A Study of the Japanese Question in Continental United States, Hawaii and Canada* (New York, 1914), p. 99; *San Francisco Chronicle*, June 25, 1912; Kiyoshi Kawakami, "How California Treats the Japanese," *The Independent*, vol. 74 (May 8, 1913), p. 1020; "Visit with Mr. George Shima, 'Potato King' of California," interview, July 14, 1924, pp. 1–3, Survey of Race Relations, Stanford University, Hoover Institution Library.

66. Ichioka, *Issei*, p. 61.

67. Ichioka, *Issei*, pp. 147, 148.

68. Kesa Noda, *Yamato Colony, 1906–1960* (Livingston, Calif., 1981), p. 18.

69. Noda, *Yamato Colony*, p. 18.

70. Ichioka, *Issei*, p. 148; Noda, *Yamato Colony*, pp. 10, 18, 40, 65, 174; Ito, *Issei*, p. 132.

71. Ichioka, "Early Japanese Immigrant Quest for Citizenship," pp. 10, 11, 17; Yamato Ichihashi, *Japanese in the United States* (New York, 1969), p. 298; *Ozawa vs. United States, Decision of the Court*, November 13, 1922, reprinted in appendix, Eliot G. Mears, *Resident Orientals on the American Pacific Coast: Their Legal and Economic Status* (New York, 1927), pp. 509, 513, 514.

72. Ichihashi, *Japanese in the United States*, pp. 321–322; Jerrold Takahashi, "Changing Responses to Racial Subordination: An Exploratory Study of Japanese American Political Styles," unpublished Ph.D. thesis, University of California, Berkeley, 1980, p. 107.

73. "American-Born Japanese in Interstitial Position Says League President,"

Japanese American Courier, April 17, 1928; "Life History of Kazuo Kawai," March 2, 1925, p. 17, Survey of Race Relations, Stanford University, Hoover Institution Library; "Interview with Mr. S. Nitta," January 7, 1925, p. 2, Survey of Race Relations; Yuji Ichioka, "A Study in Dualism: James Yoshinori Sakamoto and the *Japanese American Courier,* 1928–1942," *Amerasia,* vol. 13, no. 2 (1986–87), p. 57.

74. *Japanese American Courier,* January 21, 1933; Ito, *Issei,* pp. 274, 449, 497; "Life History of Dr. Peter S——— of Los Angeles," pp. 2–3, 1925, Survey of Race Relations, Stanford University, Hoover Institution Library; "Interview with Yamato Ichihashi," p. 1, Survey of Race Relations; "Life History of a Japanese Man at Santa Paula, California," December 29, 1924, p. 2, Survey of Race Relations; S. Morris Morishita, in Smith, *Americans in Process,* p. 112; Hosokawa, *Nisei,* p. 136.

75. Fred Korematsu, "Views from Within," A Symposium on the Japanese American Internment Experience, University of California, Berkeley, September 19, 1987; Kay Yasui, " 'Jap!' 'Jap!' 'Jap!,' " *Pacific Citizen,* January 15, 1931; interviews with Mary Tsukamoto and Donald Nakahata, in John Tateishi, *And Justice for All: An Oral History of the Japanese American Detention Camps* (New York, 1984), pp. 5, 36, respectively; Toyo Tanaka, "How to Survive Racism in America's Free Society," in Arthur A. Hansen and Betty F. Mitson (eds.), *Voices Long Silent: An Oral Inquiry into the Japanese American Evacuation* (Fullerton, Calif., 1974), pp. 84, 90; "An American Born Japanese in America," an interview with J. Sato, pp. 2–3, Survey of Race Relations, Stanford University, Hoover Institution Library.

76. Report on Vocational Guidance Issue by Kojiro Unoura, in *Japanese American Courier,* September 10, 1938; Mears, *Resident Orientals,* pp. 199, 200.

77. John Modell, *Economics and Politics of Racial Accommodation: The Japanese of Los Angeles, 1900–1942* (Urbana, Ill., 1977), pp. 132, 137–138; Yori Wada, "Growing Up in Central California," *Amerasia,* vol. 13, no. 2 (1986/7), p. 12; "Interview with Miss Esther B. Barlett of Y.W.C.A.," December 12, 1924, p. 5, Survey of Race Relations, Stanford University, Hoover Institution Library.

78. Aiji Tashiro, "The Rising Son of the Rising Sun," *New Outlook* (September 1934), pp. 36, 40.

79. *Japanese American News (Nichi Bei),* in Bradford Smith, *Americans from Japan* (New York, 1948), pp. 244–245.

80. Ichioka, "Study in Dualism," p. 59; "Life History of Kazuo Kawai," pp. 5, 12, 13, 15–17.

Chapter 11. Between "Two Endless Days"

1. Abraham Cahan, *The Education of Abraham Cahan,* translated by Leon Stein, Abraham P. Conan, and Lynn Davison (Philadelphia, 1969), p. 184. The phrase "two endless days" comes from the definitive study and classic by Irving Howe, *World of Our Fathers: The Journey of the East European Jews to America and the*

Life They Found and Made (New York, 1983) (p. 12), which I found indispensable and inspirational. For important analyses that focus on Jewish women, see Sidney Stahl Weinberg, *The World of Our Mothers: The Lives of Jewish Immigrant Women* (New York, 1988), and Susan A. Glenn, *Daughters of the Shtetl: Life and Labor in the Immigrant Generation* (Ithaca, N.Y., 1990).

2. Mary Antin, *The Promised Land* (New York, 1980; originally published in 1911), pp. 5, 22; Howe, *World of Our Fathers*, p. 10.

3. Sydelle Kramer and Jenny Masur (eds.), *Jewish Grandmothers* (Boston, 1976), p. 64; Golda Meir, in Maxine Schwartz Seller (ed.), *Immigrant Women* (Philadelphia, 1981), p. 37; Glenn, *Daughters of the Shtetl*, p. 43; Ronald Sanders, *Shores of Refuge: A Hundred Years of Jewish Emigration* (New York, 1988), p. 213; Cahan, *Education*, pp. 158, 182.

4. Song, "Purim Gifts," in Mark Slobin, *Tenement Songs: The Popular Music of the Jewish Immigrants* (Urbana, Ill., 1982), p. 155.

5. Abraham Cahan, *The Rise of David Levinsky* (New York, 1960; originally published in 1917), pp. 59–61; Anzia Yezierska, *Children of Loneliness* (New York, 1923), p. 152; Mary Antin, in Howe, *World of Our Fathers*, p. 27; Antin, *Promised Land*, p. 142.

6. Cahan, *Education*, pp. 187, 186; Glenn, *Daughters of the Shtetl*, pp. 46, 47; Weinberg, *World of Our Mothers*, p. 73; Elizabeth Ewen, *Immigrant Women in the Land of Dollars: Life and Culture on the Lower East Side, 1890–1925* (New York, 1985), p. 54.

7. Antin, *Promised Land*, pp. 168–169; Cahan, *Education*, pp. 195, 188.

8. Sanders, *Shores of Refuge*, p. 66; Milton Meltzer, *Taking Root: Jewish Immigrants in America* (New York, 1976), p. 36; Cahan, *Education*, pp. 214, 215, 196; see also Howe, *World of Our Fathers*, pp. 39–41.

9. Howe, *World of Our Fathers*, p. 12; Cahan, *Education*, p. 196. My thanks to Larry Friedman for the phrase "countryless people" to describe the Jews.

10. Cahan, *Rise of David Levinsky*, pp. 86, 87; Sanders, *Shores of Refuge*, p. 161; "The Life Story of a Polish Sweatshop Girl," in Hamilton Holt (ed.), *The Life Stories of Undistinguished Americans as Told by Themselves* (New York, 1906), p. 36.

11. Klaperman, quoted in Stephen Steinberg, *The Ethnic Myth: Race, Ethnicity, and Class in America* (New York, 1981), p. 82.

12. For statistics, see Glenn, *Daughters of the Shtetl*, p. 47; Thomas Kessner, *The Golden Door: Italian and Jewish Immigrant Mobility in New York City, 1880–1915* (New York, 1977), p. 33; Weinberg, *World of Our Mothers*, p. 76; Howe, *World of Our Fathers*, p. 59.

13. Glenn, *Daughters of the Shtetl*, pp. 54, 137–138; Deborah Dash Moore, *At Home in America: Second Generation New York Jews* (New York, 1981), p. 29; Meltzer, *Taking Root*, p. 65; Cahan, *Rise of David Levinsky*, p. 93.

14. Cahan, *Rise of David Levinsky*, pp. 512, 93; Meltzer, *Taking Root*, p. 64; Kramer and Masur (eds.), *Jewish Grandmothers*, pp. 131, 132.

15. Isaac Raboy, in Irving Howe and Kenneth Libo (eds.), *How We Lived: A Documentary History of Immigrant Jews in America, 1880–1930* (New York, 1979), p. 29.

16. Moses Rischin, *The Promised City: New York's Jews, 1870–1914* (Cambridge, Mass., 1977; originally published in 1962), pp. 79, 82–83.

17. Rischin, *Promised City*, pp. 84, 87; Howe, *World of Our Fathers*, p. 152.

18. Howe, *World of Our Fathers*, p. 212.

19. Howe, *World of Our Fathers*, pp. 72, 184, 239, 213; Cahan, *Rise of David Levinsky*, p. 459.

20. Raboy, in Howe and Libo (eds.), *How We Lived*, p. 26; Rischin, *Promised City*, p. 55; Michael Kraus, *Immigration, The American Mosaic* (New York, 1966), p. 168.

21. Anzia Yezierska, in Howe and Libo (eds.), *How We Lived*, p. 19.

22. Milton M. Gordon, *Assimilation in American Life: The Role of Race, Religion, and National Origins* (New York, 1964), pp. 186, 187; Nathan Glazer, "The American Jew and the Attainment of Middle-Class Rank: Some Trends and Explanations," in Marshall Sklare (ed.), *The Jews: Social Patterns of an American Group* (Glencoe, Ill., 1958), p. 142.

23. Miriam Shomer Zunser, *Yesterday* (New York, 1939), p. 169; Cahan, *Education*, p. 5.

24. Rischin, *Promised City*, p. 55.

25. Cahan, *Rise of David Levinsky*, pp. 97, 107.

26. Howe, *World of Our Fathers*, p. 80.

27. Howe, *World of Our Fathers*, p. 60.

28. Glenn, *Daughters of the Shtetl*, p. 92; Rischin, *Promised City*, pp. 63, 67.

29. Glenn, *Daughters of the Shtetl*, p. 95; Cahan, *Rise of David Levinsky*, p. 443.

30. Cahan, *Rise of David Levinsky*, pp. 201, 90–91.

31. Cahan, *Rise of David Levinsky*, pp. 151; Glenn, *Daughters of the Shtetl*, p. 94; Ray Stannard Baker, in Howe and Libo (eds.), *How We Lived*, p. 153.

32. Glenn, *Daughters of the Shtetl*, pp. 100, 104, 101; Meltzer, *Taking Root*, pp. 111–112; Bella Feiner, in Ewen, *Immigrant Women in the Land of Dollars*, p. 245.

33. Glenn, *Daughters of the Shtetl*, pp. 90, 94, 64; Rischin, *Promised City*, p. 61; Howe, *World of Our Fathers*, p. 81.

34. Glenn, *Daughters of the Shtetl*, pp. 101, 152; Marie Ganz, in Howe and Libo (eds.), *How We Lived*, p. 136; Yezierska, *Children of Loneliness*, p. 158.

35. Mollie Linker, in Kramer and Masur (eds.), *Jewish Grandmothers*, p. 95; "Polish Sweatshop Girl," p. 43.

36. Glenn, *Daughters of the Shtetl*, p. 103; Anzia Yezierska, in Kramer and Masur (eds.), *Jewish Grandmothers*, p. 45; Morris Rosenfeld, poem, in Howe and Libo (eds.), *How We Lived*, p. 157.

37. Meltzer, *Taking Root*, pp. 111–112; "Polish Sweatshop Girl," p. 44.

38. Glenn, *Daughters of the Shtetl*, pp. 49, 19, 21, 22, 26; Fannie Shapiro, in Kramer and Masur (eds.), *Jewish Grandmothers*, p. 10.

39. "Polish Sweatshop Girl," pp. 42, 46.

40. Glenn, *Daughters of the Shtetl*, pp. 80, 87, 138–139.

41. *Jewish Daily Forward*, March 26, 1911, in Howe and Libo (eds.), *How We Lived*, p. 185; Rischin, *Promised City*, p. 253; Meltzer, *Taking Root*, pp. 231, 233.

42. Mothers' laments, "Mamenyu! Including an Elegy to the Triangle Fire Victims," in Slobin, *Tenement Songs*, p. 134; poem by Morris Rosenfeld, in Howe, *World of Our Fathers*, p. 305.

43. Glenn, *Daughters of the Shtetl*, p. 49; reporter, in Ewen, *Immigrant Women in the Land of Dollars*, p. 260.

44. Clara Lemlich, in Howe, *World of Our Fathers*, p. 268, and in Howard M. Sachar, *A History of the Jews in America* (New York, 1992), p. 183; Benjamin Feigenbaum, in Glenn, *Daughters of the Shtetl*, p. 187.

45. Glenn, *Daughters of the Shtetl*, p. 205.

46. Glenn, *Daughters of the Shtetl*, p. 172; Howe, *World of Our Fathers*, pp. 299–300; poem, "The Uprising of the 20,000," in Barbara Wertheimer, *We Were There* (New York, 1977), p. 293; see also Ewen, *Immigrant Women in the Land of Dollars*, p. 242.

47. Howe, *World of Our Fathers*, p. 302.

48. Glenn, *Daughters of the Shtetl*, p. 169.

49. Immigrant's recollection, in Glenn, *Daughters of the Shtetl*, p. 204; Paul Novick, in Howe, *World of Our Fathers*, p. 306; Howe, *World of Our Fathers*, p. 302.

50. Immigrant, in Weinberg, *World of Our Mothers*, p. 83; Howe, *World of Our Fathers*, p. 121.

51. John Murray Cuddihy, *The Ordeal of Civility: Freud, Marx, Levi Strauss, and the Jewish Struggle with Modernity* (Boston, 1987), pp. xi, 13, 165, 166; Andrew R. Heinze, *Adapting to Abundance: Jewish Immigrants, Mass Consumption, and the Search for American Identity* (New York, 1990), p. 98.

52. Cuddihy, *Ordeal of Civility*, p. 13; Ewen, *Immigrant Women in the Land of Dollars*, p. 68; Cahan, *Rise of David Levinsky*, pp. 93, 94, 101.

53. Howe, *World of Our Fathers*, p. 128; Jewish mother, in Ewen, *Immigrant Women in the Land of Dollars*, p. 72; Cahan, *Rise of David Levinsky*, pp. 172, 93, 94, 101, 129, 176.

54. Cahan, *Rise of David Levinsky*, p. 330.

55. Howe, *World of Our Fathers*, pp. 128, 181; Heinze, *Adapting to Abundance*, p. 43; Weinberg, *World of Our Mothers*, p. 114; Meltzer, *Taking Root*, pp. 142–143; Antin, *Promised Land*, p. 188.

56. "Polish Sweatshop Girl," p. 46; Heinze, *Adapting to Abundance*, pp. 4, 15, 126, 42, 77.

57. Heinze, *Adapting to Abundance*, p. 116; *Commercial Advertiser*, September 25, 1899, and the *Jewish Daily Forward*, in Howe and Libo (eds.), *How We Lived*,

pp. 77, 78, respectively; Maurice Samuel, poem, in Howe and Libo (eds.), *How We Lived*, p. 115.

58. Cahan, *Rise of David Levinsky*, p. 404.

59. Cahan, *Rise of David Levinsky*, pp. 260, 444.

60. Cahan, *Rise of David Levinsky*, pp. 291, 327, 328, 337.

61. Statistics and quote from immigrant woman, in Glenn, *Daughters of the Shtetl*, pp. 74, 75.

62. Immigrant daughter, in Weinberg, *World of Our Mothers*, p. 105; Glenn, *Daughters of the Shtetl*, p. 67; Heinze, *Adapting to Abundance*, pp. 108, 106; Mollie Linker, in Glenn, *Daughters of the Shtetl*, p. 1, and in Kramer and Masur (eds.), *Jewish Grandmothers*, p. 100; Ruth Katz, in Kramer and Masur (eds.), *Jewish Grandmothers*, pp. 148, 149.

63. Glenn, *Daughters of the Shtetl*, p. 77; Heinze, *Adapting to Abundance*, p. 108.

64. Barry R. Chiswick, "The Labor Market Status of American Jews: Patterns and Determinants," *Ethnicity and Public Policy*, vol. 4 (1985), pp. 115–118.

65. Kessner, *Golden Door*, p. 170; Glenn, *Daughters of the Shtetl*, pp. 83, 84.

66. *Jewish Daily Forward*, in Steinberg, *Ethnic Myth*, p. 226.

67. Selma C. Berrol, "Education and Economic Mobility: The Jewish Experience in New York City, 1880–1920," *American Jewish Historical Quarterly*, vol. 65 (March 1976), p. 271; Heinze, *Adapting to Abundance*, p. 102.

68. Antin, *Promised Land*, p. 205.

69. Kessner, *Golden Door*, p. 98.

70. Steinberg, *Ethnic Myth*, p. 228.

71. Steinberg, *Ethnic Myth*, pp. 234, 242.

72. A. Lawrence Lowell, to Professor William E. Hocking, May 19, 1922; A. Lawrence Lowell, to Judge Julian Mack, March 29, 1922, in Steinberg, *Ethnic Myth*, pp. 245, 241; Marcial Graham Synnott, *The Half-Opened Door: Discrimination and Admissions at Harvard, Yale, and Princeton, 1900–1970* (Westport, Conn., 1979), pp. 27, 36, 112.

73. A. Lawrence Lowell, *New York Times*, June 17, 1922, in Steinberg, *Ethnic Myth*, pp. 241, 240; Sachar, *History of the Jews in America*, pp. 322–324.

74. Steinberg, *Ethnic Myth*, p. 248; Synnott, *Half-Opened Door*, pp. 109–110, 112.

75. Mayor James Michael Curley, in Synnott, *Half-Opened Door*, p. 77.

76. Howe, *World of Our Fathers*, p. 126.

77. John Higham, *Send These to Me: Immigrants in Urban America* (Baltimore, 1984), p. 158.

78. Higham, *Send These to Me*, pp. 109, 166, 114; Sachar, *History of the Jews in America*, p. 321; John Higham, *Strangers in the Land: Patterns of American Nativism, 1860–1925* (New York, 1966), pp. 67, 93.

79. Horace Kallen, in Steinberg, *Ethnic Myth*, p. 246; Higham, *Send These to Me*, pp. 169, 145, 135; Sachar, *History of the Jews in America*, p. 331.

80. Quoted in Gilbert Osofsky, *Harlem: The Making of a Ghetto, Negro New York, 1890–1930* (New York, 1966), pp. 88–89.

81. Moore, *At Home in America*, pp. 24, 42, 43.

82. Moore, *At Home in America*, pp. 20, 23, 28.

83. Moore, *At Home in America*, pp. 30, 38; Cahan, *Rise of David Levinsky*, p. 512.

84. Jonathan Kaufman, *Broken Alliance: The Turbulent Times between Blacks and Jews in America* (New York, 1989), p. 22.

Chapter 12. El Norte

1. Ricardo Romo, *East Los Angeles: History of a Barrio* (Austin, Tex., 1983), p. 48; Paul S. Taylor, "Songs of the Mexican Migration," in J. Frank Dobie (ed.), *Puro Mexicano* (Austin, Tex., 1935), pp. 241–243.

2. Albert Camarillo, *Chicanos in a Changing Society: From Mexican Pueblos to American Barrios in Santa Barbara and Southern California, 1848–1930* (Cambridge, Mass., 1979), p. 146; Manuel Gamio, *The Mexican Immigrant: His Life Story* (Chicago, 1931), p. 15.

3. Romo, *East Los Angeles*, p. 45.

4. Mario T. García, *Desert Immigrants: The Mexicans of El Paso, 1880–1920* (New Haven, Conn., 1981), pp. 37, 39.

5. Romo, *East Los Angeles*, pp. 36, 52.

6. Romo, *East Los Angeles*, pp. 32, 37; Lawrence A. Cardoso, *Mexican Emigration to the United States, 1897–1931* (Tucson, Ariz., 1980), pp. 6, 75; Merle E. Simmons, *The Mexican Corrido as a Source for Interpretive Study of Modern Mexico* (Bloomington, Ind., 1957), p. 348.

7. García, *Desert Immigrants*, pp. 204–205.

8. Romo, *East Los Angeles*, p. 43; Gamio, *Mexican Immigrant*, p. 7; Cardoso, *Mexican Emigration*, p. 74.

9. Romo, *East Los Angeles*, p. 48; García, *Desert Immigrants*, p. 41; Gamio, *Mexican Immigrant*, p. 2.

10. Gamio, *Mexican Immigrant*, pp. 46, 67.

11. Gamio, *Mexican Immigrant*, p. 7; Romo, *East Los Angeles*, p. 45; Simmons, *Mexican Corrido*, p. 142.

12. Gamio, *Mexican Immigrant*, pp. 69–70; Camarillo, *Chicanos in a Changing Society*, p. 156; García, *Desert Immigrants*, p. 39; Romo, *East Los Angeles*, pp. 57, 40.

13. Romo, *East Los Angeles*, pp. 32, 36; David J. Weber, *Foreigners in Their Native Land: Historical Roots of the Mexican Americans* (Albuquerque, N. Mex., 1973), p. 260; Mario Barrera, *Race and Class in the Southwest: A Theory of Racial Inequality* (Notre Dame, Ind., 1979), p. 71.

14. Manuel Gamio, *Mexican Immigration to the United States* (Chicago, 1930), pp. 91–92.

15. Cardoso, *Mexican Emigration*, p. 82; Romo, *East Los Angeles*, p. 52; Barrera, *Race and Class in the Southwest*, p. 75; Mark Reisler, *By the Sweat of Their Brow: Mexican Immigrant Labor in the United States, 1900–1940* (Westport, Conn., 1976), p. 269; Ernesto Galarza, *Barrio Boy: The Story of a Boy's Acculturation* (Notre Dame, Ind., 1971), p. 200. Reisler's study is solidly researched and useful.

16. Marilyn P. Davis, *Mexican Voices, American Dreams: An Oral History of Mexican Immigration to the United States* (New York, 1990), p. 8; Taylor, "Songs of Mexican Migration," pp. 222–224.

17. Gamio, *Mexican Immigrant*, p. 124.

18. Barrera, *Race and Class in the Southwest*, p. 86; Camarillo, *Chicanos in a Changing Society*, p. 172; Gamio, *Mexican Immigrant*, pp. 97–98.

19. Barrera, *Race and Class in the Southwest*, p. 89; Camarillo, *Chicanos in a Changing Society*, pp. 211–212, 176; García, *Desert Immigrants*, p. 87.

20. Vicki L. Ruiz, "A Promise Fulfilled: Mexican Cannery Workers in Southern California," in Ellen Carol DuBois and Vicki L. Ruiz (eds.), *Unequal Sisters: A Multi-Cultural Reader in U.S. Women's History* (New York, 1990), p. 265; Edith Summers Kelley, "The Head-Cutters," in appendix, Vicki L. Ruiz, *Cannery Women, Cannery Lives: Mexican Women, Unionization, and the California Food Processing Industry, 1930–1950* (Albuquerque, N. Mex., 1987), pp. 125–127.

21. Barrera, *Race and Class in the Southwest*, p. 98; Evelyn Nakano Glenn, "Racial Ethnic Women's Labor: The Intersection of Race, Gender and Class Oppression," *Review of Radical Political Economics*, vol. 17, no. 3 (1985), p. 95; García, *Desert Immigrants*, pp. 94, 76.

22. Barrera, *Race and Class in the Southwest*, p. 91; Reisler, *Sweat of Their Brow*, pp. 101, 100–102.

23. García, *Desert Immigrants*, pp. 57, 68; Reisler, *Sweat of Their Brow*, p. 97.

24. Gamio, *Mexican Immigrant*, pp. 15–16, 150; Galarza, *Barrio Boy*, p. 190.

25. Carey McWilliams, *Factories in the Field: The Story of Migratory Farm Labor in California* (Santa Barbara, Calif., 1971), pp. 127–128, 131; Reisler, *Sweat of Their Brow*, p. 87; Abraham Hoffman, *Unwanted Americans in the Great Depression: Repatriation Pressures, 1929–1939* (Tucson, Ariz., 1974), p. 10; Cardoso, *Mexican Emigration*, p. 25.

26. David Montejano, *Anglos and Mexicans in the Making of Texas, 1836–1986* (Austin, Tex., 1987), pp. 172, 184–185, 199; Paul S. Taylor, *An American-Mexican Frontier* (Chapel Hill, N.C., 1934), p. 102.

27. Taylor, *American-Mexican Frontier*, p. 143.

28. Montejano, *Anglos and Mexicans*, pp. 200, 219, 218.

29. Montejano, *Anglos and Mexicans*, pp. 202, 204.

30. Gamio, *Mexican Immigrant*, pp. 150–151.

31. Barrera, *Race and Class in the Southwest*, pp. 78, 79.

32. Devra A. Weber, "Mexican Women on Strike: Memory, History and

Oral Narrative," in Alelaida R. Del Castillo (ed.), *Between Borders: Essays on Mexicana/Chicana History* (Encino, Calif., 1990), p. 183; Elizabeth Martinez and Ed McCaughan, "Chicanas and Mexicanas within a Transnational Working Class," in Del Castillo (ed.), *Between Borders,* p. 47.

33. Galarza, *Barrio Boy*, pp. 261–262; Gamio, *Mexican Immigrant*, p. 56.

34. Gamio, *Mexican Immigrant*, p. 86; Reisler, *Sweat of Their Brow*, p. 89.

35. Laura H. Parker, "Migratory Children," *National Conference of Social Work Proceedings* (1927), p. 304; California Commission of Immigration and Housing, *Annual Report* (1927), p. 18; see also Reisler, *Sweat of Their Brow*, pp. 84, 85.

36. Reisler, *Sweat of Their Brow*, p. 235.

37. Reisler, *Sweat of Their Brow*, p. 240.

38. Weber, "Mexican Women on Strike," pp. 186, 192.

39. Gamio, *Mexican Immigrant*, pp. 149, 147.

40. Montejano, *Anglos and Mexicans*, p. 250.

41. Gamio, *Mexican Immigrant*, p. 177.

42. Montejano, *Anglos and Mexicans*, pp. 226–227, 221, 194.

43. Sarah Deutsch, *No Separate Refuge: Culture, Class, and Gender on an Anglo-Hispanic Frontier in the American Southwest, 1880–1940* (New York, 1987), p. 141; Rosalinda M. Gonzalez, "Chicanas and Mexican Immigrant Families, 1920–1940: Women's Subordination and Family Exploitation," in Lois Scharf and Joan M. Jensen (eds.), *Decades of Discontent: The Women's Movement, 1920–1940* (Westport, Conn., 1983), p. 66.

44. Montejano, *Anglos and Mexicans*, pp. 192–193; Taylor, *American-Mexican Frontier*, p. 194.

45. Montejano, *Anglos and Mexicans*, p. 160; García, *Desert Immigrants*, p. 117.

46. Taylor, *American-Mexican Frontier*, p. 204; Galarza, *Barrio Boy*, p. 211.

47. Gamio, *Mexican Immigrant*, pp. 222–223; García, *Desert Immigrants*, p. 125.

48. Gamio, *Mexican Immigrant*, pp. 44, 132; Deutsch, *No Separate Refuge*, p. 139; George Sanchez, " 'Go After the Women': Americanization and the Mexican Immigrant Woman, 1915–1929," in DuBois and Ruiz (eds.), *Unequal Sisters*, p. 260.

49. Reisler, *Sweat of Their Brow*, pp. 152, 155.

50. Reisler, *Sweat of Their Brow*, pp. 153, 155, 156, 205.

51. Reisler, *Sweat of Their Brow*, p. 156.

52. "Present and Future," *Saturday Evening Post*, vol. 202 (March 15, 1930), p. 28; "Singling Out Mexico," *New York Times*, May 16, 1930.

53. Taylor, *American-Mexican Frontier*, p. 289; García, *Desert Immigrants*, pp. 104, 101.

54. Reisler, *Sweat of Their Brow*, pp. 169, 207, 173.

55. Reisler, *Sweat of Their Brow*, pp. 176, 175.

56. Reisler, *Sweat of Their Brow*, p. 13.

57. Taylor, "Songs of Mexican Migration," pp. 232–233.

58. Hoffman, *Unwanted Americans*, pp. 47, 84; Taylor, "Songs of Mexican Migration," pp. 232–233.

59. Camarillo, *Chicanos in a Changing Society*, p. 163; Hoffman, *Unwanted Americans*, p. 95.

60. Carey McWilliams, "Getting Rid of the Mexican," in Wayne Moquin (ed.), *A Documentary History of the Mexican Americans* (New York, 1972), p. 297; Reisler, *Sweat of Their Brow*, p. 203.

61. Galarza, *Barrio Boy*, p. 200.

62. Camarillo, *Chicanos in a Changing Society*, p. 62; Galarza, *Barrio Boy*, p. 206; Arnold De Leon, *The Tejano Community, 1836–1900* (Albuquerque, N. Mex., 1982), pp. 180–181.

63. Gamio, *Mexican Immigrant*, p. 28; De Leon, *Tejano Community*, p. 160.

64. Camarillo, *Chicanos in a Changing Society*, p. 169; Galarza, *Barrio Boy*, p. 201.

65. De Leon, *Tejano Community*, p. 65; Galarza, *Barrio Boy*, p. 201.

66. Gamio, *Mexican Immigrant*, p. 26.

67. Galarza, *Barrio Boy*, p. 239.

68. Galarza, *Barrio Boy*, pp. 12, 19, 23, 42.

69. Galarza, *Barrio Boy*, pp. 237, 49.

70. Montejano, *Anglos and Mexicans*, p. 31; Gamio, *Mexican Immigrant*, p. 13; Reisler, *Sweat of Their Brow*, p. 113.

71. Gamio, *Mexican Immigrant*, pp. 182, 104.

72. Galarza, *Barrio Boy*, p. 183; Camarillo, *Chicanos in a Changing Society*, p. 149; García, *Desert Immigrants*, pp. 228–229; Gamio, *Mexican Immigrant*, p. 94.

73. Galarza, *Barrio Boy*, p. 12.

Chapter 13. To the Promised Land

1. Zora Neale Hurston, *Jonah's Gourd Vine* (New York, 1990; originally published in 1934), pp. 147–148; song, in *Chicago Defender*, May 28, 1917, quoted in Allan H. Spear, *Black Chicago: The Making of a Negro Ghetto, 1890–1920* (Chicago, 1967), p. 135.

2. Gilbert Osofsky, *Harlem: The Making of a Ghetto, Negro New York, 1890–1930* (New York, 1966), p. 17. This is the best book on the subject.

3. Emmett J. Scott, *Negro Migration During the War* (London, 1920), pp. 41, 48; Florette Henri, *Black Migration: Movement North, 1900–1920* (New York, 1976), p. 72; Arna Bontemps and Jack Conroy, *Anyplace but Here* (New York, 1945), p. 163.

4. Scott, *Negro Migration*, pp. 42–43.

5. Bontemps and Conroy, *Anyplace but Here*, p. 163; Zora Neale Hurston, *Dust Tracks on a Road* (New York, 1991; originally published in 1942), p. 7; Langston Hughes, "New York," *Phylon*, vol. 11, no. 1 (1950), p. 14; Henri, *Black Migration*, p. 51.

6. St. Claire Drake and Horace R. Cayton, *Black Metropolis: A Study of Negro Life in a Northern City* (New York, 1962), vol. 1, p. 60; Ray Stannard Baker, "The Negro Goes North," *World's Work*, vol. 34 (July 1917), p. 315.

7. Spear, *Black Chicago*, p. 135; Scott, *Negro Migration*, pp. 17–18. The studies by Spear and also Drake and Cayton are the standard works for the black community of Chicago.

8. Emmett J. Scott (ed.), "Letters of Negro Migrants of 1916–18," *Journal of Negro History*, vol. 4 (July and October 1919), p. 413.

9. Scott (ed.), "Letters of Negro Migrants," p. 459; Spear, *Black Chicago*, p. 133; Baker, "Negro Goes North," p. 314.

10. Osofsky, *Harlem*, pp. 24, 26.

11. Osofsky, *Harlem*, pp. 21, 24–25.

12. Spear, *Black Chicago*, p. 137.

13. Osofsky, *Harlem*, pp. 21, 22; Ray Stannard Baker, *Following the Color Line* (New York, 1964; originally published in 1908), p. 112; Baker, "Negro Goes North," p. 316; Bontemps and Conroy, *Anyplace but Here*, p. 163.

14. Osofsky, *Harlem*, p. 23; Scott, *Negro Migration*, p. 31; Scott (ed.), "Letters of Negro Migrants," pp. 329, 438, 298.

15. Osofsky, *Harlem*, p. 21; Richard Wright, "Introduction," in Drake and Cayton, *Black Metropolis*, p. xvii; Toni Morrison, *Jazz* (New York, 1992), pp. 33, 7.

16. Baker, "Negro Goes North," p. 319.

17. Spear, *Black Chicago*, pp. 136–137; Hurston, *Jonah's Gourd Vine*, p. 151.

18. James R. Grossman, *Land of Hope: Chicago, Black Southerners, and the Great Migration* (Chicago, 1989), p. 110; Osofsky, *Harlem*, p. 31. Grossman's is a human portrait of these migrants in Chicago.

19. Scott, *Negro Migration*, p. 102.

20. Drake and Cayton, *Black Metropolis*, p. 177.

21. Spear, *Black Chicago*, pp. 22, 140, 202.

22. Spear, *Black Chicago*, pp. 209, 210.

23. Drake and Cayton, *Black Metropolis*, p. 181.

24. Spear, *Black Chicago*, pp. 29, 39.

25. Spear, *Black Chicago*, pp. 151, 157–158.

26. Drake and Cayton, *Black Metropolis*, p. 305.

27. Drake and Cayton, *Black Metropolis*, p. 306.

28. Spear, *Black Chicago*, p. 163.

29. Spear, *Black Chicago*, p. 211.

30. Spear, *Black Chicago*, p. 213.

31. Drake and Cayton, *Black Metropolis*, p. 66.

32. Claude McKay, "If We Must Die," in Langston Hughes and Arna Bontemps (eds.), *The Poetry of the Negro, 1746–1949* (Garden City, N.Y., 1951), p. 333.

33. Spear, *Black Chicago*, p. 221; Drake and Cayton, *Black Metropolis*, p. 80.

34. Osofsky, *Harlem*, pp. 94, 95.

35. Osofsky, *Harlem*, pp. 105–110.

36. Osofsky, *Harlem*, pp. 105, 130, 122.

37. Osofsky, *Harlem*, p. 136.

38. Osofsky, *Harlem*, pp. 127, 122; Edmund David Cronon, *Black Moses: The Story of Marcus Garvey and the Universal Negro Improvement Association* (Madison, Wis., 1966), p. 70. Cronon's biography is a useful narrative.

39. Marcus Garvey, "The Negro's Greatest Enemy," *Current History*, vol. 28 (September 1923), pp. 951–953.

40. Garvey, "Negro's Greatest Enemy," pp. 953–954.

41. Cronon, *Black Moses*, p. 206.

42. Cronon, *Black Moses*, pp. 176, 39, 65, 68; Amy Jacques-Garvey (ed.), *The Philosophy and Opinions of Marcus Garvey* (New York, 1925), p. 140.

43. Cronon, *Black Moses*, pp. 52, 114.

44. Garvey, "Negro's Greatest Enemy," p. 955; Cronon, *Black Moses*, pp. 136, 142.

45. Cronon, *Black Moses*, p. 136.

46. Osofsky, *Harlem*, pp. 123, 128.

47. Nathan Huggins, *Harlem Renaissance* (New York, 1971), p. 24; Osofsky, *Harlem*, p. 181.

48. Langston Hughes, *The Langston Hughes Reader* (New York, 1958), p. 369.

49. Robert Bone, *The Negro Novel in America* (New Haven, Conn., 1958), p. 45; Hughes, *Hughes Reader*, p. 341.

50. Bone, *Negro Novel*, p. 53; Huggins, *Harlem Renaissance*, p. 58.

51. Huggins, *Harlem Renaissance*, p. 59; Hughes, "I, Too, Sing America," in Hughes and Bontemps (eds.), *Poetry of the Negro*, p. 97.

52. Langston Hughes, "The Negro Artist and the Racial Mountain," *The Nation*, vol. 122, no. 3181 (June 23, 1926), pp. 692–694.

53. Hughes, "Negro Artist and Racial Mountain," pp. 692–694.

54. Hughes, "Afro-American Fragment," in Hughes and Bontemps (eds.) *Poetry of the Negro*, p. 102; Huggins, *Harlem Renaissance*, pp. 179, 82.

55. Hughes, "The Negro Speaks of Rivers," in Hughes and Bontemps (eds), *Poetry of the Negro*, pp. 105–106.

56. Claude McKay, *Home to Harlem* (New York, 1928), pp. 44, 15, 106, 156, 160–187.

57. McKay, *Home to Harlem*, pp. 226–229, 267.

58. Arna Bontemps, "Introduction," in Jean Toomer, *Cane* (New York, 1969; originally published in 1924), p. viii.

59. Toomer, *Cane*, pp. 17, 82, 21.

60. Toomer, *Cane*, pp. 8–13, 51–67.

61. Toomer, *Cane*, p. 71.

62. Toomer, *Cane*, pp. 91–130.

63. Toomer, *Cane*, pp. 157–238, 191.

64. Darwin Turner, "Introduction," in Jean Toomer, *Cane* (New York, 1975;

originally published in 1924), p. x; Bontemps, "Introduction," pp. xiii–xv; Hughes, *Hughes Reader,* p. 380.

65. Hurston, *Dust Tracks on a Road,* p. 121; Robert E. Hemenway, *Zora Neale Hurston: A Literary Biography* (Urbana, Ill., 1977), p. 31.

66. Zora Neale Hurston, *Their Eyes Were Watching God* (New York, 1978; originally published in 1937), p. 34.

67. Hurston, *Their Eyes Were Watching God,* pp. 31, 29, 30, 38.

68. Hurston, *Their Eyes Were Watching God,* pp. 48, 49, 87, 110, 111.

69. Hurston, *Their Eyes Were Watching God,* pp. 146, 171, 172.

70. Hurston, *Their Eyes Were Watching God,* pp. 192, 218, 236, 284.

71. Hurston, *Dust Tracks on a Road,* p. 151.

72. Hughes, *Hughes Reader,* p. 383.

73. Harvard Sitkoff, *A New Deal for Blacks: The Emergence of Civil Rights as a National Issue: The Depression Decade* (New York, 1978), pp. 35, 36. Sitkoff's study and Raymond Wolters, *Negroes and the Great Depression: The Problem of Economic Recovery* (Westport, Conn., 1970), are the two most useful books on the subject.

74. Sitkoff, *New Deal for Blacks,* pp. 37, 39.

75. Wolters, *Negroes and the Great Depression,* pp. 91, 92.

76. Sitkoff, *New Deal for Blacks,* pp. 54, 55, 56–57.

77. Francis L. Broderick, *W. E. B. DuBois: Negro Leader in a Time of Crisis* (Stanford, Calif., 1966), p. 189; Wolters, *Negroes and the Great Depression,* p. 250.

78. Sitkoff, *New Deal for Blacks,* pp. 251, 252, 254; Wolters, *Negroes and the Great Depression,* pp. 236–240, 258; Broderick, *DuBois,* pp. 165–179.

79. Sitkoff, *New Deal for Blacks,* pp. 179, 183, 186.

80. Sitkoff, *New Deal for Blacks,* pp. 69, 72, 97, 95.

Part IV: The Ashes at Dachau

1. M. F. Ashley Montagu, *Man's Most Dangerous Myth: The Fallacy of Race* (New York, 1942), pp. 179–180; Ruth Benedict and Gene Weltfish, *The Races of Mankind* (New York, 1943), p. 31.

2. Gunnar Myrdal, *An American Dilemma: The Negro Problem and Modern Democracy* (New York, 1962; originally published in 1944), pp. 1004, 1021.

3. Richard Polenberg, *One Nation Divisible: Class, Race, and Ethnicity in the United States since 1938* (New York, 1980), pp. 47, 71; Myrdal, *American Dilemma,* p. 1009; Harvard Sitkoff, *A New Deal for Blacks: The Emergence of Civil Rights as a National Issue: The Depression Decade* (New York, 1978), p. 311.

4. Arthur Hertzberg, *The Jews in America* (New York, 1989), p. 294; "The Hidden Heroes," *New York Times,* December 7, 1991.

5. James H. Cone, *Martin & Malcolm & America* (New York, 1991), p. 5.

6. Perry Miller, *Errand into the Wilderness* (New York, 1964), pp. 1–15; Howard M. Sachar, *A History of the Jews in America* (New York, 1992), pp. 487, 535;

Ronald Sanders, *Shores of Refuge: A Hundred Years of Jewish Emigration* (New York, 1988), p. 513; Hertzberg, *Jews in America*, p. 299.

7. Hertzberg, *Jews in America*, p. 299; Aaron Zeitlin, in Irving Howe, *World of Our Fathers: The Journey of the East European Jews to America and the Life They Found and Made* (New York, 1976), p. 626.

8. Jonathan Kaufman, *Broken Alliance: The Turbulent Times between Blacks and Jews in America* (New York, 1989), p. 50; Lou Potter, *Liberators: Fighting on Two Fronts in World War II* (New York, 1992), p. 242.

9. Chester Tanaka, *Go for Broke: A Pictorial History of the Japanese American 100th Infantry Battalion and the 442d Regimental Combat Team* (Richmond, Calif., 1982), p. 117.

10. Interview with Rudy Tokiwa, September 6, 1992; Report on Japanese Americans in Jerusalem, reunion between members of the 442nd Regiment and former Dauchau inmates, CBS News, May 3, 1992.

Chapter 14. Through a Glass Darkly

1. Commission on Wartime Relocation and Internment of Civilians, *Personal Justice Denied: Report of the Commission on Wartime Relocation and Internment of Civilians* (Washington, D.C., 1982), p. 265.

2. Commission on Wartime Relocation, *Personal Justice Denied*, pp. 269, 270, 272.

3. Lawrence Fuchs, *Hawaii Pono: A Social History* (New York, 1961), p. 302; Andrew Lind, *Hawaii's Japanese: An Experiment in Democracy* (Princeton, N.J., 1946), p. 64.

4. Jacobus tenBroek, Edward Barnhart, and Floyd Matson, *Prejudice, War and the Constitution: Causes and Consequences of the Evacuation of the Japanese Americans in World War II* (Berkeley, Calif., 1970), p. 117; Bradford Smith, *Americans from Japan* (Philadelphia, 1948), pp. 171–172; Lind, *Hawaii's Japanese*, p. 63.

5. Dennis Ogawa, *Kodomo no tame ni: For the sake of the children* (Honolulu, 1978), pp. 279–280; Lind, *Hawaii's Japanese*, p. 42.

6. Commission on Wartime Relocation, *Personal Justice Denied*, pp. 55, 64, 73.

7. Commission on Wartime Relocation, *Personal Justice Denied*, pp. 56, 71–72, 80; Lind, *Hawaii's Japanese*, p. 49; Roger Daniels, *Concentration Camps USA: Japanese Americans and World War II* (New York, 1971), p. 62; tenBroek *et al.*, *Prejudice*, p. 75; Gary Y. Okihiro and Julie Sly, "The Press, Japanese Americans, and the Concentration Camps," *Phylon*, vol. 44, no. 1 (1983), pp. 66–69.

8. tenBroek *et al.*, *Prejudice*, pp. 79–80.

9. tenBroek *et al.*, *Prejudice*, p. 80.

10. tenBroek *et al.*, *Prejudice*, p. 83; Commission on Wartime Relocation, *Personal Justice Denied*, pp. 70–71.

11. Commission on Wartime Relocation, *Personal Justice Denied*, pp. 78, 79.

12. Commission on Wartime Relocation, *Personal Justice Denied*, pp. 111, 121; Congressman Robert Matsui, speech in the House of Representatives on the 442 bill for redress and reparations, September 17, 1987, *Congressional Record* (Washiongton, D.C., 1987), p. 7584; Monica Sone, *Nisei Daughter* (Boston, 1953), p. 158.

13. Yasui and Tsukamoto, interviews, in John Tateishi, *And Justice for All: An Oral History of the Japanese American Detention Camps* (New York, 1984), pp. 73, 12, 74; Commission on Wartime Relocation, *Personal Justice Denied*, pp. 139, 142, 147.

14. Yasui, interview, in Tateishi, *And Justice for All*, p. 76.

15. Commission on Wartime Relocation, *Personal Justice Denied*, pp. 160, 172, 176; Miyo Senzaki, interview, in Tateishi, *And Justice for All*, p. 104.

16. Lind, *Hawaii's Japanese*, p. 161.

17. Shig Doi, interview, in Tateishi, *And Justice for All*, pp. 165–166; Chester Tanaka, *Go for Broke: A Pictorial History of the Japanese American 100th Infantry Battalion and the 442d Regimental Combat Team* (Richmond, Calif., 1982), p. 100.

18. Shig Doi, interview, p. 161; Lind, *Hawaii's Japanese*, p. 158; Commission on Wartime Relocation, *Personal Justice Denied*, p. 260; Tanaka, *Go for Broke*, p. 171.

19. Lind, *Hawaii's Japanese*, pp. 161–162.

20. "A Memo to Mr. Hitler, Hirohito & Co.," *Chinese Press*, May 8, 1942.

21. "First Chinese WAAC: New York's Emily Lee Shek," *Chinese Press*, September 25, 1942; Victor and Brett de Bary Nee, *Longtime Californ': A Documentary Study of an American Chinatown* (New York, 1972), pp. 154–155; Diane Mark and Ginger Chih, *A Place Called Chinese America* (Dubuque, Iowa, 1982), pp. 97–98.

22. "Give 'Em Wings: The Story of the Part Played in Aircraft by L.A. Chinese," *Chinese Press*, April 2, 1943; "Chinese Career Girls: They Help Run the Vital 'Behind-the-Line' Business of the United States at War," *Chinese Press*, May 29, 1942; "Women in the War," *Chinese Press*, March 26, 1943.

23. Rose Hum Lee, "Chinese in the United States Today: The War Has Changed Their Lives," in *Survey Graphic*, October 1942, pp. 419, 444.

24. Franklin D. Roosevelt, "Message from the President of the United States Favoring Repeal of the Chinese Exclusion Laws," October 11, 1943, in appendix, Fred Riggs, *Pressures on Congress: A Study of the Repeal of Chinese Exclusion* (New York, 1950), pp. 210–211.

25. Alison R. Bernstein, *American Indians and World War II: Toward a New Era in Indian Affairs* (Norman, Okla., 1991), p. 24; John Collier, "The Indian in a Wartime Nation," *Annals of the American Academy of Political and Social Science*, vol. 223 (September 1942), p. 30.

26. Tom Holm, "Fighting a White Man's War: The Extent and Legacy of American Indian Participation in World War II," *Journal of Ethnic Studies*, vol. 9, no. 2 (summer 1981), pp. 73, 74.

27. Bernstein, *American Indians*, pp. 43, 35, 42; Collier, "Indian in a Wartime Nation," p. 29.

28. Bernstein, *American Indians*, p. 45; Holm, "Fighting a White Man's War," p. 71.

29. Bernstein, *American Indians*, pp. 48, 49.

30. Bernstein, *American Indians*, pp. 53–55.

31. Bernstein, *American Indians*, pp. 58, 60.

32. Evon Z. Vogt, *Navaho Veterans: A Study of Changing Values* (Cambridge, Mass., 1951), p. 64; Leslie Marmon Silko, *Ceremony* (New York, 1978), p. 43.

33. Bernstein, *American Indians*, p. 51.

34. Bernstein, *American Indians*, pp. 70, 68, 86; Collier, "Indian in a Wartime Nation," p. 31.

35. Holm, "Fighting a White Man's War," p. 74.

36. Raul Morin, *Among the Valiant: Mexican-Americans in WWII and Korea* (Alhambra, Calif., 1966), p. 15.

37. Carey McWilliams, *North from Mexico: The Spanish-Speaking People of the United States* (New York, 1968), pp. 266–267.

38. Marilyn P. Davis, *Mexican Voices, American Dreams: An Oral History of Mexican Immigration to the United States* (New York, 1990), pp. 171, 126.

39. Mario García, *Mexican Americans: Leadership, Ideology & Identity, 1930–1960* (New Haven, Conn., 1989), p. 166.

40. McWilliams, *North from Mexico*, p. 260.

41. García, *Mexican Americans*, p. 2; Morin, *Among the Valiant*, pp. 111–114, 91.

42. McWilliams, *North from Mexico*, p. 271.

43. McWilliams, *North from Mexico*, p. 261; Carlos Muñoz, Jr., *Youth, Identity, Power: The Chicano Movement* (London, 1989), pp. 38–39.

44. Gunnar Myrdal, *An American Dilemma: The Negro Problem and Modern Democracy* (New York, 1944), p. 1007; Harvard Sitkoff, *A New Deal for Blacks: The Emergence of Civil Rights as a National Issue: The Depression Decade* (New York, 1978), pp. 301, 324.

45. John Hope Franklin, *From Slavery to Freedom: A History of Negro Americans* (New York, 1967), pp. 581, 586.

46. Richard Polenberg, *One Nation Divisible: Class, Race, and Ethnicity in the United States Since 1938* (New York, 1980), p. 76; Sitkoff, *New Deal for Blacks*, p. 324.

47. Sitkoff, *New Deal for Blacks*, pp. 324, 318; Myrdal, *American Dilemma*, p. 1006; Polenberg, *One Nation Divisible*, p. 71.

48. Sitkoff, *New Deal for Blacks*, p. 301; Polenberg, *One Nation Divisible*, p. 70; Howard Zinn, *A People's History of the United States* (New York, 1980), p. 411.

49. Sitkoff, *New Deal for Blacks*, p. 300.

50. Sitkoff, *New Deal for Blacks*, p. 314; Jacqueline Jones, *Labor of Love, Labor*

of Sorrow: Black Women, Work, and the Family from Slavery to the Present (New York, 1985), p. 233.

51. Sitkoff, *New Deal for Blacks*, p. 320; Franklin, *From Slavery to Freedom*, pp. 578–579.

52. Jones, *Labor of Love, Labor of Sorrow*, p. 254.

53. Polenberg, *One Nation Divisible*, p. 75; Carey McWilliams, *Brothers under the Skin* (Boston, 1964), p. 9.

54. Jones, *Labor of Love, Labor of Sorrow*, pp. 234, 235.

55. Abraham Lincoln, "First Inaugural Address," in *The Annals of America*, vol. 9, *The Crisis of the Union: 1858–1865* (Chicago, 1968), p. 255; Bernstein, *American Indians*, p. 35; Francis L. Broderick, *W. E. B. DuBois: Negro Leader in a Time of Crisis* (Stanford, Calif., 1966), p. 196.

56. Frank Chuman, *The Bamboo People: The Law and Japanese-Americans* (Del Mar, Calif., 1976), pp. 209–218; Kazuo Ito, *Issei: A History of Japanese Immigrants in North America* (Seattle, 1973), p. 585.

57. Fred Powledge, *Free at Last? The Civil Rights Movement and the People Who Made It* (Boston, 1991), pp. 28–29; Chuman, *Bamboo People*, p. 312; Robert Wilson and Bill Hosokawa, *East to America: A History of the Japanese in the United States* (New York, 1980), p. 279.

58. Poem by Kiyoko Nieda, in Lucille Nixon and Tomoe Tana (eds. and translators), *Sounds from the Unknown: A Collection of Japanese American Tanka* (Denver, 1963), p. 49.

59. David Reimers, *Still the Golden Door: The Third World Comes to America* (New York, 1985), pp. 83, 70, 67, 71.

60. Matsui, speech, p. 7584; Congressman Norman Mineta, interview, March 26, 1988; Warren Furutani, testimony, reprinted in *Amerasia*, vol. 8, no. 2 (1981), p. 104.

61. "Text of Reagan's Remarks," reprinted in *Pacific Citizen*, August 19–26, 1988, p. 5; *San Francisco Chronicle*, August 5, 1988, and August 11, 1988.

62. *Brown et al. v. Board of Education of Topeka et al.*, reprinted in Clayborne Carson *et al.* (eds.), *The Eyes on the Prize Civil Rights Reader* (New York, 1987), pp. 64–74; "The Atlanta Declaration" of the NAACP, reprinted in Carson *et al.* (eds.), *Eyes on the Prize*, p. 82; Robert Williams, quoted in Carson *et al.* (eds.), *Eyes on the Prize*, p. 36; the implementation decision, in Carson *et al.* (eds.), *Eyes on the Prize*, pp. 95–96.

63. Harvard Sitkoff, *The Struggle for Black Equality, 1954–1980* (New York, 1981), pp. 41–42, 52; Norman W. Walton, "The Walking City: A History of the Montgomery Boycott," *Negro History Bulletin*, pt. I (October 1956), pp. 18–19.

64. Martin Luther King, Jr., *Stride toward Freedom: The Montgomery Story* (New York, 1958), pp. 12–13; Stephen B. Oates, *Let the Trumpet Sound: The Life of Martin Luther King, Jr.* (New York, 1982), p. 16.

65. King, *Stride toward Freedom*, pp. 47–48; Oates, *Let the Trumpet Sound*, p. 112. See Gloria Steinem, *Revolution from Within* (Boston, 1992).

66. Sitkoff, *Struggle for Black Equality*, pp. 86, 90; student quoted by James Farmer, in Francis L. Broderick and August Meier (eds.), *Negro Protest Thought in the Twentieth Century* (New York, 1965), p. 372; Oates, *Let the Trumpet Sound*, p. 154; Guy and Candie Carawan, *Songs of the Southern Freedom Movement* (New York, 1963), p. 61.

67. Sitkoff, *Struggle for Black Equality*, p. 109; Powledge, *Free at Last?*, pp. 256, 262.

68. Martin Luther King, Jr., "I Have a Dream," reprinted in Broderick and Meier (eds.), *Negro Protest Thought*, pp. 400–405.

69. Jonathan Kaufman, *Broken Alliance: The Turbulent Times between Blacks and Jews in America* (New York, 1989), pp. 14, 17. For this discussion on Jews, I am indebted to this informed and passionate study of the Jewish involvement in the Civil Rights Movement.

70. Kaufman, *Broken Alliance*, pp. 20, 17, 28, 63, 64, 81, 91.

71. Kaufman, *Broken Alliance*, pp. 95, 83, 84, 96, 212; see Alan M. Dershowitz, *Chutzpah* (Boston, 1991), pp. 65–80.

72. Kaufman, *Broken Alliance*, pp. 96, 30, 63.

73. Kaufman, *Broken Alliance*, pp. 104, 130, 132, 77.

74. See Stokely Carmichael and Charles Hamilton, *Black Power: The Politics of Liberation* (New York, 1967); Frantz Fanon, *The Wretched of the Earth* (New York, 1966); Martin Luther King, Jr., *Where Do We Go from Here: Chaos or Community* (New York, 1967), p. 55.

75. Nathan Glazer, "Negroes and Jews: The New Challenge to Pluralism," in Jack Salzman (ed.), *Bridges and Boundaries: African Americans and American Jews* (New York, 1992), pp. 101–104.

76. Kenneth B. Clark, *Dark Ghetto: Dilemmas of Social Power* (New York, 1965), pp. 1, 12, 10.

77. James H. Cone, *Martin & Malcolm & America: A Dream or a Nightmare* (Maryknoll, N.Y., 1991), p. 223; Martin Luther King, Jr., *Why We Can't Wait* (New York, 1964), pp. 80, ix; King, *Where Do We Go From Here*, p. 6.

78. Cone, *Martin & Malcolm & America*, pp. 1, 42, 213, 222.

79. William Julius Wilson, *The Truly Disadvantaged: The Inner City, the Underclass, and Public Policy* (Chicago, 1987), p. 109; King, *Stride toward Freedom*, p. 72; Nicholas Lemann, *The Promised Land: The Great Black Migration and How It Changed America* (New York, 1991), p. 6.

80. Donald J. Bogue, *The Population of the United States* (New York, 1985), pp. 584, 11, 45; *Social Security Bulletin, Annual Statistical Supplement, 1983*, p. 248; Leslie Dunbar, *The Common Interest: How Our Social Welfare Policies Don't Work and What We Can Do About Them* (New York, 1988), p. 103.

81. *Social Security Bulletin*, vol. 45, no. 4 (April 1982), p. 8; U.S. Department of Health and Human Services, *Aid to Families with Dependent Children: 1979 Recipient Characteristics Study*, pp. 3, 17; Carol B. Stack, *All Our Kin: Strategies for Survival in a Black Community* (New York, 1975), p. 51; William Julius Wilson and Kathryn N. Neckerman, "Poverty and Family Structure: The Widening Gap

between Evidence and Public Policy Issues," in Sheldon H. Danziger and Daniel H. Weinberg, *Fighting Poverty: What Works and What Doesn't* (Cambridge, Mass., 1986), p. 235; Bogue, *Population*, p. 603; *Social Security Bulletin*, vol. 45, no. 4 (April 1982), p. 5; United States Commission on Civil Rights, *Unemployment and Underemployment among Blacks, Hispanics, and Women* (Washington, D.C., 1982), p. 51; Bogue, *Population*, p. 166; Lenore Weitzman, *The Divorce Revolution* (New York, 1985); Wilson, *Truly Disadvantaged*, pp. 72–92.

82. Dunbar, *Common Interest*, pp. 165–167.

83. John Reid, "Black America in the 1980s," *Population Bulletin*, vol. 37, no. 4 (December 1982), p. 7; Barry Bluestone and Bennett Harrison, *The Deindustrialization of America: Plant Closings, Community Abandonment, and the Dismantling of Basic Industry* (New York, 1982), p. 270; Andrew Hacker, *Two Nations: Black and White, Separate, Hostile, Unequal* (New York, 1992), p. 101; Wilson, *Truly Disadvantaged*, pp. 12, 90–91.

84. Isabel Wilkerson, "How Milwaukee Boomed but Left Its Blacks Behind," *New York Times*, March 19, 1991, pp. A1, A16.

85. Jimmy Morse, interview, in Dunbar, *Common Interest*, pp. 89–94; Illinois Advisory Committee to the United States Commission on Civil Rights, *Shutdown: Economic Dislocation and Equal Opportunity* (Washington, D.C., 1980), pp. 8, 32–34; Report of the Congressional Office of Technology Assessment, reported in *New York Times*, February 7, 1986. For the welfare argument, see Charles Murray, *Losing Ground* (New York, 1984).

86. Darryl Swafford, quoted in Jacob Lamar, "Today's Native Sons," *Time*, December 1, 1986, p. 28; Danny Coleman, quoted in Lamar, "Today's Native Sons," p. 29.

87. William Raspberry, "Beyond Racism (Cont'd.)," *Washington Post*, November 19, 1984; "Asian-Americans: Are They Making the Grade?" *U.S. News & World Report*, April 2, 1984, pp. 41–47; "The Changing Face of America," Special Immigrants Issue, *Time*, July 8, 1985, pp. 24–101; "Asian-Americans: The Drive to Excel," *Newsweek on Campus*, April 1984, pp. 4–15; "Asian-Americans: A 'Model Minority,' " *Newsweek*, December 6, 1982, pp. 40–51; "America's Super Minority," *Fortune*, November 26, 1986.

88. Ronald Takaki, "Have Asian Americans Made It?" *San Francisco Examiner*, January 10, 1984; Ronald Takaki, "Comparisons between Blacks and Asian Americans Unfair," *Seattle Post-Intelligencer*, March 21, 1985.

89. Paul Ong, "Chinatown Unemployment and the Ethnic Labor Market," *Amerasia*, vol. 11, no. 1 (1984), p. 45.

90. Peter Kwong, *The New Chinatown* (New York, 1987), p. 36.

91. Alexander Reid, "New Asian Immigrants, New Garment Center," *New York Times*, October 5, 1986; Thomas Kessner and Betty Boyd Caroli, *Today's Immigrants, Their Stories: A New Look at the Newest Americans* (New York, 1981), p. 257.

92. Nee, *Longtime Californ'*, pp. 282, 285.

93. Murray, *Losing Ground*, p. 55; CBS, *Sixty Minutes*, "The Model Minority," February 1, 1987; Ronald Takaki, "Asian Americans in the University," *San Francisco Examiner*, April 16, 1984; Raspberry, "Beyond Racism (Cont'd.)"; Bluestone and Harrison, *The Deindustrialization of America*; Barbara Ehrenreich, *Fear of Falling: The Inner Life of the Middle Class* (New York, 1989), p. 15.

94. Peter Schmeisser, "Is America in Decline?" *New York Times Magazine*, April 17, 1988; Wilson, *Truly Disadvantaged*, p. 65; President Ronald Reagan, speech to a group of Asian and Pacific Americans in the White House, February 23, 1984, reprinted in *Asian Week*, March 2, 1984; Ronald Takaki, "Poverty Is Thriving under Reagan," *New York Times*, March 3, 1986; Ronald Reagan, quoted in James Reston, "Reagan Is the Issue," *San Francisco Chronicle*, September 13, 1984. This disciplining also includes the middle class; see Chris Tilly, "U-Turn on Equality: The Puzzle of Middle Class Decline," *Dollars & Sense*, May 1986, p. 11 ("middle-class" income is defined as between 75 percent and 125 percent of median household income); Bob Kuttner, "The Declining Middle," *Atlantic Monthly*, July 1983, pp. 60–72; Barbara Ehrenreich, "Is the Middle Class Doomed?" *New York Times Magazine*, September 7, 1986, pp. 44, 50, 62; Tom Wicker, "Let 'Em Eat Swiss Cheese," *New York Times*, September 2, 1988; Don Wycliff, "Why the Underclass in Still Under," *New York Times*, November 16, 1987; Murray, *Losing Ground*, pp. 32, 55, 146, 220, 227.

95. William Broad, "Swords Have Been Sheathed But Plowshares Lack Design," *New York Times*, February 5, 1992, pp. A1, A8.

96. Bruce Johansen and Roberto Maestras, *Wasi'chu: The Continuing Indian Wars* (New York, 1979), pp. 154–166; Anthony Lewis, "The Cost of Reagan," *New York Times*, September 7, 1989.

97. James S. Olson and Raymond Wilson, *Native Americans in the Twentieth Century* (Urbana, Ill., 1986), pp. 144, 152, 153, 163–164.

98. James E. Young, "Living at the Scene of the Crime," review of Charles Hoffman's *Gray Dawn: The Jews of Eastern Europe in the Post-Communist Era* (New York, 1992), *New York Times Book Review*, September 6, 1992, pp. 12–13; interview with Soviet lawyer in Moscow, June 1990; interview with Barbara Budnitz, August 22, 1992; Steven Erlanger, "As Ukraine Loses Jews, the Jews Lose a Tradition," *New York Times*, August 27, 1992.

99. Interview with Sofiya Shapiro (pseudonym), August 30, 1992.

100. Statistics from Natasha Kats of the Bay Area Council of Soviet Jews, San Francisco, interview, August 28, 1992; interview with Barbara Budnitz, August 22, 1992.

101. Interview with Sofiya Shapiro (pseudonym), August 30, 1992; interview with Barbara Budnitz, August 22, 1992.

102. Al Kamen, "Irish Will Win 'Green Card' Sweepstakes," *San Francisco Chronicle*, July 29, 1991; Richard Lacayo, "Give Me Your Rich, Your Lucky...," *Time*, October 14, 1991, p. 27.

103. Wilma Randle, "The Changing Face of the Work Force," *San Francisco*

Examiner, January 7, 1990; David Hayes-Bautista, Werner Schink, and Jorge Chapa, *The Burden of Support: Young Latinos in an Aging Society* (Stanford, Calif., 1988), pp. 35–36.

104. Hayes-Bautista *et al.*, *Burden of Support*, p. 85.

105. Hayes-Bautista *et al.*, *Burden of Support*, p. 54.

106. "The Economic Crisis of Urban America," cover story, *Business Week*, May 18, 1992, pp. 38, 40, 43.

107. Gregory Lewis, "L.A. Riot Area Likened to Third World Nation," *San Francisco Examiner*, May 31, 1992; April Lynch, "Southland's Hopes Turn to Ashes: Promise Eroded by Recession, Ethnic Tensions," *San Francisco Chronicle*, May 22, 1992.

108. Langston Hughes, "Lennox Avenue Mural," in Langston Hughes, *The Langston Hughes Reader* (New York, 1958), p. 123.

109. "Beyond Black and White," cover story, *Newsweek*, May 18, 1992, p. 28.

110. Sara Rimer, "Watts Organizer Feels Weight of Riots, and History," *New York Times*, June 24, 1992, p. A9; Richard Rodriguez, "Horizontal City," *This World*, San Francisco Chronicle, May 24, 1992, p. 16.

111. Martin Luther King, Jr., quoted in Willie L. Brown, "Riots Echo Decades-Old Anguish of Dispossessed," *San Francisco Examiner*, May 3, 1992, p. A13; interview with Sister Janet Harris, in *Los Angeles Times*, May 13, 1992, p. T11.

112. "$150 Billion a Year: Where to Find It," *New York Times*, March 8, 1990; Ann Markusen, "Department of the Peace Dividend," *New York Times*, May 18, 1992.

113. Broad, "Swords Have Been Sheathed," pp. A1, A8.

114. Perry Miller, *Errand into the Wilderness* (New York, 1964), pp. 1–15; William Shakespeare, *The Tempest* (New York, 1904), Act V, sc. i, 184–185; Langston Hughes, "Let America Be America Again," in Langston Hughes and Arna Bontemps (eds.), *The Poetry of the Negro, 1746–1949* (Garden City, N.Y., 1951), pp. 106–107.

115. Herman Melville, *Moby-Dick, or the Whale* (Boston, 1956; originally published in 1851), pp. 105, 182, 253, 322.

116. Gloria Anzaldúa, *Borderlands, La Frontera: The New Mestiza* (San Francisco, 1987), first page of preface, p. 87.

117. Steinem, *Revolution from Within*, p. 107; Mitsuye Yamada, "Invisibility Is an Unnatural Disaster: Reflections of an Asian American Woman," in Cherrie Moraga and Gloria Anzaldúa (eds.), *This Bridge Called My Back: Writings by Radical Women of Color* (New York, 1983), p. 40; Audre Lorde, "Good Mirrors Are Not Cheap," in Lorde, *From a Land Where Other People Live* (Detroit, 1973), p. 15. My thanks to Henry Louis Gates, Jr., for bringing my attention to this poem in *Loose Canons: Notes on the Culture Wars* (New York, 1992), p. 192.

118. Carlos Fuentes, *The Buried Mirror: Reflections on Spain and the New World* (Boston, 1992), p. 348; Reese Erlich, "Alice's Wonderland," an interview with Alice Walker, *Image*, San Francisco Examiner, July 19, 1992, p. 12; Paula Gunn Allen,

interview, in Laura Coltelli (ed.), *Winged Words: American Indian Writers Speak* (Lincoln, Nebr., 1990), p. 17; Herman Melville, *Redburn* (Chicago, 1969; originally published in 1849), p. 169, also quoted in Gates, *Loose Canons,* pp. 116–117, and Michael Paul Rogin, *Subversive Genealogy: The Politics and Art of Herman Melville* (New York, 1983), p. 69.

119. Allan Bloom, *The Closing of the American Mind: How Higher Education Has Failed Democracy and Impoverished the Souls of Today's Students* (New York, 1987); Patrick Buchanan, speech at the National Republican Convention, 1992, quoted in Garry Wills, "The Born-Again Republicans," *New York Review of Books,* September 24, 1992; Arthur M. Schlesinger, Jr., *The Disuniting of America: Reflections on a Multicultural Society* (Knoxville, Tenn. 1991).

120. Rodney King's statement to the press, *New York Times,* May 2, 1992, p. 6; interview with Toni Morrison, *Time,* May 22, 1989, p. 121; Black Elk, *Black Elk Speaks: Being the Life Story of a Holy Man of the Oglala Sioux,* as told to John G. Neihardt (Lincoln, Nebr., 1988), p. 43.

121. Joy Kogawa, *Obasan* (Boston, 1982), opening page; Lincoln, "First Inaugural Address," *The Annals of America,* vol. 9, 1863–65: *The Crisis of the Union* (Chicago, 1968), p. 255; Walt Whitman, *Leaves of Grass* (New York, 1958), pp. 9, 10, 38.

INDEX

INDEX

INDEX

Tashiro, Aiji, 275
Taylor, Graham D., 240
Taylor, Zachary, 175
Tempest, The, 24–52, 191
  see also Shakespeare, William
Terán, Manuel Mier y, 173
Terrecowah, Chief, 103
Texas, 172–3, 179–81, 184, 314, 318–22, 327–8
Their Eyes Were Watching God (Hurston), 364–6
Third World, 408
Time, 2
tobacco, 35–6
Tocqueville, Alexis de, 80–1, 92, 107, 109
tongs, 216
Toomer, Jean, 361–4
Topsell, Edward, 52
Trail of Tears, 93–7
Treaty of Dancing Rabbit Creek, 90
Treaty of Guadalupe Hidalgo, 176, 191–2
Treaty of New Echota, 94–6
Triangle Shirtwaist Factory fire, 294–5, 303
Trilling, Lionel, 308
Truman, Harry, 384, 400
Tuchman, Barbara W., 16
Tucker, William, 36
Turner, Darwin, 364
Turner, Frederick Jackson, 10, 225, 228
Turner, Nat, 6, 116
Tuskegee Institute, 136–8

underclass, 7, 412
Union Pacific, 146
United Auto Workers, 368–9
United Nations Charter, 399
Universal Negro Improvement Association, 355–7
University of California, Berkeley, 4
University of Minnesota, 4
University of Wisconsin, 4
Up from Slavery (Washington), 355
Uprooted, The (Handlin), 6

Vallejo, Francisca, 167–9
Vallejo, Guadalupe, 169–70
Vallejo, Mariano, 167–70, 180
Vallejo, Rosalie, 170
Vallejo, Salvador, 167–9, 180
vaqueros, 12, 184–5
Vaughn, Alden T., 57
Verdugo, Julio, 183
Vesey, Denmark, 114
Vespucci, Amerigo, 31
Vietnamese, 7

Vikings, 21–3
Villa, Pancho, 314
Vinland, 21–3
Virgin of Guadalupe, 335
Virginia, 1, 17, 26, 28–33, 52–68
  tobacco in, 35–6
Voluntary Relocation Program, 418
Voorhis, Jerry, 393

Walker, Alice, 427
Walker, David, 106–7, 410
Walker, Francis Amasa, 231–4, 417, 418
Wallace, Mike, 416
Wampanoags, 10, 25, 37–40
War for Independence, 14
Warren, Earl, 381
Washington, Booker T., 136–8, 345, 355
Watts riot, 5, 409–10
Waymouth, George, 30, 31
Weaver, Robert C., 398
Weber, Max, 225
welfare, 8, 411–3
West Indies, 58
Wexler, Mollie, 292
Wheatley, Phillis, 72–4
White, Richard, 98, 244
Whitman, Walt, 12, 428
Wilcox, George, 252
Williams, Eugene, 351
Williams, Roger, 24, 29, 38
Willkie, Wendell, 374
Willoughby, Charles, 383
Wilson, William Julius, 412
Winthrop, John, 7, 30–1, 42, 44, 50, 58, 176
Wishart, David, 100
women, *see* African Americans; Chicanos; Chinese; Indians; Irish; Japanese; Jews
Wonder-working Providence (Johnson), 43
Wong, Ah So, 211–2
Wong, Chin Foo, 201
Wood, William, 39
World of Our Fathers (Howe), 6
World War I, 279, 342, 348
World War II, 8, 310, 369, 373–99, 413, 426
  and African Americans, 395–9
  and Chicanos, 392–5
  and Chinese, 385–7
  and Indians, 387–91
  and Japanese, 401–2
  and Jews, 310, 373–7
Wounded Knee, 228–30

505

507

ABOUT THE AUTHOR

R ONALD TAKAKI is one of the foremost nationally recognized scholars of multicultural studies. The grandson of Japanese immigrant plantation laborers in Hawaii, he holds a Ph.D. in American history from the University of California, Berkeley, where he has been a professor of Ethnic Studies for over two decades. He served as the department chairperson and also the graduate advisor of the Ethnic Studies Ph.D. program. The Berkeley faculty has honored Professor Takaki with a Distinguished Teaching Award, and Cornell University has appointed him to be the prestigious Messenger Lecturer for 1993. He was instrumental in the establishment of Berkeley's American Cultures Requirement. Takaki is the author of the critically acclaimed *Iron Cages* and the prize-winning *Strangers from a Different Shore*, which the *New York Times Book Review* selected in 1989 as one of the year's Notable Books.